THE OXFORD HANDBOOK OF

CHORAL
PEDAGOGY

THE OXFORD HANDBOOK OF

CHORAL

PEDAGOGY

Edited by

FRANK ABRAHAMS

and

PAUL D. HEAD

OXFORD
UNIVERSITY PRESS

OXFORD
UNIVERSITY PRESS

Oxford University Press is a department of the University of Oxford. It furthers the University's objective of excellence in research, scholarship, and education by publishing worldwide. Oxford is a registered trade mark of Oxford University Press in the UK and certain other countries.

Published in the United States of America by Oxford University Press
198 Madison Avenue, New York, NY 10016, United States of America.

Library of Congress Cataloging-in-Publication Data
Names: Abrahams, Frank, editor. | Head, Paul (Paul D.), editor.
Title: The Oxford handbook of choral pedagogy /
edited by Frank Abrahams and Paul D. Head.
Description: New York : Oxford University Press, [2017] |
Includes bibliographical references and index.
Identifiers: LCCN 2016025406| ISBN 9780199373369 (cloth : alk. paper) |
ISBN 9780199373383 (oxford handbooks online : alk. paper)
Subjects: LCSH: Choral singing—Instruction and study.
Classification: LCC MT875 .O94 2017 | DDC 782.5071—dc23
LC record available at https://lccn.loc.gov/2016025406

3 5 7 9 8 6 4 2
Printed by Sheridan Books, Inc., United States of America

To the loving memory of Robert Page (1927–2016), who was influential in the development of many choral conductors and whose support and sound advice was consistent for many years.

CONTENTS

PRACTICE

Acknowledgments

THE editors thank the authors for their timely and scholarly contributions to this text. We are grateful to the reviewers who read early versions of each chapter and provided critiques that made each chapter better. Special thanks to Christopher Filice, Allison Griffiths, and Daniel Wells who worked as assistants to the editors, facilitating correspondence and document formatting. We also appreciate the support and guidance from Norm Hirschy at Oxford University Press. Finally, we thank Ellen Abrahams and Carol Head for their support throughout the writing, production, and publication process.

LIST OF CONTRIBUTORS

Daniel Abrahams studied music education at Temple University and completed a master of instrumental conducting degree at the University of Nebraska at Omaha. He holds a Ph.D. in music education from Oakland University in Rochester, Michigan. Abrahams is assistant professor of music education at the University of Arkansas, and has presented research at numerous, state, national, and international conferences. He has contributed several book chapters in edited publications. His research interests include the acquisition of learner agency and the use of reciprocal teaching in classroom music and ensembles. His dissertation research examined how pedagogy fosters personal and musical agency among beginning instrumental conductors.

Frank Abrahams is Professor of Music Education at Westminster Choir College of Rider University in Princeton, New Jersey. A native of Philadelphia, he holds degrees from Temple University and New England Conservatory. Dr. Abrahams has pioneered the development of a critical pedagogy for music education and has presented research papers and taught classes in the United States, China, Brazil, Taiwan, Hungary, Israel, Italy, and the United Kingdom. He is senior editor of *Visions of Research in Music Education* and has been on the editorial board of the *Music Educators Journal*. With Paul Head, he is co-author of *Case Studies in Music Education* and *Teaching Music Through Performance in Middle School Choir*. He is also author of *Planning Instruction in Music* with co-author Ryan John.

Susan Avery is an Associate Professor of Music Education at Ithaca College, where she has been on the faculty since 2000. Before that, she was a choral music educator in the public schools for 24 years. Her work has been published in NAfME's *Music Educators Journal* and NYSSMA's *School Music News* and she co-authored a chapter in the book *Community Music Today*. She has presented at state, division, and national levels on diverse topics such as choral curriculum and assessment, adult music literacy, and cognitive apprenticeship. She also adjudicates and provides clinics in choral work throughout New York State.

Charles Beale : Born in London in 1964, Dr. Charles Beale was a Cambridge organ scholar, and is a choral conductor, a jazz pianist and a passionate campaigner for music education and on LGBTQ issues. Key research interests include choral singing, jazz, and music education. Central to the invention of ABRSM Grade exams for beginner jazz musicians, he was nominated for a UK Jazz Parliamentary Award for services to jazz education in 2005. Beale is published by Oxford, Hal Leonard, Faber and ABRSM

Publishing, and co-authored Oxford's "Popular Voiceworks," which won the MRA award for "Best Pop Music Publication" in 2008. Since 2007, he has been Artistic Director of the 270-strong New York City Gay Men's Chorus, and oversees their Youth Pride Chorus and pop a cappella ensemble. He gives frequent clinics and workshops internationally, most recently in Hobart, Tasmania; Denver, Colorado; New York, and London.

Richard Bjella : Director of Choral Studies at Texas Tech University, Richard Bjella has distinguished himself as a conductor, clinician, choral pedagogue, and choral arranger. He also served as Director of Choral Studies at the Lawrence Conservatory of Music for 25 years. The choirs have appeared at Regional and National ACDA conferences. Bjella was appointed Artistic Director of the San Antonio Chamber Choir in 2014. Bjella has presented over 400 festivals and workshops at several ACDA conventions, colleges, and universities, and in 32 states and several foreign countries. Bjella was awarded the prestigious Morris Hayes Lifetime Achievement Award (2013) from WCDA.

Deborah Bradley was Assistant Professor in Music Education at the University of Wisconsin-Madison from 2006 to 2010. She taught at the University of Toronto Faculty of Music from 1997–2005, and from 2010–2014, after retiring from UW-Madison. She is a leading scholar in anti-racism and critical multiculturalism in music education; her work is published in such Journals as *Philosophy of Music Education Review, Journal of Aesthetic Education, Music Education Research,* and *Action, Criticism, and Theory for Music Education.* She has also published several book chapters, including a chapter in the 2012 *Oxford Handbook of Philosophy of Music Education.*

Simon Carrington has enjoyed a distinguished career as singer, double bassist, and now conductor. He was a creative force for 25 years with the internationally acclaimed King's Singers, which he cofounded at Cambridge University in 1968. Coming to the United States in 1994 he was successively director of choral activities at the University of Kansas and New England Conservatory, then professor of choral conducting at Yale and director of the Yale Schola Cantorum. Now a Yale professor emeritus he maintains an active schedule as a freelance conductor, leading workshops and master classes round the world. In 2014 he received an honorary doctorate from New England Conservatory.

Duane Cottrell is Associate Professor of Choral Music Education at the University of Delaware, where he conducts three ensembles and teaches undergraduate and graduate courses in choral conducting, literature, and methods while also supervising student teachers. His ensembles have appeared at ACDA and NAfME conferences, and he has presented interest sessions on vocal pedagogy at national and division conferences of ACDA. His writing has been published in the Choral Journal and The Choral Scholar. Dr. Cottrell received his DMA at the University of North Texas where he studied choral conducting with Jerry McCoy and voice science with Stephen Austin.

Craig Denison is Assistant Professor in Music Education and Choral Music at Indiana University of Pennsylvania. He serves the American Choral Directors Association as the National Chair of Repertoire and Resources for Boychoir. Dr. Denison regularly presents workshops and conducts honor choirs at state and national conferences. Previous positions include Artistic Director for Florida's Singing Sons, Music Director for the Colorado Children's Chorale, Conductor of The American Boychoir, and Founding Director of Schola Cantorum at Westminster Choir College of Rider University. Dr. Denison holds a Ph.D. from the University of Miami.

J. Donald Dumpson, **Ph.D.** is an experienced educator and performer, with over 30 years of experience as a producer, conductor, and music minister. He is president and CEO of Diverse Arts Solutions, a division of J. Donald Dumpson Productions, LLC; is the founding director of the Philadelphia Heritage Chorale; and currently serves as minister of Music and Arts at Arch Street Presbyterian Church in Philadelphia. Holding a Bachelor's, Master's, and Ph.D. in Music Education, all from Temple University, his dissertation is titled: "Four Scholars' Engagement of Works by Classical Composers of African Descent: A Collective Case Study."

Dr. Colin Durrant is conductor of the University of London Chamber Choir and Imperial College London Choir. He has held various positions in universities in London and the USA and has published many articles on choral conducting and music education. His book *Choral Conducting: Philosophy and Practice* appeared in 2003 and is used widely in universities around the world (the second revised edition coming next year). Colin Durrant has led conducting and choral singing workshops in the United States, Australia, Singapore, Taiwan, China, Hong Kong, Malaysia, and Kenya as well as in Europe and the UK. He is a member of the Voice Care Network of America.

Liz Garnett is a choral clinician and musicologist whose research and praxis both explore the theme of music and its social meanings. She studied at the Universities of Bristol and Southampton (Ph.D.: "Constructions of Gender and Musical Style, 1790–1830"). She taught at Colchester Institute's School of Music and Performance Arts for four years, before moving to Birmingham Conservatoire, where she served as Head of Postgraduate Studies until 2009. She is the author of *The British Barbershopper: A Study in Socio-Musical Values* (2005) and *Choral Conducting and the Construction of Meaning: Gesture, Voice, Identity* (2009).

Mary Goetze is Professor Emerita from the Indiana University Jacobs School of Music where she taught in the music education, choral, and general studies departments. She founded the Indiana University Children's Choir and the International Vocal Ensemble, an ensemble that focused on songs from outside the western art tradition. She is the co-author of *Educating Young Singers: A Choral Resource for Teacher-Conductors*; two series books, *Share the Music* and *Spotlight on Music*; and numerous chapters, articles, DVDs, compositions, and arrangements. In her retirement, she advocates for justice reform and offers a songwriting class for inmates in the local jail.

Arreon Harley, Director of Music and Operations was appointed to the Cathedral Choir School of Delaware in June, 2013. He began singing with Doreen Falby and the Peabody Conservatory's Children's Chorus at the age of seven. When Arreon's voice changed, he began to sing with the Columbia Pro Cantare, under the directorship of Mrs. Frances Dawson. Arreon graduated with honors from Goucher College in Baltimore, Maryland, with bachelors degrees in music theory and composition and vocal performance (opera). There he studied piano with Dr. Lisa Weiss, voice with Mrs. Betty Ridgeway, and conducting with Dr. Elisa Koehler. He received masters of music degrees in choral conducting and vocal performance from the University of Delaware. Arreon studied choral conducting with pedagogue Dr. Paul Head and continues to study voice with Dr. Noel Archambeault. Arreon has had the opportunity to conduct in venues such as St. Peter's in Vatican City, The Kimmel Center for the Arts in Philadelphia, and the Joseph Meyerhoff Symphony Hall in Baltimore.

Scott Harrison is currently Director of Queensland Conservatorium Griffith University, following a career teaching in primary, secondary, and tertiary environments. He has over 20 years of experience in performance of choral, opera, and music theatre works as both singer and musical director. Scott is a former coeditor of the *International Journal of Music Education*, and recipient of an Australian Award for University Teaching. He has grants from the Australian Office for Learning and Teaching and the Australian Research Council on Assessment in Music, One-To-One Pedagogy in Music, and Musicians' Careers.

Paul D. Head serves as the director of choral studies at the University of Delaware, where he conducts the internationally renowned University of Delaware Chorale, the community-based Schola Cantorum, and the Symphonic Chorus, which performs frequently with the Delaware Symphony Orchestra. Dr. Head is a native Californian where he taught in the public schools for eight years before completing his Master of Music in Conducting and Music Education degree at Westminster Choir College of Rider University and a Doctor of Musical Arts in Conducting from the University of Oklahoma. His choirs have toured extensively throughout the United States, Canada, Asia, and Europe and have received consistently high acclaim for their musical artistry. Dr. Head maintains an active presence as conductor and guest clinician, as well as researcher and pedagogue. His work is published in several books and publications, notably *The School Choral Program; Teaching Music Through Performance*, and as coauthor with Frank Abrahams for *Case Studies in Music Education*.

Dr. Eduardo Lakschevitz is Associate Professor of Music History at the University of Rio de Janeiro (UNIRIO), where he chairs a Graduate Program in Music Education. Active as a teacher, conductor, and clinician, he has conducted workshops for teachers, musicians, and corporate leaders in several Brazilian states, as well as in the United States. His main research relates to the connections between music making and corporate management, a work he has been developing with large Brazilian companies for the past 20 years. His choral compositions, articles, and arrangements have been recorded and published in Brazil, Venezuela, United States, Slovenia, and Germany.

László Norbert Nemes , has been director of the International Kodály Institute of the Liszt Ferenc Academy of Music since 2008. At the Institute Dr. Nemes currently lectures in Kodály's educational philosophy, teaching methods according to the Kodály Concept, and conducts the choral ensemble formed from students of the Kodály Institute. For twelve years he worked as the Associate Conductor of the Hungarian Radio Children's Choir and since September 2014 he has been artistic director of the New Liszt Ferenc Chamber Choir of the Liszt Academy. In recognition of his artistic activities, he received the Bartók-Pásztory Award. As a music pedagogue and conductor, Dr. Nemes has held workshops and master classes in four continents from Australia to South America. Since 2012 he has been guest professor and academic consultant at the Central Conservatory of Music in Beijing. László Norbert Nemes is Vice President of the International Kodály Society.

Matthew Owens is Organist and Master of the Choristers of Wells Cathedral (since 2005), Conductor of Wells Cathedral Oratorio Society, and a former President of the Cathedral Organists' Association (2010–2013). He has directed choral workshops and summer schools throughout the UK and abroad (recently in Australia, China, Germany, Hong Kong, Luxembourg, New Zealand, and the United States) and has made over 30 CDs as a conductor with major labels including Hyperion and Signum. He has conducted over 180 premieres (ranging from John Rutter to Sir Peter Maxwell Davies) and his own choral compositions are published by Oxford University Press and Novello.

Anthony Rafaniello serves as Director of Choral Activities and Advisor of the Academy of the Performing Arts at Cranford High School in Cranford, New Jersey. He maintains one of the top high school choral programs in the state, directing six ensembles and teaching Advanced Placement Music Theory. Mr. Rafaniello's students are consistently selected for state, regional, and national honor choirs. In demand as a pianist, he serves as the resident accompanist for the New Jersey All-State Mixed Chorus. Mr. Rafaniello holds degrees in music education and sacred music from Westminster Choir College, Rider University, and Teachers College, Columbia University.

Martin Ramroth is a teacher of music and English, as well as conductor and Director of Choral Activities at Landesmusikgymnasium Rheinland-Pfalz in Montabaur, Germany. His choral ensembles Mädchenchor laFilia, Kammerchor Art of the Voice, and the alumni ensemble EXtraCHORd have repeatedly won national and international awards and acclaims, including two first and three third prizes at the German National Choral Competition. He maintains an active presence as conductor, guest clinician, and adjudicator throughout Germany. His choral compositions and arrangements have been published with Bosse Verlag, Edition ferrimontana, Carus Verlag, and Santa Barbara Music Publishing.

Paul Rardin is Elaine Brown Chair of Choral Music at Temple University, where he conducts the Concert Choir, teaches graduate conducting, and oversees the seven-choir program at Temple's Boyer College of Music and Dance. He is also Artistic Director of Mendelssohn Club of Philadelphia. Rardin previously taught at the University of Michigan, where for six years he conducted the UM Men's Glee Club, and at Towson University. Rardin has served as a guest conductor for all-state choirs in 16 states, for divisional honor choirs for the ACDA and Music Educators National Conference, and for Manhattan Concert Productions at Lincoln Center, and his choirs have twice performed for ACDA division conferences.

Dennis Shrock is author of *Choral Repertoire* and *Choral Monuments* and also editor of *Choral Scores*, all published by Oxford University Press. In addition, he is author of several books for GIA, including *Performance Practices in the Baroque Era* and *Performance Practices in the Classical Era* as well as *Handel's Messiah, a Performance Practice Handbook*. He has held several faculty positions, has served as Artistic Director of the Santa Fe Desert Chorale and Canterbury Choral Society of Oklahoma City, and has given lecturers for the American Choral Directors Association and at academic institutions such as Yale University and the University of Southern California.

Mollie Spector Stone serves as the Director of World Music at Chicago Children's Choir, and the Assistant Director of Choral Activities at University of Chicago. In the summers, she teaches across the United States, Europe, and Africa with the organization Village Harmony. Ms. Stone earned her doctorate in conducting from Northwestern University, and has pursued extensive research on how black South Africans have used choral music in the struggle against HIV. Through a grant from the Henry J. Kaiser Family Foundation, Stone created teaching DVDs to help American choral directors learn black South African choral music in the oral tradition.

Jason Vodicka is Assistant Professor of Music and Coordinator of Music Education at Susquehanna University and is also Music Director of the Harrisburg (PA) Choral Society. For nine years he was a choral director at Pennsbury High School in Bucks County, Pennsylvania. His research focuses on engagement and the use of dialogue in the choral rehearsal. He holds a doctoral degree in conducting from the University of Georgia and two degrees in music education from Westminster Choir College where he is a member of the summer session faculty.

Patrice Madura Ward-Steinman is Professor of Music Education at the Indiana University Jacobs School of Music. Dr. Madura is the author, coauthor, or editor of seven books: *Getting Started with Vocal Improvisation* (1999), *Becoming a Choral Music Teacher* (2010), *Music Education in Your Hands* (with Michael Mark, 2010), *Madura's Danceland* (2010), *Advances in Social-Psychology and Music Education Research* (Ed.) (2011), *Contemporary Music Education* (with M. Mark, 2012), and *Vocal Improvisation Games for Singers and Choral Groups* (with J. Agrell, 2014.) She has published in the *Journal of Research in Music Education, Bulletin of the Council for Research in Music Education, International Journal of Music Education, Psychology of Music, Philosophy of Music Education Review, Journal of Historical Research in Music Education*, and *Choral Journal*.

Professor Graham Welch holds the UCL Institute of Education Established Chair of Music Education (since 2001). He is a Past President of ISME, (2008–2014), Chair of SEMPRE and past Co-Chair of the ISME Research Commission. He holds Visiting

Professorships at the Universities of Queensland (Australia) and Liverpool, and is a former member of the UK AHRC Review College for Music. Publications number approximately 350 and embrace musical development and music education, teacher education, the psychology of music, singing and voice science, and music in special education and disability. He is Chair of the new Paul Hamlyn Foundation National Working Group on music education in the UK from 2015.

David Westawski is the Director of Choirs at West Windsor-Plainsboro High School South, Princeton Junction, New Jersey, where he conducts four curricular choirs and three extracurricular a cappella groups. Previously, David spent 12 years at Robbinsville High School as choir director and musical director for the spring musicals. David earned his bachelor's degree in music education with a concentration in voice from Temple University and his Master of Music Education degree from Westminster Choir College. In addition to his teaching duties, David is the Director of Liturgical Music at Queen of the Universe RC Church in Levittown, PA.

John Wilson is the choral director at Bridgewater-Raritan High School where he conducts seven ensembles. His choirs have consistently received superior and first-place ratings in festivals throughout the state, earning praise most recently for performances of Gustav Holst's *Hymns from the Rig-Veda*. Mr. Wilson's ensembles have performed at major venues in the New York/New Jersey area under the baton of Ryan Brandau, Alan Raines, Lee Nelson, and Andrew Megill. John is also an Associate Director at the prestigious Princeton Girlchoir organization, where he conducts the high school-aged Cantores ensemble. During the summers of 2014 and 2015, Mr. Wilson served on the faculty at Westminster Choir College's High School Vocal Institute, where he conducted the women's choir. He will be joining the Vocal Institute faculty once again in 2016. John was also a conducting fellow at the 2014 Yale School of Music Choral Conducting Workshop, held in Norfolk, Connecticut, where he worked with Simon Carrington. In June of 2014, Mr. Wilson worked with Harold Farberman, Guillermo Figueroa, and Eduardo Navega at Bard College's Orchestral Conducting Institute. At Rutgers University, John teaches courses in music education as a part-time lecturer. In addition to his work as a teacher and conductor, John is also active as a professional singer. He has performed as a soloist in G.F. Handel's *Israel In Egypt* with the Westminster Chamber Choir and Orchestra in Princeton.

Nana Wolfe-Hill is Associate Director of Choral Activities and Assistant Professor at Wingate University where she conducts two women's choirs and teaches conducting and music education courses. She holds a Doctor of Musical Arts in choral conducting and a Master of Music in collaborative piano performance from the University of North Carolina-Greensboro, as well as a Bachelor of Music in vocal music education from St. Olaf College. Prior to her appointment at Wingate University, she conducted choirs at Lakeville High School in Minnesota, and with The Greensboro Youth Chorus in North Carolina. Currently, she is the NCACDA Repertoire and Chair for Women's Choirs.

Anthony Young is Head of Classroom and Choral Music activities at St. Laurence's College in South Brisbane, Australia, which has a strong male singing tradition, supported by 6 choirs involving 150 singers aged 10 to 17. He recently completed doctoral studies in music education at the Queensland Conservatorium Griffith University and holds a Masters in Music Studies together with degrees in law and literature. A teaching award winner, he is involved in curriculum design and assessment at the state and national level. His research has been published widely in professional and academic outlets.

THE OXFORD HANDBOOK OF

CHORAL
PEDAGOGY

INTRODUCTION

FRANK ABRAHAMS AND PAUL D. HEAD

As we, the editors and contributing authors of this volume, set off in an effort to engage our colleagues as potential contributors to a compendium on the topic of choral pedagogy, a common response was that of curiosity and intrigue.

"What do you mean, *exactly*, when you speak about the idea of choral pedagogy? Is this about teaching? About the voice? Or are you looking for scholarly research related to pressing issues such as individualized instruction, trends in standardized testing, or the perils of maintaining a choral program under the inherent burden of curriculum design in the age of the Common Core?"

A quick keyword search of the Oxford University Press database will identify over fifty volumes that are in some way related to the subject of music, with more than a half-dozen of these dedicated specifically to thoughts on teaching or making music, such as the two volumes of *The Oxford Handbook of Music Education* (McPherson & Welsh, 2012), or volumes with a broader scope such as entitled *The Oxford Handbook of Children's Musical Cultures* (Campbell & Wiggins, 2013), as well as very specific collections of essays like that defined with titles like *The Oxford Handbook of Computer Music* (Dean, 2011).

But back to the question at hand; what exactly is choral pedagogy? Is this a study of musical practice grounded in the plethora of conducting books that have been accumulating on the shelves of our conservatories and universities since World War II, or should this be a research-based endeavor where the author is charged with establishing a hierarchy of philosophical and sociological constructs that take place within the choral ensemble. If you consider recent trends in self-publication, it would be impossible to present an exhaustive survey of recent publications in even a single genre. Consider, for example the myriad of choral methods books that typically limit themselves to the more perfunctory and organizational elements of the choral program: basics in vocal production, rehearsal technique, planning tours, and dealing with administration. While these texts may dedicate a chapter or two to philosophical foundations and sociological trends, substantive discussion of such issues are beyond the scope and intent of what often become the principal resources for "training young conductors."

For those preparing to become conductors of school choirs, there are typically courses in choral methods with comprehensive curricula pertaining to establishing and maintaining a choral program, where there are multiple choirs and students earn grades and graduation credits for participation. Some of our colleagues learned to be a conductor by *participating* in a choir and mimicking the mannerisms of a particular conductor they admired. Some serve in apprentice roles to conductors of church and school choirs where they help with the routine managerial tasks as well as assist with the conducting. Perhaps they will be fortunate enough to enjoy an internship in a church as an assistant minister of music, or as a choral scholar in a community group, or at least realize their talents in the fleeting weeks of college when they student teach. At the graduate level, there exists a field of study where one can earn a master's or doctoral degree. Often these programs include opportunities where candidates combine coursework with practical experience in various types of graduate assistantships, though it is particularly noteworthy that at the graduate level, the academy makes a clear distinction between those who will become researchers, those who will focus on pedagogy, and those who will become practitioners or performers. The curricula of graduate programs have become so carefully defined that the music education student may scarcely have an opportunity to sing in a choir, while the conducting student may be completely lacking in skills related to research and publication. But are they not *all* students of choral pedagogy?

Several authors in this volume cite Patricia O'Toole's landmark article, "I Sing in a Choir But I Have 'No Voice'" (O'Toole, 2005) renowned as one of the first formal challenges to teacher-centered instruction, examining the time-honored tradition of the authoritarian, all-knowing conductor whose charge was to "train" the choir while disseminating wisdom as related to all things interpretive. But as the times have changed, and as the notion that "children should be seen and not heard" has given way in the wake more Socratic and constructivist paradigms that lend themselves to increasingly diverse populations, there have been more complex and challenging questions related to issues such as gender bias, elitism, or even basic survival skills in the age of assessment at a time when many "choral pedagogues" feel completely adrift when asked to provide evidence of achievement or measurable progress that aligns to current trends in student and teacher accountability.

In this light, choral pedagogy is an interdisciplinary field of study that includes all of the aforementioned experiences—coursework, participation in choirs as a singer, and serving as an apprentice to an established conductor. An important distinction, however, is that choral pedagogy focuses on singers and conductors who work together in a community of practice called "the choir." The field considers sociotransformative constructivist ideologies, critical pedagogies, voice pedagogy, voice science, psychology, sociology, and philosophy filtered through a lens of teaching and learning, or perhaps even more importantly, how they relate to one another in the ever-evolving realm of choral music education.

The choral landscape is changing. The traditional school, church, and community choirs that replicate works of the western canon, including new compositions by living composers, are only part of the picture. In the United States, the popularity of television shows such as *GLEE, The Voice*, and *The Sing-Off* have challenged traditionally time-honored concepts of choral tone, repertoire, and identity, while at the same time placing an emphasis on the attainment of musical experience devoid of a traditional instructor or mentor. Virtual choirs sing on the Internet and the singers never meet the conductor or each other synchronously face-to-face. Frequently, the choral performance seeks to appease the visual senses beyond the traditional auditory event, which requires many choir members to possess more than just a beautiful singing voice, but be able to move, dance, and act as well. In many venues, costumes, lighting, and stage sets are an integral part of the final performance in an attempt to reach overstimulated audiences in the age of multimedia. YouTube provides accessibility for all to see and hear multiple performances by choirs and their conductors singing in live, unedited performances of varied repertoires where even the most remote middle school choir can gain an international reputation—flattering or otherwise—almost overnight. On the technological front, the ability of an engineer to autotune sound has shaped a consumer's expectation of what is acceptable tone quality and has opened dialogue about what a choral sound should be. Conducting and teaching world music means learning to produce tone in different ways in order to be authentic when performing music that was isolated within the bounds of sustained oral traditions as recently as a generation ago.

As this volume has evolved, we are reminded again and again of the perceived chasm between the contrasting ideologies represented by our leading practitioners and our most prolific academic researchers, and the ongoing disparity within our professional organizations that suggest a lack of understanding between one camp and the other. How frequently do we encounter a graduate student who has a sudden epiphany in an educational foundations course: "I've done that for years, but I had no idea I was doing something of any pedagogical or philosophical significance. In fact, I was just doing what I remembered from high school!" What fuels this perception that musicians don't have time to give careful consideration to process, while "academics" isolate themselves from making music?

In these pages, you will find a broad spectrum of perspectives from the contributing authors. Some are renowned for their ability to internalize—or even memorize—a lengthy and complex musical score, where an intense sense of musicianship becomes the springboard to creating a highly effective educational environment. Conversely, we also have authors who have spent much of their lives focused on a single attribute of the way students learn, the way communities are formed, and the way humans disseminate information to create a transformative experience. And, of course, a few contributors live with one foot in each world, embracing a mission to close the gap between philosophy, research, and practice. Or more concisely, they are driven by the desire to create a holistic approach to choral pedagogy grounded in sound philosophical foundations that leads to heightened aesthetic experiences.

In the end, we believe it is the disparity defined by these distinctly varied approaches to scholarship that makes this volume so unique, resulting in something of a dialogue between those who see the process from the outside in, and those who approach the process inside out! Some chapters are clearly steeped in research, with numerous references related to a plethora of readings that will lead the scholar to further study, while other contributors provide historical, sociological, and contextual insights that document what will be revelatory to some, but common knowledge to others. And finally, a few other chapters unfold in the form of longitudinal or qualitative studies, providing valuable insights as to how we have arrived where we are today. This book finds its voice in amalgamation of all three perspectives.

A final thought on this topic recalls the landmark volume entitled *Choral Conducting: A Symposium* (Decker & Herford, 1973) by Harold Decker and Julius Herford; a smaller, but highly regarded collection of essays on the state of the Choral Art as it was observed in 1973. Of particular intrigue in that volume was a chapter by Howard Swan who sought to define the five schools of choral singing in America, implying a geographical organization of approaches to the choral instrument—in terms of vocal production, interpretation, and even the essence of the various choral communities. This elicits two reactions from the editors of this book, the first being that while there have been many books in recent years that have collected essays dealing mainly with methodology, we are not aware of anyone since Decker and Herford who has attempted to document the broader pedagogical state of the choral art.

But even more striking is the realization that much has changed since *Choral Conducting: A Symposium* was written, largely driven by technology that allows us to transcend previously impenetrable barriers in the search for repertoire, recordings, and even live video of choirs from all over the world with a few clicks of the mouse. Some suggest the unintended consequence of this phenomenon has been a sense of conformity as pedagogical approaches have become increasingly—if not generically—uniform, due to this global body of shared knowledge and information.

Acknowledging that all things pedagogical are also in perpetual transition, we hope this volume might serve as bookmark in the evolutionary timeline of choral artistry, which may well be of greater intrigue to future generations as an artifact of the state of the choral art in 2015, just as chapters in Decker and Herford's volume provide an invaluable glimpse into the minds of the leading pedagogues of their era.

ORGANIZATION OF THE VOLUME

Determining organizational divisions within this handbook is reflective of the complexity of defining choral pedagogy itself. Is the primary theme in the study of choral pedagogy theory or practice? The obvious answer to that question is a resounding . . . "Yes!"

It bears repeating at this juncture that even those chapters grounded in philosophical ideals find their full realization in the actuality of making music. While the essence of a volume dedicated to the philosophy of music education may well be rooted in foundational principles detached from practice, the pedagogical nature of this compendium finds commonality in the sense that all roads lead to what ultimately happens in the rehearsal room—that is, theory and practice are inextricably linked!

Acknowledging that the headings of "Theory" and "Practice" are largely arbitrary, the reader will find the chapters in the first half of the book grounded in philosophical or historical foundations that either represent the evolution of Choral Artistry as we know it today, or alternatively, challenge the paradigms of tradition in the rehearsal room. Ward-Steinman's chapter documenting the proliferation of popular choral music inspired by media productions such as *The Sing Off* and *GLEE* shakes the very foundations of choral programs built on the canon of Western European classical repertoire, but in the end, the author is forthright in the acknowledgment that while she doesn't "much care for contemporary rock music . . . [she admits that] there is no doubt that some of the contemporary commercial and a cappella music is excellent and appropriate for young singers, and therefore, deserves our attention as choral directors."

Several authors in this section present challenges to traditional rehearsal paradigms, from the pragmatic and logistical in Abraham's chapter on "Going Green" documenting that resources are transitioning from paper and pencil to iPads and Smartboards, to Head's chapter that documents the gradual transition of the authoritarian model of conductor as a benevolent dictator, to more recent phenomena such as those delineated by Ward-Steinman, where learning is student-centric, from the genesis of composition to the end product of competitive performance.

In the second subsection under Theory, several authors examine the role of personal identity within the context of the choral endeavor. These chapters are well represented in a quote from Garnett's chapter, "Choral leaders manage and guide the processes by which individuals are constituted as singers and by which groups of singers are constituted into ensembles, but the methods are only effective through the active complicity of those individuals." How often have we heard the adage, "Oh, you teach music! Well at least your students want to be there." The discussion of meaning and identity strips away the simplistic assumptions of such a statement to reveal the implicit complexities of the choral community. Additional chapters address the unique implications of working with ensembles organized on gender-based criteria, and the explicit and implicit ramifications of such decisions. Here again, we hope the reader will wrestle with the pragmatic traditions in the greater context of the underlying sociological and philosophical foundations.

The first half of the book concludes with four chapters that seek to integrate theory with cultural and historical perspective. Stone and Lakschevitz's two chapters provide fresh insights on the choral traditions of South Africa and Brazil, while Durrant and Ramroth's chapters provide a sociological context to elucidate the ever-evolving choral traditions of Western Europe. Given that many trace the genesis of most choral traditions back to the emergence of polyphony in Europe, these authors reexamine these traditions as they exist today.

While many of the authors in the first half of the handbook are active practitioners as well, the second half of this volume shifts the focus from underlying philosophical and sociological perspectives that might be best defined as "the view from the podium," or more concisely, attempts to document the state of the Choral Art in this second decade of the 21st century, as portrayed by those charged with the organization and artistic direction of ensembles on a daily basis.

On the pragmatic end of the spectrum, several authors discuss recent perspectives on repertoire, programming, and perceptions of vocal production and choral tone—all timely topics in an era where globalization has had a vast impact on choral traditions the world over. Today's young conductor can hardly comprehend the notion of multi-cultural music, but instead, has come to expect an intermingling of musical tradition where a Balinese folk song may be paired with an opera chorus, or a "new world motet" from Latin America. In the age of the iPod shuffle feature, the idea of distinct genres and ethnicities has large disappeared.

Finally, the nucleus of this section of the book consists of a collection of chapters authored by conductors with established reputations in their respective fields, ranging from college glee clubs, to professional choirs, to ensembles closely aligned with creating communities for fellowship and moral support. To this end, Charles Beale "unpacks" (his vernacular) the growing tradition of LBGTQ (Lesbian, Bisexual, Gay, Transgender, Queer) choirs, while Arreon Harley uses his program in an urban community choir as a paradigm for initiatives that provide a safe haven and a social support system for disadvantaged youth who are seeking opportunities for a better future—by singing in the choir!

Conclusions

At the risk of redundancy, the editors wish to remind the reader that the principal aim of this endeavor is to establish a point of departure in the discourse—if not the definition— of the discipline we have come to identify as choral pedagogy. As this handbook has taken shape, we are intrigued with the dance that takes place between time honored traditions that have informed the way experts rehearse their choirs, and the ongoing research related to all things philosophical, psychological, and sociological, acknowledging that the "successful choral rehearsal" is most frequently defined in terms of personal investment and engagement on the part of the participants. We want to believe that music making is life changing, and anecdotal evidence—in particular, ensemble participants coming back day after day, week after week—suggests that indeed, this is true. This volume is intended to pursue the investigation of cause and effect, practice and outcome, intended objectives and realized performance. We hope the reader will move beyond the arbitrary classification of each individual chapter and instead, embark on a journey of thoughtful contemplation when considering those chapters that grapple with the construction of identity in immediate succession to those that turn theory into practice.

Finally, we would like to reiterate that this volume is far from exhaustive or conclusive, nor should it be, nor could it be. There is much work to be done in the field of scholarly research on world perspectives; a tradition that is more often than not defined by oral tradition outside the western hemisphere. Furthermore, with broad educational reforms sweeping through communities all over the globe, discourse related to "traditional paradigms" and "identity and meaning" represents a much broader discussion pertaining to the rapid evolution of social and philosophical norms in today's global community. In the last place, we hope this handbook will encourage, inspire, or even provoke a desire for additional inquiry in the ongoing quest to define and refine the study of choral pedagogy.

REFERENCES

Campbell, P. S., & Wiggins, R. (2014). *The Oxford handbook of children's musical cultures.* New York: Oxford University Press.

Dean, R. T. (2011). *The Oxford handbook of computer music.* New York: Oxford University Press.

Decker, C., & Herford, J. (Eds.). (1973). *Choral conducting: A symposium.* New York: Meredith Corporation.

McPherson, G. E., & Welsh, G. F. (2012). *The Oxford handbook of music education* (Vols 1 & 2). New York: Oxford University Press.

O'Toole, P. (2005). I sing in a choir but "I have no voice!" *Visions of Research in Music Education, 6.* Retrieved from http://www.rider.edu/~vrme/

THEORY

PART I

CHALLENGING TRADITIONAL PARADIGMS

CHAPTER 1

....

CRITICAL PEDAGOGY AS CHORAL PEDAGOGY

....

FRANK ABRAHAMS

THE organization of the typical chorus is conductor centered. The conductor often has the autonomy to select and program repertoire, select the singers, hire the accompanist, and design the scaffolds, sequence, schema, or strategies to teach the music. During prerehearsal preparation and study, the conductor formulates an interpretation of the music and communicates that to the members of the choir throughout the rehearsal process. Critics often judge the quality of the performance on how authoritative the conductor's interpretation was and how well the singers operationalized the conductor's gestures, transforming the signals into sound.

College students learning to be conductors master the catalog of gestures and learn the skills necessary to communicate musical ideas to the singers. Nonetheless, once these are mastered, the novice conductor often replicates or reproduces the affect, warm-up exercises, and rehearsal schema they remember from their time in the choir with a conductor whom they particularly admired. Sometimes, those familiar with the novice conductor's teacher will say that the young conductor is a carbon copy of the teacher.

A survey of conducting textbooks confirms that little has changed in the ways that conductors learn their craft. That is, student conductors learn through a traditional mentor-apprentice model either in a conducting class or privately. Students preparing to be music teachers in schools or choirmasters in church often learn on the job, but find that the choirs they have are not like those they had when they were in college. The singers do not have the skills and lack the discipline to produce the quality they remember from their own background. Many beginning conductors do not handle the power that the position of conductor warrants well and the choral experience becomes about rules and procedures rather than a journey that the conductor and singers take together toward the acquisition of choral agency.

In this chapter, I posit a model that confronts traditional approaches to choral pedagogy and particularly the relationship between conductor and singer. As a prescription to combat the marginalization of singers, the pressures of politics, and the misguided and inappropriate uses and abuses of power, I suggest conductors use the tenets of critical pedagogy to inform their decisions. Best practices would include using reciprocal teaching and rehearsal strategies that focus on opportunities for conductors and singers to collaborate in ways that enable constructivist practice, singer and conductor agency, and each individual in the group, including the conductor, acquiring a critical consciousness.

ORIGINS OF CRITICAL PEDAGOGY

Critical pedagogy is a perspective on teaching and learning that emerged from a postmodern philosophy called critical theory. This ideology originated in Germany during the 1920s at the New School for Social Research in Frankfurt. There, Fromm, Adorno, Horkeimer, Marcuse, Lowenthal, Pollack, and Weber developed theories that challenged the accepted sources and solutions to the ills of contemporary society (Giroux, 1983; McLaren, 2003). As a group, they were influenced by the writings of Marx on social transformation and Kant on personal critique, as well as Hegel's philosophical perspective relative to the emergence of spirit. The theorists also considered the work of Freud in psychology and socialist suppositions (Abrahams, 2004).

In the 1960s, Paulo Freire (1970) applied the principles of critical theory to education when he began teaching the illiterate of Brazil to read. He believed that students came to learning experiences with knowledge they gleaned from their own life experiences. Freire used that knowledge as a bridge to new learning. Most significantly, he shifted from the traditional paradigm of teacher as the only source of knowledge and information, whose responsibility it was to fill the tabula rasa of the student, to one where teacher and student worked together to co-construct new knowledge. This was quite controversial in Brazil.

While Freire may or may not have known of Dewey's work in the United States in the early part of the 20th century or Vygotsky's theories applied in Russia during the 1930s and 1940s, his ideas were consistent with constructivist strategies (Vygotsky, 1978, 1986), use of generative themes (Bruner, 1966), and democratic practice (Dewey, 1916/ 2005). Freire's students learned from each other, and the teacher learned from the students as well.

Freirean pedagogy has been applied to many learning domains. There are examples in language literacy (Billmeyer, 2003; Palincsar & Brown, 1984), in mathematics (Gutstein, 2005) in theatre (Boal, 1993) as well as other disciplines. There are five tenets in critical pedagogy for music education (Abrahams, 2005):

1. Education is a conversation where students and their teachers pose and solve problems together. Teaching from the principles of critical pedagogy includes dialogue, discussion, and conversation. While this is sometimes problematic in choir, as students want to sing in rehearsal and do not wish to talk, it is possible to have such conversations in an online discussion board outside the rehearsal.

Sometimes these conversations are better outside the rehearsal because students have time to be thoughtful in responding. In addition, every single member of the choir has an equal opportunity to respond. Within the confines of the rehearsal period, only a few may be recognized to offer a response. Vodicka (2009) confirmed that students were interested in having a dialogue and not just singing. He found that in his high school choir

students were eager to renegotiate the roles of student and teacher in the classroom, preferring to have a more active role in the creation of knowledge. They articulated a need for teachers to honor students' worlds, basing classroom materials and activities in students' actual lives in order to stimulate interest and create meaning. This was carried out most often through dialogue, which . . . was also effective in teaching musical skills. (p. viii)

2. Education broadens the student's view of reality. For critical pedagogy, the goal of teaching and learning is to change the way that both students and their teachers perceive the world. Sometimes this happens as students acquire agency. For Dewey (1916/2005) an agentive person was "one who is "bound up with what is going on: its outcome makes a difference to him or her" . . . [and] implies interest and ownership of the outcomes; people who act with personal agency act with concern, interest, aims, purpose, intent and motivation (Dewey, pp. 124–125, as cited in Blair, 2009, p. 179). Freire (1973), although he did not use the term "agency," called this the acquisition of a critical consciousness. This connects to the next critical pedagogy tenet.

3. Education is empowering. Such empowerment comes when singers are able to construct meaning on their own and can navigate the scaffolds and schema that are part of the conductor's rehearsal planning. As mentioned above, this fosters the acquisition of a critical consciousness or agency.

4. Education is transformative. For conductors using a critical pedagogy approach, learning takes place when both the conductors and the students can acknowledge a change in perception. It is this change or transformation that teachers can assess. For the choir, this happens during the rehearsal process and in the moments of the performance. In 2009, Vodicka studied the efficacy of choral pedagogy as the pedagogical framework for his high school choral program. He discovered that as students became more agentive and could self-identify their own musical strengths and weaknesses, their "perceptions of the group improved dramatically and the group dynamic as a whole greatly changed for the better" (p. vii). In Silvey's (2005) study on the types of knowledge gained through learning Benjamin Britten's *Rejoice in the Lamb*, high school students found that by interacting meaningfully with this piece of music a transformation occurred. They began to see themselves as interacting with the score (connecting word to world) and becoming personally a part of its performance.

5. Education is political. There are issues of power and control inside the classroom, the rehearsal hall, inside the school building, and inside the community. Those in power make decisions about what is taught, how often choirs meet, how much

money is allocated to each school subject or program, and so forth. Those who teach the critical pedagogy model resist the constraints that those in power place on them. They do this first in their own classrooms and rehearsals by acknowledging that children come to class with knowledge they gain from the outside world, which knowledge needs to be honored and valued.

ISSUES OF CRITICAL PEDAGOGY

Issues of marginalization and "othering"

High on the agenda of critical pedagogues is a concern for the equity of sexes and the unfair treatment of minorities. That inequality and unfair treatment results in marginalizing specialized groups and othering, or excluding, those that are not part of the dominant group, which is the one in power. Issues of conductors privileging men over women or repertoire by men over women are discussed in the literature (see O'Toole 1993–1994, 1998). One clear example is the assumption that all students celebrate Christmas and therefore repertoire that represents other religious practices is not present on December holiday concerts (Abrahams, 2009). As a high school teacher, I clearly remember having the ability to send an unlimited number of young men to audition for specialized festival choirs, but restricted to a small number of sopranos and altos, usually young women. Thus it was not unusual for a young man of limited talent and potential to be selected for such groups when young women of considerably more ability were not even allowed to audition. O'Toole (1998) found that the national average for girls to boys auditioning for honor choirs is 4 to 1. O'Toole's research exposed these inequities, noting a bias in the way male conductors cause young women to doubt their self-worth by enacting choral policies that sort students inequitably. Many of us know instances if the number of singers exceeds the space on stage, it is often the sopranos and altos who are eliminated or "excused" from the performance. Such examples of hegemonic practice among choral directors are common. While such situations are not obvious issues of pedagogy, they contribute to an unspoken hidden curriculum that favors one sex over another and one voice part over another. When these practices influence decisions by conductors relative to who sings and who does not and who composes the literature to be studied, they are indeed issues of pedagogy and specifically critical pedagogy.

Males feel just as marginalized, but often by their peers who tease them and challenge their masculinity (Abrahams, 2012). Demorest (2000) investigated male participation in chorus and found that boys did not like the repertoire choices and did not have experience listening to male choral singers. Mullaney (2011) and Freer (2007) studied the theory of possible selves as a remedy for the missing males. Missing males, in particular, was the topic of research by Koza (1993). Others (Siebenaler, 2006) looked at the need males have for positive support. Seminal studies by Adler (2002, 2005), Harrison (2001, 2003), and Harrison, Welch and Adler (2012) provide a wealth of research on the topic.

Issues of power

Power is the ability to control or influence others in a particular way. It may result in causing or preventing a particular action. Regelski (2005) suggested that accepting authority without questioning is a natural desire of the human psyche. In fact, when the dominant class controls, shapes and manipulates the beliefs of subordinate groups to ensure that dominant views become common-sense and taken for granted it is known as hegemony.

The choral rehearsal presents a unique set of problems as the choral experience is usually focused on repertoire rather than a specific skill set. Since each piece the choir sings presents its own unique challenges, no one size fits all. For some ensemble conductors, the performance is the be all and end all of the choral experience. Learn the notes, sing the rhythms, unify the vowels, tune the chords, and spin the phrase. For those conductors, typical or traditional routines and procedures work well.

Those who advocate critical pedagogy are concerned with those issues, too, but also have a concern for the ways in which the choral experience adds value to the singer's life. Allsup (2003) pointed out that the issues of power become especially apparent when determining which music to sing and warns conductors not to impose the dominance of one culture over another. Shor (1992) criticized traditional educators for presenting a canon of works not as historical choices of the privileged, but as "universal, excellent, and neutral" (p. 32). Vodicka (2009) suggested that it was in critically analyzing, by the conductor, of the systems of political power inherent in the structure of school and in the texts choir members were singing that critical pedagogy was engaged.

Writing about the ways conductors abuse their power, Patricia O'Toole crafted several thought provoking articles (1993–1994, 1998) that examined the role of the male conductor from a feminist perspective. In "I Sing in a Choir but I Have 'No Voice'" (1993–1994), she discussed the unpleasant experiences she had as a member of a chorus where the conductor believed he was the all-knowing leader and used intimidation to motivate the female singers, who he thought to be intellectually challenged. She criticized the traditional notion that it was the mixed choir of soprano, alto, tenor, and bass that was the preferred model, especially in schools, and argued for the choir of female voices to replace that paradigm. She abhorred the practice of privileging the male singers, because they were fewer in number, to ensure a high-quality performance. Citing Foucault as her philosophical framework, she unpacked the traditional model of conductor and chorister in thought-provoking ways.

Vodicka (2009) noted, "In public school performance-based ensembles, education is usually limited to skill-building and rote learning a limited number of selections for a concert with very little critical thinking ever taking place" (p. 2). Authoritarian conductors, albeit unintentionally, may inhibit a singer's ability to think critically. Vodicka wrote:

> School-age musicians have little reason to think critically; often, they blindly follow the artistic intentions and motives of a director who unknowingly brings their own

biases to the process. Because critical thinking is not taking place, true learning that goes beyond rote learning is not taking place. Further, because student interaction is so severely limited, students are not able to construct meaning as part of a social structure. (p. 2)

In September of 2011, Aaron Peisner, an undergraduate at Wesleyan University, organized a group of 22 volunteers to sing in a choir as part of his senior honors thesis. His goal was to investigate the efficacy of critical pedagogy by changing the traditional power structures of conductor and singer and establishing a spirit of democracy and dialogue. He hoped to give each member of the ensemble an equal opportunity to contribute to the musical decisions that would influence the preparation and performance of the repertoire. In his own reflection after the concert he wrote:

> Before singing through a new piece of music, I would ask the singers to scan the music and discuss sections that looked tricky with the people standing next to them. After first reading through a new piece of music, I would tell the singers to find a space with their sections to work on their notes. Sometimes after running through a song, I would ask the singers to take a few minutes to go over their mistakes with the people next to them, and surely enough, they often sang their parts correctly the next time. The group learned the music quickly and sounded fantastic. Throughout the rehearsal process, I made sure to ask the singers questions about how they thought we sounded, or people had suggestions for solving particular problems. Inviting them to share their opinions established a rehearsal environment that was open to dialogue.
>
> Listening to the recording of the show a few weeks later, I was struck by how wonderful the choir sounded. . . . I was proud, as were all the singers in the group. Being able to contribute to the rehearsal process led to a sense of ownership of the music and camaraderie among the singers. Many of the singers in the group tell me that singing in my thesis choir was one of their greatest musical experiences at Wesleyan, and I am convinced that . . . the collaborative rehearsal process played a crucial role in enhancing the overall experience. (Peisner, 2011, pp. 11–21)

The Orpheus Chamber Ensemble is one of the few professional ensembles—except for groups like the King's Singers or instrumental trios, quartets, and groups of similar size—that applies the ideas of critical pedagogy, and particularly that of shifting power and applying democratic practice. Founded in 1972 by cellist Julian Fifer, the goal of the Orpheus Chamber Ensemble is to bring democracy, personal involvement, and mutual respect into an orchestral setting. As Fifer said, "In order for everyone to be able to communicate more effectively, it seemed necessary to do without a conductor" (Seifter, 2001, ¶3). In place of a conductor, Orpheus applies a system of collaborative leadership that provides opportunity for each member to participate in decision making and management.

Instead of focusing solely on perfecting his or her own approach to performance, each musician takes a personal interest in perfecting the performances of their colleagues and the overall sound of the orchestra. It is therefore not uncommon for a violinist to comment on the playing of a flutist or the timpani player to comment on a cellist's approach to phrasing or bowing. In an orchestra with a regular conductor, not only would such crossing of organizational lines be unwelcome, it would be unthinkable. As cellist Eric Bartlett stated:

> When there's an important concert, everybody feels it, and everybody goes into it doing their absolute best work, giving it their utmost concentration, playing off of each other, and making sparks fly. For the most part, in a conducted orchestra, you play a more passive role. Not only is less expected *of* you, but less is expected *from* you. You have to play extremely well, but you're not playing off of your colleagues— you're playing off of that one person in front of the orchestra holding the baton. I don't see that people in regular orchestras are emotionally involved in the same way. Everybody plays well, they do a very good job, but the level of individual emotional involvement isn't there. (Seifter, 2001, ¶ 7)

Seifter (2001) concludes:

> With no conductor to act as a filter to the *what* and the *why* behind the group's decisions, the members of Orpheus are uncommonly energized and responsive to the needs of the organization and to the desires of its leaders. Turnover is extremely low, and employee loyalty is extremely high. The result is a better product, increased customer satisfaction, and a healthier bottom line. (¶ 8)

Issues of politics

The issues of politics become apparent in choosing literature. Allsup (2003) suggested that while the music of diverse cultures might be worthy of study, he cautioned that such a decision must be made by carefully considering the political ramifications of privileging one culture over another. Including high art in the curriculum can be either an effort to control culture or an effort to "uplift and transform" depending on the analysis of power that supports it (Allsup, 2003, p. 8).

To provide support for conductors, Ryan John and I (2015) provided a template for building collaboration, creativity, critical thinking, and communication into rehearsals by engaging choral singers in many aspects of the artistic processes of creating, performing, and responding. Included were many sample objectives choral teachers might consider when designing their curriculum so that they could balance the criteria of their own evaluation with the goals for their students that a critical pedagogy approach would advocate (see Abrahams & John, 2015).

To consider the issue of politics from a different angle, in recent years the evaluation of teachers has been a high priority of schools in the United States. In many states, teachers, including school choral teachers, must set objectives that measure student growth and learning. A primary condition of a teacher's continued employment is that students meet those objectives. While there are different models of teacher evaluation among states (Danielson, 2013; Marzano & Toth, 2013), teachers are held accountable for the performance of their students. This causes concern for advocates of critical pedagogy and alarm for the conductors of school choirs. Many fear that if they share their power as conductor with the singers by collaborating on issues of musical interpretation, or empowering them to learn things on their own or construct their own meanings, there is a chance that the students may not meet the preset objective, thus affecting the ability of the conductor to receive a positive evaluation. If the authorities that assess the conductor's work do not support the tenets of critical pedagogy, that could significantly disadvantage the conductor. Thus the conductor is faced with an ethical dilemma.

Issues of agency

Apfelstadt (1989) stated that if the teacher is always the one responsible for making decisions in the choral rehearsal, the students become like mindless drones that have no reason to utilize independent thought or critical thinking. It is important that students not only make decisions in the rehearsal, but that they realize they are involved and acting critically. Students need, Apfelstadt believed, a chance to make decisions on their own and to take ownership for their own music making. That, she claimed, would foster their becoming self-sufficient or agentive musicians. One way to develop these traits in student-musicians is through collaborative work. This collaboration can take place on many levels, but probably the most important for critical pedagogy is between the singers and the conductor.

While a comprehensive review of textbooks on conducting and rehearsal technique is beyond the scope of this chapter, most of the historical textbooks (e.g., Rudolf, 1950) and iconic textbooks (e.g., Green, 1961) focus on the conductor's gestures and comment on musicianship, leadership, and motivational skills. Unfortunately, most do not address collaboration with the ensemble members in ways that this chapter suggests. However, Rudolf did acknowledge the role of conductor as teacher when he wrote:

> If education is the art of opening people's minds, then the conductor's function in rehearsal must be called educational, not in the sense of formal teaching but of bringing to the fore all the best qualities latent in his musicians. To accomplish this he must be regarded by his group as *primus inter pares* [first among equals]. (Rudolf, 1950, p. 392)

Lisk (2006) developed Rudolf's statement further. In his conducting text, he discussed the importance of the musical mind and suggested a method of teaching that encouraged students to "ask thoughtful questions and make responsible decisions" (p. 19). He quoted Frank Wilson, a neurologist, who wrote:

> Your training in music must from the very beginning deliberately guide you toward the goal of making your own independent judgments about the quality of your

playing. There is a serious threat to your growth if this does not occur because if someone with greater knowledge must always approve your interpretation, your music ultimately can only be imitative. If this happens, you've missed the boat! (p. 18)

While Lisk is not a critical pedagogue, he did recognize the importance of students constructing meaning on their own and discussed the importance of conductors providing opportunities for them to make their own musical decisions, believing that such decision making nurtured musical independence.

One of the most prolific writers in choral music is James Jordan (2007, 2008; Holt & Jordan, 2008). An analysis reveals that the texts are a compendium of prescriptions to solve various vocal or choral issues as they manifest themselves in the rehearsal process. Most are written from the perspective of the conductor and what he or she might do to provide a remedy when such problems or musical situations when they appear.

However, in his two-volume text on the choral rehearsal (2007, 2008), he invited colleagues to author several chapters. Eugene Migliaro Corporon is one author who contributed to Jordan's text *The Choral Rehearsal: Volume 2—Inward Bound*. In a chapter titled "The Quantum Conductor" he wrote:

> The simplified goal of the rehearsal is to "transfer ownership" from you to your singers. The idealized goal of the rehearsal is to discover how a piece works—the goal is not to fix problems. The discovery process will expose problems, which in truth, can only be solved by the singers. You can facilitate that process by offering solutions. Your singers must take the action to implement the change that is the only way to improve. It is important to understand that the rehearsal is the place to do the work together that cannot be done alone. (Corporon in Jordan, 2008, p. 189)

While it is doubtful Corporon identifies himself as a critical pedagogue, the desires to transfer ownership, to problematize the issues in the music, and to find solutions through dialogue and discourse with the singers are consistent with the tenets of critical pedagogy. However, this is rare. The authors of most texts discuss techniques such as engaging the singers by using various motivational techniques, pacing the rehearsal so that singers remain focused and connected, and adopting a charismatic aura (see Boonshaft, 2002, 2006, 2009 as typical examples).

CRITICAL PEDAGOGY IN THE REHEARSAL

I have found that several rehearsal strategies, adapted from the literature on language literacy have been effective pedagogical tools with adolescents singing in school choirs. These strategies empower students to contribute to the rehearsal as individuals and in groups and are consistent with the principles of critical pedagogy. In short, they become agentive and able to use their agency to foster their own musical learning.

Reciprocal teaching

With the overall goal of fostering agency and the acquisition of a critical consciousness among singers, I developed several strategies to engage students in the decision making and construction of meaning inside the choral rehearsal. One involved adapting the strategies of reciprocal teaching. Palincsar and Brown (1986) developed the strategies at the University of Michigan to assist teachers as they help children find meaning in the literature they were reading. The strategies are predicting, questioning, clarifying, and summarizing. It is reciprocal in that both teachers and students apply the strategies. Both ask questions of each other. Sometimes students provide the clarifying explanations or answers and sometimes students engage in the summarizing.

In music education, Daniel Abrahams (F. Abrahams & D. Abrahams, 2012) used reciprocal teaching to help his high school band students find the musical meanings in the scores they were playing. As a result, he added connecting to the list of strategies. Consistent with the research, he found that the strategies of reciprocal teaching promoted the characteristics of critical consciousness and promoted critical thinking, collaboration, creativity, and communication—components of "21st Century Skills" (Partnership for 21st Century Skills, n.d.).

With Daniel Abrahams (F. Abrahams & D. Abrahams, 2012), I used reciprocal teaching to help students in choir and band construct meaning of the musical line and form in the compositions they were singing and playing. By engaging the ensemble members in conversations that included predicting, questioning, clarifying, summarizing, and connecting, we both found that our students gained a deep understanding of the inherent artistic processes embedded in the music, and that brought about a more sophisticated performance. Such a deep understanding is a critical element of what Freire (1973) described as a critical consciousness. For those who advocate critical pedagogy, the acquisition of a critical consciousness is a goal of education.

In 2010, I applied reciprocal teaching in a high school honors choir I was conducting in the community music school affiliated with my college. To better prepare the students to sing *Three Russian Folksongs* by Rachmaninoff with the Community Orchestra, I developed ways to engage the students in the five elements of the reciprocal process. Throughout the rehearsal period, I used many of the rehearsal strategies above as we posed and solved musical problems together. This was consistent with Freire (1970) who wrote, "Students, as they are increasingly posed with problems relating to themselves in the world and with the world, will feel increasingly challenged and obliged to respond to that challenge" (p. 81). Knowledge is therefore not kept theoretical or objective but made real and consequential through problem-posing education.

Sometimes the singers called attention to the challenges inherent in the music, and at other times I asked clarifying questions or requested students to summarize what we had learned together at the end of each rehearsal. When dealing with musical issues— which included intonation, Russian diction, rhythmic precision, and so forth—they suggested solutions and contributed ideas based on their own knowledge of singing and of choral technique, and I suggested prescriptive measures based on mine. For example, singers discussed what the tempo should be on the middle section. Each student offered an idea of what it should be and why. In the end, it was clear that most felt a brisk tempo would work best. On their own, students investigated Rachmaninoff and listened to his symphonies, concertos, solo piano works, and other choral works, most notably *The Bells,* to acquire a sense of his compositional style and to find consistencies in his style across his compositional output. This is an example of how students constructed new knowledge, and they shared that information on individual blog entries they posted on a choir discussion board online. I read each posting and made a comment, asked for clarification, or posed a question. In the end, I found that, like Daniel Abrahams, students knew the work more thoroughly than other pieces we prepared; there was a level of critical consciousness demonstrated in the vocabulary students used in their blogs and when discussing various issues in rehearsal. In addition, I found that the strategies of reciprocal teaching engaged students in creating, performing, responding, and connecting (National Coalition for Core Arts Standards, 2014), although they had not been developed at the time of the study. Looking now at the benchmarks and rubrics for those standards, the Rachmaninoff project, rich with reciprocal teaching, would have enabled singers in the choir to meet the rubrics and assessments that are embedded in the National Core Arts Standards document.

From the perspective of critical pedagogy, the Rachmaninoff project addressed all the tenets of critical pedagogy. The experience empowered musicianship (tenet 3). It broadened students' view of reality (tenet 2) in that through the reciprocal teaching strategies they came to understand the piece in the context of Rachmaninoff's compositional output and the social conditions in Russia described in the texts of the three folk songs. Since the texts dealt with infidelity and spousal abuse, there were opportunities for discussions that centered on how we all felt about such issues as the subject of an artistic statement by a recognized and respected composer. We talked about whether the texts made the pieces inappropriate choices for the choir to sing (tenet 4). Issues of politics (tenet 5) within the context of the songs and within the context of our own performing them became topics that evoked impassioned dialogue, discussion, and responses from the students (tenet 1). Should we be singing about such things in choir?

General rehearsal strategies

What Would You Do? While preparing college students or members of a community choir to perform the choral finale of Beethoven's *Symphony No. 9,* the conductor might ask singers to consider the order of the sections in the final movement. She or he might pose the question, "Would the piece be stronger if Beethoven had ended with the fugue, instead of the material he chose?" Using audio editing software, interested singers might reorder the sections and consider the impact. In the end, I suspect they will decide that Beethoven made the right choice, but perhaps not. Engaging singers in this type of problem solving and discourse is typical of activities one finds in rehearsals informed by the ideas from critical pedagogy.

Circle All Around. In this strategy, the chairs in each section are arranged in two circles—one outer and one inner—so that students in each circle face each other. This forms a partnership of two. Together, and informally, each set of partners scans the music to identify rehearsal or performance challenges and brainstorms a solution together. They predict those issues they may encounter that might hinder the group's performance. The conductor then asks representatives of the group to clarify their issues and summarize the solutions. Asking probing questions, the conductor helps the group to connect the issue, the solution, and the music. Then, when the group sings the music, students check their predictions against the reality of what happens. A brief discussion follows. In some instances, there is need for refocusing, refining, and remediating, which the conductor moderates. The Circle All Around strategy empowers musicianship and allows each singer to accept ownership and responsibility for ensuring that musical challenges are identified and conquered. Sometimes the conductor also identifies challenges, but after presenting the challenge, calls on students to suggest remedies. Individuals are often asked what they will do specifically to make something better. The strategy engages problem posing, problem solving, and dialoguing, which are key strategies in a critical pedagogy environment.

That's Me. I use this strategy whenever there is a musical theme that moves from one part to another. When a section of singers have the theme, they stand to sing. Sometimes I will have the accompanist play the choral parts and singers jump up when they have the theme and proclaim, "That's me!" This engages critical listening and helps singers see the form and texture of the piece. At times, I use a recording for students to listen to. From a lens of critical pedagogy, it fosters musical independence or empowerment.

Catch Me Being Good. This is a strategy for motivation and encourages student input. As the choir sings, I walk through the rows of singers and find the "best" singer in each section. They collaborate with the conductor to judge an activity called *So You Think You Can Sing.* This strategy compliments students, showing them that they are valued as individuals and not merely members of a larger group. Honoring the individuality of singers is a principle of critical pedagogy philosophy.

So You Think You Can Sing. I select four judges from the choir to listen with the conductor as the entire choir, or a particular section of the choir, sings. Each judge must give a positive and a negative criticism and suggest a remedy to make the negative into a positive. This engages critical listening and higher order thinking. This strategy fosters singer agency and engages critical consciousness. As mentioned earlier in this chapter, the acquisition of a critical consciousness was a goal Freire (1973) identified as significant in the development of his students.

In 2009 Vodicka, as part of a study about using critical pedagogy as the curricular framework, taught his high school choir to sing Schubert's *Mass in G major.* Throughout the process, he asked students to keep a personal journal that included their own goals for rehearsals, processed their feelings, self-assessed their progress, and analyzed their daily performance. Instead of teaching the notes by rote, his usual practice, he required them to learn the notes independently. They had to find ways to do that. The students decided to organize themselves into four teams to help each other with the challenges of mastering the pitches and rhythms. Vodicka wrote,

> It was surprising to me to see the level of musicianship displayed by each of the four groups. The intelligent musical conversation occurring within each group was like nothing I had ever seen from these students. I was unaware that they were capable of working in this way. Pounding out notes on the piano year after year had not allowed the students to engage in higher-level thinking. Working in that manner had not allowed me to assess what the students comprehended about the music. My initial reaction was frustration. Why had these musically intelligent students not been using all of their knowledge and talent in every rehearsal? I quickly realized that it was because I had simply never asked them to. (p. 59)

Because of the study, Vodicka (2009) found that applying critical pedagogy as the curricular framework to be a positive experience. He noted that the choir's overall musicianship improved, that students were more motivated and connected with the Schubert mass in ways that suggested musical agency, and they acquired a critical consciousness. This also fostered the abilities of the choir members to meet the expectations of the 21st Century Learning and Innovation Skills (Partnership for 21st Century Skills, n.d.) of collaboration, communication, creativity, and critical thinking. Vodicka attributes the application of the tenets of critical pedagogy to his success and the successes of his singers.

Conclusion

Critical pedagogy is a perspective that informs the ways conductors think about the choral rehearsal and school choral program. To implement the perspective, conductors must be willing to release from their routine practice many of the time-honored and traditional paradigms that have long been associated with the responsibilities of the conductor and the expectations both conductors and singers have for each other. The conductor needs considerable confidence in his or her musicianship and a belief in the potentials of the singers to be able to do this. Research shows, however, that adopting critical pedagogy as the framework for decision making yields positive results. These include the acquisition of a critical consciousness, the ability to create meaningful teaching and learning experiences, and the attainment of agency.

Critical pedagogy is sometimes called radical pedagogy and a pedagogy of resistance. When it frames the choral pedagogy, it opens choral experiences to the opportunities of transformative teaching and sensitizes everyone to the negative issues of power, marginalization, hegemonic practice, and political issues that constrain the artistic processes of creating, performing, and responding and inhibit the artistic spirit from reaping the benefits of choral singing it their fullest. What follows is a template to aid conductors when they plan a rehearsal.

Ensemble Rehearsal Plan

Title of Piece: _____

Conductor's name: _____   Ensemble name: _____

Composer/arranger: _____   Grade of Piece: _____

Learning Goals

What Learners will . . .

Be able to do (behavioral):

Understand (cognitive):

Encounter (experiential):

Construct meaning (constructivist):

Technical Skills (intonation, posture, breath, phonation, balance, bowing for strings, stick-ing for percussion, diction for singers)

Musical Concepts (*melody, rhythm, harmony, form, timbre, texture*)

Empowering Musicianship (*historical perspective, stylistic integrity, musical artistry*)

Ensemble Rehearsal Plans

Process

Partner: (Differentiate instruction by collaborating with ensemble members predicting the performance challenges. Pose problems and brainstorm solutions together. Encourage students to respond.)

Present: *(Sequence of the rehearsal steps. Present the steps to scaffold and allow time for students to practice independently on their own. Differentiate instruction through* questioning, clarifying, summarizing, *and* connecting.)

Personalize: (Make the learning personal to the students. Provide opportunities for ensemble members and their conductor to collaborate as musicians to create a musical experience and "add value" to their lives.)

Perform: (Demonstrate teaching music when students perform.)

Assessment

Formative

Summative

Integrative

From: Abrahams, F., & John R. (2015). *Planning instruction in music: Writing objectives, assessments, and lesson plans to engage artistic processes.* Chicago, GIA (pp. 182–183).

REFERENCES

Abrahams, F. (2004). The application of critical theory to a sixth grade general music class [Electronic Version]. *Visions of Research in Music Education*, 6. Retrieved from http://www-usr.rider.edu/~vrme/

Abrahams, F. (2005). Transforming classroom music instruction with ideas from critical pedagogy. *Music Educators Journal* 92(1), 62–67.

Abrahams, F. (2009). Hosanna, Hanukah, and hegemony: Anti-Semitism in the music classroom. In E. Gould, J. Countryman, C. Morton, & L. S. Rose (Eds.), *Exploring social justice: How music education might matter* (pp. 325–342). Toronto: Canadian Music Educators' Association.

Abrahams, F. (2012). Changing voices-voices of change: Young men in middle school choirs. In S. D. Harrison, G. F. Welch, & A. Adler (Eds.), *Perspectives on males and singing* (pp. 79–94). New York, NY: Springer.

Abrahams, F., & Abrahams, D. (2012). The impact of reciprocal teaching on the development of musical understanding in high school student members of performing ensembles: An action research. In K. Swanwick (Ed.), *Music education: Major themes in education: Vol. 3* (pp. 239–259). New York, NY: Routledge.

Abrahams, F., & John, R. (2015). *Planning instruction in music: Writing objectives, assessments and lesson plans to engage artistic processes*. Chicago, IL: GIA.

Adler, A. (2002). A case study of boys' experiences of singing in school. Abstract of unpublished doctoral dissertation. Retrieved from http://post.queensu.ca/~grime/v11n1.html

Adler, A. (2005, September). Let the boys sing and speak: Masculinities and boys' stories of singing in school. Keynote address for the Boys and Voices Symposium, Melbourne, Australia.

Allsup, R. E. (2003). Transformational education and critical music pedagogy: Examining the link between culture and learning. *Music Education Research*, 5(1), 5–12.

Apfelstadt, H. (1989). Musical thinking in the choral rehearsal. In E. Boardman (Ed.), *Dimensions of musical thinking* (pp. 73–82). Reston, VA: Music Educators National Conference.

Billmeyer, R. (2003). *Strategies to engage the mind of the learner*. Omaha, NE: Dayspring Printing.

Blair, D. V. (2009). Learner agency: To understand and to be understood. *British Journal of Music Education*, 26(2), 173–187.

Boal. A. (1993). *Theatre of the oppressed* (C. A. McBride, Trans.). New York, NY: Theatre Communications Group.

Boonshaft, P. L. (2002). *Teaching music with passion: Conducting, rehearsing and inspiring*. Galesville, MD: Meredith Music Publications.

Boonshaft, P. L. (2006). *Teaching music with purpose: Conducting, rehearsing and inspiring*. Galesville, MD: Meredith Music Publications.

Boonshaft, P. L. (2009). *Teaching music with promise: Conducting, rehearsing and inspiring*. Galesville, MD: Meredith Music Publications.

Bruner, J. (1966). *Toward a theory of instruction*. New York, NY: W. W. Norton.

Corporon, E. M. (2008). The quantum conductor. In J. Jordan (Ed.), *The choral rehearsal: Vol. 2: Inward bound* (pp. 175–204). Chicago, IL: GIA.

Danielson, C. (2013) *Enhancing professional practice: A framework for teaching* (2nd ed.). Princeton, NJ: Danielson Group.

Demorest, S. M. (2000). Encouraging male participation in chorus. *Music Educators Journal*, 86(4), 38–41.

Dewey, J. (2005). *Democracy and education.* New York, NY: Barnes & Noble Books. (Original work published 1916.)

Freer, P. K. (2007). Between research and practice: How choral music loses boys in the "middle." *Music Educators Journal, 94*(2), 28–34.

Freire, P. (1970). *Pedagogy of the oppressed.* New York: Continuum.

Freire, P. (1973). *Education for critical consciousness.* New York: Continuum.

Giroux, H. A. (1983). *Theory and resistance in education: A pedagogy for the opposition.* South Hadley, MA: Bergin and Garvey.

Green, E. A. H. (1961). *The modern conductor: A college text on conducting based on the principles of Dr. Nicolai Malko as set forth in his* The Conductor and his Baton. Englewood Cliffs, NJ: Prentice-Hall.

Gutstein, E. (2005). *Reading and writing the world with mathematics: Toward a pedagogy of social justice.* New York, NY: Routledge.

Harrison, S. (2001). *Why boys limit musical choices.* GRIME Newsletters. Retrieved from http://post.queensu.ca/~grime/v1on1.html

Harrison, S. (2003). *Musical participation by boys: The role of gender in the choice of musical activities by males in Australian schools* (Unpublished doctoral dissertation), Griffith University, Australia.

Harrison, S. D., Welch, G. F., & Adler, A (Eds.). (2012). *Perspectives on males and singing.* New York, NY: Springer.

Holt, M., & Jordan, J. (2008). *The school choral program: Philosophy, planning, organizing, and teaching.* Chicago, IL: GIA.

Jordan, J. (2007). *Evoking sound—the choral rehearsal: Techniques and procedures.* Chicago: GIA.

Jordan, J. (2008). *Evoking sound—the choral rehearsal: Inward bound, philosophy and score preparation.* Chicago: GIA.

Koza, J. (1993). The "missing males" and other gender issues in music education: Evidence from the *Music Supervisors' Journal,* 1914–1924. *Journal of Research in Music Education, 41*(3), 212–232.

Lisk, E. S. (2006). *The creative director: Conductor, teacher, leader.* Galesville, MD: Meredith Music Publications.

Marzano, R. J., & Toth, M. D. (2013). *Teacher evaluation that makes a difference: A new model for teacher growth and student achievement.* Alexandria, VA: Association for Supervision & Curriculum Development.

McLaren, P. (2003). *Life in schools: An introduction to critical pedagogy in the foundations of education* (4th ed.). New York, NY: Allyn and Bacon.

Mullaney, T. W. (2011). *The impact of critical pedagogy on the development of possible musical selves in middle school male choral singers: A case study* (Unpublished master's thesis). Westminster Choir College of Rider University, Princeton, NJ.

National Coalition for Core Arts Standards. (2014). National Core Arts Standards. Retrieved from http://nccas.wikispaces.com/.

O'Toole, P. (1993–1994). I sing in a choir but I have "no voice!" *The Quarterly, (4–5),* pp. 65–76. Retrieved from http://www-usr.rider.edu/~vrme/

O'Toole, P. (1998). A missing chapter from choral methods books: How choirs neglect girls. *Choral Journal, 39*(5), 9–31.

Palincsar, A. S., & Brown, A. L. (1984) Reciprocal teaching of comprehension-fostering and comprehension-monitoring activities. *Cognition and Instruction 1*(2), 117–175.

Palincsar, A. S., & Brown, A. L. (1986). Interactive teaching to promote independent learning from text. *The Reading Teacher, 39*(8), 771–777.

Partnership for 21st Century Skills. (n.d.). Framework for 21st century learning. http://www.p21.org/about-us/p21-framework

Peisner, A. (2011). *Between order and chaos: An exploration of power dynamics and democratic rehearsal techniques in school choirs* (Unpublished undergraduate thesis). Wesleyan University, Middletown, CT.

Regelski, T. (2005). Critical theory as a foundation for critical thinking in music education [Electronic Version]. *Visions of Research in Music Education, 6*. Retrieved from http://www-usr.rider.edu/~vrme/

Rudolf, M. (1950). *The grammar of conducting*. New York, NY: Schirmer.

Seifter, H. (2001). The conductor-less orchestra. *Leader to Leader, 21*. Retrieved from http://www.seifterassociates.com/uploads/4/0/5/9/4059165/drucker_foundation_-_the_conductorless_orchestra.pdf

Shor, I. (1992). *Empowering education: Critical teaching for social change*. Chicago, IL: University of Chicago Press.

Siebenaler, D. J. (2006). Factors that predict participation in choral music for high school students. *Research and Issues in Music Education, 4*(1), 1–8. Retrieved from http://www.stthomas.edu/rimeonline/vol4/siebenaler.htm

Silvey, P. (2005). Learning to perform Benjamin Britten's *Rejoice in the Lamb:* The perspectives of three high school choral singers. *Journal of Research in Music Education, 53*(2), 102–119.

Vodicka, J. (2009). *The impact of critical pedagogy on a high school choir* (Unpublished master's thesis). Westminster Choir College of Rider University, Princeton, NJ.

Vygotsky, L. S. (1978). *Mind in society: The development of higher psychological processes*. Cambridge, MA: Harvard University Press.

Vygotsky, L. S. (1986). *Thought and language*. Cambridge, MA: MIT Press.

CHAPTER 2

CHORAL PEDAGOGY RESPONDS TO THE MEDIA

American Idol, Glee, The Voice, The Sing-Off, *and . . .*

PATRICE MADURA WARD-STEINMAN

POP choral music has changed during the 21st century due to the enormous popularity of commercial network TV shows such as *American Idol, Glee, The Voice, The Sing-Off*, and the *Clash of the Choirs*. Our choir students watch these shows and are influenced by them in terms of vocal tone, repertoire, showmanship, and competitive spirit. As a teacher, how might I respond? Should the media shape/influence choral pedagogy, or should traditional pedagogy develop the pop-influenced singer? This chapter will address these questions and will include viewpoints of competition-winning show choir directors and leaders in the field of choral music who have witnessed the effects of these media on choral interest, enrollment, attitudes, and achievement in school choral programs.

Although each of these shows has a somewhat different musical focus, such as solo versus choral singing, or fictional versus reality show, the common denominator is the genre of vocal popular music. And while popular music does have its place in school music programs, choral music teachers have been trained to provide a balance of musical styles in the school curriculum. With the impressive popularity of these TV shows, students are increasingly joining school choirs but with the expectation that school music will mirror what they observe on TV. Certainly the boost in motivation to participate in choral music programs is one that no music teacher would disparage, and there is evidence that real changes are occurring in the numbers of young people drawn to enroll in choir as a result of their enthusiasm for these shows. The multiple-award winning TV series, *Glee*, in particular, has made show choir appear to be the "cool" place to be, even for teenage misfits (Kidder, 2013). However, cognitive dissonance is to be expected when throngs of new choral "Gleeks" find that preparation for an outstanding musical performance requires hard work and time commitment, rather than what may appear on TV to be practically spontaneous. This unrealistic understanding of what it takes to be successful in music has been a common concern of experienced choral teachers who work with these media-influenced students seeking the *Glee* experience. On the other hand, some teachers find the harsh criticism of the TV judges to be detrimental to the average singer, who may never participate in choir because of these judgments.

Criticism by many choral teachers revolves around the "quality" of the music produced in these TV shows, and the emphasis on entertainment over educational value. Due to increasingly sophisticated choreography, pop choral arrangements are now often simpler than those written for concert choirs from earlier decades, although some advanced show choirs do perform complex choral arrangements (Weaver & Hart, 2011). Steve Zegree (2012) emphasized that when he auditioned singers for *Clash of the Choirs*, strong singing and musical ability were the primary criteria, and after the singers were selected they were taught to dance, and were the eventual champions of the competition. Regarding the uneven quality of music performed on commercial network TV, it stands to reason that entertainment for as wide a general audience as possible is its goal.

Another potential misunderstanding of media-influenced students is what constitutes a good, healthy choral sound. The *Glee* singers are not actually teenagers although they play them on TV, and our students will want to emulate their more mature, professional, and sound-engineered (and autotuned!) voices (Amerind, http://www.facebook.com/groups, ACDA). A number of pop stars with vocal injuries necessitating surgery can be used as examples of reasons to learn to sing in a healthy manner. "Cross-training" (Eilers, http://www.facebook.com/groups, ACDA) can help students realize aspects such as vowel modification and registration for different styles of singing and ultimately make them more marketable (Amerind, http://www.facebook.com/groups, ACDA).

The *Choral Director* magazine surveyed hundreds of choral directors and found that 77% of them watched these shows, and they perceived that the vast majority of their students did too (www.choraldirectormag.com/1620/articles/survey/glee). These shows have both benefits and drawbacks. The largest benefit seems to be the publicity for choral music and the resulting influx of students into choral programs where we have the precious opportunity to teach them how to broaden their knowledge and skill of beautiful, healthy choral singing. Choral directors may need to exercise a delicate balancing act between motivating through encouragement, enthusiasm, and open-mindedness and teaching about healthy singing, pedagogically-appropriate repertoire, and realistic approaches to achievement and competition.

CHALLENGES THAT CHORAL DIRECTORS FACE

In preparation for writing this chapter, I asked members of the ACDA Facebook Group to respond to the following prompt: "Tell me what you think about how choral pedagogy should respond to the influence of *Glee, The Voice, The Choir,* and *American Idol.*"

A lively and assertive discussion ensued from October 15th through 21st, 2013. The first topic focused on healthy singing, with comments ranging from blatant opposition to belting (e.g., "The only quality of a belt is the quality of the doctor you need for the vocal problems it caused") to an open-minded view (e.g., "You need to pair up with a voice teacher who is familiar with that approach to singing . . . there are different versions of healthy singing. There are distinct differences when it comes to the pharyngeal voice (see blogs.voices.com), in registration, vowel modification, and vocal closed phase in classical vs non-classical singing."

The use of microphones also sparked debate, with comments ranging from, "When the mikes take over the stage, you can kiss good singing good-bye," to "Using microphones actually helps the singers. They are able to sell the quality of a belt while being able to use a high mixed voice with a longer closed phase in the vocal folds."

The second hot topic was regarding popular music, with comments such as, "Years ago ACDA was throwing too much weight behind the swing choir/show choir movement; great music should always be at the forefront before the fluff," contrasted with "Don't disregard popular music. There's garbage classical music as well as excellent contemporary pop," and "Young people aren't going to stop participating in programs that provide them with opportunities to sing popular styles of music. We can either decide to step in and be involved, thereby ensuring that the singing is done in a healthy, supported manner, or we can let others do it without that)."

One topic that generated unanimous agreement among ACDA members was the unrealistic nature of *Glee*. Concerns included the "harmful" aspect of high school students wanting to emulate the more mature voices featured on *Glee*, as well as the unrealistic notion that perfect sight-reading and choreography happen spontaneously.

I posed the same question to the Vocal Jazz Educators Facebook page on the same date which resulted in a different tone of responses, as might be expected from directors whose focus is on popular singing style. The prompt: "Please tell me what you think choral pedagogy's response to *Glee*, *The Voice*, and *American Idol* should be" yielded positive comments, suggesting 1) that these shows stimulate interest in choir; 2) that *Pitch Perfect* and *The Sing-Off* portray the "chemistry of real-world groups and how people work together;" 3) that *The Sing-Off* and *Pitch Perfect* encourage participation in contemporary a cappella groups that focus on songs that students know and are excited about, while allowing the director to teach good vocal habits and how to write their own arrangements (see acatribe.com); 4) that "*The Voice* uses a blind audition process, so that the judges are focusing on the voice, and not on the way the contestants look. I think that's another important takeaway for students;" 5) the opportunity to converse with the students about the healthy use of the voice, using good and bad vocal models from these shows; and finally, 6) that because our teacher training doesn't include how to work with popular music styles with the same depth as classical styles, music educators are naturally resistant to it, but they shouldn't be. Teachers need "research-based, pedagogically sound methods."

IMPACT OF CONTEMPORARY MEDIA-DRIVEN MUSIC SHOWS

The impact of these popular vocal music TV shows and movies staggers the mind of the traditionally-trained choral music director. The earliest of these, *American Idol*, was an interactive talent show which arrived in the summer of 2002 as a reality show on the Fox TV network. It was the top-watched show for people aged 18–49 from season three to season ten (see www.realitytvworld.com/news/american-idol/sixth-season-finale-averages-pver-30-million-viewers-5225.php), and was the most watched TV series by all American viewers, averaging 27 million (see today.msnbc.msn.com/id/16563051).

The next interactive reality talent contest on NBC TV was the *Clash of the Choirs*, which was short-lived, only running for one season (four episodes) in 2007. It featured five 20-voice choirs from different cities, each directed by a different celebrity, and the public voted online and by phone. One of the four episodes of *Clash* had a viewership of 8 million, mostly adults, aged 18–49. Two other interactive singing competitions followed; first, *The Sing-Off*, which premiered in 2009, and *The Voice* in 2011, both on NBC. *The Sing-Off* featured a cappella groups and ran for four seasons, while *The Voice* continues as of this writing. All of these US TV shows feature pop music, pop star judges, public voting, and grand prizes that range from cash (to the contestant or to a charity) to a recording contract (en.wikipedia.org). A theatrical release in 2012, *Pitch Perfect*, which now has a sequel, focused on the contemporary a cappella movement, and became the second highest grossing musical comedy film of all time.

The teen comedy-drama, *Glee*, which focuses on the show choir concept, began airing on the Fox TV network in May of 2009 and ran through 2015. It was strategically scheduled to air after *American Idol*, which provided a ready audience for it, attracting more than 14 million viewers. The featured popular tunes were available for downloading after each hour-long show, resulting in more than 16 million downloaded songs and 25 *Billboard* Hot 100 hits. The *Glee* Facebook page has more than 15 million fans and continues to grow (Weaver & Hart, 2011).

A BRIEF HISTORY OF POP VOCAL GROUPS

Billboard magazine, founded in 1894, has been influential in preserving the history of pop singing groups. *Billboard* published records of best-selling sheet music and records, as well as most-played music in juke boxes and by disc jockeys, in lists like "Top 100" and "Hot 100." Jay Warner (2000), in his book, *The Da Capo Book of American Singing Groups*, cites *Billboard* lists in his documentation of the history of vocal harmony groups as applied to popular song back to the mid-19th century, including minstrel show vocal groups, glee clubs, and barbershop quartets. By the early 1890s, vocal harmony groups began recording, and with the advent of radio and big band jazz, the extended harmo-nies of the 1930s began to phase out barbershop groups in favor of jazzier groups such as the Boswell Sisters, Mills Brothers, and Ink Spots. African-American quartet singing reached its zenith between the mid-1940s and late 1950s when it dominated the com-mercial gospel field (Allen, 1991). Warner considers the 1940s through the 1960s to be the "glory days of vocal groups" (p. xii). The Contemporary A Cappella (CAC) ensemble is a direct descendant of the pop vocal harmony groups, and represents one stream of media-influenced vocal music.

Warner (2000) proceeds to detail over 350 pop vocal groups from the 1940s to the 1990s, and includes a section on "The 'Acappella' Era," which provides a welcome expla-nation of the various spellings of the term. In 1960, Times Square Records owner Irving "Slim" Rose was the first to use the term a cappella for advertising the new style of recorded pop singing groups without accompaniment, but chose to spell it "acapella." By 1964, the accepted spelling changed to "acappella" and represented a rebellion against the instrumental and psychedelic bands of the British invasion. This spelling has often persisted, despite every music teacher's attempt to correct it on student papers, even with the newly-formed and correctly-spelled A Cappella Education Organization (ACEO).

The show choir movement represents a second popular choral music stream. According to Colleen Hart, co-author of *Sweat, Tears, & Jazz Hands*, a show choir "is a mash-up between a standard choir, a dance team, and a drama club, which competes with similar groups throughout the country" (Weaver & Hart, 2011, p. ix). Owing its beginning to the influences of vaudeville and *The Fred Waring Show*, the earliest swing choirs began to emerge around 1949. In 1950, George Krueger created the first popu-lar music glee club at Indiana University, called the Singing Hoosiers, and many other Midwestern college groups followed suit. It wasn't until the late 1960s and 1970s that high school swing choirs transformed into dancing and costumed show choirs that competed, with obsessive hubs in the Midwest and southern California. High school show choirs have continued to grow in popularity, and have a large presence throughout much of the United States.

GLEE AND SHOW CHOIRS

In 2009, Fox Broadcasting Company took the show choir concept and turned it into the TV sensation, *Glee*. The music was intended to support the drama and the emotional state of misfit teenagers who are enrolled in choir. The teenage drama is not unlike what high school students actually experience, and this explains much of the success of the show. What *Glee* doesn't reveal is the reality of the commitment required to sustain long rehearsals, sleepless road trips, injuries, illnesses, and the demands of balancing show choir with homework. *Glee* makes choral performance appear spontaneous, yet each episode required at least ten days to shoot due to music and dance rehearsals. Music was prerecorded by the cast before the choreography was learned. As Weaver and Hart

(2011) explain, "although real-life show choirs worked for decades to strike a perfect harmonized balance between pop culture and traditional choral ensembles, in just two seasons *Glee* figured out a way to nail it every week . . . *Glee* is show choir's idol" (p. 139).

While the show choir is perhaps the most natural fit for media-influenced pop music singers, most university choral music education curricula fail to prepare future teachers to direct show choirs. Alan Alder (2012) conducted a comprehensive study of the "profile of the ideal show choir director" who can simultaneously create an artistic product while keeping students interested in choral music. His study is particularly valuable from the standpoint of extra-musical knowledge needed to direct a show choir, including budget and fund-raising, choreography, props, costuming, makeup and hair, sound reinforcement, competitions, and the challenges of singing while dancing. These aspects will not be unpacked here, but the conductor interested in these important extra-musical aspects, as well as lighting, staging, and more, should also see Steve Zegree's (2010) *The Wow Factor*.

I conducted a survey of the 20 top-ranked show choir competition winners in Indiana over a five year period regarding their opinions of the influence of *Glee, The Voice, The Sing-Off*, and *American Idol* on their choral programs (2013). Three main influences emerged as themes: 1) an increase in interest and enrollment in choral programs, greater audience enjoyment, and increased publicity; 2) a concern regarding the influence of these shows on healthy vocal/choral tone quality; and 3) a concern about the "unrealistic" portrayal of how to achieve success as a show choir and solo singer. These consistently successful show choir directors offered the following comments on the influences of these shows on their students.

On negative vocal influence: "The kids are more interested in singing as a 'cool' activity and are willing to give it a try—especially males. What I feel is detrimental is that they deal with only one type of vocal singing, and it elevates unhealthy singing. Every year I retrain entering freshman in regards to this, and the response is not always positive!! It has become an expectation that you need to sing in a certain way to be 'good.' I see this in the show choir competitions as well. There are judges who think this is the way to sing and give you negative feedback when your soloist does not belt" and "I think that *The Voice* and *American Idol* have given many kids an undue degree of confidence in their vocal ability. There seems to be an opinion that raw talent is all one needs to be successful, and many kids seem offended by the suggestion of voice lessons. I think this attitude is encouraged by these shows."

On pedagogical opportunities: "Students can learn a lot from mic technique, stage presence and performance technique from the shows;" "I think that some of the vocals are good models for pop music but not for good choral singing. However, I don't think it has hurt my program in any way. I think it has helped it and as far as I'm concerned, that's all that matters. Because then I can teach and mold them in my classroom;" and "I use it as a springboard into discussions of overall vocal health. I give the examples of singers who have had vocal surgeries. It also helps me explain that they can get popular music everywhere they go, so I put a much stronger emphasis on concert choir music because, for the most part, my class is the only place they'll get that type of music."

On the unrealistic nature of *Glee*: "I think some people think that what we do in rehearsals is as automatic as it appears on *Glee*. I even had a sub in the department say to me, 'Your job must be so much fun—just like *Glee* every day!' Dislike!"; "I don't think they are helpful, other than the fact that they are promoting music. They are completely unrealistic. For example, last year I had a freshman girl's mother, who had been to three competitions with us, ask me why we did the same show every weekend. She said that she watched *Glee* and those kids did a new show every week;" "These shows are a double-edged sword. The benefits are that they bring singing and choral music to the public and the media. The downside is that they usually represent what we do totally wrong—you never see *Glee* doing fundraising, rehearsing as a choral ensemble, rehearsing the band, or fitting costumes. The vocal shows encourage singing that is not always appropriate for all age levels and yet everyone wants to be an IDOL!"; and "I feel that the shows portray an inaccurate perception of rehearsal procedures and social dynamics within the ensemble. This is for an obvious reason—15 minutes of vocalizing and sight-singing doesn't make for compelling television. Also, I believe that manufactured drama between the characters on television programs has the unintended effect of producing similar situations in the classroom. Anecdotally speaking, I have had more 'drama' in the past two years than I had in the previous ten. I don't think the slight uptick in interest that might be attributable to the success of the shows is worth it. Those who join choir because it looks cool on television have no idea what it takes to be a serious music student. I am just finding that many who join because of media influence aren't interested in learning music literacy, studying classical literature, or quite frankly, working very hard." Clearly, there are mixed emotions regarding the pros and cons of these shows. While there is real evidence that high school students are enrolling in choir in greater numbers due to the media, their show choir directors face greater challenges in teaching the realities of building a successful choral ensemble. Those challenges include not only finding ways to motivate "Gleeks" to work hard at developing their musical skills, but also keeping abreast of new styles of singing.

Alder (2012) makes the point that students often know the desired sound for popular singing, but not how to produce it in a healthy way, while their teachers often know classical singing techniques, but not approaches to healthy pop singing. The show choir directors in his study reported that they taught singing the same way as they did in their concert choirs, but Alder observed that the show choirs sang noticeably brighter in tone color. Perhaps, if an authentic pop sound is important, teachers need additional study of healthy singing techniques in a variety of styles, rather than just the traditional.

CONTEMPORARY A CAPPELLA

Brody McDonald (2012) is at the forefront of the contemporary a cappella movement, and he devotes a chapter of his book, *A Cappella Pop*, to healthy singing in that style. He bemoans the vocal tension heard in most rock and pop singing, and while he states that an authentic style is important to pop music, he advises pop singers in the following approaches to singing: 1) be aware of any discomfort in the voice and avoid it, 2) properly warm up the entire range of the voice, 3) use resonance rather than tension to create a full and exciting sound, and 4) sing in your comfortable range. Diana Spradling (2007), in *Jazz Singing: Developing Artistry and Authenticity*, also stresses the importance of developing resonance in the tone to help the singer project "with ease (musical freedom)" and achieve authenticity in styles including R&B, gospel, rock, pop, folk, funk and jazz (p. 21).

Because a cappella music often is comprised of "cover tunes" (existing pop songs), a certain sense of authenticity is important. McDonald recommends learning the original song accurately before adding any embellishments, but not emulating the exact sound of the original singer, as no two voices are alike. When performing, he advises sticking to the original on the first verse and gradually add new ideas during other verses. Those changes might include runs (pop version of a melisma), altering the range or direction of the melody, altering the rhythm on a repetition, or simple improvisations.

The authors of *The A Cappella Book* (Chin & Scalise, 2012) also address the soloist's tone quality. They advise choosing someone other than a "belter" for effective solos in CAC (Contemporary A Cappella) groups. They explain that "Big, and big alone, will only get you so far" (p. 54). They encourage a voice that has a unique texture, and a singer who can use a wide range of dynamics and can create the unexpected in a song.

COMPETITION

While many choral directors feel that competition should be left to the football or basketball teams (Zegree, 2010), others thrive on it. I will not repeat all of the pros and cons of school music competitions that can be found in most choral methods books, but rather provide insights from choral educators regarding their experiences competing on these TV shows. Steve Zegree, long-time choral director of Western Michigan University's Gold Company, and later of the Indiana University Singing Hoosiers, had the unique opportunity to serve as choirmaster for the *Clash of the Choirs*. This TV show featured a competition among five auditioned choirs, each led by a celebrity. Nick Lachey's group, mentored by Zegree, won the competition. In Zegree's book, *The Wow Factor*, he detailed how his group won the competition: the audition process, repertoire choices, rehearsal structures, arranging considerations (including orchestrated accompaniments), the balance of choral versus solo singing, the four-night broadcast experience, stage presence, and work ethic. His philosophy on media-driven choral competitions is worth repeating here:

> As a self-proclaimed "pied piper" of bringing as many people to quality music as possible, I viewed *Clash of the Choirs* as a chance to expose an enormous mass market to the joys of group singing. My thought is that, as a result of this show, even

if just 1 percent of the 12 million viewers on Thursday night became motivated to join a school, church or community choir, we now have a least 120,000 more people throughout the country participating in your choirs, and that is a remarkable recruiting statistic that is hard to match. (p. 175)

Another award-winning ensemble featured on NBC's *The Sing-Off* is Eleventh Hour from Kettering-Fairmont High School in Ohio, directed by Brody McDonald. In his book (2012), he defines contemporary a cappella as "the new chamber music" (p. 17). He identifies all of the skills that members of a cappella ensembles develop, including collaboration, improvisation, evaluation, emulation, independence, tuning, keeping time, and visual presentation. He believes that contemporary a cappella music participation is "for everyone" because it can be performed with virtually any song, any size ensemble, any experience level, and any gender combination. He also elaborates on the topics of set lists, vocal percussion, bass line singing, booking gigs, microphone technique, effects pedals, and making a recording. McDonald explains the rigors of preparing his high school students to win, along with ten other groups, the opportunity to perform on *The Sing-Off*'s second season. He summarized the pros and cons of the experience: the pros were mostly for that season's ensemble, and included the understanding of the value of dreaming big, instant credibility, financial gains through performances and CDs, and industry contracts for his students as they pursued careers as professional musicians; cons included "living in the shadow" of the group, oversaturation of attention, and emphasis on the past.

Chin and Scalise, co-founders of The A Cappella Blog and co-authors of *The A Cappella Book* (2012), state that "no competition supersedes Varsity Vocals' International Championship of Collegiate A Cappella (ICCA)," which began in 1996 and has featured groups from around the world. The Best of Collegiate A Cappella (BOCA), which began in 1999, also "marks the best-respected, most objective proving ground for recorded a cappella" (p. 187). These competitions help groups avoid mediocrity because of their serious emphasis on appropriate song selection for the group, the set structure, and on a perfect performance.

THE VOCAL ATHLETE

One of the most pervasive controversies regarding the media-driven music shows is vocal technique and health. *The Vocal Athlete*, by LeBorgne and Rosenberg (2014) presents an overview of scientific knowledge of the singing voice in both classical and "Contemporary Commercial Music" (CCM) singing. They acknowledge that there is a critical need for research on the effectiveness of both approaches to singing, because our current practices are primarily based on tradition, our training, and trial and error. The CCM approaches are being systematically explored as the industry demands and injuries of 21st century vocalists multiply. One study (Donahue, LeBorgne, Brehm,

& Weinrich, 2013, as cited in *The Vocal Athlete*, p. 111), reported that, of 188 freshman musical theater majors who were screened for laryngeal abnormalities, more than 85% suffered from vocal folds trauma due to dehydration and reflux. The awareness and prevention of these vocal difficulties and potential for more serious injuries must be paramount in the minds of choir directors.

The authors of *The Vocal Athlete* address the strong influence that musical shows such as *Glee*, *The Voice*, and *American Idol*, have had on singers' interest in contemporary vocal styles, and belting, in particular. They report that 34% of university voice teachers have had no experience with singing commercial music styles nor methods unique to teaching them. The authors present an overview of 30 years' worth of historical and pedagogical approaches to belting, as this style of stage singing is so common in practice. The belting theories and pedagogies of Jo Estill (creator of Estill Voice International), Jan Sullivan (*How to Teach the Belt/Pop Voice*), Larra Henderson (*How to Train Singers*), Jeannette LoVetri (creator of Somatic Voicework certification), Robert Edwin (provides specific vocalizes to achieve a belt), Seth Riggs (creator of Speech Level Singing certification), Lisa Popeil (creator of Voiceworks Method), and Mary Saunders-Barton (creator of Bel Canto/Can Belto) are detailed. I add Randy Buescher (Your True Voice Studio) to this list of contemporary singing pedagogues. Although these methods require more research to determine the long-term effects of belting on vocal health, they are based on extensive teaching and performance practice. Faculty and graduate students looking to conduct important research topics will find, in this book, a comprehensive review of literature on topics related to belting, such as laryngeal action, formants, intensity, vibrato, timbre, nasality, and registration.

The authors based their warm-up exercises for CCM on five principles of exercise science for muscle strengthening (LeBorgne & Rosenberg, 2014). These principles are intensity, frequency, overload, specificity, and reversibility. As breath control is paramount to singing in any style, respiratory muscle strength training can adhere to the principles of exercise science and reduce laryngeal tension. Similarly, the principles of exercise science can be applied to larynx and glottal efficiency, albeit with some alterations for the unseen vocal mechanism. Exercises for a minimum of three days per week, with enough repetition for muscle memory and strengthening, are as effective for the voice as for the rest of the physical body. Slow increases in difficulty continue to strengthen the voice in a healthy manner. The concept of specificity refers to the different voice registers on which the singer consciously focuses, while reversibility refers to the ability to balance and control extremes in range and color. Internalization of these principles requires much repetition as the singer learns in three stages: the beginning trial and error stage assisted by the teacher's feedback, the stage of increased refinement assisted mostly by the singer's own "feel" for doing it correctly, and the final stage when the skill has become automatic.

The accompanying book, *The Vocal Athlete: Application and Technique for the Hybrid Singer* (Rosenberg & LeBorgne, 2014), defines the hybrid singer as "the vocal athlete who is highly skilled in performing in multiple vocal styles possessing a solid vocal technique that is responsive, adaptable, and agile in order to meet demands of current and ever-evolving vocal music industry genre" (p. ix). The book presents sixty vocal exercises advised by a cast of contributors whose expertise included speech pathology, voice and speech therapy, communication science and disorders, physical therapy, performance psychology, musical theater, choral music, and vocal pedagogy. Several exercises address each of the following: laryngeal strength and coordination, registration and vocal tract modification, and specific vocal styles such as musical theater, rock, and belting.

REPERTOIRE

Beyond passionate discussions about the value of popular versus classical music in the surveys of choral directors, little reference has been made to the musical characteristics of the extant repertoire for popular music ensembles. A few comments found on a ChoralNet online discussion group on March 4, 2014, are notable:

"The problem stems from singing material that has a very limited range, and more often than not, a range that is compressed from roughly A below middle C to an octave above middle C. This limited and lower range is sung in a belting tone which has at least three drawbacks: 1) it forces vocal production; 2) there is no development of the upper register; and 3) it is more difficult to hear your own vocal pitch and balance. Pop repertoire has its place in the curriculum; however, great care and training with widespread selection of repertoire must be the key to total choral training;" and "What has gotten my attention are the choral parts to a recently written musical. The women's parts were all written in the chest voice belt range, and men's were all written in the treble clef. It was all in the high baritone range, or even higher. No bass part to speak of."

To verify these observations, I reviewed 40 new pop choral arrangements. My criterion for review was that the arrangement noted on the cover was featured on *Glee*, *The Sing-Off*, or *Pitch Perfect*, or was *A Contemporary A Cappella Selection*. Eight different choral arrangers were represented in the selected pieces (see dekesharon.com). They were approximately equally divided between SATB and single-gender choir arrangements. I played through and sang each piece at the appropriate tempo marking.

I found that most of the arrangements are characterized by extensive use of repetition within parts, the simplest of melodies, and a rock beat; but at the same time they are rhythmically challenging to read due to the surprising exclusion of piano reductions, and to the common problem of attempting to notate the rhythm of recorded pop melodies. Frequently I noticed that the text-setting was contrary to natural rhythmic flow. Notably, some of the arrangements were true gems, thus affirming that it is not the style but rather the piece of music that is worthy of study.

Technically speaking, the *Glee* arrangements were either individual songs or "mashups" of several tunes. For the most part, vocal ranges are quite limited, with women's particularly low, and men's quite high. Parts are evenly balanced between unison lines, duets, and simple, repetitive homophony, with frequent solos. The pieces are primarily in major keys, with key signatures of no more than three sharps or three flats, and in duple meter. The text is primarily adolescent in nature, often with an upbeat message or longing for love.

The arrangements that were featured in the movie *Pitch Perfect* were also a mix of individual songs and mash-ups. Some had piano accompaniment, but most were true to the movie's a cappella theme. Six voice parts are common, arranged as either six-part homophony, or four-part vocal accompaniment supporting a solo or duet. Ranges are much wider than the *Glee* pieces, particularly for the basses who are imitating an actual bass instrument in a cappella music (the alto 2 serves as the "bass" in treble music). Vocal accompaniments use a wide variety of scat syllables to imitate instruments, including vocal percussion. Some arrangements are extremely simple and homophonic, while others have six independent lines, both rhythmically and melodically, and are quite challenging. A variety of major and minor keys are utilized, and duple meter predominates. Texts should be carefully examined as some are less than desirable for younger choirs because of sexual and drug insinuations.

The smallest collection was from *The Sing-Off*. True to the show, all were a cappella arrangements, featuring accessible four-part pieces or six parts supporting a solo or duet of a pop tune. Rhythmically independent lines would make these arrangements appropriately challenging to singers. Ranges are extremely low in some arrangements, but appropriate in others. Many arrangements from the series, *A Contemporary A Cappella Selection,* are familiar songs by pop and jazz artists, as well as Christmas carols. Although attractively written, the choral teacher should be wary of the ranges of high school students, because many bass parts require a low E, and the soprano parts are rarely written in the head voice range.

Summary and Recommendations

In this chapter I have presented the issues concerning the influences of the shows *Glee, American Idol, The Voice, The Sing-Off, Clash of the Choirs,* and *Pitch Perfect* on choral singers and choral pedagogy. I have watched the shows, listened to recordings of each show's "hits" and read choral arrangements based on them, surveyed winning show choir directors and professional choir directors for their opinions, and reviewed the literature. The identified benefits and drawbacks of the influence of the shows can be summarized in the following paragraphs, followed by recommendations for choral directors.

The positive influences can be summarized into five main themes: 1) Choral enrollment increases, 2) enhanced teaching opportunities, 3) development of new musical skills, 4) contemporary repertoire, and 5) competition opportunities. *Choral enrollment increases* are related to student interest in popular music ensembles, perceived as a "cool" activity as well as a place for "misfits," and to increased publicity for and promotion of choral music. *Enhanced teaching opportunities* include molding students who wouldn't normally have joined choir into healthy singers, and to use the shows' good and bad vocal examples as springboards for discussion about healthy singing. The *musical skills that develop* through show choir and the contemporary a cappella ensemble include stage presence, microphone technique, aural skills, independence, intonation, keeping time, and improvisation. *Contemporary repertoire* that students know and like can be at motivator and plenty of excellent educational arrangements are available. Finally, the positive aspects of *competition* include working to achieve an outstanding performance, and to realize that excellence in performance can lead to financial rewards and a career in contemporary music.

The negative influences also fell into five major themes: 1) Unhealthy singing, 2) unrealistic expectations, 3) directors' lack of knowledge about contemporary vocal production, 4) questionable repertoire, and 5) competition stresses. These five themes contain numerous concerns. *Unhealthy singing* concerns included belting, vocal tension, emulating mature singers whose voices are engineered for the TV shows, injury, and surgery. The *unrealistic expectations* are with regard to an influx of students who want the "Glee" experience without putting in the necessary work and time to be a successful musician. The *knowledge that many traditional choral directors lack* includes pedagogically-sound contemporary singing techniques, sound reinforcement, vocal percussion, vocal bass lines, choreography, singing while dancing, making a recording, booking gigs, and aspects of producing a show (budget, fundraising, props, costumes, makeup, hair, lighting, staging, and set lists). *Concerns about repertoire* include the emphasis on popular music over classical music and on entertainment over educational value, simplistic arrangements, limited ranges, text setting, and appropriate texts for adolescents. *Competition concerns* include judges who want to hear unhealthy belting, and the constant pressure to continue to "win." Other negative influences included harsh and discouraging TV judges, the overemphasis on raw talent, and increased "drama" in the classroom.

These five pros and five cons regarding the influence of popular vocal music TV shows on choral programs elucidate the challenges directors face and work to balance. With these in mind, I suggest that choral directors strive to focus on the positive aspects and work to overcome the negative aspects through the following recommendations.

There are many contemporary aspects of choral music that traditional directors know little about. I suggest four main areas of study, with the first being the major concern as expressed in this chapter—vocal training for 21st century commercial music. Healthy and informed approaches to belting, singing while dancing, emulating pop singers, improvising to pop songs, choosing appropriate pop repertoire, mastering vocal percussion, and bass line singing may benefit our students. Several approaches exist from which to choose, and all were identified earlier in this chapter and are cited in *The Vocal Athlete* (LeBorgne &Rosenberg, 2014). It may be in our students' best interests to hire contemporary commercial music experts who can assist us in preparing them for wherever their talents, opportunities, and preferences take them. It goes without saying that we also need to notice when students experience periods of vocal fatigue and determine the appropriate course of action (e.g., whether hydration is all that is needed for recovery, or if vocal rest may be necessary). Fatigue may be a sign of the emergence of a serious vocal problem which may require an expert medical doctor's help.

In fact, systematic research is needed on all kinds of singing, and faculty and graduate students should consider collaborating with voice/speech pathologists and therapists on studies which can inform our profession about healthy approaches to singing contemporary commercial music. It is natural to teach as we've been taught, and to believe in the "truths" that our mentors taught us, but it is better to stay attuned to and create new knowledge.

Second, choral teacher preparation courses are needed that include the practical aspects of show production. Many new teachers will direct show choirs and/or contemporary a cappella groups. These practical aspects include budget, fund-raising, publicity, choreography, props, lighting, staging, costuming, makeup, hair, competition and travel. A successful high school show choir director would be an invaluable resource for these topics, as well as the books by McDonald (2012), Zegree (2010), and others referenced in this chapter.

Third, sound technology is indispensable for all of the types of music discussed in this chapter. Sound reinforcement systems, microphone technique, effects pedals, and recording techniques are usually supervised by an experienced sound technician, or sometimes by a relatively inexperienced but eager student technician. Nevertheless, choral directors need to take responsibility for acquiring a basic knowledge of sound technology for many reasons: they may be involved in sound equipment purchases, they will need to be able to communicate with the sound technician about the quality of amplified sound that they prefer, and they may need to adjust the sound during the unexpected absence of a sound engineer during rehearsal.

In the end, if these media-driven music shows bring students to our choirs, as evidence shows is true, then we should welcome them with open arms and minds, and teach them to be good musicians, despite the many challenges. To keep our young people singing, we must carefully build bridges between their music and ours, and wisely select repertoire that fuels the spirit and educates the mind. We must embrace and lead.

References

Alder, Alan L. (2012). Successful high school show choir directors: Their perceptions about their teaching and administrative practices. Ball State University, Muncie, Indiana. *ProQuest Dissertations and Theses A&I*, 382.

Allen, Ray (1991). *Singing in the spirit: African-American sacred quartets in New York City*. Philadelphia: University of Pennsylvania Press.

Chin, Mike, & Scalise, Mike (2012). *The a cappella book*. Self-published (http://acappellablog.com/book).

Glee and the real music classroom (2010, August 17). *Choral Director Magazine* Retrieved from http://www.choraldirectormag.com/1620/articles/survey/glee-and-the-real-music-classroom-2/.

Kidder, Lisa D. (2013). *Share the Glee*. Chicago: Triumph.

LeBorgne, Wendy D. & Rosenberg, Marci (2014). *The vocal athlete*. San Diego, CA: Plural.

Madura Ward-Steinman, Patrice (2013). *Characteristics of high-achieving secondary school show choir directors* [Raw data file available from pwardste@indiana.edu].

McDonald, Brody (2012). *A cappella pop: A complete guide to contemporary a cappella singing*. Van Nuys, CA: Alfred.

Rosenberg, Marci, & LeBorgne, Wendy D. (2014). *The vocal athlete: Application and technique for the hybrid singer*. San Diego, CA: Plural.

Sharon, Deke (2016). *The heart of vocal harmony: Emotional expression in group singing*. Montclair, NJ: Hal Leonard.

Spradling, Diana R., & Binek, Justin. (2007). *Jazz singing: Developing artistry and authenticity*. Edmonds, WA: Sound Music.

Warner, Jay (2000). *The Da Capo book of American singing groups*. Boulder, CO: Da Capo. Originally published in 1992 as *The Billboard book of American singing groups*.

Weaver, Mike, & Hart, Colleen. (2011). *Sweat, tears, and jazz hands: The official history of show choir from Vaudeville to Glee*. Montclair, NJ: Hal Leonard.

Zegree, Steve (2010). *The wow factor: How to create it, inspire it, & achieve it*. Montclair, NJ: Hal Leonard.

Discography

American Idol, 10th Anniversary: The Hits, Volume I (2011). [CD] New York: RCA/Jive Label Group.

Evolution. Eleventh Hour. (2008). [CD]. Produced, Engineered, and Mixed by John Gentry. New York: Naked Voice Records.

Glee: Volume 6, Season Two. (2011). [CD]. New York: Columbia Records.

Glee encore (2011). [TV series episode.] Beverly Hills, CA: Twentieth Century Fox.

Pitch Perfect: Original Motion Picture Soundtrack. (2012). [CD]. Santa Monica: Universal Music Enterprises.

The Sing-Off: The Best of Season 2. (2011). [CD]. New York: Sony Music Entertainment.

The Voice: Season 1, The Highlights. (2011). [CD]. New York: Universal Republic Records.

CHAPTER 3

···

THE CHORAL EXPERIENCE
Turned Inside Out

···

PAUL D. HEAD

To this day, I have vivid recollections of my undergraduate conducting professor lead-ing a discussion about the qualities of the effective conductor, touting the familiar adage that "the role of the conductor is that of a benevolent dictator." The intended message was, in fact, altruistic and deliberate. At the end of the day, one person in the rehearsal room is charged with making musical decisions, and if everything is in place, the mem-bers of the ensemble will accept rehearsal directives as undisputable truths that will ulti-mately lead to choral excellence.

This was near the end of an era when legendary conductors like Arturo Toscanini, Leopold Stokowski, and Eugene Ormandy were very much in the collective conscious-ness of conducting students everywhere. Innumerable anecdotes inspired by quotations from the podium served to offer informal guidelines that shaped the ideology of a gen-eration of conductors in training.[1]

> Why do you always insist on playing when I'm trying to conduct?
> *Eugene Ormandy*

> I don't mean to make you nervous, but unfortunately, I have to.
> *Eugene Ormandy*

> God tells me how the music should sound, but you stand in the way.
> *Arturo Toscanini*

In the context of choral pedagogy, statements such as these were uttered in an era when the systematic study of conducting and rehearsal technique was still an emerg-ing phenomena. The postwar era brought the baby boom with its increased demand for public schools, teachers to staff them, and university music education programs to prepare those teachers. A few Lutheran college choirs in the Midwest had once defined the American choral tradition. These programs had now become the gold standard for building excellent high school programs, a tradition that would flourish through from the 1960s through the 1980s throughout the nation.

But much has changed since Toscanini was an icon and the Lutheran choir was the sole harbinger of the state of the choral art. Today, we live in an age when cyber-communities have largely replaced local bowling teams, religious communities, and other opportunities for humans to interact—in a physical space—with one another. Eric Whitacre's foray into the realm of virtual choirs has yet to supersede the desire for people to travel a few miles for making music with others in real time in a real space. But at the same time, technological advances ranging from social media to a plethora of options for 24/7/365 connectivity have placed extraordinary demands on people in the realm of time management. "I would love to sing in the community choir, but I simply can't find the time!"

Additionally, the time-honored traditions of the high school and university chorus are being challenged as well. Ask a young person if they have a choral music program at her school, and she is more likely to cite participation in a student-run a cappella group than membership in the formal choral organization on campus. Students will enthusiastically report that they sang all the way through high school and college, then go on to admit that they didn't realize the school had "a choir," nor have they ever participated in an ensemble led by a "conductor."

This chapter focuses on the ever-evolving role of the conductor, acknowledging both the challenges to traditional paradigms (which in turn, are causing many to rethink the preparation of pre-service teachers); the effect that technological advancement (I use the word advancement with admitted skepticism) has had on the traditional norms of community—musical or otherwise; some specific strategies for encouraging musical ownership during and outside the rehearsal; and finally, the emergence of musical communities that function without a designated leader or the pedagogical expertise of a professional conductor.

THE HISTORICAL ROLE OF THE CONDUCTOR

Having graduated from undergraduate school in the mid-1980s, I look back on that decade as a significant turning point in the history of choral music education. There was a tacit expectation that conducting students would maintain a sense of reverence for the great conductors who had gone before—not only the orchestral greats mentioned above, but for the acknowledged leaders in educational institutions as well, including well-established and highly regarded high school and college conductors.

At that time, a book entitled *The Choral Experience: Literature, Materials, and Methods* (Robinson & Winold, 1992) was very much in vogue, and somewhat unique given the inclusion of a chapter that traced the historical development of the conductor from the Renaissance to "the present day." Particularly telling is this definition of "the conductor in the twentieth century":

> The conductor in the twentieth century has emerged as a virtuoso in his own right. The demands which the composer has placed upon the conductor of contemporary music have required a program of extensive training. (p. 44)

Robinson and Winold (1992) go on to discuss the requisite training and discipline necessary to attain the expertise that makes one worthy of standing in front of an ensemble, yet within that stream of consciousness, they offer this remark that foreshadows the trends of the decades to follow:

> As the leader of a communicative-education experience, the choral conductor must be trained as a facilitator—one who is able to create and control a special kind of learning environment and evoke an empathic response from the participants in the choral experience. (p. 44)

A decade-and-a-half later, a landmark publication entitled *In Quest of Answers: Interviews with American Choral Conductors* (Glenn, 1991) sought to reveal insights from thirty-four conductors had been identified by the editor/interviewer as leaders in the choral profession. Not surprisingly, the question "What are the most important musical and personal qualifications for a successful conductor?" elicited a broad range of responses, each of which not only represents a diverse ideological perspective, but collectively, the evolving perceptions of what conductors do. Consider the following responses, particularly in regard to the conductor's role on the podium:

> A conductor's first duty is to his composer, and his composer's welfare. After that comes the chorus and the orchestra, and long, long after these comes the conductor. I don't think Szell had a great deal of charisma in the "beautiful people" sense of the word, but he had an incredible mind and enormous intellectual energy. That has to be there.
>
> *Margaret Hillis* (Glenn, 1991, p. 110)

> The most important musical qualifications are the ability and facility to study the score . . . The conductor should have a rich musicological and historical background. It would be wonderful if our performers and conductors had the sort of richness of background that Hindemith had and also had his facility for score reading, either at the keyboard or away from the keyboard.
>
> *Robert Shaw* (Glenn, 1991, p. 118)

> Probably of equal importance to musicianship is leadership ability. An effective conductor must be a good leader . . . Of course, what goes into effective leadership is a complex thing. It involves many skills, abilities and personal traits. Along with this, there must be an enthusiasm for people, an enthusiasm for choral music, and above all, and enthusiasm for life.
>
> *Dale Warland* (Glenn, 1991, p. 120)

> A conductor must be a warm person. Carl Jung, the noted psychologist, speaks of our "feeling function." I would deem it important that we in our profession have a high feeling-function.
>
> *Weston Noble* (Glenn, 1991, p. 115)

And finally, two additional perspectives that again, seem forward-looking:

> The conductor should have musicianship, intelligence, a passion to communicate through word and gesture, and an understanding of how people learn.
>
> *Joseph Flummerfelt* (Glenn, 1991, p. 109)

> It is important that a choral conductor be an outgoing person a person who cares about people, who is interested in people, who is open to people, who is responsive to them and interacts with well with them.
>
> *Lloyd Pfautsch* (Glenn, 1991, p. 117)

Now, nearly a quarter-century later, it would be interesting to recreate this exercise in an effort to document the pervasive ideologies at play in the present day. Interestingly, today's conducting pedagogues seem to be gravitating to the metaphysical and psychological realm:

> Perhaps no area of my personal conducting pedagogy has grown as much as my appreciation and understanding of the importance of an awareness of one's soul and spirit before any conducting study begins. While many believe this is not the stuff of beginning conducting study, I now strongly disagree. Humanness brought to conducting through careful thought and study allows gesture to be expressive and compelling because it is developed from an understanding of self. Without this, there can be no meaningful gesture, and there will never be beautiful sound. (Jordan, 2009, xxx)
>
> Our conducting must grow beyond the merely technical to become a personal language of gesture, born from the kinesthetic experiences unique to each choir, which elicits a physical and musical response from the singers. The physical impetus of the conductor must be given an inner context with which to resonate in the singer.
>
> Our rehearsal style must evolve into a realm of creating experiences, both affective and physical, and into a safe place to experience emotional bonding, intimacy, and vulnerability. We must be more intentional in providing life-lessons and personally expressive explorations. We must encourage our singers to be participants in the creative process as opposed to merely being reactive to the conductor's creativity. (Boers, 1998, p. 74)

All this considered, we live in a time of many dichotomies where initiatives like the constructivist classrooms and problem-based learning have been heralded as teaching innovations, regardless of discipline, to foster increased student engagement. But at the same time, sweeping reforms tied to standardized testing focused on the "Core Curriculum" leave teachers little time for teaching beyond the test.

With the recent reworking of the National Association for Music Education (NAfME) National Standards, we see music educators searching for equilibrium in the assessment-engagement conundrum, while at the same time, students in our classrooms are arriving with different expectations as to what their "expert facilitator" should provide.

Assuming the dual role of editor of, and a contributing author to, this handbook, I have been intrigued not only with the diversity of conceptual ideas related to the idea of choral pedagogy, but even more so by the linear nature of these writings that present an overview of what's happening in the choral rehearsal today. Bjella and Goetze delve in repertoire and programming as the basis for curriculum. Abrahams identifies specific rehearsal strategies based on "critical pedagogy," and Madura traces the development of ensemble singing in the media that may or may not resonate with those who identify themselves as choral professionals, but has had an undeniable and profound effect upon those people seated in our rehearsal rooms.

What I find most intriguing, however, is that none of these circumstances live in a vacuum. In the same way that a typical sixteen-year-old listens to music in "shuffle mode" on his mp3 player (implying that they have little or no desire to make a distinction between genres previously labeled as classical or popular, serious or commercial, traditional or world) most are inclined to say that a musical experience is a musical experience—simple as that! If there is a definition related to hierarchy, it's more likely to be something to effect of, "I get it and I like it," or "this sounds like music written by dead white guys, and I really don't care for that."

It bears stating the obvious that in most middle class homes, a 48" television now occupies the place where the family piano once stood, and the time allotted for lesson preparation has either been redistributed to preparation for advanced placement exams, or forfeited to interactive video gaming, which in itself demands a level of engagement and interaction than was not required of those who sat docilely in front of the television just a generation or two ago.

It is at the nexus of these varied perspectives and parameters where today's conductor and choral educator finds the greatest challenge. Unattainable norms are set forth by pristine digital recordings and overproduced Hollywood television programs, while choral directors are greeted with singers who are seemingly disenfranchised, apathetic, or simply shell-shocked by the constant overstimulation of life in the 21st century.

As so well identified by the aforementioned authors, there is an increasing preponderance of conductors who are responding to challenge with artistic innovation, while replacing or reinventing traditional authoritative leadership with a process more closely aligned to Socratic principles. Professional ensembles like Voces Nordicae in Sweden, Voces 8 in the United Kingdom, or Conspirare in the United States emulate the concept of the shuffle mode when pairing music from the Renaissance with creative settings of popular tunes that find commonality in thematic substance and poetic intent. Now that the iPod generation has entered the ranks of influential choral directors, this has become an increasingly common approach to programming for school, community, and even church choirs. In this realm, Gorecki pairs with Gospel, Brahms segues to the The Beatles, and Rachmaninov is mirrored in songs by Regina Spektor.

While perhaps an unintended consequence, this eclectic approach to programming provides innumerable possibilities for teachable moments, as clear delineations of genre, style, ethnicity, and performance practice give way to the collaborative imagination of the performers. Consider Bjella's program examples where *Carmina Burana*, Medieval chant, and Bobby Mcferrin are assembled into a seamless expression of "Mirrored Messages." Or Craig Hella Johnson's affinity for crafting sophisticated arrangements of folk and pop music that illuminate the poetic essence of paired compositions by Mendelssohn or Bach. For the iPod generation singer, not only does this juxtaposition seem unremarkable, but provides the conductor with an opportunity to exploit a thoughtful setting by a contemporary songwriter, while facilitating inquiry and discussion that might help the singer find parallel meanings amidst musical settings perceived by students as archaic, or shrouded in the mystery of a foreign language or an unfamiliar style.

This leads to the mechanics of the engaging choral rehearsal itself. Though the lens of critical pedagogy, Abrahams provides several concrete examples of facilitating an environment where singing participants assume an active role in making musical decisions, ranging from guided discussion in response to thought-provoking prompts, to peer listening exercises where students are charged with making concrete evaluative remarks as related to musicianship and interpretation.

Creating an Environment That Fosters Student Engagement

> Give the pupils something to do, not something to learn; and the doing is
> of such a nature as to demand thinking; the intentional noting of connec-
> tions; learning naturally results. (Dewey, 1916, p. 154)

I have known many choral directors who believe collaborative rehearsal in the classroom begins with the selection of repertoire, facilitating a process where students peruse the music library with the objective of assembling a program that "the students will buy in to."

While I appreciate the intent of such an exercise, this seems something akin to asking a calculus class to submit a list of their favorite equations and theorems, regardless of anticipated learning outcomes at the end of the course. The selection of repertoire represents the very foundation of a comprehensive curriculum (Head, 2011). Extensive discussion about the strategies for choosing repertoire is beyond the scope of this article, except to reinforce the pervading concept that pedagogues and educational theorists dating back to John Dewey and beyond are adamant that student engagement begins with assuring that the content presented is worth the pursuit of the inquiry, and that the method of delivery must be varied and thoughtful in acknowledging that every person learns differently and at a different pace. Music teachers are often reticent to give serious consideration to differentiated instruction beyond meeting the criteria mandated for the learning disabled. But true artistry in teaching begins with curricular design of a nature that demands thinking. In this case, this involves thinking about vocal production, historical context, cultural influence, musicological influence, varied textures, and stylistic nuances, and in the end, the unique aesthetic response each student will derive from the encounter with a particular composition.

I was teaching high school when NAfME (then MENC) first published the national standards for music education. I could recount innumerable stories of grieving and angst amongst my colleagues serving as high school choral directors, staring blankly at standards number three (Improvising melodies, variations, and accompaniments,) and four (composing and arranging music within specific guidelines) (Music Educators National Conference, 1994).

I agreed with my peers that teaching a classroom of seventy-five ninth graders to compose a sonata seemed a bit beyond the reality of this "performance-based" class, but at the same time, I thought we were a bit hasty in dismissing what I believed to be the implicit nature of these directives. Improvisation is largely concerned with the development of aural skills, understanding the basic tenants of tonality, and teaching students to listen to one another. Truth be told, singers in my ninth grade chorus were improvising all the time, albeit as a result of their inability to sing the notes printed on the page. My personal objective was to empower a student to know when she was singing the indicated pitch, and in many cases, to develop a sense of pitch acuity that would allow her to distinguish dissonance from consonance. And so it is that the core of studying improvisation is the ability to grasp theoretical principals, while developing the aural skills to put those to work.

My approach to teaching composition was a similar endeavor, noting that in the same way John Grisham writes in a discernibly different style than Shakespeare, so it is also with the compositional stylings of Mozart, Palestrina, Whitacre, Brahms, and Britten. Despite the requirement to compose in music school, I certainly never considered myself a composer, though I did come to know a great deal about compositional practice and how that relates to analysis and interpretation. A sixteen-year-old chorister may know nothing of the evolution of church modes into tonal counterpoint, but may quickly acquire the curiosity and vocabulary to describe the architecture and voicing of a William Byrd motet, and the resultant aesthetic affect of his profound compositional practice.

In this light, it is intriguing to witness the emergence of the new, expanded iteration of the National Standards (NAfME, 2014), which are not only delineated by five subheadings (General Music, Composition/Theory, Music Technology, Guitar/Keyboard, Harmonizing instruments, and Ensembles), but the nine original standards have been reorganized and expanded under the nomenclature of "Essential Questions" such as "How do musicians generate creative ideas?" Or "How do musicians improve the quality of their creative work."[2] The now antiquated headers of "Improvisation" and "Composition" have been woven into a complex matrix that appears to replicate what highly effective choral directors have been doing all along—requiring the singers to move beyond rote learning while meeting specific task-oriented criteria as put forth by the conductor. Alternatively, the engaging rehearsal requires a commitment to kinesthetic involvement (Stand up, breathe, and sing!) and cognitive investment (creating an environment where students are required to reconcile the marriage of music and text in an effort to grasp the lingual nuance of the composer)—all the while succumbing to an elevated aesthetic experience (practice and thoughtful investigation learning to the desired outcome: feeling).

Perhaps this is the foundation of criteria stated near the bottom of the NAfME Standards rubric suggesting a level of mastery, which states, "[The performer will] demonstrate an understanding and master of the technical demands and expressive qualities of the music through prepared and improvised performance of a varied repertoire representing diverse cultures, styles, genres and historical periods in multiple types of ensembles" (NAfME, 2014). Is this not an appropriate learning goal that should appear at the top of every lesson plan?

Over time, I have come to refer to this process—approaching the rehearsal as an opportunity to instill a sense of investigative curiosity in my students—as "reverse engineering." First conceived as a way to teach score analysis to graduate students, I have found that adopting a similar approach with lesser-experienced adolescent singers to be equally effective—if not even more so.

At first one may not immediately recognize the subtleties that transform a typical sequence of rehearsal activities into an exercise of reverse engineering, as that represents more of an ideology or ethos than simply a bag of tricks. And in fact, conceptually it is quite simple, defined by a two-part process: The conductor presents the music at hand in a way that allows the singers to immediately recognize the profundity of a composer's work as an interpretive artist. This requires that the singers' first experience with the piece is meaningful and relevant, and thus it is necessary for the conductor to find a way to present the most compelling elements of the composition within the first fifteen minutes of rehearsal. Sing a recurring melodic pattern first taught in the warmups. Sight-read a simple chordal section of the work that is especially illustrative of the text. Speak the text in rhythm of a fugal section while the piano plays the parts so the singers can hear the unfolding chord structure in a participatory way. There are hundreds of examples, but the point is that the first experience with a new composition must be directed toward fostering curiosity and desire amongst the singers to come back for more.

Sandra Snow (2011) does well to capture the essence of this process with her thoughts on improvisation in the choral rehearsal:

> Making an explicit focus on the conductor-teacher as facilitator of student learning, conductor-teachers shift responsibility to the ensemble member for understanding of the score.
>
> Shifting the role of the conductor-teacher to that of active facilitator does not imply that singers are fully responsible for decisions regarding music. After all, the conductor-teacher is the one with the background and experience, and who has studied the music closely. Neither does facilitating mean reorienting the experience to the verbal domain; that is, to talk about the music incessantly rather than experience it directly.

> Facilitating instead involves an ongoing commitment to guiding singers to musical understanding by stimulating musical thinking, reflecting actively on musical actions, and providing meaningful ways for singers to experience musical ideas. (p. 55)

This, in fact, is the departure point for the reverse engineering process, as one plans subsequent rehearsals with careful attention to the detail of the architecture and structure of the piece. Decisions as where to begin, how long to drill, which pairings of voices to rehearse, whether to begin with rhythm or pitch, and so on, are all critical not only for the pacing of rehearsal, but for pulling the singers deeper into a cognitive relationship with a work that is becoming increasingly meaningful to them on an aesthetic level.

WRITTEN INTERACTION WITH
THE CHORAL ENSEMBLE

It is at this point that I start writing to the choir, and ask them in turn to write to me. A simple gesture, but one that never fails to elicit a layman's analysis—albeit, at first, frequently misinformed or unwieldy—from the singers, while allowing the conductor to adapt subsequent rehearsal procedures on the basis of one-on-one communication with each singer.

There are many fine models of this tradition, perhaps the most highly celebrated being that of Robert Shaw with his collection of letters that spanned the entirety of his career, most of which began with the peculiar, but congenial salutation, "Dear People" (Blocker, 2004).

For those unfamiliar with these literary gems, they are a source of inspiration to the conductor of any choir, as many an epistle dealt with matters of the incredibly mundane and perfunctory:

> In the last three weeks I've been reminded of the importance of the time-consuming nonmusical mechanics of building and maintaining a chorus. Chief case in point would be the business of increasing membership, and the operation is as far removed from the golden glow of art as one could get. (p. 6)
>
> We will give always proportionate (that is, rhythmic) time value to the various portions of speech sound that make up a word. That is to say hummed consonants and the final vowel sounds in diphthongs will always have an actual rhythmic allotment, varying up to ½ of the full time value, and depending upon tempo and style. (p. 14)

To the Julliard Chorus:

> The problem of discipline in a school situation is a thoroughly confusing one. Somehow, both professional and completely amateur regimens are easier to handle.

The professional's pay stops, and the amateur simply drops out. But a school is more complex. One contracts to take certain courses, and if they are ensemble courses with performance as their objective, then attendance must be counted one of the contractual obligations . . . And it seems reasonable to me that those who break that contract-of-sorts should not expect the benefits of credit and/or performance. If that is unfair, I'd like to know it. (p. 9)

But many of his letters were much more substantive and introspective, as he took the time (that he never had in rehearsal) to give the singers a glimpse of insight into the conductor's process. More often than not, these musings found their way into matters of philosophy, religion, and the incessant waves of change that were slowly eating away at the time-honored reverence for tradition, for culture, for art:

Regarding Mendelssohn's *Elijah*
Mendelssohn's audience was not a congregation of believers in a house of worship, but paying customers, very probably, of a minority upper economic class. His "chorales" were not, then, impulsive and commonly bonded responses to a religious drama, but further sermonettes and homilies delivered by angelic mini-hosts of angels in very proper Victorian measures and nuances.—at their worst a sort of Hallmark get-well card. (p. 305)

Regarding Verdi's *Ave Maria*
It seems to me that there are three major performance problems: the first and most obvious is that of keeping the performance "in tune": staying on a C major base of C = 523.3 while accommodating the constant switching of harmonic polarities occasioned by the affluence of accidentals (something like 135 on the first two pages). For singers, A-sharp simply is not B-flat; and in theory, at least, if we sang the wrong sequence of the "just" intervals versus "tempered" (keyboard) intervals, we could stray so far from C major—and from each other—that we'd never find our way home. (p. 330)
What are the meanings of art? What is it trying to tell us of man? What is man trying to tell us of himself? . . . what may be the function of influence of art in a world gone schizophrenic, paranoid, masochistic? (p. 357)

By nearly any account, Shaw's disposition on the podium was more closely aligned with the old school conductors cited at the front of this chapter, but similarly, his "force majeure" was most certainly motivated by his deep musical convictions, and his unrelenting desire to share his aural perceptions with the other musicians in each musical endeavor. When his demeanor on the podium was brash, the corresponding letter was often swimming in humility. When his rehearsal directives seemed unattainable, his rehearsal notes frequently celebrated a tone of compassion and empathy. Many in my generation have found inspiration in these letters as we do our best to find a source of wisdom and the requisite vocabulary to express our innermost thoughts about music, meaning, and mortality.

I have written to my choir since I first began teaching high school, and have rarely, if ever, regretted the investment of time required to commit my musical and philosophical ideals to paper. Where my own writing may be lacking in the theological or philosophical depth of Mr. Shaw, I have found my students particularly responsive to corollaries drawn between "the great composers" and modern icons who garner admiration and praise in the Arts and Entertainment pages of the *New York Times*. For that, I am deeply indebted to my own children, who have been patient enough to say, "Dad, you gotta hear this. This is really profound!" From this, I learned that while profundity may be in the ears of the beholder, finding common denominators between Madonna and Mozart is not as difficult as one might imagine.

What I don't recall is when I first asked my choir to write to me. It may well have been inspired by a professor in graduate school named Michael Rogers who once stated that the essence of helping students understand theory has not so much to do with revelatory discourse, but more about asking the right questions. Thought-provoking questions that cannot be dissuaded or deflected with a simple yes or no answer. When asked what constitutes a "good question," he merely replied, "It's always a work in progress—you keep refining and rephrasing until you begin to elicit thoughtful responses and substantive remarks."

And so I started asking my singers questions; my college singers, my community singers, the participants of rigorously auditioned all-state choirs, and the members of less confident groups of seventh- and eighth-graders participating in a community music festival. It turns out, that while the vocabulary may vary, nearly everyone has something to say about how music is meaningful, and why. And in the rare instances when that does not occur, that in itself provides insight regarding one's teaching effectiveness—a cue to consider a different approach in subsequent rehearsal.

In accordance with the simple wisdom of Michael Rogers, the most difficult part of the equation is asking the right question, particularly as the conductor comes to develop a relationship of trust with the singers. If the engagement is of a limited timespan, such as an honor or festival choir, I have found inquiries of a general nature to be sufficient, such as "Now that you've sung through all the music once, and we have identified that it is the composer's job to portray a musical interpretation of the text, which composer did the best job in getting it right? Cite examples in the score where it's clear the composer had a deep affinity for the text."

Or after a few guided discussions about compositional and stylistic elements, I might ask, "Choose a piece in your folder where you can readily identify an element or device that defines the composer's character and style." This is a particularly interesting question if you program pieces on a similar theme, but from different eras or by different composers; an excellent opportunity to ask the students to compare and contrast.

To be certain, there are many teachers who are exceptionally skilled at asking great questions and facilitating in depth discussions within the course of the rehearsal, but what is critical here is the written response. A verbal discussion not only tends to draw on responses from the more outspoken or extroverted participants, but even then, they are likely to be guarded when sharing their opinions amidst their peers. But when they write, they have the freedom to speak with more candor and introspection.

The guiding principle for this exercise is a simple, but an important mantra that frames the entire rehearsal experience. "You never know when somebody around you is having a musical experience." This, in fact, represents the very essence of elevated ensemble singing. When a large percentage of the members of the ensemble come to realize that the efforts of each singer contributes to someone else's evolving relationship with the choral art, each rehearsal activity shifts away from serving one's own needs to consideration for the livelihood of the entire ensemble.

Once the singers have committed their observations, reactions, and inspirations to paper, it is imperative that the conductor read every comment, and that this becomes immediately evident to the singers, ideally in the subsequent rehearsal. While there will undoubtedly be a great deal of repetition, and in many cases, the singers may simply be paraphrasing something that was said during rehearsal, even the paraphrase may shed an insight given that each person comes to the study of art with an individual perspective on life, religion, culture, poetry, and all things philosophical. But equally important is how these insights and reflections are shared.

For example, after combing through the responses from the previous rehearsal, the conductor might have highlighted a dozen particularly unique or otherwise distinctive responses to a question about Brahms' *O Schöne Nacht*. Having identified the composer's celebrated tendency of placing the piano and the choir in rhythmic opposition to one another, an appropriate prompt might be, "How has the composer employed the piano to help the singers understand his sentiments related to the poignancy in the text? The words alone suggest a simple love story, but the piano provides additional information. What, how, and why?"

A few typical responses from high school singers:[3]

> The piano almost never lines up with the singers, creating a sense of opposition or argument between the two.
>
> As the piano rolls through the opening measures, I can hear longing in the simple hanging chords.
>
> Even though I don't speak German, I can tell from the piano part when the boy starts running toward the girl.
>
> I love Brahms because even when we're in ¾ time, there are many times when I can't tell what meter we're in unless I'm looking at the music.
>
> There's something about the way Brahms uses harmony—I can never quite tell if the song is happy or sad. Maybe it's just melancholy!

Over time, the singers come to learn that they can even challenge the assumptions or assertions of the conductor:

> I think the music gets too crazy when we speed up in the middle. I'm a pianist, and I want to hear every detail in the piano part, but I get lost when the tempo is too fast.

Or maybe even this:

> Actually, I don't really care for the Brahms. I like it better than when we started, but I think the music get's sort of cheesy when the girls are singing about the birds.

At the beginning of the next rehearsal, without saying a word, I simply pull out a stack of papers with highlighted excerpts representing a variety of opinionated responses; the greater the diversity of the sampling the better, even if they are in complete opposition to my own interpretation of the music. All remarks are made without personal attribution, and if two participants have stated opposing opinions of the same musical element, it's best to read those back to back. In an honor choir setting, there may be two or three hundred responses to choose from and there will only be time to read ten or twelve excerpts in any give rehearsal session, but it quickly becomes evident to the singers that the conductor has read every response and has given consideration to every opinion. To that end, there have been many instances when I have altered an interpretation or realized a nuance in the score that I had missed before noting what a sixteen-year-old tenor has found clearly notated on the page.

Another variation on this exercise is to compile a bulleted list of response excerpts to be distributed by email or shared on a message board, but again, the responses are anonymous and seemingly random in an effort to present varied perspectives and ideologies. But in the end, the value to the conductor (and thus, to the singers) is two-fold; gathering tangible evidence as to what degree the singers understand the musical experience in progress, and of even greater importance, providing the opportunity for students to hear what their peers are thinking, reinforcing the mantra once more—"You never know when somebody around you is having a musical experience."

As a sense of community and mutual trust develops over the course of time, I have found that members of the choir are willing not only to speak in a voice that reveals their personal ideologies and perspectives, but once realizing that their "voices have been heard," they are willing to take more risks in the reverse engineering process. Of course, this requires a reciprocal effort on the part of the conductor, who leads by example in the depths of his writings to the choir and the aforementioned mode of rehearsal organization that lead the singers to musical discovery. At the same time, the effort to compose increasingly challenging questions—as related to specific repertoire—that will encourage thoughtful responses is absolutely paramount. Questions for an advanced ensemble that meets over an extended period of time might look like this:

On Poulenc's *Chansons françaises*:

> These pieces of a folk-song nature are among the most lighthearted of anything Poulenc has composed, and yet they were conceived at the end of World War II at a time when much of France lay in destruction and despair. (Some of you may remember *Un soir de niege*, a composition of a very different character, but published the same year.) What might have been Poulenc's intent in creating these settings? Can you think of other composers who have created works that seem to contradict the era or culture in which they lived? Can you think of a composer/artist who is doing that now?

On Bruckner's *Os Justi*:

> This year we have sung both Brahms and Bruckner. Brahms had an affinity for vocal chamber music with voice accompanied by piano, while Bruckner found much of his identity in his role as a church organist. Can you find evidence of this in his *Os Justi*? Be specific in identifying compositional devices that suggest the composer was an organist.

On Whitacre's *Leonardo Dreams of His Flying Machine*:

> We've talked a bit about how Whitacre has "quoted" Monteverdi in his compositional style of this piece. Identify a few places that you think the work sounds like Monteverdi, and a few others that are quintessential Whitacre. For a bonus point, explain why the composer would use this stylistic approach with this particular text.

It bears revisiting Rogers's caveat that the only way to develop the skill of asking thought-provoking questions is the pursuit through trial and error. And since repertoire changes from one season to the next, one has few opportunities to recycle good questions, particularly when it involves the elements of compare and contrast. But the intent remains constant in the charge to the singers to grapple with elements of score study in a communal way. Not only will this reveal one's musical experience, but additionally, this invites the singer to develop a personal relationship with the score and the words that inspired it. The ability to identify compositional process as a mode of interpretation gives the singer the opportunity to consider the artwork within a broader literary context.

In many instances, participants in these exercises have begun their statements with a disclaimer such as, "I don't consider myself a religious person, but . . .", only to go on to present some astounding revelation about the composer's ability to create a work that reflects the depths of the composer's faith. Or even more interesting is when we study a work on a sacred text composed by a confirmed atheist or agnostic, yet the composition is highly effective in communicating the implicit and explicit elements of that text. Such situations allow us to objectify the compositional process to some degree, which in turn, gives the singer the freedom to arrive at a unique and personal interpretation of his or her own. In other words, the singer is given the freedom of developing a relationship with a text that may, in fact, be in opposition with his own personal philosophical or religious values. We are studying the art—with an awareness of the underlying ethos, but devoid of personal indoctrination.

Clearly, by the end of the process, the ensemble will need to agree on matters of tempo, articulation, text inflection, and the corresponding elements of ensemble performance. But in the end, these are mere surface details as compared to the process of reverse engineering the score in an effort to help the singer develop a personal relationship with the music, keeping in mind that the conductor now has the added benefit of an entire team of investigative researchers who are scouring the score in the pursuit of revealing the composer's intent. I can scarcely think of a time when I have not experienced a new revelation with a composition that was spawned by a singer's momentary insight. Even the seasoned musician has much to learn from youthful eyes and a fresh perspective.

THE A CAPPELLA PHENOMENON: THE TRAIN IS LEAVING, WITHOUT THE CONDUCTOR!

When I first assumed my current post at The University of Delaware in 1997, I stumbled into an unanticipated hurdle in time-honored recruitment procedures. It seemed that students, especially non-music-major students, were reluctant to commit to the week regimen of curricular mandated rehearsals until they had the results from the audition "that really mattered"—the coveted honor of being invited to participate in an a cappella group.

At the time, I was vaguely familiar with the a cappella tradition, in particular, that of the legendary groups from the eastern Ivy League schools like Yale and Princeton, but I had no idea that the tradition had become such a phenomenon. As registered student organizations within the university community, these groups held a status similar to that of a fraternity, and appropriately so, as their mission was as often as not one of social interaction, superseding the musical or artistic agenda.

It seems hardly a coincidence that this was the era when MySpace and Facebook were becoming the main conduit of communication which, in time, would result in unprecedented opportunities like-minded musicians to find one another from coast to coast. It was in this environs that the Contemporary A Cappella Society of America (CASA) was born:

> Deke Sharon is commonly referred to as the father of contemporary a cappella, and while he may have bestowed that title upon himself, the name rings true. In 1990, Deke started the Contemporary A Cappella Society of America (CASA) out of his dorm room at Tufts. The organization's mission was (in part) to foster communication between all of the disparate a cappella groups popping up across the country.
>
> In the mid-nineties, collegiate a cappella exploded from an Ivy League curiosity to a full-blown coed pursuit. "We went from two hundred and fifty groups to more than twelve hundred and fifty." Deke says. He credits the growth spurt to a number of factors, from Boyz II Men to the Internet. (Rapkin, 2008, p. 79)

By 1996, the predecessor of the International Championship of Collegiate A Cappella (ICCA) contest had formed, which now functions as the Superbowl of college vocal groups, including several "playoff" rounds that lead to the final competition in Lincoln Center in New York City. Intended or otherwise, the consequence of this has been evidenced in a renewed purpose amidst these traditionally fraternal organizations. Motivated by the allure of becoming grand national champions, social interaction and simplistic arrangements have given way to disciplined and rigorous rehearsals and vocal arrangements that are frequently as complicated as vocal jazz.

In the context of pedagogy, and particularly in regard to fostering an environment where the participants assume full ownership of the process, the a cappella phenomenon has had a tremendous impact on the expectations singers bring into the rehearsal room. Joshua Duchan's (2012) efforts have resulted in a landmark scholarly publication that chronicles the evolution of a cappella while working to identify commonalities in pedagogical process, such as that documented below:

> Unlike a traditional Western choir, in which all the singers follow the direction of the conductor, the Fallen Angels [an a cappella group at Brandeis University,] rehearsal shows how collegiate a cappella groups distribute power more broadly. They more closely resemble an adolescent rock band model, in that important musical aspects are self-taught and the learning process is a peer-based experience. (p. 97)

One could argue that the a cappella and "serious music" populations on our college and high schools campus are not one and the same. The most serious music schools and conservatories often have strict policies that forbid "serious music students" from participating in student-led ensembles, but in other instances, the entire musical reputation of an educational institution may have more renown from its a cappella culture that the curricular choral program. In any event, conductors and teachers will need to reconcile these heightened expectations for student engagement, as well as a culture that encourages students to compose, arrange, improvise, and imagine! As has been said many times regarding repertoire, we must make sure that the music making in our rehearsal room meets or surpasses what is happening in our singers' everyday lives.

Conclusion

At this time when the very mores of our public schools and higher education institutions are under unprecedentedly intense scrutiny in this age of assessment and economic challenge, there is little doubt that traditional paradigms in music education will be questioned as well. Is our work meaningful? Relevant? Integral to the total education of the human being?

In this environment, the only constant is change, which will require future choral pedagogues to give careful consideration to the most meaningful aspects of choral artistry, and in particular, how we will empower our singers with the gift of musical curiosity.

Notes

1. Quotations from Ormandy and Toscanini: www.searchquote.com
2. See http://www.nafme.org/my-classroom/standards/.
3. Summarized and collected from conducting this exercise with all-state and honor choirs.

REFERENCES

Abrahams, F. (2011). Teaching and learning music through performance in middle school choir. In F. Abrahams & Paul D. Head (Eds.), *Teaching music through performance in middle school choir* (pp. 5–21). Chicago, IL: GIA.

Blocker, R. (Ed). (2004). *The Robert Shaw reader*. New Haven, CT: Yale University Press.

Boers, G. (1998). "This is not your father's automobile." *Choral Journal, 38*(10), 73–74.

Dewey, J. (2005). *Democracy and education*. New York: Barnes & Noble Books. (Original work published 1916.)

Duchan, J. (2012). *Powerful voices: The musical and social world of collegiate a cappella*. Ann Arbor, MI: University of Michigan Press.

Glenn, C. (Ed.). (1991). *In quest of answers: Interviews with American choral conductors*. Chapel Hill, NC: Hinshaw Music.

Head, P. (2008). The Search for Healthy and Appropriate Repertoire: Three Perspectives. In Michele Holt & James Mark Jordan (Eds.), *The school choral program: Philosophy, planning, organizing, and teaching* (pp. 133–146). Chicago, IL: GIA.

Head, P. (2011). Hearing between the lines: Promoting choral artistry in rehearsal and performance. In Frank Abrahams (Ed.), *Teaching music through performance in middle school choir* (pp. 29–37). Chicago, IL: GIA.

Jordan, J. (2007). *Evoking sound—the choral rehearsal: Techniques and procedures*. Chicago, IL: GIA.

Jordan. J. (2009). *Evoking sound: Fundamentals of choral conducting* (2nd ed.). Chicago, IL: GIA.

Music Educators National Conference. (1994). *National standards for arts education*. Reston, VA: Music Educators National Conference.

National Association for Music Education. (2014). National core music standards. Retrieved from http://www.nafme.org/my-classroom/standards/core-music-standards/

Rapkin, M. (2008). *Pitch perfect: The quest for collegiate a cappella glory*. New York, NY: Gotham.

Robinson, R. & Winold, A. (1992). *The choral experience: Literature, materials, and methods*. Prospect Heights, IL: Waveland. (Originally published Harper & Row, 1974).

Rogers, M. (1984). *Teaching approaches in music theory: An overview of pedagogical philosophies*. Carbondale, IL: Southern Illinois University Press.

Snow, S. (2011). Brainstorming for improvisation: Developing imaginative teaching strategies in the choral rehearsal. In Heather Buchanan, et al. (Eds.), *Teaching music through performance in choir: Vol. 3*. Chicago, IL: GIA.

CHAPTER 4

GOING GREEN

The Application of Informal Music Learning Strategies in High School Choral Ensembles

FRANK ABRAHAMS, ANTHONY RAFANIELLO,
JASON VODICKA*, DAVID WESTAWSKI,
JOHN WILSON

THIS chapter describes a collaborative project that studied the applications of informal music learning within the context of high school choral ensembles. For a 12-week period, the conductors of four high school choirs assigned students to small groups. The conductors charged each group to copy a Christmas carol of their choice from a recording or to create a new arrangement inspired by the recording without intervention from their conductor. The promise was to perform those carols at a public concert during the December holiday season. The team of conductor/researchers met face-to-face at the beginning of the semester to fine-tune the research design, procedures and methodology. The overarching research question addressed the efficacy of informal learning as a pedagogy to nurture the students' musicianship in choir. It also sought to uncover changes in perception on the part of both students and teachers relative to the school choral program. Data consisted primarily of interviews, video recordings, and reflective journals. Results showed that working informally to copy an arrangement from a recording had a positive impact on group cooperation, peer-directed learning, autonomy, leadership, and personal musical identity. It also served as a catalyst to change the culture of the ensemble because it changed perceptions of both students and teachers relative to musical skill and ability.[1]

The work of Lucy Green (2002; 2008) and others (Batt-Rawden & DeNora, 2005; Folkestad, 2006; Jaffurs, 2004) call attention to the power of informal learning to engage students in authentic music making and thereby empower their musicianship. Green wondered what would happen if students in general music classes were divided into cooperative learning groups and charged with copying a recording with minimal intervention from the music teacher. Research convinced her that meaningful and long-lasting engagements with music informally could be significant. She cited the many instances where popular musicians worked on their own in garage bands copying recordings. The Beatles started that way, as did the Rolling Stones and others. She reported success when general music students copied popular recordings and also when they copied recordings of classical music. She concluded that the process connected well to students, and increased motivation in and attitudes about the efficacy of school music classes. The geniuses at Apple computer call their music composition program "GarageBand" to reference that exact process of students working on their own, in their home garage, to create musical compositions. GarageBand comes as a standard program on every Macintosh computer.

Green (2007) identified five main characteristics that delimit informal learning practices. They are:

1. that learners always start with music that they know and like;
2. that the main learning practice involves copying recordings of real music by ear;
3. that learning takes place alone and, crucially, in groups of friends, mostly without adult guidance or supervision;
4. that learning is not progressively structured from simple to increasingly complex, but holistic, idiosyncratic, and haphazard; and
5. that listening, performing, improvising and composing are all integrated throughout the learning process. (p. 3)

The motivation for this study was to examine the efficacy of informal music learning when applied to the students in high school choral ensembles. These students are ones who chose to participate in a school music experience rather than the general population Green studied in the United Kingdom.

Research Questions

Sociologists (Green, 2005b; Martin, 1995; Finnegan, 1989; Negus, 1999; DeNora, 2000 and 2003; Clayton et al., 2003), note that current interests in music focus on how one applies discourse to construct musical meaning and how the media and the institution of schooling influence face-to-face interaction with music as a domain of study. Green (2005b) noted:

What people say about music, the uses to which they put it in their ordinary lives, and their music-making practices are all receiving interest from researchers and scholars, alongside questions about the structures and processes of the music industry and broadcasting corporations and perhaps to a lesser extent, of education. (p. 1)

To frame the research, we chose to ask foreshadowing questions (Malinowski, 1992) because we predicted that the outcomes would be positive. They were:

1. To what extent do informal music learning experiences facilitate group cooperation, peer-directed learning, autonomy, leadership, and personal musical identity among student members of school choral ensembles?
2. To what extent do informal music learning experiences bridge the gap between music students sing in choir and the music students listen to and enjoy outside school?
3. To what extent do informal music learning experiences influence the music teacher's perception of the skills his or her choral students possess?
4. To what extent do informal music learning experiences empower student musicianship and transform or change the culture of the choral ensemble?

Definition of Informal Music Learning

Some researchers (Jorgensen, 1997; Ziehe, 1986) suggest that informal learning is a function of both the place where the learning occurs and the process by which it happens. Ziehe (1986) contends that when learners are aware that learning is taking place it is "common." When the learners are unaware that learning is taking place, the learning is dubbed "uncommon." This happens when students learn by participating in an activity. Learning a new dance by watching others at a club is one example of uncommon learning. Jorgensen (1997), referencing ideas of Rousseau and Dewey, noted that teachers create the situations whereby students learn. She contended that those situations may be formal or informal but that together, they constitute "education." It is *formal* when the learning is teacher centered and *informal* when it occurs in ways that mirror learning outside of school. Without the teacher present, Folkestad (2006) added, the learner is often unaware that learning is taking place. Rolf (1991, cited in Lilliestam, 1996) added that when situated outside the school, informal learning as pedagogy shifts the power from the teacher to the student.

In this study, we acknowledged that informal learning occurs when there is no formal teacher guidance, direction, or formal evaluation from a teacher. Jaffurs (2004) stated that being able to work with and collaborate with other musicians is an important aspect for developing musicality. Informal learning builds both community and musicianship. The informal situation fosters an environment that facilitates a passion for learning and music making. Zimmerman (2001) reinforced this point by stating that what is important is how people relate to the music, not the specific aspects being studied within the music.

Significance of the Study

The research of Green (2002, 2006, 2007, 2008) and others (Goodrich, 2007; Heuser, 2008) confirms that students have the ability to copy arrangements from recordings in ways that are both literal and creative. Their research verifies that when students have a part in determining what they will be learning, the learning is more significant, meaningful, and long-lasting. It was the contention of the research team that information gleaned from this study could inform choral directors to consider yet another dimension to the ensemble experience.

Theoretical Framework

Based on findings from her 2002 study of popular musicians, and believing that music classes in British secondary schools were not engaging students, Green (2008) developed a curriculum for informal music learning for use in school music programs. She applied her ideas at 21 secondary schools and studied the results. Her population included 32 classroom music teachers, and over 1,500 students, most of whom were ages 13 and 14. Data included observations, video and audio recordings, and field notes. Her method was to infuse the music classes with an informal music curriculum that had seven stages:

> Stage 1 involved pupils choosing a piece of music, listening to it in friendship groups and copying it by ear on selected instruments;
> Stage 2 required pupils to create a version of a funk track by ear through listening and copying fifteen riffs (provided separately and in combinations). Worksheets with note names were provided to assist pupils if needed;
> Stage 3 was a repeat of Stage 1;
> In Stage 4 pupils composed, rehearsed and performed their own music, directing their own learning in friendship groups;
> Stage 5 was about songwriting with a band of peer musicians or community musicians;
> Stage 6 provided pupils with recordings of five pieces of familiar classical music. In friendship groups pupils had to listen, discuss, select, copy, arrange, rehearse and perform the music as an ensemble.
> Stage 7 was similar to Stage 6, except the classical music provided was unfamiliar to the pupils. (Green, 2008, pp. 193–194)

In self-selected friendship groups, students learned to listen to, interpret, analyze, and perform popular music by copying a recording of their choice. Students learned to work together, build relationships with colleagues, and did not rely on the guidance from their teachers. As a result, students became more attentive listeners. Green (2008) stated that just sitting and listening to music is not enough for informal music learning to stimulate student learning. Green's work suggested that having the students copy recordings of popular music in order to play it motivated them to listen to music analytically. Students became increasingly able to listen for: (a) detail, (b) quality, (c) texture, (d) harmony, (e) instruments, and (f) structure. This was a key finding that informed our study as well.

When applying Green's research to our study, we noted some differences. Green worked with general music students—that is, students who were required to be present in music classes. Our study focused on students who freely selected to be in the school ensemble program. The school choral ensembles in our study were even more specialized, as those students were accepted into the ensembles by competitive audition. Therefore the issues Green faced with motivation did not exist for us.

Throughout Green's research, one finds themes of musical autonomy (Green, 2006) and of the values of peer-directed learning (2008). In one study (2008), she noted that students prefer and are more comfortable helping each other rather than asking the teacher for guidance. Students felt less anxious and were more willing to explore and go beyond the boundaries usually set by teachers in formal music classrooms. This contributed to a feeling of student empowerment. Green (2009) also spoke to the issue of musical leadership. Although students work cooperatively in friendship groups, leaders emerge. We were curious to see if we would find similar themes.

Research Protocol

In the fall 2009, and acting as the senior researcher, Frank Abrahams invited four high school choral directors to participate as research fellows in a study to investigate the efficacy of Green's theories when applied to the high school choir. Each was his former student and had similar approaches to music teaching and learning. In addition, each had a similar number of years teaching. It was by chance that all were male. Abrahams invited two female teachers to participate but they declined. To assist, Abrahams assigned a research assistant to each conductor. An administrative assistant worked with him.

As a group, we all met together early in the fall on campus. We reviewed the research that Lucy Green conducted with general music students in the United Kingdom and each conductor received a copy of Green's texts, *How Popular Musicians Learn* (2002) and *Music, Informal Learning, and the School: A New Classroom Pedagogy* (2008). As a team, we decided that each conductor would choose one of the ensembles at his school, and assign them to small groups. Abrahams would ask each group to find a Christmas carol or holiday song on YouTube and copy the arrangement, adapting it for performance by the group in the upcoming December holiday concerts. All agreed to provide the students with time to complete the project at school but not to participate with the students while they were working. The conductors would ask students to keep personal journals. The conductors would also keep a journal and there would be periodic video recording of sessions when students were working together. Once the project was completed, Frank would visit each site to conduct semistructured interviews with each teacher and the students who participated in the study. In all, 80 students participated and arranged 20 songs.

Consistent with qualitative research methodology (Charmaz, 2006; Strauss & Corbin, 1990), we applied methods of open and axial coding (Plano, Clark, & Creswell, 2010) to sort, categorize and analyze the data. During the process of open coding, concepts, categories and properties were developed. These categories were consistent with Green's (2008) themes of group cooperation, peer-directed learning, autonomy, leadership and personal musical identity. To these categories, we added change in perception on the part of both students and teachers.

As a result of axial coding, we identified individual and group autonomy as a central phenomenon (Plano, Clark, & Creswell, 2010) for discussion later in the chapter. Insights from selective coding grounds the conclusions presented at the end.

Triangulation (Stake, 2010; Denzen, 1970); catalytic validity (Brown & Tandom, 1978; Reason & Rowan, 1981; Cohen, Manion, & Morrison, 2007); and member checks (Stake, 2010; Lincoln & Guba, 1985) provided trustworthiness for the study. Multiple times, we heard the same or similar comments from students and teachers across sites (triangulation). We noted "ah ha" moments from each conductor (catalytic validity). These are evident throughout the discussion of the data. Frank wrote the draft of the study and sent a copy to each teacher and to the research assistants to confirm accuracy (member checks). He then made changes as appropriate.

PRESENTATION, ANALYSIS, AND DISCUSSION OF THE DATA

Jason's story

Jason chose his most advanced ensemble, the chamber choir, to participate in the study. He grouped them into smaller choirs of about six singers each. Each small group selected a song on their own to transcribe and perform in the December holiday concert. The following is a transcription of one group's practice session.

They play the first run through.

STUDENT A: Is that the tenor or is that the bass? That last note. Cuz that's the lowest pitch that I can hear. The lowest pitch that I can hear is the one that I could hear you singing. I don't think there's a bass part there, at that part.

STUDENT C: If there isn't a bass part, can you . . .?

STUDENT A: I can sing that, I can find that low note, I'm saying that that's the lowest part I can hear on this recording and that was the one that [Student C] was singing most of the time. If that's the case then, if tenors and basses are in unison there?

STUDENT C: You can just make it up.

STUDENT B: Yah!

STUDENT C: As long as it like, works.

STUDENT A: When in doubt, I'll just sing what [Student C is] singing, cuz that's what I can hear. I cant hear any bass part.

STUDENT F: Hmm?

Another run through of the CD.

STUDENT A: I'm going down at the end.

STUDENT B: I mean, should we like, write it out what we think it is?

STUDENT A: No!

STUDENT C: I feel like that'd take a long time though.

STUDENT C: I could write it as, we could do it. We just don't know if we'd have time.

STUDENT A: I have no idea!

STUDENT B: I guess we'll just do it again.

STUDENT A: If I had another lyric I'd just try to put it together.

They listen to the recording again.

STUDENT F: Uhm, can we play the part with the solo again? Because the rest is the main chorus and the fa la la's.

STUDENT C: The solo's like the holly . . . something something . . .

STUDENT A: There's like a girl and then a guy and that's it.

STUDENT C: And then the second part is with "the rising of the sun and the running of the deer."

STUDENT A: I'm convinced there is no bass part. If it is, then it's just the same as [what] the tenors are singing. I'm convinced there is no bass part.

STUDENT C: I know.

STUDENT B: Or its like so low it isn't even audible.

STUDENT F: Can you play it again?

STUDENT C: Yah.

STUDENT A: I'm convinced there is no bass part from like, halfway to the end. Like, until the last part, like I can't hear it.

STUDENT B: Now you can.

STUDENT A: No not here, but like toward the end.

They listen to the CD.

STUDENT F: The second part of the solo is "the rising of the sun."

STUDENT C: Right, but what's the first part?

STUDENT F: "The holly bears the berry, and red as any blood, then Mary bore sweet Jesus Christ . . ." its like, there are more verses than that, and I think they are trying to splice that together. I don't know if all of what I said was on there, but you can just sing out and pick a different verse. Uhm, and then, after the solo its just the fa la la's?

STUDENT C: Yah!

STUDENT F: And the chorus. (Audio transcription from October 20, 2009)

The transcript, typical of each of the rehearsals, shows that the students are all working cooperatively together (*group cooperation*). In this instance, particularly with Student C, they are making independent as well as group (*peer-directed*) musical decisions. Student

A has difficulty hearing a particular part and the other members of the group help him to find his notes (*peer-directed learning*). Student C emerges as the leader (*leadership*) in this session, but each student does contribute to the good of the whole group.

In lieu of personal journals, Jason's students posted comments on a group blog he set up on a social networking site on the Internet. As a catalyst for responses, Jason posted prompts to help students focus their posts. These included:

> How did you choose your piece of music? What about your piece did you keep the same? What did you change and why? How was this project problematic? What was easy? What was more difficult than using a printed score? What was easier than using a printed score? What was more difficult about not having a teacher? What was easier about not having a teacher? What advice would you give to your choir teachers about how to approach music in the future? How much did you use a keyboard? Do you think this could work with a less experienced choir or only an advanced group? What was the most valuable part of this experience? How have you changed because of this experience? (Jason's website)

Posting the prompts enabled students to write freely and provide valuable insights. Some excerpts follow:

Student 1

Sometimes it was hard to separate the harmonies. I, in particular, had a lot of trouble with this, as it is hard for me to just hear something once and then sing it. During practice, we were fortunate enough to have music theory students and people who were amazing at hearing the notes in our group to pick out the parts. They could then sing them back to us and play them on the keyboard (*Peer-directed learning*). What may or may not be surprising, is that we were really focused during our rehearsal time. We knew what we had to do and we went straight at it, while still having a good time (*group cooperation*).

Student 2

We were able to focus in on these problems easier without a teacher because we knew what we were not comfortable on and what needed more focus (*autonomy*). Overall, this experience shows to teachers that students can learn in a nontraditional manner. The most valuable part of this experience to me was seeing the great amount that we are capable of by ourselves that I wouldn't have known before. Because of this experience I pay more attention to the different voice parts that are in a song not just the melody (*student change in perception*).

Student 3

My group chose to learn and perform the *Holly and the Ivy* by AWKapella. We chose this recording because it is a classic holiday song, and at first listening the parts sounded well represented. One of our difficulties as we dug into the project was hearing the alto, tenor, and bass parts, as well as figuring out the starting key and key changes. Eventually we listened to the recording enough that we got some parts, and made it up in areas where we couldn't hear the recording well (*group coopera-tion* and *peer-directed*). Reading music is very important, but learning by ear is not a choral faux pas. Our work in these projects demonstrates the value of listening by ear. Perhaps all choral directors, or anyone aspiring to be a choral director, should develop warmups that intensely focus on strengthening the ear. These projects have given me confidence about our ability to learn challenging pieces (*personal musical identity*).

John's story

Like Jason, John chose his top choral ensemble to participate. He divided them into five small groups and charged them with selecting a Christmas song to copy. Three groups chose traditional carols to copy. The other two groups chose more general Christmas songs. Unlike Jason's students, most of the students in John's cohort met outside of school at individual homes to complete their arrangements. This was not the inten-tion of the study. Instead, the study was to apply informal music learning strategies as part of the in-school experience. Nonetheless, data gleaned from student journals con-firm findings that support goals of group cooperation, peer-directed learning, auton-omy, leadership, and personal musical identity. Therefore the data are included in the analysis.

In her journal, one student described the process her group used to complete their transcription. She wrote:

> We decided that we wanted to rearrange the harmonies of the chorus. Instead of rewriting them all at once, we rewrote one part at a time based off the melody. Once we put all parts together, some notes were conflicting because we had just written them to agree with the melody only, so we had to adjust some of them. (Student A journal entry 3)

In another entry she wrote:

> Instead of getting much work done, we contemplated the direction of our arrange-ment. It seemed as though the new harmonies we had written were too troublesome for people to learn. After much discussion as to how we would approach the situa-tion, we talked for some time about the shape of the piece. (Student A journal entry 5)

Then, she wrote:

> We progressed further in harmonizing and blending our voices, which did not come easily. We focused mostly on a section of the piece that involves voice parts begin-ning at different measures but ending at once. Rhythmically it was challenging but eventually we accomplished our goal. (Student A journal entry 7)

Not all of John's students found the task easy. Student B wrote:

> By this point, I began to realize that trying to learn a piece of choral music without some sort of visual aid was a real challenge for me. Excluding rock songs, learning a piece by ear is not necessary a strong point for me. (Student B journal entry 4)

Concerning personal musical identity this student also noted:

> While we were there [at rehearsal], we decided that the best way to "make it our own" was to merge it with another song. We chose *God Rest Ye Merry Gentlemen,* and listened to a few recordings of it to get some ideas. (Student B journal entry 2)

Different students contributed to the arrangement in different ways. Student C wrote the transitions and commented:

> On my own, I created a possible transition from *Carol of the Bells* into *God Rest Ye Merry Gentlemen.* I had the sopranos and altos hold out the line "on, on they send, on without end" while the tenors sing the next line and basses sing dings and dongs. It was a simplistic way of making the transition but I felt that we might be able to build off of it. (Student C journal entry 4)

To connect to personal musical identity, she continues:

> To come up with my idea, I used a guess and check style. I went through a number of different approaches, with varying chords and tempos, before coming to the one that I will present to my group tomorrow. I did not have a clear thought for the transition but messing around with various notes was useful in that it got me thinking and allowed me to be open to a number of possibilities instead of going in feeling that there was only one correct way. (Student C journal entry 4)

This is consistent with what Green (2007) found popular musicians would do in their garages. In addition, it became apparent that Student C had become the group's leader (*leadership*). As time went on, the instances of peer-directed learning became apparent. Student C comments:

> Today was amazing. [Student D] and I were able to figure out how to fit in *God Rest Ye Merry Gentlemen.* To put it together still involved a good amount of guess and check, but there was definitely an improvement from the last time. (Student C journal entry 8)

We see in Student E the emergence of a personal musical identity as well as a sense of autonomy. In his journal, he wrote:

> We met after school, this time in the choir room. We continued working on parts and sang together with the CD. I began to feel more confident on my part, especially since

I am not used to hearing the tenor line in a song. Towards the end of the meeting, a few of us stayed in the choir room and played around with some harmonies for *God Rest Ye Merry Gentlemen*. I found a few that fit and I plan on sharing them at the next meeting. (Student E journal 3)

One student wrote of her own personal method of creation that she called "guess and check" (Student C) but which clearly connected to her sense of personal empowerment (*personal musical identity*) and facilitated a change in her own perceptions of her musical abilities. In the end, all five groups did produce something for performance. This evidenced an ability to work together and to meet a goal (*group cooperation* and *peer-directed*). The fact that most did not follow the instructions for the study in a curious way suggests autonomy.

Dave's story

At Robbinsville, a student explained the process. He said:

> Mr. Westawski put us into groups and sent us off to practice rooms to arrange a pop song of their choice. We all worked together, and we figured out the voice parts. We chose a song by Lincoln Park. Actually, I know everything about them already and so I was like hey, I know it. So I became the leader but each member of the group came up with their own voice parts. Then, we taught it to the rest of the choir.

As with all of the other groups, one student emerged as the leader (*leadership*). However at this school, each group taught their arrangement to the entire choir. When interviewed about what it was like to teach the arrangement to the group, the student leader revealed some noteworthy insights. He said:

> [Teaching the other students] was a lot harder. It was like a different perspective (*change in student perspective*) 'cause when you teach and stuff, it's like we joke around. When I was sitting there, it was like "stop!" It was annoying. And it pissed me off when people wouldn't get it right.

Dave spoke about the connection of the informal learning experience to the formal learning in the classroom (*change in teacher perception*). At their interview with me, several students talked about how much longer it took to get the song ready when they worked on their own than when they worked with their teacher in the formal rehearsal. Dave said:

> They would find the problem and not know exactly what is was or how to fix it, go through the things we talk about in class all the time, and eventually hit on the right one whether it be a vowel shape or a tuning issue or whatever the case was. They found it on their own, but it took a little bit longer than if I had been in the front of the room. But they got the answer themselves at the end of it.

All throughout the process, I heard them using terms and terminology from class and exercises from class. They didn't even realize, a lot of the time, that so much of what we do on a daily basis, whether it be warmups or actually rehearsing pieces, they were pulling out from somewhere to put that together. So it's kinda cool to watch on the sidelines. Every method that we do during the class period they could pull from to put together that piece on their own. (Interview with Dave)

I asked Dave's students if they noticed any change in their teacher's teaching style since the completion of the informal learning project? One student said:

I think like in the beginning of the year it was always like counting notes and this is what you have to do and we're doing it exactly like what's on the page because that's how it's written. And now, we are more independent and we learn more stuff on our own and we have more freedom (*autonomy*). (Student interview)

Another student responded that their teacher did not change. Instead they (i.e., the students) changed (*student change of perception*). I asked them to describe in what ways. A student responded:

He looks at us like we're not stupid (*all laugh*) (*change in student perception*). My focus has improved because of working with the group (*group cooperation* and *peer-directed learning*). I listen to other parts better. I listen to my own part better (*personal musical identity*), more than I did at the beginning of the year. (Student interview)

Another student said:

I think that as a choir we matured (*change in student perception* and *connection to research question 4*) since the beginning of the year. We sing better together and listen more to each other. (Student interview)

I asked how did the two pieces that you worked on together help that? A student answered:

Working on our own we had to listen to each other and it made us understand better and be more musicians ourselves (*personal musical identity*).

I asked, "Was one of you more in charge?" As in all the other groups, they said, "Yes!"

Dave agreed that the challenge for him was to find ways to add value to what the students could do on their own (*change in teacher perception*). He said, "Rather than assuming the choir can't do anything, I better teach you your part. How do you tap into that as a conductor knowing what they are capable of doing? [This study showed that students] don't really need the traditional means and methods. They can do far more on their own" (interview with Dave).

Anthony's story

Anthony invited his separate men's and women's ensembles to participate in the research study. The men copied two arrangements, and the women transcribed one.

In addition to student journals, Anthony conducted a short video interview with each student who participated. In response to a question asking about the positive aspects of the project, a student answered:

> Well, you really have to know the music and so you really know it especially when I was singing the song, I felt as though I knew the music much better than any other piece that I've done because we created the piece (*peer-directed, autonomy*, and *personal musical identity*). It also forces you to look at how the parts really work together and what each part does (*change in student perception*).

He continued:

> You need to make the piece and teach the piece to other people (*peer-directed learning* and *leadership*).

In answer to a question asking what the student believed were the positive aspects of the informal learning project, another student spoke to the issue of change in perception. He said:

> I feel it helps us grow musically and for anyone who really enjoys arranging, composing, and performing it helps you understand the process you go through making sure all the touches are like neat and fine. Then you actually get to perform or see your finished product and you feel kind of like a sense of pride and you understand what a composer actually goes through. (Student 4 video interview)

When asked if the student felt hindered without input from the teacher, he responded:

> No, I don't think we felt any, or I didn't, because we had at least one trustworthy member of our group (*leadership*) that kept us going and I felt that we had like a good group discussion like we always heard everyone's side (*group cooperation*). It was basically like a class but it was sort of all of us teaching the class (*peer-directed learning*) at like one point or another. (Student 4 video interview)

Some months later, I visited several of the schools to interview the students and their teacher. I was curious to find out if the ensemble culture changed because of the study. These data were needed to answer research questions 2 and 3. I also wanted to ask how the individual students changed and whether the teacher felt that he changed or whether the students noticed a change in the teacher. When I asked the teachers how they felt that they changed because of what their students accomplished, John said:

> It was a good situation. People all played to their strengths and so it was just nice to see strengths come out from everybody. There were some cool things that happened corporately. Lisa's group decided originally to do *Carol of the Bells* and then they decided to layer on *God Rest Ye Merry Gentlemen*. And they just did it, put it together and it was fantastic. So, it was nice to see that cohesion. In other groups there were folks looking to one person for guidance. It was so cool. (Interview with John and his students, June 3, 2009)

This speaks to the issue of musical autonomy. I asked whether he changed in any way after the experience. He responded:

> Just that I realized that they have really long memories. We didn't originally record these, then one day I said, "we need to record these," so we just did it, and it was fantastic. That confirms my suspicions that there is some really good musicians in here and some pretty awesome musical thinkers. (Interview with John and his students, June 3, 2009)

This comment may suggest that students tend to remember what they do on their own more so than what teachers do with them, which in turn connects further to issues of musical autonomy. The analysis of data revealed and confirmed the same themes found in Green's (2007) research. They are: group cooperation, peer-directed learning, autonomy, leadership, and personal musical identity.

> Jason's students (Interview with Jason and his students, June 1, 2010) told me that they felt a great sense of accomplishment (*autonomy*) upon completing their song. Jason stated that he wondered what might happen if he gave them a legitimate choral piece to learn informally (*teacher change in perception*).

Autonomy

Because of axial coding, the theme autonomy emerged as a central phenomenon. Autonomy was closely connected to the theme of personal musical identity and issues of changes in student perception. One example happened at Dave's school. Before the interview, I heard the students rehearsing with student teachers from a local college on pieces that they were preparing for a concert. There were intonation issues, uniformity of vowel issues and more. However, when the students sang their own arrangements, these issues disappeared. The high school students suggested that one reason might be that they were reading from notation for the formal choral pieces and learned their own arrangements by ear (*autonomy, personal musical identity*). Regarding autonomy, one of Dave's students said:

I think that as a choir we matured (*autonomy, change in student perception*, and *connection to research question 4*) since the beginning of the year. We sing better together and listen more to each other. (Student interview)

I asked how did the two pieces that you worked on together help that? A student answered:

Working on our own we had to listen to each other and it made us understand better and be more musicians ourselves (autonomy and *personal musical identity*). (Student interview)

As a result, a student at Dave's school shared:

I try to listen a little bit more to Mr. Westawski when he gives us directions. I try to look at my music more to make sure I know what I am doing. (Student interview at Dave's school)

CONCLUSIONS

Green (2006) writes:

By paying attention to how children learn informally in music, whether it is applied to popular or classical or any other music, I wish to suggest, we allow an engagement with musical inherent meanings as a *theoretical aspect of virtual musical autonomy* from social contexts. When they engage with music's materials themselves, especially through aural, informal learning practices, pupils are touching on an aspect of inherent meaning that is virtually freed for a moment from social context. They are bringing inherent meanings into being and are able to imbue the music with a new *delineated* content of their own. They touch a quality of musical experience which, precisely because of its fleeting freedom from delineation, at the same time exposes the inevitability of delineation. (p. 113)

We found this to be true as well. Students took ownership for the arrangements they created. Teachers validated their work by including the performances in the December concert programs and permitting students to do an arrangement for the spring concert. At each site, students said in our group interview that they wanted to do at least one piece of their own making at every concert. Several of the conductors agreed that this would be a good and worthwhile practice.

As stated previously, four questions framed the research.

Research Question 1

To what extent do informal music learning experiences facilitate group cooperation, peer-directed learning, autonomy, leadership, and personal musical identity among student members of school choral ensembles?

As with Green's (2002, 2008) research with general music students, members of the school ensembles reported that they felt positive about their music learning experiences. They documented this in journals (John's students, Dave's students), in online blog postings (Jason's students), and in video interviews (Anthony's students). This was confirmed when watching video recordings of their rehearsals and in reading the teacher's personal journal. Students found members of the groups to be cooperative for the most part (*group cooperation*) and the learning in groups to be helpful (*peer-directed*). Frequently, students helped each other (*peer-directed learning*) and assumed roles of authority (*leadership*). In all, the experience provided students with a sense of accomplishment, ownership, pride, and a desire to do the project again in the future (*autonomy*). In interviews, journals and blogs, students reported that they felt the arrangements were representative of who they are as musicians (*personal musical identity*). Many students reported that they came to realize how much is involved in creating a musical arrangement even when there was a recording to serve as the model, and had a new respect for the musical arrangements of others (*student change of perception*). Live interviews, interviews on video recording, online blogs, and personal journals provided the triangulation of data. Instances of change in perception by students and their teachers such as John's comments relative to how impressed he was with what his students accomplished (*teacher change in perception*) were instances of the "ah ha" moments that define catalytic validity. Students in their blogs, interviews and journals provided instances of "ah ha" moments as well. An example of this was one of Dave's students who said that because of this experience she realized that she could learn from someone other than the teacher (*change in student perception*). In fact, she realized that all could learn from each other (*peer-directed*).

Research Question 2

To what extent do informal music learning experiences bridge the gap between the music that students sing in choir and the music they listen to and enjoy outside school?

In all instances, students chose the music to transcribe and arrange without input from their teacher. Anthony reported that at his school the students chose music that he would not have considered when selecting music for the ensemble to perform. He expressed pleasure in the breadth that brought to the choral program. Dave and Jason concurred (personal correspondence). Students were asked to transcribe a Christmas carol or song and all found interesting versions on YouTube to transcribe; *Carol of the Bells* seemed to be most popular with separate groups from three schools choosing it. When asked in interviews and on blogs if they enjoyed the informal learning project, all were unanimous in responding "Yes!" They felt pride that their teacher believed enough in their abilities to complete the project successfully and expressed gratitude to their teachers for including the finished products in the winter concerts.

Research Question 3

To what extent do informal music learning experiences influence the music teacher's perception of the skills his or her choral students possess?

Throughout this process, students worked without input from their teacher. Most groups reported that a leader emerged from inside each group to ensure that the group kept moving forward. This represented a shift in the power structures within the choral classroom. In addition, it showed the students that their teacher had the confidence that they had the ability to complete the informal music-learning project successfully. This was consistent with every teacher at every school. Students commented in journals, blogs, and interviews that they appreciated that responsibility and the trust their teachers showed them.

Each teacher believed that his students would be able to complete the project and each teacher was certain that the results would be of a high level. This may have been because the teachers chose their best students to participate and in this sense the project differed significantly from Green's (2002, 2008) experiences with general music students. John noted that he was particularly surprised that students were able to recall their arrangements when asked to record them several months after the performance. Dave's students performed their arrangements for me when I visited the school six months after the public performance. As with John's students, Dave's singers remembered exactly how to sing the arrangement. In both instances, there were no printed scores. Students learned everything aurally and recalled it from memory.

Regarding one the pieces the students arranged, Dave said:

> If I actually saw that in print, I don't think I would have picked it. I would have looked at all those inner voices and said "No way!" And, that would have been a shame because of what they were able to do on their own. I would have limited them by looking at that score and thinking that they were not ready for or not capable of [meeting the challenges]. That could limit what I am going to choose music-wise because they obviously can get that stuff down without having a score in front of them (*change in teacher perception*). (Interview with Dave)

This was an important insight for him. Dave agreed that the challenge for him was to find ways to add value to what the students could do on their own (*change in teacher perception*). He said, "Rather than assuming the choir can't do anything, I better teach you your part. How do you tap into that as a conductor knowing what they are capable of doing? . . . [This study showed that students] don't really need the traditional means and methods. They can do far more on their own" (interview with Dave).

Dave also spoke about the connection of the informal learning experience to the formal learning in the classroom *(change in teacher perception)*. At their interview with me, several students talked about how much longer it took to get the song ready when they worked on their own than when they worked with their teacher in the formal rehearsal.

I asked Dave's students if they noticed a change in their teacher because of the informal music learning project. One student responded:

> I think like in the beginning of the year it was always like counting notes and this is what you have to do and we're doing it exactly like what's on the page because that's how it's written. And now, we are more independent and we learn more stuff on our own and we have more freedom *(autonomy)*. (Student interview)

Another student responded that their teacher did not change. Instead they (i.e., the students) changed *(student change of perception)*. I asked them to describe in what ways. A student responded:

> He looks at us like we're not stupid *(all laugh)* *(change in student perception)*. My focus has improved because of working with the group *(group cooperation, peer-directed learning)*. I listen to other parts better. I listen to my own part better *(personal musical identity)*, more than I did at the beginning of the year. (Student interview)

Research Question 4

To what extent do informal music learning experiences empower student musicianship and transform or change the culture of the choral ensemble?

Students felt that they became more aware of the process that composers follow to produce a piece. As a result, they had a new found respect for the music of others that they were singing or playing in the ensemble. One of Anthony's students summed it best when she said in her video interview:

> I think that it helps each of us individually a lot. I was an Alto I for this, so I had to listen for a part that wasn't there. Usually, you have maybe at the most a melody and then maybe a little bit of harmony but there's no alto I in a piece. So I feel like having us search for that really helped me grow as a musician and it helped me grow in choir too, because now I can listen for things that maybe don't come so easily.

Students from every school and in each group mentioned the importance of leadership as part of the culture of the ensemble. In nearly every instance, a leader emerged from the group to help guide and shepherd the ensemble toward performance. With very few exceptions, students felt that that project brought them closer together, despite minor instances of disagreement during the process, and all were proud of their public performance. Most felt that the project challenged and improved their musicianship and predicted that such improvement would be beneficial to their choir and band in the future:

> One noted changes in perception on the part of the students at varying points during the project. For example, one of Dave's students said that because of this experience she realized that she could learn from someone other than the teacher (*change in student perception*). In fact, she realized that all could learn from each other (*peer-directed learning*). (Student interview)

In the interviews I did at their schools or in their personal journal, each teacher remarked either that they were pleased with the results and proud of how well their students worked together and met the expectations of the project. All have agreed to include an informal learning experience where students do their own transcriptions in future concerts.

Dewey (1899, 1902, 1914) argued for a student-centered pedagogy. Freire (1970, 1973) advocated that students bring materials of their own to the classroom for teachers to use as the basal teaching texts. Swanwick (1999) urged music teachers to teach music musically. Green (2002, 2006, 2007, 2008) suggested that informal music learning has curricular applications that enhance motivation and nurture both musical and social skills.

Generating theory

This research posits a theory for informal music learning as a strategy for music teaching and learning in high school choral ensembles. Specifically, informal engagements with musicking (Small, 1998) should be included alongside the traditional ensemble experience with the music teacher at the core. When students are empowered by their conductors to choose music they like, and bring music from their engagements outside the school, they have "voice." Music teachers do not always hear these voices. Instead these conductors are intent on training singers to respond only to the gestures and verbal instructions of their conductor without student input. Informal music learning experiences provide a process for self-created arrangements that student members of school ensembles produce independently of their music teacher. Next, when engaging in this process, students in school ensembles focus, become leaders, and produce musical products of high quality worthy of public performance. Students, working independently and with minimal intervention from their teacher, become better musicians. They take ownership and feel empowered. Their musical contributions broaden the culture of the ensemble.

Returning to the issue of relevancy, the informal music-learning project did indeed empower student musicianship. Group cooperation and peer-directed learning contributed to students' abilities to create original transcriptions and arrangements. In one instance, the project inspired a student to complete his own arrangement independent of the group. Several teachers shared insights that confirm such empowerment caused a change or transformation in their students and in them. The students shared similar insights. In all instances, the teachers who participated in the study changed their strategies and expectations because of the work produced independently and informally by the students. Power relationships inside the rehearsal changed, as well as a mutual respect for the abilities of students by their teachers and from the students to their teachers. Students recognized that it was because of the fine programs to which they belonged that they acquired the skills needed to arrange their pieces. By allowing students to pick their own music to arrange and perform, teachers honored their students' personal musical preferences and taste. That was a positive step toward linking the music that students enjoy outside of school with the music they perform in school.

Future research might replicate this study with students in middle school ensembles or with students who are not in top performing groups in the high school. Individual action research studies, as originally proposed for this project, would inform teachers of the efficacy of informal music learning in their own programs as well as add to the literature. Policy for curriculum might be developed to ensure that students do have regular opportunities for informal music learning in school ensemble programs and that teachers are prepared to facilitate such musical endeavors.

Notes

* At the time of this study, Jason Vodicka was a choral director at Pennsbury High School, Fairless Hills, Pennsylvania, USA and David Westawski was a choral director at Robbinsville High School, Robbinsville, New Jersey, USA.
1. The Center for Critical Pedagogy at Westminster Choir College, where the senior researcher serves as director, provided support for this research. Research fellows included Anthony Rafaniello, Jason Vodicka, David Westawski, and John Wilson. Research assistants for this project included Jacob Ezzo, Chad Keilman, Louis Spinelli, and James Stirling.

References

Abrahams, F. (2005a). The application of critical pedagogy to music teaching and learning. *Visions of Research in Music Education*, 6. Retrieved from http://www-usr.rider.edu/~vrme/v6n1/visions/Abrahams%20The%20Application%20of%20Critical%20Pedagogy.pdf

Batt-Rawden, K., & DeNora, T. (2005). Music and informal learning in everyday life. *Music Education Research*, 7(3), 289–304.

Brown, D., & Tandom, R. (1978). Interviews as catalysts. *Journal of Applied Psychology*, 63(2), 197–205.

Charmaz, K. (2006). *Constructing grounded theory: A practical guide through qualitative analysis*. Thousand Oaks, CA: Sage.

Clayton, Martin, Herbert, Trevor, & Middleton, Richard (Eds.). (2003) *The cultural study of music: A critical introduction*. New York and London: Routledge.

Cohen, L., Manion, L., & Morrison, K. R. B. (2007). *Research methods in education*. New York: Routledge.

De Nora, T. (2000). *Music in everyday life*. Cambridge, MA: Cambridge University Press.

De Nora, T. (2003). *After Adorno: Rethinking music sociology*. Cambridge, MA: Cambridge University Press.

Dewey, J. (1899). *The school and society*. Chicago: University of Chicago Press.

Dewey, J. (1902). *The child and the curriculum*. Chicago: University of Chicago Press.

Dewey, J. (1916). *Democracy and education*. New York: Macmillan.

Finnegan, R. (1989). *The hidden musicians: Music-making in an English town*. Cambridge, UK: Cambridge University Press.

Folkestad, G. (2006, July). Formal and informal learning situations or practices vs. formal and informal ways of learning. *British Journal of Music Education*, 23(2), 134–145.

Freire, P. (1970). *Pedagogy of the oppressed*. New York: Seabury.

Freire, P. (1973). *Education for critical consciousness*. New York: Continuum.

Goodrich, A. (2007). Peer mentoring in a high school jazz ensemble. *Journal of Research in Music Education*, 55(2), 94–114.

Green, L. (2002). *How popular musicians learn: A way ahead for music education*. Burlington, VT: Ashgate.

Green, L. (2005b). The music curriculum as lived experience: Children's "natural" music learning processes [Electronic version]. *Music Educators Journal*, 91(4), 27–32.

Green, L. (2006). Popular music education in and for itself, and for "other" music: Current research in the classroom. *International Journal of Music Education*, 24(2), 110–118.

Green, L. (2007). *Group cooperation, inclusion and disaffected pupils: Some responses to informal learning in the music classroom*. Paper presented at the 2007 Research in Music Education Conference, Exeter, UK. Retrieved from http://eprints.ioe.ac.uk/1113/1/Green2008Group177.pdf

Green, L. (2008). *Music, informal learning, and the school: A new classroom pedagogy*. Burlington, VT: Ashgate.

Heuser, F. (2008, September). Encouraging change: Incorporating aural and informal learning processes in an introductory music education course. *VRME: Visions of research in music education*, 12, 1–9. Retrieved September 8, 2008, from Westminster Choir College of Rider University Web site: http://usr.rider.edu/~vrme/

Jaffurs, S. E. (2004, December). Developing musicality: Formal and informal practices. *Action, Criticism, and Theory for Music Education*, 3(3), 2–17.

Jorgensen, E. R. (1997). *In search of music education*. Urbana, IL: University of Illinois Press.

Lilliestam, L. (1996). On playing by ear. *Popular Music*, 15(2), 195–216.

Lincoln, Y. S., & Guba, E. G. (1985). *Naturalistic inquiry*. Thousand Oaks, CA: Sage.

Lostetter, K. (2009). *The application of informal learning principles in an eighth grade saxophone sectional: a case study* (Unpublished master's thesis). Rider University, Lawrenceville, New Jersey.

Malinowski, B. (1992). *The Argonauts of the western Pacific*. London: Routledge.

Martin, P. (1995). *Sounds and society: Themes in the sociology of music*. New York: Manchester University Press.

Negus, Keith. (1999) *Music genres and corporate cultures*. London: Routledge.

Plano Clark, V. L., & Creswell, J. W. (2010). *Understanding research: A consumer's guide*. Upper Saddle River, NJ: Pearson.

Reason, P., & Rowan, J. (1981). Issues of validity in new paradigm research. In P. Reason & J. Rowan (Eds.), *Human inquiry: A sourcebook of new paradigm research* (pp. 239–262). New York: John Wiley.

Small, C. (1998). *Musicking: The meanings of performing and listening.* Hanover, CT: Wesleyan University Press.

Stake, R. E. (2010). *Qualitative research: Studying how things work.* New York: Guilford.

Stauffer, S. L. (2002). Connections between the musical and life experiences of young composers and their compositions [Electronic version]. *Journal of Research in Music Education, 50*(4), 301–322.

Strauss, A., & Corbin, J. (1990). *Basics of qualitative research: Grounded theory procedures and techniques.* Newbury Park, CA: SAGE.

Swanwick, K. (1999). *Teaching music musically.* New York: Routledge.

Ziehe, T. (2003). *Ny ungdom. Om ovanliga läroprocesser* [New youth. On uncommon learning processes]. Stockholm: Norsteds.

Zimmerman, M. P. (2001). *On musicality & milestones.* M. R. Campbell (Ed.). Urbana-Champaign: University of Illinois.

CHAPTER 5

"LET THE WHOLE WORLD REJOICE!" CHORAL MUSIC EDUCATION

The Kodály Perspective

LÁSZLÓ NORBERT NEMES

> "We must look forward to the time
> when all people in all lands
> are brought together through singing,
> and when there is a universal harmony."[1]

ZOLTÁN Kodály (1882–1967), one of the most outstanding figures of 20th-century Hungarian musical art, musical research, and music education, was the founder of the 20th-century Hungarian choral tradition and choral movement. In his lifework choral compositions fill a prominent place as he composed a great number of choruses for children's, female, male, and mixed choirs, altogether 160 a cappella pieces (Bónis, n.d.). His compositions and other creative achievements together with his intellectuality and teachings influenced not only his contemporaries but have continued to live in the works and in the thinking of succeeding generations. From a wider perspective, over the course of his long life, Kodály, both figuratively and literally, worked for the establishment of 20th-century Hungarian musical culture that embraced fundamentally new ways of thinking about Hungarian national music and about music education for both professional musicians and the general public. His achievements in the field of choral music cannot be separated from his concept of music education, the understanding of which requires a comprehensive understanding of his philosophical thinking.

The aim: Hungarian musical culture. The means: making the reading and writing of music general, through the schools. At the same time the awakening of a Hungarian musical approach in the training of both artists and audience. The raising

of Hungarian public taste in music and a continual progress towards what is better and more Hungarian. To make the masterpieces of world literature public property, to convey them to people of every kind and rank. The total of all these will yield
the Hungarian musical culture which is glimmering before us in the distant future.
(Kodaly, 1974, p. 160)

Kodály's above program, dated from year 1947, summarizes all the goals that he
throughout his long life so passionately worked and strived for from the moment that
he set out for his first folksong collecting journey. He and his friend Béla Bartók with
their never-fading efforts recaptured the most ancient layer of Hungarian musical culture, the Hungarian peasant songs that "express the most of our nation's soul in the
most perfect form" (Kodály, 2007c, p. 25). The discovery of this repertory enriched and
greatly influenced both Kodály's and Bartók's musical world. As a profound source of
inspiration, folk music influenced the style of both Kodály's and Bartók's compositions and laid the foundations for the creation of a new Hungarian classical musical
style[2] that, as Kodály stated, "shows the fertilizing influence of this newly rediscovered
ancient musical language. These songs give the foundations and the fertile soil for our
new music" (Kodály, 2007a, p. 25). For Kodály, the Hungarian peasant song does not
only "echo the life of the village but it is the mirror of the Hungarian soul" (Kodály,
2007a, p. 34).

> Although it (Hungarian folksong) is a living tradition only for the peasant commu-
> nity, all Hungarians have a connection with it. It is like a great collecting valley; dur-
> ing the past one thousand years many brooks have run into it. Regardless of social
> status all Hungarians left their mark in it. Therefore it is the mirror of the Hungarian
> soul. (Kodály, 2007c, p. 20)

When Kodály in his program writes about the "awakening of Hungarian consciousness in education" he again refers to the peasant songs that "have sprung from the depth
of the Hungarian soul for one thousand years and show the eternal and unchanged face
of the nation" (Kodály, 2007a, p. 54). Kodály believed that "national musical culture is
based on the healthy relationship of folk music and art music" (Kodály, 2007a, p. 221).
He wrote that Hungarian art music of the 19th century "tried to imitate different foreign
musical forms" and therefore it could not create new and original pieces (Kodály, 2007a,
p. 221). Nevertheless, Kodály's devotion to Hungarian traditional music never diminished his devotion to European culture as proven by his own compositions which, from
the stylistic point of view, create "Hungarian music of European significance," a bridge
between the European art music traditions and Hungarian traditional music (Kodály,
2007a, p. 122).

> [...] Hungary is an organic part of Europe, therefore it has to live according to its
> traditions as well. A nation standing in the buffer-zone between East and West can
> have one purpose in life: to belong to both and to reconcile and to melt together their
> differences in itself. From this viewpoint the Hungarian nation that is not European

at the same time is worthless and for us Europeanness without being Hungarian at the same time is also worthless. (Kodály, 2007a, p. 78)

As is the case with the country, the future of choral music also depends on whether we shall be able to become more Hungarian and more European at the same time. (Kodály, 2007a, p. 56)

Kodály, through his musical talent, managed to enrich Hungarian music literature with "more Hungarian and more artistic musical masterworks" (Kodály, 2007a, p. 55). As a composer, he achieved his first great success in 1923 when his oratorio *Psalmus Hungaricus*, composed in honor of Budapest's celebration of its 50th anniversary, received its premiere performance; 1923 is also generally considered to be the birth of Hungarian choral music. At the performance of *Psalmus Hungaricus* Kodály was greatly inspired by the sound of a children's choir performing the treble part, mesmerized by the children's "aptitude and unspoiled musical taste" (Kodály, 2007c, p. 10). From 1925 Kodály's creative work focused on choral music for children.[3] His scholarly essays from this period clearly show that he dedicated a lot of thought and time to the realization of a music pedagogical program with strong emphasis on choral music. From 1929 to 1935 more than a dozen pieces for children's voices were composed and more and more concerts for children's and youth choirs were organized in Budapest and in the country. These concerts led toward the establishment of the so-called "Singing Youth" movement. The "Singing Youth" concerts were festivals of songs (not competitions!) organized for the participating choirs usually culminating in the performance of a large-scale choral piece performed by all choirs together (Kodály, 2007a). This was the time period when, besides many new Hungarian choral works, music periodicals such as Singing Word (Énekszó)[4] and Singing Youth (Éneklő Ifjúság)[5] were published by the Hungarian Choir Publishing House (Magyar Kórus Lap és Zenekiadó).[6] These pioneer years of Hungarian choral music mark Kodály's recognition of the need for music education that could successfully lead Hungarians toward active cultivation of music and consequently, toward the understanding reception of musical art as summarized in his manifesto entitled *Internal Mission of Music*:

> Our task can be summarized in one word: education. [. . .] To drive the Hungarian masses closer to higher art music. [. . .] To make the thirsty souls know and love the great works of musical art that can be often accessed with so simple tools. (Kodály, 2007a, p. 49)

Kodály recognized that children's choirs and choral music could become the greatest tool in the creation of a renewed musical life. In his 1929 article "Children's Choruses" Kodály began to formulate his ideas about the possible ways to raise the standard of musical instruction in schools. The essence of his music education concept is rooted in the recognition of the importance of art and music in the education of all people.[7] In his writings, topics such as education of the whole person, spiritual nourishment, spiritual enrichment, order, discipline, and the shaping of the personality through valuable music are frequently recurring ideas. He felt strongly that it was the duty of schools to provide young people with enjoyable and meaningful musical experiences that would have the potential to enrich their lives:

> It is every child's birthright to be given into his hand the small key that can open, if so he wishes, the magic garden of music that multiplies the value of his whole life. (Kodály, 2007a, p. 73)

In the article *Children's Choir* Kodály speaks about the importance of school music education,[8] and underlines the impact of musical learning both on the emotional and cognitive development of young people. He was aware of what science nowadays so convincingly proves: music learning is an agent not only for musical development but it has a significant transfer effect on nonmusical endeavor as well. Music has the power to touch the lives of all young people in many positive ways and therefore it should, according to Kodály, be placed at the center of children's education.

> ... with music we do not only learn music. Singing sets you free, it gives you self-confidence, it releases you from inhibitions and fears. It helps concentration, it enhances you physically and emotionally, it energizes and enables you to approach your work in a positive manner, makes you more focused and more disciplined. Singing has an holistic impact on the person. It makes school life enjoyable. It develops social competence. [...] it creates the foundations for musical understanding which makes the person's whole life more beautiful and rich. [...] music education does not only teach music. These children (learning music in singing primary schools) have greater numeracy skills because numbers are not abstract patterns for them since they feel them in their body together with rhythm. They learn how to read faster because they feel the musical structure in the sentence. The precision required in musical notation conditions their handwriting ability, which becomes nicer and more accurate [...]. They learn correct spelling earlier, and musical notation has a beneficial effect on their ability to form letters [...]. Finally: the child's self-esteem grows since he is in possession of a skill that is not looked down upon by adults [...]. (Kodály, 2007a, pp. 304–305)

The most important principle of Kodály's music educational concept as highlighted in the article above is singing.

> If one were to attempt to express the essence of this education in one word, it could be—singing. (Kodály, 2007c, p. 152)

One of the greatest achievements of Kodály-inspired music education was the founding of singing primary schools throughout the country that still offer daily music education and choral music education to their pupils. Singing in Kodály's educational concept plays a prominent role for various reasons. First of all Kodály was convinced that musical culture can only be obtained through regular musical practice and in-depth musical understanding, and that musical reception is the direct consequence of active musical experiences. Kodály was deeply concerned by the growing popularity of musical programs on the radio that over the decades pushed people from active music-making toward passive music listening. Kodály believed that passivity, the lack of musical practice, weakens the audience because it weakens the audience's relationship with valuable music. The balance of musical practice and listening can be created only in a healthy musical environment (Kodály, 2007a). He felt strongly that one can only understand the human value of music by learning the language of music through active participation in music-making begun during early childhood years. The language of music can never be fully understood by listening to lectures or reading literature popularizing musical art:

> Anyone who has not been prepared for it will not understand much of it (the symphony), nor will the belletristic pseudo-professional literature, so fashionable with us now, take him nearer to it. To this end a gradual conditioning to the elementary phenomena of music, beginning in childhood, is needed together with practice over many years; a systematic education in listening to music, which can only be based upon tuition at the primary and secondary school. The start must be made as early as in kindergarten, because there the child can learn in play what would be too late to learn in the elementary school. (Kodály, 1974, p. 128)

Singing—according to Kodály—is the most useful tool in making people sensitive for musical reception:

> "Those who have learned to sing first, and only then to play an instrument, will catch the "melos" of any music much more quickly" (Kodály, 2007a, p. 192).

The essence of Kodály's music educational program is choral music education that embraces the whole nation and aims at making the great masterworks accessible to everyone, and this is laid down in his article entitled "Musical Life in a Provincial Town."

> "What is to be done? To get the greatest possible mass of people into direct contact with really valuable music. How can this be achieved? Through choral singing" (Kodály, 2007a, p. 72).

Kodály was convinced that choral music education has to be started in the schools in order to take full advantage of its educational benefits:

> "Choral singing is the most rewarding subject, [. . .] the choir of any school can reach the level at which it becomes suitable for an educational role within the school. And one step further: it can be of significant value in public musical life as well" (Kodály, 1974, p. 121).

In Zoltán Kodály's concept of music education, choral singing creates unique opportunities to experience the beauty and the revitalizing power of classical music through many joyful communal experiences. Common singing in schools can lead young people to the decision to perform with community choirs in their later years, and stay in touch with active music-making this way.

> "If we do not organize children's choirs properly, our adult choirs will increase neither in number nor in quality. A grown-up person will in any case sing differently if he has the opportunity to preserve the fervent enthusiasm of singing from his childhood" (Kodály, 1974, p. 121).

In choral music education Kodály also saw a unique potential for the creation of valuable community bonds and the development of community consciousness that could enhance the formation of a society based on mutual respect and solidarity. As he wrote:

> "Is there anything more demonstrative of social solidarity than a choir? Many people unite to do something that cannot be done by a single person alone however talented he or she may be" (Kodály, 1974, p. 121).

While the nineteenth-century choral life of Hungary can be mainly characterized by the male choir tradition of the *Liedertafel* movement, based on the German example, Kodály promoted the formation of mixed choirs:

> The male choral society is doomed to be at a stand in the vestibule of art forever because of its limited vocal range and artistic qualities. Great composers wrote either little or nothing for male choirs. [. . .] They (the choral works) should not settle only for half of the tools for artistic representation, the darker and less colorful half: the male voice. [. . .] the female voices give the choir brightness, gaiety, warmth and other forms of expression that lacks in the male voice. (Kodály, 2007a, p. 52)

Kodály strongly felt that the newly formed choirs have to be provided with new Hungarian choral compositions of high artistic merits written by Hungarian composers. As a composer, Kodály did not leave the male choirs without repertory of high quality despite his preference for mixed choirs:

> If the male choirs asked what to do in order to become yielding trees and to rightfully occupy a plot in the garden of Hungarian life, the answer would be simple: add more art and more Hungarianness. (Kodály, 2007a, p. 53)

In Kodály's thinking, the new musical audience, together with the newly created Hungarian classical music, would form the pillars of the new and flourishing musical culture of the country. The new foundations laid for school music education and the gradually increasing number of school choirs supported Kodály's great vision of the singing Hungary.

> I dedicated a lot of my time to the writing of choral music for children and to the compilation of school textbooks. I believe that I shall never feel sorry for the time

thus taken away from the writing of greater compositions. I feel that I did as useful work for the community as I would have done had I written more symphonic works. And sometimes I could take delight in the exhilaratingly beautiful performances of simple schoolboys that were of the highest artistic level, conducted by class teachers who are not even considered to be artists. (Kodály, 2007a, p. 199)

In his train of thoughts, the music education of the musical elite and the audience always forms an inseparable unit:

"We have brought up a musical elite but we have forgotten to bring up an audience that needs the work of the musical elite" (Kodály, 2007a, p. 73).

In regards to the training of the musical elite, the professional musicians, Kodály throughout his life stood for a comprehensive training encompassing a thorough general musicianship training, resulting in a cultivated hearing and a cultivated intellect. In one of his writings, he warns his readers that only intelligent people can become good musicians:

"Only an intelligent person can be a good musician. Music is such a difficult job that every branch of it demands thorough intellectual preparation. [...] The age of uneducated musicians has expired" (Kodály, 2007a, p. 251).

He confessed that as a young teacher at the Music Academy[9] he waged a Sisyphean battle against ill-trained musicians and the main reason why he undertook the leadership of the Music Academy for a short time period in 1919 was his determination to improve the general musical training of students (Kodály, 2007a). At several places he bitterly acknowledged that a great number of musicians graduating from the Music Academy lacked the most important of all musical skills: the fine inner hearing that enables musicians to write and to read music with security:[10]

Brilliant pianists are unable to write down or to sing faultlessly a simple one-part tune after hearing it fifteen or twenty times. How do they expect to imagine an intricate piece of several parts if their internal ear is so undeveloped? They only play with their fingers and not with their heads and hearts. (Kodály, 1974, p. 196)

According to Kodály, musical reading and writing skills can be acquired only if singing forms the basis of music education:

Place the instrument into the child's hand only after he has learned how to sing. His inner hearing abilities can be developed only if the first images of sound are shaped from his own singing and are not connected to either visual or kinesthetic experiences. [...] The child, who studies a musical instrument before studying singing usually remains unmusical for his entire life. This is why one can hear so many skilled pianists who have no idea about the essence of music. (Kodály, 2007a, p. 206)

Singing is an essential tool that trains inner hearing the most efficient way. The essence of inner hearing is the ability to hear the sound of a musical piece inside the head without any mechanical (instrumental) support when reading from the score.[11]

From time to time Kodály, with firm belief, and occasionally with passionate exaggeration or subdued temper, speaks about the cardinal faults of professional musical training. He confesses that the training of technical skills should always be preceded by and later be developed in harmony with the development of the musician's intellect and hearing abilities:

> We have to correct one old, cardinal mistake of our music education. We are breeding nimble fingers, but in the wake of the running fingers the spirit is dragging itself on legs made from lead. Whereas the spirit should head the line. (Kodály, 2007a, p. 192)

In his famous speech delivered at the year closing ceremony of the Music Academy in 1953 Kodály cites various passages from Schumann's *Musikalische Haus- und Lebensregeln* (Music Rules at Home and in Life) for special emphasis:

> "You must not know your pieces only via your fingers; you must also be able to hum them away from the piano. Teach your imagination so that you can recall not just the melody of a composition but also the harmony that goes along with it."
> "You must reach the stage when you can understand music by just seeing it on the page."
> "If someone places a composition in front of you for you to play, and you have never seen it before, read it through first."
> "Sing regularly in a choir, especially the middle parts. This makes you musical."
> "Somebody once opined that a consummate musician is one who, on first hearing a complex orchestral work, can visualize it as if it were before him. This is the highest level imaginable." (Kodály, 2007a, pp. 273–278)

In Kodály's thinking the good musician possess a refined musical taste as well (Kodály, 2007a). In his writings expressing the foundations of his music educational principles the question of artistic value of the pedagogical repertory taught in schools constantly occupies a prominent place. He is strongly convinced that refined musical taste can be shaped only if the teaching material is of the highest artistic value at all times:

> Let us stop the teacher's superstition according to which only some diluted art-substitute is suitable for teaching purposes. A child is the most susceptible and the most enthusiastic audience for pure art. [. . .] only art of intrinsic value is suitable for children. (Kodály, 1974, p. 122)

In his writings, Kodály made clear he did not live in the illusion that musical pulp fiction and music of dubious quality would one day just disappear. He had a great faith in new school music education and believed that, even if bad taste in adults could hardly be cured, good taste cultivated during the early years cannot be spoiled later on:

> Why can't we at once give good music to those who are not yet aware of what is good or bad? The person, whose taste is still untainted, will by all means appreciate good music. If he has got to know and got to like good music, bad music will hardly get near him. [...] It is therefore important to start nurturing (children) with good music already in the school or what is even better in the kindergarten. [...] I do not feel sorry about the time (spent writing music for children), because even if I wrote fewer pieces, I could in some ways contribute to the increasing number of those who appreciate good music. (Kodály, 2007a, pp. 188–189)

Musical material worthy of the status of teaching repertory can be found among the folksong repertory and the great classical masterworks according to Kodály. The use of folksongs are promoted by him for their high aesthetic, cultural, and national value and for their relative simplicity. Kodály also believed that if Hungarians did not want their folk music repertory to be lost for the next generations then folk music had to become an integral part of the school music repertory. Kodály was also aware that the traditional children's songs selected from the folksong repertory and sung in the children's mother-tongue are the closest natural musical expression of all children, and that therefore they were highly suitable for teaching purposes. Through the singing of folksongs, children could be guided with ease toward the understanding and learning of the basic musical concepts such as pulse, tempo, rhythm, meter, form, and melody. According to Kodály, the study of folksong repertory would create in children a better understanding of for-eign musical cultures as well.[12] When Kodály refers to selecting suitable repertory from the great classical masterworks for teaching purposes he frequently mentions the names of G. P. Palestrina and J. S. Bach. In his writings the music of Palestrina and Bach appear as the works of a great epoch of choral art that should be in the focus of study not only for composers but for Hungarian choirs including school choirs as well:

> "We should not abstain from Bach or Palestrina; the great foreigners only help the unfolding of our own national spirit" (Kodály, 2007a, p. 53).

In his essay entitled "Hungarians in Music" he clearly describes two of the most impor-tant influences of his own art: the monophonic musical culture—the world of pentatonic music discovered in Hungarian and Finno-Ugric folk music—and the great European vocal tradition exemplified by the music of Bach and Palestrina. When looking behind the word-by-word meaning of his sentences on this topic one can almost feel that Kodály suggests a musical program for composers of his and subsequent generations.

> One of our hands is held by the Nogaj-Tartar, the Votyak and the Cheremish people, the other hand is held by Bach and Palestrina. Are we going to be able to connect these two distant worlds? Can we one day stop tumbling on a ferry boat between the cultures of Europe and Asia, and become a bridge or even better, a dry land that

is connected to both? This would be a task great enough for another 1000 years. (Kodály, 2007b, p. 260)

In Palestrina's art Kodály found "pure sobriety" (Kodály, 2007c, p. 93) that according to him can only be found in the works of the greatest artists. The music of Palestrina and J. S. Bach had a great influence on the development of Kodály's polyphonic style as well. Lajos Bárdos, Kodály's composition student, choral conductor, composer, and theorist, pointed out how the in-depth study of this repertory occupied a prominent place not only among Kodály's scholarly interests and but in his teachings as well:

> Zoltán Kodály created the Hungarian polyphony. [. . .] he recognized that the real language of the choir is polyphony. [. . .] He (the singer) prefers singing a melody to accompanying one. According to our knowledge Kodály was the first (in Hungary) to introduce the teaching of the Palestrina-style for composition students. And of course Bach's style as well. (Bárdos , 1974, p. 154)

The study of Palestrina and Bach leads Kodály, according to his own remarks, to the "acquisition of self-control and responsibility in the writing of each single note" (Kodály, 2007c, p. 127). In Palestrina's music Kodály marveled at the "degree of responsibility not to be found anywhere else" (Eősze, 2000, 85). About J. S. Bach's music he writes the following in his letter to Pablo Casals: ". . . whose (Bach's) pieces represent the unbreakable unity and perseverance" (Kodály, 2007b, p. 410). The words responsibility, unity, and perseverance in Kodály's thinking are the most important attributes of an ideal musical epoch characterized by the artifact of counterpoint. In his article from 1917, Hungarian musicologist Antal Molnár (Dalos, 2007, p. 246) refers to Kodály's polyphonic style as "Hungarian counterpoint." Lajos Bárdos in his essay previously cited claims that Kodály became the creator of "Hungarian polyphony" (Bárdos, 1974, pp. 115–210). Their opinions are compared in the chapter entitled "Hungarian Counterpoint" in Anna Dalos's book *Forma, harmónia, ellenpont (Form, Harmony and Counterpoint)* (Dalos, 2007). According to Dalos' viewpoint the pieces of *Bicinia Hungarica* and examples of the two-part singing exercises in the *Choral Method* series clearly display Kodály's stylistic imagination about the so-called "Hungarian counterpoint" (Dalos, 2007, p. 263). In an interview published under the title *Music Education and Singing Primary School* Kodály indeed refers to his pedagogical compositions as preparatory exercises to the great works of Renaissance polyphony (Kodály, 2007c).

Kodály's pedagogical compositions are available in two different editions. Both Editio Musica Budapest and Boosey & Hawkes published all of Kodály's singing exercises. The English language edition appears under the title *Choral Method Series* suggesting that the exercises are to be used in a choral setting. Because these instructive exercises can be used for the practicing of sight-reading in any given situation this title can be somewhat misleading; however it reflects on Kodály's great devotion to improve the standard of Hungarian choral music education through the general improvement of amateur and professional musicians' sight-singing abilities.

The singing exercises serve two equally important goals as expressed in Kodály's article "Musical Life of a Provincial Town":

> "The training of elites and the education of masses must form an inseparable, integral part, and the result can only become invaluable if the balance of the two prevails" (Kodály, 2007a, p. 73).

The article cited above was written in 1937, the year when Kodály wrote the first volume of *Bicinia Hungarica* (Hungarian two-part songs), the first volume in the *Choral Method* series. In the years to follow, compositions written by Kodály with pedagogical purpose appeared one after the other.[13]

1937 *Bincinia Hungarica Volume 1 (two-part exercises)*
1941 *Let Us Sing Correctly*
1941 *15 Two-Part Singing Exercises*
1941 *Bicinia Hungarica Volumes II. III.*
1942 *Bicinia Hungarica Volume IV.*
1943 *333 Reading Exercises*
1944 *Pentatonic Music Volume I.*
1946 *24 Little Canons on the Black Keys*
1947 *Pentatonic Music Volumes II. III. IV.*
1954 *55, 44, 33 Two-Part Singing Exercises*
1954 *Tricinia (Three-Part Exercises)*
1954 *Epigrammes*
1962 *50 Nursery Songs (see 333 Singing Exercises)*
1963 *66 Two-Part Singing Exercises*
1965 *22 Two-Part Singing Exercises*
1967 *77 Two-Part Singing Exercises*[14]

The volumes of the *50 Nursery Songs* together with *Pentatonic Music I-III, 333 Reading Exercises, Let Us Sing Correctly*, selections from *Bicinia Hungarica*, the *15 Two-Part Exercises*, and *77 Two-Part Exercises* are suitable for introduction into sight-reading through unison and easy two-part material, whereas the volumes of *Tricinia, 22* and *33 Two-Part Exercises*, and *Pentatonic Music Vol. IV.* offer numerous musical challenges of melody, rhythm, polyphony, harmony and intonation for university students as well. While most of the two-part exercises exhibit the stylistic features of Baroque and Renaissance imitative counterpoint, several pieces in the volume of the Epigrams and the Tricinia (three-part songs)—the most challenging collections of the singing exercises—are musically enriched by the chromatic melodic and harmonic language of the late Romantic style. They can be best regarded as an introduction to the challenges of intonation of chromatic melody and harmony. They were composed during a period in Kodály's late life when he, presumably under the influence of the new European trends, composed some of his technically most challenging choral works.[15]

Search among the volumes of *Choral Method* from the sheer viewpoint of difficulty clearly shows that some of these short compositions are appropriate for teaching purposes at different levels. Erzsébet Hegyi states that "if we are able to meet all the musical and intellectual requirements which Kodály poses for us in his vocal series (the so-called 'Choral Method') composed with a pedagogical purpose for future musicians, then we may claim we are conversant in all the four components of the conception of a good musician (the well-trained hearing, intelligence, heart, and hand)" (Hegyi, 1985, p. 36). Professor Hegyi's thoughts clearly place Kodály's *Choral Method* series into perspective. With systematic study of these compositions from elementary to post-secondary level, students can obtain fluency in sight-reading and can develop stylistic knowledge that will enable them to accurately read the masterworks of vocal polyphony at first sight not only because of getting each interval of the melodic progression right but because of the gained stylistic understanding. Through creative teaching techniques applied to the methodological approach to the singing exercises, musical skills other than singing at sight such as part-singing, sing-and-play, melodic and harmonic hearing, rhythmic skills, improvisation, intonation, reading in C-clefs, transposition, melodic transformation, dictation, musical memory, and skills to analyze music can equally be developed to the highest degree. Sol-fa singing should be used throughout all the volumes combined with singing with letter names in order to develop thinking both in the relative and absolute systems.

Kodály's pedagogical compositions can also be regarded as the most valuable introduction to Kodály's ideas regarding teaching methodology and choral music education. Kodály presented basic guidelines for music teachers and choral conductors in the preface and epilogue of *Bicinia Hungarica*, in the preface of *Let Us Sing Correctly*, *15 Two-Part Singing* Exercises, the *333 Reading Exercises*, the *24 Little Canons on the Black Keys*, and in the methodological references to the second, third and fourth volume of *Pentatonic Music*. These writings together with the collection of several of Kodály's essays written between 1929 and 1967[16] and published in *Visszatekintés (In Retrospect)* contain Kodály's various ideas for teaching in their purest form (Kodaly, 2007a, 2007b, 2007c).

For the purpose of musical reading, Kodály suggests the use of relative solmization that assists students in the acquisition of the clear understanding of the tonal function of each single note both in the melodic and harmonic context. Relative solmization, Kodály suggests, is also a helpful tool when reading C-clefs and doing transposition.

> "Reading in different clefs and transposition do not create problems anymore if we approach them with this kind of preparation. Because solmization includes and substitutes the naming of the degrees of the scale" (Kodaly, 2007a, p. 69).

Kodály did not only experience the educational benefits of the sol-fa method but knew the international literature on the systematic use of solmization in music education as well (Kodaly, 2007a). He found that sol-fa is a helpful tool that has the power to teach musical reading in an efficient and, probably more importantly, musical way:

> Solmization is the best foundation for score reading. Is it possible to imagine someone acquiring education in literature or even just a small measure of knowledge

without being able to read? Well, musical knowledge cannot be acquired without a musical score. (Kodaly, 2007a, p. 222)

The methodology for the teaching of musical reading through solmization was fully developed by one of Kodály's highly talented students, Jenő Ádám, whose book entitled *Systematic Singing Instruction on the Basis of Relative Sol-Fa* (1944) became a model for music textbooks written for the Hungarian primary schools for several decades (Szőnyi, 1983). Although Kodály-based music education is most frequently (I believe wrongly) identified with sol-fa singing, at many places Kodály points out the importance of rhythm education and believes that rhythm should be introduced to pupils prior to learning melodic concepts.

> "... clumsiness in rhythm and general uncertainty are the chief causes of poor reading. Thus rhythm should always be our first consideration" (Kodaly, 2007a, p. 128).

Kodály's singing exercises, with the exception of the nine pieces in the volume of *Epigrams,* are written for a cappella singing. The development of the security of singing without instrumental support forms the foundation of choral music education according to the Kodály Concept:

> "... the ear will only be able to fully take in polyphonic music if the parts are learned unaccompanied (without instrumental support) whilst listening to another part" (Kodaly, 2007a, p. 218).

According to Kodály's conviction a cappella singing leads to the achievement of fine intonation in vocal performance. Kodály also believed that singing continuously supported by instrumental accompaniment does not only hinder the development of sensitivity toward the beauty of monophonic melody,[17] but with the support of the well-tempered piano, even a perfectly tuned instrument, choral intonation cannot be adequately trained.[18] The clarity of a cappella singing is not to be achieved through the tempered system but through intonation according to the acoustically pure, "natural" intervals that are enriched by the appearance of combination notes and overtones.[19] He, in his forward to *Let's Sing Correctly* also asserts that:

> "... those who always sing in unison never learn to sing in correct pitch. Correct unison singing can, paradoxically, be learned only by singing in two parts: the voices adjust and balance each other" (Kodaly, 1952, p. 3).

Kodály was convinced that the security of intonation has a great impact on the richness and beauty of the choral sound. Lajos Bárdos in his analysis of Kodály's "Children's Choruses" warns choral conductors that because "choirs occasionally sing works with piano accompaniment there is no other way but to acquire both the skill of acoustically clear a cappella singing, and the skill of singing in equal temperament when accompanied by the piano. The same ability is needed in pieces conceived in the equally tempered dodecatony" (Bárdos, 1979, p. 43). Bárdos in his analysis indicates the differences between the acoustic and equal temperament of intervals—the difference between the narrow major second (re-mi in a major key), the wide major second (do-re in major), and the diminished third (enharmonic to the major second), as well as the wide and narrow chromatic steps. He states that "when everybody acquires the nuances of pure intonation, fewer choirs will sing out of tune" (Bárdos, 1979, p. 43). Miklós Szabó points out that the demand for acoustically clear intonation follows logically from Kodály's fundamentally tonal way of thinking. "In a complex series of harmonies or in an enharmonic modulation the singer must often correct his part instinctively and with great sensitivity. If he does not do so the chord of resolution—mostly a major triad—will lose its brightness or will be out of tune" (Szabó, 1983, p. 16).

In regards to sequencing the repertory of musical studies Kodály suggests the use of pentatonic material in the beginning in order to establish the pillars of tonality and to enhance fine intonation of the scale:

> "The scale [. . .] will be clear only if the pillars have been laid in advance. These are d r m s l (the notes of the pentatonic scale)" (Kodály, 2007a, p. 84).

He believed that in-tune singing of the semitones creates the greatest difficulties for young people:

> "Let's give the child melodies without semitones first, only after having moved in them securely we can carefully introduce the semitones" (Kodály, 2007a, p. 125).

In the preface of *Let's Sing Correctly* Kodály suggests several ways to introduce semitones (mi-fa, ti-do) through a series of intonation exercises (Kodály, 2007a).

Kodály's inspirational and charismatic guidance in regards to the establishment of vocal-based music education in the training of amateur and professional musicians through all institutions of music education from the kindergarten to the music colleges contributed to the establishment of a new subject in music education in the Hungarian school system: *solfège*, the training of music students' general musicianship through singing and other forms of music-making encompassing all areas of musical knowledge and skill development such as singing, rhythm, meter, form, melody, intonation, polyphony, harmony, notation, sight-reading, dictation, transposition, improvisation, and memory. The subject of solfege involves aspects of music theory (harmony, polyphony and form) as well placing a strong emphasis on ear-training:

> "The sole purpose of music theory is not the information about concepts and (theoretical) knowledge but primarily the training" (Kodály, 2007a, p. 11).

Zoltán Kodály's philosophy of music education and choral music education has had a lasting impact on Hungarian music education system from the kindergarten until the music academy level. The education system developed on its basis by his colleagues has been attracting the attention of the whole world far beyond Hungary, from Australia to America, for several decades. Kodály was fully aware that his dream about the singing Hungary could be successfully realized only if there could be sufficient time allocated for music in the schools, adequate pedagogical repertory nurturing musical sensitivity, and well-trained musician-teachers[20] who could implant into the pupils a lifelong interest in valuable music that makes them quality-sensitive in their musical choices.

> "I see three reasons for the failure of music education in the schools. There has not been enough competent teachers, pedagogical repertory, and time" (Kodály, 2007a, p. 74).

More than anything he was concerned about the personality of the teacher without whom the best pedagogical methods, school curricula or even the most carefully constructed and valuable textbooks remain useless.

> "The finest curricula and the wisest regulations issued from above are of no value if there is nobody to put them into practice with conviction and enthusiasm. Souls cannot be reshaped by administration" (Kodály, 1974, p. 147).

But how should music be taught according to the Kodály Concept? How should the souls be shaped through music education?

> "... a music lesson that is led properly is not a burden but the source of refreshment, joviality, and happiness" (Kodály, 2007a, p. 74).
> "The singing class should be about mainly practical music-making, refreshing musical experiences as opposed to scholastic argument" (Kodály, 2007a, p. 69).
> "It is not technique that is the essence of art, but the soul. As soon as the soul can communicate freely, without obstacles, a complete musical effect is created" (Kodály, 1974, pp. 121–122).

Communal music-making and singing in itself is a special source of joy according to Kodály's words. In his concept the goal of school music and choral music education is twofold: (1) to make pupils appreciate valuable music by giving them a key to understanding of music through several positive and enjoyable experiences, but more importantly (2) to regard these enjoyable musical experiences as an invaluable source for the healthy maturity of the human personality. In Kodály's thinking high quality music education has the potential to create the foundations for a more complete and happier future. Since singing is a keystone in his educational concept, the key to the future is possessed by the new generation of music educators and choral conductors.

> "What will be the future? A fairy garden or wilderness? It is up to us. It depends on whether there will be enough working hands. Enough choral conductors with well-trained intelligence and heart, who notice what has to be done and are capable of carrying it out" (Kodály, 2007a, p. 56).

Notes

1. Kodály (1941, p. 3).
2. "... the folksong showed us the way towards the independence of our literature and music so that we can safeguard our authenticity" (Kodály, 2007a, p. 202).
3. "Villő" (Strawguy) and "Túrót eszik a cigány" (see the Gypsy Munching Cheese), both based on folk tunes, were the first two of his choral pieces written for children's voices. Four years later, on April 14, 1929 a historic concert of Kodály's Children's Choruses was organized in the Great Hall of the Music Academy with the participation of 700 pupils from seven different Budapest schools performing thirteen of Kodály's choral works.
4. "Singing Words" published between 1933 and 1948 and edited by György Kerényi and another of Kodály's composition students at the Music Academy, Gyula Kertész.
5. Ibid.
6. Ibid.
7. "Already in my childhood I felt that a good piece of music leaves behind some kind of a "plus," a kind of surplus of spiritual nourishment. [...] The consequence of being nourished on good art is spiritual health" (Kodály, 2007a, p. 213).
8. "It is the duty of the state [...] to regularly develop the structure of education" (Kodály, 2007a, p. 45).
9. Kodály became teacher at the Music Academy in Budapest in 1907 at the age of 25.
10. "The old Music Academy trained a few fine instrumentalists, but it could not give to them the foundations of general music education: musical reading. Diplomas in music education were given out in great numbers to those who were incapable of reading music without an instrumental support" (Kodály, 2007a, p. 215).
11. "Those, who cannot hear the music inside when looking at a musical score, cannot be recognized as musicians, only a half-ready dilettante or a dabbler" (Kodály, 2007a, p. 254).
12. "Of course, every school should deal with Hungarian folk music as thoroughly as with the mother-tongue itself. Only then can the pupil reach a proper understanding of foreign music" (Kodály, 1974, p. 123).
13. For detailed analysis of Kodály's pedagogical compositions see M. Ittzés (1999), 22 zenei írás. Kecskemét. Hungary: Kodály Intézet.
14. See Mihály Ittzés's article.
15. "Mountain Nights II-V" (1955–1962), "Meghalok, meghalok" (1957), "Fancy" (1957), "Gyászének" (1959), "Media vita in morte sumus" (1960), "An Ode for Music (1963)."
16. "Gyermekkarok" (Children's Choirs) being the earliest (1929), "Válogatott biciniumok" (Selected Bicinia) being the latest (1967) of these essays.
17. "Continual piano accompaniment (1) deprives the child of the pleasure and profit of independent singing. Anyone who always walks with crutches will never be able to walk without them" (Kodály, 1974, p. 150).
18. "... what do we want with the tempered chords in a cappella singing?" (Kodály, 2007a, p. 61).
19. "The proof and reward of correct singing is beauty of sound caused by the appearance of combination tones, and in the higher registers, by the increased brightness of the overtones" (Kodály, 1952, p. 3).
20. "... series tasks can be undertaken only by professionals with serious training" (Kodály, 2007a, p. 11).

References

Bárdos, L. (1974). *Tíz újabb írás*. (L. Nemes, Trans.). Budapest: Zeneműkiadó.

Bárdos, L. (1979). On Kodály's children's choruses - part two. *IKS Bulletin, 4*(2), pp. 36–43.

Bónis, F. (n.d.). Pillantás az alkotóműhelybe: hat Kodály-kórus. *Forrás*, pp. 40–44. Retrieved from http://www.forrasfolyoirat.hu/0712/bonis.pdf.

Dalos, A. (2007). *Forma, harmónia, ellenpont - Vázlatok Kodály Zoltán poétikájához*. Budapest: Rózsavölgyi és Társa.

Eősze, L. (2000). *Örökségünk Kodály - válogatott tanulmányok*. Budapest: Osiris.

Hegyi, E. (1985). High-level musicianship in focus. *IKS Bulletin, 10*(2), p. 36.

Kodály, Z. (1941). *Bicinia Hungarica I*. New York, NY: Boosey and Hawkes.

Kodály, Z. (1952). *Let us sing correctly: Preface*. London: Boosey & Company, Ltd.

Kodály, Z. (1974). A hundred year plan. In F. Bonis (Ed.), *The selected writings of Zoltán Kodály* (pp. 160–162). Budapest: Corvina.

Kodály, Z. (2007a). *Visszatekintés I*. F. Bónis, (Ed.), L. Nemes, (Trans.). Budapest: Argumentum.

Kodály, Z. (2007b). *Visszatekintés II*. F. Bónis, (Ed.). (L. Nemes, Trans.). Budapest: Argumentum.

Kodály, Z. (2007c). *Visszatekintés III*. F. Bónis, (Ed.), L. Nemes (Trans.). Budapest: Argumentum.

Molnár, A. (1917). Magyar kontrapunkt. *Zenei Szemle, 1*(4), p. 120.

Szabó, M. (1983). Problems of interpretation in Kodály's choral music. *IKS Bulletin, 8*(1), p. 16.

Szőnyi, E. (1983). *Kodály's principles in practice*. Budapest: Corvina Kiadó.

PART II

CONSTRUCTION OF IDENTITY AND MEANING

CHAPTER 6

FOSTERING MUSICAL
AND PERSONAL AGENCY

Considering the Conductor

DANIEL ABRAHAMS

CONDUCTORS are teachers who engage with ensemble members in ways that help them solve musical problems, test hypotheses, and be musical decision makers. However, there often comes a time when the conductor must step in and, using his or her greater knowledge and judgment, say, "It needs to happen this way, because this is authentic to the performance practice." During the concert, the role of the conductor shifts from pedagogue to musical leader and professional conductor.

As the artistic leaders of their ensembles, conductors are responsible for decisions about programming and musical interpretation. The conductor also diagnoses problems and prescribes solutions (Wis, 2007). However, conductors displaying an attitude of superiority and dominance toward their ensemble are capable of inflicting emotional, physical, and psychological damage making it difficult to produce expressive and beautiful music (Durrant, 2003, p.7).

Long-accepted practices in the Western art music community place conductors within sociocultural and historical expectations and traditions created by institutions and ensemble members (O'Toole, 1993; Morrison & Demorest, 2012; Shively, 2005). Students experiencing teacher-conductors who emulate traditional or professional ensemble conductors become accustomed to being passive receivers of information, memorizing what the conductor tells them, which in turn inhibits students' opportunities to discover the why and construct understanding for a meaningful performance experience. As music education philosopher Bennett Reimer (1989) explained:

> When performance group directors or classroom teachers are directing the music of students but make all the decisions *for* them . . . those *directors* are creating, but their students are surely not. The students have been forced to be artisans, used for making art but permitted no involvement in artistic creation. (p. 69)

For amateur choirs in schools, conductors can move away from the caricature of the dictatorial male figure with white hair waving his arms madly about on the podium. They should immerse students in multiple musical experiences and practices such as conducting, composing, arranging, and teaching, thereby helping students enhance their musical and self-knowledge (Elliott, 1995; Shively, 2005).

The school ensemble *teacher-conductor* (Shively, 2005) should develop each individual ensemble member's consciousness or humanness through dialoguing (verbal and musical) and reflective practice in the performance of music. Teacher-conductors establish a community of practice through "inducting students into the way of life of a music culture; of engaging students in a living encounter with the knowing, beliefs, plans and values of a Music" (Elliott, 1995, p. 206). Through dialoguing and reflective practice, students' personal and musical agency emerges as they enter into the new community of practice and begin to take ownership of their learning processes. As teacher-conductors:

> We cannot simply focus on developing their abilities as singers or players; we must also help them understand the creative process from the inside out so that they can move from being musical *for* us, to being musical *with* us, to ultimately, being musical *without* us. (Wis, 2007, p. 14)

Recently, conductors seem to have shifted their approach on the podium from the traditional conductor-centric viewpoint of music making to one where they provide ensemble members opportunities to take on more responsibility in the process of musical decision-making and offer input into the rehearsal process. The conductor now functions as a facilitator, or guide, assisting individuals and the ensemble as a whole to achieve mutually beneficial goals. The conductor and ensemble members act as musical collaborators in the process of making music leading to a deeper and more meaningful experience for all (Wis, 2007, p. xi).

The teaching of choral conducting seems to consist of several components: The teaching of executive skills such as conducting the fermata or cuing with the left hand; the acquisition of habits of mind and disposition of a conductor, including general leadership characteristics such as decision making; and the fostering of conductor's personal and musical agency. This means that the student "feels" like they can do it and can "be" a conductor. Many good texts deal with the teaching of executive skills (Durrant, 2003; Jordan, 2009; Kaplan, 1985; Green, 2004; Rudolf, 1995). The *Musician's Soul: A Journey of Examining Spirituality for Performers, Teachers, Composers, Conductors, and Music Educators* (Jordan, 1999); *The Art of Conducting* (Hunsberger & Ernst, 1992); and *The Complete Conductor* (Demaree & Moses, 1995) all contain chapters that assist novice conductors in fostering the habits of mind of conductors. This chapter will focus on the other aspects of learning to conduct that foster musical and personal agency.

I propose a conducting pedagogy framed in the perspective of constructivism where the goal is to foster habits of mind that contribute to a novice conductor acquiring personal and musical agency. In this approach, in addition to acquiring the executive skills that are basic to conducting technique, and learning the qualities of successful leaders, beginning conducting students engage in meaningful experiences or episodes representing authentic conducting activities during each class session. According to Cummings-Potvin (2007), tasks deemed meaningful encourage learner agency. Within each conducting episode, students need opportunities to engage in reflective practice involving problem solving, goal setting, self-assessment, self-evaluation, self-reaction, initiative, and decision making. By engaging in reflection, they become more open to learning. Because they are more open to learning (supported by their engagement in reflection on the experiences), they remove the barriers--and take action to problem-solve. Because they are open to more learning, they become more passionate about learning, their goals, music, and conducting practice--which lead them into the next experience (making them eager to pursue the next challenge).

This process of *engagement, reflection on their engagement,* and *openness* encourages conducting students to want to learn more--to experience more challenging aspects of conducting. In the process of working through each episode, learners develop a sense of agency, because at each step they realize they can succeed. Their success in each episode motivates them to want to engage with the next challenge/episode.

RELATED LITERATURE
AND THEORETICAL FRAME

There are multiple viewpoints about what makes a good conductor, the skills desired for competency as a conductor, and how we teach students to become good conductors. Choral conductor and educator Collin Durrant suggested it might be easier to reach agreement on what a good musician is than what a good conductor is (1994, p. 57). To determine the skills needed for effective conducting, some researchers (Boardman, 2000; Chapman, 2008; Silvey, 2011a) focused on undergraduate conducting curricula. Others (Neidlinger, 2003; Orzolek, 1996; Yontz, 2001) looked to interdisciplinary techniques from dance and theatre for ways to address personal traits, expressive technique, and communication skills needed to be an effective conductor.

Several researchers (Boardman, 2000; Chapman, 2008; Getchell, 1957; Grashel, 1991; Manfredo, 2008; Runnels, 1992; Silvey, 2011a) studied undergraduate conducting from a curricular perspective. Undergraduate conducting curricula gained prominence because conducting is often the performing medium for many graduates of teacher preparation programs. However, there has never been a standardized curriculum for the teaching of conducting. Through surveys of undergraduate conducting instructors, researchers inquired about the executive skills considered important in teaching novice conductors. Some (Leppla, 1989; Miller, 1988; Neidlinger, 2003; Orzolek, 1996; Powell, 2008; Runnings, 2006; Yontz, 2001) examined the application of interdisciplinary approaches such as acting, dance, and movement training to the teaching of conducting as a response to a perceived lack of emphasis on teaching expressiveness and creativity in undergraduate conducting curriculum (Running, 2009). James Jordan (2011) wrote a text that applied Laban movement to conducting. Others (Bergee, 2005; Byo, 1990; Byo & Austin, 1994; Fredrickson, Johnson, & Robinson, 1998; Manternach, 2012; Silvey, 2011b), examined nonverbal communication skills in novice conductors with the expectation that they could predict how student conductors would act under certain situations.

Constructivism as a learning theory

Constructivism is an ontological and epistemological student-centered perspective of teaching and learning where we impose and construct our own understanding of the world through socially situated experiences. This brings about multiple meanings or perspectives of a concept or event (Brooks & Brooks, 1999; Fosnot, 2005). The learning process is self-regulating, where learners come to reconcile the differences between prior knowledge and new knowledge and construct understanding through dialogue and reflection within a community of practice.

A constructivist perspective acknowledges that people make sense of the world through the construction of their own understanding. Boardman (2002) suggested "humans do not find or discover knowledge, but rather construct or make it" (p. 3). Learning occurs when people engage with experience and connect new knowledge with prior knowledge by making connections. It is through these connections that people construct ideas and figure things out for themselves. Shively (2015) insisted that active engagement by the learner is key to constructing knowledge. However, he suggests we must consider which activities are most meaningful as not all actions are equal.

There is a wide array of viewpoints concerning constructivism. Peter Webster (2011) conducted an extensive review of the literature surrounding music education scholarship on constructivism, as well as examining the general constructivist literature. Webster saw the following principles within most descriptions of constructivism:

- Knowledge is formed as part of the learner's active interaction with the world.
- Knowledge exists less as abstract entities outside the learner that are absorbed by the learner; rather, it is constructed anew through action.
- Meaning is constructed with this knowledge.
- Learning is in part a social activity. (p. 36)

Wiggins (2015) provided the following guidelines about learning and learners:

- Learners actively engage in real life, relevant, problem-solving experiences that enable them to construct and act on their own understanding.
- Learners work with "big ideas" or "primary concepts" in ways that foster thinking.
- Learning experiences are contextual and holistic in nature.
- Learners have opportunities to interact with peers and teachers.

- Learners' own ideas are central to the learning/teaching process.
- Learners are aware of goals and of their own progress toward those goals.
- Assessment of learning is embedded in and emerges from the learning experiences. (p. 26)

Like Boardman (2002) and Webster (2011), Wiggins (2105) suggested active engagement on the part of the learner within contextual and relevant experiences is key to constructing knowledge. For learning to occur, experiences must be meaningful and relevant to the participants. If they cannot make sense of the experience, learning cannot happen.

Constructivist Strategies Applied to the Teaching of Conducting

The focus of a constructivist approach to teaching conducting is centered in a context of how students learn rather than the content and skills they need to master, which implies they are talking about conducting. While such content and skill is important and is included, it is the challenge of the conducting teacher to foster the abilities of the conducting students to make and construct meaning. When the students can say, "aha, I can do that!" we can claim that they have agency. These learning environments include opportunities that are collaborative, democratic, active, authentic, and connect to a community of practice. To these, we add problem solving, reflection, and the importance of prior experience.

Teaching conducting through this perspective begins with the whole or big idea, and expands to include the parts. Such big ideas might include, the tempo, meter, or dynamics of a particular piece of music. The smaller parts include the physical gestures conductors use to express those larger ideas to their choir. A constructivist teacher acknowledges that learning is intellectual because the mind is self-organizing and culturally influenced. Understanding the intellectual tools of a culture such as language, numbers, or conducting gestures is a key component of the approach. Ideas continually evolve and are always under construction. Students, in response to what occurs in the rehearsal hall, come to this state of agency by constructing new meanings and conquering tasks that are more complex.

Bruner (1960) a constructivist psychologist, contributed the concept of the spiral curriculum as a model for general education. In this model, concepts are introduced in their simplest form and upon mastery, are represented in a progression from simple to complex. This may take a period of years or, in the college classroom, may occur during the semester. For example, in general education a student may learn their city's history in grade 4, their state history in grade 8 and United States history in grade 10. At each stage, the historiography is more sophisticated. In music, a young child may learn the names of the notes, later on how those notes form scales, and later on how those scales connect to tetra chords, the overtone series, and the notes combining harmonically to form chords. Applying Bruner's notion of the spiral curriculum to conducting pedagogy includes cyclical episodes where students revisit musical concepts and conducting skills multiple times, but at a more sophisticated level, where something new is added each time.

For example, dynamics are always present in a musical performance. New conductors learning a beat pattern for the first time are not usually thinking about dynamics, although they understand dynamics and are aware of the concept of dynamics. So on one pass around the spiral, students think about why and how they might incorporate dynamic changes and add them to the affect of the gesture. Now the challenge is a physical one, because they know why dynamic changes are necessary and how to execute and create dynamic change as ensemble members; they also know what it sounds like when they hear it in a musical performance, and they can conceive it when they see it in print.[1]

Active-apprenticeship

Rogoff (1990) suggested, "The notion of apprenticeship as a model for children's cognitive development is appealing because it focuses our attention on the active role of children in organizing development" (p. 39). Children discover what a culture is about through their interaction with other others (Bruner, 1966; Rogoff, 1990; Vygotsky, 1978). The tools and practices used by experts to attain knowledge and negotiate problematic situations are sometimes ignored; however, "to make a real difference in students' skill, we need both to understand the nature of expert practice and to devise methods appropriate to learning that practice" (Collins, Brown, & Newman, 1989, p. 455). Bruner (1996) concurred with Collins, Brown, and Newman (1989) suggesting, "If pedagogy is to empower human beings to go beyond 'native' predispositions, it must transmit the 'toolkit' the culture has developed for doing so" (p. 17). Apprenticeship "offers direct exposure to real conditions of practice and patterns of work" (Schön, 1987, p. 37), affording learners insight into methods needed to be successful within a domain. For these reasons, learners enter into the practice of conducting through a framework of apprenticeship.

Cognitive apprenticeship consists of: modeling, coaching, scaffolding, articulation, reflection, and exploration (Collins et al., 1989). Observing experts modeling their processes within conducting affords learners an opportunity to experience, in a holistic approach, the desired outcome of the learning. Through modeling "the expert seeks to transmit a skill he has acquired through repeated practice to a novice who, in his turn, must then practice the modeled act in order to succeed" (Bruner, 1996, p. 53).

Learners then attempt the activity with coaching or scaffolding (Bruner, 1996; Schön, 1987). Support from the teacher provides guidance to learners for finding solutions to problematic musical and conducting situations. "Coaching would consist in observing student performance, detecting errors of application, pointing out correct responses" (Schön, 1987, p. 39). Teacher and learner enter into what Rogoff (1990) describes as shared problem solving. Learners not only have access to the skills, but also to the inner thoughts of the teacher, as assistance may be covert on the part of the teacher helping learners determine what kind of questions to formulate or how to begin the process of solving a situation. Support is then faded as learners acquire expertise of the activity and move through the zone of proximal development (Vygotsky, 1978) as "the interplay between observation, scaffolding, and increasingly independent practice aids apprentices in developing self-monitoring and correction skills and integrating the skills and conceptual knowledge needed to advance toward expertise" (Collins et al., 1989, p. 456).

Membership within multiple communities (Bruner, 1996; Wenger, 1998; Wenger et al., 2002) provides learners access to many experts, past and present, helping refine their musicianship (Elliott, 1995). Learners engage in an apprenticeship with the conducting teacher who acts as a broker (Wenger, 1998; Wenger et al., 2002). "Knowledge brokers . . . have membership in multiple communities" (Wenger et al., 2002, p. 154), and assist learners in accommodating similar interpretations, moving them from one cultural practice to a culture or community of conductors through modeling, coaching and fading. As a member of an instrumental ensemble, a second community, learners are able to observe the conductor performing the desired task contextually in practice. Lastly, within a conducting community of practice, learners refine ideas socially by observing, dialoguing, and scaffolding among peers, past and present. This notion of multiple experts is enhanced by Internet resources where learners can search, observe, and possibly scaffold in the desired outcomes leading to multiple perspectives for solving conducting situations.

Discussing the role of the teacher in a constructivist classroom, Shively (2005) suggests, "This approach also demands a much higher level of preparation and much greater musicianship on the part of the teacher" (p. 183). With that notion, I have become more comfortable within my own musicianship, flexible in my decision making, receptive to the possibility of multiple perspectives, and reflective in my approach to teaching conducting.

Creativity cannot be conceptualized as being the sole prerogative of the teacher-director, the students being artisans who only carry out his or her artistic wishes. The students must share in the creativity, under the insightful, unifying governance of the teacher (Reimer, 1989, p. 193).

My conducting classroom, at times, resembled what Schön (1987) described as a traditional *practicum* experience. It was a setting designed for the task of learning a practice. In a context that approximates a practice world, students learned by doing, although their doing usually fell short of real-world work. They learned by taking on projects that simulated and simplified practice; or they took on real-world projects under close supervision. The *practicum* was a virtual world, relatively free of the pressures, distractions, and risks of the real to which, nevertheless, it referred (p. 37).

My classroom also transformed into a laboratory for musical imagination (Greene, 1995) where I facilitated the goal of learners' proving or disproving of hypotheses with opportunities provided for the construction of their own meaning within conducting. Learners interacted with each other, bringing prior knowledge into a relationship with new knowledge, becoming an "apprentice, experimenter, interviewer, investigative reporter, and researcher" (Wink & Putney, 2010, p. 9). I served as a guide and facilitator, scaffolding learning when necessary (as I was the more skillful practitioner) in my relationship with the learners ensuring what Dewey (1916) called active engagement with appropriate authentic experiences so that the learners could take ownership of their outcomes.

Community of practice

Lave and Wenger (1991) and Wenger (1998) described a *community of practice* as a group of people with a shared passion for what they do in common, and as they interact, learn how to do it better. For Wenger (1998), what distinguished one community of practice from another was the mutual goals and expertise of the community that, among other things, created a separate identity for its members. Elliott (1995) suggested a similar notion as "musical practices swirl around the efforts of practitioners who originate, maintain, and refine established ways and means of musicing, as well as cherished musical histories, legends, and lore" (p. 67).

Music practitioners (Elliott, 1995) have a shared expertise in what they do and when grouped together share a passion to interact and create an experience for themselves and others through performance (a level of understanding transferred from musician to audience). There is a shared understanding (Rogoff, 1990) of the performance goals and needs to create an artistic experience.

The concept of musical practitioners engaged in communities of practice extends beyond the ensemble, as they are involved in multiple communities. "Individuals rarely owe allegiance to any single institution: one 'belongs' to a family of origin and one by marriage, an occupational group, a neighborhood, as well as to a more general group like a nation or a social class" (Bruner, 1996, p. 30). American musicians might be members of a community of western art music, a community of composers, a community of arrangers, a community of a school music program, a musical community of their cultural heritage, a musical community of their main performance instrument, and possibly a community of conductors. These communities play an active role in the practitioner's/learner's establishing understanding in the commonalities within each community entered.

Vygotsky (1978) and others (Bruner, 1996; Lave & Wenger, 1991; Rogoff, 1990) suggested that learning is a social process between learners and individuals or groups of more capable peers providing guidance or collaboration––a community of practice (Lave & Wenger, 1991; Wenger, 1998). Learners demonstrate varying levels of expertise within each community, which accounts for learners needing assistance in one community, while in another offering someone else assistance. Therefore a learner's zone of proximal development is fluid not only between a community of practice (Wenger, 1998), but among individuals within multiple communities, and possibly among communities as a whole.

Learners within the practice of instrumental conducting engage in multiple communities of practice sharing the communities of their school, music major, western art music, instrumental ensemble member, and conducting students. The entry point or bridge into conducting practice is the instrumental ensemble, where learners first engage in the practice of conducting as what Lave and Wenger (1991) describe as legitimate peripheral participants observing conductors in practice from the boundary of the culture. "This central concept denotes the particular mode of engagement of a learner who participates in the actual practice of an expert, but only to a limited degree and with limited responsibility for the ultimate product as a whole" (Lave & Wenger, 1991, p. 14). Learners, as members of ensembles, enter into an apprenticeship of observation (Lortie, 1975) with the ensemble conductor. From the beginning instrumental conducting class, learners enter into a new apprenticeship, where, acting as a *broker* (Wenger, 1998; Wenger, McDermott, & Snyder, 2002), a more-experienced other (conducting teacher or other ensemble conductors) scaffolds the apprentice's (learner's) journey from a community of the ensemble member into a conducting community of practice. As Schön (1987) explained, senior practitioners initiate learners into the practice by practicing the making or performing at which they seek to become adept assists students.

"The customs, methods, and *working* standards of the calling constitute 'tradition,' and . . . initiation into the tradition is the means by which the powers of learners are released and directed" (Dewey, 1974, p. 151). It is through learning by doing (Dewey, 1933, 1934, 1938; Elliott, 1995; Schön 1983, 1987) with a coach (Bruner, 1966; Schön, 1983, 1987) providing the freedom to learn, that a learner initiates into the "traditions of the calling" (Schön, 1987, p. 17).

Problem solving

Learners engage in problem solving through a series of reflective processes to gain understanding of experiences and in the process become more aware of their knowings (Blair, 2012; Butke, 2006; Dewey, 1910; 1933, 1938, 1976; Fendler, 2003; Marquart & Yeo, 2012; Osterman, 1990; Schön, 1983, 1987; van Manen, 1990, 2002; York-Barr et al., 2006). "Reflection is viewed as an active thought process aimed at understanding and subsequent improvement" (York-Barr et al., 2006, p. 4). Reflecting on experiences is not a new concept. Socrates, quoted by Plato (2012) in *Apology*, described the notion of a reflective process in his famous quote "The unexamined life isn't worth living" (p. 34). Socrates suggested there was room for interpretation of meaning behind every experience. It is through interpretation of our experiences that life becomes worth living (Robinson, 1997).

The foundational framework of reflective practice can be traced back to Dewey (1910, 1933, 1938) who viewed learning as a reflective process of interactions between individuals and their environment requiring a scientific process of describing, questioning, generating hypotheses, and testing hypotheses arising from an experience. According to Dewey (1933), reflective thinking occurred after a pre-reflective situation or "perplexed, troubled, or confused situation" (p. 106). Learning through problem solving engages problematic situations within a context authentic to a practice providing stimulus for thought where learners, having the information needed to deal with situations, are responsible for developing, testing, and validating their solutions (Dewey, 1966). Within Dewey's theory, reflective thought occurs within the following phases:

> *Suggestions*, in which the mind leaps forward to a possible solution;
> *Intellectualization* of the difficulty or perplexity that has been *felt* (directly experienced) into a *problem* to be solved, a question for which the answer must be sought;
> *Hypothesis*: The use of one suggestion after another as leading idea to initiate and guide observation and other operations in collection of factual material;
> *Reasoning*: The mental elaboration of the idea or suppositions as an idea or supposition (in the sense in which reasoning is a part, not the whole, of inference); and
> *Testing* the hypothesis by overt or imaginative action. (Dewey, 1933, p. 107)

Schön (1987) suggested, "Real world practice doesn't present itself as problems but as messy situations" (p. 4) and described Dewey's pedagogy as contextual situations, or experiences, that are problematic in nature and presented to learners where solutions are constructed from familiar theories formed from prior knowledge, past experiences, and known techniques. For Schön (1983, 1987), learners always created situations that involved learning by doing or action and that reflective practice involved intuitive knowledge generated by practitioners based on those experiences. He identified and described two forms of reflection: *reflection-in-action*, referring to the process of observing one's own thinking and action as they occur in order to make adjustments; and *refection-on-action*, referring to the process of "looking back at what we have done to discover how our knowing-in-action may have contributed to an unexpected outcome" (Schön, 1987, p. 26).

Reflection

York-Barr et al. (2006) suggested reflection as, "an active thought process aimed at understanding and subsequent improvement" (p. 4). In the conducting class, students engaged in problem solving through a series of reflective processes to gain understanding of experiences and in the process become more aware of their own musical knowledge. For example. . . .

Constructivism suggests that each person creates their own version of the world containing knowledge, concepts, and ideas based on their experiences within their environment. Learners continually reevaluate their prior knowings and experiences against new knowledge.

Reflection in the conducting class should be an ongoing planned activity. Students construct knowledge by investigating problematic conducting situations within musical contexts, and then, through reflection, naming and reframing those situations by testing and retesting their solutions based on their prior knowledge and experiences as music practitioners. Reframing occurs when learners challenge their beliefs, ideas, or assumptions about a problematic situation in a new or different way and in the process change its meaning. Reflection provides opportunities for students to know when and how to make musical judgments by challenging their prior knowings about conducting and past conducting experiences. The process of reflecting on previous experiences makes them feel aware and responsible for their own learning—a process of becoming agentive.

The role of prior experience

Novice choral conductors enter the conducting classroom with a wealth of prior experiences. Participation as singers in school, church, and community choral ensembles of various sizes and configurations results in direct and indirect contact with choral conductors. Through participation in ensembles, novice conductors, usually only a few yards away from the conductor while participating as members of the ensemble, "construct" what it is to be a conductor (Shively, 2007). Individual perspectives vary based on individual experiences with conductors and become the grounding for any preconceptions students hold about conducting. As ensemble members, they only receive a partial view of what it is to be a conductor. Novice conducting students are not always privy to the observed conductors' thoughts and reflections behind their actions, which makes the students capable of identifying various conducting gestures, but unable to describe the decision-making skills used by expert conductors in practice. Students do not know when to use certain gestures, the reasoning behind why conductors might use certain gestures in certain musical situations, or understand what it takes to make decisions about which gestures to use. Working with experienced conductors through the rehearsal process provides opportunities for those learning to conduct to clarify and challenge previous conceptions of what it means to conduct a choir. They observe the conductor's gestures and musical decisions and engage as a shared participant in the music making.

BECOMING AGENTIVE

Because of the spiral nature of the planned conducting experiences, learners exist in multiple phases of the agentive process at any given time. There is an overlapping or spiral approach to learners becoming agentive. Even though students may feel uncomfortable during certain conducting situations, they are still capable of investigating possible solutions, and even though not fully in control over their situation, believe they can succeed in future conducting experiences.

Student agency propels or deters learning and the way in which educators recognize and respond to student agency is important. Bruner (1996) wrote, "Perhaps the single most universal thing about human experience is the phenomenon of 'Self,' and we know that education is crucial to its formation. Education should be conducted with that fact in mind" (p. 35). He identified agency, reflection, collaboration, and culture as important to the way teachers teach and students learn, and defined agency as taking control within your own thinking. Key to students becoming agentive in choral conducting is the ability and opportunity to make decisions, strategize, and create frames that enable understanding.

Agency is described by Blair (2009) as "the ways people act and interact within sociocultural settings . . . [and] implies students moving from powerless to a sense of control and a hope for the future, their own future" (pp. 179–180). Wiggins (2011) defined agency as "the intentionality and control an individual feels she has over her own circumstances in a particular situation or at a given time in that situation" (p. 91). I define agency as the power of an individual (or group) to enter into and follow through with a desired activity through decision making, strategies, and creating frames (complex schemas used to filter and create meaning built on prior knowings and beliefs), that enable understanding. Students perceive themselves as agents or participants (as opposed to spectators) when they take ownership or control of their outcomes within an activity.

In order for students to be able to learn how to conduct, they must believe that they are capable of conducting and that their ideas and contributions to the practice of conducting are valued. Without personal agency, students become nonparticipants in the learning process.

Personal agency and musical agency

Both *personal* and *musical* agencies are important traits for conducting students to acquire. Personal agency is the sense of control students feel when they take ownership of particular situations or within a particular situation. It is rooted in the phenomenon of the self where students become empowered such that they are capable of following through with a desired activity (Bruner, 1996; Rogoff, 1990). Students need personal agency to be capable of recognizing their own musical skills and knowledge and feel confident in their abilities to use that knowledge and those skills while engaging in music making (Wiggins, 2011).

In examining the role of learner agency within the context of music education, Blair (2009) suggested that two fundamental areas of agency emerge. First, students want to accomplish learning tasks by discovering things for themselves. She suggests students want to function as musicians in ways that provide opportunities to participate with others as composers, listeners, and performers. Secondly, she stated students want respect and value as productive members within the community of practice.

In choral conducting classroom students, like the participants in Blair's (2009) study, appear to manifest ownership through their desire to participate musically with others as conductors. Through socially situated experiences solving real-life problems within the context of the conducting class, students apply conceptual understandings to new musical contexts, allowing them to relate to others (peers, the musical ensemble, and audience) in new musical ways.

Musical agency is rooted in one's prior musical experiences and their membership with varied communities of practice. It is how learners function as music makers and articulate ideas through music. According to Wiggins (2016), musical agency occurs when students feel they can act on their own musical ideas and ideas about music. Fostering musical agency fuels learners' desire to learn more within the conducting classroom, while ignoring musical agency hampers music learning.

For example, not all learners become personally and musically agentive quickly and some require extra guidance in self-directing their learning, and developing an awareness of their beliefs about their abilities, and about their role in choosing to learn or choosing not to learn. Students come into the conducting classroom with varied ensemble experiences and sometimes without lifelong ones. Lack of prior experiences observing choral conductors in practice contributes to a devaluing of the domain, leading students to less motivation and less engagement in the process of learning to conduct. Students might choose to not learn because of possible feelings of inadequacy due to a self-perceived lack of knowledge. Lack of confidence in one's ability to conduct, lack of knowledge about conducting, and lack of prior experiences with choral conductors slow the learning process and inhibit students from becoming agentive.

Conducting Pedagogy in Action

From 2011 to 2013, I engaged in a qualitative study where, as a teacher-researcher, I analyzed experiences of students and teachers in an undergraduate conducting course. I was interested in seeking understanding of challenges, frustrations, and successes as we negotiated their learning to become conductors and my learning to teach conducting (Abrahams, 2013).

My own reflective teacher-journal and classroom observations, video recordings of classroom experiences, student reflective journals, and follow-up email member checking with students served as data.

The 15 participants across the two years of the study (six in 2011–2012 and nine in 2012–2013) were in their junior year of undergraduate preparation as music education majors or in their senior year as performance majors. The combined demographic consisted of students experienced with conducting and conductors as well as those new to conducting. The setting of this study was an undergraduate conducting classroom where I was the primary instructor for two years. Data were collected over four semesters, with two sets of students each taking Conducting I and Conducting II class, with the two-course sequence running from September through April. The conducting class took place on Monday and Wednesday weekly for 112 minutes. It was a part of the students' normal semester course schedule.

With the goal of fostering personal and musical agency, I designed episodes that were authentic to the practice of conducting. These actively engaged learners in problem solving and reflective practice. Within each class session, students took turns conducting an ensemble comprised of members of the class. At the conclusion of each conducting episode, students received instructor and peer feedback. Class members constantly switched roles between conductor and evaluator. After each week, students and teacher wrote reflective journals about their weekly conducting experiences. Students created their own personal conducting websites that provided space for them to upload videos of their conducting episodes from class and post self-reflections. Each student brought her or his own uniqueness to the class. Greene (1995) suggested, "There are always roads not taken, vistas not acknowledged. The search is ongoing. The search must be ongoing; the end can never be quite known" (p. 15). For these reasons, I did not know what I might find.

Early in the term, I selected *Chester,* by early American composer William Billings, for them to conduct because it is a four-part homophonic setting and a good example for teaching the four-beat conducting pattern. As part of the students' preparation for the Billings, I had them develop two personal goals for improving their technique and two musical goals toward improving musicality. Throughout their conducting, I wanted them to refer back to their goals to help them focus on what they perceived as needing work. They had difficulty setting musical goals. This was a problem for the entire class.

At the end of each semester, I collected and coded data. The emergent theme of becoming agentive in the process of learning to conduct seemed to follow a similar process of feeling powerless, gaining control, and becoming hopeful as described by Blair (2009). As they learned to conduct, I could observe students acting on their self-awareness of problematic conducting situations that they realize during reflective practice. Problem solving through real life experiences of preparing a score and then communicating musical ideas to the ensemble were valued but also deemed challenging by students. Nonetheless, these episodes appeared to promote the agentive process making the journey to become a conductor a meaningful one.

Jacob's [2] reflections learning to conduct *Chester* by William Billings were typical of all in the course. In his journal (September 30, 2012) Jacob wrote:

> So far, *Chester* was the most difficult and complex piece of music we have looked at. I really thought I had a good idea of how to show the theme of revolution and pride by using dynamics, to show tension in the conducting, and how the climax of the song should work. As I practiced through the week, I found myself slipping in to a three pattern often as I tried to work with the other musical elements (*identification of problematic situation*). As I stepped onto the podium for this take, I was thinking about how the music would begin and develop and forgot to count to four. I slipped in to a three pattern very early and could not get back on track; this was a quick crash and burn.

Jacob conducted the excerpt a second time with adjustments and commented:

> The second take of *Chester* went smoother than the first. I actually made it all the way through the piece. I did not seem to bounce my arms as much on the down beat,

which had been an issue (*identification of problematic situation*). Earlier in the week while conducting this piece, I was not floating all the way through beat 2 and 3 on the phrase release (*identification of problematic situation*). I did a better job in this take. I once again slipped in to a three pattern but recovered well, though I gave away my mistake by laughing and shaking my head (*identification of problematic situation*). At the beginning of this take, I felt I was focusing on counting and was using too much of an ictus, which was another issue I had worked on through the week (*identification of problematic situation*). I began to correct the sharp ictus and then lost the focus on the dynamics. Luckily, the class knew what dynamics I wanted, but I do not think I actually showed them very well. We have discussed in class how the conductor must be a master of multitasking, and I experienced this first hand during this take. As soon as I corrected one mistake, I found myself slipping in another area (*Identified problematic situation*).

Aware that multitasking is an obstacle toward success, Jacob *developed a plan for success*. He conducted the excerpt a third time finding some success in his third attempt:

The third take of *Chester* was finally the one I felt confident and satisfied with. I was very frustrated with myself at this point, and before the take, I took a deep breath, refocused, and just did what I had practiced all week. I felt I used a smoother ictus to show legato, I imagined pulling my hands through tar to help show tension, and felt I prepped and showed clear dynamics throughout the piece. A couple of things I notice in the video: it seems like I sped up the tempo a few times during crescendos, and I have a kind of hitch or hesitation on one of the last beats that I do not remember doing.

He concluded his reflection with a *self-evaluative statement* of his experience: "I know things will not always be perfect, but those little mistakes make me feel less confident about this take. It was sufficient, but not great."

Novice conductors do not always execute conducting episodes as planned. Schön (1983, 1987) describes the process of *reflection-in-action* as observing ones own thinking and action as they occur in order to make adjustments. In those problematic situations, students seem to reflect-in-action and make adjustments that appear to help maintain engagement in tasks. For instance, Jacob was frustrated with himself because his in-class conducting did not match his expectation and set goals; however, he seemed motivated and continuously engaged in trying to succeed. Even though the mistakes seem to make Jacob feel less confident, it appeared that he was able to see the possibility of success, which seemed to keep him engaged in the task. Other problems students identified were more generic. Another student, Kayla, identified eye contact as a problem. In her journal (November 25, 2012), toward the end of the fall term Kayla shared:

I was truly disappointed with the eye contact in this conducting episode (*identification of problematic situation*). As far as keeping my head out of the music, I felt I did rather well, especially in keeping eye contact at all the major cue points. However, I fell back into my habit of only looking at half of the ensemble again.

She framed her problem:

> I'm not sure if this is because I tend to concentrate only on the soprano line, or if it is just that I don't like the [singers] on the left side of the class (of course, this is not the case).

Kayla strategized a plan to remedy the situation:

> I definitely need to work at listening to the bottom three voices and not base my listening solely on the soprano voice (*strategizing a plan for success*). I definitely feel this is what is causing me to continually look to my right, and it is something that will definitely need to be fixed for future conducting episodes.

She concluded her journal entry with a *self-evaluative statement*:

> I think my progress as a conductor has been consistently improving. Every week I feel like I improve upon my technique and presence on the podium. I have also done a good job of improving upon showing music with my whole body and not just my right arm. I feel like I use my face, style of pattern, and use of my left hand better than I did at the beginning of the semester, but I still need to further exaggerate these gestures at times. We have not had the opportunity to work on long pieces, but for what has been expected of us I feel like I have done very well.

After reading Kayla's reflection, I reexamined her conducting video. Paying close attention to Kayla's eye contact, I noticed her head slightly turned to the side. This could be what she perceived as favoring one side of the ensemble; however, I recall perceiving her action as her listening to the ensemble. In Kayla's reflection, she mentioned needing to concentrate on listening to the bottom voices of the score. The way her head cocked to the side seemed to suggest she was listening to the tenor and bass line. By turning her head to listen more intently for the nonmelodic line, Kayla looked as if she was favoring the soprano voices.

Kayla's reflection suggested a progression through a three-phase agentive process. She seemed to enter into a process of metacognition, or thinking about her own thinking, where she expressed concern for her ability to achieve self-established goals. Kayla's ownership of her thinking processes seemed to be a product of her awareness of problematic situations. Significantly, Kayla's perceived self-confidence in her ability to use her musical skills and knowledge while engaged in conducting was evidence that she was becoming agentive personally and musically.

Awareness of problematic conducting situations engaged these students in taking corrective actions through hypothesizing, testing their hypotheses during home practice, and validating their solutions by observing other conductors during class and during ensemble rehearsals demonstrate solutions to similar problematic situations.

As a result of their corrective actions, these students generated self-evaluative statements that expressed their needs, or goals, to gauge their future conducting experiences.

Goal setting fueled their motivation to remain engaged in the process of learning even when solutions to problematic situations failed and they appeared frustrated. Setting goals towards future conducting experiences expressed a level of confidence in their musical skills and knowings and their newly acquired skills in conducting created a sense of openness, as there ceased to be confining barriers in the way of their completing their conducting episode.

Responding to their self-evaluative statements, the learners expressed their feelings regarding their abilities to achieve their future conducting goals. These statements provided value to the concepts experienced in the conducting classroom. When these learners valued the concepts and activities during their conducting experiences, they remained engaged and motivated towards learning and became more passionate about self-assessing, about music, and about their career goals leading them into the next experience. They appeared more eager to pursue the next challenge.

These students engaged in metacognitive processes continually reflecting on their knowings and abilities to conduct. Their reconciliation of problematic situations leading to openness towards the possibility of success, value, and respect within the practice of conducting seemed to lead to their realization of new problematic situations. The construction process in these students appeared recursive, or a process that a procedure goes through when one of the steps of the procedure involves invoking the procedure itself.

My analysis and interpretation of the data about the agentive processes of these students suggests they experienced moving from feeling powerless in their problematic situation to moving to a sense of control and finally becoming hopeful about future conducting episodes with more challenging concepts and skills that would eventually bring them back to feeling powerless within the next conducting episode. The recursive processes of identifying problematic situations, acting on awareness through problem solving, and becoming open to possibilities of successful conducting experiences assists learners in thinking about and taking ownership for their processes of learning. As a result, these students became aware of their own musical skills and knowings and confident in their abilities and actions in using those musical knowings and skills while engaged in conducting; in moving from ensemble member through conducting student to conductor they became personally and musically agentive.

Implications for Practice and Connecting to Choral Pedagogy

Agency as a choral singer and as a choral conductor are two co-constructed goals that are part of a journey toward choral excellence. When empowering students to become agents taking ownership of their learning processes, choral conductors plan lessons and their singers experience those lessons. As teacher-conductors, we traditionally plan our rehearsals by mapping out what we are going to rehearse for each class and what we expect our singers to achieve. Instead we might plan our rehearsals not only from the perspective of what we will teach, but from the perspective of what is happening to our singers while engaged in rehearsal. How do our singers learn within our rehearsals? As can be noted from the study above, it is engaging in experiences, reflecting on those experiences, and creating openness towards learning that leads to learners' desire to engage in new experiences that are more challenging. This is what should happen in any student-centered experience and how we, as choral conductors, should view learner agency—through the lens of the learning experience.

If choral conductors rehearse in a student-centered manner, then planning shifts focus to the singers' needs and to fostering their personal and musical agencies. Rehearsal experiences become episodes comprising basic concepts that spiral repeatedly, building on increasing difficulty. During each rehearsal, singers actively engage in experiences that are authentic to the choral art. As singers rehearse, they reflect on the experiences and in the process take action to problem-solve and become more eager to pursue the next challenge leading them into the next rehearsal.

As this process evolves, choristers are immersed in multiple musical experiences at multiple levels of difficulty. This provides opportunities for them to exist in multiple agentive stages. By reflecting on their experiences within the rehearsal they remove the barriers that keep them from succeeding. In the end, they take ownership of their actions and of the actions of the ensemble as a whole. They are valued as a member of the choir and, in the process become agentive.

Conclusions

Learning to conduct is about envisioning musical possibilities through a synthesis of all other musical knowledge and understanding, and in the process creating a unique musical experience. Reflective practice provides opportunities for conductors and their singers to use their imaginations to envision possibilities, pose and solve problems together, and test hypotheses. As a result, all become open to the notion that there are multiple solutions to meet the challenges in a musical score and in the process they foster their personal and musical identity. Thus, they achieve a state of musical and personal agency and as agentive conductors, they contribute to performances that are vibrant and exciting for themselves and for those who hear them.

Learning to conduct a choir is about becoming a musical leader entrusted to provide singers opportunities to question their prior knowledge, solve musical problems, and reflect on their actions. The journey to become an agentive choral conductor develops musicianship and decision-making skills. In addition, in the process of becoming, novice conductors acquire confidence and competence in their own musical and conducting abilities and attain personal and musical agency.

Notes

1. This is similar to Boardman's (1988) application of Bruner's theories to general music planning and teaching.
2. The participant names have been changed.

References

Abrahams, D. A. (2013). *Fostering musical and personal agency in beginning conductors.* Unpublished doctoral dissertation, Oakland University, Rochester, MI.

Bergee, M. J. (2005). An exploratory comparison of novice, intermediate, and expert orchestral conductors. *International Journal of Music Education, 23*(1), 23–36.

Blair, D. V. (2009). Learner agency: To understand and to be understood. *British Journal of Music Education, 26*(2), 173–187.

Boardman, E. (1988). The generative theory of musical learning. Part II. *General Music Today, 2*(2), 3–6.

Boardman, E. (2002). The relationship of musical thinking and learning to classroom instruction. In E. Boardman (Ed.), *Dimensions of musical thinking and learning* (pp. 1–20). Reston, VA: MENC, The National Association for Music Educators.

Boardman, S. M. (2000). *A survey of the undergraduate instrumental conducting course in region seven of the national association of schools of music* (Unpublished doctoral dissertation). University of Georgia, Athens, GA.

Brooks, J. G., & Brooks, M. G. (1999). *In search of understanding: The case for constructivist classrooms.* Alexandria, VA: ASCD.

Bruner, J. (1960). *The process of education.* Cambridge, MA: Harvard University Press.

Bruner, J. (1996). *The culture of education.* Cambridge, MA: Harvard University Press.

Byo, J. L. (1990). Recognition of intensity in the gestures of beginning conductors. *Journal of Research in Music Education, 38*(3), 157–163.

Byo, J. L., & Austin, K. R. (1994). Comparison of expert and novice conductors: An approach to analysis of nonverbal behaviors. *Journal of Band Research, 30*(1), 11–34.

Chapman, C. C. (2008). *An investigation of current instruction practices for the undergraduate instrumental conducting students concerning left hand technique and facial gestures* (Unpublished doctoral dissertation). University of Washington, Seattle, WA.

Collins, A., Brown, J. S., & Newman, S. (1989). Cognitive apprenticeship: Teaching the craft of reading, writing, and mathematics. In L. B. Resnick (Ed.), *Knowing, learning, and instruction: Essays in honor of Robert Glaser* (pp. 453–494). Hillsdale, NJ: Lawrence Erlbaum.

Cummings-Potvin, W. (2007). Scaffolding, multiliteracies, and reading circles. *Canadian Journal of Education, 30*(2), 483–507.

Demaree, R. W., & Moses, D.V. (1995). *The complete conductor: A comprehensive resource for the professional conductor of the twenty-first century.* Englewood Cliffs, NJ: Prentice Hall.

Dewey, J. (1910). *How we think.* Boston: D.C. Heath and Company.

Dewey, J. (1933). *How we think* (revised ed.). Boston: D.C. Heath and Company.

Dewey, J. (1934). *Art as experience.* New York: Perigee Trade.

Dewey, J. (1938). *Experience and education.* New York: Macmillan.

Dewey, J. (1966). *Democracy and education: An introduction to the democracy of education.* New York: The Free Press. (Originally published in 1916).

Dewey, J. (1976). The child and curriculum. In J. A. Boydston & J. R. Burnett (Eds.), *The middle works of John Dewey* (Vol. 2, pp. 271–291). Carbondale, IL: Southern Illinois University Press. (Originally published in 1902.)

Durrant, C. (1994). Towards a model of effective communication: A case for structured teaching of conducting. *British Journal of Music Education, 11*(1), 57–76.

Durrant, C. (2003). *Choral conducting: Philosophy and practice*. London: Routledge.

Elliott, D. J. (1995). *Music matters: A new philosophy of music education*. New York: Oxford University Press.

Fredrickson, W. E., Johnson, C. M., & Robinson, C. R. (1998). The effect of pre-conducting on the evaluation of conductor competence. *Journal of Band Research, 33*(2), 1–13.

Fosnot, C. T. (2005). Preface. In C. T. Fosnot (Ed.), *Constructivism: Theory, perspectives, and practice* (pp. ix–xii). New York, NY: Teachers College Press.

Getchell, R. W. (1957). *An investigation of and recommendation for the beginning conducting class in the college curriculum* (Unpublished doctoral dissertation). University of Iowa.

Grashel, J. (1991). Teaching basic conducting skills through video. *Music Educators Journal, 77*(36), 36–37.

Green, E. A. H., Gibson, M., & Malko, N. (2004). *The modern conductor: A college text on conducting based on the technical principles of Nicolai Malko as set forth in his The conductor and his baton* (7th ed.). Upper Saddle River, NJ: Pearson Prentice Hall.

Greene, M. (1995). *Releasing the imagination: Essays on education, the arts, and social change*. San Francisco: Jossey-Bass.

Hunsberger, D., & Ernst, R. E. (1992). *The art of conducting* (2nd ed.). New York: McGraw-Hill Publishing.

Jordan, J. (1999). *The musicians soul: A journey examining spirituality for performers, teachers, composers, conductors, and music educators*. Chicago, IL: GIA.

Jordan, J. (2009). *Evoking sound: Fundamentals of choral conducting* (2nd ed.). Chicago, IL: GIA.

Jordan, J. (2011). *The conductor's gesture: A practical application of Rudolf Laban's movement language*. Chicago, IL: GIA.

Kaplan, A. (1985). *Choral conducting*. New York: Norton.

Kincheloe, J. L. (2004). *Teachers as researchers: Qualitative inquiry as a path to empowerment*. New York: Routledge.

Lave, J., & Wenger, E. (1991). *Situated learning: Legitimate peripheral participation*. New York: Cambridge University Press.

Leppla, D. A. (1989). *The acquisition of basic conducting skills by beginning conductors: A comparison of effects of guided and unguided videotaped modeling*. Unpublished doctoral dissertation, Ohio State University.

Lortie, D. C. (1975). *Schoolteacher: A sociological study*. Chicago: University of Chicago Press.

Manfredo, J. (2008). Factors influencing curricular content for undergraduate instrumental conducting courses. *Bulletin of the Council for Research in Music Education, 175*, 43–57.

Miller, S. W. A. (1988). *The effect of Laban Movement Theory on the ability of student conductors to communicate musical interpretation through gesture*. Unpublished doctoral dissertation, University of Wisconsin-Madison.

Morrison, S. J., & Demorest, S. M. (2012). Once from the top: Reframing the role of the conductor in ensemble teaching. In G. McPhereson & G. Welch (Eds.), *Oxford handbook of music education* (pp. 826–843). New York, NY: Oxford University Press.

Neidlinger, E. J. (2003). *The effect of Laban effort/shape instruction on young conductors' perception of expressiveness across arts disciplines* (Unpublished doctoral dissertation). University of Minnesota, Minneapolis, MN.

Orzolek, D. C. (1996). The effect of imagery and movement exercises on the ability of students to conduct expressively. *Dissertation Abstracts International, 57,* 145. http://vc.bridgew.edu/cgi/viewcontent.cgi?article=1003&context=music_fac

O'Toole, P. (1993). I sing in a choir but I have "no voice!" *The Quarterly Journal of Music Teaching and Learning, 4–5(5–1),* 65–76.

Powell, S. R. (2008). *The effects of Elizabeth A. H. Green's conception of psychological conducting on the ability of beginning instrumental conducting students to communicate through gesture.* Unpublished doctoral dissertation, University of Illinois at Urbana-Champaign.

Reimer, B. (1989). *A philosophy of music education.* Englewood Cliffs, NJ: Prentice Hall.

Robinson, D. N. (1997). *Socrates and the unexamined life: The great ideas of philosophy.* Springfield, VA: The Teaching Company.

Rogoff, B. (1990). *Apprenticeship in thinking: Cognitive development in social context.* New York: Oxford University Press.

Rudolf, M. (1995). *The grammar of conducting: A comprehensive guide to baton technique and interpretation* 3rd ed. New York: Schirmer.

Runnels, B. D. (1992). *Practices in the teaching of instrumental conducting at the undergraduate level among colleges and universities in the Upper Midwest.* Unpublished doctoral dissertation, University of Missouri–Kansas City.

Runnings, D.J. (2009). Effects of an interdisciplinary method for training conductors. *Music Faculty Publications.* Paper 4. Retrieved from http://vc.bridgew.edu/music_fac/4.

Schön, D. A. (1983). *The reflective practitioner: How professionals think in action.* New York: Basic Books.

Schön, D. A. (1987). *Educating the reflective practitioner: Toward a new design for teaching and learning in the profession.* San Francisco, CA: Jossey-Bass.

Shively, J. (2005). In the face of tradition: Questioning the roles of conductors and ensemble members in school bands, choirs, and orchestra. In L. Bartel (Ed.), *Questioning the music education paradigm* (pp. 179–190). Waterloo, ON: Canadian Music Educators Association.

Shively, J. (2007). *Examining apprenticeship of observation through introduction to music education courses.* Paper presented at the Instrumental Music Teacher Education conference, Mt. Sterling, OH.

Shively, J. (2015). Constructivism in music education. *Arts Education Policy Review, 116* (3), 128–136.

Silvey, B. A. (2011a). Undergraduate music major's perceptions of instrumental conducting curricula. *Journal of Music Teacher Education, 21*(1), 27–38.

Silvey, B. A. (2011b). Effects of score study on novices' conducting and rehearsing: A preliminary investigation. *Bulletin of the Council for Research in Music Education, 187,* 33–48.

van Manen, M. (1990). *Researching lived experience.* New York: State University of New York Press.

Vygotsky, L. S. (1978). *Mind in society: The development of higher psychological processes.* Cambridge, MA: Harvard University Press.

Webster, P. (2011). Construction of music learning. In R. Colwell and P. Webster (Eds.), *MENC handbook of research on music learning,* (pp. 35–83). New York: Oxford University Press.

Wenger, E. (1998). *Communities of practice: Learning, meaning, and identity.* New York: Cambridge University Press.

Wenger, E., McDermott, R., & Snyder, W. M. (2002). *Cultivating communities of practice.* Boston: Harvard Business School Press.

Wiggins, J. (2001). *Teaching for musical understanding.* New York: McGraw-Hill.

Wiggins, J. (2011). When the music is theirs: Scaffolding young songwriters. In M. Barrett (Ed.), *A cultural psychology of music education* (pp. 83–114). London: Oxford University Press.

Wiggins, J. (2015). *Teaching for musical understanding* (3rd ed.). New York: Oxford University Press.

Wiggins, J. (2016). Musical agency. In G. McPherson (Ed.), *The child as musician: A handbook of musical development* (2nd ed.). New York: Oxford University Press.

Wink, J., & Putney, L. (2010). *A vision of Vygotsky*. New York: Pearson.

Wis, R. M. (2007). *The conductor as leader: Principles of leadership applied to life on the podium*. Chicago: GIA.

Yontz, T. G. (2001). *The effectiveness of Laban-based principles of movement and previous musical thinking on undergraduate beginning conducting students' ability to convey intended musical content* (Unpublished doctoral dissertation). University of Nebraska–Lincoln, Lincoln.

York-Barr, J., Sommers, W. A., Ghere, G. S., & Montie, J. (2006). *Reflective practice to improve schools: An action guide for educators* (2nd ed.). Thousand Oaks, CA: Corwin.

CHAPTER 7

CHORAL PEDAGOGY AND THE CONSTRUCTION OF IDENTITY

LIZ GARNETT

"One is not born, but rather becomes, woman"'

SIMONE de Beauvoir's pithy statement from *The Second Sex* is the foundation stone of modern theories of identity, which have moved away from a concept of "self" as a stable, enduring core, to one of an ongoing project, actively maintained by the subject. Self-identity is constructed through practices and discourses, maintained as coherent patterns of action and feeling within the social groups they define.

Hence it would be equally valid to state "One is not born, but rather becomes, a choral singer." Choral traditions represent communities of practice that actively maintain and promulgate musical behaviors and their associated meanings. From this perspective, the function of choral pedagogy is to transform a miscellaneous collection of human beings into a unified ensemble populated by individuals who all self-identify as choral singers. It defines the vocal and conceptual elements that a participant has to master to count as a competent member of that community, and presents a range of established methods through which to train new arrivals in the acquisition of these elements.

The aim of this chapter is to provide insights into these processes of identity-formation in order to inform the way choral leaders deploy and develop their repertoires of choir-training techniques. Many western choral traditions maintain a genuinely inclusive ethos, built on beliefs in the naturalness and universality of singing together.[1] At the same time, they maintain their heritage—and, indeed, attain their best results—through stringent disciplinary regimes, which in turn can lead to criticisms of exclusionary and elitist practices. It is possible to negotiate a path through this contradictory ideological landscape without either diluting artistic standards or alienating those one would wish to engage, but it is not always a simple process. Critical analysis of the ways that choral identities are formed will allow the choral leader to be more strategic and self-aware in their praxis and the ethical commitments they reflect.

The chapter will start with an outline of key concepts in theories of identity, and how they can help us understand the processes by which choirs inculcate their members into their particular choral culture. It will then examine in detail three areas particularly salient for the choral leader. The first is the phenomenon of "non-singers": how they emerge as a by-product of western mythologies of talent, and what can be done to rehabilitate them. The second is the interpenetration of social and musical identity categories: how elements we may think of as "purely" musical are constructed in terms of wider social categories such as class, regionality, or race, and the implications for how we frame the choral techniques we use. The third is the relationship between individual and group: how an ensemble establishes a corporate, supra-personal identity, and ways to facilitate the lowering of individuals' ego boundaries to allow this.

The emphasis throughout will be less on the description of techniques than on how to use the discipline's established methods effectively and inclusively.[2] This chapter draws on these methods to illustrate the processes it discusses, but does not attempt to duplicate their function. Rather, it aspires to send choral directors back to their disciplinary forerunners with a clearer sense of how to use the fruits of their experience without inadvertently reproducing implicit and unwanted cultural hierarchies.

THE PROJECT OF THE CHORAL SELF

The identity of the choral singer is constituted within the context of, and through the same processes as, the self as a whole. Choir is in some ways a distinct social environment, separated from daily life by location and activity; self-identification as a choral singer is likewise a discrete element of one's overall sense of identity. At the same time, people's understanding of choral music as an art and as a social activity is formed within their experience of their wider cultural milieu. Several key concepts are useful to clarify the workings of these processes, and thus to unpick the role of choral pedagogy in producing proficient and well-adjusted singers.

First, is the idea of identity as *performative* (Butler, 1990). Both our experience of ourselves and other people's conception of who we are come through what we do. Everybody's daily life is built upon myriad iterative practices—habits—that through repetition provide a sense of coherence and continuity to their lived experience. We learn these habits through interaction with our cultural environment: through direct social contact with our family, neighbors, and peers; and through exposure to the products of mediated culture—television, radio, newspapers. Many are picked up without conscious awareness of their acquisition, while others are imposed as we learn standards of acceptable and unacceptable behavior through parental discipline, school rules, and peer pressure. Bourdieu (1984) uses the term *habitus* for the cultural environment that forms these basic patterns of behavior.

Our learned behaviors are not random, but are organized by cultural discourses into more-or-less stable constellations of practices, which are understood as identity categories: gender, religion, ethnicity. The discourses of identity are ideological, in that the social groups they define have access to different levels of power, both in terms of relative economic advantage and different levels of cultural prestige.

The extent to which individuals experience their relationship with these different axes of identity as salient to their sense of self will depend in the first instance largely on their habitus, but it is not a passive process. In a world shaped by migration, social mobility, and the mass media, individuals will find themselves interacting in multiple social contexts, with different and sometimes conflicting ethics and expectations, and they will need actively to develop their sense of self in dialogue with these competing claims on their allegiance and ways of being.

The subject thus creates and maintains his or her identity *reflexively* (Giddens, 1991), through an ongoing internal autobiography in which they make sense of their own experience. Through this personal narrative, people ascribe meaning to the events in their lives in terms of the cultural discourses available to them, and establish a sense of continuity in the trajectory of their lived experience. This reflexive project will be particularly intense at times of change or upheaval, as the subject decides how to construe a move into new social contexts: whether as a progression or departure from previous commitments, and whether to cling to old forms of behavior or abandon them in favor of new ones.

Hence the self is neither as "free" as ideologies of Western democracies might suggest nor as pre-determined as a Marxist analysis would contend. Both the patterns of behavior available to us and the narrative structures available to make sense of them are shared cultural artifacts, formed and maintained within contexts of power, authority and control. They are inscribed upon us through the social environments in which we act and interact. At the same time, they are not monolithic. Dominant ideologies spawn countercultures which offer both discursive critique and active forms of resistance. Even in the absence of outright opposition, individuals will often have a range of narrative and behavioral possibilities accessible to them through their habitus, although the degree of flexibility available will be more or less limited by their social status.

Individuals also have the opportunity to adopt certain ways of being temporarily or intermittently. Many people engage in activities that are bracketed off from their daily lives by their placement in distinct social spaces with distinct social groups, often articulated by specific forms of attire, language use, and norms of behavior. Bourdieu refers to these sub-sets of life as *fields*, while Giddens refers to them as *lifestyle sectors*. These activities are secondary forms of identity in that participants are less likely to use them as identity markers in other contexts, but they nonetheless take on a significant role in their personal narratives. People invest a lot of time, attention, and emotional commitment to their chosen lifestyle sectors, and may construe their development within that field in terms of a distinct career (Stebbins, 1996; Elkington and Stebbins, 2014).

These lifestyle sectors may be experientially separate from the wider culture in which they subsist, but they are still embedded within it, and draw upon its discourses in developing their sector-specific norms. Hence, whilst adherence to a particular field may be self-selecting in a way that primary identity categories are not (one can choose whether or not to be a biker; one cannot choose whether or not to be white), access to that field may not be equally open to all from that wider culture.

Choral singing operates as such a lifestyle sector: a slice of identity that people don for the duration of choral activities. It may interpenetrate with their wider life to some extent (inviting family members to concerts; socializing with choir members between choral activities), but it is a clearly defined world, with its own particular habits and values. Choral pedagogy thus emerges as the set of formal methods for constituting choral singers. The knowledge-base is well-developed, with clear procedures for inculcating both the patterns of desired behavior and the moral order that sustains them and gives them meaning. It also produces some unintended consequences.

Singers, Non-Singers, and Talent

We shall start by considering the "non-singer": the individual who self-identifies as unable to sing. The most important task of choral pedagogy is arguably to avoid producing this self-identification in children and to reverse it in adults. As a cultural category it is a product of deeply ingrained beliefs about the nature of "talent" and "musicality."[3] It is created by exclusionary discourses wielded by authority, but once internalized it is actively maintained by the non-singer.

Many adults who self-identify as non-singers can identify the moment at which they learned that they "could not sing" (Whidden, 2008; Pascale, 2002). The tale is one of discovery or revelation, of being told for the first time by an authority figure that they were failing at something they were previously unaware of being unable to do. The stories are also tales of practical exclusion, of being set apart from those who "can" sing, whether being told to mime rather than sing out loud, or a physical removal from the activity. Other "non-singers" tell of how they adopted the label for themselves through observing their social milieu; their stories are of people they knew who were celebrated as "talented," and from whom the "non-singers" felt different.

Once someone has accepted or assumed their designation as a "non-singer," they maintain that identity through both their behaviors and their personal narratives. They may also find themselves managing contradictions between their narratively maintained identity and behaviors that contradict it. "Non-singers" may in fact sing routinely in daily life—in the shower, along with the radio, with their children—but they categorize these activities as "not really" singing, as they are informal, private, and therefore immune from the judgment of others.

The categories of "singer" and "non-singer" were once standard in the educational literature. Rutkowski's (1990) overview of mid-20th-century pedagogical vocabulary gives the following terms for children with imperfect control of their voices: "nonsingers," "problem singers," "inaccurate singers," "dependent or lazy singers," "near singers," "partial singers," and "monotones." Her summary of Joyner's (1969) study of 11-year-old boys illustrates the problems associated with this literature:

> "Normal singers" were those who could sing in a low and high key; "Grade A monotones" were tuneful in the low key but not in the higher key; "Grade B monotones" were those who were erratic at both pitch levels; "Grade C monotones" are always untuneful.

The classifications usefully analyze the way children develop control over different vocal registers sequentially, but at the same time impose an overarching division into "normal singers" and "monotones." The use of the word "normal" is striking: one would gather from the taxonomy of "monotone" types that incomplete skill-acquisition is in fact a normal condition for this cohort of boys. By applying it instead to those with more secure skills, the term operates ideologically, pathologizing the "monotones" as aberrant rather than merely unskilled.

Underpinning these essentializing categories is the discourse of talent. To call someone "talented" is both to observe a degree of proficiency in what they do and to ascribe an inherent aptitude as the source of that proficiency. This is a pervasive cultural mythology, although there is little if any evidence that either technical or expressive skills are hereditary. As Sloboda (2005) stated: "Many people mistakenly assume that intuitive behavior must be innate. This is a major fallacy. Any well-practised habit eventually becomes automatic" (p. 268).

Studies of expertise across different disciplines have shown that the only identifiable differentiator between a casual or moderately capable executant and those at the top of their field is the sheer amount of time spent engaged in it. Mastery emerges after 10,000 hours of focused practice, which is typically double the time invested by the merely capable (Ericsson & Charness, 1994). Sloboda and Davidson's (1996) study of young musicians also finds no empirical basis for two other elements of the myth of talent: that musical excellence is by definition rare, and that it is heralded by developmentally precocious displays of musical capacity. Instead, they find that the best predictors for success in young musicians are kindliness in their initial teachers and parental support for their musicianship. Like Whidden's (2008) and Pascale's (2002) studies of "non-singers," they found that people who self-identify as "unmusical" commonly reported negative emotional experiences of music in early pedagogical situations. Notwithstanding these findings, the cultural conception of "talent" continues to consider it a quality that is inborn, bestowed upon the "gifted" by fate or genetics. If the years of effort are observed, they will be construed as evidence of this predetermined capacity, rather than as the source of acquired skill.[4]

Practical ramifications

The implications for choral leaders are far-reaching, both in the classroom and for those working with adults. The language we use with and about the singers in our care is not just descriptive, it is also productive. The labels we apply can give permission for a child to consider themselves as destined for success or cause them to consider themselves as categorically excluded from the ranks of the world's singers.[5]

Abandoning an outmoded pedagogical vocabulary is, on the face of it, a simple enough task. Other areas of the curriculum manage perfectly well without their equivalents of "non-singer" after all. This will not be enough, however, to counteract the exclusionary effects of the discourse of talent, given the extent to which it structures belief about musical activity in culture at large. If a school presents a habitus in which singing is kept separate from the rest of the curriculum, only led by music specialists, while other classroom teachers either opt out or are excluded from singing this will shape children's beliefs about musical capacity far more deeply than the specific vocabulary used in music sessions (Pascale, 2002).

England's "Sing Up" program presents an extensive case study in the attempt to avoid producing non-singers.[6] With the central ambition to give every child in primary school the opportunity to sing every day, it promoted singing as a learning activity across the curriculum, with two main strategies. The first was in providing training for generalist teachers so that they could feel confident using songs routinely in class, and the second was the development of a wide range of materials (songs, lesson plans, activity packs) designed specifically to link with subjects right across the country's national curriculum.

Impact studies assessing the effectiveness of the program (Welch, Himonides, Saunders, & Papageorgi, 2010; Saunders, Papageorgi, Himonides, Rinta, & Welch, 2011) found that the standard demographic categories for social science research (gender, race, class/prosperity, urban/rural locations) were relevant for the baseline assessments, but substantially less so when measuring development in singing skills as the program progressed. Rather, the primary differentiator for the success of the interventions was the extent to which schools' senior management teams supported the program. "In schools where singing was seen as important," Welch (2009) reported, "we tended to find more advanced singing development being evidenced" (p. 10). These findings are instructive in the way they demonstrate both how one's general habitus affects one's engagement with singing, and how the specific social world of the school can inflect this. To be effective, it needs to be valued as part of the school's wider culture, not fenced off into a music-specialist ghetto; however inspiring an individual teacher may be, their effectiveness is limited in isolation. These findings are also supported by Ashley (2011).

Leaders of adult choirs face the challenge of the legacy left by divisive practices of the past. It is possible to ignore the problem, as people who volunteer to join choirs are a self-selecting pool who already identify as "singers," but in an era of aging choirs and declining participation in community leisure (Putnam, 2000), the great untapped pool of self-identified "non-singers" is a much-needed resource for adult choirs.

In this context, it is worth observing the strategies of various choirs and choral organizations which have positioned themselves as more or less countercultural to what
they deem "traditional" choirs. I have written elsewhere, using analyses borrowed from
the sociology of new religious movements, about how the barbershop movement can
be characterized as a kind of musical "sect," counter-poised against the "church" of the
musical mainstream (Garnett, 2005). This comparison is also apt for other choral subcultures that share certain features in the way they go about recruiting those who self-
identify as unable to sing, and reclaiming them as musically active participants.

First, these "new choral movements" operate with a proselytizing zeal, offering
not just a musical experience but a promise of personal well-being. There is a heavy
focus on outreach, with the emphasis on choir as a means of individual transformation and interpersonal connection. The Natural Voice Practitioners Network website,
for example, states that, "Singing creates a sense of wellbeing, brings communities
together and gives us the opportunity to create sounds of power and beauty" (http://
www.naturalvoice.net/). Second, they promote a strongly egalitarian ethos, appealing
for anyone to join, regardless of previous experience, and actively removing barriers to entry. Hence, Rock Choir™ reassured potential members that, it "is for all ages
and all levels of experience. Even if you have not sung in public before you can do
it in Rock Choir as there is no audition and no requirement to read music" (http://
www.rockchoir.com/who-is-rock-choir-for.html/). Choice of repertoire is part of
this ethos, with a strong commitment to vernacular musics (particularly world music
and/or commercially popular music) as opposed to the posited elitism of "traditional"
(that is, classical) choral music.

There is also a more-or-less explicit critique of "traditional" choirs, placing their offer-
ings in direct contrast to those attributes of the mainstream deemed to be off-putting
to newcomers. New choral movements present themselves as friendly, accessible and
entertaining, implying—if not always directly articulating—that traditional choirs are
standoffish, elitist, and dull.[7] For example, All Sorts Choir from Scotland presents itself
as "an adult mixed-voice choir with a difference," whose "aim is to make choir music
exciting and fun. . . . [U]nlike the majority of traditional choirs we don't just stand up in
lines and sing" (https://projects.handsupfortrad.scot/scotlandsings/link-pages/allsorts-
performing-choir/).

Through such evangelistic tactics, these new choral movements position themselves
as "rescuing" adult non-singers from the damage inflicted on them in youth by a snooty
and uncaring classical tradition. Those church choirs and classical choral societies who
are struggling for members would no doubt find this characterization unfair; indeed,
from ethnographic research, I would observe that friendliness is almost invariably in
good supply across all choral genres. Moreover, the childhood experiences that produced the self-identity of "non-singer" were far more likely to have been associated with
classroom music such as folk songs or hymns than classical music per se. However, this
does illustrate how the ideological "lines of coherence" that delineate available identity
categories are established using culturally-available discourses. The prestige of Western
art music is conflated with the institutional authority of those who made the judgments

that excluded people from singing, while popular repertories are cast in the role of a musical Everyman, on the side of the underdog.

These recuperative strategies have been highly successful in recruiting to new choral movements those with a fear of singing. They are problematic, though, in the way they are predicated on increasing barriers between choral genres. At the same time they offer self-identified "non-singers" support to rediscover their voices, they risk discouraging their newly reclaimed singers from venturing further into the varied choral landscape, and thereby make recruitment harder for choirs associated with the classical tradition.

None of these tactics, however, are beyond the reach of a choir of any genre. It is worth recalling that the British choral society movement of the 19th century, whose descendants are now being cast as the out-of-touch establishment, itself shared many of the features of today's choral movements. In an era of great economic inequality it was one of the few social arenas that genuinely mixed social classes, and through the *sol-fa* methods developed by Glover and Curwen, made music literacy accessible on an unprecedented scale.[8] Mass participation established the canonical works of Bach and Handel as vernacular musics.[9]

The task for choirs wishing to attract adult novices is thus both practical and ideological. At a practical level, they need to provide the kind of vocal and musical training that their target cohort missed out on in youth once identified as "non-singers." This is not such an insuperable task as it may sound. As members of their culture, the recruits will have a well-developed competency in understanding music (Sloboda, 2005); what they will lack are habits and techniques that experienced choristers take for granted, and without which newcomers will find participation difficult and baffling—that is, there is a greater need for en explicit choral pedagogy to help newcomers overcome the practical barriers to entry than may be immediately obvious to those who have never doubted their capacity to sing.

The ideological task is to reappropriate the concept of choir as a socially accessible lifestyle sector. This includes, but goes beyond, the practical provision of training. It also involves, as the new choral movements have demonstrated, positioning choral participation as a transformative experience. Generating choral participants from adult "non-singers" is not merely a matter of remedying a skill deficit, it is a matter of redeeming emotional damage sustained in childhood. As such, it will be useful to examine in greater detail the way choral practice draws on ideological discourses from wider culture in constructing and maintaining its identity categories.

MUSICAL IDENTITIES, SOCIAL IDENTITIES

While choral singing as a lifestyle sector is largely separate from everyday life as a social world and sphere of activity, the meanings it creates and maintains are constructed within wider cultural discourses. The musical and extramusical dimensions of identity interpenetrate, each domain being understood to an extent in terms of the other. Choral singing's compulsory and forbidden forms of vocal behavior are routinely articulated in terms of wider cultural categories such as accent or genre. At the same time, the characteristic musical behaviors of the different parts in a choral texture are extrapolated out to subsume the entire personhood of the singers on that part, forming tradition-specific stereotypes.

The choral practitioner needs an awareness of these processes because the specific forms of alienation reported by those who drop out of choir, or who feel put off from joining in the first place, are often experienced in terms of a failure of identification: the feeling that "it's not for people like me."[10] Such remarks may frustrate choral leaders who wish to foster an inclusionary ethos in their ensembles, but their own successful inculcation into a choral culture may often obscure their perception of the implicit cultural hierarchies intuited by those who perceive themselves as "outsiders."

Accent, genre, and cultural hierarchies

The voice is a primary means by which people construct both a sense of self and a range of social and musical allegiances. The connection between voice and self is such that the word indicates not just vocal sound, but a person's unique contribution to culture: the "voice" of the poet, the novelist, the composer.[11] At the same time, we learn to use our voices within the culturally-constructed collections of practices understood as identity markers: class, educational background, and regionality are all inscribed upon and inferred from our voices.

When people join a choir, the first thing they are asked to do is change how they use their voices. The preferred norms of vowel shape and placement in choral singing vary according to nationality and genre, but are invariably configured to privilege accents that enjoy greater cultural esteem. Writers on choral practice routinely warn against pronunciation "problems" (Kaplan, 1985, p. 55),[12] and the avoidance of "colloquial" and "regional" accents (Hylton, 1995, p. 21). Singers who use such word sounds are seen as either willfully deviant from the normative, with their accents described as "mannerisms" (Garretson, 1974, p. 56) or "peculiarities" (Coward, 1914, p. 86), or simply not trying hard enough, with their "slovenly" and "lip-lazy" habits (Garretson, 1974, p. 56). Choral methods require singers from backgrounds other than middle-class middle England or middle America to erase the audible traces of their social origins in order to align themselves with a universalized choral identity, and do so in terms which range from the casually dismissive to the deeply judgmental.

As well as seeking to modify these social or demographic identity markers, choral pedagogies also come into conflict with people's existing forms of musical identification, whether these are formally taught or informally learned. Many writers consider the styles of voice production associated with popular musics not simply as different traditions, but as faults that need to be corrected when singers partake in what Neuen (2002) referred to as "legitimate" choral singing (p. 45). Knight (2000), for instance, mandates that "pop-orientated singers wishing to join choirs and operatic societies must be expected to show goodwill towards the unfamiliar style. They are entitled to be greeted with reciprocal goodwill as individuals, but musically they must change, not seek acceptance as they are" (p. 6).

Discourses such as those of accent and genre allow hierarchies in wider culture to act as obstacles to access to choral music for those who already lack cultural capital. Choral leaders need to find ways to "check their privilege" and consciously counter rather than inadvertently reinforce the exclusionary power of these discourses.

To do this by trying to be "purely" musical in approach, by trying to strip off cultural meanings in an attempt to avoid evoking these extramusical associations, rarely works. Theoretical or technical language is after all itself a marker of cultural prestige. Avoiding wider discourses also impoverishes the experience, since musical understanding relies on clusters of connotations that bring richness and depth to the experience (Green, 1988; Garnett, 1998). Without contextual and associative reference singers find it harder to connect emotionally and imaginatively with the music they sing.[13] Moreover, people still bring their cultural competence to bear on their perception of an ensemble's activities. In a workplace choir I observed, for example, it was not the predominantly classical repertoire that produced anxieties about social and musical identities, but exercises designed to work on vowel placement and a legato vocal line, which elicited the question: "Do we have to sound posh?"

A more productive strategy is to reframe hierarchical exclusionary practices as informed decisions about style: to treat language, genre and accent as axes of exploration rather than rigidly located boundaries of the acceptable.[14] To relativize the concept of "correct" is to exploit choral music's status as a lifestyle sector—a distinct world with its particular modes of being—while recognizing that individuals will routinely move through a variety of such social environments, adapting to the norms and expressive registers of each as they go. It is possible to teach people appropriate vocal techniques for a particular repertory or performance tradition without implying (or indeed stating) that the way they use their voices in other social and musical contexts is wrong. Flexibility of style, and therefore also of technical control, becomes an act of informed empathy, performers aligning themselves with each other and with the music's identity commitments to create a convincing imaginative world.

Voice-type and personality

Voice classification is a central part of most choral pedagogies. This is often presented as a quasi-scientific process, but in fact the only aspects of voice which are genetically determined are the thickness of the vocal folds (and therefore weight of the voice) and the outer limits of range (Wright, 2014). Choral traditions take these basic physiological elements and build upon them a complex set of beliefs about the character and behaviors expected from the owners of voices in each particular range. These expectations are derived in part from the role of that voice in the musical texture ("supportive altos", for instance), but are generalized out to apply to people's overall character. The process of classification may be systematic in its methods, but it is as much a dialogue between the individual's experience and habitus to date and the vocal and emotional behaviors encoded within a particular choral tradition as it is an act of objective assessment.[15]

Probably the most developed example of this is the Fach system used in German opera houses. This uses a detailed taxonomy of voice types to classify both roles and singers as a practical tool to build repertory companies.[16] Each voice category is defined by range and timbre, by the character types of the roles it applies to, and the physical appearance of the singers needed for those roles. It thus offers both an in-depth analysis of the musical constructions of identity in that particular tradition, and an ongoing demonstration—in its use in the preparation of young singers for the profession—of how an ostensibly "natural" attribute like the voice is formed within the cultural expectations of specific traditions.

Choral genres generally use categories that are less narrowly defined than the Fach system, but their expectations of those who fall into the categories are no less absolute. Indeed, they are arguably more controlling, since they lack the Fach system's pragmatic artificiality. Opera producers know that few voices fit the categories exactly, but still value the system as a tried-and-tested method for managing a busy schedule; choral practitioners typically treat their typologies as natural and essential attributes of those they apply them to.

The arbitrary nature of these stereotypes becomes apparent when one moves between different choral genres. Voices of broadly the same pitch range play rather different musical roles in the textures of different choral traditions, and consequently encounter quite different expectations of their associated personalities. Even the ostensibly natural element of range shows significant variation in definition: what is unusually high for a female barbershop tenor is perfectly normal for a classical soprano, and what is low for a classical alto is routine for a female barbershop bass.

These belief systems are thus, like the ideology of talent, productive rather than merely descriptive. They can also be useful. Voice-part stereotypes provide holistic structures of understanding through which individuals can develop a relationship with their voice and their expressive behaviors that makes sense in the context of a particular genre. They are part of the cultural infrastructure that allows us to make sense of music and of ourselves as musicians.

They also have dangers, however. Stereotypes can make the experience of a voice that changes over time harder to manage.[17] They can act as obstacles to participation if the characteristics ascribed to a singer's range conflicts with the self-identity they maintain in their overall internal life-narrative. They can interfere with choral blend if the sections are overly identified with their voice-part at the expense of the choir as a whole.

Again, supporting flexibility is a good way to deal with these risks. Encouraging singers periodically to sing a different part from usual gives them a chance to explore different parts of their voices and different expressive modes as well as facilitating a broader musicianship.[18] Developing an awareness of historical perspective is also valuable. While the same part labels may be used in repertories written 200 years apart, the vocal and expressive ways of using the self they encode can be quite different: being a soprano in Bruckner is a significantly different experience from being a soprano in Monteverdi. The "self" who sings is in part brought into being by the repertories sung.[19] This dialogic relationship between performer and musical content is also relevant to constituting a choir as an ensemble with its own, suprapersonal, identity.

CORPORATE IDENTITY AND THE LOSS OF SELF

A central challenge in forming a choir is how to coordinate a diverse assortment of people to operate as a coherent ensemble. Many of choral pedagogy's standard methods are designed specifically to induce uniform patterns of vocal and musical behavior among disparate individuals. Indeed, the literature reserves some of its most censorious comments for those who insist on singing with those traits which in a solo context act as markers of individual expressiveness: vibrato, portamenti, rhythmic flexibility or a prominent singer's formant. This tension between the need for soloists to develop a distinctive performing identity and the choral requirement for blend underlies the conflicts between voice teachers and choral directors documented by Ekholm (2000): each appears to be waging a campaign to deliberately undo central elements of the other's specialism.[20]

Approaching the challenge in such an adversarial mode, however, makes the task harder than it needs to be. To attempt ensemble cohesion through the suppression of "disagreeable excesses of individuality" (Coward, 1914, p. 25) risks entrenching positions, inviting singers to incorporate this conflict of musical imperatives into their personal identity narrative. More effective is to find ways to encourage people to identify with the group, to adopt it as an identity category with which they align themselves and thus diminish conflict between self-as-individual and group needs (Brewer & Garnett, 2012). This in turn creates an environment in which the director can manage their singers' attention such that their individual internal narratives shift from a central, actively maintained focus to the periphery of their awareness.

Identity narrative and choir mythologies

Just as individuals' self-identities are maintained reflexively through an internal autobiography, groups develop and maintain a continuity of experience through shared narratives. Long-standing members reminisce to newcomers; landmark anniversaries are celebrated; in-jokes are repeated. The narratives are rehearsed through formal or semiformal channels (officers' reports at the AGM, choir newsletters, notices and announcements) and through the informal exchanges of social interactions. This process will happen whether or not the director participates actively in it, but not to participate is to relinquish a significant form of influence on the choir's artistic and ethical agendas.

The iterative patterns of a choir's activities also bind the group together in shared experience, both musical and extramusical. Some forms of behavior are explicitly invested with meanings to articulate group identity, such as wearing visible tokens of belonging or the marking of occasions with particular pieces of music. But the simple routines of regular rehearsal form the experiential substrate of what it is to be part of that choir. There are thus opportunities for the director to consciously deploy standard pedagogical methods in service of the ensemble's identity by framing their use in terms of the choir's shared narratives and values. Any repeated activity can accrue the resonance of ritual if invested with choir-specific meanings.[21]

Rehearsal strategies that give singers the opportunity to listen are particularly valuable as rituals around which to build the choir's sense of corporate self, for several reasons. Purposeful listening supports the development of musicianship by giving singers insight into the wider musical texture beyond their own part. This awareness in turn builds a sense of the music itself as a distinct identity with whom the performers need to empathize for the performance to work. And listening activates the mirror neurons, the unconscious mechanism that underlies both skill acquisition and the "chameleon effect" by which people become more alike in social interactions.[22]

Flow and flux

A flow state is one in which the subject is completely immersed in an activity, losing all self-consciousness, with action and awareness completely merged (Czikszentmihalyi, 1990; De Manzano, Harmat, Theonell, & Ullén, 2010). This concept is important for educators because it relates both to the development of complex, high-level skills and to high levels of personal satisfaction.

There are several conditions required to induce a flow state, all of which are available to musicians, and all of which can be facilitated or hindered by the choral practitioner through their choice of rehearsal tactics. The activity needs to be intrinsically rewarding; it needs to be clearly defined, such that participants know whether they have achieved it or not; related to this, there needs to be direct and immediate feedback, so that participants can adjust what they do in real time; and participants need to have a sense of personal control over what they are doing. Most importantly, there needs to be a balance between the activity's challenge and its achievability: if it is too far beyond the skills of the participants, they will become anxious, but if it is too easy they will become bored.

Difficulty level is clearly central to decisions that directors make in both long-term planning and moment-to-moment rehearsal management. Apt choice of repertoire to stretch but not overwhelm a choir largely determines success over a season, while the capacity to anticipate and respond to the choir's needs in real time makes the difference between the singers feeling secure or frustrated.

Feedback is also important: the rehearsal process is essentially one of iterative feedback on a choir's successive attempts at vocal and musical tasks. There are different forms of feedback, however, and some are more useful than others in fulfilling the other criteria to create a flow state. Stopping the choir to give spoken instruction will always be a part of the conductor's toolkit, but it does not give the same immediate and ongoing response as real-time interactions with the singers while managing and molding the music as it unfolds. Singers also receive aural and kinaesthetic feedback from their immersion in the sound, and gain both more intrinsic satisfaction and more personal control over what they do when given the opportunity to respond to it. Almost every conducting manual warns the director against talking too much in rehearsal; the psychology of flow gives another good reason to follow this advice.

Flow is a state experienced by individuals. It can optimize both the learning process and the personal satisfaction experienced by singers, but it does not by itself guarantee interconnection within the ensemble. A singer in a flow state will feel at one with the music, but whether this loss of self-consciousness connects them to the whole choir will depend on how much their internal representation of the music embraces the full texture. This is in part a matter of musicianship, but it is also a function of the interpersonal relationships within the choir.

Flux is a state experienced by a group. Like flow, it involves a sense of losing the self, but rather than being lost in an activity, the individual becomes merged into the collective (Bradley, 1987; Bradley & Pibram, 1998). It is a highly-charged state emotionally, associated with feelings of euphoria and overwhelming love; for this reason it is also sometimes referred to as "communion."[23] The key dynamic in creating a flux state is the combination of specific relationship and power structures within the group. The relationship structure is characterized by all members of the group having access to, and affective bonds with, all other members. The presence of cliques, or allegiances that create "us versus them" relationships within the group, will mitigate against the experience of communion. The power structure is characterized by a strong top-down hierarchy through which the leader exerts control over all members. Both elements are needed to create flux: the relationship structure generates the emotional energy that is experienced as euphoria, while the power structure maintains the coherence of the group. The two dimensions work in tandem. Emotional energy without control creates chaos; top-down discipline without internal affective bonds produces tyranny.

These structures can be observed in standard choral practice. Consider, for example, the use of space in a rehearsal room. There are many different ways to organize choral seating/stacking, but all the standard models ensure that every singer shares communicative space with the conductor, while preventing sub-groups of singers from setting up shared communicative spaces that exclude others. They thus set up both the interactional structure to generate flux and the top-down power-structure to contain it. [24]

The flux/control matrix allows choral practitioners to analyze and adjust their rehearsal strategies in each of its two dimensions. Rehearsal tactics that require singers to connect with different members of the ensemble build social attachments as well as increased aural acuity; it is neither possible nor desirable to prevent friendship groups evolving within a choir, but it is important for the musical bonds to transcend social preferences. At the same time, the level of rigor in choral discipline needs adjusting proportionately to the emotional tone of the room. Excitement needs to be channeled if it is to produce music rather than mere hubbub, while applying an authoritarian approach to a subdued ensemble will simply make them retreat further.

CONCLUSION

Choral pedagogy can be seen as a "technology of the self"—that is, a set of methods by which people make changes to their external and internal states in order to transform themselves into a desired state (Foucault, 1988). Choral leaders manage and guide the processes by which individuals are constituted as singers and by which groups of singers are constituted into ensembles, but the methods are only effective through the active complicity of those individuals. To become a choral singer involves not only physical participation in technical and musical tasks, but emotional and imaginative participation in the flow of the musical content and in the life of the ensemble. Rehearsals teach not only the skills required to take part, but also the discourses that allow individuals to integrate the identity of singer into their personal narrative projects of the self and that allow the group to collaborate in the project of the choir's corporate identity.

Much of what choral leaders need to achieve in order to produce convincing musical performances from capable ensembles are already built into the habits, practices, and discourses of the traditions in which they operate. In that sense, this chapter's analyses could be seen as simply illustrating theories of identity developed in other realms of experience with examples from choral cultures. Theory says identity is constructed through discursively-bundled packages of behavior patterns; choral pedagogy has a standardized repertory of methods for creating uniform vocal production. Theory says that flux's euphoric merging of egos is potentiated by a comprehensive network of bonds within a group; choral pedagogy teaches blend. The aim of the chapter, after all, has not been to extend established practice, but to deepen insight into it.

This is not to say, however, that choral practitioners should take this analysis as an invitation to simply continue with business as usual. The lines of coherence as currently drawn carry considerable risks, both for individuals and consequently also for the ensembles that rely on the successful co-option of new members for their continued existence. The literature and habitus of western choral culture are infused with exclusionary discourses that conflate social and genre identity markers with moral inadequacy; it is not surprising therefore to see the alienation evinced by those choirs and choral movements that position themselves in opposition to the "traditional." The mythology of talent has an even higher casualty rate in its systematic production of self-identified "non-singers."

These are problems that cannot be solved solely from within the choral rehearsal. People bring their belief structures and expectations from their wider habitus to choir; people who are already alienated from singing and/or choral music are necessarily even harder to reach. But they are problems that need to be addressed in the rehearsal room if choral pedagogy is to minimize the hazards potential singers have to negotiate in learning to identify with a choir. For, whilst all choral traditions are framed by the wider cultural contexts from which they draw their members, their status as distinct lifestyle sectors does give choral leaders space within which to make strategic decisions about how best to use the methods and discourses available to them.

This chapter has discussed the "project of the choral self" in terms both of the individual who becomes a choral singer and the corporate identity of the choir that emerges from the collaboration of many such selves. The discipline of choral pedagogy is likewise maintained through both praxis and the reflexive narratives represented by volumes such as this one. This chapter contributes to our shared disciplinary identity by facilitating the ongoing discursive project to position choral singing as an inclusionary and accessible artform.

NOTES

1. By "western choral traditions" I refer to the collection of culturally dominant practices based in churches, schools, and concert halls in the first world. They maintain their cultural dominance through a combination of a partly professionalized leadership; institutional support (from churches, schools, universities, etc.); the wider prestige associated with the classical canon; and the propagation of their values through published literature. I am referring to them in the plural, however, as despite the continuity of practice implied by these common factors, there is still a variety of distinct strands of practice, such that a singer with experience in one may need to make significant adjustments to both musical and nonmusical habits to fit into another.

2. There is a well-developed literature going back to the early years of the 20th century on the practical methods for training choirs, which reflects the depth and nuance of western choral traditions. There is also a more recent, more explicitly scholarly literature in choral pedagogy, which, while equally practical in intent, aims to substantiate the common knowledge of the discipline that the practitioner literature presents in largely anecdotal forms with more systematic study. For a more detailed overview of these bodies of knowledge, and a discussion of the relationship between the two, see Garnett (2009).

3. Welch (2009) asserts that the "ascribed musical identity as a 'non-singer,' 'tone-deaf,' or 'tone-dumb'" is "found in virtually all cultures." Ethnomusicological studies, however, show that in many cultures active musical participation is the norm (Turino, 2008; Hill, 2012). The concept of congenital musical incapacity may exist in all cultures, but the level of its prevalence in the West is unusual.

4. Kingsbury's (1988) ethnographical study of a specialist music college gives a detailed analysis of how "talent" is a socially negotiated quality, the label bestowed upon learners by experts as a recognition of achievements to date. The young musician needs the approval of those whose authority they respect to consider themselves "talented," and the ascription provides both the motivation and the obligation to put in the hard work required to realize the potential.

5. Peterson (2002) found increased motivation and persistence in school choirs where success was attributed to effort rather than innate ability.

6. The National Singing Programme "Sing Up" was launched by the Department for Education in 2007, and ran with direct state funding until 2011. Since then, it has been run

as a not-for-profit organization, with support from the DfE, but funded largely by membership subscriptions from participating schools. At the time of writing (2014), the only research into the program's impact dealt with the initial phase; it is too soon at any rate to assess its longer-term impact.

7. See also the tensions between show choirs and "traditional" choirs reported in by Russell (2006).

8. Russell (1987) gives a detailed analysis of the social composition of choral societies in Victorian and Edwardian England. While social hierarchies from wider society were still clearly in evidence (along both class and gender lines), this was nonetheless a far more socially mixed milieu than most of that era. Both the egalitarian impulse and the underlying cultural politics shine through the writing of Coward (1914)—a text which bears study not just as a historical document of a particular era, but as a repository of practical advice from a distinguished and insightful choral conductor.

9. Notwithstanding the inappropriateness of such forces in the eyes of today's specialists in historically-informed performance.

10. See, for example, Maxted (2014).

11. Barthes (1977) theorizes the intersection between individuality and cultural meanings in vocal timbre; see also Dunn and Jones (1996).

12. See also Darrow (1975), pp. 150–151, which gives a summary of pronunciation "errors," many of which are related to variations in accent.

13. Carter (2005) promotes the use of methods derived from drama as a means actively to foster this kind of emotional connection.

14. This approach uses the "inner game" principle of Will; see Green & Gallway (1986).

15. See Garnett (2005), Chapter 8 for a detailed discussion of this process.

16. Cotton (2007) gives a useful critical overview of this system and its impact on the development of young opera singers.

17. The voice changes at puberty and their impact on self-identity has received a considerable amount of scholarly attention (for example, Ashley, 2009; Welch & Howard, 2002). There is a smaller body of work on the effects of aging on the voice, and this mostly concerns physiological changes and how to manage them rather than questions of musical identity (see Butler, Lind and Van Weelden, 2001).

18. Not all repertoire allows for this, of course, but there are more opportunities than is often supposed.

19. See Cone (1974) and Pabich (2012) for, respectively, work-based and listener-based discussions of this idea.

20. See also Ford (2003).

21. A striking example of this process is Seth's (1999) fictional account of a string quartet's practice of playing a slow, unison scale at the start of rehearsals: a basic technique for building the ensemble's sound becomes a meditative practice that lets the distractions of the outside world fall away and both the symbol and vehicle for a sense of ensemble "unity" that goes beyond technical coordination to imaginative and emotional connection.

22. See Iacoboni (2009) for an overview of mirror neuron research and its implications for both socialization and learning. The term "chameleon effect" was coined by Chartrand and Bargh (1999).

23. There are echoes here of the new choral movements discussed earlier. The evangelistic testimonies of those recruiting to choirs are often couched in the terms of a flux experience: "It energises me, it connects me. I love the power" (Maxted, 2014).

24. The creation of shared communicative spaces through physical positioning is discussed by Kendon (1990); see Garnett (2009), pp. 160–162 for a discussion of how they emerge in different choral layouts.

References

Ashley, M. (2009). *How high should boys sing? Gender, authenticity and credibility in the young male voice*. Farnham, UK: Ashgate.

Ashley, M. (2011). The canaries in the cage: Lessons in the role of leadership and pedagogy in conducting from the widening young male participation in chorus project. In U. Geiser & K. Johansson (Eds.), *Choir in focus 2011* (pp. 89–103). Göteborg, Sweden: Bo Ejeby.

Barthes, R. (1977). The grain of the voice. (S. Heath, Trans.) In S. Heath (Ed.), *Image music text*. London: Fontana.

Bourdieu, P. (1984). *Distinction: A social critique of the judgement of taste*. London: Routledge.

Bradley, R. T. (1987). *Charisma and social structure: A study of love and power, wholeness and transformation*. New York: Paragon.

Bradley, R. T., & Pibram, K. H. (1998). Communication and stability in social collectives. *Journal of Social and Evolutionary Systems, 21*(2), 29–81.

Brewer, M., & Garnett, L. (2012). The making of a choir: Individuality and consensus in choral singing. In A. de Quadros (Ed.), *The Cambridge companion to choral music* (pp. 256–271). Cambridge, UK: Cambridge University Press.

Butler, A., Lind, V. R., & Van Weelden, K. (2001). Research on the aging voice: Strategies and techniques for healthy choral singing. *The Phenomenon of Singing, 3*, 42–50.

Butler, J. (1990). *Gender trouble: Feminism and the subversion of identity*. New York: Routledge.

Carter, T. (2005). *Choral charisma: Singing with expression*. Santa Barbara: Santa Barbara Music Publishing.

Chartrand, T. L., & Bargh, J. A. (1999). The chameleon effect: The perception-behaviour link and social interaction. *Journal of Personality and Social Psychology, 76*(6), 893–910.

Cone, E. T. (1974). *The composer's voice*. Berkeley: University of California Press.

Cotton, S. (2007). *Voice classification and Fach: Recent, historical and conflicting systems of voice categorization* (Doctoral dissertation). University of North Carolina, Greensboro.

Coward, H. (1914). *Choral technique and interpretation*. London: Novello.

Csikszentmihalyi, M. (1990). *Flow: The psychology of optimal experience*. New York: Harper & Row.

Darrow, G. F. (1975). *Four decades of choral training*. Metuchen, NJ: Scarecrow.

De Beauvoir, S. (1949). *The second sex* (C. Borde & S. Malovany-Chevallier, Trans.). Paris: Gallimard.

De Manzano, Ö., Harmat, L., Theonell, T., & Ullén, F. (2010). The psychophysiology of flow during piano playing. *Emotion, 10*(3), 301–311.

Dunn, L. C., & Jones, N. A. (1996). *Embodied voices: Representing female vocality in Western culture*. Cambridge, UK: Cambridge University Press.

Ekholm, E. (2000). The effect of singing mode and seating arrangement on choral blend and overall choral sound. *Journal of Research in Music Education, 48*(2), 123–135.

Elkington, S., & Stebbins, R. (2014). *The serious leisure perspective: An introduction*. New York: Routledge.

Ericsson, K. A., & Charness, N. (1994). Expert performance: Its structure and acquisition. *American Psychologist, 49*(8), 725–747.

Ford, K. (2003). The preference for strong or weak singer's formant resonance in choral tone quality. *International Journal for Research in Choral Singing, 1*(1), 29–47.

Foucault, M. (1988). Technologies of the self. In L. H. Martin, H. Gutman, & P. H. Hutton (Eds.), *Technologies of the self: A seminar with Michael Foucault* (pp. 16–49). Amherst: University of Massachusetts Press.

Garnett, L. (1998). Musical meaning revisited: Thoughts on an "epic" critical musicology. *Critical Musicology Journal.* Retrieved from http://www.leeds.ac.uk/music/Info/critmus/articles/1998/01/01.html

Garnett, L. (2005). *The British barbershopper: A study in socio-musical values.* Aldershot, UK: Ashgate.

Garnett, L. (2009). *Choral conducting and the construction of meaning: Gesture, voice, identity.* Aldershot, UK: Ashgate.

Garretson, R. L. (1974) *Conducting choral music* (3rd ed.). Boston, MA: Allyn & Bacon.

Giddens, A. (1991). *Modernity and self-identity: Self and society in the late modern age.* Cambridge: Polity.

Green, L. (1988). *Music on deaf ears: Musical meaning, ideology, education.* Manchester, UK: Manchester University Press.

Green, B., & Gallwey, W. T. (1986). *The inner game of music.* New York: Anchor Press/Doubleday.

Hill, J. (2012). Imagining creativity: An ethnomusicological perspective on how belief systems encourage or inhibit creative activities in music. In D. J. Hargreaves, D. Miell, & R. MacDonald (Eds.), *Musical imaginations: Multidisciplinary perspectives one creativity, performance, and perception* (pp. 87–106). Oxford: Oxford University Press.

Hylton, J. (1995). *Comprehensive choral music education.* Englewood Cliffs, NJ: Prentice Hall.

Kaplan, A. (1985). *Choral conducting.* New York: Norton.

Kendon, A. (1990). *Conducting interaction: Patterns of behaviour in focused encounters.* Cambridge: Cambridge University Press.

Kingsbury, H. (1988). *Music, talent, and performance: A conservatory cultural system.* Philadelphia: Temple University Press.

Knight, V. (2000). *Directing amateur singers.* West Kirby: Jubal Music Publications.

Maxted, A. (2014, January 11). Join a choir. *The Guardian.* Retrieved from http://www.theguardian.com/lifeandstyle/2014/jan/11/join-a-choir-do-something

Neuen, D. (2002). *Choral concepts: A text for conductors.* Belmont, CA: Schirmer/Thomson Learning.

Pabich, R. (2012). Learning to live music: Musical education as the cultivation of a relationship between self and sound. In W. Bowman & A. L. Frega (Eds.), *The Oxford handbook of philosophy in music education* (pp. 131–146). Oxford: Oxford University Press.

Pascale, L. (2002). *Dispelling the myth of the non-singer: Changing the ways singing is perceived, implemented and nurtured in the classroom* (Doctoral dissertation). Cambridge, MA: Lesley University.

Peterson, C. (2002). Recruiting for choral ensemble by emphasizing skill and effort. *Music Educators Journal, 89*(2), 32–35.

Putnam, R. D. (2000). *Bowling alone: The collapse and revival of American community.* New York: Simon & Schuster.

Russell, D. (1987). *Popular music in England, 1840–1914: A social history.* Kingston: McGill-Queen's University Press.

Russell, M. (2006). "Putting Decatur on the map": Choral music and community in an Illinois city. In K. Ahlquist (Ed.), *Chorus and community* (pp. 45–69). Urbana: University of Illinois Press.

Rutkowski, J. (1990, Spring). The measurement and evaluation of children's singing voice development. *The Quarterly*, *1*(1–2), pp. 81–95. (Reprinted with permission in *Visions of Research in Music Education*, *16*(1), Summer, 2010). Retrieved from http://www-usr.rider.edu/~vrme/v16n1/visions/spring10

Saunders, J., Papageorgi, I., Himonides, E., Rinta, T., & Welch, G. (2011). Researching the impact of the National Singing Programme "Sing Up" in England. Choir Schools' Association (CSA). Retrieved from http://www.singup.org/fileadmin/singupfiles/previous_uploads/IoE_Diverse_approaches_to_successful_singing__COP_.pdf

Seth, V. (1999). *An equal music*. New York: Broadway.

Sloboda, J. (2005). *Exploring the musical mind: Cognition, emotion, ability, function.* Oxford: Oxford University Press.

Sloboda, J., & Davidson, J. (1996). The young performing musician. In I. Deliège & J. A. Sloboda (Eds.), *Musical beginnings: Origins and development of musical competence* (pp. 171–190). Oxford: Oxford University Press.

Stebbins, R. (1996). *The barbershop singer: Inside the social world of a musical hobby.* Toronto: University of Toronto Press.

Turino, T. (2008). *Music as social life: The politics of participation.* Chicago: University of Chicago Press.

Welch, G. F. (2009). Evidence of the development of vocal pitch matching ability in children. *Japanese Journal of Music Education Research*, *39*(1), 38–47.

Welch, G. F., & Howard, D. M. (2002). Gendered voice in the cathedral choir. *Psychology of Music*, *30*(1), 102–120.

Welch, G. F., Himonides, E., Saunders, J., & Papageorgi, I. (2010). Researching the impact of the National Singing Programme "Sing Up" in England: Main findings from the first three years. Children's singing development, self-concept, and sense of social inclusion. Retrieved from http://www.singup.org/fileadmin/singupfiles/previous_uploads/IoE_Sing_Up_Phase_4_Evaluation_.pdf

Whidden, C. (2008, Spring). The injustice of singer/non-singer labels by music educators. *GEMS – Gender, Education, Music & Society*, *5*.

Wright, A. (2014, April). *Vocal technique for conductors.* Presented at the meeting of the British Kodály Academy Spring Course, Derbyshire.

CHAPTER 8

CHORAL PEDAGOGY AND THE CONSTRUCTION OF IDENTITY

Boys

SCOTT HARRISON AND ANTHONY YOUNG

CONDUCTORS have complained of "missing males" for over a century (Richards, 1922; Harrison, 2006, Harrison et al., 2012; Swanson, 1960; Freer, 2007; Ashley, 2009). Early texts lamented boys leaving choirs to work in factories or mines to support their families, while more recent research documents the physiological and sociological challenges facing the adolescent male singer (Collins, 2012). In current times the importance of information technology cannot be underestimated: while it provides instant access to an impressive array of approaches, methods, and models of male singing, it also provides instant access to innumerable activities which might, in the current context, be more attractive than singing. Clearly, for a long time in our culture, there have been plenty of reasons for men not to sing.

SOME PRELIMINARY THOUGHTS

Accordingly, the first question the choral pedagogue should ask is "why sing?" If, as the data indicate, students are abandoning singing during adolescence, is this simply a natural concomitant of time and place? Further, is the teaching of adolescents to sing in group settings worth the effort of working against what appear to be Western cultural norms? Given the ease with which pedagogues and students could be culturally complicit in the decay of group singing, choral directors must be certain of its value if they are to successfully resist the dominant discourse of silenced singers. This chapter seeks to encourage choral directors to interrogate and clarify their reasons for running a male chorus.

One of the most important reasons for running an adolescent male chorus is to create a supportive peer group, or a safe village for the singers (Collins, 2009). Adolescents tend to form subcultures in their schools and in society. Music students form subcultures of their own and these subcultures prove to be important vehicles for support and growth (Adderley, Kennedy, & Berz, 2003, p. 191). Accordingly, choral directors should nurture male singing groups so as to provide a safe place where adolescents can belong.

Choral communities like adolescent male choruses make it possible for individuals to develop and broaden their conceptions of male identity in the presence of supportive peers. During adolescence, boys can become reluctant to do anything different from their peers. If their peers don't do much, they can end up with narrow unhealthy self-concepts. As Swain (2003) suggests, "It is the peer group, rather than individual boys, that is the bearer of gender definitions"—boys need to gain power and status through "intense maneuvering and negotiation" and this power is sustained through performance (p. 302). Swain also suggests that ". . . there were serious risks involved for anyone not conforming to the group norms" and there was a need to conform "in order to be safe" and to avoid rejection and/or peer-group ostracism (p 308). The chorus has a role to play in reinforcing healthy concepts of male identity and should broaden these concepts for those within the group and those exposed who interact with it.

By way of example, Miller (2008) recalled that his (female) high school choral conductor would identify athletes who had high social capital, and would subsequently convince these students that being a member of the choral group was as prestigious as being on an athletic team. Her logic was that well-developed bodies would produce relatively mature voices and would give kudos to the group. As a result, as Miller contends, ". . . as an unathletic fourteen-year-old my location in the concert choir was between the co-captain of the football team and a leading basketball player" (p. 18). Miller's conductor seemed to be recruiting influential sporting peers, partly so that the choral program would be seen as a safe activity rather than one which would lead to ostracism. As well, she seemed to be making the singers more athletic, the athletes more musical, and the whole ensemble more broad-minded. This approach finds support in the work of Harrison (2004, 2012). Surely, the creating of broad, healthy conceptions of male identity is a laudable reason for men to sing.

While Miller's choral director may have assisted in broadening the concept of masculinity in the school, unreflective application of these sorts of approaches can narrow concepts of masculinity by perpetuating outdated and misogynist approaches to gender identification and singing. For the last two centuries, some research has dealt with the problem of "missing boys" by trying to make chorus less "feminine" and more "masculine" and this has led to some blunt approaches with limited progress as a consequence (Koza, 2010, p. 61). A young men's chorus should be an opportunity to form reliable, committed, supportive, cooperative young adults who are comfortable with their identity free of the gendered confines attributed to singing.

The development of identity among choristers is strongly connected with the meaning of the text in the repertoire being sung. Making meaning with music is another powerful reason for running an adolescent male chorus. Recent research has no doubt moved the debate beyond Roe's recommendation that the music "thrill the red-blooded [*sic*] male" and his admonition to avoid singing about "birds daisies and butterflies" (Koza, 2010, p. 55). Furthermore, the choice of music should speak to matters that are important and educational in the social and cultural worlds of the singers. Works that express outdated positions or concepts can be problematized as opportunities for learning. Similarly, a vacuous song can be recognized as such.

Choral directors should aim for singers to develop a love of music and singing: repertoire planning should contain carefully planned physical and musical challenges that students can enjoy meeting. Programming music that boys cannot convincingly perform is a sure way to disappoint all concerned, and careful repertoire choice is essential as a result. Music should be chosen with a full knowledge of the physiological development of the singers so that they can perform with competence, confidence, and joy. Apart from obvious considerations such as range, styles requiring a highly specialized vocal aesthetic might be unachievable. For example male opera choruses, which require very mature vocal timbres, are unlikely to be rewarding for adolescent singers—they will be physiologically incapable of sounding like "the real thing." Similarly, some styles of popular music may put unachievable expectations on young voices. There are few experiences more embarrassing for an adolescent singer than performing current popular music unconvincingly, especially to peers. There are implications here for choral directors in careful choice of performance opportunities. It is important, especially at the outset to carefully choose supportive audiences and to remember that the rehearsal, the community singing, is a reward in itself. Programs run solely to prepare for performances can collapse after a bad performing experience. It is much more sustainable to think of the rehearsal as a destination in itself, and the performance as "the icing on the cake." Joyful successful music making must be a core aim of the successful director of young men's singing groups.

So far, this chapter has advocated that a successful director of adolescent male choirs will have clear sociological goals, will be orientated towards an inclusive choral identity, and will aim to sing meaningful achievable repertoire with confidence and joy. Achieving these goals necessitates considerations of pedagogy with an emphasis on social capital, rehearsal strategies, physiology, kinesthetic learning, role models, repertoire, and musicianship.

PEDAGOGICAL APPROACHES

Once the choral director has a clear purpose in mind for the ensemble, the next key requirement is the management of successful rehearsals. The test of the success of any rehearsal is whether the people present want to attend the next one, and, build membership through encouraging peers to attend. This section of the chapter aims to propose practical pedagogical applications of the research that have been suggested to promote rehearsal success.

Adolescent singers initially need to trust that the conductor knows and understands what is happening to them. Often the choral conductor is the only source of personalized knowledge of voices and singing. The choral conductor who shares this knowledge with the singers will empower them to sing with freedom and confidence. The admonition that males should not sing during voice change remains a prevalent narrative (Friar, 1999). Research—and practical application—in the United States have established that it is not only safe to sing throughout the voice change, but beneficial (Friar, 1999; Cooksey, 2000b) and it is the duty of choral directors to promulgate this knowledge.

Physiology

White and White (2001) summarize the physiological changes that occur. They state:

> The muscles and cartilage of the larynx change in position, size, strength and texture; accordingly, the singing voice changes in range power and tone. At the onset of puberty . . . physiological changes occur in the organs, muscles, cartilage, and bones that support the phonatory process. The epiglottis grows, flattens and ascends, the neck usually lengthens. The chest cavity grows larger, especially in males. As the skeletal structure of the head grows, the resonating cavities increase in size and change in shape. More important, the larynx grows at different rates and in different directions according to gender. The male larynx grows primarily in the anterior- posterior (front-to-back) direction, leading to the angular projection of the thyroid cartilage, the Adam's apple, a visible indication of the impending voice change. In fact, the male's vocal folds lengthen four to eight millimeters. (White & White, 2001, pp. 39–40)

This description aligns with that of Thurman and Klitzke (2000) and Ashley (2009). Ashley (2009) and Cooksey (2000a) describe how this feels for boys. Ashley says that a "rapid increase lung volume and weight (indicative of changes in muscle mass affecting in turn the mass of the vocal folds) [indicates the] end of the treble career" (p. 44). Furthermore, he explains that:

> Boys experience increasing muscular difficulty in controlling their voices at around age thirteen or fourteen. This is fundamentally no different to general adolescent clumsiness and the difficulty some boys have at the same age of controlling limbs that have suddenly changed length. The vocal folds at this stage become quite rapidly more massive, stiffer and rectangular in shape and this change outpaces the boy's ability to adjust the way he controls their movement. The result is not infrequently a flip between child and emergent adolescent pitch during speech, the 'cracking' or 'squeaky' voice that can embarrass boys at this age. (p. 47)

Cooksey (2000a) notes:

> When a young man sings in his upper range, then, his vocal folds cannot thin out as much as before, but his habitual prepubertal brain program will lengthen them for those pitches anyway. The result is excess effort in the larynx and excess vocal fold and shear forces. If male voices shift suddenly from lower or upper registers to the falsetto [boys] commonly shut off their voices and say that their voice 'cracked' or 'broke.' (pp. 827–828)

Cooksey further explains why boys voices can sound as if they "crack" and he attacks the term "broken voice." He explains that during puberty "voice function . . . becomes confused, and unintended surprise sounds and out-of-tune singing can be expected in boys" who are vocally inexperienced, continue to use "prepubertal brain programs" or "continue to do all or nearly all of their singing in their falsetto register after their laryngeal anatomy has proceeded through several of its growth stages" (pp. 827–828). Cooksey's observation partly explains the culture-wide folklore about adolescent boys communicating in monosyllables and grunts (Roberts, 2005). Adolescent boys are therefore likely to be unwilling to speak at length out of fear of the sounds their unruly voices will make. Someone who is unwilling to speak will be naturally unwilling to sing.

There is little doubt that the body of evidence suggests that voices change dramatically–sometimes at an erratic rate–through a set of predictable stages during adolescence, but continuing to sing during the voice change is not physically damaging (Phillips, 1996). Cooksey (2000a) concurs and suggests that unhealthy voice use such as yelling is more dangerous than singing. Phillips and Aitchison (1997) assert that "singing is a learned behavior and can be effectively taught as a developmental skill" and that "total range may be improved with instruction, especially for boys" (p. 195). Choral directors are in an ideal position to assist in this process by training boy voices so that they can have more confidence in controlling them and less fear in using them. Choral directors who both literally and physically give boys a voice will be rewarded with loyal singers in their ensembles.

Friar (1999) (amongst others) recognized the preeminence of John Cooksey in researching this area. In 2000, Cooksey brought together his own research and a number of other studies including The London Oratory School Study (1992–1994), and the Cambridge Study (1996). Cooksey (2000b) concluded that "Voice maturation . . . proceeds at various rates of velocity through a predictable, sequential pattern of stages" and that "individual growth rates and distribution of voice 'types' are highly variable" (p. 733).

Cooksey's stages are set out in Table 8.1 as readers will note that his descriptors are commonly described in the literature.

Cooksey's earlier material found that:

1) Pubertal stages of development closely parallel the stages of voice mutation. Singing is most limited at the climax of puberty.

Table 8.1 Cooksey's Voice Classification

Voice maturation stage / Voice classification	Voice classification			Tessitura	Range	Quality
Pre-mutational	Unchanged			D4-C5	A3-E5	Full, rich soprano. The "pinnacle of development."
Stage 1	Early mutation	Midvoice I	Beginning of change	D4-B4	G3-D5	Breathy, strained upper range; little resonance or "body" in lower range
Stage 2	High mutation	Midvoice II	Middle of change	A3-F4	F3-B4	Loss of agility, falsetto emerges, uniquely beautiful and rich if in range
Stage 3	Mutation climax	Midvoice IIA	Climax of change	F3-D4	D3-F4	Evolution of modal register into baritone range, retention of stage 2 quality
Stage 4	Post-mutation stabilization	New baritone	Tapering period	D3-A3	C3-D4	Light and husky, approximating mid-baritone, difficulties with 4ths and 5ths
Stage 5	Post-mutation settling and development	Settling baritone	Expansion/ development	C3-B3	A2-E3	Body, resonance and power increase, agility recovered, adult qualities emerge

Table extracted from (Cooksey, Voice Transformation in Male Adolescents, 2000, pp. 721, 722) and (Ashley, John Cooksey's "eclectic" scheme, 2014).

2) Voice mutation proceeds at various rates through sequential stages which affect singing differently in each stage. The onset of voice transformation is variable.

3) Mutation can start as early as age 12 and end as late as 17.

4) The first stage of voice mutation is indicated by an increase in "breathiness and strain" in the upper registers.

5) The lower register is generally more stable throughout the mutation than the upper.

6) The most noticeable changes occur in the Midvoice I, Midvoice II and Midvoice IIA stages.

7) Register definitions (modal, falsetto, whistle) become clear during the high mutational period.

8) Age and grade level are not reliable criteria for voice classification.

9) The average speaking fundamental frequency lies near the bottom of the voice pitch range.

Further sonographic analysis justified Cooksey's findings and his additional observations include:

1) Total pitch range compass is the most important vocal criterion in determining voice maturation stage.
2) Other criteria include tessitura, voice quality (increased breathiness and constriction in the Midvoice IIA state), register development, and average speaking fundamental frequency.
3) Adult voice quality should not be expected from the early adolescent male voice, even after the settling baritone classification has been reached.
4) The width of the comfortable singing pitch range (tessitura) remains fairly stable throughout the stages of voice change.
5) Increase in height seems related to the most extensive voice maturation stages while increase in weight accompanies the settling baritone classification. (Cooksey, 2000, pp. 727–734)

In spite of his very comprehensive work, Cooksey's view that there are fixed stages of vocal development is not completely uncontested (White & White, 2001). Indeed, the six stages described make the allocation of singers to choral parts problematic. One approach to this issue is the Cambiata approach founded by Irvin Cooper and developed by Collins which divides the voices into treble, Cambiata I, Cambiata II and Baritone.

Ashley (2014a) counsels that choral directors should be aware of, but not restricted by the ranges and stages described by the various researchers. He contends that Cooksey does not take into account the effect of training voices during adolescence and finds, "boys who sing a lot (such as choristers) have much bigger ranges and retain their treble voices for longer than is suggested by Cooksey. They are usually also better able to manage the transition to new voices, having some understanding of the need to develop control of *passaggio*" (Ashley, 2014b). He quotes Henry Leck who contends,

> If you keep coming down across the break enough, it disappears. The students that leave my choir (especially the basses) can sing soprano, alto, tenor, or bass. It drew me to the conclusion that, in reality, a bass range is not the range of a man's voice at all. It is only the lower register. Nearly every male who is allowed to keep singing in his high voice is able to keep that voice. So it is not a boy's "changing" voice, it is a boy's "expanding" voice. It is not an unchanged treble voice becoming a tenor or a bass. It is an unchanged treble voice adding a lower register. (Leck, 2009, p. 49)

Ashley (2014) also claims that the "vocal agency" of the singers must be taken into account. He observes "a boy's body is his own and his voice is very much an expression of his body and indeed soul . . . Boys confident of their own ability, secure in their self-esteem and strong in agency might sing in different sections of the choir at the same concert!" This author, together with Ancell (2010), recommends Leck's approach. A number of boys will approach a male chorus partly so that they can get better at singing their own music. Technical work in rehearsals, which yields dividends for the boys in their singing lives outside the chorus, can materially improve their loyalty to the group. They value the way chorus membership empowers them to sing their own music and are happy to contribute to the ensemble in return.

Overall, choral directors need to be willing to accommodate a choral group that will change in its composition every rehearsal and need to work steadily to improve the range and technical skill of the singers over time. They should know about tessituras, growth spurts, breathiness, strain, the modal pitch of speech, and increases in weight and height and should develop a shared understanding with their choristers. This does not suggest that rehearsals consist of long technical dissertations by the choral director while the singers sleep. Instead, technical material should be taught in the context of singing repertoire and exercises, when relevant to what is sung. In this way the material will be remembered because it was learned experientially. Conductors should develop enough practical knowledge about singing to aurally diagnose technical difficulties and propose effective solutions within rehearsals. Alternatively, singing teachers with a good knowledge of vocal technique can attend rehearsals, provide advice, lend a diagnostic ear, and assist individual singers, without disrupting rehearsal flow.

Rehearsal Strategies

Once there is a shared understanding of the physiology of voice change, choral directors need to ensure that rehearsals are cherished events for all concerned. Koza (2010) examines the "missing males" issue and criticizes the way a number of historical approaches dealt with the assumption that singing in Western culture had become seen as a feminine activity. Some authors suggested that the way forward was to create a masculine construction of singing and to make rehearsals as masculine and sport like as possible. Koza suggests that:

> The problem was presumed to be improper placement of singing at the feminine end of the masculine/ feminine polarity; the polarity itself was un-questioned. The proposed solutions involved changes in perceptions about singing or voices but not about gender or sexual orientation.

The key to recruitment and retention lay in identifying what is masculine and then linking the "masculine" to singing. Although several references openly argued that singing is masculine, and one suggested that it is both masculine and feminine, no text recognized that like mathematics, sports, and needlework, singing is not intrinsically gendered (p. 59).

Roe (1983) advised "get the coach to back the choral program if you can" (p. 17). Ashley (2009) coached rugby himself and the boys in his choral outreach program "are content to go out to primary schools . . . *as long as the lesson they are missing is not double sport*" (p. 17). He advises "boys will sing provided they are not asked to choose between choir and sport, an unfair choice that youngsters should not have to make (p. 103)." Clearly the assumption here is that the dominant "male" activity, sport, will always triumph over the marginalized "female" activity, singing. Surely, both music and sport are admirable activities and neither men, nor women, should be denied access to either activity.

The authors reflect that in a contemporary context, issues of gender and sport have become conflated. To suggest that boys should not have to choose between sport and singing ignores the fact that girls are just as likely to have competing sporting and musical interests. To try to turn choral rehearsals into something they are not, "sport lite" is probably not going to convince sportsmen to sing. If they want to play real sport they will do so. Many choristers may also join choral groups simply because they reject some aspects of sports. However, many aspects of good sport coaching are applicable to choral training and can make for better choral results and more enjoyable rehearsals: sports have games, music has concerts; sports have training, music has rehearsal. This suggests that choral directors might be better off allying themselves with the sports departments in their institutions rather than setting up in competition. Choral directors should aim to do what will produce the best choral result and this will often suggest sports-like rehearsal strategies simply because they are effective. Overall, as choral directors, the aim should be to examine the parts of practice that are choral and the parts that are cultural. There may be aspects of "choral culture" (LeBorgne & Rosenberg, 2014) that are holding up progress and need to be abandoned, and there may be practices from other disciplines that need to be adopted.

Accordingly, Harrison (2005) admits, "examples of effective practice in exploring the complementary nature of the two activities (sport and singing) are scarce, but isolated instances can provide useful illustrations for . . . improving the plight of music in relation to status and participation" (p. 56). Harrison counsels, "sport can be harnessed as a motivational tool in music, but this needs to be executed with caution so as to avoid entrenching stereotypes" (p. 57). Choral rehearsals can benefit in many ways from being sport-like and active. Voice pedagogues already use the term "vocal athlete" (LeBorgne & Rosenberg, 2014). Sessions that start with "warm-ups" which are physical align well with physical education. These sorts of activities are good for singing and may well encourage the participation of both boys and girls. The material following examines what has been suggested as appropriate for adolescent boy choirs, but the reader is encouraged to ask whether these activities are simply good choral work in their own right, and whether it is right to deny these approaches to female singers simply because of gender stereotypes.

Role models

Given that adolescents are experimenting with possible future selves, singing older peers can strongly influence younger singers. Ashley uses Mechling's term "fratriarchy" "to reflect the fact that it is the community of older brothers rather than adults who are the main influences on boys' identity and aspirations" (Ashley, 2009, p. 156). Younger students look up to singing elders and will emulate their behaviour. Ashley notes that the younger boys seek reassurance that plenty of other boys sing and that "those boys that do are 'normal'" (p. 157). White and White recommend the use of "role models" as does Roe (1983, p. 176) but given Ashley's work, it appears that the most effective role models would be good young singers of an age that they could be big brothers of the students, preferably with some social capital. The author has found that having older boys from the senior choir attend middle school choir rehearsals is beneficial to the sense of esprit de corps amongst the middle school singers. Giving leadership roles to the more senior members of the group also encourages the students to take more ownership over the fortunes of the program. For example, if rehearsals begin with technical work ("warm-ups") for which a consistent ritual of exercises is used, older students can run the technical work session leaving the conductor free to check on individual students. If conducting is taught in rehearsals, students can have the opportunity to conduct the group. The authors have observed that responsible use of student leadership in appropriate roles encourages a more productive working environment in the rehearsals.

Almost by definition, boys undergoing voice change need to find the rehearsal experience emotionally supportive so that they are free to take risks with their voices without fear of ridicule (Thurman & Welch, 2000; Oakes, 2008). Parker (2007) notes that "teens are vulnerable in the classroom" but "if an environment is deemed safe and trustworthy . . . the singing experience will be one that fosters growth of individuals and their voices." The authors suggest respect as a core attribute of rehearsal discourse and this respect must be modeled by the director and enforced amongst the choristers (Young, 2009).

Kinaesthetic learning

Incorporating physical movement in rehearsal is widely supported in the literature. Kodály and Dalcroze teachers have used movement, games, dances, clapping, and hand signs for many years. Cooksey (2000) recommends using "physical gestures that serve as a visual-kinaesthetic metaphor for some aspect of the vocal skill being targeted" such as "pretending to throw a frisbee, spreading open arms down and away with voicing or turning hands in rapid circles in front of the abdomen" to encourage "active breath support and healthy voice use" (p. 829). Eichenberger (2001) developed this approach and pioneered linking movement to effective conducting gestures. Castles (2009) notes that "boys like action" (p. 40) and moving in rehearsals to help with beat, rhythm, vocal technique, phrasing, and style is now well established (Menehan, 2013). The authors have incorporated considerably increased movement into rehearsals and found this to improve singing and attitudes to music (Young, 2009).

Perhaps it is an accident of teacher training but in many contexts teachers trained in teaching elementary or primary school are sometimes more confident using movement than those trained in secondary or college contexts. Accordingly, it can be the case that students, at the time in their development when they most need to move, are confronted by teachers who are themselves uncomfortable with movement, dancing, and games. Some might argue that they do not want to use movement, as they want choral singing to be taken more seriously. Movement should be taken very seriously so that it is effective; games have rules that must be followed. Ashley validates the value of singing as social play (Ashley, 2009). It is important to remember that music is "played" music and that the verb "to play" has joyful connotations.

Moreover developing a shared sense of how the body sings through instruction in body mapping can, at a technical level, encourage singers to keep their knees unlocked, their hips free, and their bodies aligned; a valuable outcome (Conable, 2000). The foregoing may appear to be an avocation of making rehearsals more sport–like but it is actually recommending empowering singers to have comprehensive knowledge of how their bodies work so that they can develop confidence and facility with their voices. Young men are more likely to be involved in choral rehearsals if they can perceive that they are growing in knowledge, skill, and ability, and if the learning is embodied in physical experience.

Musicianship

Accordingly, it is essential to teach musicianship in male chorus rehearsals. Most choral groups sing in parts and part-singing is indispensable when boys are at the peak of voice change and have to deal with a decreased range. Cooksey (2000a) complains "most published unison songs have pitch ranges that are too wide or the appropriate ones are in keys that force many changing voices into pitch ranges that they are incapable of singing without excess vocal effort" (p. 824). Restricted range necessitates enabling students to take another part, but conductors should be familiar with groups being unable to hold parts because of underdeveloped aural skills. Often one part disappears as boys drift to another, even if they had reasonably developed part-work skills when singing as trebles. Of course, boys who start singing just before their voices change, as is the case when boys begin singing on arriving in middle school, may have to be taught part-singing from scratch. Singers are under an increased cognitive load as they have to manage an unruly voice and it is reasonable in these circumstances to sing simpler, more manageable two-part music. Nothing will make rehearsal more tedious than fruitless repetition (note bashing) of parts that the students cannot hold. Singing manageable music successfully with growing vocal technique, a respectable sound, emotional engagement, and convincing performance skills will be much more rewarding.

Choral directors will encounter singers who cannot match pitch but wish to sing. The quest for good intonation during the voice change is "an achievable challenge rather than a quixotic goal." The word "closer" will be more encouraging and effective than "wrong." It is important that teachers have aural and vocal solutions for the hard-working struggling student and also have motivating strategies for the less involved student (Young, 2006, p. 20). Sometimes, simply placing a student in a section with singers at the same stage of voice change will be enough. Also a student might find it easier to match the pitch of a motif than to match an individual note. If the voice is not damaged, out-of-tune singing is caused by either insufficient musicianship or lack of coordination. Once the teacher has discovered the source of the challenge, musicianship training should be implemented or the usual physical causes of out-of-tune singing, such as poor breath management, bad body alignment, tight jaw or tongue should also be checked.

The authors have found that the elementary school sequence of teaching musicianship skills works very well for adolescents (Herboy-Koscar, 1984). Depending on the stages of voice change in the group, it may then be possible to sing a major scale in two- or three-part canon on a chosen vowel. Once the singers can hold a scale in parts, they should be ready to sing homophony. All of these activities can be incorporated into warm-ups, technical work, and repertoire. If the choral director explains this process, the singers can enjoy their growing mastery of the skill.

Musicianship can also include teaching music literacy. The debate about teaching music literacy has filled many other texts and will not be canvassed here. The position of the authors is that if literacy is taught in the context of music making it is enjoyable and rewarding. Many music literacy pedagogies advocate the "sound before symbol" approach in line with the reality that we speak before we read (Houlahan & Tacka, 2009). This would suggest that choruses commence with rote learning music and move to reading from printed choral music as the musical concepts intended to be taught become familiar. This is not to suggest a privileged position for notated music. In the interests of authenticity and sensitivity to cultural context, the choral director must decide which music to teach from notation and which music to teach aurally. Music from a written tradition should be read as such. However, it would be unfortunate to have students learn from a printed score music that is from an oral tradition. Teaching a range of music in different ways powerfully enhances the rehearsal experience. Singers will listen far more intently if they know they must rely on their ears to learn a piece and they will develop their aural skills and musical memory. This has implications for the choral director in terms of being able to provide an appropriate model.

Students who learn to sight sing have a broader range of music making possibilities open to them. If working in a context where teaching notation is practical, inner hearing, Tonic solfege, French time names, together with Curwen hand signs can all assist in making the learning of music literacy more straightforward and accessible in a rehearsal context. Clearly approaches will vary in different contexts. In a community choir rehearsing for a short period once a week, progress may need to be gentle but in an educational context, with substantial time available, a methodical, sequential approach would be appropriate. Indeed, if timetabled class time were given to the chorus (as a normal subject), it would be unfortunate to have to say to a prospective singer ". . . you will take my class for three years but will not learn how to read." Surely, literacy should be taught in this context for its value in cognitive development as well as for its ability to enable the students to interact with a wider range of music. In a society that privileges literacy, teaching literacy, done effectively and enjoyably, should make chorus membership more attractive.

Rehearsals need to be carefully planned by a choral director who has made the time to choose appropriate repertoire, to analyze the aural and physiological demands of the repertoire, and to plan exciting fulfilling rehearsals filled with focused learning experiences. Rehearsals should not be allowed to bog down. Freer (2007) recommends" a change of activity focus or location in the room about every twelve or thirteen minutes." Kodály teaching methodology recommends that music lessons comprise a number of short focuses (Klinger, 2014). In addition, Freer suggests that teachers "take advantage of research suggesting that competition and timed activities promote learning in male students" (p. 29). Rehearsals need to be brisk and businesslike with a sense that each session has yielded a number of noticeable improvements. This places a heavy burden on the conductor to have solutions for the challenges faced by the group and also to educate the group so that it can perceive and enjoy when progress is made.

Within rehearsals, drill and skill should be adopted and drill and kill avoided. If a musical section is to be repeated there must be a clear goal in doing so. Bromfman (2009) cites "research in motor learning in relation to skill acquisition." He finds that "for optimal physical learning to occur, repetition should ideally consist of a variety of similar tasks that are related to, but not an exact replication of the skill to be learned" (p. 61). Thurman (2000) reminds us that the brain learns by "target practice" and the adolescent male needs opportunities for continual "target practice" throughout the voice change process (p. 196). Kodály methodology suggests that each learning focus end with a reinforcement stage that is a repetition of the skill learned in a new way (Klinger, 2014).

For example, students may sing known repertoire or a simple canon while walking on the beat into a different space in the rehearsal room. While walking they can collect a new piece of choral sheet music. This approach saves rehearsal time, frees the bodies, encourages part independence and makes the singers more able to deal with the different acoustic properties of different spaces. The fact that the students can negotiate movement around the space while singing the repertoire also demonstrates in-depth mastery of the music. This approach is more interesting than standing and singing the material repeatedly for no shared purpose.

Similarly, if a section of repertoire is being sung with insufficient breath support, the singers can sing the section to the voiced fricative consonant "th." This will encourage balanced airflow while simultaneously ensuring that the tongue is not retracting into the throat as a result of tongue root tension. Singing a section detached to "doo" is commonly used to get a large group to sing more accurately in tune and in time while ensuring that the vowel does not spread and the tongue does not retract. Developing these strategies relies on a good knowledge of the music and a good knowledge of applied vocal technique (Jordan, 2009).

In summary

There is a wealth of material available on rehearsal strategies and planning and the director should develop a methodology to suit the context. Many of the techniques described here are simply good pedagogy, regardless of gender. The authors are drawing on their own experiences in the field, alongside their own in-field research, and the existing research of those who have gone before—Cooksey (2000a, 2000b), Young (2006, 2009, 2012), Welch (2010), Freer (2007), Harrison (2005, 2006), and Ashley (2009). Identities are formed through these pedagogies, drawing on gender-specific concerns—the voice change, employment of role models, reference to sporting analogies and team-work, and where appropriate, selection of repertoire and rehearsal strategies.

The authors recommend developing a technical regime, or series of warm-ups that will help build the voices and that the singers understand. These exercises can be led by choir members who are willing to take on extra responsibility. These members might be older peers or might be receiving private voice instruction and be perceived to have appropriate knowledge and authority. This approach develops peer leadership and enhances the ownership of the group by its members. The exercises need to go beyond warming up the vocal apparatus and extend to actually improving singing. Of course, breath support, body alignment, musicianship, range extension, messa-di-voce, diction, and such matters are important to all singers. As well, having students leading the technical exercises enables the conductor to be vigilant in looking individually for students exhibiting the typical technical problems that present in this stage of voice development such as jaw jut, leading with the chin, poor posture, swallowed tongue, tight knees and locked lower abdominal muscles.

Regardless of context, consistently applied head-to-chest voice exercises will make the biggest difference to male singers at this stage. Cooksey (2000a) recommends vocalizing downward from falsetto, through the *passaggio* into the chest voice. He states, "physically efficient register transitions can be facilitated by vocalizing from the upper range downward. These register transition processes can produce a very consistent, efficiently produced tone throughout the singer's pitch range" (p. 828). This approach conforms to Leck's (2009) advice cited earlier. Downward sighs form an important part of the voice development regime advocated by Westminster Choir College (Haasemann & Jordan, 1989). Blackstone (1998) also supports the use of head voice for settling voices. Cooksey suggests that these exercises be refined into descending 5-note and 3- passages as the voices develop but the author has warned previously to avoid tension while singing through the passaggio (Young, 2012). Ancell's (2010) "loo-law" exercise provides an excellent steppingstone between sighs and the 5-note patterns described above.

CONCLUSION

Overall, the authors of this chapter have argued that one approach to keeping boys singing is to empower them by educating and training them. It recognizes the value of peer learning and developing shared understandings in the pursuit of musical and personal goals. It proposes that young men who become able, skilled and confident as choral singers should be powerful advocates for our ensembles and influential agents for developing broadened concepts of masculinity so that healthy conceptions of manhood can be nurtured.

References

Adderley, C., Kennedy, M., & Berz, W. (2003). "A home away from home": The world of the high school music classroom. *Journal of Research in Music Education, 51*(3), 190–205.

Ashley, M. (2009). *How high should boys sing? Gender; authenticity and credibility in the young male voice.* Farnham, UK: Ashgate.

Ashley, M. (2014a). John Cooksey's "ecclectic" scheme. Notated version by Henry Leck. Retrieved from http://www.martin-ashley.com/wp-content/uploads/2012/06/P1211-Cookseys-ecelctic-scheme.pdf

Ashley, M. (2014b). Range. Retrieved from http://www.martin-ashley.com/teacher-pages/range

Blackstone, J. (Writer-Director). (1998). *Working with male voices* [Motion Picture]. United States: Santa Barbara Music.

Bromfman, J. (2009). Repeating with variety: Implementing motor learning theory in the middle school choral rehearsal. *Choral Journal, 50*(1), 61–63.

Castles, A. (2009). Oh boy(s)! Ideas for engaging boys in music. *Music In Action, 7*(2), 40.

Collins, A. (2009). A boy's music ecosystem. In S. D. Harrison (Ed.), *Male voices: Stories of boys learning through making music* (pp. 33–47). Melbourne, Australia: ACER.

Conable, B. (2000). *The structures and movement of breathing: A primer for choirs and choruses.* Chicago: GIA.

Conable, B. (n.d.). Teaching tips for choral directors. Retrieved from Andover Educators. http://bodymap.org/main/?p=286

Cooksey, J. (2000a). Male adolescent transforming voices: Voice classification, voice skill development, and music literature selection. In L. Thurman, G. Welch, & J. Ostrem (Eds.), *Bodymind and voice: Vol. 3* (pp. 821–841). Minneapolis: Fairview Voice Centre.

Cooksey, J. (2000b). Voice transformation in male adolescents. In L. Thurman, G. Welch, & J. Ostrem (Eds.), *Bodymind and voice: Vol. 3* (pp. 718–738). Minneapolis: Fairview Voice Centre.

Eichenberger, R. (2001). *Enhancing musicality through movement.* Santa Barbara: Santa Barbara Publishing.

Freer, P. K. (2007). Between research and practice: How choral music loses boys in the middle. *Music Educators Journal, 94*(2), 28–34.

Friar, K. K. (1999). Changing voices, changing times. *Music Educators Journal, 86*(3), 26–29.

Haasemann, F., & Jordan, J. (1989). *Group vocal technique.* Chapel Hill, NC: Hinshaw Music.

Harrison, S. D. (2005). Music versus sport: A new approach to scoring. *Australian Journal of Music Education, 1*, 56–61.

Harrison, S. D. (2006). Engaging boys in a sequential, voice-based music program. *The Bulletin of the Kodaly Music Education Institute of Australia*, 6–13.

Harrison, S. D., G. Welch, & A. Adler, Eds. (2012). *Perspectives on males and singing* Dordrecht, The Netherlands: Springer.

Henry, W. (2001). Vocal development in general music: Bringing two worlds together. *General Music Today, 15*(1), 4–8.

Herboy-Koscar, I. (1984). *Teaching of polyphony, harmony and form in elementary school.* Kecskemét, Hungary: Zoltán Kodály Pedagogical Institute of Music.

Houlahan, M., & Tacka, P. (2009). *From sound to symbol*. Oxford: Oxford University Press.

Jordan, J. (2009). *Evoking sound*. Chicago: GIA.

Klinger, R. (2014). *Lesson planning in a Kodály setting*. Los Angeles, CA: Organization of American Kodály Educators.

Koza, J. E. (2010). Big Boys Don't Cry (Or Sing): Gender, misogyny and homophobia in college choral method texts. *Visions of Research in Music Education, 16*(5), 48–64.

LeBorgne, W., & Rosenberg, M. (2014). *The vocal athlete*. San Diego: Plural.

Leck, H. (2009). The boy's expanding voice: Take the high road. *Choral Journal, 49*(11), 49–60.

Menehan, K. (2013, June 21). Movement in rehearsal. Retrieved from Chorus America https://www.chorusamerica.org/singers/movement-rehearsal

Miller, R. (2008). Acknowledging an indebtedness. *Choral Journal, 49*(5), 16–22.

Oakes, V. (2008). The developing male voice: Instilling confidence in the young male singer. *Choral Journal, 28*, 116–118.

Parker, E. C. (2007). Intrapersonal and interpersonal growth in the school chorus. *Choral Journal, 48*(2), 26–31.

Phillips, K. (1996). *Teaching kids to sing*. New York: Schirmer.

Phillips, K., & Aithchison, R. (1997). Effects of psychomotor instruction on elementary general music students' singing performance. *Journal of Research in Music Education, 45*(2), 185–196.

Richards, H. (1922). *Church choir training*. London: Joseph Williams Limited.

Roberts, A. (2005). Boys, and how we can reach them. *Visions: BC's Mental Health and Addictions Journal, 2*(5). Retrieved from http://www.heretohelp.bc.ca/ visions/men-vol2/boys-and-how-we-can-reach-them

Roe, P. F. (1983). *Choral music education*. Englewood Cliffs, NJ: Prentice-Hall.

Swain, J. (2003). How young schoolboys become somebody: The role of the body in the construction of masculinity. *British Journal of Sociology of Education, 24*(3), 299–314.

Swanson, F. J. (1960). When voices change: An experiment in junior high school music. *Music Educators Journal, 46*(4), 50.

Thurman, L. (2000). Human-compatible learning. In L. Thurman, G. Welch, & J. Ostrem (Eds.), *Bodymind and Voice: Vol. 1* (pp. 188–301). Minneapolis: Fairview Voice Center.

Thurman, L. (2000). The astounding capabilities of human bodyminds. In L. Thurman, G. Welch, & J. Ostrem (Eds.), *Bodymind and voice: Vol. 1* (pp. 18–26). Minneapolis: Fairview Voice Center.

Thurman, L., & Klitzke, C. (2000). Highlights of physical growth and function of voices from prebirth to age 21. In L. Thurman, & W. Graham, *Bodymind and voice: Vol. 1* (pp. 696–703). Minneapolis: Fairview Voice Center.

Thurman, L., & Welch, G. (2000). Sunsets, elephants, vocal self-expression and lifelong learning. In L. Thurman, & G. Welch, *Bodymind and voice: Vol. 1* (pp. xi–xxiv). Minneapolis: Fairview Voice Center.

Welch, G. (2010). Yes, we can! *Sing Up*. Retrieved from http://www.singup.org/ knowledge-hub/how-tos-guides/yes-we-can/

White, C. D., & White, D. K. (2001). Commonsense training for changing male voices. *Music Educators Journal, 87*(6), 39–53.

Young, A. (2006). Classroom strategies for changing voice boys. *Australian Kodaly Bulletin*, 17–23. Retrieved from http://kodaly.org.au/assets/Australian_Kodaly_Bulletin_2006.pdf

Young, A. (2009). The singing classroom: Singing in classroom music and its potential to trans-form school culture. In S. D. Harrison (Ed.), *Male voices: Stories of boys learning through making music* (pp. 62–78). Camberwell, Australia: ACER.

Young, A. (2012). The courage to sing: Reflections on secondary school singing. In S. D. Harrison, G. Welch, & A. Adler (Eds.), *Perspectives on males and singing* (pp. 311–324). Dordrecht, The Netherlands: Springer.

CHAPTER 9

CHORAL PEDAGOGY AND THE CONSTRUCTION OF IDENTITY

Girls

MATTHEW OWENS AND GRAHAM F. WELCH

GIRL choristers have become an established part of the English choral tradition in the last twenty years (Welch, 2011), notwithstanding earlier examples, such as in the 16th century nunneries prior to the Reformation and, sporadically, in the 20th century (Mould, 2007), including Bradford and Leicester. Currently, the majority of cathedrals in the United Kingdom have female as well as male choristers. These are usually in same sex choirs that perform separately unless for special occasions, such as major feast days. Nevertheless, despite this shift from the previous all-male cathedral choir hegemony, there has been, and continues to be, much debate about the role of girls' choirs, the resulting potential/actual impact on boys' choirs and the overall impact (real and imagined) on the English choral tradition—which its itself a relatively recent phenomenon from the late 19th century, at least in terms of quality (Day, 2014). The identity and development of both types of choir is of significant interest and, while there is a considerable body of literature regarding boys' choirs, there has been, to date, relatively little research undertaken specifically with regard to girls' choirs in the United Kingdom.

One defining aspect of the musical identity of girls' choirs can be their sound in comparison with boys' choirs. Although there is considerable overlap acoustically in terms of their sung vocal products, making it possible to mistake girls for boys, there can also be distinctive differences in chorister tone color that are discernible to the professionally experienced listener. Typically, in the untrained child's singing voice, gender characteristics become more and more evident perceptually around the age of eight years. Consequently, it is usually possible for the listener to identify whether the untrained child singer is male or female at this age and older, but this judgment is often more problematic with trained voices unless the listener is experienced (e.g., Howard, Syzmanski,

& Welch, 2002; Sergeant, Sjölander, & Welch 2005; Sergeant & Welch, 1997; Sergeant & Welch, 2009; Welch & Howard, 2002).

When educating and training cathedral girl choristers, the first author of this chapter occasionally encounters the question: "Are you trying to make them sound or sing like the boy choristers?"—that is, "Is the male chorister the ideal acoustic model?" The answer to this, in our view, is an emphatic "No." Personal experience and empirical data suggest that the professional sociocultural context—including the religious rituals, the acoustic characteristics of the performance spaces, the sacred music repertoire, the underlying similarities and differences in anatomy and physiology of the choristers' vocal instruments, the expectations of the clergy and congregations—collectively combine to constrain possible variations in choral behaviors (Small, 1999; Welch, 2012).

Nevertheless, the shaping of the choir's vocal products is also related to the professional biography of the choral director. Despite customarily being inducted into the choral tradition for many years, often as a chorister and organist, the choral director will bring his or her own personal preferences (and idiosyncrasies) to the roles of expected musical practices, rehearsal behaviors, and ideal musical outcomes. Although there is a commonality of professional expectation across the sector, not least because of the constraints of the cultural expectations of the music and its performance, the actual process of developing a choir in rehearsal and performance over time allows the individual director opportunity to shape the vocal products in ways that can be discernible to the experienced listener.

A Comment on the Relevance of the Authors' Professional Backgrounds

In designing the content of this chapter, the authors have drawn on their complementary professional experiences as well as other sources. In particular, the first author has spent much of the past two decades working in three different cathedrals with choristers of both sexes and has a wide range of other choral experience in community settings. The second author has spent nearly four decades as a teacher and researcher of children's singing development. The latter has included, since the mid-1990s, ongoing investigations into the nature of trained chorister development in children and adolescents, with an ongoing longitudinal study of female chorister development at Wells Cathedral. Female choristers have been a particular focus for investigation because this group has been significantly underresearched and underreported (until very recently) compared to boys.

In terms of the particular focus for this chapter, the first author has been working with boy and girl choristers for twenty years, both separately and together, and has sought to develop them, first and foremost, as singers, rather than as boys or girls with gender-specific vocal outputs. In these years, he has observed, firsthand, several differences in the approach, learning, and output of the two sexes through working in three different institutions: Manchester Cathedral in England; St Mary's Episcopal Cathedral, Edinburgh, Scotland; and Wells Cathedral in England. Unusually for the United Kingdom, at Manchester and Edinburgh, the treble/soprano line is made up of boys and girls singing together. In contrast, at Wells there are two separate treble/soprano lines. Throughout these different working contexts, there has been a continued emphasis on enabling the participant children to become competent and motivated professionals, irrespective of sex. This approach appears to be commonplace, at least according to data from related interviews with other directors across the UK who share this professional cathedral music role.

As Sub Organist, Manchester Cathedral (1996–1999), the primary duty was to accompany the cathedral choir for its regular services. This enabled direct experience of the mechanics of the life of the cathedral choristers on a daily basis. Originally conceived as a boys-only treble line since the choral foundation began in 1848, the choristers at Manchester became mixed (boys and girls singing the treble line/soprano together) from 1993.[1] Choristers then and now are educated at Chetham's School of Music, one of the nine government-funded specialist schools for music, drama, and the arts in the United Kingdom. Five of these specialize in music. Chetham's also acts as the choir school to Manchester Cathedral.[2] At Manchester, the choristers customarily sang the following services each week: Choral Evensong on Tuesday (treble voices), Wednesday (full choir), Thursday (treble voices), Saturday (full choir); and a Choral Eucharist on Sunday morning—a total of five services, which is a relatively light schedule in comparison with many other cathedral and collegiate choirs in the United Kingdom. In the full choir services, the choristers at Manchester sing with six to nine professional and semi-professional men.

As Sub Organist, there was also opportunity to direct the Manchester Cathedral Voluntary Choir, which comprised only boy choristers and men.[3] The Voluntary Choir's regular schedule consisted of two rehearsals per week with one sung service of Choral Evensong on a Sunday. This experience in Manchester provided regular opportunities to work with two different types of treble voice line, one mixed, the other single sex.

Subsequently, the first author was appointed Organist and Master of the Music, St. Mary's Episcopal Cathedral, Edinburgh (1999–2004). The Choir of St. Mary's Episcopal Cathedral, Edinburgh, is the only choir in Scotland to maintain the daily Anglican choral tradition.[4] The foundation goes back to 1879 and is one of only three mixed treble voice cathedral choirs in the United Kingdom (the others being Manchester Cathedral and Brecon Cathedral in Wales). Children who are successful at audition for the choir receive a scholarship to attend St. Mary's Music School, one of the five government-funded specialist music schools in the United Kingdom which also acts as the choir school to St Mary's Episcopal Cathedral—a similar setup to Manchester. The role of Organist and Master of the Music at St. Mary's required sole responsibility for the education and training of this mixed treble line. The choir sings seven services a week: Choral Evensong on Monday (treble voices), Tuesday (full choir), Wednesday (men's voices), Friday (full choir, unaccompanied), and Sunday afternoon (full choir). It also sings two services of Choral Eucharist each week, on Thursday evening and on Sunday morning.[5]

The treble line at Edinburgh became mixed in 1978 and developed relatively early on the following criteria in terms of gender balance: the girls would number no fewer than one quarter of the treble line and not more than one third, thus always ensuring that the boys were in the majority. This was an interesting perspective on a mixed treble line as it was clearly felt, at least in the early years of the choir's existence, that there was no need for total equality in terms of numbers between the sexes and so, to some degree, the authorities sought to ensure that the boys continued to form the main body of the treble line.[6] Since 2005, however, this policy has changed and the numbers are now more equal.

Working for over five years with this mixed chorister line has allowed insightful comparisons with the *separate* treble lines of boys and girls in subsequent employment at Wells Cathedral as Organist and Master of the Choristers, Wells Cathedral (2005–present). Unlike Edinburgh and Manchester, Wells Cathedral Choir is one of the oldest music foundations in the world. Boy choristers first sang at Wells in 909 AD (the year of the foundation of the Diocese), and the full choral tradition stretches back over 800 years. Despite such an established history of a male-only choir of boys and men, girl choristers were introduced into the foundation in 1994, but as a separate entity. Twenty years on, they are now a well-established part of the Choir of Wells Cathedral.

The choristers at Wells are educated at Wells Cathedral School, which was founded at the same time as the Cathedral itself. Today, the school is an independent school that acts as the choir school to the cathedral, and—coincidentally, along with Manchester and Edinburgh—is also a specialist music school.[7]

At Wells, the boy choristers sing the majority of the eight weekly choral services. The general working pattern for the girls is currently to sing Tuesday Evensong, Friday Evensong, alternate Saturday Evensongs, and either Eucharist or Matins on a Sunday (i.e., three to four services per week). As with the boy choristers, the girls are required for additional services (e.g., Advent, Christmas, Easter, Remembrance Day) and other events such as concerts, broadcasts, recordings, tours, and outreach projects. Most of the time, the girl choristers sing with the Vicars Choral,[8] but at other times may join with the boy choristers, forming what is known as *The Great Choir*. Occasionally, the older boys and girls will work together.[9]

The working practice and the constituency of the girls' choir at Wells have evolved over its twenty years of existence. From early on in the girls' choir's history until September 2009, it offered places to girls from School Year 4 (age 8–9) until School Year 9 (age 13–14). At the end of Year 9, the girls could retire,[10] or they had the option to stay on for up to two further years until Year 11 (i.e., age 16), should it be mutually agreeable. Part of the decision process regarding this possible extension included an assessment of whether or not the individual girl would cope with the enhanced demands and rigor of academic work at the school alongside being a cathedral chorister. Having girls stay on until age 16 had some significant advantages, such as an increased level of vocal power and collective expert musicianship in the girls' treble line. In addition, there could often be an enhanced sense of family, through the oldest girls having a well-developed sense of pastoral care and responsibility.

Nevertheless, in 2009 a decision was taken to do away with this possible extension period and make the age range of the girls the same as that of the boys (i.e., School Years 4–9 [age 8–14). There were various reasons for this decision, which were primarily concerned with the issue of the wide age range of the girls at this crucial educational and developmental stage. Having such a wide age and experience range within the girls' choir was not necessarily musically or pedagogically helpful in the following ways:

- The younger girls could rely too heavily on the older girls, musically and vocally.
- With a group ranging from eight- to 16 year-olds, there was a need to strike a somewhat difficult balance in educating and stimulating the younger members of the choir while maintaining the interest of the older ones. This can be an issue also with the subsequent reduced age range of years 4–9, but it can become acute with the spread from Years 4–11.
- Given the relatively limited number of services, assigning solo work could be difficult in that there was a natural tendency to favor the older girls, who were often singing so well and able to deliver a great deal on little rehearsal. On the other hand, there was also the need to encourage the younger choristers and to promote future soloists.
- There was a question of the girls' treble line having an unfair advantage over the boys' treble line, since the girls could sing to a much more accomplished level, given the musical experience and vocal power of the older girls. This had the potential to cause a corporate feeling of low self-esteem amongst the boys and might have led to challenges in recruitment.

The first author feels that, as a result of the aforementioned changes made at Wells Cathedral in 2009, the current arrangements work well for both the boy and the girl choristers.

THE WIDER IMPACT OF THE INTRODUCTION OF GIRLS' CHOIRS

There is no doubt that the relatively recent advent of female choristers has changed the identity of the United Kingdom's cathedral choirs. Originally, the majority of ecclesiastical foundations in the country had one treble line of boys with one choirmaster. This is still the case in a number of foundations, such as the cathedrals of Chichester; Christ Church (Oxford); Hereford; St. Paul's (London); Westminster (London, Roman Catholic), and in the Royal Peculiars of St. George's Chapel (Windsor);Westminster Abbey (London); St. James's Palace (London); and Hampton Court (London).[11] This is also the case for the choirs of Magdalen College and New College (Oxford), and King's College and St John's College (Cambridge). This membership pattern that has been in place for centuries and, nowadays at least (Day, 2014), continues to be perceived as effective: one director with one choir.

With the modern introduction of girl choristers in England in the early 1990's different types of internal musical direction have evolved in different cathedral foundations.[12] In the cathedrals of Durham, Salisbury, Wells, and York, for example, the Director of Music[13] has overall responsibility for both the boy and the girl treble lines. Normally, this will mean sharing the education and training with a deputy or deputies (and often the conducting in performances) of whichever treble line is on duty that day. As a result, there may be (or not) challenges in terms of the consistency in choral pedagogy practices between individuals and, possibly, in terms of vocal and musical output. This may be one of the reasons that, in some foundations with two treble lines, the Director of Music is principally in charge of the boy choristers (i.e., the original historically-established choir) as, for example, in the cathedrals of Ely, Exeter, Lincoln, Norwich, and Southwark, where the girls' treble line is customarily directed by an Assistant Director of Music.[14]

Personal experience suggests that, if there are multiple directors, the boy choristers will generally perform best for their own assigned director, or pack leader, whereas girls are more accepting of others, even though they too will normally work at their full capacity for *their* perceived pack leader, rather than for a deputy or deputies. In one sense, this could be compared with a substitute teacher entering a normal classroom situation, where it may be more difficult to assert authority and to inspire learning than is found to be the case with the regular teacher.

In reflecting on our experiences with boy and girl choristers, there is a realization that, whichever group is the focus, *continuity* is one of the key factors in nurturing development. As far as female choristers are concerned, it is also our experience that constant reiteration and modeling of good vocal and musical practice is more likely when the director (pack leader) sees the girls for longer and for more sustained periods, thus developing a stronger relationship with the group as a whole, as well as a greater understanding of individuals and their vocal strengths and developmental needs within the group. Empirical research data suggest that the characteristics of effective singing pedagogy with children include continuity; a confident and competent vocal model (whether adult or peer); sustained and positive experiences; musically informed feedback instantly provided against shared and explicit criteria for success; and achievements being recognized, valued, and celebrated (Saunders et al., 2011).

ARE THERE DIFFERENCES IN GIRLS' AND BOYS' VOICES?

Childhood and adolescence are marked by physical growth and this is also evident in changes in the underlying anatomy and physiology of the voice (for reviews, see Welch & Howard, 2002; McAllister & Sjölander, 2013). Compared to an adult, a child's vocal

instrument is smaller, its structure is less developed, and the resultant pitch products tend to be higher and less complex acoustically. However, children are capable of
achieving similar loudness levels to adults by using relatively more breath (with related
increases in subglottic pressure—see Stathopoulos, 2000). Nevertheless, there are differences between boys and girls in overall physical size of the vocal instrument, even
though overall body height is similar from age eight to twelve years (Stathopoulos &
Sapienza, 1997). For example, although the length of the vocal folds (the vibrating tissue that is the voice source within the larynx) gradually increases across childhood,
and with relative stability (i.e., much slower growth rates) from around the ages of four
to the onset of puberty, girls tend to have shorter vocal folds than boys (Titze, 1994).
The vocal folds grow in length from between 4 mm to 8 mm at birth to 21 mm in adult
females and to 29 mm in adult males (Kent & Vorperian, 1995). This physical difference implies that boys should exhibit lower pitched speaking voices, assuming similar
body height, but generally this has not been supported by the available research data
(Titze, 1994; Stathopoulos, 2000; Sataloff, 2000) until very recently. However, analyses
of data from a large-scale research study of children's singing in the United Kingdom
that included the assessed speaking behaviors of 11,000+ children aged five to eleven
years has revealed: (1) a common bias in both sexes for their spoken pitch to be centered around middle C (c4, 256Hz) or below; (2) younger children having higher average vocal pitch than older children, with spoken pitch lowering by approximately ¾ of a
tone from age 5+ to 10+, in line with vocal fold (voice source) growth within the larynx,
but that (3) girls have a higher average speaking pitch of ²/₃ of a semitone, implying that
they have slightly smaller vocal folds, on average, than boys (Welch et al., 2009).

Concerning singing development and competency, there are well-established gender
differences reported in the literature on untrained children's singing, with girls customarily being more advanced than boys for each age group (e.g., Sergeant, Sjölander, &
Welch, 2005; Sergeant & Welch, 2009; for an overview, see Welch et al., 2012). However,
in terms of untrained children's singing development within an appropriately nurturing
environment, such as was provided from 2007–2012 by the UK Government's national
"Sing Up" program, both girls and boys are equally capable of improving their singing
skills (Welch et al., 2010; Welch et al., forthcoming), even though gender differences
tend to persist. Overall, there is a consensus in the literature on untrained children's
singing that girls tend to achieve singing competency at a younger age than boys. The
other side of this trend is reflected in the relative proportions of children who have difficulties singing in tune, with boys outnumbering girls by a ratio of approximately 3 to 1
in each age group (Welch, 2006).

Gender differences are also evidenced in vocal studies of more experienced child
singers. For example, research into 11-year-old experienced singers from a Stockholm
music school found that mean formant values F1 and F2 (i.e., significant harmonic
components in vocal timbre) for both speech and singing were significantly higher for
girls than for boys (White, 1999). Such gender differences in the sung vocal products
of trained child singers have also been evidenced in studies of choristers in Europe,
but the listener's accurate perception of these is contexualized by the nature of the

particular musical example, the listener's acoustic environment, their musical biography, the choir membership of the individual choristers, and whether or not listeners are hearing an individual child or a group (e.g., Howard et al., 2001; Howard & Welch, 2002; Mecke & Sundberg, 2010; Sergeant & Welch, 1997; Welch & Howard, 2002). In general, more naïve listeners, in terms of their degree of experience of this skilled performance group, are less likely to be accurate in assigning gender accurately; trained female choristers from the age of eight through their early teens have often systematically been mistaken as male in empirical research studies, particularly if the girls have been inducted into a choral repertoire by a male director with a significant depth of experience of working with boys.

DIFFERENCES IN VOICE AND TIMBRE: THE IMPACT OF THE DIRECTOR

The existence or not of noticeable gender differences in children's singing is perhaps less important than the impact of the biography and expectations of the choral director on the ways that choristers perform. It has been noted, for example, across the past two centuries that certain directors of music within the English choral tradition favor a particular personal style of performance that appears to be distinctive and persistent over time (Day, 2014).

Compare, for example the Choir of King's College, Cambridge under the direction of its three most recent conductors: David Willcocks (1957–1974), Philip Ledger (1974–1982) and Stephen Cleobury (1982–present). Each has produced a different sound with the same forces, albeit with different personnel. Similarly at St. John's College, Cambridge, the sound of the boy choristers changed dramatically from the tenure of George Guest (1951–1991) to Christopher Robinson (1991–2003). Furthermore, recordings of three well-known collegiate boys' choirs in Oxford (Christ Church Cathedral, Magdalen College, and New College) in 2014 reveals that there are three distinct sounds under three different directors. And, in London, the treble lines of St. Paul's Cathedral, Westminster Abbey, and Westminster Cathedral are all quite individual. There is a very particular sound and identity associated with the boys of Westminster Cathedral Choir, which has been attributed partly to the repertoire that they sing (with a particular emphasis of the large amounts of repertoire in Latin, which—with its open vowels and long *cantabile* lines—can lend itself to a brighter, more Italianate sound) and partly from the building in which they sing.

How much do these choirs reflect the choir trainer, the building,[15] and the overall musical forces?[16] Concerning the construction of identity of girl choristers, the first author took the opportunity afforded by the writing of this chapter to listen back to the sound of three recordings that had been made with the girl choristers and Vicars Choral of Wells Cathedral (derived from separate discs of Burgon, Bednall, and Davison).[17] In listening to these discs, it was noticeable that they all bore the hallmarks of what each conductor was personally aiming for. However, even though they all had a particular performance stamp on them, the voices also all sounded slightly different. This is only to be expected, given that there were a number of different personnel involved in the recordings, within both the girl choristers and the Vicars Choral. Thus, the actual vocal products reflects the voices in combination of individual singers within the group that are being shaped by the approach of the director, which itself may vary over time.

Another influence is the fact that the boys and the girls at Wells Cathedral sing with 12 men. This, in itself, helps form the identity of the choristers at Wells, for a balance must be achieved between them and the alto, tenor, and bass parts of the choir. It may well be that the number and quality of the adult male singers will also have an effect on the sound of the boys or girls on the treble line. At present, this is under-researched.

In the United Kingdom, some cathedral girls' choirs have been criticized for sounding weak and lacking in substance (the common term used is "girly") and it has been argued that girls who are singing at the same ages as boy choristers (normally 8–13 years) are not capable of producing the same sound or power as boy choristers. Empirical data to support this supposition is contested but personal experience indicates that were one to have an average 9 or 10-year-old girl singing next to an average 9 or 10-year-old boy, one would immediately hear more power and projection from the boy. This can be particularly apparent in solo work. Experience suggests that girls' voices normally only gain this kind of vocal strength at, or just after, the onset of puberty.

It is hypothesized that the reason for this apparent gender difference in the vocal power of young choristers of similar ages relates to an underlying gender difference in children's normal voice use. Untrained girls' voices tend to exhibit higher formant frequencies and have breathier voices compared to untrained males of the same age due to the underlying pattern of coordination of the vocal folds in speech (sometimes referred to at the onset of female puberty as a glottal chink). There is an incomplete closure of the posterior part of the glottis that results from relative weaknesses in the interarytenoid muscles (for an overview, see Gackle, 2014). This behavior is likely to carry over from speech to singing (Sergeant & Welch, 2008, 2009). Breathy voices generally are acoustically less efficient and less powerful, and exhibit a greater spread of harmonic energy. Thus relatively novice female choristers will bring their customary voice use to singing tasks and it is only after sustained vocal training in the choir that their voices become more acoustically efficient. On the other hand, by the age of eight boys tend to have less breathy voices anyway and so will have an initial advantage in terms of focused vocal energy in singing from their underlying habitual voice use. This gender difference in relative vocal power may be one of the main reasons that some cathedral choirs in the United Kingdom have chosen to have older girl choristers: Ely (age 13–18), Winchester (age 12–17), Worcester (age 13–18), and the Girls' Choir at Bath Abbey (age 11–18) are some examples.

Nevertheless, the advantage of girls starting to sing as choristers at the age of seven or eight is that they generally become musically very proficient during their years in the choir, particularly in becoming good sight-readers (and perhaps related to the general gender bias toward girls in reading development—e.g., Logan & Johnston, 2009). They also gain a considerable amount of confidence from an early age, which stands them in good stead for their later musical and vocal development. There was direct evidence of this musical and vocal grounding when, in October 2014, the 20th anniversary of the founding of the Girl Choristers at Wells was celebrated. Many former girl choristers returned to sing in a special service of Choral Evensong, alongside the current girl choristers and Vicars Choral. With extremely limited rehearsal time and demanding music (much of it new and unknown to most of the former girl choristers, and which included a challenging, newly commissioned work) the former girl choristers read the pieces fluently and performed them musically at the first rehearsal. This demonstrated a considerable level of musicianship that will have undoubtedly come from daily and consistent work from a young age, as cathedral choristers.

Some Vocal Production Issues

Vowels

There are some commonly misformed vowels, which—in the experience of the first author (and, for some reason, increasingly so in the last few years) are more prevalent in girls' singing than that of boys. These are just a few examples (British English):

1. the 'a' of 'father,' which can often sound as often sounds as an 'er' vowel, as in 'learn';
2. the 'o' of 'love' (or the 'u' of 'but') which also often sounds as an 'er' vowel;
3. the diphthong of 'mouth,' which can sound more like a 'a' vowel (as in 'math');
4. the 'i' of 'King' (often sounds as an 'a' vowel).

In examples 1, 2, and 3, this is nearly always likely to be because the tongue position is incorrect, being too high. In example 4, the fault is normally the soft palate not being raised sufficiently.

Various factors may be behind such types of vowel production for the director, such as an increased listening to popular music by young people. For example, a survey for British Music Rights of n=773 young people in 2008 reported that they were, on average, listening to music more than six hours a day, either in the background or as the main focus for their attention (BMR, 2008). A follow-up survey in 2013 reported that young people have, on average, 4,000 tracks in their music library, with 2,800 being carried with them on their MP3 players (Bahanovich & Collopy, 2013). Also, there has also been a general shift reported in the use (and deference toward) received pronunciation in British English over the past decade or so (e.g., Wells, 1999). At the same time, there has been a corresponding acceptance of regional accents, such as in the media, with strong regional accents on television and film—including children's television. The linguistic cultural soundscape has changed and it may be that girls are more attuned perceptually to contemporary linguistic practices as they are more proficient at singing at an earlier age than boys (Welch et al., 2012), suggesting that—as a group—they engage more in this kind of activity than boys.

Consonants

Given the impact of sociocultural experiences on promoting gendered behavior in children (e.g., Karsten, 2003; Martin & Ruble, 2004), it is likely that both girls and boys enter the role of chorister with particular gender traits. Anecdotal evidence suggest that novice female choristers appear to be particularly feminine and less physical in their behavior, whereas boys have a tendency towards favoring physicality. As singing, arguably, is a highly physical activity, the amount of time needed by the director to shape choristers' sung products may be unequal between the sexes. For example, the various types of consonants often need more encouragement with girls in order to achieve the desired effect.

- Unvoiced consonants: Experience suggests that girls sing with naturally more sibilant non-voiced consonants ("t" and "s") and need to be encouraged (more often than boys, and with more insistence) to sing them shorter and with appropriate abdominal region breathing. Other unvoiced consonants ("p," "f," "th" as in "thirty," "ch," "sh," and "k") also need greater breath support. In contrast, once boys have the concept, they normally need less encouragement to deliver the physical actions.
- Voiced consonants: Constant reinforcement is needed to make sure that the resonating consonants (particularly "d," "g" as in "judge," "l," "ng," "th" as in "there," "v," and "z") are formed with appropriate breath support and resonance.

With reference to most consonants, it is generally a question of engaging the singers to enjoy the physical sensation of making the sounds and communicating the text, although this is not necessarily gender specific.

OTHER CONSIDERATIONS

Warming-up

The warm-up exercises that are used for the female choristers at Wells are almost identical to those for the male choristers. Girls, however, often need specific encouragement to use their abdominal region musculature rather more than boy choristers, as suggested above. Where aural exercises are included in the warm-up, girls can be slightly quicker than the boys in their responses and achievement of overall accuracy.

Sense of pitch

Craft knowledge suggests that a key element in the education of choristers is the development of a good sense of pitch. This can be fostered in a variety of ways. For example, many choir directors will play a chord or give a note at the beginning of a warm-up or rehearsal and continue to give notes frequently. This, arguably, appears to offer little by way of stimulation of an awareness of pitch among the choristers and may develop quickly into a form of constant spoon-feeding. An alternative successful approach is to request that a specific note be sung at the beginning of a specific warm-up or piece of repertoire. Experience suggests that a significant number of choristers will respond to the invitation and be able to sing the requested pitch correctly (both boys and girls). Another way in which a good sense of pitch can be nurtured is to use the piano as little as possible during a rehearsal or—in the cathedral—have notes given as infrequently as possible in order to stimulate the aural senses.

Sight reading

It may be an overgeneralization, but experience of working with both boys and girls of the same age range suggests that girls tend to sight-read pieces more quickly than boys (which is in line with a reported gender bias in general reading competency). In addition, directors of music who are colleagues from other cathedrals have often commented that boys seem to be more willing to attempt something and get it wrong, whereas girls may be more cautious. This may not be the case, however, if the group is made to feel comfortable with making mistakes as part of the learning process.

Repertoire

At Wells, there is no conscious distinction between the type of repertoire that the boys and girls sing. Given the right circumstances, both boy and girl choristers are equally capable of tackling demanding repertoire. At Wells, there may be a perception that the girl choristers often tackle more difficult repertoire, but this is simply because—with fewer services to sing—their rehearsal to performance ratio is greater than that of the boys, thus giving the girls more time to learn what is arguably more difficult repertoire.

In supporting two treble lines within one institution, there is the possibility that one group or the other will not sing some of the classics that one may expect to encounter as a chorister during their customary time in the choir from the ages of eight to 13. One might argue, however, that girl choristers—unlike boy choristers—may have the opportunity to sing some of these so-called classics when they are older. As such, the identity of a cathedral girls' choir may be partly formed through the singing of what might be viewed as more specialized repertoire.

Non-musical identity

The group identity of boy and girl choristers is not necessarily identical, despite the common role. This can be examined when an individual, small group, or even the whole group becomes upset by a particular external factor or occurrence within or without the choir. Such events appear to affect girl choristers and their performance more than it does the boys. An example of this might be a family death, which may induce an element of collective distress within a girls' choir, but would generally only affect an individual and perhaps a close friend within a boys' choir. Similarly, a school incident (e.g., playground fall-out) will often affect the girls' performance more than the boys.

Cathedral choristers across the UK are some of the few children, along with child actors, who undertake professional work and responsibilities. They are also acting as a team working within an historic and culturally important part of the UK's heritage, and it is therefore important that they look and feel professional. One example relates to personal appearance. For example, in shaping the visual identity of the female choristers at both Edinburgh (a mixed-voice treble line) and subsequently at Wells Cathedral (a separate girls' choir), the director required hair to be worn up (off the collar/ruff), and that no makeup or jewelry should be worn. This was unpopular in some circles in both institutions when it was first introduced, including the comment from one chorister parent that "the director is depriving the girls of their femininity." Nevertheless, it was important to remember that there was (and still is, in some quarters) considerable opposition to girls singing in cathedral choirs. As such, looking less professional than their male counterparts was considered an unnecessary reputational risk.

In a short space of time, in both institutions, the girls' parents, the congregation, and other observers subsequently expressed a liking for this visual identity and commented how much more professional the girls looked than some of their counterparts in other choral foundations. One of the most interesting changes of opinion was that of the girl choristers themselves who—quite early on—also agreed that they looked smarter and, therefore, reportedly felt more professional than their colleagues in other choirs. Thus, part of the issue of professional identity appears to be inextricably linked with pride in team appearance. In addition, the discipline underpinning of this consistency of collective uniformity is likely further to exemplify a serious team at work.

There are other factors in the construction of identity of girl choristers and, of course, attitudes vary from choir to choir. At Wells, the girls from the outset wanted to be treated exactly the same as the boy choristers. When the girls' choir was formed in 1994, the girls were asked what kind of robes they would like; the presumption by the cathedral authorities was that they would want something different from the boy choristers in order to mark them out—such as the tabard, as worn by girl choristers at Salisbury Cathedral. This proved not to be the case. The new girl choristers requested exactly the same robes as the boy choristers—the traditional cassock and surplice.

CONCLUDING COMMENTS

In summary, although there are likely to be both similarities and differences between individual singers, choirs, and director of music expectations, the past two decades in the United Kingdom have demonstrated that female choristers are at least as capable musically and vocally as their male counterparts. As such, they have been able to make a full contribution to ensuring the continuance and development of the choral tradition. Moreover, these two decades have seen a shift from a sense of girl choristers being a novelty to a presence that is much more mainstream, with the majority (n=33) of cathedrals (2014) now having girls' as well as boys' choirs, compared to a small minority who have continued with boys only (n=7), in addition to the continuance of the two mixed sex choirs.

Accordingly, despite the relative recency of girl choristers, at least in the modern era, both sexes appear here to stay in UK cathedrals. Foundations and directors need to continue to nurture girls' choirs and to give them a strong identity, while ensuring the continued support for their boys' choirs (which, some would argue, are in a more fragile state, at least in terms of recruitment in some parts of the United Kingdom). Cogent arguments need to be proffered to ensure that cathedral chapters (the cathedrals' decision making bodies) do not mix their treble lines on cost-cutting or ideological grounds, as this will likely weaken the distinctive contributions that each group can make to the quality of the musical repertoire that is being performed regularly. It would also reduce the overall number of children singing in the United Kingdom's cathedrals, which would be highly regrettable in the authors' view. Nevertheless, there is a lot more research to be undertaken on the nature and development of girls' choirs, including evaluation of appropriate generic and specific pedagogical methods for each sex, not least because the widespread introduction of girls' choirs has challenged the status quo and made more public the role of the cathedral chorister and their valuable professional contribution to the musical life.

NOTES

1. As far as we are aware, there has never been a strict policy regarding the balance between boys and girls at Manchester Cathedral. At the beginning of the academic year in 2014 (21 years after it became mixed) it should be noted that there were 11 girls and one boy.
2. Chetham's School of Music www.chethams.com
   - Elmhurst School of Dance www.elmhurstdance.co.uk
   - St Mary's Music School www.st-marys-music-school.co.uk
   - The Hammond School www.thehammondschool.co.uk
   - The Purcell School www.purcell-school.org
   - The Royal Ballet School www.royalballetschool.co.uk

- Tring Park School for the Performing Arts www.tringpark.com
- Wells Cathedral School www.wellscathedralschool.org
- Yehudi Menuhin School www.yehudimenuhinschool.co.uk

3. It is now a mixed adult choir.

4. The choir sings during school term times and at special festivals such as Christmas and Easter, and for two weeks in the summer, during the Edinburgh Festival. Often visiting choirs will be in residence at other times.

5. To reduce the weekly workload, the music from the Thursday Eucharist is nearly always repeated at the Sunday Eucharist.

6. There was a concern that boys would begin to leave the choir if the girls became the majority.

7. Of the five specialist music schools in the UK, just three act as choir schools to cathedrals. The other two specialist music schools—the Purcell School and the Yehudi Menuhin School—are "purely" specialist music schools.

8. The Vicars Choral, more commonly referred to in other cathedrals as "lay clerks," are the men who sing the alto, tenor, and bass parts of the choir. At Wells, they are made up of nine professional men and three choral scholars, who are normally postgraduate.

9. This organization of the chorister membership is often for practical reasons, as the choristers at Wells are formed from two different parts of the school, which are timetabled differently. The school has pupils from Nursery (aged three) until Sixth form (aged 18) and the choristers are drawn from across the Junior School and Senior School.

10. This is also the official retirement age for the boys at Wells, although a number of the boys have to take "early retirement" owing to voice change.

11. A Royal Peculiar is a parish or a church that is exempt from the jurisdiction of the diocese in which it lies and, therefore, not subject to the jurisdiction of the Bishop or Archdeacon. Instead, it is under the direct jurisdiction of the monarch.

12. For a history of the girl chorister see Mould, 2007, p. 76, pp. 257, and 267–270.

13. The Director of Music may be called Organist and Master of the Choristers, Organist and Master of the Music, Organist and Director of Music, Master of the Music, or something similar, depending on the choral foundation and the duties required.

14. The Assistant Director of Music may be called Assistant Organist, Sub Organist, or something similar, depending on the choral foundation and the duties required.

15. The acoustics in which a choir sings can have a fundamental effect on the vocal production if the choir trainer allows it to. For example, if one relies on a vast reverberant space to "aid" the singers, then there is a danger that they will not sing with a sound technique.

16. This includes the number and proficiency of singers on the alto, tenor, and bass lines, and also the type of organ used to accompany the choir: a smooth English romantic organ may encourage vocal production which is distinct from the sound which neoclassical organs (some of which can be overly aggressive) may encourage.

17. These discs are: Geoffrey Burgon, Wells Cathedral Choir, Matthew Owens (conductor) *Sacred Choral Works*—Hyperion Records CDH55421—recorded in 2006; David Bednall, Wells Cathedral Choir, Matthew Owens (conductor), *Hail, gladdening light and other choral works*—Regent Records REGCD247—recorded in 2006; and Gary Davison *Sacred Choral Music*—Regent Records, recorded in 2014 and released in 2015.

References

Bahanovich, D., & Collopy, D. (2013). *Music experience and behaviour in young people: Winter 2012–2013.* Bedford: Music and Entertainment Industries Research Group, University of Hertfordshire. https://musikwirtschaftsforschung.files.wordpress.com/2013/03/uk-music-survey-2013-research-report-final.pdf

British Music Rights. (2008). *Music experience and behavior in young people: Main findings and conclusions.* Bedford: Music and Entertainment Industries Research Group, University of Hertfordshire. http://www.songwriters.ca/ContentFiles/ContentPages/Documents/S.A.C.%20Proposal/Hertfordshire%20University%20Study%202008.pdf

Day, C. (2014). Cultural history and a singing style: "The English Cathedral Tradition." In G. F. Welch, D. M. Howard, & J. Nix (Ed.), *The Oxford Handbook of Singing.* New York: Oxford University Press. Published online, August 2014. http://www.oxfordhandbooks.com/view/10.1093/oxfordhb/9780199660773.001.0001/oxfordhb-9780199660773-e-021?rskey=iip5Dy&result=1

Gackle, L. (2014). Adolescent girls' singing development. In G. F. Welch, D. M. Howard, & J. Nix (Ed.), *The Oxford Handbook of Singing.* New York: Oxford University Press. Published on line, August 2014. http://www.oxfordhandbooks.com/view/10.1093/oxfordhb/9780199660773.001.0001/oxfordhb-9780199660773-e-22?rskey=oylgwt&result=1

Howard, D. M., Barlow, C., Szymanski, J., & Welch, G. F. (2001). Vocal production and listener perception of trained English cathedral girl and boy choristers. *Bulletin of the Council for Research in Music Education, 147,* 81–86.

Howard, D. M., Szymanski, J., & Welch, G. F. (2002). Listeners' perception of English cathedral girl and boy choristers. *Music Perception, 20*(1), 35–49.

Howard, D. M., & Welch, G. F. (2002). Female chorister development: a longitudinal study at Wells, UK. *Bulletin of the Council for Research in Music Education, 153*(15), 63–70.

Karsten. L. (2003). Children's use of public space: The gendered world of the playground. *Childhood, 10*(4), 457–473. doi: 10.1177/0907568203104005

Kent, R. D., & Vorperian, H. K. (1995). Development of the craniofacial–oral–laryngeal anatomy: A review. *Journal of Medical Speech–Language Pathology, 3*(3), 145–190.

Logan, S., & Johnston, R. (2009). Gender differences in reading ability and attitudes: Examining where these differences lie. *Journal of Research in Reading, 32*(2), 199–214.

Martin, C., & Ruble, D. (2004). Children's search for gender cues: Cognitive perspectives on gender development. *Current Directions in Psychological Science, 13*(2), 67–70. doi: 10.1111/j.0963-7214.2004.00276.x

McAllister, A., & Sjölander, P. (2013). Children's voice and voice disorders. *Seminars in Speech and Language, 34*(2), 71–79.

Mecke, A.-C., & Sundberg, J. (2010). Gender differences in children's singing voices: Acoustic analyses and results of a listening test. *Journal of the Acoustical Society of America, 127*(5), 3223–3231. doi: 10.1121/1.3372730

Mould, A. (2007). *The English chorister: A history.* London: Hambledon Continuum.

Sataloff, R. T. (2000). Vocal aging and its medical implications: What singing teachers should know. Part 1. *Journal of Singing, 57*(1), 29–34.

Saunders, J., Papageorgi, I., Himonides, E., Rinta, T., & Welch, G. F. (2011). *Researching the impact of the national singing programme "Sing Up" in England: Diverse approaches to successful singing in primary settings.* London: International Music Education Research Centre, Institute of Education.

Sergeant, D. C., Sjölander P. J., & Welch, G. F. (2005). Listeners' identification of gender differences in children's singing. *Research Studies in Music Education*, 24(1), 28–39.

Sergeant, D. C., & Welch, G. F. (1997). Perceived similarities and differences in the singing of trained children's choirs. *Choir Schools Today*, 11, 9–10.

Sergeant, D. C., & Welch, G. F. (2008). Age-related changes in long-term average spectra of children's voices. *Journal of Voice*, 22(6), 658–670.

Sergeant, D. C., & Welch, G. F. (2009). Gender differences in long-term average spectra of children's singing voices. *Journal of Voice*, 23(3), 319–336.

Small, C. (1999). Musicking—the meaning of performing and listening: A lecture. *Music Education Research*, 1(1), 9–21.

Stathopoulos, E. T., and Sapienza, C. M. (1997). Developmental changes in laryngeal and respiratory function with variations in sound pressure level. *Journal of Speech, Language, and Hearing Research*, 40(3), 595–614.

Titze, I. R. (1994). *Principles of voice production*. Englewood Cliffs, NJ: Prentice-Hall.

Welch, G. F. (2006). Singing and Vocal Development. In G. McPherson (Ed.), *The child as musician: A handbook of musical development* (pp. 311–329). New York: Oxford University Press.

Welch, G. F. (2011). Culture and gender in a cathedral music context: An activity theory exploration. In M. Barrett (Ed.), *A cultural psychology of music education* (pp. 225–258). New York: Oxford University Press.

Welch, G. F., Himonides, E., Saunders, J., Papageorgi, et al. (2010). *Researching the impact of the National Singing Programme "Sing Up" in England: Main findings from the first three years (2007–2010). Children's singing development, self-concept and sense of social inclusion.* London: International Music Education Research Centre, University of London, Institute of Education.

Welch, G. F., Himonides, E., Saunders, J., et al. (forthcoming). Children's singing behaviour and development in the context of *Sing Up*, a national programme in England.

Welch, G. F., Himonides, E., Saunders, J., et al. (2009). *Researching the second year of the National Singing Programme in England: An ongoing impact evaluation of children's singing behaviour and identity.* London: International Music Education Research Centre, University of London, Institute of Education.

Welch, G. F., & Howard, D. (2002). Gendered voice in the cathedral choir. *Psychology of Music*, 30(1), 102–120.

Welch, G. F., Saunders, J., Papageorgi, I., & Himonides, E. (2012). Sex, gender and singing development: Making a positive difference to boys' singing through a national programme in England. In S. Harrison, G. F. Welch, & A. Adler (Eds.), *Perspectives on Males and Singing* (pp. 37–54). New York: Springer.

Wells, J. C. (1999). British English pronunciation preferences: a changing scene. *Journal of the International Phonetic Association*, 29(1): 33–50.

White, P. J. (1999). Formant frequency analysis of children's spoken and sung vowels using sweeping fundamental frequency production. *Journal of Voice*, 13(4), 570–582.

CHAPTER 10

COLLABORATION AND MEANING MAKING IN THE WOMEN'S CHORAL REHEARSAL

NANA WOLFE-HILL

FROM TERMS TO CONCEPTS

THE words *feminist* and *feminism* provoke wide-ranging emotional and intellectual responses—both positive and negative. Many individuals align themselves with tenets of feminism (e.g., equal rights), even though they would not label themselves as feminist (Redfern & Aune, 2010). This chapter provides an opportunity for readers to move beyond the common polarized reactions to these terms and engage thoughtfully with the concepts *behind* the terms. The material and research within this chapter have affected me personally, challenged my thinking, and offered suggestions for new ways of rehearsing and being. Listening to the voices of women about their experiences has been humbling and rewarding in my journey as a conductor and teacher.

INTRODUCTION

In conjunction with the feminist movement from the 1960s through the 1990s, some educators fused aspects of feminist theory and gender research with pedagogical approaches in the classroom.[1] Lamb, Dolloff, and Howe (2002) expound:

> The development of feminist theory and gender research has resulted in an expansion in our conceptions of what "matters" in school and university classrooms. What

matters is not only the musical content of our programs but our pedagogy—how we interact musically and personally with our students, the way we design our musical environments to be inclusive of and to provide opportunities for all students. (p. 660)

The impact of the values of feminism on education developed into *feminist pedagogy*, which explores an inclusive and empowering manner of teaching.

This chapter focuses on what matters—pedagogy and its influence on singers. An overview of the inception of feminist pedagogy and its main tenets lays the groundwork for a qualitative research case study with Professor Whitley's collegiate women's choir. Professor Whitley was selected for this study because she is a nationally renowned conductor whose rehearsal approaches align with the values of feminist pedagogy. Professor Whitley is a senior level faculty member at a Research 1 university in the United States. Under her direction, the women's choir has become one of the premier choirs at the university and has been featured at state, regional, and national ACDA conventions. The study illustrates nontraditional rehearsal methods rooted in values of feminism and it demonstrates ways in which those methods affect female singers as individuals and musicians. The methods presented are collaborative in nature: inviting the thoughts and opinions of singers through discussion, inviting singer decision making through sound, and giving singers opportunities to reflect upon multiple meanings and making meaning. A substantive portion of this chapter's content is derived from a previous research project, which follows the guidelines set up by the Institutional Review Board pertaining to the protection of research participant identity (Wolfe, 2015). Consequently, the names of the research participants are pseudonyms.

Feminist Pedagogy

The inception of feminist pedagogy

The feminist movement advocates for equal rights for all people with particular support for marginalized populations (e.g., women); respects myriad differences among people, such as gender, sex, sexual orientation and identity, race, ethnicity, social class, religion, exceptionalities, and age; and welcomes varied and even conflicting voices. Feminist pedagogy emerged from these values of the feminist movement and their application in education. Several works of literature were influential in the inception of feminist pedagogy (Belenky, Clinchy, Goldberger, & Tarule, 1986; Gilligan, 1982/1993; Noddings, 1984). Previous to the publication of these works, women and feminine qualities were often excluded in research and in theoretical discourse. Because of their absence in preceding research and theory, works by Belenky, Clinchy, Goldberger, and Tarule (1986), Gilligan (1982/1993), and Noddings (1984) focus on women and/or feminine qualities. Men, however, are not excluded: Some men develop, learn, and function in the ways presented in these seminal works, which may differ from conclusions found in previous research and theories (Gilligan, 1982/1993, p. xiii; 2011, p. 25). In addition, women do not necessarily develop, learn, and function in the same way as one another. Groundbreaking research by authors such as Belenky and Gilligan challenges former long-standing perspectives and reveals various ways of development and learning for both men and women. For the purposes of this chapter, I give a brief overview of the results of research by Belenky et al. that pertain to teaching approaches in the classroom (1986).

Women's Ways of Knowing presents the results of a qualitative research study conducted by four women psychologists who interviewed 135 female students (high school, college, or recent alumnae) and 45 mothers from various social classes and races (Belenky et al., 1986). The study explored "how women's self-concepts and ways of knowing are intertwined" and "how women struggle to claim the power of their own minds" (p. 3). In addition, they examined how the institutions of the family and the school "promote and hinder women's development" (p. 4). Aspects of the Belenky et al. study particularly pertinent to the present case study addressed the inclusion of personal experience in learning, the midwife-teacher model, and connectedness within the learning process.

Belenky et al. (1986) stated, "Most of the women we interviewed were drawn to the sort of knowledge that emerges from firsthand observation" (p. 200), even though the majority of their institutional education emphasized abstract or out-of-context learning. Although many of the women did not oppose an abstract approach to learning, they preferred to "start from personal experience" (p. 202) and to "make meaning of their experiences" (p. 203). The participants named out-of-school learning as the most powerful in their lives (p. 200), but the most empowering courses they attended helped them "translate their ideas . . . [from] private experience into a shared public language" (p. 203). Giving women time to explore the connections between firsthand experiences and constructing new knowledge may be a more beneficial educational approach for women (p. 229).

Most of the research participants "lacked confidence" in themselves as thinkers (Belenky et al., 1986, p. 193). This struggle, according to the study, was directly related to suppressing one's thoughts and ideas. The authors presented a new model of teaching called the midwife-teacher model that addressed this struggle:

> Many women expressed . . . a belief that they possessed latent knowledge. The kind of teacher they praised and the kind for which they yearned was one who would help them articulate and expand their latent knowledge: a midwife-teacher. Midwife-teachers are the opposite of banker-teachers. While the bankers deposit knowledge in the learner's head, the midwives draw it out. They assist the students in giving birth to their own ideas, in making their own tacit knowledge explicit and elaborating it . . . They support their students' thinking but they do not do the students' thinking for them or expect the students to think as they do. (pp. 217–218)

The midwife-teacher model opposes the banker-teacher model because it encourages students to voice and develop their own ideas, rather than simply giving ideas to students.[2]

The midwife-teacher model encourages dialogue and community within the classroom, which can result in connectedness through shared knowledge construction. In community, rather than a hierarchy, "people get to know each other. They do not act as representatives of positions or as occupants of roles but as individuals with particular styles of thinking" (Belenky et al., 1986, p. 221). Teachers and students alike, "engage in the process of thinking, and they talk out what they are thinking in a public dialogue" (p. 219). Watching professors solve and fail to solve problems within a shared knowledge construction process gives the research participants healthy "models of thinking as a human, imperfect, and attainable activity" (p. 217).

Belenky et al. (1986) purported that traditional education "do[es] not adequately serve the needs of women" (p. 4). They concluded that,

> [E]ducators can help women develop their own authentic voices if they emphasize connection over separation, understanding and acceptance over assessment, and collaboration over debate; if they accord respect to and allow time for the knowledge that emerges from firsthand experience; if instead of imposing their own expectations and arbitrary requirements, they encourage students to evolve their own patterns of work based on the problems they are pursuing. (p. 229)

Based on the results of their study, Belenky et al. (1986) illustrated how some women may benefit from classrooms that are less hierarchical than the traditional model. Professors within these classrooms incorporate nonhegemonic pedagogical approaches, such as the inclusion of personal experience in learning, the opportunity to voice and develop student ideas, and co-constructing knowledge with teachers and students through dialogue. The results of this study by Belenky et al. (1986) align with values of feminist pedagogy.

Characteristics of feminist pedagogy

Feminist pedagogy is often misconstrued as "curriculum reform, analysis of girls' and women's experiences in educational environments, teaching about women, teaching feminist ideas, and teaching done by self-identified feminists" (Crabtree, Sapp, & Licona, 2009, p. 2). Feminist pedagogy includes advocacy for women *and* promotes the inclusion and liberation of all people—particularly those who are marginalized. In addition, feminist pedagogues move toward the following five aspects in praxis: equalization of power, collaboration, affective learning, inclusiveness of diversity, and social responsibility (Crabtree et al., 2009; Kimmel, 1999; Shrewsbury, 1997). Inclusion of diversity and social justice are not directly studied in this case study or included in this chapter: Such topics are addressed in the choral music profession through publications pertaining to repertoire selection (Holt & Jordan, 2008; Wahl, 2009) and community engagement (Saltzman Romey, Sweet, & Wanyama, 2009).

Equalization of power

Moving toward an equalization of power counteracts the hierarchical construct of the teacher-dominated classroom and teacher-student relationship by empowering each individual to express his or her voice (Shrewsbury, 1997, p. 168–169). Rather than the teacher being treated as the only person that brings knowledge to the classroom, each individual, student and teacher alike, is considered knowledgeable based on the intellectual and experiential insights they bring. The teacher invites students to share their voices to enhance the learning of all present (including the teacher) and encourage the development of students as individuals. All persons are invited to talk and listen to one another, to express their inner selves, and to honor each individual. This respectful relating leads to collaboration.

Collaboration

Collaboration is multidimensional in the feminist classroom, involving (but not limited to) curriculum, method, and community. The presumed responsibility of the teacher is to create, compile, and/or organize the curriculum of a course. In contrast, feminist pedagogues invite "students to participate in decisions about the content and process of the class, asking for feedback about the class and teaching methods throughout the course, and co-teaching the course" (Kimmel, 1999, p. 65). Students are given greater levels of involvement and responsibility regarding almost all aspects of the course. As a result, they use high-level cognitive skills and "develop skills of planning, negotiating, evaluating, and decision making" (Shrewsbury, 1997, p. 169). Being involved in a course to this degree not only engages students intellectually, but also creates a space for relationships to develop among students and between student and teacher. This sense of "connectedness" (Shrewsbury, 1997, p. 171) caused by collaborative decision making and feedback, combined with the autonomy of each person sharing their voice, inspires community in the classroom.

Inclusion of affective learning

At a feminist practice conference in 1994, a pedagogical group decided on the major tenets of feminist pedagogy and agreed that "emotions are central to learning" (Kimmel, 1999, p. 67). Kimmel stated that, "Inclusion of the affective domain is part of a student-centered education movement that focuses on student development as part of the instructional mandate" (p. 67). Intellectual and emotional development are intertwined. To separate them in the classroom negates a part of the student. Since feminist "teachers demonstrate sincere concern for their students as people and as learners," they seek to support students as whole individuals (Crabtree et al., 2009, p. 4–5). Fostering the integrity of the student—the person inside and outside of the course, the emotional and cognitive growth, the individuality and membership of a team—allows students to be "wholehearted" learners in the classroom (hooks, 1994, p. 193).

Seeking to define feminist pedagogy

At its core, feminist pedagogy is a "movement against hegemonic educational practices that . . . reproduce an oppressively gendered, classed, racialized, and androcentric social order" (Crabtree et al., 2009, p. 1). Feminist pedagogues seek the wholehearted development of individuals through learning environments that are "cooperative rather than competitive, attentive to student experiences, and concerned with the personal and relational aims and sources of knowledge" (Maher & Tetreault, 1992, p. 58). Feminist pedagogy is simultaneously caring, holistic, inclusive, engaging, empowering, and liberating for all individuals.

Based on the extensive qualitative research study by Belenky et al. (1986), I purport that incorporating the values of feminist pedagogy into the women's choral rehearsal could benefit women singers as individuals and musicians. These values challenge traditional hegemonic methods that may not serve female singers well (Koza, 1994, p. 74). With the exception of O'Toole's dissertation (1994), I have not found any other studies that examine the effects of the incorporation of the values of feminist pedagogy into the choral rehearsal. Additional research is needed.

CASE STUDY OVERVIEW: FEMINIST PEDAGOGY IN THE WOMEN'S CHORAL REHEARSAL

While researching feminist pedagogy, I crossed paths with two conductors who were former students of Professor Whitley. I shared the concepts of my research with them and they both felt that Professor Whitley's teaching reflects feminist pedagogy. They encouraged me to contact her. When I met with Professor Whitley, she and I confirmed that her philosophy and methods align with feminist pedagogy. As a result, she agreed for her collegiate Women's Ensemble to be the case study site.

The fieldwork for the study consisted of two 80-minute rehearsal observations; one three-hour interview with Professor Whitley; and nine 80-minute individual interviews with undergraduate and graduate female singers with varying musical experience (non-music and music majors). The initial data collection totaled 18 hours.[3] The singers were contacted via an online survey forwarded to them by Professor Whitley's graduate assistant (Wolfe, 2015, Appendix C). The survey determined if singers were experts who had participated in previous choirs and could compare their experience in Women's Ensemble with past experiences. 12 singers that completed the survey were considered experts and invited to participate. Of the 12, nine women responded to the invitation: Alicia, Anna, Delaney, Dorothy, Hannah, Lilia, Natalia, Maeve, and Sarafina. I hired someone unrelated to the research participants to transcribe the interviews in which pseudonyms were used. I reviewed each transcription with the recording, edited the transcriptions for accuracy, coded each portion of the transcriptions and rehearsal observations, and organized the data based on themes.[4]

Collaboration and meaning-making were two themes evident throughout each singer interview and are discussed in this chapter. The conductor's perspective of her philosophy and methods are presented, followed by the singers' perspectives of methods and selected common effects of those methods on the singers.

Collaboration in the choral rehearsal: conductor perspective

Conductor philosophy

> Professor Whitley: In broad strokes, I want students to see me as approachable. I want them to know that I am there to collaborate and to facilitate. I am not there to tell them how to do it. I want them to be able to leverage their own knowledges and experiences and grow that in the context of community—the idea that corporate expertise is always stronger than any single person's.

At the heart of Professor Whitley's philosophy is the belief that singers in the choir are knowledgeable and individually valuable. Knowledge is defined in a broad sense: Regardless of a singer's musical expertise, students are considered knowledgeable through their various talents, their intellectual pursuits, and life experiences.[5] Rather than a classroom focused on the conductor sharing his/her knowledge and creating the music based on the conductor's interpretation alone, Professor Whitley invites singers to creatively engage in the music-making process and actively share their various ways of knowing. This approach does not negate the knowledge or preparation of the conductor. Professor Whitley enters the rehearsal with a thorough preparation of the score, her conducting gesture, the rehearsal procedure, etc. In addition, she approaches the music-making process in ways that give students opportunities to lead, to make their own musical choices, and to share their thoughts about the music-making process.

This philosophy manifests in Professor Whitley's rehearsal through myriad approaches:

- rehearsing and performing selected repertoire without a conductor;
- ensemble rehearsal formations that decenter the conductor;
- discussing the reasoning behind various conductor decisions (e.g., soloist selection and voice placement);
- collectively deciding on criteria for selecting soloists and voting on soloist selection;
- encouraging students to lead portions of the rehearsal;
- singing in the choir when graduate students conduct;
- initiating discussion regarding interpretation and meaning of the music by inviting the thoughts and opinions of the singers; and
- asking thought-provoking questions to help students make musical decisions (Wolfe, 2015, p. 102).

Each of the listed approaches influences singers positively and aligns with feminist pedagogy. The last two approaches—initiating discussion by inviting the thoughts and opinions of singers and asking thought-provoking questions to help students make musical decisions—were the methods most thoroughly discussed by the interviewees and, therefore, are examined in this chapter.

Conductor overview of method

PROFESSOR WHITLEY: What if you are presented with a student who says, "Why are we singing that phrase in that way because to me it looks like actually this is an intensity in the composition, not a retreat?" . . . what if, in fact, we don't take a defensive posture and [instead] say, "Let's try it that way. Let's sing it that way. What do we think about that?" Am I willing as a teacher to shift my view because of the input of an ensemble member? I hope so. And that is a very different thing, isn't it, than what we think of as a democratic classroom? So the idea that students vote on where the breath happens, that is a misunderstanding, I think, of an inclusive classroom that allows for the views of students to be expressed.

NANA: [How do you] help create that inclusive environment?

PROFESSOR WHITLEY: You have to provide that opening for them to participate, so there has to be an invitation. That can be a direct invitation in the form of a question. It can be an indirect invitation, which is to say that they know that their thoughts are valued and I will hear them. If they put their hand up, they will be recognized. And that informal invitation comes over a period of time because you have to set up a situation of safety and trust in order for that to happen.

Professor Whitley described rehearsal collaboration as inclusive, where students' thoughts and ideas are welcomed, heard, and considered in the music-making process. She differentiates this inclusive environment from a democratic environment. A democratic environment gives each participant the opportunity to vote on every decision. In a choral rehearsal setting, an exclusively democratic approach could prove to be inefficient and laborious. Contrastingly, an inclusive environment intentionally invites students to participate more fully in the music-making process. Through thought-provoking questions, students are invited to discuss musical ideas and think about the music more deeply rather than simply respond to what they see in a conducting gesture, what they are verbally told by the conductor, and/or what they see in the musical score.

Collaboration in the choral rehearsal: student perspective

Method 1: Collaboration through inviting discussion. Each interviewed singer described the collaborative process through discussion within the rehearsal. Dorothy and Lilia recounted specific examples of these conductor-initiated conversations:

DOROTHY: [Professor Whitley] will say, "Let's try this sound with this piece of music," or maybe "Let's try this or maybe I like that better." So, it is like she has that structured, formulated plan of what she wants it to sound like, but it is almost like she is still playing devil's advocate in her mind . . . And she will even ask us, "Do you like that sound better? Good. Me too." So it is a collaborative environment. Yes, she is leading, but she is also asking our input as well.

LILIA: A lot of times she asks us for opinions about, "Okay, how should this sound and why?" . . . There is always that sense of democracy. A lot of times we make musical decisions together . . .

Professor Whitley has a clear sense of her musical options as a conductor and leans toward her preferred interpretive decisions. Nevertheless, she includes the singers in the interpretive process by inviting their input. Dorothy described an experimentation process in rehearsal. Professor Whitley has a rehearsal plan, but allows time for the ensemble to sing portions of the music multiple ways asking for feedback. Dorothy and Lilia both gave a picture of a conductor who knows what "she wants," but still felt they were included in a process where some musical decisions were made "together." Lilia believed the process had a *sense* of democracy. Although it is not a true democracy, these descriptions point toward a collaborative environment where singers feel included in making musical decisions.

Method 2: Collaboration through inviting decision making through sound. Asking thought-provoking questions encouraged students to make their own musical decisions. Answers to these questions were evidenced by a change in singing. Natalia described an example of a question that provoked students to think about the musical composition in a different way and respond through singing:

NATALIA: We will sing it once and then she says, "Now can you look in this section and see where your color may change?" And then she just has us do it. So, it is involving us almost entirely . . . It is just [like] saying, "Use your musicianship, please."

Professor Whitley posed a question asking about where an appropriate color change should occur based on the composition. She gave the singers an opportunity to choose and then had them sing again. To Natalia, it was a reminder to use her "musicianship" and an opportunity to share her thoughts through her singing.

I observed this pedagogical approach multiple times throughout each rehearsal. Below is one example:

Professor Whitley said, "Think through this section. Are [the phrases] all equal? We will sing through it and be ready to answer that question after we sing." They sang through to the end. "Very nicely done. How many measures comprise a phrase, 2 or 4?" Many singers answered "4." "So, what's going to help you know how to sing this section?" A few students responded. "How about harmony? Texture? Where you are in your range? . . . Let's sing again and change it with those things in mind."

She asked questions to help the singers engage with the composition at a deep level, but did not dictate for the singers how they should interpret the music. Rather than giving them specific verbal direction, she asked singers to think about aspects of the composition and how that could affect their sound. This approach invited the singers to be more thoughtful about the music and allowed them the freedom to make their own musical decisions based on the composition.

Impact of collaborative methods on singers

Each singer experienced positive outcomes on her musicianship resulting from rehearsal approaches that invite discussion and decision making through sound. The common effects illustrated in this chapter are increased mental engagement, confidence in one's abilities, ownership of the musical product, and increased musicianship.

Increased mental engagement

Anna, Dorothy, Natalia, and Sarafina described an increased mental engagement with the music after thought-provoking questions were posed in rehearsal. Dorothy described an increased sense of mental engagement in general terms: She said, "[Collaboration] makes me think more about how music can be performed in different way." In the following examples, Anna expressed a greater understanding of the music, while Natalia and Sarafina exemplified heightened creativity.

> NANA: How does [being allowed to have an opinion] make you feel?
> ANNA: I like it a lot better "cuz it helps me understand things better because then I actually get it rather than memorizing something."
> NATALIA: And when she says that it makes me realize, "Okay, switch your brain back on. You are a talented musician. What choices would you make in this piece?"
> SARAFINA: And she will many times say, "So, this word here, how can we color this differently?" And then we make a musical choice together and I think that making musical choices is a right brain activity. Instead of saying, "This note could really use some vibrato. Sing more vibrato here. This note could be straight, just sing this note straight," [Professor Whitley says something like,] "What do you think the color is on the word serene? . . . Sing it!"

Anna felt that her understanding of the music increased when she was asked her opinion. Simply memorizing a response or doing what she was told did not give her understanding. Having an opportunity to choose helped her get it. When Professor Whitley asked questions, Natalia was reminded to think critically about the music and sing with intention. This interaction helped bring her musicianship from a posture of going through the motions of learning the notes to creating expressive music. Sarafina delineated the difference between the effects of a conductor telling singers what to do versus a conductor inviting singers' choices in the music-making process. She experienced the use of primarily left-brain activity when being told by a conductor what/how to sing. In contrast, when she was asked a question that invited her to make a decision and sparked her imagination, her whole mind was fully engaged. With all four women, the inclusive decision-making process produced mental engagement through opportunities to make decisions, enhanced understanding of the music, and/or imaginative creativity.

Confidence

The collaborative and inclusive environment of Women's Ensemble gave Alicia, Delaney, and Lilia a sense of confidence.

> ALICIA: Whenever [Professor Whitley said], "I could not decide if I want this cut off here." or "Here, can we please sing it both ways?" as a conductor, I feel relieved . . . It is nice to know I have room to experiment with that before I make the decision because I feel that the perfectionist in me says that you need to make a decision now so you look prepared in front of people.
>
> DELANEY: It has brought up my confidence as a musician especially because I am so new. I don't really have very much experience, so it is nice to still be respected and know that I can make my choices . . . That really boosted my confidence and it helps me feel that I belong here and this is what I am born to do.
>
> NANA: What has that [collaborative] process taught you about your own intuition, your own thoughts, your own musicianship?
>
> LILIA: To trust it. I think that people don't realize that their creative instincts are usually valuable. Even if it is different from someone else's . . . that doesn't mean that it is wrong . . . I think that we probably all feel like really good musicians in her choir because she wants us to make decisions and she wants us to do what we think we should do with the sound.

Although Alicia did not use the word "confidence," I believe the meaning of her statement points toward confidence. For Alicia, seeing Professor Whitley experiment in rehearsal gave her confidence to experiment within her own rehearsals, rather than feeling the need to be prepared with all of the right answers. She believed this freedom counteracted her struggle with perfectionism. For Delaney, having the opportunity to make decisions and share her thoughts (regardless of her level of experience) made her feel respected and boosted her confidence. In addition, it gave her a sense of belonging and assurance in her career path. Because Professor Whitley asked for her thoughts, Lilia felt her thoughts were valuable. The freedom to make creative choices gave Lilia the opportunity to trust her own musicianship. Her descriptions of trusting her musicianship and feeling like a good musician implied her sense of confidence grew from the collaborative process in Women's Ensemble. The confidence that Alicia, Delaney, and Lilia have gained stemmed from experiencing a process that incorporated the freedom of choice in music-making, from making musical choices of their own, and from feeling that their choices and opinions are valued.

Ownership

Delaney, Dorothy, and Natalia spoke of taking ownership in rehearsal through making their own musical choices:

> DELANEY: . . . a lot of times when you are a musician you just listen to the conductor, and the conductor is right. They are always going to be right. But when she asks <u>you</u> how to do it right, you think, "What can I do to make it better?"

DOROTHY: [Professor Whitley] asked the choir, "How should this sound? What do you want the audience to be feeling here? . . . What do you think it should sound like?" So again, making it a more collaborative, more empowering environment, ownership for the choir.

NATALIA: It makes me feel that your input into what this choir is doing is very important . . . So it does give you a sense of ownership.

Delaney described how asking questions of the singers moved the responsibility of the music-making from the conductor to the singers. She now thinks about how "I" can make it better. Dorothy saw that specifically asking for singers' thoughts was empowering and ownership-giving for the choir. Natalia felt that she was given a sense of ownership when her input in musical decision making was invited and valued. Giving students opportunities to make music-making decisions empowered them to take ownership of the musical process and product.

Increased musicianship

Among other research participants, Anna, Dorothy, Hannah, and Sarafina talked about the freedom to make their own choices within Women's Ensemble. They connect the act of individual decision making with their growth in musicianship.

NANA: [W]hat teaching approaches do you feel have influenced you most as a musician?

ANNA: One would definitely be Professor Whitley's way of just letting us come to our own conclusion about how we want to let it sound.

NANA: How does that process influence you as a musician?

DOROTHY: Makes me think more about how music can be performed in different ways and that there is not one right answer . . . I am able to make decisions as a musician . . . in that it is not just one right way.

HANNAH: I think the amount of trust that is in the way Professor Whitley teaches helps me grow as a musician on my own versus [in] previous choirs they plot out everything they want you to do . . . I think to make those decisions on your own is really when you are becoming more of a musician.

SARAFINA: She gives you room to explore and make corrections on your own without being nit-picky . . . she lets you be a musician . . . She has the confidence that you are there to do your job.

These four women expressed the importance of being able to make individual musical choices as a member of an ensemble. Anna and Sarafina took ownership of their music-making by drawing conclusions or making corrections on their own. Dorothy described how having a choice helped her think about her musical options. Hannah described how this collaborative process was different from her previous choirs where she was told what to do and she did it. In Women's Ensemble, she connected more to the music because she was making decisions and, as a result, was becoming more of a musician. Having a choice in rehearsal combined with feeling trusted to make good musical decisions by the director positively influenced each of the singers as musicians.

Multiple meanings and meaning making: conductor perspective

Conductor philosophy

Professor Whitley described the exploration of the intertwining meaning of text and music as a vehicle to understand others: in history, in other cultures, and from various backgrounds. It was a way to understand oneself in context of others, rather than as separate individuals. It was a path, in Professor Whitley's words, to learn respect for difference:

> I think for them to understand that singing is a way that they understand themselves in the world is really important. You know, when they sing something very unfamiliar to them, if set up in the right way, they can be very reflective about the fact that they don't really know anything about that world. I think, it teaches them a process for respect, for being respectful of differences. It is an ongoing process that says, "Here are my experiences, here are my experiences that are very different. How do I fit into this? Do I fit into it?"

This philosophy reiterated the aspect of feminist pedagogy that encouraged activism in the world. I see it as the first steps towards social justice—becoming aware of different groups or peoples and respecting those differences. When exploring these differences and meanings, singers are given the opportunities to become aware of their own thoughts and perspectives contextually.

Conductor overview of method

Professor Whitley believed it is important to draw attention continually to the interpretation of the relationship between text and music within the rehearsal in order for personal connections to occur:

> [I]n an ongoing way, you have to connect the text to music over and over again . . . [w]e have to discuss what all those possibilities could be. We often come up with more than one view about what text could mean and I think that is really a positive and healthy thing actually. So, let's look at this range of possibilities and as the individual singer you are going to express the one that makes the most sense to you. It does not matter if people have different views because what comes out is thoughtful.

Professor Whitley encouraged the exploration of multiple meanings. Among these various meanings, students had opportunities to make individual connections with the text and chose which of the multiple meanings made the most sense to them. Singers who were mentally and emotionally engaged with the music, as a result, were thoughtful in their singing.

Multiple meanings and meaning making: student perspective

The following excerpts display various ways in which students are given opportunities to connect with the meanings of the text and music.

> After reading [through the text and program notes in the score], Professor Whitley said, "Why does the pianist have to play that repetitive note so much [she sings it]? I am going to have you show the text with your bodies . . . They all pointed to East, West, North, South, as in the text. Professor Whitley asked, "What do we create? Balance, symmetry, the circle of life. What could that repetitive G mean with that image in mind?"
>
> SINGER: "I learned in my Asian studies class that Om is the center."
>
> PROFESSOR WHITLEY: "I love it when we have cross-class connections! Will you go, 'Om'?" [All the women chanted, "Om."] It's like a meditation bell. This is the same way she grows this composition. The phrasing is not traditional. Why are some phrases long and some short?"
>
> ANOTHER SINGER: "We read that it was like a dance. Some movement is longer and some shorter. It reflects movement."
>
> ANOTHER SINGER: "In Buddhism, they believe that you are reincarnated until you reach Nirvana. The section where we escalate could be the end of life. The one where you soar, you finally reach it." [All exploded in affirming comments and cheering.]

Through questions, Professor Whitley invited the students to make connections with a culture and tradition that may not be their own. By opening up the discussion to the singers (as opposed to telling them the meaning the conductor thought of), students created connections with various meanings. Realizations regarding the meaning(s) of the composition by students caused excitement within the ensemble.

Lilia compares her experience in Women's Ensemble with her past experiences:

> LILIA: I would say for 90% of the music we do in Women's Ensemble, we know exactly what it is about or where it came from . . . Not just because we are being told how to sing it, but we relate it to something and I think that all choirs do that somewhat but we are very thorough about it in Women's Ensemble . . . Sometimes she will just give us a little bit of a thought prompt like, "Can you think about this or this when you are singing this?' Or she will say, "What does that mean to you?" Or she will just bring our attention to the text and the musical meanings of different parts. And sometimes when we make certain musical decisions, we really pick a piece apart and analyze it. I think, "Oh my gosh . . . I wish we could tell the audience everything that we have thought about and all the musical decisions because I think that would will help them connect to it more too."

Lilia said that 90% of the time in Women's Ensemble, they relate it to something. This in-depth reflection was different than what she had experienced in previous choirs. From her examples of questions that follow this statement, it seems that this relating through thought-provoking questions helped instigate meaning making for her. These connections and decision-making processes were exciting to Lilia: She wanted to share them with the audience, so that they could connect in the same way.

Impact of exploring multiple meanings and meaning making on singers

Self-expression, improved performance experiences, and relationships with and understanding others were three affirmative benefits of exploring multiple meanings and meaning-making in the rehearsal for the interviewed women.

Self-expression

In their interviews, Alicia, Delaney, and Sarafina shared personal and difficult experiences in their lives. They described how exploring the meanings of music gave them opportunities to express those intimate parts of themselves:

> ALICIA: There is a song called "The Kiss" and I think it is about somebody's kiss not being as great as [they] had hoped for . . . Professor Whitley said, "Maybe you had a great first kiss, but maybe it doesn't have to be a kiss. Maybe you have had something in your life that you really hoped would have been great and it ended up just being a huge disappointment." All of this hung around my wedding. I mean, it's a happy day. I look back on it, but I can never look at those pictures without thinking of the pain . . . as soon as she said it, I thought, "Oh great! I have it! And every time I sang that song, there was emotional connection there."

In other portions of the interview, Alicia shares certain aspects of the events surrounding her wedding that were heartbreaking and disappointing. After Professor Whitley asks a question to help the students personally connect to the meaning of the music, Alicia is able to connect with that painful, personal experience. Connecting with her experience helps Alicia engage in singing the piece and express deep emotion.

> NANA: Do you feel, as a woman, that it has been important to you to have experienced this [pedagogy in Women's Ensemble]?
>
> DELANEY: . . . [I]t helps me express my own emotion that I pent up during the day. I feel better after I sing. I feel better after I can connect with music . . . I think as a woman, most people expect you to [pent up emotion] because if you are too expressive, they say things like, "You are such a girl." But if I want to be respected, then you have to hold your head up high and keep charging forward or you are not going to get anywhere. Especially men—if you show your emotion all the time, they are not going to respect you and I definitely need respect here if I want to succeed and be the best teacher I can be.

Delaney feels that being overly expressive is not respected in the academic world, even in the field of music. To be respected as a musician and succeed in music as a profession, she believes emotional suppression is necessary. The emotional connection helps Delaney tap into her own suppressed emotion and release it through singing. It helps her "feel better."

> SARAFINA: I think one of the reasons why I like music so much is that it forces me . . . to be more emotional [Tears come to her eyes.]—that I am not very good at doing [laughs uncomfortably] . . . So, my mother . . . died when I was 18 . . . and I think when she died, then I closed myself off to that part of music-making. And I was really good at the analytical stuff, so that is what I excelled at. And with Women's Ensemble, it has helped me heal somewhat or at least opened up a way for me to explore that emotional side that I am really good at cutting off in any other circumstance . . . I think it has pushed me to explore . . . those emotional boundaries and the space to feel that and not be so ashamed to cry when it touches you.

To avoid the pain of her mother's death, Sarafina tends toward technical aspects in music, such as analysis and theory. The exploration of emotion and personal connection with the texts in Women's Ensemble gives Sarafina a safe space to experience her grief. This release of emotion through singing, discussion, and tears play a part in her healing.

Improved performance experiences

Delaney and Lilia described improved aspects of performance resulting from the exploration of meanings.

> LILIA: I feel like certain pieces in my musical life have been transformed by knowing what they were about and especially pieces that maybe I did not connect to initially and then you find out what it is about or you just analyze it a little bit and then it just brings new life to it and it is certainly much more enjoyable to perform and easier to deliver accurately.
>
> DELANEY: If there is no passion, you are just really analytical and, "This is this part, and this is this part and I need to get this note," but when you are most passionate and you feel it, your performance is better because when you think too hard you are going to make more mistakes. But when you are feeling it and you feel good about it, it changes the meaning of everything. It is not, "I am supposed to do this here." Instead, "Oh of course this goes here because it is portraying this feeling."

Lilia believed her performances were more meaningful and enjoyable because she had the opportunity to explore the multiple meanings of the music. Delaney said this connection to meaning made her feel good in performance. Both Lilia and Delaney talked about how the accuracy of their performance was influenced. Lilia believed the music was easier to deliver accurately and Delaney said that she made fewer mistakes. For Lilia and Delaney, one could deduce that the technical aspects of music come more easily to them because of their personal connection to meaning.

Relationships with and understanding others

Anna, Hannah, Lilia, Natalia, and Maeve experienced the ways in which a deep connection with the music impacted how they thought about and related with others. Lilia and Natalia recognized a change in their thinking, while Anna and Hannah described its influence on how they relate to others.

> NANA: You mentioned in class how she will bring your attention to the text or the musical meaning. Do you mean she is helping you connect to it personally?
>
> LILIA: Yeah, sometimes. But sometimes in a more worldly sense or both, like in a more generalized, "What would this mean to this group of people?" . . . We did this piece my freshman year . . . about freedom . . . liberty and diversity . . . I remember us having a big discussion about all these cultures and why they come together and it was a piece that was supposed to reflect on a bigger society.
>
> NATALIA: . . . it makes me realize things about people or different times or different situations that I have never been in and they change my way of thinking about certain things.

Discussions about text that refer to culture and a bigger society have helped Lilia connect with the world. When Natalia connects to the meaning of a piece, it changes her way of thinking. She learns about other people in situations different from her own. The process of digging deeper into the possible meanings of the text through discussion gave both of these women a broader worldview.

Anna, Hannah, and Maeve felt that aspects of their personal growth (also) resulted from hearing other women and discussing as an ensemble.

> ANNA: It makes me more open to other people's opinions and their perspectives. Just because I see something one way it doesn't mean everyone else does.
>
> MAEVE: You learn from what each person has to say and it is like every person's input is valued in a way.
>
> HANNAH: Any kind of collaborative process is good for team building—learning how to be a team player, understanding how people work together, and how we make decisions. That is just good for life.

Discussions in Women's Ensemble helped Anna be more open to other's perspectives. Maeve felt she learned from the other singers (as well as the conductor). Hannah was learning to be more of a team player. Through listening to others and making decisions as a group, these three women in their understanding of others, their understanding of music through others, and their understanding of being a member of a team.

CONCLUSION

When asked to give advice to conductors of women's choirs, Delaney responded:

> You acknowledge that this is a great group of women and once you acknowledge that, you can achieve a lot of great things ... When you embrace all the women in your group they are going to feel better about themselves. I feel so much better because [Professor Whitley] embraces all of us as musicians. So if you are in charge, especially of a women's group, and you take in all these people and you accept them as musicians, they are going to feel so much better and they are going to want to do more.

Delaney summarized the overall sense I received from listening to these women's voices. The women in this study feel embraced as people and respected as musicians by Professor Whitley through collaborative rehearsal methods. By inviting singers into the decision making process through thought-provoking questions that initiate group discussion or individual responses through sound, singers in the study experienced an increase in mental engagement, confidence in their abilities, ownership in the music-making process, and improved musicianship. The women in the study also benefit-ted from the exploration of multiple meanings and meaning-making via collaborative methods: It gave them opportunities for self-expression, improved performance experi-ences, and a capacity to understand and relate with others.

Feminist pedagogy embodies a midwife-teacher approach that challenges traditional hegemonic structures through new ways of being, thinking, and doing (Jorgensen, 2003). Based on my research, I maintain that incorporating feminist values into the choral rehearsal can transform singers and conductors into engaged individuals whose wholehearted energies spill over into the collective music-making process. Most impor-tantly, feminist pedagogy can be a catalyst for encouraging and empowering women as holistic individuals, leaders, and musicians.

NOTES

1. For more information regarding the three waves of feminism and its historical influence on music education, see Lamb, Dolloff, and Howe (2002).
2. Educator and philosopher Paulo Freire originally introduced the banker-teacher model analogy.
3. In addition, each singer read the data analysis and participated in a follow-up interview to give feedback. Follow-up interviews totaled 4 hours.
4. For interview questions, see Wolfe, 2015, Appendix G.
5. Valuing knowledge that originates from various personal experiences reiterates results of the research study by Belenky et al. (1986).

References

Belenky, M., Clinchy, B., Goldberger, N., & Tarule, J. (1986). *Women's ways of knowing: The development of self, voice, and mind*. New York: Basic Books.

Crabtree, R. D., Sapp, D. A., & Licona, A. C. (2009). Introduction: The passion and the praxis of feminist pedagogy. In R. D. Crabtree, D. A. Sapp, & A. C. Licona (Eds.), *Feminist pedagogy: Looking back to move forward* (pp. 1–22). Baltimore: The John Hopkins University Press.

Gilligan, C. (1982/1993). *In a different voice: Psychological theory and women's development*. Cambridge, MA: Harvard University Press.

Gilligan, C. (2011). *Joining the resistance*. Malden, MA: Polity.

Holt, M., & Jordan, J. (Eds.). (2008). *The school choral program: Philosophy, planning, organizing, and teaching*. Chicago, IL: GIA.

hooks, b. (1994). *Teaching to Transgress: Education as the practice of freedom*. New York: Routledge.

Jorgensen, E. R. (2003). *Transforming music education*. Bloomington: Indiana University Press.

Kimmel, E. (1999). Feminist teaching, an emergent practice. In Davis, S. N., Crawford, M., & Sebrechts, J. (Eds.), *Coming into her own: Educational success in girls and women* (pp. 57–76). San Francisco, CA: Jossey-Bass.

Koza, J. E. (1994). Getting a word in edgewise: A feminist critique of choral methods texts. *The Quarterly Journal of Music Teaching and Learning*. 5(3), 68–77.

Lamb, R., Dolloff, L., & Howe, S. W. (2002). Feminism, feminist research, and gender research in music education. In Colwell, R., & Richardson, C. (Eds.), *Handbook of Research on Music Teaching and Learning* (pp. 648–674). New York, NY: Oxford University Press.

Maher, F., & Tetrault, M. K. (1992). Inside feminist classrooms: An ethnographic approach. *New Directions for Teaching and Learning* 49(Spring), 57–74. Retrieved from http://onlinelibrary.wiley.com/wol1/doi/10.1002/tl.37219924907/abstract

Noddings, N. (1984). *Caring: A feminine approach to ethics and moral education*. Berkeley: University of California Press.

O'Toole, P. A. (1994). *Redirecting the choral classroom: A feminist poststructural analysis of power relations within three choral settings*. (Doctoral dissertation). University of Wisconsin, Madison. Retrieved from ProQuest Dissertations and Theses Global (Order No. 9426965).

Redfern, C., & Aune, K. (2010). *Reclaiming the F word: The new feminist movement*. London, England: Zed.

Saltzman Romey, K., Sweet, E., & Wanyama, S. M. (2009). Building bridges: Choruses engaging communities. In J. Conlon (Ed.), *Wisdom, wit, and will: Women choral conductors on their art* (pp. 73–100). Chicago, IL: GIA.

Shrewsbury, C. M. (1997). What is feminist pedagogy? *Women's Studies Quarterly*, 25(1–2), 166–173.

Wahl, S. L. (2009). *By women, for women: Choral works for women's voices composed and texted by women, with an annotated repertoire list*. Doctoral dissertation. University of Michigan, Ann Arbor. Retrieved from ProQuest Dissertations and Theses (Order No. 3379284).

Wolfe, N. F. (2015). *Where practice meets philosophy: Feminist pedagogy in the women's choral rehearsal*. Doctoral dissertation. University of North Carolina, Greensboro. Retrieved from ProQuest Dissertations and Theses (Order No. 3708256).

CHAPTER 11

CHORAL PEDAGOGY AND THE CONSTRUCTION OF MEANING

FRANK ABRAHAMS AND DANIEL ABRAHAMS

INTRODUCTION

CHORAL pedagogy is grounded within a community of practice. The conductor's goal is to create an ensemble where singers become members of a community through situated experiences in rehearsal. The process involves the journey from novice chorister to expert. It is framed in the educational theories of Lev Vygotsky (1978) and his conception of the zone of proximal development; the ideas of Bruner (1996) and others (Wood, Bruner, & Ross, 1976; Stone, 1993) regarding scaffolding, and our own ideas, which we call socio-transformative apprenticeship (Abrahams & Abrahams, 2016).

Constructivism is a theory about knowledge and learning and not necessarily a theory about teaching practice. As Fosnot (1996) noted:

> Although constructivism is not a theory of teaching, it suggests taking a radically different approach to instruction from that used in most schools. Teachers who base their practice on constructivism reject the notions that meaning can be passed on to learners via symbols or transmission, that learners can incorporate exact copies of teachers' understanding for their own use, that whole concepts can be broken down into discrete sub-skills, and that concepts can be taught out of context. In contrast, a constructivist view of learning suggests an approach to teaching that gives learners the opportunity for concrete, contextually meaningful experience through which they can search for patterns, raise their own questions, and construct their own models, concepts, and strategies. The classroom is seen as a minisociety, a community of learners engaged in activity, discourse, and reflection. (p. ix)

Two important notions orbit around the simple idea of constructed knowledge. The first is that learners construct new understandings using what they already know. There is no *tabula rasa* on which new knowledge is etched. Rather, they come to learning situations with knowledge gained from previous experience, and that prior knowledge influences what new or modified knowledge they will construct (Boardman, 1988).

The second notion is the Deweyian idea that learning is active rather than passive (Dewey 1938). Hoover (1996), suggested that learners apply current understandings, note relevant elements in new learning experiences, and judge the consistency of prior knowledge. Emerging constructs, based on that judgment become new knowledge. For conductors, a constructivist approach to choral pedagogy facilitates the abilities of singers to glean meaning that is deep and significant and contributes to lifelong pleasurable experiences as choir members.

MEANING: MAKING MEANING AND FINDING MEANING

How do singers construct meaning?

The answer lies in pedagogy that is grounded in the theory of constructivism and the branch called sociotransformative constructivism. Singing in choir and the act of conducting the choir are social processes where collaboration between the group and individual singers and between the conductor and choir occur. Vygotsky (1978) suggested that learning occurs within a *zone of proximal development* or "the distance between the actual developmental level as determined by independent problem solving and the level of potential development as determined through problem solving under adult guidance or in collaboration with more capable peers" (p. 86). In choir, singers construct meaning through these social interactions.

The British scholar Vivien Burr (1995), inspired in part by the writings of Kenneth Gergen (1985), described four key assumptions that contribute to the construction of meaning. The first centers on the idea that one adopt a critical stance toward ways of understanding the world and us in the world. She wrote:

> For example, just because we think of some music as 'classical' and some as 'pop' does not mean we should assume that there is anything in the nature of the music itself that means it has to be divided up in that particular way. (p. 3)

A second assumption is that the ways we understand the world are historically and culturally specified. We come to understand the world because of where and when we are. Forms of knowledge in any culture are artifacts of time and geography. This is particularly true for singers and their conductors trying to be authentic when interpreting the composer's intentions in a choral score.

The notion that social processes sustain knowledge is the third assumption—that is, people are constantly engaged with each other:

> It is through the daily interactions between people in the course of social life that our versions of knowledge become fabricated. Therefore, social interaction of all kinds, particularly language, is of great interest . . . The goings-on between people in the course of their everyday lives are seen as the practices during which our shared versions of knowledge are constructed. (p. 4)

Finally, knowledge and social action go together. Although we may define a number of possible constructions of the world, a prevailing construction does have an effect on the way we act in society and the meanings we deduce from those actions.

Burr cites seven ways that her views differ from traditional psychology. Her comments on language are particularly relevant to the ways choir members make meaning, as the essence of choral performance lies in the understanding and communication of text.

- Anti-essentialism: there are no essences inside things or people that make them what they are
- Anti-realism: denial that knowledge is a direct perception of reality; there is great suspicion of the notion of an objective fact
- No notions of discovering the "true" nature of people and social life: attention should be placed on historical study of ever-changing nature and social life
- Language as a precondition of thought: language is a key to understanding thinking and this provides a framework for understanding meaning making
- Language as a form of social action: language is more than a vehicle for expressing ourselves, it is seen as a form of action for construction
- Focus on interaction and social practices: it is not the social practices themselves that are of interest, it is the interaction of these practices
- Focus on process: emphasis is not on static entities such as personality traits or memory models, but on the dynamics of process found in social interaction (pp. 5–8).

Having examined a multitude of differing perspectives among constructivists, Shively (1995) frames his conception of constructivism as follows:

1. Learning is the process of making meaning out of one's experiences; it is knowledge construction
2. Learning should always be grounded in a constructivist approach
3. Learning is enhanced by engaging learners in experiences reflecting practitioner culture

4. Learning is enhanced by engaging the learners in experiences involving individual and group knowledge construction

5. Learning is enhanced by engaging learners in experiences reflecting multiple perspectives

6. Learning is enhanced by the individual distributing the process of knowledge construction and the resultant knowledge base among other individuals and artifacts

7. Learning is enhanced by experiences encouraging the reflexive use of a learner's knowledge base. (pp. 76–77)

Frank Abrahams (2005) offered a perspective on constructivism as a strong partner to critical pedagogy. Citing the work of Freire (1970) as inspirational for critical pedagogy, he reminded us that:

> Critical pedagogy is concerned not only with the students and the change that occurs in them as a result of the learning, but also with the change that occurs in the teacher. In critical pedagogy, not only do the teachers teach the students, but also the students, in turn, teach the teacher. This effects a transformation of both students and teachers. (p. 13)

This is a critical point that sometimes is missed in the literature. Critical pedagogy, for Abrahams, is based on the sociotransformative constructivism of Rodriguez and Berryman (2002) (a type of social constructivism that deals with the multicultural dimension) and experiential learning theory. Experiential learning, according to Abrahams, adds the element of critical feeling and action. Both elements contribute to the abilities of singers and their conductor to make meaning.

How does the construction of meaning contribute to what singers find meaningful?

Singers in choir belong to a community of practice (Lave & Wenger, 1991; Wenger, 1998). They are a group of people bounded by a shared passion for what they do in common, and as they interact as a choir, they learn how to do it better. Wiggins (2009) described a musical community of practice in this fashion:

> Members engage with a wide variety of music (perform, listen, create), explore that music in a variety of contexts (cultural, historical, personal), conceive and contribute ideas (musical and verbal), make decisions (musical and social), evaluate one another's musical ideas and products, and learn to value a wide range of musical ideas and products (produced by both professional musicians and peers). (p. xiv)

It is membership in such communities of musical practice that singers find meaningful.

Research on meaningfulness in musical ensembles

Researchers have investigated participants' perceptions of meaning in a variety of music ensembles. Most of these studies have focused on the perceptions of choir members, but have also examined the perceptions of general music and instrumental ensemble participants. Farrell (1972) and Hylton (1980) conducted early studies of perceptions of meaning among ensemble members.

Farrell (1972) investigated how urban adults perceive the meaning of recreational vocal music experiences. She noted that singers who felt an attachment to and pride for the group and had the desire to "learn, excel, and produce good artistic music" (pp. 72–74) found the choral experience to be meaningful. Hylton (1980) was among the first music researchers to look directly at what public school music students perceive as meaningful about their participation in choir. His findings suggested that when conductors honor and acknowledge the individual needs of the singers, the choir members find the choral experience to be meaningful. According to Sugden (2005), multiple meanings derived from participant's choral experiences included musical-artistic, psychological, communicative, and social achievements.

In her analysis of these two studies, Cape (2012) noted that:

> Whereas Hylton found achievement to be the most salient dimension of meaning for choir students, Sugden found the musical-artistic dimension to be strongest. Sugden considers that contemporary teachers may place greater emphasis on their students' musical-artistic development, or that students are involved in more varied types of musical activities, thus supporting the notion that context may play a role in students' perceptions. (p. 51)

Looking at one high school choral program she deemed to be exemplary, Arasi (2006) discovered that the personality of the conductor was a significant influencer for singers in the choir—that is, singers were more likely to find the school choral experience to be meaningful when they liked the conductor's personality. Adult singers, on the other hand, appreciated conductors who challenged them to think critically, to be creative, and contribute to their overall self-confidence as members of the choir. Cape (2012) concluded that such intrinsic and extrinsic influences of participation in the choral program included "the desire to achieve excellence; the ability to analyze critically and evaluate vocal music; the ability to appreciate diverse cultures and music genres; and enriched [sic] of socialization and personal growth" (Arasi, 2006, p. 192).

Adult singers from a study by Rensink-Hoff (2009) acknowledged the impact and leadership of the conductor as the second most important motivational factor for participation in choir. Bell (2000) examined the attitudes of adult singers and the conductor's influence on that experience. Singers rated the personal and behavioral skills of the conductor higher than the musical and technical skills. According to participants, the five most important conductor actions were (a) gives clear and understandable directions, (b) instills confidence in singers, (c) selects appropriate repertoire, (d) identifies and

corrects errors, and (e) has enthusiasm. Bell's (2000) study acknowledged the importance of the conductor and his or her impact on the choral experience. The rehearsal
behavior of a choral conductor may affect the sense of place and meaningfulness of
singers.

Finding agency

We consider the acquisition of singer agency to be an important outcome of choral pedagogy. Wiggins (2011) defines agency as "the intentionality and control an individual
feels she has over her own circumstances in a particular situation or at a given time in
that situation" (p. 91). Bandura (2000) suggested that people work together to "to secure
what they cannot accomplish on their own" (p. 75); collective agency is where people
share beliefs in a collective power to achieve desired results. This is consistent with, and
particularly relevant to, many of the goals of a choral experience.

Blair (2009) suggested that two fundamental areas of agency emerge within the practice of music education, which we adapt for the choral experience. Firstly singers desire
to enable and further their own understanding, or more simply, to grow as vocalists and
musicians and to accomplish that learning by discovering things for themselves. This
"own understanding" implies ownership or control within the learning process. In the
choral rehearsal, this is confirmed in the students' desire to function as musicians—to
participate with others as composers, listeners, and performers. Through these kinds
of experiences, they are able to a) apply conceptual understanding to new musical contexts and b) relate to others in musical ways. The authentic nature of participating in
such roles is critical, for it is in solving problems in real-life contexts that learning has
meaning.

Secondly singers desire to be respected and valued as members of a choral ensemble.
Students seek to have their musicianship honored, to have their musical ideas known,
valued, even celebrated. In a sense, the conductor facilitates a process of enculturation
for singers as they become respected and valued members of the choir.

APPLICATIONS FOR CHORAL PEDAGOGY—
SOCIOTRANSFORMATIVE APPRENTICESHIP

John Dewey (1938) offered a different perspective predicated on learners being active
participants in the learning process rather than passive receivers of knowledge. In the
choir, singers engage, reflect, and act on their experiences, and in the process knowing and meaning become embodied, contextual, and socially constructed—that is, they
acquire agency and become "agentive." The pragmatic and progressive educational pedagogy of Dewey favored experiential learning and rejected the empiricist viewpoint that

children arrive at school as blank slates. The same is true for the singers in the choir. While they may not be able to decode the notation or play their parts on a piano, they have heard music, singing, and choral singing in many diverse circumstances. They elect to join the choir because they found those experiences to be pleasurable. Even the youngest singers in our choirs know what they like, know when the choir sounds wonderful and when something, because perhaps it is out of tune, seems wrong. Learning occurs when singers experience some form of change resulting from their singing in the ensemble.

The roles conductors and singers play inside the community of the choral experience can be described as one of master and apprentice. In the traditional sense, the conductor is the master and the singers are the apprentices. We advocate a model of apprenticeship we call sociotransformative apprenticeship where by the roles of conductor and singer are reconceived and redefined. Bruner (1996) suggested, "If pedagogy is to empower human beings to go beyond 'native' predispositions, it must transmit the 'toolkit' the culture has developed for doing so" (p. 17). Apprenticeship "offers direct exposure to real conditions of practice and patterns of work" (Schön, 1987, p. 37) affording learners insight into methods needed to be successful within a domain. For these reasons, learners enter into the choral experience through a framework of apprenticeship.

Sociotransformative apprenticeship is a model of apprenticeship consisting of *dialogic conversation, authentic activity, metacognition,* and *reflexivity* that occur through the natural social interaction of mentor (i.e., conductor) with apprentices, the singers, as well as between apprentices and mentor in groups inside the choir rehearsal bringing about a sense of critical consciousness among the participants.

As the mentor, the conductor provides the necessary scaffolds for singers until, over time, singers become capable of completing activities alone without assistance. From this process, singers develop socially, both person-to-person (interpsychologically) and individually within themselves (intrapsychologically) (adapted from Vygotsky, 1978). Collins, Brown, and Newman (1989) suggested that once learners, in our case the singers, master concepts with appropriate scaffolding, the scaffolding fades away and singers can apply these concepts to a new contextual situation on their own. We believe that this contributes to a lifelong commitment to choral singing.

ENACTING THE MODEL

The principles of reciprocal teaching, when applied to the choral rehearsal, provide the strategies for a choral pedagogy where the making of meaning and the finding of meaningful experiences are central goals. Reciprocal teaching consists of five components. They are: predicting, questioning, clarifying, summarizing, and connecting. Each, when integrated separately or collectively into the choral rehearsal, engages students in the critical thinking processes that foster the making of meaning.

Predicting provides opportunities for singers along with the conductor to form hypotheses regarding musical and technical issues that might cause difficulties when rehearsing and performing music.

Questioning is a catalyst for deeper understanding providing opportunities for singers and the conductor to think about what they don't know, need to know, and would like to know.

Clarifying assists singers along with the conductor by consider the reasons why the music is difficult to understand. Members of the choir consider roadblocks within the music and take necessary actions to restore meaning.

Summarizing provides opportunities for the singers along with the conductor to identify and integrate the most important information within the music.

Connecting interconnects all of the strategies. Members of the choir make connections and apply them to their music making, ensuring that singers are using high-level thinking and understanding the musical concepts within the music they are rehearsing.

Sociotransformative Apprenticeship in Action

In 2010, Frank Abrahams applied the components of reciprocal teaching and the principles of sociotransformative apprenticeship to design scaffolds as he prepared high school students to sing a performance of *Three Russian Folksongs* by Sergei Rachmaninoff with a local community orchestra.[1] The singers, all members of the Westminster Conservatory Youth Chorale, met weekly at Westminster Choir College in Princeton, New Jersey. The singers were selected by competitive audition. Most brought extensive choral experience to the ensemble, and most play musical instruments. They also voice privately and participate in their school choirs. However, while not a typical situation, they were an appropriate choice for the application of a sociotransformative apprenticeship choral pedagogy.

During the period of study, Frank infused summarizing, clarifying, predicting, questioning, and connecting through conversations and other activities into the context of the ensemble rehearsals. Discussions were deliberately kept short so as not to compromise the intention of the rehearsals, which was to make music and not talk about it. Leading questions, however, were typical.

We describe the process in the form of a first-person narrative which excerpts from the complete study.

The *Three Russian Folksongs*, Op. 41, by Sergei Rachmaninoff were composed in 1926 for Leopold Stokowski and the Philadelphia Orchestra; they were the last choral pieces the composer wrote. Although they were originally set in Russian and scored for alto and bass voices only, I decided to have the entire choir sing in English and in unison.

In *clarifying* this with the choir, I explained that because of the dark narrative texture, because the compositions were folk songs that would normally be sung in unison and by any voice part, and because of the complex and subtle accompaniment by a very large orchestra, I believed that having everyone sing would make it easier for the choir to be heard and understood by the audience. Of the songs, Vladimir Wishau wrote, "[As the music] moved along in its simple, folk like fashion, I grew numb. My soul could take no more, and tears began to flow! Only a man who loves his fatherland could compose this way. Only a man who in his inmost soul is a Russian. Only Rachmaninoff could have composed this!" (Van Ausdall, 1974).

In the first rehearsal, singers listened to the recording and followed the score. A discussion followed where I asked singers to *clarify* for me their overall impressions as well as their impressions about the style, harmonic language, and orchestration. Then they were asked *(questioning)* to *predict* what challenges they would face as they prepared the pieces for performance. One singer, Clara (all singers' names have been changed to protect their identities) *predicted* that diction would be a priority so the audience would understand the story of each song. She noted that the texts were stories told in the first person. She *clarified* her statement by explaining that in the third song, a young wife was speaking to someone worried that her husband would return home and beat her in retaliation for her seemingly unfaithful behavior at a dinner party. In the second song, the main character yearns for her lost lover, Johnny. Kieran *predicted* that the timing would be a challenge and Jenna suggested that the complex intervallic relationships throughout would be difficult to navigate. The singers were asked *(questioning)* to *summarize* the problems and to suggest solutions that would address the issues and provide the strategies to meet the challenges. This was a first step toward *connecting*.

I presented a brief account of Rachmaninoff by discussing his style and the color and texture of the music. I also talked about the texts. At the second rehearsal, we began with the third folksong, singing it on solfège syllables. Then we read text aloud as fast as possible, each person reading it at their own pace so as to get the words "into the mouth." Next, singers were instructed to silently read the words as fast as possible, with dynamics, until they came to the hardest line for them to read. They were to read that line aloud, with everyone choosing their own hardest part. This was a surprise. Singers chose parts to read aloud that I would not have *predicted* would be hard for them. As a consequence, I *questioned* them, and they *summarized* and *clarified* why they were hard. Diane said that the line she chose, "A ay lulee ay da lushenkee lee!" was difficult because it was the one line that was not in English. Several other singers confirmed that they had difficulty with this text as well.

Next, we *connected* the tune. Singers were directed to audiate the melody, but to sing aloud what they thought was the hardest part. As a pre-step, they were asked to scan the music and *predict* which line that would be. Singers did not share their answers at this time with me or with the rest of the choir. Instead, they were asked to confirm or *summarize* what they found after the exercise was completed. The instructions continued, "If the whole piece is hard, then sing the whole thing. If none of it is hard, then you won't sing at all. But sing as fast as you can. Then find a friend near you and sing to your friend the hardest part. Afterwards, switch, and your buddy will sing his or her hardest part to you." A discussion followed to *clarify* and to *summarize* what the hardest parts were as there was no consensus. I asked, "What makes the part hard?" Again, there was no consensus.

I then asked what strategy we should use to make "A ay lulee ay da lushenkee lee" perfect. Travis suggested that not everyone was pronouncing the words the same. He *predicted* that identical pronunciation would be the solution. I decided that it should be *ayee* not *eye*.

I asked the singers to take a pencil and circle the hardest dynamic. This required singers to make *connections* and value judgments. I asked for *clarification*, "Is there anything anyone needs to hear, if so Ryan [the accompanist] will play it." Again, it was "Ay loo lee." *Questioning* followed. What makes that hard? What is the difficult interval? Rickey offered that the intervals of a second were challenging. The choir sang from the beginning and missed the phrase "my jealous husband." I stopped and asked *(questioning)* what had to be circled. They *clarified* the correct parts. I *predicted* that we would have significant articulation issues when we were joined by the orchestra.

Singers broke into groups by sections to repair the issues they had identified. Afterwards, singers were asked what they learned. *Summarizing,* they suggested: "Be aware of the notes after the page turn." Many agreed that this was a problem. "Page 29 is not as easy as it looks" was contributed. Then, I asked the singers to sing the entire song at performance level.

At the third rehearsal, I began with the question *(questioning* looking for a *prediction),* "What kind of a sound are we looking for when we know this was written for Russian altos?" Laurie responded, "Very dark." I asked *(questioning* looking for a *prediction),* "If we are going for a very dark sound, what would one do to the vowels?" "Close them," Mike answered. "Use a lot a schwa [the neutral vowel] vowel," Mateo added. "Make lots of space in the back of the throat by imagining a golf ball or something," Andrew remarked. Some other choir members suggested more air; another said adding weight and not tightening the throat. All of these answers served reciprocal teaching through *questioning, predicting, clarifying,* and *connecting.*

I continued the discussion with the statement that color is often used as a metaphor for tone quality. To develop that idea, I asked *(questioning),* "What does a dark sound look like?" "Burgundy," Ari suggested. I continued, "Change your image of your own body weight. Add pounds to your body weight. Think about the instrument as being supported by something larger than you might be. Think about those large green exercise balls. Think about sitting on one of those to support the sound. The color of Ben's sweater [one of the staff in the room] is an example of the burgundy color we seek."

One of the interns, Dan (his real name) who worked with me at rehearsals, felt that the tone was tight. So, the choir began a discussion of thinking about the whole body. My sense was that the sound was not connected to support and therefore would not be heard over the orchestra. "How do we do this?" I asked. Jason suggested that we think about the cello and bowing a cello. *Questioning* continued. I asked, "Do any of your voice teachers talk to you about support and connecting to the breath? What do they say?" Lindsay answered, "Breathe low." I requested that the members who were taking voice lessons talk to their voice teachers about how connect the sound to the breath.

As the dialogue continued, Cory suggested that we were not taking in enough air. However, my concern was what they would do with the air once they took it in. I *clarified* as follows:

> Singing is a whole body experience. We talked about the way the conductor should be and the way the gesture should be, but you need to ask your voice teachers about "singing on the breath" and "engaging the support." See what they say about these two items.

One alto asked about "resistance." We talked about tension, that there must be tension in certain places. Dialogue centered on the phenomenon that no one could see our voices or hear them the way that we do. "When you watched the conductor, you noticed that he was conducting with a low gesture," I remarked, "and you noticed body posture. You must connect to that as well."

More *questioning* followed. "Can you find 'Lo the berries blue and red' and see how you might attend to the articulation of the second eighth note in each group? What might be a suggestion? What is the problem? Why am I stopping?" Rita remarked that "the notes are getting smaller." "What must we do?" I asked. Rita answered, "Enunciate!" I asked, "If you were going to put a marking on those eighth notes, what marking might it be?" Jackie said "Marcato!" I waited for singers to put the marking in their scores. "We want to emphasize the second eighth note. Watch what happens when Ryan emphasizes the second and fourth eighth notes." *Questioning* continued: "What else will help the articulation?" David suggested "Shadow vowels." He added, "While it won't help the eighth notes, it will help final releases." These are examples of choristers taking information they know from previous encounters in the choir and applying them to the piece they are currently rehearsing. In reciprocal teaching, this exemplifies *connecting* and is clear evidence that singers are synthesizing information and engaging cognitive and constructivist processes that facilitate their abilities to make meaning (McCarthy, 1987, 2000).

Together, we identified the following patterns:

1. The roles of conductor as mentor and singer as apprentice were constantly shifting. It should be noted that all of these strategies—questioning, predicting, clarifying, summarizing, and connecting—included both the conductor and the singers. There were instances where the conductor did predicting that sometimes proved correct and sometimes not. One instance of that was when the choir was asked to articulate aloud only the hardest text. They chose the one line that was not in English and was contrary to what I had thought they would select. However, the important point here is that we were all learning together with the roles of mentor and apprentice shifting throughout. As their conductor, I was continually learning as well. By asking them questions that engaged them in the processes of clarification and summarization, I was able to gain insights into their musical understanding each step of the way. As I result, I could instantly adjust my responses and

re-clarify and re-question to help the singers make the connections that would enable them to make meaning of the music.

2. Singers were always searching for and making connections. In each of the activities, singers connected newly acquired knowledge with prior knowledge. This was achieved through their questioning and subsequent clarification of questions. Reciprocal teaching was the catalyst for them to connect concepts learned in the rehearsal with those they constructed on their own away from school.

We also identified the following themes:

1. Reciprocal teaching differs from what a good teacher normally does in the routine and daily interactions of rehearsing with choirs and orchestras. Specifically, good teachers always question and clarify. A goal of good teaching is for students to make connections. So, what makes this different? Reciprocal teaching requires that the conductor think more about the types of questions asked, often framing them in advance rather than constructing them in the moment. This results, we discovered, in a more thoughtful and purposeful question and in more thoughtful and significant pre-rehearsal planning. We found that in preparing our rehearsals, we spent dedicated time formulating *questions* and *predicting* answers. We spent directed time thinking about how to *clarify* and to *connect* concepts, and how to remedy issues we identified that might be problematic *(predicting)*. We were deliberate about how we would *summarize* and where in the rehearsal summary would occur and found that it happened more frequently throughout the rehearsal than in the traditional closure of the rehearsal.

2. While the literature on reciprocal teaching focuses on the results one sees in students, we found that reciprocal teaching also impacts the conductor's understanding of the material and of the tools singers need to achieve understanding.

3. Reciprocal teaching empowered singers to express their opinions and insights freely. One of the patterns discussed above is that of the shifting roles of apprentice and mentor. When singers took responsibility for their own learning through questioning and clarifying, they began to build trust and respect for one another's opinions and insights. Singers relied on the feedback of their peers, positive and negative, to meet the common goal of improving performance. As a result, singers became more comfortable opening themselves up to making decisions that they believed were in the best interest of the society of the ensemble.

NOTE

1. Adapted from Abrahams, F. & Abrahams, D. (2010), The impact of Reciprocal Teaching on the development of musical understanding in high school student members of performing ensembles: An action research. *Visions of Research in Music Education, 15*. Retrieved from http://www-usr.rider.edu/~vrme/. Used by permission.

References

Abrahams, F. (2005). The application of critical pedagogy to music teaching and learning: A literature review. *Update: Applications of Research in Music Education*, 23(2), 12–22.

Abrahams, F., & Abrahams, D. (2010). The impact of reciprocal teaching on the development of musical understanding in high school student members of performing ensembles: An action research. *Visions of Research in Music Education*, 15. Retrieved from http://www-usr.rider.edu/~vrme/

Abrahams, F., & Abrahams, D. (2016). Child as musical apprentice. In G. E. McPherson (Ed.), *The child as musician: A handbook of musical development* (2nd ed., pp. 538–550). Oxford: Oxford University Press.

Arasi, M. T. (2006). *Adult reflections on a high school choral music program: Perceptions of meaning and lifelong influence*. (Unpublished doctoral dissertation). Dissertation, Georgia State University, Atlanta, GA.

Bandura, A. (2000). Exercise of human agency through collective efficacy. *Current Directions in Psychological Science*, 9(3), 75–78.

Bell, C. L. (2000). *An examination of adult amateur community chorus and choral conductor rehearsal behavior, with implications for music education*. (Unpublished doctoral dissertation). Columbia University, New York, NY.

Blair, D. V. (2009). Learner agency: To understand and to be understood. *British Journal of Music Education*, 26(2), 173–187.

Boardman, E. (1988). The generative theory of musical learning, Part 1: Introduction. *General Music Today*, 2(1), 4–30.

Bruner, J. (1996). *The culture of education*. Cambridge, MA: Harvard University Press.

Burr, V. (1995). *An introduction to social constructionism*. London: Routledge.

Cape, J. (2012). *Perceptions of meaningfulness among high school instrumental musicians*. (Unpublished doctoral dissertation). Arizona State University, Tempe, AZ.

Collins, A., Brown, J. S., & Newman, S. (1989). Cognitive apprenticeship: Teaching the craft of reading, writing, and mathematics. In L. B. Resnick (Ed.), *Knowing, learning, and instruction: Essays in honor of Robert Glaser* (pp. 453–494). Hillsdale, NJ: Lawrence Erlbaum.

Dewey, J. (1938). *Experience and education*. New York: Macmillan.

Farrell, P. (1972). *The meaning of the recreation experience in music as it is defined by urban adults who determined singer typal profiles through q-techniques*. (Unpublished doctoral dissertation). Pennsylvania State University, State College, PA.

Fosnot, C. T. (1996). Constructivism: A psychological theory of learning. In C. T. Fosnot (Ed.), *Constructivism: Theory, perspective, and practice* (pp. 8–33). New York, NY: Teachers College Press.

Freire, P. (1970). *Pedagogy of the oppressed*. New York: Herder and Herder.

Gergen, K. (1985). The social constructionist movement in modern psychology. *American Psychologist*, 40(3), 266–275.

Hoover, W. A. (1996). The practice implications of constructivism. *SEDL Letter*, 9(3). Retrieved from http://www.sedl.org/pubs/sedletter/v09n03/practice.html

Hylton, J. B. (1980). *The meaning of high school choral experience and its relationship to selected variables*. Doctor of Education Dissertation, Pennsylvania State University.

Lave, J., & Wenger, E. (1991). *Situated learning: Legitimate peripheral participation*. New York: Cambridge University Press.

McCarthy, B. (1987). *The 4MAT system: Teaching to learning styles with right/left mode techniques*. Barrington, IL: Excel.

McCarthy, B. (2000). *About teaching: 4MAT in the classroom.* Waucaonda, IL: About Learning, Inc.

Rensink-Hoff, R. (2009). *Adult community choirs: Toward a balance between leisure participation and musical achievement.* (Unpublished doctoral dissertation). University of Western Ontario. Canada.

Rodriguez, A. J., & Berryman, C. (2002). Using sociotransformative constructivism to teach for understanding in diverse classrooms: A beginning teacher's journey. *American Educational Research Journal, 39*(4), 1017–1045.

Schön, D. A. (1987). *Educating the reflective practitioner: Toward a new design for teaching and learning in the profession.* San Francisco: Jossey-Bass.

Shively, J. (1995). *A framework for the development and implementation of constructivist learning environments for beginning band classes.* (Unpublished doctoral dissertation). University of Illinois, Urbana-Champaign.

Stone, C. A. (1993). What's missing in the metaphor of scaffolding? In E. A. Forman, N. Minick, & C. A. Stone (Eds.), *Contexts for learning: Sociocultural dynamics in children's development* (pp. 169–183). New York: Oxford University Press.

Sugden, N. L. (2005). *Meaning of the choral experience and musical self-concept of secondary choral music participants.* (Unpublished doctoral dissertation). Indiana University, Bloomington, IN.

Van Ausdall, C. W. (1974). *Rachmaninoff: Three Russian Songs*, Op. 41. [CD] Album liner notes. New York: RCA Red Seal ARL 1-0193. Stereo.

Vygotsky, L. (1978) *Mind in society: The development of the higher psychological processes.* Cambridge, MA: Harvard University Press.

Wenger, E. (1998). *Communities of practice: Learning, meaning, and identity.* New York: Cambridge University Press.

Wiggins, J. (2009). *Teaching for musical understanding* (2nd ed.). Rochester: Center for Applied Research in Musical Understanding.

Wiggins, J. (2011). Vulnerability and agency in being and becoming a musician. *Music Education Research, 13*(4), 355–367.

Wood, D., Bruner, J. S., & Ross, G. (1976). The role of tutoring in problem solving. *Journal of Child Psychology & Psychiatry & Allied Disciplines, 17*(2), 89–100.

PART III

WORLD PERSPECTIVES

CHAPTER 12

THE FRAMING OF CHOIRS AND THEIR CONDUCTORS

A UK Perspective

COLIN DURRANT

"ONCE in royal David's city" heralds the real beginning of Christmas for many religious and nonreligious people across the globe. The sounds of a solo boy treble singing the well-known carol's first verse conjures up warm glows, mince pies, mulled wine, snow, and all the other trappings associated with a northern hemisphere Christmas. Choral singing is an accepted part of Christmas and is to be found not only at King's College Chapel Cambridge, but also in streets, shopping malls, railway stations, and other churches across the UK and, of course, in many other countries as well. Many of the carols stem from English folk song traditions as well as from Victorian hymnody. "In the Bleak Midwinter," written by the 19th century English poet Christina Rossetti, with beautiful settings by Gustav Holst and Harold Darke, resonates in the summer sunshine of countries in the southern hemisphere each December as much as in the northern, along with reindeer, robins, and snow on their Christmas cards. The English (and yes, it is largely English rather than British) choral tradition is recognized widely. To believe, however, that this is representative of a wide practice that exists today is misleading. It is a fragment of an elitist model of choral singing perpetuated by an intellectual Christian minority. It is not necessarily to be found in most of our schools for most of our children.

The tradition as recognized worldwide is rooted in the music of the Church since the middle ages and more particularly since the reformation. As its counterpart in Germany, the Reformation required composers to write music in the vernacular—in English as opposed to Latin. Under Elizabeth I, composers such as William Byrd, Thomas Tallis, Thomas Weelkes, Thomas Morley, and Orlando Gibbons supplied the new Anglican rite with an immense amount of beautiful anthems and canticle settings. This was indeed the Golden Age of English choral music (Le Huray, 1978).

During the 19th century, church services included a good deal of hymn and psalm singing involving the whole congregation, where participation was the essence of Protestantism. The singing methods put forward by John Curwen and Sarah Glover during the latter half of the 19th century aimed to improve the standard of singing and sight singing in the English churches. Indeed, Curwen's tonic sol-fa scheme had an impact also on music education in its wider sense, in schools and churches and leading to large-scale singing festivals throughout the land. This in turn led to the emergence of community choral societies in most towns in England, where performances of the great oratorios of Handel, Haydn, and Mendelssohn were commonplace, as well as works of now lesser-known English composers. As with the development of singing practices in North America and other parts of northern Europe, notably Scandinavia and Germany, so England and Wales with the male voice choirs in the mining communities heralded a renaissance of community choral singing during the 19th and early 20th centuries. Contemporary writers use the word "ennoble" to suggest that choral music had the potential to elevate people in taste and status. Its pedagogy was not just a musical one. Curwen's aim was both to improve the standard of singing and enhance the moral standing of the working class (Durrant, 2003; McGuire, 2006). He was himself a congregational minister and a reformer. His work promoted a strong temperance movement and evangelical development of working clubs and societies as well as sight singing and, in turn, the flourishing of moral probity. Church attendance was at its high point during the 19th and early 20th centuries in Britain. People went to church and people sang.

The growth of robed church choirs in towns and villages following the "Oxford Movement" from 1834 created a demand for music—and not always of high quality (Fellowes, 1969). On the shelves of countless churches today plentiful disintegrating copies of anthems, psalms, and settings of Victorian and Edwardian composers can be found that are no longer in use.

At this time there was an overt evangelism of singing and its relationship to the culture, society, and moral standing of its people. However, since the death of Purcell in 1695, England suffered a plethora of mediocre composers. Routley (1966) even refers to the "vulgarity" and "cult of amateurism that ensured mediocrity would be accepted" in the churches in the land. He also suggests that it was the dominance of the sol-fa sight singing movement even during the early years of the 20th century that "settled choral taste into a strictly 18th–19th century rut" (p. 18). It was only the renaissance of the early twentieth century that found a new vitality in choral and other composition. C. Hubert Parry, Charles Villiers Stanford, and Arthur Sullivan (although he died in 1900) were prominent in this renaissance, notably in their choral and, in the case of Sullivan, operatic works. Major composers like Edward Elgar (with his most anti-Protestant Catholic of works *Dream of Gerontius*), Ralph Vaughan Williams, and latterly Benjamin Britten contributed not just to the sacred and secular choral repertoire but also to the resurgence of English music generally following two centuries of mediocrity.

New choral music provided challenge for both singers and their conductors. Indeed Elgar's oratorio had a difficult birth, due primarily to the complexity of the choral writing in comparison to what had gone before as well as its overt Catholic text, which was not to everyone's more protestant taste. *Gerontius* demands a lot technically and expressively from singers and conductor. Later choral compositions, notably William Walton's *Belshazzar's Feast*, used challenging harmonies and rhythms that English choirs of the time (the 1930s) had not previously encountered. Nowadays choirs can expect irregular meters and rhythms and atonal harmonies and this commands a level of skill that challenges singers and conductors. Even local community choirs can expect to include contemporary music in their repertoire, with English composers such as John Rutter, John Tavener, Bob Chilcott, James Macmillan (sorry—Scottish) and Gabriel Jackson providing accessible, well-crafted, and musical additions to the choral repertoire.

PERCEPTIONS OF THE ENGLISH CHORAL TRADITION

Although the intention of this chapter is to explore the framing of choirs and their conductors from a UK perspective, it is often the case that to view it from the outside can illuminate some of its characteristics, traits and idiosyncrasies. After all, choral singing is a global phenomenon and western European choral music is not just the preserve of Western cultures and countries. Some of the best choirs are to be found in Asia, for example, with the Philippines having a strong choral tradition performing as much Western classical repertoire as indigenous.

My experience in conducting and carrying out research with university choirs in the United Kingdom is documented elsewhere (Durrant, 2011, 2012) and reveals some interesting contrasts and challenges that face students joining from other cultures and countries. Further research, through unstructured interviews with overseas student singers and conductors studying in the UK, has been carried out since: some of the findings are presented. Some students are on masters' programs specifically in choral conducting, but most are undergraduates or postgraduates on non-music programs. In the University of London Chamber Choir (ULCC) at the time of writing, for example, are two students studying veterinary science, one from Singapore and the other from the United States. Other student singers from Germany and The Netherlands have also contributed to ongoing research.

A doctoral student from the Philippines on presenting himself recently at an audition for ULCC, for example, found the level of sight-singing skill required excessively challenging. His tenor voice was bright and strong and certainly acceptable for admission to the choir in terms of vocal sound, yet the dependence on reading the music rather than learning by heart was a deterrent for him and for the conductor. A Japanese student was accustomed to rehearsing at his previous university choir in Japan for some ten hours a week, rather than two or three in his London choir. Again, the expectation on personal learning of the music was greater than the ability to read at sight. Yet this custom of sight-reading is prevalent in the United Kingdom, and not only for singers. Even in our cathedrals it would not be uncommon for the men singers to rehearse a piece just once before performing it in a service. Our professional orchestras are among the least rehearsed in the world: it is not unusual to employ an orchestra for one rehearsal only for a major choral oratorio performance, for example. But, their sight-reading is among the best.

The perception of the English choral tradition from a conducting student from Malta (studying on a masters' program in the United Kingdom) was "first and foremost cathedral choirs" and felt that choral singing was "in the blood of most people," this being very different from her own country. Similarly, a conducting student from Singapore thought that the cathedral tradition was "grounded" and part of the "deep culture" of England. He talked of the "clear and precise diction and very bright sound" of the choirs with "smooth long lines." Both referred to the perception that choral singing is noncompetitive (as compared with Singapore particularly) and people sing because they want to. Indeed, it is noticeable that within Europe choral singing is a more deep-rooted part of the culture in the northern countries (Scandinavia, Germany, and the United Kingdom) rather than in the southern countries. In Malta, for example, singing in schools is normally only practiced in preparation for religious events such as saints' days. While in Malta as with many European contexts, the main choirs might well be associated with the Church, this is not so in, for example, Singapore, where most people's singing comes from the schools. The Ministry of Education supports choirs here, and a highly organized quasi-competitive festival is held as part of their co-curricular studies (Wang, 2010). One student commented that school students in Singapore often joined choirs "out of necessity" as a requirement for co-curricular activity participation and not because they really had a burning desire to sing. The perception is that in Singapore the results matters, whereas choral singing in the United Kingdom stems more from within the culture. These are perceptions—not necessarily reality or universal truths.

Two American students studying in London and singing with the university chamber choir likewise (and independently) stated that the all male boy choir dominated their perceptions of the English choral tradition. One even referred to "boys between the ages of 12 and 17 singing John Rutter in some beautiful cathedral," using "less vibrato and more pure sound." Certainly, vibrato is not found as much in English choirs generally as compared with North America. Fern (a female American singer) referred to a more operatic approach to sound back home—"this ridiculous vibrato"—which she didn't find in the United Kingdom choirs. This poses the question do we ourselves (female sopranos) model our singing on the boys choir sound? Singing students from Singapore and the Netherlands endorsed this perception of English boy choirs.

As mentioned, much of the English choral tradition is rooted in the church. Historically, this has been the preserve of boys and men and it is only in the last thirty or so years that girls have been admitted to our cathedral choirs—and then usually singing in separate choirs from the boys (Welch et al., 2012).

Andreas, from Germany, felt that there was not so much attention to style and authenticity issues in England as there is in Germany—with a certain sound for a baroque piece being quite different from a romantic piece. He feels that people don't understand the style and rhythmic changes, for example, in early music:

> Using vibrato in baroque music seems so wrong for me. If we have a classical piece we sing it in a classical way, and I didn't see those differences in style even with choirs at Westminster [Abbey] and St Paul's [Cathedral].

However, he also notes that (as in the UK situation) many conductors in Germany are trained firstly as organists and musicologists and rooted in the Church traditions. Thomas, a student singer from Sweden, also came to singing through the Church and he himself plays the organ, pointing out that most choir conductors will start from this tradition. While coming from a small town in central Sweden, it was evident that singing was a fairly common phenomenon in his country, and he stated that there was no equivalent there to the cathedral and college chapel tradition found in England. Also the music sung was generally more rooted in Swedish folk song. Indeed, in Sweden it is estimated from an earlier study that a large proportion of people do sing in choirs—some 600,000 out of a population of 8.9 million (Durrant, 2003).

This church-based tradition suggests that, while choral leaders have much musical knowledge and understanding, in rehearsals their lack of vocal pedagogy may potentially limit the vocal development of singers. This contrasts, perhaps, with American choral conductors who are more likely to be trained in conducting and vocal pedagogy before they are let loose on school and college choirs. Fern mentioned that her most rewarding experience vocally was with conductors who had that understanding of vocal pedagogy, whereas her church conductor was "full of passion but not a good conductor or singer."

Greg, another American student in London, noted a difference in approach to learning the style in music. Referring to a motet by William Byrd, he said that he is more likely to be rehearsed with a more analytical approach:

> Like count it out . . . we would like do it very mechanically for a while, and then something would lock and oh, I feel this now.

He suggested it became more of an instructional theory lesson back home, whereas there might be more responsibility laid at the feet of the individual singer in the United Kingdom as well as more awareness of musical style and its vocal implications. The practice generally in his experience through school and college in the United States was of a more atomistic approach.

Two Singaporean students singing in London told of their introduction to choral singing in their schools. Chris started when she was 12 and then joined an a cappella group when she was 17 before coming to university in London. Kun also first of all sang in his school choir. Both commented on their perceptions of the English choral tradition (much in line with others from overseas) but spoke of their surprise at the level of sight-singing expected of them in their choir in London. Generally in Singapore, school choirs learn their music in vocal parts separately to start with and from memory before coming together as an ensemble. They commented on the advantages to learning the notes securely, but that they had little sense of the music and its expressive character for a long time in the rehearsal process. It was as if musicality was added as icing on the cake towards the end of preparation. While this appeared to be general practice, particularly in the lead-up to the school choir festival where there tended to be a competitive edge, this was considered to be an efficient and perhaps economical way of operating. Chris suggested that in her choral singing there was more emphasis on getting the right notes and being grounded in the musical technique, whereas in England she felt that people started young and "there is more musical expression and feel for the music . . . there is more of a tradition here . . ." In her chamber choir "we start from a higher musical level" and "we pay more attention to the text and the meaning of the music." Chris reported that she often felt pressured in her Singapore school choirs because of the competitive element in the festivals—"there were a lot of expectations, but it was a good experience." This pressure when competing in school festivals was also noted by Yeung (2007) in her study on choral singing in Hong Kong. (As an adjudicator in these, I can attest to the pressure engendered by the conductors on their choirs and also on themselves on such occasions.)

Felicia from the Netherlands had sung in choirs, including the national youth choir, from the age of ten. Her parents were musical and she felt her experience was probably not very different from many singing in her chamber choir from the United Kingdom. She stated that her conductor in the Netherlands "was very much influenced by the boy choir tradition of England and into that boy choral sound." She was also taught with solfège, though does not find it useful now. She felt that the level of sight-singing here was similar to her experience previously, suggesting perhaps that there was a northern European norm of musicianship in choral singing that was not just English.

Of course, it is tempting to make overall generalizations on approach to musical style between cultures or countries, when it might well be attributable to the individual conductors and their own priorities rather than to a particular musical practice within a country or culture.

One essential difference between certain university choirs, for example, is that in the North America and some Asian and European situations, students gain academic credit for singing in the choir. This is largely not the case in the United Kingdom, where choirs are more normally extracurricular. This perhaps extends from the public school context, where choirs are part of the corporate culturalization of students, along with team sports, rather than part of the serious academic study.

X-FACTOR AND POSH: CHORAL SINGING NOW

The question as to whether choral singing is in a healthy state occupies music educators throughout the western world and that is certainly the case in the UK. Recent initiatives, some government induced, have at least created an awareness of choral singing and the part it can play in the lives of young people. Other studies have highlighted the benefits of singing in terms of well-being as well as culturally and socially (Clift & Hancox, 2010). While there are still issues as, for example, of adolescent boys singing that challenge the minds and practices of teachers, it is at least on the agenda. Many of these issues are tackled elsewhere and need not take too much space here, though pedagogically this is indeed significant (see the work of Cooksey, 1992, for example).

In the United Kingdom, as I suspect elsewhere in the world, talent shows and X Factor-like programs are as prevalent on our televisions as cookery and border control programs. Yet a lot of these focus on the individual and their range of emotional reactions from ecstasy to anguish, rather than actual vocal and musical quality. The media is dependent on there being failures as much as winners. It is the crying and jubilation that interest the audience. In schools, this then presents a very real challenge to teachers in encouraging their young people to engage in collaborative singing classes in contrast to the media-driven image-dominated so-called talent shows. The cult of celebrity pervades and clouds the essence of collaborative singing endeavors, where the whole is greater than the individual.

In primary (up to Year 6, aged 10–11) and secondary schools (Year 7 and upwards, aged 11–18) singing in our state schools is patchy and dependent on the enthusiasm of the individual teacher (as reported by our national inspection system OFSTED—the Office of Standards in Education for England and Wales). It can occur in ordinary time-tabled music classes as a singing session, certainly in the earlier years, where it might be used more informally as a learning tool, or in more formalized optional extra-curricular choirs if there is a teacher with the skill and determination to lead this. In independent schools (termed rather bizarrely "public schools" in the United Kingdom) singing is more accepted and prevalent and occurs in chapel for services and other extra-curricular settings. In less common situations, there may well be individual singing lessons in the same way a student might have clarinet lessons.

The occurrence of singing in schools normally takes the form of three main modes: (1) class singing—where mere participation in the timetabled activity within the non-optional music classroom is the intent rather than (regrettably) any developmental vocal or musical learning; (2) choral practice—where the activity is run in the manner of a choral rehearsal, usually extracurricular, with associated instruction to correct errors and work towards a performance, and; (3) vocal study—in rarer circumstances where individual students may have individual voice lessons.

Over the last decade, the UK government has supported and indeed advocated a revival of singing through such funded initiatives as "Sing Up," the National Music Plan and the chorister outreach program, monitored by the government inspection body "OFSTED." There have been a number of advocates for this, though in the recent years of economic downturn, inevitably it is the arts subjects that are susceptible to reduction in public funding and therefore official interest. In addition, the media has given attention to singing through such popular reality television programs like Gareth Malone's *The Choir*. Although, this may well have given singing more "street cred," it has not in itself ensured greater participation in singing in schools, churches and communities. Official OFSTED reports (2012; 2013) have consistently referred to a paucity of singing particularly in state secondary schools (though with notable exceptions). The reasons for this are largely the low expectations of singing from the teachers themselves. Attitudes that singing is just not cool still prevail and therefore engender a reluctance often bordering on alienation. While there are no easy answers, part of the problem is lack of knowledge of singing and vocal issues, in particular surrounding the male (and female) adolescent changing voice. But my own theories put forward the fact that there is not enough opportunity for teachers to gain vocal knowledge, to be trained in choral conducting and therefore gain insight into why they are leading singing or how they do it, and choose appropriate musical material for those they teach, lead, and conduct (Varvarigou & Durrant, 2010).

An earlier study (Turton & Durrant, 2002) revealed that adult reflections of and attitudes toward their secondary school singing experience was, on the whole, negative. Yet, these people (randomly selected for interview) believed (1) that singing was inherently worthwhile activity, (2) that it contributed to personal confidence and corporate identity, and (3) that they would have liked to receive vocal training and development rather than just have a singalong. The participants in this study, on reflection, wanted to learn to sing. As with the more recent OFSTED findings, low expectations are commonly found in the timetabled secondary school classroom. The implications are that more professional development in leading singing activity and understanding the nature of vocal development is essential for motivating class singers, as well as inspiring them to belong to choirs and other choral groups.

It should be noted that in England and Wales, music is taught as a compulsory subject up to and including Year 9, and then as an optional examination subject. The curriculum content is wide and does not per se stipulate singing classes or equivalence to choral singing. This contrasts with the North American situation where choir is usually an elected class in many schools. Choir in the United Kingdom operates as an extracurricular, optional activity.

In churches and cathedrals much of the choral tradition is still maintained with the (sometimes) daily singing of services in the Anglican rite. The larger cathedrals and college chapels will have a choir, often men and boys and, more recently an additional choir with girls and men. This means that choristers will have daily rehearsals usually early in the morning before main schooling and one before the evening service. The repertoire is large and challenging with a range of music from early Elizabethan to contemporary. This, however, is the preserve of a small elite with choristers often having to board away from home, sometimes from the age of seven. It is a precious but rarefied environment and regarded as "posh" and "for grannies" by those not engaged in this tradition (Ashley, 2009). As we listen to the famous carol service from King's College Chapel, it should be remembered that this is the result of hard work and an often punishing schedule for (in this case) a committed group of highly musical, highly intelligent, highly motivated auditioned boys and male choral scholars. The schools where choristers are educated are normally fee-paying, thus suggesting that the partakers will, for the most part, be also well off. This is neither typical nor indicative of the singing population and culture in the UK.

In churches, cathedrals, and college chapels, choral conductors would normally and firstly be organists, with some form of diploma (usually the Fellowship diploma of the Royal College of Organists for the prestigious positions) required to hold the job. This seems to be the case in other European countries, as gleaned from the participants in the research—notably the Netherlands, Germany, and Scandinavia. Practice in other churches is variable, led by an organist who may well not be able to conduct or lead from the front, but more likely from the keyboard. Or in some cases and in smaller churches, there is no choir at all. Newer traditions, as can be found in the more Pentecostal and evangelical churches, may well have vibrant gospel and more pop orientated singing groups.

EXTRACURRICULAR: PUBS, CLUBS, ROWING AND SINGING

Most choirs in the United Kingdom and, I suggest in many parts of Europe, are dependent on people's goodwill and enthusiasm to turn up to rehearsals. Church and community choirs usually rehearse one evening each week in preparation for concerts or sung services. Some choirs will operate on a less regular basis, with perhaps intensive rehearsals leading up to a specific event such as a Christmas carol service. Apart from cathedrals and college chapels and professional choirs where singers are obliged to turn up, sometimes daily, other choirs are amateur and extracurricular. Schools choirs, as mentioned, are not usually part of the mandatory curriculum and the expertise and enthusiasm of the individual teacher as well as the cultural norms and ethos of the particular school will determine the success of the choir.

Maria, a student conductor from Malta, spoke of her frustration at getting her singers to attend rehearsals. Similarly, a well-established conductor of a very able adult community chamber choir in the Cambridge area of England reported that she found it challenging and frustrating that her singers were not always regular and reliable in attendance. The internal perception then of choral singing is an amateur one—that is, essentially for the love of it—when you can. One British axiom is that we are "jolly good amateurs."

This then suggests that conductors themselves may behave in different ways in different countries and traditions according to common practice. Students from Singapore have often referred to the conformist nature of their society and that expectations from school students who are members of the choir are high in terms of commitment. The Singapore Youth Festival is an example of a systematic and highly organized festival where, on alternate years, some 130 secondary school choirs come to perform in turn a program of three pieces, including a compulsory set one. These choirs operate as part of co-curricular activities that students have to opt into. If they choose choir, then there are obligations to attend and perform and, if required, to attend additional rehearsals near the performance time (Wang, 2010). There is no equivalent in the United Kingdom;

in Singapore, with a population of some five million, approximately 6,000 secondary school students sing in the festival. That is indeed a significant number.

In the increasingly global environment, where it is now not unusual for students to study overseas, it is good for young singers to experience new choirs and different choral practices and traditions. Gaining insight into other ways of rehearsing and performing is valuable. However, in order for this to be a positive learning experience, conductors need to be aware of basic principles on which their work can be optimally effective.

PEDAGOGICAL TRANSFORMATION

My own research interest over the years has been particularly concerned with the conductor and the teaching and training of conductors (Durrant, 1998, 2003; Varvarigou & Durrant, 2010). In various studies, it became clear that choral conducting in the United Kingdom until some 20 years ago was pedagogically unsound. Teachers in schools, for example, would mostly be qualified to at least a first degree in music or education. This would not necessarily mean that they would have received any courses or studies in conducting or choral conducting. Yet they would be expected and assumed to be able to train and conduct their school choir and, in the case of fee-paying independent schools, often the chapel choir. This contrasts to the state of play normally found in North America, where those intending to teach are educated to a specialist level in choral pedagogy or in band pedagogy for band directors. While music teachers in the United Kingdom will likely have some instrumental or vocal specialization, it is rare to find one who has specialized in conducting (Varvarigou, 2009).

My own findings from teaching courses and leading workshops in the United Kingdom is that conductors may well have general musical qualification, but may also be amateur in that their main profession is entirely outside the realm of music. They do it through their own passion and commitment, or because there is no one else to do it. Generally in community choirs, the situation is difficult to ascertain, as there is not one professional body where choral conductors are obliged to, or feel the compelling need to, belong. The *Association of British Choral Directors* does not, for example, have the proportional membership of the *American Choral Directors Association*. Many major British choral conductors, including most of the cathedral directors, do not belong.

Today, various research studies by experienced practitioners (including my own) have contributed to an improving situation, with more choral conducting courses taking place within the higher education sector as well as through independent bodies such as the *Association of British Choral Directors*. A growing awareness of the impact good choral education can make to the state of singing is happening in the United Kingdom, although there are still pedagogical, developmental and cultural issues and challenges that we face. However, some of these issues and challenges are to be found across the world where choral singing is within a more formal setting, as is the case in schools, colleges, churches, and certain community contexts and not just in the United Kingdom.

Successful and effective choral singing requires effective and successful choral conducting and leadership, which, in turn requires a pedagogy that is founded on essential
musical and communication skills. In a previous study (Durrant, 2009), I concluded
that musical knowledge in the context of choral conducting incorporates:

a knowledge of choral repertoire appropriate for the singers;
  a knowledge of the voice, including some physiology, in order to be able to promote healthy singing;
  a knowledge of the expressive intentions of the music through its text and musical
structures;
  a technical knowledge that enables the conductor to hear and therefore provide
feedback to the singers, as appropriate, to enhance the musical and singing experience.

But, above all, the efficient and effective communication of this knowledge through
conducting and rehearsing and an awareness of the ability level of the singers are paramount attributes. This moves on from the previous model of effective choral conducting
put forward in Durrant (2003), where I proposed three main elements that contribute to
an effective conductor's personal constructs: (1) philosophical principles underpinning
the role (knowing and understanding the music and its aesthetic potential); (2) musical-
technical skills (aural skills and being able to indicate tempo, dynamics, etc.), and; interpersonal skills (communicating and being positive towards the singers).

The model of an effective choral conductor is founded on the premise, firstly, that
people all over the world sing—it is an elemental part of the human condition (biologi-
cally, psychologically, and sociologically) and, secondly, that people learn more effectively in a positive, safe environment (Durrant, 2003; Thurman & Welch, 2000). While
much singing takes place without a notated score, it is often inextricably linked with
sociocultural events and ceremonies, be it at a football stadium or Indonesian temple
ceremony. In terms of choral pedagogy, we are more likely to refer to more formal settings where singing takes place—possibly for a ceremony or event, or just as likely for
leisure and pleasure.

This then translates into a pedagogical model for teaching conductors with the ultimate aim of enhancing the choral experience for singers. Let us look into the constituent
elements of the effective choral conductor a little more. From talking with student singers and others, it is evident that in the conductor they appreciate: (1) their knowledge of
the music and the voice, (2) their efficient and effective rehearsing, and (3) their passion
and enthusiasm.

Choral repertoire and vocal impact. Our personal quest for finding newly composed
or previously undiscovered choral music has never been easier. We have access to such
websites as CPDL where older scores have been edited and uploaded for public use. So
there is a vast range of styles, genres, and arrangements available for us. Depending on
the size, constituency, and aims of the choir, repertoire will be chosen accordingly—
sometimes with a planning committee with larger groups, but normally in all cases following the recommendations and advice of the choral director. In most cases, budget

considerations have to be taken into account, especially if new music is to be purchased or an orchestral accompaniment to be employed. But whatever the considerations, it is surely most important that music is chosen appropriately for the singers. And by this I mean for their level of musical ability and vocal development. During adolescence in particular, choosing repertoire appropriate for the developing voice is of supreme importance. This is dealt with extensively elsewhere, but in short, judicious choice of music that fits the voice is more likely to engage young singers than repertoire that is out of range and vocally uncomfortable, whatever the music.

I have witnessed (and led a workshop with) a choir of some 70 largely black American junior high students from a socially deprived urban area, singing a three-part arrangement of Vivaldi's *Gloria*. They sang this with equal enthusiasm as they did a gospel song. The music fitted their voices at their stage of development with soprano, alto, and baritone parts. The result was total commitment to the activity and a sense of choral identity and positive attitude. I have also witnessed young singers being forced into singing (or belting) unison show songs, where, for some, the vocal range was totally unsuited to their tessitura at their stage of development. The result was vocal stress and frustrated, disillusioned singers.

Cooksey's work (1992) on the boys' changing voice has implications for the choral conductor. Ashley's (2009) more sociological research into boys' attitudes towards singing in relation to the paucity of experience in some schools suggests that far too many teachers in the United Kingdom know little about the voice, its properties, and vocal development.

In informal discussion with a group of adult singers in an amateur rural English choir, I found a high level of frustration as the choir conductor had indicated that he wanted to do Handel's *Messiah* with them. They felt overpowered by this decision and realized that vocally and musically the challenge was daunting. While *Messiah* is indeed a profound work, it was not an appropriate choice in its entirety for this particular group of some 20 amateur singers. The choice made some leave the choir. It was more about the conductor wanting to conduct rather than lead and develop the singers vocally and musically from where they were. While not criticizing the musical ability of the conductor, it was his knowledge of the choral repertoire being appropriate for that particular choir that was called into question.

While it is not expected, nor the custom in the United Kingdom, for choral conductors to act as singing teachers, it is extraordinary that conductors will be appointed to positions on the strength of their keyboard playing as much as their vocal knowledge. One would expect an orchestral conductor to have a working knowledge of orchestral instruments even if not being a player of each one. But as the voice is a precious and personal instrument—one that is tied in to our psyche and emotional lives—it is imperative that some knowledge of vocal development is gained for the choral conductor to be effective in teaching and making music with their singers. Most choral conductors work with amateur and often young developing singers; most choral rehearsals are concerned with teaching and leadership and not just making beat patterns in the air. So it is in the treatment of our singers through nonverbal and verbal communication that we can enhance their vocal experiences (Durrant, 2003). It is not uncommon to find, even in our cathedrals, choral conductors showing their lack of vocal knowledge in rehearsals, evidenced through inappropriate language and behavior, and through inappropriate and vocally unfriendly conducting gestures. Although I am sure the same is to be found elsewhere, a lack of systematic and structured conducting tuition has led choral conducting practice itself to be patchy and lacking in vocal awareness.

Efficient and effective rehearsing. This chapter does not set out to take on the mantle of how to conduct or how to rehearse, but it is worth considering what is effective and how singers get the most from rehearsals and performances. Rehearsing choirs is a craft skill utilizing verbal and nonverbal communication. Gesture is an elemental nonverbal part of conducting and its shape and communicative properties need to be in context and related to musical meaning (Durrant, 2009; Hatten, 2004; Ford, 2001).

> One significant consideration for the conductor is the cooperative meanings of the image—the gesture—and the verbal instruction. The craft of conducting is to ensure the interpreted meanings of both coincide, otherwise the conducted will receive confusing subliminal messages. (Durrant, 2009, p. 330)

It will send out confusing messages to the singers if on the one hand conducting gestures are large and emphatic, while on the other hand verbal instruction is asking for a *piano* and *legato*. Efficient and effective rehearsing makes the singers feel good about themselves, gives them challenges and approval when the challenges are met. At the beginning of the chapter on rehearsing in *Choral conducting: Philosophy and practice* (Durrant, 2003, p. 105), I make reference to two styles of rehearsing by two eminent conductors: the one making the singers feel secure and confident while the other castigated the choir for not knowing the notes, thus creating a feeling of insecurity and negativity. (The fact that one conductor was English and one American was not, I hope, an indicator of national traits.) But, it is so easy to create a negative atmosphere in rehearsal—probably less easy to create a positive one.

Passion and enthusiasm. From my own experiences of teaching and conducting together with a variety of research studies, it is evident that conductors need to show a commitment both to music and to those they are conducting in order to be truly successful (Ashely, 2001; Durrant, 2000, 2003, 2009). Passion and enthusiasm invigorate singers. Conductors should examine ways of communicating their own passion and commitment to singers. Thurman (in Thurman & Welch, 2000) refers to "human-compatible" and "human-antagonistic" behaviors. He suggests we can impact negatively not only upon singers' attitudes to singing but also disable their means of improving and learning effectively.

> It is therefore incumbent on the conductor to adopt a "human-compatible," as opposed to a "human-antagonistic" style of behavior in music-making processes in order to get the best out of the participants. This includes providing safe,

free-from-threat learning and singing environments as well as encouraging cooperative rather than competitive actions from participants. (p. 162)

This means that a behavior that constantly admonishes rather than supports singers
can compromise efficient singing and expressive intentions. Many traditional modes of
conducting behaviors are associated with "telling off," belittling people, and thus creating a threatening situation where effective learning is unlikely to take place. Singers have
commented when passion and enthusiasm are more apparent in the rehearsal than rep-
rimand, as they then associate with this and the music's essential meaning. As a general
means of communication we can open and extend our arms as a sign of welcome, or
we can cross or fold them as a sign of noncommittal or "fed-up-ness" (Durrant, 2009).
Conductors can make their singers feel good or bad about singing and about themselves.

There are distinct, specific and also covert meanings in gestures. The teacher standing in the front of a class with folded arms, together with a particular expression is
giving a subliminal message to the students. A conductor beginning a choir rehearsal
with arms extended, coupled with a warm smile, gives a message of welcome to the
singers, as if to embrace them and invite them to sing. (p. 331)

There are profound implications for conductor education therefore. While choral and
vocal knowledge along with musical and technical skills form the backbone of creating a
musical situation, it is the communication of the music's expressive intentions and character that will make the experience special. Referring back to some of the student singer
comments—it was a surprise to some that musical meaning and emotional import comes
from the conductor's engagement with and enthusiasm for the music and was part of the
rehearsal process from the beginning and not just an "add-on" when the notes had been
learned. The music is more than the notes. How then is this element taught?

Varvarigou (2014) has demonstrated that cooperative learning, particularly peer
feedback, can have a distinctive and positive role to play in conductor education.
Throughout teaching conducting courses, the feedback and general comments from the
singers can impact significantly on the conductors' development, as she reports. Many
such comments are to do with the nature and level of communication—does the conductor look at us? When the conductor smiles—it makes such a difference! Your gesture
is telling us one thing and your verbal instruction another.

CONCLUSION

This chapter has intended to present an aspect of the framework of choral singing and
conducting in the United Kingdom. It has taken the views of overseas student singers
and conductors to create a broader dimension to the discourse. The more traditional
and historical perspective has impacted on these views: yes, the United Kingdom has

a fine cathedral choral and college chapel tradition that should not just be preserved in aspic, but nurtured and disseminated as widely as possible beyond the cathedral precincts. This is where non-church choirs can play a role in performing some of the finest choral music by United Kingdom composers, especially, for example, from our golden age of Elizabethan composers (both Elizabeth I and II).

Pedagogically, choral singing and choral conducting are receiving a renaissance at the time of writing—though there is still a long way to go. Choral conducting courses are emerging both within the higher education sector and individual organizations. The quality of these, however, is dependent on those teaching on them. Where these are founded on research into human learning and understanding of choral music—its style and aesthetic character, vocal knowledge, the development of appropriate musical and technical skills and communication—then they are likely to be more effective and successful. Where courses concentrate on beat patterns at the expense of the music or are based on the whims and prejudices of incompetent and malpracticed tutors, then they will ultimately lead to dissolution and poor practice—and poor or nonexistent singing. That is a phenomenon to avoid anywhere, and is not peculiar to the United Kingdom.

References

Ashley, M. (2009). *How high should boys sing? Gender, authenticity and credibility in the young male voice.* Farnham, UK: Ashgate.

Ashley, M. (2011). The canaries in the cage: Lessons in the role of leadership and pedagogy in conducting from the widening young male participation in chorus project. In U. Geisler & K. Johansson (Eds.), *Choir in Focus 2011* (pp. 89–103). Göteborg, Sweden: Bo Ejeby.

Clift, S., & Hancox, G. (2010). The significance of choral singing for sustaining psychological well-being: Findings from a survey of choristers in England, Australia and Germany. *Music Performance Research, 3*(1), 79–96.

Cooksey, J. (1992). *Working with the adolescent voice.* St Louis, MO: Concordia.

Durrant, C. (1998). Developing a choral conducting curriculum. *British Journal of Music Education, 15*(3), 303–316.

Durrant, C. (2000). Making choral rehearsing seductive: Implications for practice and choral education. *Research Studies in Music Education, 15,* 40–49.

Durrant, C. (2003). *Choral conducting: Philosophy and practice.* New York: Routledge.

Durrant, C. (2009). Communicating and Accentuating the Aesthetic and Expressive Dimension in Choral Conducting. *International Journal of Music Education, 27*(4): 326–340.

Durrant, C. (2011). Engineering, settling baritones, and sexuality: The togetherness of choral singing. In In U. Geisler & K. Johansson (Eds.), *Choir in Focus 2011* (pp. 48–63). Göteborg, Sweden: Bo Ejeby.

Durrant, C. (2012). Male singing in the university choir context. In S. Harrison, G. Welch, & A. Adler (Eds.), *Perspectives on Males and Singing* (pp. 109–123). New York: Springer.

Fellowes, E. (1969). *English Cathedral Music* (5th ed.). London: Methuen.

Ford, J. (2001). Implications for non-verbal communication and conducting gesture. *Choral Journal of the American Choral Directors' Association, 42*(1), 17–23.

Hatten, R. S. (2004). *Interpreting musical gestures, topics, and tropes*. Bloomington: Indiana University Press.

Le Huray, P. (1978). *Music and the Reformation in England, 1549–1660*. Cambridge: Cambridge University Press.

McGuire, C. E. (2006). Music and morality: John Curwen's tonic sol-fa, the temperance movement, and the oratorios of Edward Elgar. In K. Ahlquist (Ed.), *Chorus and Community* (pp. 111–138). Urbana: University of Illinois Press.

OFSTED (2012). *Music in schools: Wider still and wider: Quality and inequality in music education, 2008–2011*. Office for Standards in Education Report 110158. Manchester, UK: Office for Standards in Education.

OFSTED (2013). *Music in schools: Promoting good practice*. Music Education Council. Manchester: Office for Standards in Education.

Routley, E. (1966). *Twentieth century church music* (Rev. ed.). London: Herbert Jenkins.

Thurman, L., & Welch, G. (2000). *Bodymind and voice: Foundations of voice education*. Collegeville, MN: The VoiceCare Network.

Turton, A., & Durrant, C. (2002). A study of adults' attitudes, perceptions and reflections on their singing experience in secondary school: Some implications for music education. *British Journal of Music Education, 19*(1), 31–48.

Varvarigou, M. (2009). Modelling effective choral conducting education through an exploration of example teaching and learning in England (Unpublished doctoral thesis). University of London Institute of Education.

Varvarigou, M. & Durrant, C. (2010). Theoretical perspectives on the education of choral conductors: A suggested framework. *British Journal of Music Education 28*(3), 325–338.

Varvarigou, M. (2016). "I owe it to my group members . . . who critically commented on my conducting"—Cooperative learning in choral conducting education. *International Journal of Music Education, 34*(1), 116–130. ijm.sagepub.com.

Wang, S. (2010). In pursuit of musical excellence: A case study on the Singapore National Youth Orchestra (Unpublished MA dissertation). Institute of Education, University of London.

Welch, G., Saunders, J., Papageorgi, I., Himonides, E. (2012). Sex, gender and singing development: Making a positive difference to boys' singing through a national program in England In S. Harrison, G. Welch, & A. Adler (Eds.), *Perspectives on Males and Singing* (pp. 27–43). New York: Springer.

Yeung, F. (2007). To compete or not to compete: A study in choral singing activities in Hong Kong with respect to the participation in the Hong Kong Schools Music Festival (Unpublished MA dissertation). Institute of Education, University of London.

CHAPTER 13

STRIVING FOR AUTHENTICITY IN LEARNING AND TEACHING BLACK SOUTH AFRICAN CHORAL MUSIC

MOLLIE SPECTOR STONE

THIS chapter examines best practices for learning and teaching choral music from other cultures by using as an example the challenges facing non-South Africans striving to perform traditional Black South African folk and religious choral music with authenticity and integrity. Traditional Black South African folk and religious choral music, which I will refer to as Black South African choral music throughout this chapter, refers to the syncretic folk and religious choral tradition that has continued to evolve and flourish from the end of the 19th century until the present day. Until the fall of apartheid, this repertoire was performed primarily by Black South Africans in their native languages with traditional dance movements. For the purposes of this chapter, I am not including in this definition the modern tradition of Black South African composed songs, which use tonic sol-fa notation, or songs from the *isicathamiya* tradition.

Music educators are expected to put together concert programs that represent a number of cultures, yet often lack the time necessary to learn enough about these traditions to create powerful, authentic performances (Campbell, 2003). In order to do justice to another culture's music, music educators would be well served to

- study how to produce, model, and instruct students in using the proper vocal tone
- find and share both poetic and word-for-word translations of the music's lyrics
- learn and impart information about the language and the significance of the text

- study pronunciation and strategize how to address unfamiliar sounds in rehearsals, and
- research the social, political, and religious contexts in which the culture's music is sung and discuss the significance of how this music functions within its culture today (e.g., black South Africans have adapted many anti-apartheid songs for the current struggle against HIV/AIDS).

Sharing the language, history, and continued development of a musical tradition helps singers gain a deeper understanding of the ways choral music can function within society.

I first developed an awareness of the importance of learning multicultural music as a young singer in the Chicago Children's Choir, an organization founded during the civil rights movement in 1956 to bring together children from different racial, religious, and socioeconomic backgrounds through the pursuit of musical excellence. In 1996, I went on tour as a singer with Chicago Children's Choir to South Africa, and my understanding of music was forever changed.

In preparation for the tour, the choir learned South African songs that had been transcribed and published in the United States and Europe. Although the director had taught the choir that Black South African choral music played a powerful role in the anti-apartheid struggle, we failed to discover any of this power in the arrangements we learned in advance of our tour. When we arrived in South Africa, we could not believe how different the music sounded from what we had prepared. In our scores, the rhythms had been greatly oversimplified. Our pronunciation was uninformed. Our vocal tone was much brighter and weaker than the powerful sound of a South African choir singing in Black South African languages. We had not fully comprehended the interplay between the voices within the call-and-response structure that defines South African choral music, and we missed the subtle complexities of the cross-rhythms created by the traditional dance movements that arrangers were unable to capture with notation (Bradley, 2006).

At a Black school in one of the townships outside of Cape Town we performed these songs, and our audience of Xhosa schoolchildren politely applauded. Then our conductor, Bill Chin, turned to the audience and asked if they would sing the songs for us "the correct way," which to our complete shock, is exactly what they did. Within moments, the audience was dancing, singing, harmonizing, and ululating with more power than any of us could have imagined. They moved up to the edge of the stage, and extending their hands, pulled us down to the floor to sing and dance with them. All at once, the line between performer and audience had completely dissolved.

We sang and danced for nearly an hour with no end in sight, and I remember gazing back up at the stage at our risers, the piano, and the conductor's music stand, wondering what they were doing there. The South African song we had sung so lifelessly from the stage just moments earlier had suddenly been transformed into the most powerful music I had ever experienced.

Once my fellow singers and I had been dragged against our will from the concert hall to depart for our next destination, I sat in the bus stunned and in silence. I felt like I had been given the most tremendous gift, yet I felt deeply betrayed and embarrassed. How was it that we, who came from the most privileged country in the world, could not learn how to sing a South African song properly?

Years later in my graduate conducting program, I watched my colleagues spend countless hours researching whether a Bach cantata should be performed with three people singing each voice-part or just one, in an effort to perform the piece authentically. I learned to write poetic and word-for-word translations of Latin, German, French, and Italian texts on every page of every score from which I performed; it was not unusual for the conductor to stop in the middle of rehearsal to quiz us about the text's meaning. We learned to write extensive program notes about the social and historical context in which each classical piece we studied was composed and first performed.

Multiple studies have shown that learning music helps students excel in other academic areas (Ruppert, 2006). By extension, learning music from other cultures can open students' minds to learning about other parts of the world. South African music is what first awakened my interest in history, politics, and social change. Seeing how South Africans adapt the songs of the anti-apartheid struggle to combat HIV/AIDS led me to take classes in biology and global health. Learning the dance movements to South African folk songs gave me an incentive to become more physically active and develop coordination and strength. Trying to understand the metrical and rhythmic complexity of South African songs made me think about music in a more mathematical way. After my first choir tour to South Africa, I bought a "teach yourself Zulu" book and cassette and became passionate about studying a foreign language.

PAVING THE ROAD TOWARD AUTHENTICITY

Striving for authenticity in learning and teaching any new type of music is a journey. When teaching a song from another culture, music educators are advocates for that song's tradition, translators for that culture's musical language, and ambassadors for the culture itself when they perform for an audience. Because of this tremendous responsibility, teachers should clearly state that their first priority in learning the music of another world tradition is to honor its culture. This should take precedence over any other reasons for choosing a song—whether it be to help singers develop a certain musical strength, explore a new skill, or because it fits well in a holiday concert.

The intention of this chapter is to help choral directors recognize the value and the challenges of striving to teach music from other cultures authentically. Through the lens of teaching traditional Black South African choral music, I will highlight key strategies for addressing these challenges and introduce important resources to help music directors teach Black South African music in the oral tradition. Finally, I will provide a detailed example teaching process for introducing a Black South African choral song to a choir.

THE IMPORTANCE OF THE AUTHENTIC LEARNING EXPERIENCE

When working on music from other cultures, one of the best ways to honor the music and its culture of origin, and also to ensure a more authentic performance, is to create an authentic learning experience for the singers (Goetze & Fern, 1999). The learning process itself can impart a great deal of information about the values of a culture, as well as its ideas about the role of music in society. Traditional Black South African choral music is taught orally. Singers look at each other, rather than at a piece of paper. They stand side-by-side, rather than sitting in chairs. They watch how everyone in the group moves so they move together as a community. Giving one's singers the opportunity to learn in the oral tradition can both strengthen the singers' aural skills and help them to listen and actively pay attention to their fellow singers.

As the value of including performances of world music on concert programs is increasingly recognized (Anderson, Moore, & Music Educators National Conference, 1998), the demand for accessible arrangements of music from these cultures has also risen. But making world music more accessible can strip the music of its essential features. The act of simplifying music from other cultures can play into racist perceptions that Black South African cultures are primitive and simplistic when in reality the music is often too complex for our Western notation system (Stone, 2004). Unfortunately, scores are not necessarily valid resources merely because they have been published. It is shocking that numerous South African choral scores are sold at major choral conventions without accompanying translations or background information about the songs and their cultures of origin. Texts are too often rife with incorrect lyrics and misspellings. Many scores are published with nothing but the Western arrangers' names on them, failing to credit the original sources. (Even when there is no known composer of a song from an oral tradition, it is both honest and essential to credit the ensemble or person from whom the song was learned.)

In my experience, when learning traditional Black South African choral music it is best to not use a score. Teachers of music from folk traditions around the world acknowledge the limits of Western notation in conveying their repertoire. Ukrainian teacher N. Tarnawsky (personal communication, August 29, 2014) asserted that for so many traditions, a score is only ever truly an approximation. These approximations serve as a mere skeleton of a song's overall structure and are meant to be used as a framework for those who already have extensive knowledge of, and experience performing, the tradition's music and who know how to appropriately ornament and fill in the subtle complexities of music from within the genre. A simplified score or arrangement misrepresents the song and the culture. Although slight modifications occur as songs pass orally from village to village in South Africa, Western arrangements sometimes lack the context to truly capture the spirit of traditional Black South African choral music.

Also inappropriate is the use of literal transcriptions to teach traditional Black South African songs to choirs. Often, the rhythms are so syncopated that the notated music appears to be extremely complicated; in reality most singers could learn by rote with just a few repetitions. Black South Africans approach syncopation with a relaxed feel, whereas the Western impulse would be to emphasize offbeats. It is difficult, perhaps impossible, to accurately interpret the feeling of South African rhythms transcribed into the Western notation system. The complexity of a score in which nearly every note is tied to another—as well as across each bar line—forces singers to spend excessive time deciphering the score rather than the music. The use of a score for South African music is inefficient and deprives educators of the opportunity to learn and teach the music authentically.

Adding movement, a necessity in authentic performance, is challenging because it is difficult to convey traditional movements in Western notation. At times, the movements occur in a different meter than the singing, and when the movement is omitted, essential cross-rhythms are lost. Singing Black South African choral music without the dance movements is, as one South African singer in University of Cape Town's Choir for Africa put it, "like performing Handel's *Messiah* or Bach's *B minor Mass* without instruments" (University of Cape Town Choir for Africa Singer, personal communication, 2000). The dance movements are not optional choreography but an essential element of the music. The acts of performing the movements and singing the notes are obligatorily concurrent, and every member of the ensemble should participate.

In addition to rhythm and movement, there are other musical elements of Black South African choral music that cannot easily be captured on the written page. The nature of slides between pitches, harmonies that fall between major and minor, distinctive tuning, dark vocal tone, consistent use of vibrato to sustain energy through the ends of phrases, power behind the sound, and fluidity of key are all difficult to understand without referencing a recording or live performance. To better understand and teach these concepts, music educators can seek out other resources, including guest artists to work with their singers, recordings, videos, and other multimedia resources (e.g. teaching DVDs).

RESOURCES

There are various methods for utilizing resources to help create more authentic learning experiences and performances. Because the West exports a huge volume of music abroad, much of the rest of the world may believe that in order to be marketable and to sustain a living with their music, they must westernize their repertoire to appeal to audiences abroad (Green, 2011). I have not found this to be the case. Instead, by insisting on learning music from other cultures authentically, music educators can help break down these misconceptions, and encourage musicians from other cultures to regain a sense of pride in their own music amidst the destructiveness of global commercialism (M. C. Brass, personal communication, August 29, 2014). Many teachers who lead singing programs in countries abroad remark how amazed and honored local residents are to see foreigners taking the time to study their languages and singing traditions well enough to perform their music. These performances often change long-held attitudes of locals towards Americans and other foreigners (M. C. Brass, personal communication, August 29, 2014).

Short of traveling to South Africa and visiting a number of South African choirs, guest clinicians, who are native to South Africa and familiar with the choral music there, can be wonderful resources. In addition, there are a number of multimedia resources readily available to help choral directors and their singers to learn and perform South African songs authentically (see resources at the end of the chapter).

In addition to teaching DVDs, a multitude of videos and recordings exist online. In situations where there are multiple recordings of the same song, music educators may choose to model based on a recording they feel is most powerful or most relatable to the voices of their singers (it is sometimes easier to have a model closer in age or physicality to the singers). Listening to a number of recordings can provide a better sense of the range of sounds and movements used by different choirs. A famous South African touring choir that performs with a sound system in a megavenue will sound quite different than a choir of schoolchildren performing in a classroom in the townships. Listening to a variety of sounds can also make it easier to discern more authentic singing from more westernized singing.

Teaching Toward an Authentic Performance

Teachers of world music often find the need to tailor their approach based on the challenges presented by a particular song. Clinicians, when teaching music from Black South African cultures, often introduce, and return repeatedly to, key concepts that help foreigners distinguish between techniques that are appropriate for the culture in which they are singing and techniques the singers use in their own everyday choral singing. I refer to these concepts as *keys*, and I utilize them to help singers develop strategies to avoid predictable pitfalls in performing music from other traditions.

Example reaching plan

Whether beginning with a lecture on the cultural history or playing a recording or singing the song, it is helpful to prepare by writing the song's lyrics on a board so the singers are able to look up throughout the learning process. Singers should learn the song standing, so they are ready to move. When introducing the song's background, it is important to explain where the song is from, the language it is sung in, and if possible, to show a map of South Africa that indicates which language is spoken in each region.

As soon as work begins on text, music teachers should provide word-for-word and poetic translations, identifying some of the key words in the song so the singers can use them as landmarks to aid in memorization. Sometimes a folk song's meaning is not entirely apparent from a mere translation, so additional explanation of the text's historical or cultural context may also be necessary.

Next, teachers should begin work on pronunciation, spending extra time on unfamiliar sounds like the clicks found in Xhosa and Zulu. In reviewing pronunciation, it is often helpful to speak the text slowly, asking the singers to repeat each line and only speeding up when they feel comfortable.

Once singers feel comfortable with the text, teachers can introduce each voice part, usually beginning with the melody, or *call* within the call-and-response structure. It is most helpful to teach each part one at a time, combining them before working on the next part. Adding a part at a time allows the harmony to unfold in a compelling way. All singers should learn each voice part as the song is taught, so they understand how the parts fit together. I highly recommend avoiding using the piano to teach notes. South Africans do not use pianos in their traditional music and therefore do not tune strictly to equal temperament. Singers will sound more authentic if they only tune to each other rather than to a piano. Teachers should model all four parts in whatever vocal range is comfortable, but they should be sure the singers perform in the correct octave.

Introducing movement

Movement in traditional Black South African choral music is compulsory, and teachers should introduce dance movements into the learning process as soon as is feasible. Depending on the complexity of the dance movements, it may be more helpful to introduce elements of the movements before teaching the voice parts. Better still would be to teach the movements along with the first voice part, so all the voices feel how their singing fits with the movements. The director, or a student with strong dance aptitude, should model the movements in front of the singers. If a mirror is available, this can improve students' understanding of how the movements fit into their own physicality. Teachers should remind singers that although dancing can be exciting, traditional South African dance movements are subtle and relaxed. It is relevant to note that singers with a wide range of disabilities are able to perform South African music beautifully: Singers in wheelchairs can often perform the upper body movements with great success, and singers with vision impairment can learn dance movements with a bit of extra guidance from a fellow singer during rehearsals.

When I teach traditional Black South African choral music, I anticipate challenges with rhythmic issues, primarily in helping singers to keep the offbeats relaxed, yet accurate. It is culturally inappropriate to westernize syncopations by putting them on the beat. Focusing on the movements can be worthwhile: Steps often fall on the beat, while offbeats occur more frequently in the vocal lines. If singers feel grounded in the steps, they have something against which to feel the offbeats. The energy in traditional South

African dance is focused downward, into the earth, where the ancestors reside, not up to heaven as in certain forms of Western dance. Physical warm-ups that give singers a feeling for this downward energy may be beneficial. Teachers can encourage their students with the key, "feel that your body is rooted in the earth."

When teaching movement, it is important the dancing not look choreographed. Each singer should move with a calm body. One should sing with passion, but make the movements appear effortless. Traditional South African dance is all about subtlety (Stone & Cuyler, 2013). Singers using too much movement risk subdividing the beat and bouncing, which is very inauthentic. Recognizing that each person's physicality is different, conductors are charged with coaching singers so that their movements work uniformly within the framework of their bodies. One of the best ways to achieve this is to encourage singers to be aware of how others in the group are moving while dancing. This creates a more authentic learning experience and helps singers achieve uniformity in movement and focus their attention and energy on each other rather than on a piece of paper or the conductor.

Introducing language

Foreigners have a tendency to introduce inappropriate diphthongs in their pronunciation of Black South African languages. To help singers strategize how to keep the vowels pure and use a darker, more covered vocal tone appropriate for this style of South African music, teachers can use the key, "keep your lips in front of your face." This helps singers avoid stretching their lips back into a smile, which alters the vowel and creates diphthongs. Another key to achieve the same effect is, "pretend to kiss a beach ball," which helps singers remember to keep their lips in the same position the entire time they sing, never allowing them to spread for [a], [e], and [i] vowels (Stone & Cuyler, 2013). When teachers regularly reiterate these keys, singers learn and internalize them, developing the ability to self-correct.

South Africans use a dark vocal tone for both speaking and singing. The traditional South African singing tone is covered and mostly in head voice. In the lower parts of the vocal range, singers may use a mixture of head and chest voice, but should always keep the sound dark and covered, rather than forward and bright. It is very important to use vibrato consistently to sustain vibrancy all the way to the end of each phrase. One can immediately tell that a choir is not South African when they hold out a phrase without sustaining the energy until the cut-off.

Conductors, instruments, and adjustments

The role of conductors. Conductors in traditional Black South African music serve a different purpose than in Western music. The conductor's role is to start and stop the song, but not to conduct it. When directing this type of South African choral music, the conductor may sing the starting pitch (determined by what is comfortable for the choir), give a breath, bring the choir in, and then join the choir in singing and dancing. Only at the end of the piece should the conductor step out again to cue the last few notes and give a cut-off.

Drums. Although some South Africans add drumming to their performances today, it is mostly in an effort to commercialize their music. Traditional Black South African choral music is sung entirely a cappella, with the dance movements providing the percussive element of the song (Bopape & Cuyler, 2004, 2008). Djembes come from an entirely different region of Africa, and adding West African drums can give the impression that the choir assumes all African cultures are the same and that it is not worth differentiating between their very distinctive musical traditions.

Making adjustments. In order to achieve the level of power of South African choirs, some Western choirs may need to adjust the keys of pieces up or down. This is an acceptable practice. In South African choral music there is a more fluid sense of key than in classical music. Songs often go sharp throughout the course of singing, especially as the song gains intensity. This is considered natural; music directors would be better served focusing on tone and pronunciation than on remaining in a particular key.

Conductors may also need to adjust the structure of the voice parts for their ensembles. Choirs comprising only high voices can use only the soprano, alto, and tenor parts of the song. Tenor parts tend to be quite high, and fit nicely into the range of women's and children's voices. It is also acceptable for men's ensembles to perform these songs, singing the top parts in falsetto.

Providing context

Amid all of the important educational concepts music teachers may address while teaching, it is always powerful to share special stories or pieces of information with singers that bring the culture and the music to life. I will often share why I chose to teach a particular song with my singers. When did I first hear it? How did it make me feel? Were there any difficulties in my first attempt to learn it? Likewise, I take time to teach my singers stories about the people who first taught me the music, as well as special pieces of information that help them develop a sense of connection to the musical tradition. Students remember these stories and facts further into the rehearsal process and realize they are on a path toward developing their own relationship with the music. For example, when I introduce South African songs in the Xhosa language, I teach the singers my favorite Xhosa word to help them get a sense of the pronunciation and vocal tone. My favorite word, *isithuthuthu* (meaning motorcycle), is something my singers never forget. They begin to develop a sense of pride in their growing knowledge of South African languages and music, and in turn, develop a sense of respect for South Africa as a whole, fostering lifelong interest and connection to another culture.

Lastly, when preparing singers to perform the music of another culture, it is essential to provide them with information about the culture's history, especially insofar as it is connected to the music they are learning. Each new song presents new opportunities to share different information, and it is valuable to draw connections between the different cultures represented by each song. One example is that South Africans and people from the nations of Estonia, Corsica, and the Republic of Georgia use their powerful polyphonic singing traditions to preserve their sense of cultural identity amid oppression. Another example is the similarity between the civil rights movement in the United States and the anti-apartheid struggle in South Africa. A third example is that Vivaldi wrote music to be sung and played by orphaned girls in the city of Venice during the early 18th century, like contemporary South Africans who compose choral music to be sung by children orphaned by AIDS. Drawing connections between the different musical traditions enriches singers' understanding of each and helps them see connections between people from different cultures and eras throughout history (Anderson & Campbell, 1996).

One of the most powerful aspects of sharing Black South African choral music with singers is imparting a sense of the historical backdrop against which the music evolved, as well as the current issues that inspire its continued development. Black South African choral music is a syncretic genre that developed as a fusion of indigenous African polyphonic singing and Western hymnody introduced by missionaries during the 19th century. With time and experience, singers will be able to identify which aspects of the music are Western in origin and which are South African. For instance, the four-part soprano/alto/tenor/bass structure is derived from Western hymnody, whereas the frequent use of parallel fourths and fifths is an element of traditional South African polyphony. Even without a score, singers can reflect on these aspects of the music to further develop their ear and their understanding of music theory and ethnomusicology.

CONCLUSION

The genre of Black South African choral music was not reserved for performers on a stage, but was lived and breathed as part of the daily life of Black South Africans of all ages—from migrant workers singing as they worked in the mines, to women singing as they worked in the fields or cooked meals for their families. Children sang as they played games, and everyone sang at weddings, funerals, and other religious services or traditional ceremonies. During times of struggle, people sang in four-part harmony as they marched in the streets to protest the government's policies. They sang in exile, in prison, and even in the face of armed police during the anti-apartheid struggle.

Schoolchildren played an important role in the anti-apartheid struggle, as they marched and sang to protest the government's attempt to enforce Afrikaans (the white language of the apartheid government) as the language of instruction in Black schools.

These protests led to the Soweto Uprisings of 1976, in which many schoolchildren were killed as they fought for the right to a better education.

The potential to use choral music to effect political and social change in society is extremely empowering to singers. Black South Africans have long adapted choral music to address the social challenges of the times, passing songs down through the generations, and from community to community in the oral tradition. During apartheid, people sang these songs to honor their leaders, condemn their enemies, mobilize communities to take action, provide comfort and support to the suffering, and assert their cultural dignity amid dehumanizing oppression. After the fall of apartheid, South Africans sang these same songs in the hopes of unifying people of all races so that they could live together peacefully as members of the new rainbow nation. Today many Black South Africans use choral music to educate people about HIV/AIDS and to break down the stigma that still surrounds the virus.

Singing choral music from other cultures provides the opportunity to create connections between people of different, and even conflicting, belief systems. Taking the time to learn to sing in someone else's language, vocal tone, phrasing is an act of solidarity. Teaching singers to put time, effort, and energy into learning to perform Black South African choral music authentically simultaneously teaches them to develop compassion for the people of that culture and creates more engaged, caring global citizens.

Multimedia Resources

In each of these resources, the viewer has the ability to hear a Black South African choir perform a song, listen to individual singers sing each voice part, receive pronunciation demonstration for the text, and view modeling for the dance movements. Each of these publications also provides translations, background information about the songs, information about the musical tradition and the culture's history, and in some cases, interviews with singers about the role that music plays in their lives and communities.

Discography

Bopape, M., Cuyler, P., & Polokwane Chorale. (2004, 2008). *The folk rhythm* (Vols. 1–2). [CD-ROM & DVD]. Marshfield, VT: Northern Harmony.

Goetze, M. & Fern, J. (1999) *Global voices in song: An interactive multicultural experience* [CD-ROM]. New Palestine, IN: MJ Publishing.

Stone, M. S., & Various Artists. (2004). *Vela vela: Striving for authentic performance in Black South African choral music* [DVD]. Chicago: Author.

Stone, M. S. & Cuyler, P., Matlakala Bopape, & Chicago Children's Choir. (2013). *Raising the bar: Traditional South African choral music* (Vols. 1–2) [Book and DVD]. Chicago: The Choral Imperative.

References

Anderson, W. M., & Campbell, P. S. (Eds.). (1996). *Multicultural perspectives in music education* (2nd ed.). Reston, VA: Music Educators National Conference.

Anderson, W. M., Moore, M. C., & Music Educators National Conference. (1998). *Making connections: Multicultural music and the national standards*. Reston, VA: Music Educators National Conference.

Bradley, D. (2006). *Global song, global citizens? Multicultural choral music education and the community youth choir: Constituting the multicultural human subject* (Doctoral dissertation). University of Toronto, Toronto.

Campbell, P. S. (2003). *Teaching music globally: Experiencing music, expressing culture*. New York: Oxford University Press.

Green, L. (Ed.) (2011). *Learning, teaching, and musical identity: Voices across cultures*. Bloomington: Indiana University Press.

Ruppert, S. (2006). *Critical evidence: How the arts benefit student achievement*. Washington, DC: National Assembly of State Arts Agencies.

CHAPTER 14

....

CONDUCTING CORPORATE
CHOIRS IN BRAZIL

....

EDUARDO LAKSCHEVITZ

FROM 1994 to 1996 I served as the director of choral activities at the Southern Baptist Theological Seminary in Rio de Janeiro, Brazil. As a young choral director, full of energy and enthusiasm, I was determined to impact the country's Protestant church music. To that end, I programmed new arrangements that mixed traditional gems from the Baptist hymnal with Brazilian urban folk and Afro-Brazilian repertoires—styles that were not usually accepted as appropriate in the Baptist services then—along with contemporary gospel music that I learned at choral conferences and other gatherings. I included body percussion and novel vocal effects to entertain and surprise audiences. The community appreciated that music, and attendance at concerts filled the halls.

One night, arriving back home from one of these events, I noticed my grandmother was still awake (It is customary in Brazil for several generations of the family to live together in same household.) I went into her room, kissed her on the forehead and asked:

> "So, Grandma. How did you enjoy tonight's music?"
>
> "If your Grandfather were here," she replied, with a look that mixed pride and a certain severity, "he would not be pleased. What you are doing with the choir . . . just doesn't seem right."

Arthur Lakschevitz, my grandfather, was the publisher of *Coros Sacros*, a hymnal that the majority of Baptist churches used in Brazil for several decades. He was a very serious musician and a meticulous choral director, who strived for artistic excellence. He valued choral music and the importance of choir in singer's lives. For him, rehearsal was mainly hard work in preparation for a performance, and choral excellence was to be attained exclusively with repertoire of the Western European tradition.

Clearly my grandmother believed that he would not approve of the music my choir performed that evening, which shows that some aspects of choral music may have changed during the past five or six decades. But what are those? How could two directors with very congruent goals and thoughts about the quality of choral music, its importance in society, the artistry involved, and the excellence sought, lead groups that delivered such different messages?

Initially this discussion should be informed by the concepts people have of the meaning of choral music. To examine its impact in past and present culture and to understand aspects that have changed in this art over the past years, one has to bear in mind that choral singing is part of society and belongs to both the participants and listeners—experts, amateurs, and consumers—that have opinions that are valid and worth consideration. An approach to contemporary choral singing must give voice to all of these actors.

In 2010 and 2011, one of the assignments for my students at the University was to go into the streets, bus stops, malls, subway stations, restaurants and any other venues to interview people, and collect their definitions for the term "choral music." When all this information was compiled in class (around six hundred responses), two main ideas emerged. First, the answers were not exclusively related to music, but associated with other factors such as fashion (people in robes), repertory (music written by people already deceased), severity (stiff people with folders in their hands), message delivered (vocal music one cannot understand), purpose (people who have nothing else to do), age (old people stuff), venues (church music), and season (Christmas music) among others. There was even one student who could not write the answer obtained, for it was just a mocking vocalization with a head tone. The second idea was the lack of unity in the answers. The term "choral music" does not convey one specific idea to everybody, although the feeling most associated with it is anachronism. The term is strongly associated with the past, as something that belongs to an age gone by. In looking at the results, students' first reaction was laughter about "how ignorant these people are regarding our art." But as discussion advanced, they started to notice that these answers should be taken seriously by choral directors. After all, most of us direct choirs of nonauditioned, volunteer, and amateur singers, and sing to non-educated audiences. If we want our art to keep flourishing, nurturing these singers and audiences becomes a fundamental part of our job, a task that, to be accomplished, demands from choral directors a more sociological view of their art.

Definition

In an earlier publication (Lakschevitz, 2009), I discussed the challenges of finding "the correct" definition for the term "choral music." Literature presents definitions that stem from the most general view, as in Wilson (1959, p. 1)[1] or Figueiredo (2006, p. 8),[2] to very specific ones associated with repertory, number of voices, conducting style, methodology, use of musical notation, tone quality, rehearsal procedures, affiliation and even visual aspects, such as uniforms, the singers position on stage or the use of choreography. Also, in order to meet editorial standards, contest rules, or criteria of school classes, age, or social function, choirs are classified in inconsistent patterns. But the use of one universal parameter seems unrealistic because groups would always overlap categories, no matter how they are organized.

Choir directors, influenced by the Western tradition, tend to think about choral music as something with very specific parameters that influence style, tone, phrase, diction, intonation, and so forth. But if a unique definition of this kind of musical production is quite hard to be determined, to define the choir simply as a group of people singing together could provide the necessary broad view to discuss this musical activity in all its contemporary colors and shapes, although this is not the most common approach. Beyond different classification attempts, the analysis of contemporary choral music must consider that it is an art form performed by people living in the 21st century.

Change

Even if a definitive description may not be possible, some ideas are present in the literature that help to place the choral experience into the context of contemporary social relationships and, consequently, have a strong impact on the lives and thoughts of choir members. For example, Topping (2002) discussed the feelings associated with change. He mentions the uneasiness that occurs in businesses, nowadays facing constant transformation. It is a situation he pictures as the "irregularly moving ground under our feet, with transition being the status quo" (p. 44). Meyer (1967) foreshadowed a "future period of stylistic stasis in the arts, characterized not by the linear and cumulative development of a single fundamental style, but by the coexistence of a multiplicity of quite different styles in a fluctuating and dynamic steady state" (p. 78). Hall (1992) spoke about identities that are not fixed or permanent, but continuously formed and transformed; and Santos (1986) studied the fast growing tendency of original facts, things, and people being replaced by their simulations, as well as the fading of a borderline between real life and its representation. Because a choir is comprised of people who sing together and take part in a society, which is larger than the choir itself, the ideas of constant change, instability, transformed identity, and representation are strong ones.

Commenting on children's choirs in Brazil, Elza Lakschevitz (2006) noted that "students sing in the choir, but also go to school, watch television, have their favorite pop artists, play sports, etc. We have to consider the effects of all these matters in their lives"[3] (p. 56). In her opinion, choral teachers must try to understand the singers first. It should be the main resource for their work. Repertory, technique, style, and all other musical choices happen later. According to her, that simple statement is not always clear for choir directors. The ideas described above are part of a singer's everyday life, and it is not likely that a singer is able to refrain from them just because he or she is joining a choral group. After all, the choir creates an environment where singers are not only able to critique peculiar features of the contemporary world, but also to promote such attitudes. Directors have to consider that, although most of the time they think of their singers solely in the context of the music, the nonmusical factors of the singers' lives ought to be the foremost consideration. When this happens, the director needs to deal with more variants and possibilities and faces situations that might even clash with the ideas considered basic and structural in their formation. Such flexibility lies in the core of contemporary choral activity.

ART WORLDS

It is my contention that the choir serves purposes that include but go beyond the making of music and the reproduction of European works of choral art. The choir is contextualized within society and functions as a mirror to preserve the past, reflect the present, and prepare musicians and nonmusicians for art forms of the future. Thus, consistent with other Brazilian philosophers (see Freire, 1970 for example), the choral experience has an agenda that is musical, but also social, political, and cultural.

To understand these ideas, one might be well-served to consider Becker's (1982) thoughts relative to the collective processes of artistic production, as he emphasizes the patterns of cooperation among individuals involved in such production, and not necessarily the results obtained, therefore leaving aesthetic judgment out of the analysis. Actually Becker treated matters of aesthetic issues from a sociological standpoint and wrote, "Art worlds produce works and also give them aesthetic value [and] treats aesthetic judgments as characteristic phenomena of collective activity" (p. 39). A more thorough look at Becker's theory is beyond the scope of this chapter, but the consideration of just some of the questions he raises in order to identify elements involved in an artistic production is valuable to understand changes happening in contemporary choral music. Analyzing a choir as an "art world," meaning one that contributes to the social, cultural, and political constructs of society, could be difficult for trained choral directors, because they are sometimes more concerned with aesthetic and technical aspects of singing and performing that are the result of traditional academic and conservatory training. Viewing the choral art through Becker's lens might promote an unsettling feeling, showing that concepts thought to be definite and inexorable might not be that significant for everybody involved in the choral activity themselves. More recent studies (see Lave & Wenger, 1991; Wenger, 1998; and Wenger, McDermott, & Snyder, 2002 relative to communities of practice) also support these ideas.

The assessment of choral music as a collective and network-shaped enterprise, leaving out aesthetic judgment or musical taste, brings to the forefront some basic questions: Who are the participants (singers, conductor, composers, arrangers, audience-members, sponsors, critics, etc.)? What are their motivations and expectations? How close is each of them to the product of that work? Which activities can be considered artistic? Who determines what is the artistic work produced? How close is one particular element in the production's network to the main artistic activity? Who are the critics and how does their opinion affect the group's musical production? How is the work supported financially and by whom?

In Brazil, a large number of corporations hire choral directors to develop group singing activities with their employees. Directors of these corporate choirs usually face situations that require the consideration of aspects that are mostly of nonmusical order. Hence, a Becker-based analysis of these ensembles can reveal certain angles through which one can look in order to understand matters that influence the social placement of choral singing, and to compare its status in society to the one it once had in the past. Although choirs in the regular schools and senior citizens' groups are starting to grow in importance in Brazil, because of the recently approved Music Education Bill and the increasing life expectancy rate, the present chapter focuses on this particularly significant aspect of Brazilian choral activity: the corporate choir.

CORPORATE CHOIRS

Although efforts were made in the past (e.g., FUNARTE's Villa Lobo's Project[4] being the most accomplished one, in the 1980's) there appears to be no current data that provides reliable information on the number of choirs and singers active in Brazil, the types of groups, or their main features and affiliation, because the stability once enjoyed by the choral music industry in the last decades of the previous century no longer remains plausible. The establishment of a choir does not require sponsorship from an institution, Western-style trained singers or directors, instruments, printed scores, or even a specific rehearsal venue. Choirs can be formed and disbanded at any time. Budgetary constraints, goals, as well as growing or decreasing interest—all of which consistent with the fast pace of the contemporary world, as discussed in the beginning of this article—impact the sustainability of a choir. Institutions traditionally involved with choral music making are experiencing its decay, as shown in the current tensions between choirs and worship teams in contemporary Protestant churches. On the other hand, in Brazil it is not unusual to find ensembles in venues such as sport's clubs and corporate offices.

Following this idea, it is common in Brazil for corporations, regardless of size, revenue, or sector, to host choirs where their workers take part as singers. In spite of the popularity of these groups in the country, there is historic precedence for this phenomenon. Fulcher (1979), writing about French Orpheonic Societies in the 19th century, cited an article published in 1854 in which the author commented: "Mr. Baron de Foument, owner of two large plants in Cercamps and Boubers, promotes daily singing lessons to his over nine hundred workers." Even twenty years earlier, Boquillon Wilhem, a music teacher and coordinator of music activities in the French public school system, included workers along with students in school choir festivals, later starting choirs exclusively with them.

Fulcher (1979) observed the relationship of the workers' music with the political ideals and actions of 19th-century Bonapartist France. She associates the great official receptivity to Wilhem's project to its potential for representing a specific ideology, showing that choral work within professional institutions can be supported by the correlations established between institutional goals and the ones of the musical ensemble: "Utopian ideas concerning the communal, harmonizing ministration of music, 'the social art,' were refocused in accordance with the Bonapartist conception of the democratic, humanitarian state" (p. 48).

The picture of choral music as a large group of singers acting uniformly, under the guidance of one only director, working toward a common goal without arguing about interpretative ideas, attitudes, and procedures is tempting. However, these ideas of control and strict obedience are not commonly remembered in the contemporary discourse that supports choral music activities in Brazilian corporations. Actually these thoughts are more connected to Industrial Age, factory-like procedures discouraged by contemporary management literature, which supports ideas of a more flexible hierarchy, horizontality, and continuous education. Instead, "Quem canta seus males espanta" (He [sic] who sings scares away his woes) is a common proverb usually quoted by Brazilian corporate directors when explaining why companies would sponsor choral singing. A project that can be implemented with low costs and small initial investment, a choir can promote moments of relaxation amidst a stressful day's work, benefiting both employers and employees, an action consistent with the growing concern—supported by unions and other types of professional associations—with workers' health and wellness. Human resources analysts also connect participation in a choral experience to modern practices of corporative governance, and view the choir as a bounded group working together to accomplish a common goal. Specifically they believe that the skills the workers learn by being in the choir contribute to the abilities of the workers to produce at a higher standard.

In addition, the organizational structure of the choir equalizes the hierarchy-based structures of the corporate environment, a fact that can be perceived in many companies where managers and directors sing side by side with factory workers, all working together as equals for a common artistic purpose. The choir fosters teamwork, requires participants to understand their work as a smaller part in a much larger process, and often makes singers deal with unexpected changes, therefore requiring flexibility from them. All of these are desired goals of modern corporate practices. In addition, the choir often reinforces the public image of a corporation, showing that the management is concerned with the social needs of the local community and with the promotion of cultural endeavors.

SINGERS

The culture of the Brazilian corporate choir represents a shift away from traditional conceptions of choral ensembles. Rehearsals and performances happen in nontraditional places, with amateur participants who usually have no prior experience. Singers and sponsors are mostly motivated to participate for reasons other than pure artistic goals. Even if looked upon with certain suspicion by classical musicians, this is a good thing, because it represents a movement toward the popularization of choral music making in Brazil, and the consequent increase of professional opportunities for choral musicians. While there are a few musical features of these groups that are consistent with a traditional view of choral music making, there are adjustments the director must make to honor the culture of the ensemble and to ensure a successful experience for all involved.

Joyce (2005) pointed out that an adult who self-identifies as a singer is an exception in contemporary urban society. In her opinion, that's a disturbing situation, for singing should be as natural an act as any other and not just for those who are formally trained. During the last century, the music industry and the popularization of recording media have caused active amateur singers to turn away from participating in live music-making. Consequently, according to Joyce, in the past century musicians and nonmusicians have become two separated groups of people. In addition, the lack of required music programs in Brazilian schools has deepened the gap between those adults who participated in choirs and those who did not. As a result, many singers in a corporate choir do not care about the type of vocal quality considered correct in the Western classical tradition, for their main reference is what they hear in the most current media.

In a corporate choir, the average singer is the non-singer type referenced by Joyce. They are volunteers who are inexperienced, and come to rehearsals for different reasons that include therapy (sometimes recommended by the company's medical services); to learn some singing techniques; to interact with their colleagues outside the work environment; or just to unwind from the daily job related stress. The only commonality among the singers is their affiliation as corporate employees. As an ensemble, they are a group of people whose musical interests are not only diverse, but also whose very idea of what a choir is may not be based on the Western traditional conceptions of choral ensembles. Consequently, the concept of persevering through the rehearsal process in order to present a fine product or concert at the end does not make much sense for these singers, who, besides, are very involved in daily corporate activities of a more pressing nature. The process itself has to be fun, rewarding, and educational.

The term "prosumer," quoted by Toffler (1980) can be useful here to explain the importance of the rehearsal process for the corporate choir singer. "Prosumer" refers to the fusion of producer and consumer into one who is involved in both process and product, a figure that emerges along with "a huge economic sector based on do-it-for-yourself rather than do-it-for-the-market" (p. 355). In the corporate choir, singers can be seen as "prosumers," who want not only to enjoy the creative process of rehearsals and concerts, but also want to be an active part in all aspects of the experience. Performances are important, but so are the meetings where they are planned and the rehearsals where they are constructed. This explains why many times corporate choirs rehearse during lunch breaks, or in the afterhours, with singers volunteering their time and wanting to provide input to the director as he or she plans rehearsals and programs.

When leading a choir in a large insurance company, I always tried to get performance opportunities for the group, contacting festivals and schools where we could sing. But everytime the choir was invited to perform, many singers would come up with excuses not to go, which would eventually cancel the choir's participation. The situation frustrated me for a while, especially because we choral directors usually understand a performance to be one the most important tools to motivate singers. One day a singer asked me to stay a little longer after practice, and said: "You don't get it. We do not want to perform in public. Our kick is to sing together here, during lunch break. That's all we want." I realized that, in a company where employees deal mostly with processes related to accidents, death, and frauds, choral music was a way to rest their minds twice a week. For a corporate choir director, understanding the singer's main goal is imperative. It might not only be the preparation of repertory for a public performance.

The singers' lack of prior choral experience presents a different set of issues that can challenge the director. Robes, tuxedos, and singing traditional European choral repertory in black folders have negative connotations for most of the singers, as do the use of head voice and melismatic passages by female voices, a practice closely associated with "church music or opera." This requires the conductor to shift perspective, focus on the singers and, as Freire (1970, p. 83) suggested, create a dialogical environment of learning and artistic creation that considers, in this case, the singer as the center of importance.

The corporate choir stands in a privileged place in Brazilian society fighting what Joyce (2005) considered a harmful feature of the binary singer/non-singer paradigm: the "significant barrier to move adults closer to transformation of their musical experiences and self-understanding as musical beings" (p. 2) A sensitive and skilled director, who understands the culture and the power of the collective nature of choral practice, enhances the chance one has to accomplish the transformation mentioned. A non-singer would perhaps never start an adventure in music making alone, but does so when feeling the safety of the larger context of a choir.

Conducting Corporate Choirs

The conductor of a corporate choir is in a precarious position and often finds himself or herself balancing the needs of the singers, all of whom are volunteers, with the artistic goals of the choir and the objectives of the corporation management. He or she is an artist working in a capitalist environment, which sometimes requires following paths that are dissonant with their own musical convictions. Thus, conductors of corporate choirs have to adapt to the individual context, understand the nature of volunteer singers, consider corporate politics, and acknowledge the hegemony that often impedes progress and impacts the musical development of the group.

Like all conductors, the directors of corporate choirs must develop techniques to motivate the singers and ensure from them a continued interest and commitment and choose repertoire for concert programs that will be interesting to the singers, but also will attract audiences. This is further complicated by the fact that the position of the director is not a tenured one, and the choir is not the principal activity of the company.

Unlike that larger-than-life authoritarian figure of the 19th century ensemble with his [sic] back to the audience who dominates the musicians (Small, 1998, p. 79), the conductor of a corporate choir cannot be the sole authority of musical interpretation, choral sound, and the re-creation of the composer's intentions. Instead, the corporate choir director's tasks include learning and choosing appropriate repertoire (mostly popular tunes) and writing the arrangements, which are often specifically designed for a particular group (usually unbalanced, and with very uneven attendance in rehearsals). Being a non-auditioned activity of often inexperienced singers, with strict deadlines to meet (typical behavior in the corporate word), repertoire must be chosen and formatted to meet the singer's characteristics, rather than in an attempt to mold a choir in order to perform a certain piece of music. The director must also apply teaching strategies that are almost exclusively rote teaching with frequent aural repetition of musical lines. The thought of a systematic music theory-training period during rehearsal—such as sight-reading or vocal instruction—is discouraged because these could have a negative impact on the singers' motivation. Singers join a corporate choir to enjoy the process of collective singing, and not to learn vocal techniques. In a corporate choir, technical training has its place only if the singers, when already involved for a longer time, request it, but never by the director's imposition.

Beyond the musical tasks, the corporate choir director is responsible for finding an accompanist, supervising the setup of amplification systems used in outdoor performances, and checking all performance venues, which often include less than ideal conditions. Even when paid professional teams are hired for these tasks, the director is ultimately responsible. There is also the responsibility to make sure the choir is functioning in accordance with the most up-to-date policies of the company. The idea mentioned above, of corporate choir being a place for the employees to relax, can be innovative at first, but diminishes choral art's transformative and educational potential. The conductor has, then, the important task of unveiling choral music's potential, which is not always clear for everyone in that community.

Finally, the director also designs recruiting programs to invite potential singers to join the group and to maintain an active choral presence in the company, which can have a positive impact on budget and the allocation of resources. The director is the principal advocate for the importance of choral singing in that organization, and must ensure that the management understands and supports the goals. Because, like many administrators, the decision makers in the companies have little or no musical background, the conductor needs to find ways to connect the goals of the choir to the goals of the company, and build relationships with all of the corporate constituencies.

Arrangements

The task of choosing appropriate repertoire for the corporate choir is no different than choosing music to sing for any ensemble. As Fernandes (2003) wrote, mistakes in this task may result in a decreased motivation and commitment to the choir on the part of the singer. An extreme situation was described by a fellow conductor, who directed the choir at the headquarters of a State Bank. One afternoon he went to rehearsal and noticed that no one was present. He was puzzled with the situation, until one choir member came to the auditorium where they usually rehearsed and said: "I must tell you that the choir will be discontinued. We haven't been enjoying the repertory you bring, and last week's song was even worse. So we got together and decided that we are no longer coming to sing in the choir."

The situation described above goes beyond the possibility of vocal health problems caused by prolonged singing of inappropriate literature. Singers who don't like the repertoire may feel disenfranchised and leave the ensemble. Choosing the best music is a crucial part of the director's work. Singing engaging repertoire that the choir and audience like may have a positive impact on recruiting and the commitment of members already in the group. Nevertheless, choosing repertory with the singer's taste in mind does not mean selecting poorly written or oversimplified Western traditional music. In many instances it means designing the appropriate arrangements and adaptations of repertory. For that matter, hiring an arranger isn't the best solution, not only for budgetary reasons but also because the director is the musician who knows best the musical strengths and weaknesses of that group. Therefore, arranging vocal music, familiarity with chord changes notation, and improvisation abilities at a harmonic instrument become skills of great importance for the corporate choir director.

In studying four different Brazilian corporate choirs, I identified issues that impact the selection of repertoire. These included the major presence of Brazilian popular songs, form, customization and text (Lakschevitz 2009).

Popular music

Singers know popular music. Using popular music is very helpful to singers for whom the corporate choir is their first choral experience. They already sing the tunes with the radio, TV or their mp3 player. Familiarity with the tunes, helps them to feel comfortable. This is consistent with Freire's ideas of building a bridge between the student's world and the knowledge developed in the education process. Bruner (1974) in general psychology and Boardman (1988–1989) in music education also advocate going from the known through the unknown to a new known.

Form

Other structural features of the repertory were that singers more easily understood songs in strophic, ternary, or rondo forms, usually tonal, and were most comfortable with pieces ranging from three to five minutes in duration. All songs were in Portuguese, and the arrangements explored ostinatos, accompanied melodies and eventual melodic imitations. These forms were closer to the usual music experience singers had as listeners and consumers and to the repertory they heard in their everyday lives. Interestingly enough, canonic pieces, sometimes referred as appropriate materials for beginning choirs, proved to be more complex to singers in these choirs.

Customization

In all groups observed, Lakschevitz (2009) found that music was customized to meet the mission of the choir, the abilities of the group, and audience appeal. Tessitura, texture, melodic contour, rhythm complexity, and form varied greatly. Even in some printed scores, instead of the term "solo" in the proper staff line, the director wrote the name of the singer who would actually sing it, which, besides displaying the proper care for each singer individually, also helped increase their sense of belonging.

Text

The manner in which singers engage with a text is a primary consideration when choosing repertoire. Words can have a deep personal connection for a singer and commitment to the meaning of the text, especially with amateur and volunteer singers, is an important consideration.

Meaning is not the only aspect that directors consider. The prosody or alignment of the words with the music, the quality and originality of the poetry, and the appropriateness to the group are considerations of note. In addition, the distribution of the text among the various vocal parts is important. Some a cappella arrangements assign certain parts to imitate the sounds of instruments, leaving the text to the sopranos. Altos, tenors, and basses sometimes resent this, as they wish to sing the melody as well. When directing a choir at a consulting company, two comments by different singers show the importance melody and lyrics have for the singers: After one rehearsal, the whole alto section stayed longer to ask me: "Why do you like the other girls [sopranos] more than us?" I was very surprised, and even a bit worried with the situation, until they explained: "They always sing correctly [sic] what is on the CD, while we always get weird parts." The other comment came from one fellow in the bass section, who said: "I really hate this tune. We almost don't sing in it." I replied that the basses were active from introduction to the end. But he responded: "No, we don't sing it. We just keep saying *la la la*." For him and his fellow basses, singing actually means singing melody and lyrics, not accompaniment parts. As discussed above, singers enjoy singing songs, and music written for them ought to consider this idea, distributing this task within the whole choir.

Rehearsals

The rehearsal is the heart of every choral experience. While there is always a concern for artistic integrity, aesthetics, and educational value, in the corporate choir, these must not replace the opportunity of the singers to have fun. The only people that struggle with their work are the ones who do not like what they do.

In the corporate choir, a choral rehearsal is more than preparing for a performance. Therefore directors must pay close attention to behavioral aspects that they take for granted when working with more experienced groups. Analysts in corporate human relations, who study workers' motivation and engagement, show that salary and benefits are not the only items that attract and retain employees. The same may be said for the choral singer in the corporate choir. While singers are interested in the performance, they are more interested in the experience they have preparing it. In fact, most of the conviviality and camaraderie among singers takes place during the rehearsal. In a corporate choir singers are very interested in how the rehearsal process makes them feel. Choral music is not the core business in the sponsoring corporations. Similarly, it is not the main activity in the singers' lives. While the musical results the choir may accomplish play a major part in how well the singers are satisfied, they do not account for the whole experience. In addition, the mere promise of a superb performance does not promote engagement by itself.

Teamwork

Enhancing the sense of teamwork heightens the singer's ownership of the music. The conductor gives directions, of course, but the singers, as inexperienced as they might be, are the ones who will actually enact them. In order to constantly stimulate singers the director is well-served to consider the performativity inherent in phrases such "sing for me," "I want it like this," or "you are doing it wrong," expressions that are off-putting to singers and reinforce hegemonic practice that deepens a sense of hierarchy. This is contrary to what is expected from the choral activity in a company.

Communication

As with all conducting, gestures delivers specific messages. Traditional beat patterns may not have meaning for the corporate choir singer. Over-repetition or exaggeration might interfere with and take away from the singers' abilities to make music.

Positive attitude

A positive and constructive attitude is essential skill to ensure the success of the corporate choir. In so many ways, the choir is a mirror reflection of the conductor, and when conductor and singers work together as partners, they realize success.

CONCLUSION

This chapter explained the nature of the corporate choirs in Brazil and explicated the challenges directors face conducting them. Work with these choirs combines musical and non-musical tasks that are aligned to goals of social, political, and cultural habitus.

It is an ensemble produced collectively by people, and their music making has to be within the context of their entire lives. This approach, then, brings the corporate choir practice closer to all other manifestations of ensemble vocal music of this time.

The concern with motivation and engagement, for instance, are two of the principal subjects identified as important characteristics of the corporate choir director, and these connect to issues of repertoire selection and the dialectic of process and performance.

In recent years, dramatic changes have affected the way people deal with time, space, and personal relationships. When one takes into account the most basic premise of choral art music being produced collectively by people, in an organized fashion, it is reasonable to suppose that the work with choirs is indeed in the midst of a changing and uncertain atmosphere. As obvious as this a might sound, it presents a challenge to choral musicians who were trained in the traditions of Western European choral music and singing. The task, therefore, is to find the proper balance between the legitimate artistic, aesthetic, and musical concepts we develop and the needs of a choral ensemble in the 21st-century corporation. It is not an exact science, and the decisions remain in our hands.

NOTES

1. When a group of people sings together simultaneously, either formally or informally, it is choral singing.
2. "Só não conheço um coro que não tenha cantores." (The only choir I don't know is the one without singers).
3. "Seus alunos cantam no coro, mas também vão à escola, assistem televisão, tem seus artistas favoritos, jogam bola etc. Temos que levar em consideração os efeitos desses fatores na vida deles."
4. "Projeto Villa-Lobos" was an initiative of the Brazilian National Arts Foundation—FUNARTE—to document choral activities in Brazil through the promotion of educational programs for conductors, composers, and singers. Mrs. Elza Lakschevitz directed the program, which lasted from 1979 to 1991.

REFERENCES

Becker, H. (1992). *Art worlds*. Berkeley: University of California Press.

Boardman, E. (1988–1989). The generative theory of music learning: Vol. 2. *Visions of Research in Music Education, 11*. Retrieved from http://www.rider.edu/~vrme

Bruner, J. (1974). *Toward a theory of instruction*. Cambridge, MA: Harvard University Press.

Fernandes, E. (2003). O arranjo vocal de popular em São Paulo e Buenos Aires. (Universidade de São Paulo, São Paulo, Brazil).

Figueiredo, Carlos Alberto. (2006). Reflexões sobre aspectos da prática coral. In: E. Lakschevitz (Org.). *Ensaios: Olhares sobre a música coral brasileira* (pp. 7–49). Rio de Janeiro: Oficina Coral, 2006.

Freire, P. (1970). *Pedagogia do oprimido*. São Paulo: Paz e Terra.

Fulcher, J. (1979). The Orpheon societies: Music for the workers in Second-Empire France. *International Review of the Aesthetics and Sociology of Music, 10*(1), 47–56.

Hall, S. (1992). *A identidade culturalna pós-modemidade*. Rio de Janeiro: OP&A.

Joyce, V. M. (2005). The subject is singing: Singing as social practice. *International Journal of Community Music*, *8*(1). Retrieved from http://www.intellectbooks.co.uk/MediaManager/Archive/IJCM/Volume%20B/08%20Joyce.pdf

Lakschevitz, E. (2006). Coro infantil. In E. Lakschevitz (Ed.), *Ensaios: olhares sobre a coral Brasileira*. Rio de Janeiro: Oficina Coral.

Lakschevitz, E. (2009). *Um canto comum: Entendendo o coro de empresa como um mundo* (Doctoral dissertation). Universidade Federal do Estado do Rio de Janeiro, Brasil.

Lave, J., & Wenger, E. (1991). *Situated learning: Legitimate peripheral participation*. New York: Cambridge University Press.

Meyer, L. B. (1967). History, stasis and change. In L. B. Meyer (Ed.), *Music the arts and ideas* (pp. 90–108). Chicago, IL: University of Chicago Press.

Santos, J. F. (1986). São Paulo: Brasiliense.

Small, C. (1998). *Musicking: the meanings of performing and listening*. Hanover, NH: University Press of New England.

Toffler, A. (1980). *The third wave*. New York: Morrow.

Topping, P. A. (2002). *Liderança e gestão*. Rio de Janeiro, Brazil: Campus.

Wenger, E. (1998). *Communities of practice: Learning, meaning, and identity*. New York: Cambridge University Press.

Wenger, E., McDermott, R., & Snyder, W. M. (2002). *Cultivating communities of practice*. Boston: Harvard Business School Press.

Wilson, H. R. (1959). *Artistic choral singing: practical problems in organization, technique, and interpretation*. New York: G. Schirmer.

....

CHAPTER 15

INVESTIGATING CHORAL PEDAGOGIES

The State of the Choral Art in Germany

....

MARTIN RAMROTH

INTRODUCTION

....

THE choral art in Germany found itself in a particularly difficult position after World War II. Music and singing had been usurped and exploited by the National Socialist regime; rituals and activities that had been used (and abused) to create a sense of community and togetherness became deeply suspicious. There was a deep distrust after the war in all musical activities that might evoke a nationalistic and totalitarian connotation.

In this process, many Germans lost their cultural identity, were alienated from, or had broken with their cultural heritage. They had lost "their song." The German Volkslied was suspected of ideology and, in due course, stigmatized and largely "discontinued."

Situation of school music education

Music lessons in German schools in the early years of the 20th century consisted largely of singing, with repertoire dominated by traditional folksong and whatever was functional to embellish ceremonies throughout the school year. While Leo Kestenberg tried to change this during the time of the Weimar Republic, his reforms of the Prussian curricula did not gain enough traction and with the Nazis' seizure of power, music lessons were dominated by singing again. Song was not only an aim, but also the method of musical instruction and it became a vehicle of indoctrination.

This changed fundamentally after the war. In Western Germany, Theodor W. Adorno promulgated his "Thesen gegen die musikpädagogische Musik" (theses against music for music teaching purposes) in 1954 and 1955. A radical change of perspective was stipulated and a rethinking of the aesthetic and ethical tenets of musical instruction as such.

Orientation toward the musical "Kunstwerk" (the masterwork) as opposed to unreflected music making in the classroom that used second- and third-rate instructional literature was called for. "Singing is not only unnecessary, it is even harmful, as it leads toward manipulation" (Gieseler, 1973) might serve as an example to illustrate the attitudes of Adorno's followers. This development culminated in the early seventies, when singing became largely neglected, or even a taboo issue.

Music instruction at public schools in West Germany (and there were very few private ones to be found) shifted toward musical appreciation, theory before practice, analysis and aesthetic appraisal before learning and experiencing by doing. Music usually became a two hours per week subject from grades 5 to 13. Later, it was not unusual to be reduced or even dropped in grades 7 to 10, and in the last three years of high school (grades 11 to 13 in most places), it was only offered as an elective. Music and the arts were, and still are, mutually exclusive subjects for those three "senior high school" years. In this process, choral singing was relegated to a secondary, extracurricular activity. More often than not, teachers added unpaid extra lessons to their timetable to make choir rehearsals possible.

Subsequently, the choral landscape at high schools in West Germany depended on the private initiative of charismatic leaders with a strong vision and talent—and a certain propensity for self-exploitation, as whatever choral program they would establish would mean unpaid extra time on top of their regular work load as music teachers, teaching music theory, history, and music appreciation.

In East Germany, however, singing remained a central and integral part of music lessons. Music became a subject that was taught once a week in most cases with singing as the primary musical activity. As with the National Socialist regime before them, the Socialist rulers also used singing as a vehicle to implement and transport their ideology.

Another specialty of the German Democratic Republic was the promotion of musical talent in so-called "Spezialschulen für Musik"—schools specializing in music. There were four of them—in Berlin, Dresden, Weimar and Halle—meant to gather new musical talent in order to train them to be professional musicians and music instructors. Quite a few more were established for the purpose of forming outstanding choirs, such as the "Jugend-Rundfunkchor Wernigerode." Obviously, music and rehearsals played a prominent part in the syllabus, but also voice training, aural skills, and music theory.

A look at the listings of the German Music Information Center for Primary and Secondary Schools Specializing in Music throughout Germany shows an astounding 426 entries (Deutsches Musikinformationszentrum, 2016). Profiles are as versatile and different as can be imagined. We find schools listed that offer more music tuition than on the timetables of the federal state in question (timetables for schools with extended music tuition) or schools that offer instrumental or vocal tuition on the grounds of a special commitment by that school in the music education area. Often, the schools will have one more music lesson than the curriculum of their state prescribes (i.e., three lessons of 45 minutes instead of two in grade 5 [age 10]). Usually these extra lessons will be used to establish or support practical music making in whatever music ensemble the school (or just one of the music teachers) has chosen to foster; be it choir, orchestra, big band, or music theater. Grades, however, will usually be determined irrespective of the student's musical achievement by written exams on music theory, history, analysis, etc. Evidently, a lot of voluntary extra time is needed to make outstanding projects possible.

In many cases, the growing importance attached to education in Germany's socio-political debates is not matched by action in everyday education at the local level. The inadequacy of music instruction in the state school system—where, particularly at the elementary level, music is far more likely than other subjects to be taught by nonspecialists or dropped altogether—is worsened by noticeable deficits in early childhood training. Only a modicum of early childhood music education is currently offered at the pre-kindergarten level for the simple reason that this area of education generally does not form part of the standard teacher-training curriculum. Ever since Germany's reunification, the accessibility of institutions outside the general school system has steadily declined. At state-subsidized public music schools (schools that provide afternoon instrumental and singing lessons) alone, there are sometimes up to 100,000 pupils on waiting lists—many of whom remain there for years—to receive reasonably priced lessons because budget cuts prevent the schools from providing sufficient staff.

The shortening of the length of secondary school education from nine to eight years ("G8"); the expansion of the amount of time spent at school each day with the introduction of all-day schools; parents' concern about their children's career prospects: all these factors have led not only to a drastic compression in the "workday" of children and adolescents, but they are also increasingly producing signs of strain. Ambitious parents often overburden their children with a barrage of subjects designed for professional qualification. Foreign languages such as English and Chinese are increasingly being taught in (private) kindergartens in lieu of music and physical education in order to groom the children for the future work environment. In coping with demands at school, children are left with little time to practice their chosen instruments.

Teachers at German high schools are often astounded to hear about the conditions of their colleagues in the United States teaching choir—and choir only—for a period each and every day, with even the possibility of having a professional pianist at their assistance. Some react with incredulity, others even with envy at such seemingly paradisiacal working conditions. On the other hand, German music teachers tend to overlook their (in the majority of cases) own privileged status as state employees on tenure ("Beamte") with paid holidays, maternity leave, and social security. As there are fewer choral and instrumental ensembles at German high schools, the ones that do exist get more attention and recognition (regardless of their musical level of achievement) as well as better performance opportunities, as the whole school takes an interest in "their" top ensemble.

Church

The Christian churches in Germany unite around one million people in choruses and instrumental groups, enriching the professional music scene, with top-calibre ensembles such as the Regensburg Cathedral Choir, the St. Thomas Choir of Leipzig, Choir of the Church of the Holy Cross in Dresden, and the Berlin State and Cathedral Choir.

These institutions belong to the oldest cultural establishment in Germany, with a history that goes back six hundred, seven hundred, and even one thousand years.

Most of the traditional boys' and men's cathedral choirs are organized as boarding school choirs. They require a particular musical and vocal ability from their singers as well as high scholastic achievements that will allow them to participate in extensive auditions and concert tours without losing out on general education.

Germany has at least 25 boys' and men's choirs, most of which are church-affiliated and financed by the churches. As the religious landscape in Germany is dominated by the Catholic and Protestant Churches with very few denominational subdivisions, these two run almost all of these traditional establishments, with the Catholic side taking the lion's share.

In quite a few of these institutions we find comparatively excellent conditions for building a strong choral program. With rehearsal sessions two to three times a week—and in most cases at least one additional voice trainer offering personal coaching—there is the chance to form a particular sound and style and to build a challenging repertoire, and opportunities for concert tours and perhaps recordings can be created. The results at the German National Choral Competition, "Deutscher Chorwettbewerb," that takes place every four years show these groups regularly in the forefront.

But also with less traditional institutions, and in the realm of church-affiliated children's, girls', and mixed youth choirs, there are some inspiring developments to be found. While some adult choirs are experiencing a decreasing number of singers, or have difficulties in replacing the singers who are retiring, a substantial number of children's and youth choirs are thriving and prospering. This may also be due to the fact that for the past 25 or 30 years the courses of study at the German Musikhochschulen have been improved to include methodology, voice training, and repertoire geared especially toward children and developing young singers. This apparently is bearing fruit in the long term as it seems to have produced viable ensembles and "choral families" in recent years.

Some of the long-established adult choirs, however, who were hoping to reinvigorate and rejuvenate their ensembles by planting a strong new program for developing young singers, had to learn that the alumni of those younger choirs were not to be integrated easily. The education and training they had received and the capabilities they had developed often made them aspire toward advanced chamber choirs or ensembles with higher artistic claims than their old parent choir had provided.

A look at the facts and figures reveals that the economic situation has left its mark on the state of the choral art—at least in the Catholic Church. The number of staff in church music within the Catholic ranks has gone down from 2039 to 1386 between the years 2002 and 2009. In the Protestant realm we find a decrease from 2073 to 1900 positions between the years 2002 to 2014 (Deutsches Musikinformationszentrum, 2015). It is evident that it will be impossible to maintain the level of musical achievement, as fewer and fewer musicians have to fulfill more and more needs. The same church musician has to take care of a growing number of parishes, with part-time employees and assistants trying to fill the gaps.

Another trend that has sprung up in the past 15 years in church-affiliated singing groups and children's choirs is the production of religiously affiliated musicals. It leads to a variety of performances on different levels, from piano-accompanied "Singspiel" to semiprofessional staging, involving costumes, lighting technology, sound equipment, effects, and professional band accompaniment. Parents and professionals are brought in to help enhance the staging of the show and take it to a new level.

Such a performance has become a popular format, as it enables ensembles to attract audiences on a larger scale and to generate quite a bit of revenue. It produces good feelings, boosts the singers' self-esteem, and captures the attention of the public. On the downside, there is the danger that it does not yield good singers nor does it promote excellent musicianship, unless the coaching of the individual singers is truly outstanding, or their artistic education is already at a very high level. In other words: the singers may learn new music, sometimes of questionable quality, and gather stage experience, but more often than not, they do not learn proper singing in the process. This obviously applies for choral ensembles in non-religious contexts, too, in which we educators should strive for a balanced and well-rounded approach in the education and training of young musicians entrusted to us.

Sometimes, after a series of successful productions and stagings in church, as well as school contexts, conductors develop symptoms of burnout, noticing that they did not manage to develop a self-sustaining, long-term choral program. This might serve as a reminder that our objective in educating singers—at any age—should not be teaching them new songs and works of art, but rather teaching them healthy singing, developing their ear, building up their endurance and resilience, as well as evolving their musical taste. Most important of all, it seems to me, to open their eyes, ears and hearts for the enjoyment and fulfillment that healthy, perceptive, and communicative singing brings to the participants in a choral ensemble performing at a high artistic level.

To sum up our look at the church-affiliated choirs:

- adult choirs of a traditional format tend to lose singers, especially in more rural areas.
- some of them counteract this tendency by merging forces or resorting to project choir formats.
- the already excellent groups are mostly getting even better.
- we see some hopeful signs with the development of new singers: quite a few successful new children's and youth choirs are being formed which may reflect improvements with training and preparation of young conductors at music colleges.
- the "singing crisis" of the late 20th century might be overcome.
- a sudden boom of musicals, bringing singing groups into the limelight, is not necessarily a blessing.

Amateur choirs

Lay choirs still constitute the predominant majority of the singing groups in Germany. Recent statistics show 1,475,300 singers organized in secular groups and

745,200 registered singers in church-affiliated ensembles in the year 2013–2014, total-ing 2,220,500 registered amateur singers. The total population in late 2013 was about 80.5 million people throughout Germany (Statistisches Bundesamt, 2016). To dem-onstrate the idea of the scale involved, extrapolations from regional polls reveal that Germany's choruses alone present more than 300,000 concerts for some 60 million lis-teners every year (Reimers, 2011).

The lay choir movement in Germany gained breadth and momentum at the begin-ning of the 19th century. It constituted a means of active recreational activities. In the evening, workers would gather in singing (glee) clubs, just as they did in the many sports clubs that began to catch on. It may be interesting to know that there was a political moti-vation for the founding of those groups: after the inner turmoil of 1815 to 1848, meeting in a sports club or singing club was the only legitimate way of gathering in larger crowds without being suspected of political or revolutionary agitation. This explains why, for about a century, the choral amateur landscape was dominated by men.

Apart from its recreational value, choral singing primarily served to educate the general public. In the 1920s it gained additional force through state reforms of music culture (the Kestenberg Reform) and through the singing movement ("musikalische Jugendbewegung" of Fritz Jöde and Walter Hensel).

In terms of quantity, Germany, after a couple of Baltic states, may well be the country with the highest number of singing clubs ("Gesang-Verein"). Based on figures published in 2014, roughly 60,000 choral ensembles organized in registered associations are home to almost three million amateur singers. Add to that an impressive number of unregis-tered groups to imagine the scope of the choral spectrum in Germany.

The number of registered choirs comprises 23,000 secular ensembles, most of which are found in the German Choral Association (DCV). There are mixed choirs, men's choirs, women's choirs, children's choirs, and youth choirs. Some 33,000 belong to Germany's two major churches, namely, the General Cecilian Society (ACV) on the Catholic side and the Association of Evangelical Church Choirs (VeK) or the Evangelical Church in Germany (EKD) on the Protestant side (Reimers, 2010).

What may set Germany apart from England or the United States is the sheer number of amateur choirs in rural areas. It is not uncommon that villages of little more than 1000 inhabitants have three different choral amateur ensembles, sometimes competing with each other, sometimes forming a "choral family" with men's, women's, mixed and children's choirs. As you will see in the "trends" section, the traditional clubs struggle with dwindling numbers of singers. This high density of choral groups makes it possible for freelance choral conductors to make a living conducting a varying number—5 to 15!—of such clubs (i.e., conducting one, two and sometimes even three rehearsals every evening).

Usually, the conductor's pay is financed by membership fees, as well as revenue from concerts. Depending on the quality of the group, most income is generated by selling food and drinks during or after concerts. Very frequently there are also other forms of fund-raising such as organizing communal events, devoid of any musical activity, such as selling mulled wine on special holidays or organizing a seasonal festival.

It is remarkable that the bulk of the traditional singing clubs perform almost exclusively a cappella literature, even though many of them operate on a rather modest musical level, frequently teaching the individual parts by rote, for instance. Notwithstanding, they serve an important cultural purpose and they also support the professional music scene, promoting a general respect and interest for well-made music and perhaps constituting the audiences to the concerts of nationally and internationally established ensembles.

Regardless of the sometimes fairly moderate achievement level, there is a well-established culture of choral competitions in Germany. This ranges from rather illustrious, notable social events in which amateur singing clubs compete for a set number of boxes of wine bottles to full-fledged and serious contests under acclaimed and distinguished adjudicators. The endeavors of the amateur groups and their conductors to attempt the highest level of music-making possible, with a high number of choristers at or approaching retirement age, is admirable and highly commendable, sometimes more so than the soaring artistic achievements of more select and highly trained ensembles.

The German Choral Association "Deutscher Chorverband" has been organizing competitive auditions for the amateur ensembles registered in their ranks for decades. Choirs would apply (and continue to do so) to attain the title of a "Masterchoir" which is obtained reaching three achievement levels: 1. District level; 2. Concert Level; 3. Masterchoir Level. Choirs are assigned different categories according to the amount of choristers and sometimes even age of the singers. Relatively recently a Pop-Jazz-Gospel and a Folksong category have been added.

Organizational structures within the Deutscher Chorverband are very well developed. Almost every singing club has their established leadership committee or board with designated functions such as president, treasurer, secretary and assistant, taking care of virtually every aspect of the management and promotion of a choral group. Due to the long-established and approved routines of the German Associations Law, it is quite easy to found a new group and conductors can find and count on plenty of support in every aspect of organization, logistics and finance. Many groups have managed to be exempted from tax in accordance with German law. The German Choral Association is also very proactive, subsidizing choirs and districts, helping choirs to settle dues with the German music rights association GEMA, and providing tailor-made insurance for singers and concert performances.

Nevertheless, it should be noted that the German amateur choir scene—especially as the traditional men's choirs are concerned—is currently going through a period of severe change and transformation. Consumer electronics, new media, devices, and gadgets have changed the way we communicate and interact and what recreational activities we choose and cultivate. Traditional singing clubs have had to realize that they compete with a host of professional entertainment programs and possibilities, and it is hardly surprising that the concert format of "Freundschaftssingen" (literally "friendship singing" of olden days, in which six to ten—or even more—regional choirs would meet in a beer tent and sing two or three songs each in folk style) is destined to die out, as it is no longer sufficient to attract a larger number of listeners, even though there may be lots of beer involved.

So male choirs—especially in rural areas—that adhere to rituals, concert formats, and repertoire that had been working for 60, sometimes even 160 years, have had to learn the painful lesson that simply carrying on as if nothing had happened won't do. They found their membership numbers dwindling, while the average age skyrocketed, and they found their audiences petering out. Different remedial strategies can be observed, from trying to merge two or three ensembles into a still viable group, to transmuting to a mixed choir—apparently an excruciating experience for some traditionalistic singers— to changing the repertoire, to drastically improving their marketing and performance formats.

On the other side of the spectrum, as has been described with choirs in religious domains, there is a trend toward more professionalization, and toward more performance-oriented choirs. These more dedicated and aspirant groups often exceed regional boundaries, and quite often operate on a project basis, meeting on selected weekends. Alumni of distinguished choral institutions get together to form semiprofessional ensembles of oftentimes astounding capabilities.

Professional level

Professional choirs in Germany encompass opera and (former) radio choirs. The number of opera choruses in Germany is striking; 83 opera houses offer about 2900 positions for singers in choral ranks. The significance of Germany's music theatre landscape becomes clear when viewed in an international context. Of the 560 permanent and professional opera houses world-wide, one out of two are in a European Union country, and one out of seven are in Germany (Bovier Lapierre, 2006).

Germany boasts seven professional broadcasting choirs (NDR, RIAS, RFC Berlin, MDR, WDR, SWR, BR) that can look back on 60 years of existence. They originally provided content for the newly emerging broadcasting services after WWII, but their objectives have shifted over time (Diwiak, 2011). They may well be seen as engines of contemporary choral music that have brought about an abundance of commissioned works, setting professional standards of performance and broadening the horizon of what is possible with the human voice. Without their existence, a lot of works by Kagel, Rihm, Stockhausen, and Nono, to name only a few, would or could not have been realized. Especially the ensembles focusing on new music, such as SWR Vokalensemble Stuttgart, WDR Chor Köln, or NDR Chor Hamburg, have expanded the gamut of vocal ensemble color, vocal technique, and vocal expression, performing what had been previously unheard of or deemed unperformable.

While these institutions, due to their fee-based public funding, have had the invaluable advantage of being able to produce avant-garde and extremely demanding contemporary works for many years and decades without having to glance at audience numbers, nowadays pressure is increasing as financial pundits, eager to minimize costs, keep on questioning the need for such extravagant productions that may cater to the tastes of only a very small number of listeners. In recent years the former radio choirs have ventured into more marketable areas, organizing and promoting their own concerts and concert tours, sometimes starting educational projects and new concert formats and trying to reach out to the general public.

However many of these choirs are struggling with recruitment problems. Due to the academic focus on soloist training, there is a distinct lack of young talent willing to blend their voices into a homogeneous ensemble sound; casting for openings can be difficult as many young singers aim for a career as a soloist. There is a slow but steady trend of realization that it would actually make sense at German Musikhochschulen to offer education programs geared toward careers as professional singers in ensembles, such as the broadcasting choirs or opera choruses. Regular, dependable payment and relatively secure, steady, and sedentary working conditions that allow or facilitate a social and family life are factors to be taken into consideration by young singers in an otherwise quite saturated market.

Organizational structures

The lack of structure, curricula, model programs, and traditions for choir and orchestral programs in the German school context has already been hinted at. Students do not get credit for the ensembles they take part in. They are usually extracurricular or free-time activities in the afternoon, like a sports or chess club would be. Many teachers, or teacher-conductors have filled the gap by building their own tailor-made framework ranging from elementary training groups, junior choirs, and senior concert choirs up to well-advanced alumni groups forming distinguished chamber choirs.

Some teachers have successfully established a system of tutors, with older, well-trained, and experienced students/choristers tutoring the younger ones. It can be stated that there is a broad variety of choral activities at German schools of varying degrees of intensity, stamina, and success. The programs that produce remarkable results invariably depend on the vision, charisma, and a certain spirit of entrepreneurship of one or two teachers who are exceptionally dedicated and put an extreme amount of time and energy into this cause. In most cases, the hours they invest are in addition to their regular teaching load in a process that could aptly be described as self-exploitation. Over the years they have established structures for finding and training new talent, often in connection with one or several regular voice trainers and a subdivision of choral groups according to their age and musical proficiency. In some places there are fruitful collaborations with state-funded public music schools, but in many cases the drive toward full-day comprehensive schools together with the curtailment of one academic year at the high school level ("G8") has led to the demise of formerly thriving programs.

The lay choir scene, by comparison, is generally well-organized in traditional associations. However its organizational structures—both its rehearsal and concert formats—must be seen as remnants of the 19th century, struggling and often failing to survive in a 21st-century environment and society that has every means of entertainment right at the tip of their remote control. In due course, we find many traditional singing groups—especially male choirs—dying a slow death. Some may manage to survive, employing modern marketing strategies and a good deal of "thinking different," as will be shown in the last section ("Trends").

An area that has not been touched upon yet is the German variety of honors choirs. Since the late 1970s, several German states—called "Länder"—have started to establish their individual "Landesjugendchor," a select state youth choir of 30 to 60 singers aged mostly 16–25, who meet two to six times throughout the year and work in a project-oriented manner, predominantly during school holidays. Some of these choirs work with frequently changing guest conductors of international acclaim; others are directed by an entrenched and proven local conductor or team of conductors. Performances are usually distinguished public concert events, not infrequently in cooperation with renowned orchestras, but also often featuring a cappella programs.

The state youth choirs are usually funded by the state government or the choral association of the respective state. Some states joined the bandwagon as late as 2008 (Hesse, Saarland, Saxony), 2011 (Berlin), and 2013 (Thuringia). Applicants go through an audition process—many of them after they have attained awards in the National Music Contest "Jugend musiziert" (for young soloists). In contrast to American contexts the connection between high school or community choirs, their conductors, and the management of the "Landesjugendchor" is quite loose, sometimes nonexistent. There is no tradition or culture of preparing singers for the auditions. Sometimes the young singers are on their own and their participation depends on private initiative. Once they have found their way into the ensemble, however, they often develop a strong group identity.

In the "California Honor Choirs 2014–2015 Handbook" I found the following regulations: "Current enrollment in and participation in the choral program at your high school or community organization is required. No director approval = No participation" (Southern California Vocal Association, 2015). This would be an excellent idea to implement on German territory, where there is quite some room for improvement.

Choral sound and rehearsal practices

Is there a particularly German sound? The short and simple answer is: if there ever was, differences between distinctive sound qualities of top-quality ensembles are getting smaller and smaller. Perhaps there is a general tendency to use less vibrato, which may be due to the fact that vibrato or an "operatic" voice projection is not one of the first aims of individual voice training. A landmark of East German choirs used to be impeccable blend and excellent enunciation. In the process of blending vocal sound qualities and prioritizing homogeneity, excellent tuning was usually achieved. The Western ensembles, in comparison, often dared to be more expressive or dramatic and show more individuality, sometimes at the expense of diction or intonation.

In looking for particular idiosyncrasies—perhaps an obsession with tone quality, pureness and blend of vowels, and the overall sound of the ensemble—the specific "Chorklang" might be stated, at least as far as the some rather advanced and successful

groups go. Some of the German groups I have observed would be much more per-
fectionist, and spend considerably more rehearsal time with the same piece trying to
synchronize every aspect of dynamics and phrasing, than, for example, their British
counterparts, who would tend to trust their musical experience, intuition, mutual
understanding, and creativity in the moment of performance.

An increasing trend for the past ten or even twenty years is also a strong concern for
tuning systems and pure or just intonation, as opposed to "equally tempered." There is
a strong discipleship advocating rehearsals without instruments, which is the predominant approach in training young conductors, including those who are studying to be
teachers and whose survival as leaders of a school ensemble will probably depend on the
clever use of an instrument.

A phenomenon you might meet much more often in Germany is the practice of working with a third-party voice trainer, contracting a distinguished "voice-builder" who
works with the choir or with sections and smaller groups strictly from the angle of vocal
technique and vocal hygiene. So, one might maintain that in Germany there is more of
an emphasis on choral voice training, "Stimmbildung," as opposed to individual singing
lessons, and it is more customary to hire a specialist other than the conductor.

Quite en vogue are also all kinds of physical activities, body-movements to support
a healthy technique, a vibrant sound, good projection, and convincing communication. You might find a lot of people in rehearsal stretching, gesticulating, walking about,
or trying to push each other around, than you would in a more civilized or restrained
country. The advent of the "functional voice training" approach as developed by Gisela
Rohmert in Lichtenberg, as well as Eugen Rabine and many subsequent followers, was
clearly influential in combining vocal production with supportive movements.

I find it quite difficult to answer the question of whether there is a chief pundit, THE
authoritative voice in choral pedagogy and rehearsal technique in Germany. From my
point of view there is no beacon or shining light in sight, as Robert Shaw might have
been for a generation of American conductors. If anybody, perhaps Eric Ericson of
Sweden best fulfills that role, as he revolutionized the choral arena in terms of style,
sound, and methodology in Europe. Conductors from all over Europe would flock to
his masterclasses, eager to put that on their resumes. So Scandinavia shaped the choral
sound and the spectrum of choral music in Western Europe to a large extent, while at the
same time the specific sound of renowned ensembles became more internationalized
and less characteristic.

Crisis?—What crisis? (current trends)

For about a decade we have seen a strong boom both with Gospel choirs and Jazz-Pop
choral groups, whereas traditional amateur choirs (especially the traditional male
choirs) are on the demise, as has been illustrated previously (Sozialwissenschaftliches
Institut der Evangelischen Kirche in Deutschland, 2009). Church choirs more often than
not are experiencing decreasing membership numbers, unless they devote themselves

toward quality and attractive and demanding programs, with all the extra effort this requires from conductor and organizers. Here, as in the field of secular amateur and semi-professional choirs, we find a trend for project choirs that require less continual commitment, but in many cases offer a superior artistic level.

The boom of religious musicals has been described in some detail in the section on church choirs. A similar trend can also be seen with musicals in school or community youth choirs. While the staging of musicals can help tremendously in heightening public awareness for singing and reaching larger audiences, more often than not teachers and choral conductors realize that a disproportionate amount of energy is drained off at the periphery and is not invested in the growth of the musicianship and the cultivation of the voices as a prerequisite for long-term growth and success.

There is a comparatively new trend to be found in German high schools, trying to introduce or reintroduce the idea that music instruction in the classroom could actually mean making music in the classroom, as opposed to teaching music appreciation, listening to, analyzing, and reflecting on music. Around the turn of the millennium, some pedagogical concepts surfaced that envisioned the concert band in a classroom ("Bläserklasse"), originally instigated and fostered by the musical instrument industry; there was also the less widely spread concept of the string orchestra in a classroom ("Streicherklasse"). Early obstacles were numerous, such as bureaucratic hurdles, including concerns over how to assign grades with this completely different approach to teaching music without written exams. But the biggest obstacle was finding teachers willing and qualified to do this without proper training in managing having a band in the classroom, which also entailed slowly establishing training courses and designing teaching material such as arrangements tailor-made for the respective ensemble situations.

In the realm of singing and choral activities, the development toward a more active approach to teaching music might have taken a little longer to emerge and thrive, since a) there were no driving forces such as the musical instrument industry who might have had a vested interest in furthering new teaching concepts requiring the use of instruments, and b) in most cases singing had always been part of the music lesson—except that there usually was no structured methodology aimed at training and qualifying singers for ensemble singing on an artistic level, and the idea of grading students for their vocal achievements was strongly frowned upon.

So, ironically, the latest concept of music-making in the classroom is the one that should have been the easiest one to implement: teaching music through singing ("Singklasse"). An influential person in this process was Ralf Schnitzer, a high school teacher in the Heidelberg area who around 1997 started to design and finally published a first concept of how to manage singing in the classroom, based on solfège (Schnitzer, 2008). Interestingly, he was inspired in this process by a choral exchange with a high school in Virginia in the United States. His many charismatic appearances at teacher training courses and workshops have helped to spread the concept and he has found many followers and emulators. A sort of second-generation publication has been issued in 2012 by two high school teachers in the Mainz area, and it is on its way to become widely used as a "textbook" in grades 5 and 6 for those willing to try this singing approach (Bolender & Müller, 2012). Workshops seem to be well-attended and in demand, and some high school music faculties have decided to implement this concept for some, if not all, of their grades 5 and 6.

It is to be hoped that—and remains to be seen—whether this will have long-lasting positive effects on the choral education and the musicianship of students, and will lead to many a flourishing high school choir, thus reviving and revitalizing the choral scene in Germany. In its best case scenario it may help to overcome the awkward starting position Germany might have had as a Nation of singers "without a song."

References

Bolender, R. and Müller, G. (2012). Gesangsklasse. Esslingen, Germany: Helbling.

Bovier Lapierre, B. (2006). Die Opernhäuser im 20. Jahrhundert. In A. Jacobshagen and F. Reininghaus (Eds.), Musik und Kulturbetrieb – Medien, Märkte, Institutionen (pp. 231–256). Laaber, Germany: Laaber Verlag.

Deutsches Musikinformationszentrum. (2015). Gründungsjahre der Kammerorchester. Retrieved from http://deutsches-musikinformationszentrum.de/downloads/statistik/43/statistik43.pdf

Deutsches Musikinformationszentrum. (2016). Primary and secondary schools specializing in music. Retrieved from http://www.miz.org/en/suche_87_0.html

Diwiak, C. (2011). Exotic figures: Broadcasting choirs today. Das Orchester, 09/2011, p. 12.

Gieseler, W. (1973). Grundriss der Musikdidaktik. Ratingen, Germany: Henn.

Reimers, A. (2010). Amateur music-making, musical life in Germany. Bonn, Germany: German Music Council. Retrieved from http://www.miz.org/musical-life-in-germany/download/05_Amateur_Music-Making.pdf.

Schnitzer, R. (2008) Singen ist Klasse. Mainz, Germany: Schott.

Sozialwissenschaftliches Institut der Evangelischen Kirche in Deutschland. (2009). Soziale Analyse der Gospelbewegung. Retrieved from http://www.ekd.de/si/projekte/abgeschlossen/analyse_gospelbewegung.html

Southern California Vocal Association. (2015). Senior high school honor choir procedures and policies. Retrieved from http://www.scvachoral.org/honor_choir_guidelines.html

Statistisches Bundesamt (2016). Bevölkerung. Retrieved from https://www.destatis.de/DE/ZahlenFakten/GesellschaftStaat/Bevoelkerung/Bevoelkerung.html

PRACTICE

PART IV

···

REPERTOIRE
AS PEDAGOGY

···

CHAPTER 16

....

THE ART OF SUCCESSFUL PROGRAMMING

Study, Selection, and Synthesis

....

RICHARD BJELLA

IT is a bit pretentious to think that one could influence the decisions of another regarding the sacred crafting of one's public program. However, with the hope that this may stir some discussion and possibly some mental embers that have been left to smolder in the same manner, we proceed.

My experience has been that too many concert programs are presented without enough concern for the overall flow, purpose, and direction of the concert itself. Often many wonderful selections are included, but rarely do they work together in tandem or with enough significant diversity and color changes to warrant the complete attention of the audience. In this age of diminishing attendance, fiscal resources, and rehearsal time, we can still bring a lifegiving performance through more study and careful selection of repertoire for that particular situation, and tap fully our ability to creatively weave the material to capture our singers and our audiences at the same time.

This chapter will look at various models for programming at all levels and discuss why certain tendencies seem to attract audiences and others tend to have them racing to get out of the hall. We will look at our likelihood to program only certain kinds of repertoire, and how we might break out of that mold and stretch our repertoire wings more completely. In addition, we will study ways to discover the strengths of our particular ensemble, and decisions that may assist in bringing forth the best results. Also addressed will be the aspect of fine tuning the concert itself, building sets of selections that can work together seamlessly. Finally we will look at ways to completely engage the audience from the moment the ensemble takes the stage until the final ovation. Discussed will be ways not to water down the repertoire, but rather increase the aesthetic experience and satisfaction in every rehearsal and performance as well. Finally, an addendum has been added with programs that I have performed for the middle level, high school, college, and professional choirs.

STUDY

We must always look first to our purpose for a concert. Asking a good deal of "why" questions is always critical to success. Why now? Why this program? Why with this particular choir? Why do it at all? If we cannot successfully answer this for ourselves, it will certainly be a tough to convince the singers. What are the suggested outcomes? How will this enhance the character of the program, of the singers, of the audience, and of course, you? The problem is the solution, as it so often seems to be for most of us. Without the truly digging in and doing the research and study, there is little of substance that will remain after the final chord.

So after setting on a course with a clear mission, we must begin early and be inclusive. Some programs will start with a single piece, others with a clear dream, sometimes with a particular need of the ensemble, or a specific event. I would encourage you to place several great recipes for success on the table before deciding the best menu for this particular occasion. Don't clear the table too early. Don't be afraid to "chase the rabbit", it will likely lead to a better diet possibility down the road for another event.

In addition to the usual sources, such as Spotify, YouTube, concerts on line, CDs, successful colleagues, and countless choral competitions to help create successful choices, don't forget cpdl/ChoralWiki, IMSLP, handlo-music.com, canadianchoralcentre.ca, madulo.com/mc/africares.html, and choirtx.com. Finally, if you are focusing on a composer, spend a week with that composer and go through all of his or her works. Even the most studied among us will find another gem of Schubert, Schütz, Stravinsky, Rossi, Scarlatti, Monteverdi, Rameau, Victoria, Rogier, Scheidt, Brahms, Fauré, Sibelius, or Mozart that has been forgotten or perhaps never realized as we were at a different place in our own study and comprehension. Revisit the masters; they will delight and inform everything!

Look carefully at how you are unfolding the different genres to a generation of singers. When was the last time a great opera chorus was utilized? Are you avoiding that beautiful folk setting from Lithuania just because you don't know the language? Have you discovered the golden nuggets of music theatre? Have you explored how chant can enhance and cleanse the palate for you, your singers, and your audience? When was the last time your singers experienced a beautiful motet of Machaut? Have you looked at all of the Bach Cantatas that require very little in the way of instrumental demands and have only a small demand on the chorus? Live in the musical cornucopia that is ours for the taking, envelop it, and let your palate be touched by the genius through the ages.

Score study itself unfolds so many stories and treasures for us all. Often, unexpected connections are found in unexpected avenues of our study. That harmonic progression in the Brahms may lead to a find of a contemporary composer with the same bent. The text to that Italian madrigal from 1580 touches the hem of a late 20th century composer as well. The folk tune melodic structure from 17th-century Latvia is surprisingly seen in an English folk song from the 19th century. The counterpoint in an Ockeghem motet may trigger a new look at a secular cantata of J. S. Bach. All of our study, however oblique, helps us in that journey towards the best piece for the ensemble.

SELECTION

An in-depth questioning of your selections will yield dividends in building a successful program. Again, we come back to the "why" of each selection on the program. Ask yourself; am I trying too hard to make the selection based upon an ill-conceived program? Am I limiting my choir by the selection I am making? What does the piece teach the singers? What will it teach me? What is the purpose?

We must know our singers, inside and out. What level of difficulty will allow for real success for the tenors in your choir? Where is the literary IQ of your ensemble? Will this piece move it forward? Do you have the likely soloists available to make this piece come to life? What is the rhythmic and harmonic level of understanding for the choir? Where does the choir live in terms of range and most especially tessitura? Can we, in the time allotted, get the voices to ring truly freely on this piece of music? These are difficult and challenging questions. If we are truly faithful to the choir in front of us, this may mean that we may throw out our favorite piece from consideration!

What of the key of the piece? What is the overall key schematic of the entire concert? How many pieces is one performing in that key? Am I living in F Major for too long? Is this setting of *I am a poor wayfaring stranger* in the best key for this choir? How many different modes are being utilized during the course of one set of music ranging from 10 to 15 minutes? Has any thought been given to connection between the pieces with instrumental interludes to help with the key evolution throughout? Is one drawn to certain keys, telling us subliminal details of the piece without our conscious mind fully knowing? The key can influence nearly everything from character, to vocal strain, to creating an affect that is perfect for the moment, to one that is too bright for the language of the poet.

What of tempi? We know that the most comfortable tempo is somewhere around 92 to the pulse. If you took the average musician and asked them to tap at about 92 to 96 beats per minute, most would be able to maintain this tempo quite well. As we move away from this "golden mean" of tempo, does our program gain strength or lose it? What is the balance of faster and slower selections of repertoire? Does the tempo of our program cause one to take notice, or is it so expected that the audience knows the tempo of any given selection before ever beginning? Is there some overriding tempo cycle to the program? Is there a living, breathing pulse to the program? How do you deal with silence in the program? Can this be cherished and nourished? Are there any clear or oblique tempo relationships between pieces within a same set of music? I think that both kinds of tempo relationships can be effective. Sameness kills energy, in all things, most especially music. Incoherent extremes in tempo for contrast's sake alone also causes us to dismiss the program or that particular set as trivial or ill conceived. Sometimes a surprising concern about tempo relationships can trigger phenomenal interest as well.

Imagine a piece beginning with a tactus pulse of 60 in duple meter, moving to a triple meter equaling 80 to the pulse, and finally a piece in 7/8 that flies at 180 to the quarter. Each drives the other through the subtle yet deeply felt tempo of 3 to 4 (60 to 80) and 3 to 1 (180 to 60) helping complete the picture.

What are your overall goals for the ensemble? When was the last time they sang a great polyphonic motet or a bi-tonal bit of Charles Ives? When did they last digest a great Bach Chorale or a Shaker tune? Why have we avoided French for so long? Can the choir truly delve into a unison chant or a thick 12-part Brummel Mass movement? What has the musical diet been during your tenure with the ensemble? What have you avoided and thus, what have your singers been denied? What are we afraid to teach and why? How many homophonic pieces are placed on the musical table every year? How many ninth chords can one choir handle and still continue to grow? What of the wealth of great counterpoint throughout the centuries? Has the choir explored a truly playful or interesting piece in mixed meter?

Consider Ockeghem's stunning *Alma Redemptoris Mater*, a striking example of great early Renaissance counterpoint. This piece, like so many others of its kind, is critical to the lifeblood of knowledge that is learned by the choir through its study and eventual performance. However, imagine that this is now a centerpiece between two much earlier works: Hildegard von Bingen's fanciful chant *O Vis aeternitatis* (for treble voices only) with 21st century saxophone improvisation, and the early *Kyrie* from *La Messe de Tournai* also presented with saxophone improvisation. Now this Ockeghem a cappella masterpiece has a frame around it that gives it special light for an audience that would likely have been left cold or completely confused by any one of these stunning pieces alone. If texture, context, key, text, tempo, and time are all a pervasive underbelly to our thinking, it is likely that something transcendent can occur in only a few minutes.

What poetry has been explored? So many of the great choral composers have savored the writings of Octavio Paz, Emily Dickinson, e.e. cummings, Robert Frost, Federico Garcia Lorca, Rumi, Henry David Thoreau, William Shakespeare, William Blake, Kahlil Gibran, Walt Whitman, Langston Hughes, Ogden Nash, or Robert Browning and so many more. Are you finding that the poetic diet is somewhat limited and you are only concentrating on lesser poets? Has the choir explored the painful *Book of Lamentations*, or the rich tapestry of the Psalm settings? Our selection of repertoire must touch the mind and heart as well as the voice of the singers.

The very practical and realistic viewpoint of limited rehearsal time is essential to balance as well as we are making our final selections. One of our most difficult tasks is analyzing carefully how long each piece will take to realize during a rehearsal cycle, especially for repertoire that is new to us. Our thorough study of the selected repertoire as well as our honest assessment of the membership of the choir will help us fully know what it takes to allow the piece to come to life.

Have we truly examined which musical elements are being addressed in each concert? Do we tend to be drawn to one kind of harmonic language? Do we truly deal with a variety of textures and timbres in our programming choices? Are we only connecting to beautiful melodies and ignoring a broad sweep of rhythms that may enhance the aesthetic?

Which musical forms are we drawn to, and, which are we avoiding? Are we truly looking at the magnitude of repertoire that can move the heart, mind, and soul? Consider taking one or two musical risks that put you outside of the repertoire you teach and conduct well. I guarantee that you will approach old favorites with a new flair of enthusiasm and understanding because of your willingness to take the risk to reach for the beyond.

Have we considered carefully the aspect of grouping pieces together? Our audiences are often completely underwhelmed at the conclusion of a two-minute selection, but may be truly moved to signal their appreciation at the end of a ten-minute segment that included three contrasting choices that fed off the energy of the other. There may be a piece that is made more complete by a pairing that unfolds. I am reminded of a pairing of Josquin's *Mille regrets (A Thousand Regrets)* with contemporary composer Eric Barnum's *The Stars Stand Up In The Air*. Both pieces are terrific on their own ground, but together they create such an emphatic impact for the audience and performers alike.

What has been the balance of accompanied repertoire with piano, versus other instruments? Is the written accompaniment one that could be changed to enhance the piece? Would it be better to leave out all of the sometimes unnecessary doubling with the voices? Can you add a colorful flute line that creates something truly unique? Have you considered using harpsichord, or organ, or guitar as an optional accompaniment? I added a string quartet to the charming French Renaissance Chanson, *Tant que vivray* by Sermisy, to bring this small strophic work to life for a 7th-and 8th-grade all-state choir. This allowed the artistry of the adult professional quartet to inspire these young artists as well. Many times adding a tasteful percussion line can add a great deal. Even something as simple as finger cymbals, or handbells, or audience percussion can add so much. We just performed Whitacre's popular *Cloudburst* with the San Antonio Chamber Choir in our *A River Runs Through Us* concert. However, we did not have the space or budget to add percussion, so the audience took on the role of the heavy rain, the loud claps of thunder, the hail, and finally the gentle wash of rain. After a minute of instruction, they were completely involved and helped create the piece.

Are there elements of key relationships, tempo relationships, melodic contouring, or the affect of the text that work together in a significant manner? For instance, the melancholy of the Latvian tune, *Kas tie tadi*, set by Steven Sametz, may find a significant partnership with Sally Terri's *Poor Wayfarin' Stranger*. Place a significant motet by Franco-Flemish composer Philippe Rogier between them (*Laboravi in gemitu*), and the musical gesture of lament and mourning reaches across nearly 500 years and within 12 minutes may have an impact that can last a lifetime. The simple grouping of pieces paired by thirds (i.e. C major, A minor, E major OR; A flat minor, C minor, E minor) can entice the ear to listen anew.

Many of us have experienced concerts that seem to go on forever. Some of us have experienced a concert that seems to last but a moment, but in reality lasted well over an hour. I think the difference may be with this sense of a heartbeat to the concert, a driving force that moves one to have no sense of time passing.

Finally, when considering your selections, buy wisely! I suggest that you follow the 80%/20% rule. Never allow yourself to spend more than 20% of your budget on music that will likely only be used once and then sit on the shelves for years. Better if you can think 90%/10% but that is fairly unrealistic with today's prices. Also continue to look for repertoire from the choral public domain library and other free sources for early music. There is always a risk with free score sites, which sometimes contain countless errors, but buying good editions for yourself can be a way to assist in correcting these mistakes. Sometimes I will buy eight different editions of a score to compare decisions made by different editors. Also, don't be afraid to make your own editions of scores. You will learn the score much more deeply, and, your singers will benefit from getting your ideas more clearly presented in an edition you create.

SYNTHESIS

Our considerably difficult yet most worthy goal is to balance unpredictability and consistency. This will help to create a sense of transcendence through not only the stunning repertoire selected, but also the manner in which it is placed and presented in the program itself. This is a tall order, and after making the careful selections for this time and for this ensemble, this final synthesis of the material into a cohesive form is critical in helping bring the music to life.

Margaret Hillis, the late great chorus master of the Chicago Symphony, said to many of us at a workshop in Ithaca, New York, "When you feel like you don't have enough time to study the score, slow down and study slower." This quip about just "make the time" is also critical to building a strong concert program as well. Let your program be your textbook for the next six to twelve weeks perhaps. Let your thoughts ferment, like any decent bottle of wine, don't rush to swallow it up. My usual mode is anywhere from 9 to 20 revisions after the final program has been decided. Sometimes small things make a huge difference in building synthesis to a cohesive program. Imagine creating a 10-second improvised soundscape that imitates nature to draw two pieces dealing with the connection to the earth together in a seamless scene.

Honor both your heart and head. You need to stay on top of the rehearsal schedule and adjust if necessary. No one ever died because a concert was five minutes shorter than originally planned. However, a bad selection or weak performance of that selection can taint the entire apple and create a toxic sense to what you tried so hard to create. Your left and right brain need to fight one other to create the best synthesis of material within the finite time frame of rehearsal that we all struggle to balance. Don't ever allow yourself to settle into just good enough. Keep your will strong and envision what can be, even if the choir has never experienced it before.

The full and complete realization that *we are a lot smarter and better than just me* changed me. Use all of your resources in and around the choir. Maximize the incredible imagination of the students that are with you on a daily basis. When was the last time you opened up a major decision to their collective ingenuity? Just three years ago we were performing at a major convention and we had one transition between a Georgian solo with a choral drone and a jazz piece by Bobby McFerrin and Roger Treece to finish the program. I could not find a way to make the transition work, but the students did. Yes, it took a bit of time, but it became a perfect ten seconds of material created by them. Do you talk about serious programming issues with your colleagues? Do you reach out to those you trust for some additional input into creating that more complete experience for all?

What is at the heart of your program? Yes, you may have a theme, you may have even put together effective sets of music, but where is it headed? How do you hope the audience feels at the beginning, in the middle, and as they leave the hall? Does the program grow to a centerpiece work? Is the audience pulled to the final breath of the concert because of how you began? It is not uncommon to try and build a concert on a theme or topic of interest. There is always a danger of working towards a theme and ignoring pieces that are best suited for a particular ensemble. As we work toward a cohesive structure for a concert, we want to make certain to always honor the particular singers with a variety of opportunities for growth, thus forcing ourselves to come to the theme too early may be a mistake.

Plan carefully the logistics to any concert. How do you unfold the package? Is it a surprise every time? Can the logistics actually help the story? We began our "Mirrored Messages" program with all of the students coming from every corner of the hall, talking to one another, and taking on character roles. Some were priests, others vagrant tramps, or street vendors. We had a good deal of flirting going on, business men next to prostitutes, young children and very old people that had lived a hard life and church bells being sounded, all to create the scene for our opening music of *Carmina Burana* from Carl Orff's 20th century work and from original music from the 13th century intermixed. The stage where the concert was held was pretentious and far removed from the audience, but this opening scene allowed everyone in the audience to feel as though they were on stage. They had something significant to latch unto and feel invited into the scene.

Can the program design, the actual quality of the paper itself, bring an immediate level of respect to the artistry on stage as well? All of us are on rather tight budgets, but can we fully explore how to make our program dollar stretch to help flesh out what the ensemble has worked so hard to create? Are there ways to have some of the design work donated? Is there a possibility that much of the work is done in house and then a higher-quality paper is utilized at cost? Can you sell tasteful ads in the program to help pay for the entire production? Many people do wish to help; they just need to be asked in a way that allows them to see the need. Have you considered ways to share the text without printing it in the program? Does a singer better share the translation while the introduction to the piece is proceeding? Or, can superscripts be presented on a projector for all to see as the ensemble is singing in Russian? Often our concert halls are not conducive to extensive reading of the program. Are the notes better presented in writing or by a singer?

Are there areas where we can help the picture with a more interdisciplinary approach to a concert? Perhaps a short discussion or lecture that touches on the life of the rural Russian peasant in preparation for the second half of the concert presenting Stravinsky's *Les Noces (The Wedding)* is the best possible manner of bringing difficult music to life. Consider presenting connections with community leaders about the health of the area river as the choir performs music that touches on the river's value to life itself. Performing music dealing with human trafficking, while having lectures presented about the widespread abuse of women throughout the world that still exists today may also motivate many others in profound ways. Perhaps a fall preview concert in a school setting is presented to your audience with several steps that allow the audience into the process of learning the music. Rather than presenting a performance, you create an "informance" to let those in attendance into all that goes into singing well and all that the students are learning.

Carefully scrutinize how much talking is going on in your concerts. Also look at the messenger. If it is just you, this may come across as self-serving and not advantageous to truly building community and connections between the audience and your ensemble. Is there another way to present the material? Can the audience see it on a screen, be given a flyer, be allowed to share individually after the concert? People come to concerts to hear great things, not to listen to us speak, so analyzing what truly needs to be said will make an enormous difference to the flow and the very integrity of the whole program. I went to a concert recently where literally 12 minutes of the concert were spent on organizing a fundraising event that had no place in this concert. I went away (and I suspect others as well) with a bitter taste in my mouth regarding this misstep in leadership. Decide carefully what is included in the program and what can be left for a committee meeting, or a pre-concert lecture.

Mentioned earlier was the aspect of allowing the music to be enhanced through careful logistics, such as the case of our *Carmina Burana* presentation and the manner in which the choir took the stage. As we think of staging the choir, it is critical to allow ourselves to let the music speak more completely through some creative staging. When I was at Lawrence University we were invited to sing at the National ACDA Convention in Oklahoma City in 2009. We performed on the final day of the convention and I knew (as I had experienced as a member of the audience for many years) that there would be a weary bunch of conventioneers after three days of listening to choirs. We decided to open that performance with *Knowee* by Stephen Leek, the brilliant Australian composer who set this selection with our four soloists having lanterns searching and calling out for a metaphorical lost aboriginal child representing the loss of the sun around the hall. The blackout, and then seeing only the single lanterns around the audience, immediately woke up a tired audience. We had another experience that came to us at Texas Tech University that involved the centerpiece to our concert called "Mirrored Messages" involving the first eight measures of the J. S. Bach chorale, *Come, Sweet Death*. I first heard this sung by the Dale Warland Singers and was completely mesmerized. After the brief presentation of the opening bars, the choir is then set free to improvise completely on each note of those measures, allowing time to hear and reflect what others are saying, interpreting syllables, and coloring every inch of these opening phrases with individual color and life. At the suggestion of Paul Head, we decided to move off the risers at that point and move independently forward, reflecting passionately this powerful text and drama. We also had red scarves for the women that had been purchased much earlier and quite frankly were not working well in performance. One of the singers came up with the brilliant idea of waiting until this moment to show the scarves and to carry and hold them with the obvious symbolism seen be all. Then, we moved to Piazzolla's blistering tango/fugue, *La Muerte Del Ángel* (*The Death Of An Angel*) that portrays the startling story of one woman trying to help in the ghettos of Rio de Janeiro who is unfortunately murdered. The scarves were used in this piece in a rather sensuous fashion imitating street life in Brazil, and then in a manner that portrayed the blood of this missionary as well. It was a simple, unchoreographed six minutes that left the audience (and the performers) completely drenched in emotion. Although this simple move caused things to momentarily move backwards musically in rehearsal, it eventually caused the entire concert to take a giant leap forward by drawing visual attention to this centerpiece through the use of the scarves and the free motion of the choir reaching far beyond the risers.

Many European choirs are exploring the use of video projections during performances. I am reminded of New York composer's Robert Convery's stunning work, *Songs Of Children* set for choir and piano trio. The children interned at Terezín Concentration Camp for Jews in World War II grace this thirty-minute work with their poetry. I often wish I had had the foresight to add slides of the horrible atrocities of the Holocaust and the deprivation within that ghetto, in particular, to allow that piece to come fully to life for the audience. When we performed John Adams's monumental work, *On The Transmigration Of Souls*, one student took it upon himself to put together a 30-minute movie to the music of this 9/11 work. For a variety of reasons we were not able to show it in the concert hall as the live performance was going on, but those that saw it before the performance in a pre-concert setting were deeply moved. The orchestra and chorus that performed it also saw it beforehand and this, perhaps more than any single thing that occurred in rehearsal, moved the ensemble forward on this most challenging work. In thinking about future concerts, we have also discussed having footage of the original presentation of a work on one screen, while another showing the performers now presenting the work in the present day. A great deal of planning goes into a project of this nature, but undoubtedly pays great dividends.

We touched on lighting with the reference to Leek's *Knowee* above. Sometimes a single candle can be used to present a chant, to focus on a soloist, to feature an instrumentalist, or to allow the audience to focus in a new way. For a concert called "A Kaleidoscope of Choirs," we began with *America*, recently set by Vince Peterson, which features an opening extended cello solo before the choir comes in. With singers coming from all areas of the hall, they enter quietly as the cellist is dimly lit with only one candle. The piece builds quite creatively, and so does the lighting to reflect the progression of singers and sound, thus creating a synergy between sight, sound, and personnel that is quite stunning.

We have all experienced holiday productions with featured lighting to accent different repertoire, but have you ever started with no light at all and presented a piece that may say more without seeing anyone? This may be a familiar piece like *Amazing Grace*, which is so personal to so many that it may say more to the audience without any visual cues. If you are able to light different parts of the concert hall, the idea of the audience being surprised by the blackout on stage, and the immediate lighting in the second balcony on the brass and then a string quartet in the organ loft without a pause can be thrilling. This kind of surround-sound effect is made so much more powerful with added lighting effects.

Many scores are calling for movement to showcase the piece. Veljo Tormis's *Raua Needine (Curse Upon Iron)* is probably one of the most dramatic and powerful pieces to consider. The composer has suggested moves throughout the entire middle section (which is largely spoken) to sense the devastation that can occur if one does not heed the warnings of perpetual war. *War Song* by Japanese composer Shin-ichiro Ikebe is also only effective with choralography, and when we finished our 2009 ACDA performance with Alberto Grau's *Arestinga*, our choralographer, Yvonne Farrow wrote:

> The movement for this work is based on the national dance of Venezuela called *Joropo*. A couples dance, it is earthy and rhythmic, centered primarily below the waist with an emphasis on footwork. Lively and syncopated, there are over 36 different steps found in this folk dance. My intent is to give you a taste of the country and its people who are of Indian, Spanish, and African descent. To me, the loose shaking of the foot represents, for this work, the 'catch' our fisherman did not bring back to his village.

So consider whether choralography will enhance or harm your program. It does take time, great patience, and a full-fledged effort to allow motions to be free and seem spontaneous as well, always honest to the score itself. There is no right answer, but seriously consider taking this programming risk.

When looking at creating a true synthesis to your program, look carefully at the long and short repertoire involved. Does it seem to balance, or is it overflowing with one composer? Is one selection dominating the set of music? Is there a lengthier piece that should stand alone and create its own set? I put together a set of music dealing with grief and despair of feeling forsaken by God and ending in almost religious ecstasy that was a bit unusual. We opened the set with the first movement from Ginastera's *Lamentations—O vos omnes* with its allusions to Argentine folk music, then proceeded to Victoria's setting of the same text and finished with Ola Gjeilo's "Dark Night Of The Soul." The first two pieces are only about six minutes long—however, Gjeilo's setting is some 13 minutes in length set with string quartet and piano and soprano obbligato. This decision seems to work because of the minimalistic quality to the Gjeilo almost making it seem shorter. In general, I like to see a similar length to the pieces within a set of music, thus allowing it to be a true partnership of time and intent.

Think carefully about the location for your concert. Are there places that best help present the repertoire you are about to unfold? I will never forget a concert in Milwaukee at a most beautiful cathedral where we tried to perform *Chichester Psalms* of Leonard Bernstein in the chamber music form from the rear balcony. This was absolutely the wrong choice for this reverberant space, and the rhythmic vitality that is so critical to the piece was completely lost in that environment. I can also remember the opposite happening while performing Tavener's haunting setting of *Svyati* in a completely dry setting and thus the silences that always give the sense of eternity with this composer were completely swallowed up.

We discussed briefly the aspect of audience involvement as it related to Whitacre's *Clouburst*. I have also had the audience create a drone while a soloist or a section sings a haunting melody. This seems to be most effective in Dorian or Phrygian mode. I will never forget when Bobby McFerrin had the entire audience sing *Twinkle, Twinkle Little Star* while he improvised above and below. He had a thousand people all singing in perfect unison. Partner songs are often a great bridge to cross as well. In her *Singing in the African American Tradition*, Ysaye Barnwell presents step-by step directions on her CD in partnering these three incredible songs—*Wade In The Water, I Wanna Die Easy*, and *Motherless Chil'*—which we performed with the audience being led by three of our singers in different parts of the hall. Nick Page from Vermont is the master at creating an environment for success with the audience as well. His book *Sing And Shine On* is most effective at demonstrating line-by-line how to teach an untrained audience to sing by rote. Consider it a goal to truly include corporate singing with the audience. They want to be involved. Figure out creative ways to make it most interesting for them and your choir. Don't forget your alumni as well if you are at a school that honors that tradition.

Conclusion

The art of successful programming is a long, arduous, circuitous, and yet most rewarding task that requires a constant study of literature of all types. There is indeed great music in all genres. Don't let your personal bias rule out the possibilities for inclusion of something you never dreamed you would perform five years ago. In this day and age, there is no excuse for not finding the right piece for the particular choir you are teaching at any given moment. I usually review over 10,000 scores for consideration per year. I could easily see myself looking at twice that many in the future, but don't forget the gems from 1380, or 1940, or 1828. Consider which parts of the world you have not yet investigated.

Your journey only begins after cutting your list down to a minor mountain of good music, then comes that full tough-love analysis of what works best in your particular situation. You are always reviewing the why, what, and where of any event. As your decisions finalize, live and study the scores deeply before making final calls on the "keeper" pile. How many different concepts are being taught every concert? How many different cultures and languages are being experienced? How many different forms and genre are being touched upon? Keep asking yourself, are these the best choices, and if so, why? Through your selections are you truly able to allow for success and growth of every singer? Will your programming selections reach the audience? Look seriously at the ones in doubt and think about the synthesis of that music within the whole program.

Allow yourself time to live and breathe in the aroma of this program. Does it truly have legs? Will it allow you to grow as a person, as a historian, as a singer, and as a conductor? Having all pieces of equal difficulty is a recipe for disaster. Just like a well-planned meal, some things take little time to prepare; others a great deal of time. They all can satisfy the appetite, but eating fast food all of the time, well . . . you get the idea.

Consider the entire gestalt of each concert from beginning to end. Engender the expertise of the members of the ensemble, close associates, and the ever present social media to assist in helping with areas you are not as well-prepared to solve as others. Love your singers, love the process, and spend a bit of time enjoying the fruits of your labor. I am always amazed when I get a letter from a former singer about an experience that in some cases happened 20 years ago, yet they are still moved by that experience. Don't ever underestimate the power of great music to change lives. When we put that same music into context that allows for full realization, the experience is profoundly held for a lifetime.

APPENDIX

Sample Programs

SPIRIT, MOVING OVER CHAOS

Wisconsin Middle Level choir – Oct. 2013

I

Spirit, moving over chaos - David Ashley White (handbells, synthesizer-drone)

    405-633 - Selah Publishing Co. wwww.selahpub.com

Dona nobis pacem - Caccini arr. James Moore (AMP 0512)

II

Tant que vivray (done in English) - Claudin de Sermisy (string quartet)

Sumer is icumen in - Bjella (violin and cello) – Carl Fischer CM9372

III

Ríu ríu chíu (up a whole step)

    http://www2.cpdl.org/wiki/images/1/10/Anonymous-Riu_Riu_Chiu-Uppsala_41.pdf

Hava Blessing - Bjella (string quartet) Carl Fischer #10443565

IV

Deep Blue - Moira Smiley (SATB) percussion, cello/bass, water jug

A RIVER RUNS THROUGH US

San Antonio Chamber Choir

Richard Bjella, Artistic Director

September 2014

HARMONY WITH NATURE

HARMONY OF THE SPHERES – JOEP FRANSSENS

BEAUTIFUL RIVER – LOWREY arr. BY WILLIAM HAWLEY

LONGING

SICUT CERVUS – GIOVANNI PIERLUIGI DA PALESTRINA (with saxophone improvisation)

O WALY, WALY – SCOTTISH FOLK SONG arr. DARYL RUNSWICK (with cello)

MYSTICISM OF WATER

EFFORTLESSLY LOVE FLOWS – AARON JAY KERNIS

CLOUDBURST – ERIC WHITACRE (shortened - with audience)

BAR XIZAM (UPWARD I RISE) – ABBIE BETINIS

Intermission

TROUBLED WATERS

WADE IN THE WATER – LUBOFF arr. NORMAN

VANRAH VARSHA – BHATIA

LOVE

IN THE NIGHT WE SHALL GO IN – IMANT RAMINSH (with cello and HS students)

WATER NIGHT – ERIC WHITACRE

SHENANDOAH – STEVEN SAMETZ

FUN ON THE WATER

OLD JOE HAS GONE FISHING – BENJAMIN BRITTEN

MOON RIVER – HENRY MANCINI arr. JOHN COATES

THE RIVER OF DREAMS – BILLY JOEL arr. Jeff Molush

PRAYER

DOWN TO THE RIVER TO PRAY – arr. M. Noia/ R. Bjella (with HS Students)

DEEP RIVER – arr. NORMAN LUBOFF

BRIDGE OVER TROUBLED WATER – PAUL SIMON arr. VINCE PETERSON

SIX DEGREES FROM JS BACH

Texas Tech University – 2013 Tour Program

Prelude

JOHANN SEBASTIAN BACH (1685–1750)   Weinen, Klagen, Sorgen, Zagen (1714)

FRANZ LISZT (1811–1886)   LISZT variations on CANTATA #12

BENJAMIN BRITTEN   (from WAR REQUIEM)

(1913–1976)   Kyrie eleison (chorale) (1961)

Matthew J. Carey, conductor

JONATHAN DOVE   (from PASSING OF THE YEAR)

(b. 1959)   Ring out, wild bells (2000)

Anthony King, David Kennedy, and Alex Kang, percussion

I

HILDEGARD von BINGEN   O vis aeternitatis (c. 1160)
(1098–1179)

JOHANNES OCKEGHEM   Alma Redemptoris mater (c. 1490)
(1410/25–1497)

UNKNOWN (13th century)   (from *LA MESSE de TOURNAI*)
                               Kyrie (*c.* 1270)
        Choral preparation by Stephanie Council

II

KRZYSZTOF PENDERECKI   (from *A POLISH REQUIEM*)
(b. 1933)   Agnus Dei (1981)

HUGO WOLF   Der Feuerreiter (1888)
(1860–1903)

III

CLAUDE DEBUSSY   (from *TROIS CHANSONS de CHARLES D'ORLÉANS*)
(1862–1918)   Quand j'ai ouy le tabourin (1908)
        Catherine Swindle, soloist

HENK BADINGS   (from *TROIS CHANSONS BRETONNES*)
(1907–1987)   Soir d'éte (1930)
        Ann Marie White, dancer
             Andrew Kreckmann, conductor

IV

RODION SHCHEDRIN   (from *THE SEALED ANGEL*)
(b. 1932)   Lord's Prayer (1988)

SERGEI RACHMANINOFF arr. Bjella   Vocalise (1912)
(1873–1943)

MODEST MUSSORGSKY arr. Bjella   (from *PICTURES AT AN EXHIBITION*)
(1839–1881)   Great Gate of Kiev (1874)
        Anthony King, David Kennedy, and Alex Kang, percussion

V

STEPHEN FOSTER (1826–1864)   Hard Times (1854/2005)
Setting by CRAIG HELLA JOHNSON (b. 1956)
        Catherine Swindle, Alicia Yantosca, Nathan Rhoden, Andrew Cravatt, soloists

Spiritual arr. ANDERS PAULSSON   Bright Morning Stars (19th
century/1998)
(b. 1961)

Katie Webb, Nathan Rhoden, Stephanie Council, Marenda Natera, Corbin DeSpain, soloists

JOHN ORFE (b. 1976)   Fire! (2010)
        Kurt Cereske, Kelsei Fortenberry, Mark Haddad, soloists
Epilogue

BRITTEN   (from *WAR REQUIEM*)
                                                 Requiem (chorale)

JS BACH   Weinen, Klagen, Sorgen, Zagen – Sinfonia in
F minor

We shall not cease from exploration
And the end of all our exploring
Will be to arrive where we started
And know the place for the first time."
— T.S. Eliot, *Four Quartets*

ALL Northwest HS Festival – 2008
Richard Bjella, conductor

I

Plaudite tympana (from Missa Salisburgensis)
        (16 part choir. 2 x 8 part choirs)   Heinrich Biber (cpdl)
        (opening section) (organ – 3 trumpets)

Lord, Thou hast been our refuge   Ralph Vaughan Williams
        (organ, three trumpets, choir octet or 16)

II
Mille Regretz   Josquin Des Prez (cpdl)

The Stars Stand Up in the Air   Eric Barnum (Walton)
        (piano)

III
Symphony of Psalms (1st movement)   Igor Stravinsky
                                       (Boosey and Hawkes)

        (piano 4 hands)

IV

Mi'kmaq Honor Song   Lydia Adams

                                  (Leslie Music Supply,Inc.)

Idumea   Ananias Davisson, 1816 (arr. Bjella) (Alliance Publications)

    Vln/ vla

Dance of Zalongo   Carol Barnett

    (piano 4 hands, hand drum. tambourine)

Mirrored Messages

Texas Tech University Choir, Richard Bjella, conductor

Clinton Barrick, accompanist

TMEA PROGRAM

February 10, 2012, 6:30 pm

Lila Cockrell Theatre

*percussion, +strings, **trumpets

I

*handbells

Carmina Burana

    +*Gauthier De Châtillon: Fas Et Nefas Ambulant (hand drum, tambourine, fiddle)

    +Anon: O Varium Fortune Lubricum

    *Fortune plango vulnera (grand casa)

    Anon: Doleo Quod Nimium

    *Orff: Carmina Burana - Cour D'Amours: Circa Mea Pectora – (grand casa, xylophone, cymbals, grand casa,)

    +*Chancellier: Bulla Fulminante (drum with sticks, fiddle)

    *+Anon: Veni, Veni, Venias ... Chume, Chume, Geselle Mîn (cello, vln), hand drum,

    *Orff: Carmina Burana - Cour D'Amours: Veni, Veni, Venias- triangle, cymbal,
        Early scores courtesy of JOEL COHEN Music Director Emeritus of
        Boston Camerata. <www.bostoncamerata.org>

        Carmina Burana – Carl Orff

            Schott Publications (female voices AP -118)/ (Male voice ED 4920-02)

            *Handbells

                (without pause)

II

From *Requiem*   Jean Richafort

    Sanctus

        Trey Davis, conductor - DMA Choral Conducting (anticipated summer 2012)

        Jean Richafort (ca. 1480-ca. 1548), *Opera omnia*, edited by Harry Elzinga in 4 volumes Vol. I - Requiem - "Sanctus"

        From *Corpus Mensurabilis Musicae* - Paul L. Ranzini, General Editor

          *handbells

From *Missa Angelorum*   Carl Rütti

    Ite Missa Est

        Escorial Edition 17–19 St George's Street, Norwich NR3 1AB, England

III

From *Reincarnations*

    The Coolin   Samuel Barber

        G. Schirmer #39970c

+O Waly, Waly   arr. Daryl Runswick (with cello)

    (performed with permission from the arranger)

        (without pause)

IV

Come, Sweet Death   **Johann Sebastian Bach**

+La Muerte del Ángel (The death of the angel)   Piazzolla arr. José Bragato

    violin, cello, piano (with choir) choral parts set by Richard Bjella

        Cat.-No. 21064 TONOS Musiekverlags GmbH, Holzhofallee 15, D-64295 Darmstadt.

V

From *Vier geistliche Gesänge*   Wolgang Buchenberg

    Ich bin das Brot des Lebens (I am the bread of life)

        Carus #7.351

Ich Bin Die Auferstehung Und Das Leben   Heinrich Schütz (cpdl)

        (I am the Resurrection and the Life)

        (without pause)

VI

** *From *ALEXANDER NEVSKY*   , Op. 78   Serge Prokofiev

    Alexander Enters Pskov

        Edwin f. Kalmus #6380

** *From *AIDA*   Giuseppe Verdi
    Triumphal scene
        Oxford University Press, John Rutter (ed.), Opera Choruses

VII

Orovela   Georgian folk tune (public domain)
*Messages   Roger Treece and Bobby McFerrin
    Messages, music by Roger Treece and Bobby McFerrin, lyrics by Don Rosler, ©
    2010 by Lindalamama Music (ASCAP); Probnoblem Music (BMI); Vocabularies
    Music (SESAC)

ACDA NATIONAL CONVENTION – 2009
LAWRENCE UNIVERSITY CONCERT CHOIR
Richard Bjella, conductor

Part 1

Knowee   **Stephen Leek (b. 1959)**
    (Sydney, Australia, 2008)
        **soloists: Rachel Niemann, Julie DeBoer, Adrienne Gallagher, Carolyn
            Grieco**

Te Lucis ante Terminum   taken from Pablo Casals (1876–1973) `
    (16th c.Catalan carol)   arrangement of *Song of the Birds*
        Small ensemble: Michael Axtell, Justin Berkowitz, Michael Burton,
            Nikolas Ross, Sanjay Seth manuscript arr. Edwin Higginbottom
                ed. by Richard Bjella
Svatba (The Wedding)   **Khristo Todorov (1927–1980)**
    (Plodiv, Bulgaria)

Part 2

Laboravi in Gemitu Meo   **Philippe Rogier (*c.* 1560–1599)**
    (Lisbon, Spain, 1587?)
Les Voici! Voici La Quadrille! (from Act 4 of *Carmen*) **Georges Bizet (1838–1875)**
    (Paris, France, 1875)

Part 3

*How Can I Cry?   **Moira Smiley (b. 1976)**
    (Indiana, 1995)
        soloists: Lacey Jo Benter, Patty LeClaire

Arestinga

> (Caracas, Venezuela, 2003

Michael Axtell, baritone

Otilio Galíndez arr. Alberto Grau

Choralograher, Yvonne Farrow

A CENTURY APART - 2006
Lawrence University Choir program

I

Exultate justi in Domino—Viadana (1560 – 1627)

Salmo 150 Ernani Aguiar (b. 1949)

II

Amor (Lamento della ninfa—Monteverdi (1567–1643)

I Gondolieri—Giovanni Rossini (1792–1868)

Viking Chorale

V

Annus novus in Gaudio (Let the New Year now begin)—(CC men) (c. 1139)

Soloists:

> Hugh Naughtin, James Antony, Evan Bravos, Jesse Weinberg, Andrew Sparks

Concert Choir men

Salva Regina—Ramona Luengen (1960–)

Cantala and Concert Choir women

VI

Absalon, fili mi—Josquin des Prez (small group) (c. 1455–1521)
> Scott Sandersfeld, conductor

When David Heard—Norman Dinerstein (b. 1937–)
> Emily Fink, soprano

VII

Ich bin die Auferstehung und das Leben (I am the resurrection and the life) Heinrich Schütz (1585–1672)

Effortlessly Love Flows (1998)—Aaron Jay Kernis (1960–)

VIII

Lamentations of Jeremiah Alberto Ginastera (1916–1983)
>   *O vos ommes qui transitis per viam*

Hard Times (1864)—Stephen Foster arr. Craig Hella Johnson (1956–)
>   Lacey Jo Benter, soloist

IX

An die Sonne (To the Sun)—Franz Schubert (small group) (1797–1828)
>   Sarah Botsford, conductor

Hymn du Soleil (Hymn to the Sun)—Lili Boulanger (1893–1918)
>   Sarah Botsford mezzo soprano

Concert Choir

February/March Texas Tech University Choir on Tour 2015

- - - W H I S P E R S - - - -

>   of the distant past

| KNOWEE | Stephen Leek |
| WHISPERS | Steven Stucky |

>   of peace

| GLORIA (from *Heiligemesse*) | Joseph Haydn |
| MISSA PAX *(Sanctus, Hosanna)* | Timothy Corlis |

>   of steadfast faith

| GEISTLICHES LIED | Johannes Brahms |
| ECCE SACERDOS MAGNUS | Anton Bruckner |

>   of longing

KAS TIE TADI	Steven Stucky
LABORAVI	Phillipe Rogier
POOR WAYFARIN STRANGER	Sally Terri

>   of grief and salvation

O VOS OMNES	Alberto Ginastera
O VOS OMNES	Antonio Lotti
DARK NIGHT OF THE SOUL	Ola Gjeilo

of hope and joy

DOMINUS REGNAVIT	Levente Gyöngyösi
PEACE LIKE A RIVER	arr. Bjella
AIN'T NO GRAVE	Caldwell/ Ivory

Alaska All-State Nov. 15–17, 2012

I

Sumer is icumen in—arr. R. Bjella (vln, c) Carl Fischer Publication CM9372

Psalm 96 – Sweelinck

http://www2.cpdl.org/wiki/images/sheet/swee-96.pdf

II

Adoramus Te, Christie—Quirino Gasparini

http://www2.cpdl.org/wiki/images/sheet/gasp-ado.pdf

Jubilate Deo (KV 117)—Mozart

III

Famine Song—arr. Matthew Culloton Santa Barbara SBMP 575

From Here on in – arr. Brumfield (4) Hal Leonard ZHL8752843

IV

O Swiftly Glides the Bonnie Boat—Beethoven (vln, c) (2) National Music Publishers CMS - 126

Loch Lomond—arr. Jonathan Quick (4) Cypress Press CP 1045

V

All My Trials—arr. Norman Luboff (3) HL 7066S (originally Walton Publications)

No Rocks a Cryin'—Rollo Dilworth (3) HL.8711307

CHAPTER 17

....

CHORAL REPERTOIRE
AS PEDAGOGY

Western Art Music

....

DENNIS SHROCK

INTRODUCTION

....

THE topic "Repertoire as Pedagogy" can be divided into two main categories: music composed to fulfill some manner of instructional mandate, and music, whatever its original intent, performed with an educational goal in mind. In the first category, the composer does not consider performance as a reason for composition or as a compositional motivator. Indeed, compositions in this category may not be meant for performance at all. Religious chants of the Medieval era and Lutheran chorales of the early Protestant Reformation, for instance, were composed for use in worship services. The chants and chorales were an integral part of sacred liturgies and, as such, they were not for performance, but for devotional purposes. The singing of chants and chorales for performance outside or beyond their intended religious services was not a consideration at the time of their composition.

On the other hand, chants and chorales, as well as compositions in other genres, may be performed apart from their intended purposes in order to accomplish another purpose, one that has an instructional or educational objective. A conductor could, for instance, desire to expose singers and/or audiences to monody and thus program chant as a vehicle for this. Or one might rehearse and perform chant along with other unison pieces in order to focus on vocal blend. Similarly, one might choose chorales, with Calvinist psalm settings, to teach precepts of the Protestant Reformation. There are a myriad of reasons for selecting repertoire and designing programs that have pedagogical purposes.

PEDAGOGICAL COMPOSITIONS

As mentioned above, religious chants were composed as a vehicle for worship. Whether Byzantine, Armenian, Russian, Ambrosian, or Gregorian, the chants were fundamental components of liturgical worship services. Some chants were set to texts of praise and adoration, some to commemorate specific days and events of the liturgical year, some were to be sung at different times of the day or night, and some were for private devotionals while others were for public ceremonies. All of the chants, however, were inextricably bound to their rites or rituals. The chants were obligatory, not optional, and were a form of prayer, not performance. With this in mind, it should be noted that the majority of chants were not composed to be sung by clergy or choirs to a congregation of listeners; the chants were sung by the clergy (including monks and nuns) for themselves.

The chants were also pedagogical in that they served a teaching purpose. Those chants of praise, including most of the psalms, were a means by which worshippers could glorify their creator. Two examples are *Cantate Domino* (Psalm 96), with the internal text "Annuntiate inter gentes gloriam ejus, in omnibus populis mirabilia ejus, quoniam magnus Dominus et laudabilis nimis" (Make known among nations his glory and among all people his wonders, for the Lord is great and greatly to be praised), and *Laudate Dominum* (Psalm 117), with the complete text "Laudate Dominum omnes gentes, laudate eum omnes populi, quoniam confirmata est super nos misericordia ejus et veritas Domini manet in aeternam" (Praise the Lord all nations, praise him all peoples, for he has bestowed on us his loving kindness, and the truth of the Lord endures forever).

Chants for the commemoration of specific days and events were important since they guided worshippers through the liturgical year—from Advent, through Christmas and Easter, to Pentecost. As examples: the Canticle of the Blessed Virgin Mary (Luke 1:46–55) that begins, "Magnificat anima mea Dominum et exultavit spiritus meus" (My soul magnifies the Lord and my spirit has rejoiced in God my savior) for Advent; "Hodie Christus natus est, hodie salvator apparuit" (Today Christ is born, today the savior has appeared) for Christmas; "O filii et filiae, rex caelestis, rex gloriae, morte surrexit hodie, alleluia" (O sons and daughters, the king of heaven, the king of glory has risen from death today, alleluia) for Easter; and "Veni sancte spiritus et emitte coelitus lucis tuae radium" (Come, holy spirit, and send forth from heaven the ray of your light) for Pentecost.

Beyond the pedagogical use of the chants as components of worship services, chants were used for a broader purpose. For instance, Pope Gregory (590–604) used chant to consolidate different factions of the church throughout Italy and Spain, and later popes continued to give prominence to the chants as a political vehicle for ecclesial unification. Pope Pius X in a *motu proprio* of 1903 called for a single book of chants to be used by the Catholic Church worldwide. The pope gave the Benedictine monks of Solesmes a mandate to prepare this book, called the *Liber usualis*, and to include in the book the basic chants for all services in the church. In effect, popes Gregory and Pius X were teaching the worshippers of diverse cultures across the world a singular protocol, one used to create a unified church.

Similar to chants, chorales in the early Lutheran Church were used as liturgical entities. As a principal part of Martin Luther's efforts to reform the Roman Catholic Church
and to make worship more relevant to and understood by the common people of the day,
music was composed or arranged in the vernacular language and in simple hymn-like
settings. Called a variety of names at first, including "geistliche Lieder" (sacred songs)
and "Kirchengesänge" (church songs), the chorales, as they later became known, were
meant to be accessible. Some of them were mere translations of well-known Gregorian
chants, for example, *Christ lag in Todes Banden* (Christ lay in death's bonds) from
Victimae paschali laudes (To the Paschal Victim) and *Komm Gott, Schöpfer, Heiliger
Geist* (Come God, Creator, Holy Ghost) from *Veni Creator Spiritus* (Come, Creator
Spirit). Other chorales were adaptations of popular secular tunes, as in, *O Welt, ich
muss dich lassen* (Oh world, I must leave you) taken from *Innsbruck, ich muss dich lassen* (Innsbruck, I must leave you). And yet other chorales were newly created. Famous
among these new compositions are *Ein feste Burg ist unser Gott* (A mighty fortress is our
God), composed by Martin Luther, and *Wachet auf, ruft uns die Stimme* (Wake up, call
the voices to us), composed by Philipp Nicolai.

Chorales and related texts for recitatives and arias in oratorio settings were also
used to contemporize biblical stories—to involve the contemporary worshipper (the
Lutheran of the 17th and 18th century) in biblical drama and to make the worshippers
feel responsible for the actions of the biblical people. The texts of these chorales, recitatives, and arias, collectively referred to as Pietistic poetry, were newly written during the
Baroque era to amplify biblical stories and to make the stories relevant to the Lutheran
theology. In the J. S. Bach *St. Matthew Passion*, for example, Jesus says at the Last Supper,
"Wahrlich ich sage euch: Einer unter euch wird mich verraten" (Truly I say to you: one of
you will betray me), after which eleven of the disciples ask, "Herr, bin ich's?" (Lord, is it
I?). Immediately following this, Bach inserts the chorale, "Ich bin's, ich sollte büssen" (It
is I, I should atone). The "I" here refers to the contemporary Lutheran. The Bach passion
oratorios, and all other passion settings of the time, were musical dramas that not only
elucidated a story, but that also taught the worshipper a personal lesson.

The passion settings themselves, all meant to be performed in a sacred setting as
part of a worship service, were didactic in purpose. The relating of Christ's suffering
was meant to deepen the faith of those who listened to the music. Most other sacred
oratorios, however, were not generally performed as part of a worship service, and
although they conveyed biblical stories (mostly about Old Testament figures such as
Jephthah, Jonah, Judith, Susanna, and Saul), they were not set to actual biblical texts,
they were not generally performed in church venues (but in special prayer halls and in
public theaters), and their purposes were more for entertainment than for education.
Even the very early Baroque-era oratorios of the Congregazione dell'Oratorio, founded
by Philip Neri (1515–1595), and the late-Baroque oratorios of George Frideric Handel,
had entertainment as a purpose for their composition. Interestingly, most of the secular oratorios of the time, composed to allegorical texts that conveyed moral or political messages, were didactic. Examples include *La vendita del core humano* (The sale of
the human heart) by Giovanni Legrenzi and *Hercules* by Handel. Even some of Handel's

sacred oratorios conveyed strong political messages. In *Judas Maccabaeus*, for example, it would have been clear to the audiences of the time that the libretto was allegorical and that the role of Judas Maccabaeus represented the Duke of Cumberland, who was to be glorified upon his victorious return from the Battle of Culloden in Scotland.

The tradition of allegorical oratorios continued in the 20th century. One such work, an interesting parallel to the Baroque-era passion settings with their insertion of chorales to the biblical texts, is the oratorio *A Child of Our Time*, composed by Michael Tippett between 1939 and 1941 and premiered in March 1944. Tippett directly modeled his oratorio on the passion settings of J. S. Bach, with recitatives, arias, choruses, and chorales. Tippett's libretto is based on the novel *Ein Kind unserer Zeit* by Ödön von Horváth (1901–1938) about the life of Herschel Grynspan, a youth who killed a German diplomat because of the Nazi treatment of Jews in Germany, and who by this action set off the Kristallnacht (the large-scale harassment and murder of Jews throughout Germany and Austria on November 9 and 10, 1938). Tippet said that he had found Grynspan to be "another of the many scapegoats I wished to commemorate: the unnamed, deranged, soldier/murderer." To take the place of chorales, Tippett chose African-American spirituals (*Steal Away; Nobody Knows the Trouble I See; Go Down, Moses; O, By and By*; and *Deep River*) to function as reflective commentaries on the oratorio's story. The spirituals, being expressions of an oppressed people, are analogous to Tippett's libretto story about oppressed Jews during the Nazi regime. *A Child of Our Time* is not, therefore, biblical or religious. Rather, it is more like the Baroque-era allegorical oratorios, all of which had texts intended to be pedagogical in their conveyance of a moralistic message.

A number of other 20th-century British composers also wrote large-scale didactic choral works, most with an antiwar theme and with combinations of texts from a variety of sources. Arthur Bliss incorporated texts from Homer, Walt Whitman, Wilfred Owen, and Robert Nichols in his choral symphony entitled *Morning Heroes*. Ralph Vaughan Williams, who worked as a battlefield medic during World War I and who was intensely bothered by Hitler's persecution of the Jews and Britain's policy of appeasement, selected and compiled a wide range of sacred and secular texts for his *Dona nobis pacem*. Included with the excerpt from the end of the Roman Catholic Mass, "Agnus Dei qui tollis peccata mundi, dona nobis pacem" (Lamb of God who takes away the sins of the world, give us peace), are biblical passages from the Old Testament (e.g., "Nation shall not lift up sword against nation, neither shall they learn war any more" from Isaiah 2:4), poems by Walt Whitman, and most poignant, part of a speech by the Quaker, John Bright (1811–1889), made in the House of Commons on February 23, 1855, that denounces Britain's participation in the Crimean War (a war that was taking place at the time).

The most obvious antiwar musical work is Benjamin Britten's epic *War Requiem*, composed for the dedication of the new Coventry Cathedral in May 1962, the old cathedral having been demolished during the Battle of Britain in November 1940. Britten was a declared pacifist who joined England's Peace Pledge Union in 1937, swearing to the oath, "I renounce war, and am therefore determined not to support any kind of war, I am also determined to work for the removal of all causes of war." As reinforcement of the oath, Britten composed his first antiwar work, *Sinfonia da Requiem*, in 1941 while he was in the United States avoiding war conflicts in England and Europe. About this work, premiered by the New York Philharmonic in Carnegie Hall, Britten stated, "I'm making it just as antiwar as possible. . . I don't believe you can express social or political or economic theories in music, but . . . all I'm sure of is my own antiwar convictions as I write it" (Carpenter, 1992, p.146). Britten later contemplated writing an oratorio entitled *Mea Culpa* about the destruction of Hiroshima and Nagasaki, and in 1948 he developed plans for a work to be called *A Ghandi Requiem*. But these works never came into being. It was in 1958, when he was approached by a committee from Coventry Cathedral, that Britten began thinking about writing his *War Requiem*. This work combines the traditional texts of the Latin mass for the dead with poetry of Wilfred Owen (1893–1918), who was killed in battle at age twenty-five, one week to the hour before the end of World War I, and who was one of the most famous antiwar poets of the 20th century. Besides using Owen's poetry as commentary to the sacred Latin texts, Britten quotes Owen as a preface to the Requiem: "My subject is war and the pity of war. The poetry is in the pity. All the poet can do today is warn."

Other didactic works have been composed to foster nationalism or to promote political ideology. The most obvious and well-known of these works were composed by Russian composers under the Communist regime. Sergey Prokofiev's *Aleksandr Nevsky*, originally composed as music for the film of the same name by Sergei Eisenstein, is about Nevsky's defeat of Teutonic invaders at the 1242 Battle on the Ice at Lake Chudskoye. Prokofiev also composed *Ballad of an Unknown Boy* in 1942 to a text by the political activist poet Pavel Antoklosky (1896–1978) about a young man who kills a fascist commander in retribution for the murder of the man's mother and sister. Prokofiev's most obvious political work is *On Guard for Peace*, composed in 1950 to texts about the protection of youth from the ravages of war. To underscore the message of the music, Prokofiev wrote, "In this oratorio I have tried to express my feelings about war and peace, and also my firm belief that there will be no more wars, that all the nations of the world will safeguard peace and save civilization, our children, and our future" (see Shrock, 2009, p. 694).

All of the works discussed above, from Gregorian chants of the Medieval era to 20th-century oratorios, were composed for purposes other than entertainment. However, works written with entertainment as their primary objective (or works with a performance history of entertainment) can also be didactic. For example, the musical theater works *West Side Story* (music by Leonard Bernstein and libretto by Stephen Sondheim—based on Shakespeare's *Romeo and Juliet*) and *Les Misérables* (music by Claude-Michel Schönberg and English libretto by Herbert Kretzmer—based on the novel *Les Misérables* by Victor Hugo) both carry with them powerful social messages. Beyond the appeal of the music and effectiveness of the staging and choreography, the entertainment value of the works is matched or superseded by the teaching quality of the libretto. In the case of *West Side Story*, it is difficult to imagine someone listening to (and watching) this musical without feeling the extraordinary injustice caused by the rivalry between the Jets and the Sharks and also the sorrowful situation that keeps two people (Maria and

Tony) of different ethnicities from being together. In *Les Misérables*, one certainly feels compassion for the unjust hardships that Jean Valjean endures, and one cannot help but empathize with the French populace as they face appalling adversities and deprivations. Furthermore, we extol Valjean's fortitude and perseverance, and we feel compatriots with the revolutionaries. Both *West Side Story* and *Les Misérables* convey meanings and promote feelings well beyond mere entertainment. The musicals serve a larger purpose because they advocate causes of social justice and human benevolence; they are pedagogical in that they teach lessons.

Pedagogical Programming

It is the lesson aspect of repertoire that makes for rich programming. This is not to say that programming for pure entertainment is unsatisfactory or worthless. Singing and listening to music for amusement has value. Laughter, escape from stress, and mindless stimulation all have positive attributes. Besides, audiences, as well as singers, often don't want (or don't think they want) to be taught a lesson, and choral directors certainly want their singers and audiences to have fun. If singers and audiences are happy, it is likely that parents, administrators, clergy, congregations, and boards of directors will also be happy, and if everyone is in this state of enjoyment, the choice of repertoire must be successful (Q. E. D., *quod erat demonstrandum*). But, entertainment as fun and pedagogy as instruction are not contradictory or incompatible, and combining both intentions can add to each of them separately. It is especially true that adding the pedagogical precept to entertainment can increase the entertainment portion of the equation (while the converse is not true). Programming repertoire for instructional purposes can be both educational and entertaining, and can make the programming experience a richer one for singers and listeners alike.

Pedagogical considerations for programming include: 1) specific musical goals that incorporate both short- and long-term growth and development, and that rely on transfer of learning; 2) recruitment and retention of singers and audiences, with acute awareness of musical accessibility; 3) knowledge and appreciation of environmental customs or expectations, including choral strengths and weaknesses; 4) psychological management of time in regards to ontology and flow; and 5) performance practices.

All these considerations of programming are pedagogical since they involve selection of repertoire, design of programming, and manifestation of music with educational purposes, purposes that advance singers, audiences, and the choral art.

1) At its most basic level of consideration, repertoire should be chosen for reasons related to specific musical, technical, religious, or social goals, and these goals should be set in accordance with specific characteristics of an ensemble. As examples: a beginning elementary school choir (private, public, or church) might be given repertoire that builds music literacy; a middle school choir could focus on music that teaches values such as teamwork and cooperation; singers in a high school choir would certainly

benefit from peak musical experiences of excellence; college and university singers could develop global awareness by singing music from foreign cultures; adult church-choir singers might broaden their horizons by incorporating music outside their liturgy; and community symphonic choirs might work to educate and further the aesthetic experiences of their audiences by performing masterworks beyond the standard fare such as the Beethoven *Symphony #9*, Handel *Messiah*, and Orff *Carmina Burana*.

It is recommended that the conductor develop a multi-year, long-range plan, with specified short-term goals that are cumulative and that serve as steppingstones toward the accomplishment of the long-term objective, and to aid in the accomplishment of the long-term target, the conductor should plan for transfer of learning (i.e., the conductor should expect and require the singers to remember specifics of the short-term goals and apply or transfer these specifics to the new goals). The transfer of learning process should (and can) exist even with a changing population of singers; as some singers leave the ensemble and others join it, the conductor should expect that the new singers will become aware of and accomplish the old or former short-term goals, even though these goals were not specifically taught to the new singers. This transfer of learning is especially apparent in schools (including colleges and universities), where singers come and go as a natural phenomenon. When the bar has been raised, so to speak, it can stay raised—as long as the conductor/teacher holds the students to the implementation of all goals.

For examples of goals and plans, I'll relate a few personal stories. Early in my career I was appointed Artistic Director of Canterbury Choral Society, a community chorus in Oklahoma City. At about the same time I was also appointed Assistant Conductor and Choral Director of the Oklahoma Symphony Orchestra. The two organizations would obviously work together. Canterbury at that time consisted of about sixty singers—all volunteers and mostly amateurs—who rehearsed for two hours on Monday evenings. Plans for vocal development were set in motion and repertoire was carefully chosen so as to provide the singers musical gratification that would keep them interested and that would encourage interest from others. I had to diligently avoid the programming of such works as the Brahms *Requiem* and Mahler symphonies so that we could focus on vocal development, and, step-by-step, progress from body preparation and vowel place-ment, with extensive calisthenics and vocal warm-ups, to efficiency of vocal production and vowel modification, and then to diction as it affected vocal production. During this process, the singers knew our focus for the year and also knew its application to the rep-ertoire we were rehearsing since I frequently stopped during rehearsal to remind them of the connections and to challenge them to transfer learning from the warm-ups to the music. With the fortunate addition of approximately twenty new singers per year, Canterbury grew to an ensemble of 150 singers and progressed to advanced musical goals. In my eleventh year as director, I was able to program the Brahms *Requiem*.

Later in my career, when I was appointed Artistic Director of the Santa Fe Desert Chorale (a professional ensemble of twenty singers drawn from across the United States), I had a mandate from the board of directors to reach out to the Hispanic com-munity. To achieve this goal, I decided not to "reach out" but to "draw in," and to do this I focused on the spiritual and historic importance of the Catholic cathedral to the people of Santa Fe (the cathedral celebrated its 500th anniversary during my tenure with the chorale). The repertoire I chose to accomplish this was a Gregorian mass, which the chorale sang as a gift to the community, and which was so well received, we repeated the mass each year to a congregation that completely filled the cathedral.

Yet later in my career, when I was appointed Director of Choral Activities at Texas Christian University, I faced an ensemble that easily learned complex repertoire but that needed to work on tuning and blend. These issues were set, in stages, as multi-year goals, and as we progressed, repertoire was chosen accordingly. At first, considerable rehearsal time was spent building chords and discerning the varying acoustical factors caused by differing chord structures. After two years, at which time I programmed Henryk Górecki's *Totus tuus* and Paul Mealor's *Ubi caritas*, the chorale needed very little work on tuning and blend. Moreover, virtually every member of the chorale, even non-music majors, could differentiate between root position, first inversion, and second inversion chords. It was time for a more comprehensive blending goal, one I called "synergy." This term, which was put in bold letters at the top of each singer's syllabus, became a mantra and another goal to be met; there was no doubt about what we were attempting to accomplish.

2) It could be argued successfully that the choice of repertoire is the single most important contributor to effective recruitment and retention of choral singers and audiences. If singers are engaged with repertoire during rehearsals and emotionally committed to it in performance, and if audiences sense this commitment and relate to the music on some tangible level, both singers and audiences will desire further experiences. Additionally, news of the favorable experiences will spread and more people will desire to be involved. Repertoire is critical to this process and should be treated as a high priority; conductors must program wisely. Herein lies the pedagogy, which is not to be comprehended as the conductor teaching while the singers and audiences learn, but the reverse: the conductor must learn from the singers and audiences. The conductor must be on the receiving end of the learning process, thinking solely of what repertoire will likely produce engagement.

The choice of repertoire to accomplish this engagement is based on an awareness of the repertoire's accessibility—the repertoire's ability to interest singers and captivate audiences. Music that is too easy to grasp will be boring, while music that is too difficult to grasp will be uninteresting and tedious. One must strike a balance, but not a balance of some repertoire that is easily accessible and some that is not. This type of balance rarely achieves positive results. The immediately accessible music loses its appeal well before performance, and the abstruse repertoire, with no tangible connection to the choristers or audience members, has no opportunity to fulfill its purpose.

When I was conducting Canterbury Choral Society, I knew that the singers, many of whom were highly educated professionals, would be positively engaged with the repertoire if they could understand it—if they had background and contextual information about the composer, performance history, text implications, cultural relationships, and other insights into the music. But there was no time during rehearsals to relate this information; we were simply too busy preparing the music. I thought about writing the information and giving it to the singers as homework, but I couldn't convince myself that this would be effective. Finally, one of the chorus members suggested that I give talks about the music the hour before rehearsals began. I did, and interest in these talks was so great that we established a once-per-month "brown-bag lecture" series. A surprisingly large number of singers attended, eating their dinners as I talked, and becoming more and more engaged with the music they were rehearsing.

Much earlier in my career, just after I graduated from Westminster Choir College and began teaching high school (a public school in Metuchen, New Jersey), I knew very little repertoire beyond the large choral/orchestral masterworks. I had had peak musical experiences as an undergraduate student singing the Mahler 2nd and 8th symphonies with Leonard Bernstein and the New York Philharmonic, the Verdi *Requiem* with Eugene Ormandy and the Philadelphia Orchestra, and the Beethoven *Symphony #9* with both Herbert von Karajan and the Berlin Symphony and Leopold Stokowski and the American Symphony Orchestra. I also knew the repertoire I had sung on tour with Westminster Choir. But none of this music was appropriate for high school singers, and, having grown up with very little choral experience, my knowledge of repertoire was exceedingly limited. I had to think fast and creatively, and I had to recruit since my initial high school choir consisted of about thirty singers, more than eighty percent of which were girls. Fortunately, I had supportive administrators who were committed to assist me in my recruitment efforts and who granted my request for a school-wide assembly. In preparation for this, I selected and secretly rehearsed a small group of singers on five different arrangements of the school's alma mater—the arrangements being in the form of a Renaissance imitative motet, a Baroque chorale with fermatas, a Classical-era setting with an Alberti bass accompaniment, a Romantic-era setting with lush harmonies, and a modern-era arrangement with the alma mater tune in inversion, retrograde, and retrograde inversion. The assembly was quite successful, in spite of the fact that it was a music history lesson. The entire student body related to the alma mater, which was sung regularly at all school gatherings and sporting events, and the students were engaged as they listened to the tune's transformation.

Also, during the months following the assembly, I learned that the singers who had been in choir before my arrival thought that madrigals were contemporary popular songs (since the Madrigal Choir at the school performed only popular music). To counter and correct this notion, I fashioned a program of historical and modern madrigals as a way of introducing the genre, demonstrating its place and use in history, and involving the students in quality repertoire that was fun to sing. The madrigal program had a pedagogical purpose.

3) Knowing what repertoire will strike the balance of accessibility (what repertoire, as mentioned above, has the ability to interest singers and captivate audiences) takes a knowledge and appreciation of environmental customs and expectations. The conductor needs to know what music the singers and audiences will relate to, and to gain this knowledge, the conductor needs to know what music the singers and audiences have experienced and received well in the past, what musical strengths and weaknesses

characterize the choir, what cultural customs may be relevant to the local population, what socioeconomic and educational conditions are prevalent, what motivates interest and drives support, and what cultural activity has in the past received the most attention. Moreover, the conductor should appreciate the process of gathering information about the environment; the conductor should be excited about becoming environmentally educated (another example of the conductor learning from his or her constituency).

When one first begins his or her tenure with an ensemble, it is helpful to assess the choir's strengths and weaknesses. Do the singers sight read poorly or well? Have they sung in foreign languages or only in English? Have most performances been with keyboard accompaniment or has a cappella repertoire been included? Has music from historic eras been a part of the programming or has the repertoire mostly been contemporary? With answers to these and other questions, the conductor can build on the choir's strengths and gradually address its weaknesses.

Of the ensembles with which I have worked, I discovered that the Metuchen High School students, with parents who were educated and culturally informed (e.g., the father of one of the singers was the poetry editor for the *New Yorker*), were intellectually curious; the Canterbury Choral Society singers had a very strong sense of belonging, with an exceptional work ethic, pioneer spirit, and can-do attitude; the Santa Fe Desert Chorale singers had advanced language skills and a bass section capable of very low tessituras, with one true basso profundo; and the TCU singers, having been trained in solfège, were excellent sight readers. As a result of these strengths, I could select cerebral programs for the high school students, physically demanding works such as the Beethoven *Missa solemnis* for Canterbury Choral Society, Russian and World repertoire for the Santa Fe singers, and harmonically complex music for the TCU Chorale.

Characteristics of the environment also play an important role in determining programs. For instance, when I was appointed Artistic Director of the Santa Fe Desert Chorale, I knew that Santa Fe was a city famous for its art, chamber music, and opera. Thousands of people, many of them well-traveled, highly educated, and culturally sophisticated, traveled to Santa Fe during the summer to view the many art galleries and to attend chamber music performances and opera productions. In order to attract these people to the Desert Chorale concerts I collaborated with the Chamber Music Festival in two concerts—one a presentation of Gesualdo madrigals and the other a program of music by the Norwegian composer Per Nørgård. Both experiences gave the chorale singers unique and exciting opportunities, and we reached out to a broader audience than that which regularly attended our sacred performances in the city's cathedral. The chorale also collaborated with the Santa Fe Opera in several productions that needed an augmented chorus and that called for singers with advanced reading skills.

I had no previous experience performing the interesting repertoire I thought the Santa Fe audiences would find fascinating; I had no background in World Music or the avant-garde. I also had no past experience with Gregorian chant. I didn't even know, at first, if I liked this repertoire. But that didn't matter. What mattered was what would interest and engage the singers and audiences.

4) Closely related to the process of discovering environmental attributes in order to program music that is accessible is the process of programming music that will engage singers and audiences psychologically—music that will create a sense of aesthetic well-being or "optimal experience," as described in the book *Flow* by the psychologist Mihaly Csikszentmihalyi. Simply put, an optimal experience is one in which a person loses his or her sense of self-awareness and is completely immersed in an activity. A sense of euphoric flow occurs because the person feels good about the activity and the time in which it occurs. The activity is simple enough to accomplish, but not so simple as to be boring—difficult enough to create challenge, but not so difficult as to prevent accomplishment. In the choral setting, it is the repertoire that determines states of flow and thus the opportunity for engagement and optimal experience. The repertoire cannot be too simple (accessible) or too difficult (inaccessible). However, the repertoire must create challenge. According to Csikszentmihalyi and many other psychologists, challenge is essential. With challenge—at the right level of engagement—it is possible for both singer and audience member to have an optimal experience, and when an optimal experience occurs, time seems to move fast. In other words, the perceived motion of time—the ontological time—seems short. It is this state of being and time that the conductor should strive for when choosing repertoire, when rehearsing it, and when organizing it in programs.

Several programming strategies can help the conductor create states of flow and short ontological time experiences: focusing the program on a singular idea or theme, organizing the music into groups with connecting key relationships, and considering the visual component of the concert experience.

Diversity in programming—a little bit of this and a little bit of that—creates a long ontological time experience, while a singularity of repertoire (by genre, text subject, historical time frame, or other unifying plan) creates a shorter ontological time experience. Think of sporting events, movies, art exhibits, and opera and musical theater productions. People are generally more satisfied with uniformity than with variety in programming. Creating a theme, which is popular with many conductors, is an obvious way to create unification. Some of my program themes, both ordinary and esoteric, have been: In Praise of the Virgin Mary; Madrigal Madness (old and new madrigals); Minstrel Merriment (a program of chansons, also old and new); Folksong Fête; Music of Old World Cultures; Music of the Americas; Missa Omnium Gatherum (a complete mass comprised of movements by different composers); Biblical Scenes (including *Jesus and the Traders* by Zoltán Kodály and the oratorios *Jonah* and *Daniel in the Lions' Den* by Giacomo Carissimi and Daniel Pinkham, respectively); Psalm Settings (exploring the music of the Calvinist Protestant Reformation); Opera Choruses; The English Countenance; Divine Diversity (divergent traditions of spiritual exploration); and Pious and Profane (a combination of sacred and secular music by the programmed composers). The repertoire in each of these theme programs, all focused on a singular idea, helped to create an aesthetic unification and a relatively short ontological time experience.

Organizing the repertoire into groups with connecting key relationships is another and very effective way of shortening the ontological time experience. A program of twelve to sixteen pieces, each separated by applause, fractures the singing and listening experience and thus lengthens the perceived time of the program. On the other hand, a program of twelve to sixteen pieces organized into four to six groups (with only four to six opportunities for applause), makes the perceived time of the program shorter. Moreover, if the pieces in each group are connected by key relationships that make them feel as one unit, the perceived time is even shorter. For example, if the first piece in the group is in C Major, the second piece is in F Major, and the third piece is in B-flat Major, the group of three pieces feels like it is one unit since C Major serves in a dominant key relationship to F Major, and F Major serves the same function to B-Flat Major. Another example, this from a Santa Fe Desert Chorale program, is a group of Russian pieces: Chesnokov's *Spaseniye sodelal* (D Major), Ippolitov-Ivanov's *Se nine Ghospoda* (G Major), Chesnokov's *Duh tvoy blagiy* (B Minor), and Gretchaninoff's *Vecheri tvoyeya tayniya* (E Major). The total real performance time of this group of pieces is fourteen minutes (as on the recording *Journeys of the Spirit* from 2003). However, the perceived time of the group is much less. Moreover, the beauty of each piece is enhanced by its juxtaposition with the other pieces.

Visual stimulation is yet another important component of programming. This is not to say that choreography (affectionately referred to as "choralography") is recommended. Such movement during singing, unless specified by the composer as integral to the musical concept of the piece, is often distracting. Staging, on the other hand, can be effective and engaging. As an example, the arrangement of singers in the ensemble can vary from group to group of repertoire in the program (for musical as well as visual reasons), and the conductor can utilize the entire performance venue, not just the stage. In the Santa Fe cathedral concerts I conducted, the singers usually began the program with a piece from the rear balcony. They would then chant as they processed to the stage, frequently stopping and singing a piece as they surrounded the baptismal font (which was in the center of the nave), chanting again as they approached the stage area, and concluding the opening group of music with a piece from the stage. The total time for this was from ten to fifteen minutes—minutes that engaged the audience members visually and that shortened their time perception. As an interesting commentary to this, a photographer of the chorale once remarked, "I always thought that choral concerts were boring, but this is high drama."

Other related factors that can appeal to audiences include facial engagement of singers while performing, short talks by the conductor to the audience, and creative arrangements of performing forces to allow audiences closer contact with singers. Facial engagement is critical in forming a close bond between performers and audiences. Even when the singers are far away from their audiences, the effect of facial enlivenment is powerful (so much so that the Santa Fe Desert Chorale singers had a clause in their contracts addressing the issue). Conductor talks also create a bond with the audience in that the audiences can gain a sense of the conductor's personality and passion for the music, and the conductor has an opportunity to educate the audience—to guide the audience members in their listening experience. Important as well is a close proximity between singers and audiences. When I conduct choral/orchestral works, for example, I have the chorus flank the orchestra so that the audience has a closer aural and visual connection to the singers. This positioning, by the way, has historical precedence: before the 20th century, choruses generally stood in front of or beside orchestras.

5) Performance practices are perhaps the most pedagogical element of programming inasmuch as singers are taught and audiences are exposed to generally unfamiliar and new manners of musical execution, executions of music that affect virtually every element of performance, including sound, meter, tempo, articulation, phrasing, and expression. As examples of these elements: the rhythms of Gregorian chant should be pliant, as indicated by the semiology of the neumatic notation, not static and organized into groups of twos and threes, with each note receiving the same amount of rhythmic time as each other note; phrasing in Renaissance-era music should be oratorical, not syllabic (i.e., notes and text syllables should be stressed or unstressed according to their place in a phrase as the text would be pronounced in natural spoken declamation); durational values of notes in Baroque-era music should be gauged according to their metric placement (many notes are shorter than their apparent value might indicate); long notes in Classical-era music should be swelled and diminished in volume (called *messa di voce*); and rubato should be a significant factor of tempo in music of the Romantic era, with expressive nuances prominently featured.

These elements of performance practice, and numerous others, are integral to the music just as hues of color are integral to paintings and architectural details are integral to buildings. Changes to the colors or architectural details alter the paintings and buildings in significant ways. Primary colors on an Impressionistic painting, for example, and exposed structural work on a Baroque building change the essence of the works. Similarly, performances of historic music according to modern-day practices alter works and prevent performers and audiences from experiencing the works as they were conceived. Performers and audiences are denied the opportunity of experiencing the greatness of the music. However, with appropriate performance practices, the music's greatness is revealed and is, therefore, likely to appeal to performers and audiences just as original and restored paintings and buildings do.

Thousands of people attend museum exhibitions of paintings by such artists as Leonardo da Vinci, Michelangelo, and Monet, and even more thousands of people flock to St. Mark's in Venice, Notre Dame in Paris, St. Peter's in Rome, and the Duomo in Florence. Would people go to see the art and the buildings if they were an amalgam of original and modern elements? Probably not. So it is with music. People have little desire to hear corrupted performances of historic music. But, music performed according to original principles and relevant practices will attract people. Given the chance, audiences would fill concert halls to hear the masterworks of Palestrina, Bach, Handel, and Brahms. Greatness is appealing if the greatness is not obscured.

Of course, fully revealing the greatness of a Palestrina, Bach, Handel, or Brahms score is a formidable task; accessing information about performance practices is not easy. Courses in the subject are not part of choral education classes, and there are few vocal and choral models to emulate (although there are many excellent instrumental models). Fortunately, however, books on the subject are becoming available (e.g., *Performance Practices in the Baroque Era* and *Performance Practices in the Classical Era*, both published by GIA), and one can glean a great deal about historic vocal timbres from listening to recordings of instrumental music played on original or reproductions of original instruments. Most performance practices, however, are based on knowledge and understandings of notation, and notation can be misinterpreted equally by players of period and modern-day instruments.

Notational meanings have changed over the years. Thus in order to do historic music justice, one must understand notation and terminology the way people of the time understood it. One must see the notation not with modern-day eyes, but with historic eyes. (To do this when I am rehearsing, I frequently put on a pair of reading glasses that I refer to as my "Baroque glasses" or my "Classical-era glasses.") As examples of changed meanings: Meter signatures conveyed tempo during the Baroque era, informing us, for instance, that the "Et incarnatus est" movement of the Bach *B Minor Mass* (with a 3/4 meter) is at a medium tempo and the immediately following "Crucifixus" movement (with a 3/2 meter) is to be considerably slower; meter signatures also conveyed patterns of metric accentuation during the Baroque and Classical eras, signifying that the downbeats of "And the glory of the Lord" from Handel's *Messiah* have a full-valued duration while the notes on beats two and three are shorter than printed; the term vivace meant vivacious and not too fast during the Classical era, indicating that the vivace at the beginning of the "Gloria" in Haydn's *Paukenmesse* is supposed to be slower than the allegro that ends the movement); and since overdotting and rhythmic conformity were prevalent practices during the Classical and Romantic eras, the dotted-eighth-sixteenth-note patterns in the "Rex tremendae" movement of the Mozart *Requiem* and the beginning of Verdi's *Va pensiero* should conform to the patterns in the orchestra. These and other understandings of notation and terminology are the performance practices that matter—that contribute to revealing an historic masterwork's greatness and that excite choristers and audiences.

To demonstrate the reality of this: In my second year at TCU, while working assiduously on tuning, I was given the opportunity to perform two Bach cantatas with the Fort Worth Symphony and the middle portion of Handel's *Messiah* with the university orchestra. I was reticent to take on these works, knowing how little experience the students had with performance practices and also knowing that we were focused on other priorities. But, the opportunity to perform historic masterworks was too great to pass up. In the beginning rehearsals, as I had the singers sing "long-short-short, long-short-short" instead of the text or solfège syllables, and as I also had the singers use their tongues to shape the melismas, the rehearsal process became fascinating and the music seemed to have a logic to it. The singers became more and more engaged and their practices spread to the orchestras. The experience was so enjoyable that the Fort Worth Symphony scheduled another concert of Baroque music the following year, and after that, a yearly series was established.

SUMMARY

There is no doubt that programming can be an arduous and lengthy process, but there is also no doubt that it can be an exciting and highly rewarding process, one that educates as well as entertains. When short-term goals are accomplished and begin to facilitate long-term plans; when singers learn to transfer elements of one objective to another; when recruitment is more about music than any other reason; when singers and audiences increase in numbers because the people are aesthetically satisfied; when a singer wants to know more about the music; when an audience member expresses gratitude for learning something he or she didn't know; when the flow of rehearsal has been such a singer can't believe that time has passed so quickly; when a program seems much shorter than the actual time it took; when an audience member comments on the exceptional look as well as sound of a program; when the rehearsal of historic music is fun instead of tedious; and when performance of more historic music is requested, the efforts of repertoire selection and programming will have been successful. Singers, conductors, and audiences will have had optimal experiences.

REFERENCES

Carpenter, Humphrey (1992). *Benjamin Britten*. Scribners.

Shrock, D. (2009). *Choral repertoire.* New York: Oxford University Press.

Shrock, D. (2011). *Performance practices in the classic era.* Chicago: GIA.

Shrock, D. (2013). *Performance practices in the baroque era.* Chicago: GIA.

CHAPTER 18

....

REPERTOIRE AS PEDAGOGY

Music of Diverse Cultures

....

MARY GOETZE

WE have become a truly multicultural nation, as borne out by the fact that non-Hispanic whites in public schools are no longer a majority in the United States. Even though the transformation of our population into a colorful mosaic has been underway for centuries, the change continues to be fraught with conflict. Any news broadcast reminds us that violence on our streets is often rooted in race and ethnic strife. Similar discord can be found on nearly every continent. In short, the world outside our rehearsal and performance venues is a troubled one.

Over its long history, tolerance and peaceful coexistence have been at heart of multicultural education. Programs abound in trying to forge relationships between disparate groups in schools and communities. In an effort to diversify classroom materials, music educators have introduced songs from around the globe, such as African or Japanese taiko drumming, Native American dances, and African American playground games. Choral musicians have also broadened the repertory to include an increasing number of multicultural selections. Yet given the rising tide of social problems, our efforts have no apparent positive effect. An honest appraisal of our practice reveals that music education in general, and western choral practice specifically, have remained fundamentally ethnocentric. In truth, teaching "their" music "our" way has done little to contribute to healing the social ills that plague our country and world, and by virtue of our imperialistic heritage, privilege, and social and economic advantages, we western art musicians may even have contributed to the problems.

In the 21st century, the music education profession has been challenged to assume a broader function than performing music for music's sake. In an article addressed to music educators, David J. Elliott (2012) suggests "that we may have unrealized opportunities and responsibilities to integrate traditional means and ends—to integrate musical processes, products, experiences, and outcomes—in the service of additional or alternative aims" (p. 21). His alternative aims for "music education as/for artistic citizenship" include putting "music to work" for the betterment of other people's lives and social well-being practice; "music-making as ethical action" for social justice; and infusing music with an "ethic of care"—care for oneself and for the health of our social communities" (p. 22).

This chapter presents one model driven by social justice rather than only musical goals. The approach evolved over 12 years during which I directed the Indiana University International Vocal Ensemble (IVE), a choir that recreated multiple styles of vocal music from outside the western art tradition (which I will refer to as "diverse music"). This personal and professional journey was shared with college-aged students, most of whom were music majors. Some were members for two semesters, while others chose to be in the group for several years of their undergraduate or graduate study. Each school year, the IVE shared two programs of music, most including sets of music from three different cultures.

I begin by discussing the multicultural goal for this ensemble, then throughout the chapter, I highlight the way it informed my approach. I examine the sources and forms of repertory, the methods I developed for presenting diverse music to singers, and the ways cultural understanding was integrated into the events at which the ensemble shared the music. A portion of the chapter will address non-*bel canto* vocal techniques and movement, aspects that are attendant to many styles of music.

ALIGNING PRACTICE WITH PURPOSE

Most choral directors have the privilege of determining the purpose of their ensembles, usually in conjunction with the context of their work—educational institution, community, or church—and the expectations others have for the choir. Prior to the epiphany that led me to transform my practice, my choral work sprang from my love of western art music and a general desire to inculcate that love in the singers in my ensemble. In truth, I gave little attention to clarifying and personalizing my purpose. Rather I carried forth the reasons and procedures that had been modeled by the conductors of the choirs in which I sang—even when the selections came from diverse cultures.

In the middle of my career, I traveled abroad to countries where I witnessed the effect of colonization by my European ancestors. Upon returning home, I saw with new eyes the continuing plight of the African Americans and Native Americans, the diversity in my community and across North America, and the struggles of newly arrived immigrants. As a choral director and teacher educator, I realized that I had played a part in privileging the dominance of western culture in music education—a practice that epitomizes colonization. I emerged with a commitment to bring the music of diverse cultures to the music students in my university in a way that would promote respect and understanding. Having experiences with diverse cultures was especially important for those students who would be teaching music to these diverse populations in schools. My goal crystallized: I wanted to provide a choral experience that would build a bridge between the singers and people from diverse cultures in ways that would honor cultures by singing their music respectfully. Once I had articulated the purpose of the IVE, my practice changed dramatically. Below I share the aspects of my work—finding repertory, rehearsing, singing, and performing—that changed as I aligned my practice with this goal.

SEARCHING FOR REPERTORY

Like most directors, I considered published "world music" or "multicultural" octavos—a section of every music catalog that seems to grow each year. Below are categories into which most notated selections can be fitted. I organized this list according to those having the most western influence progressing to the least.

- **Compositions in the style of a diverse culture**. Western composers borrow elements of diverse styles (i.e. rhythms, groove, melodic turns, and general affect) and fuse them with their own ideas, often using lyrics in the language and/or a singable translation.
- **Arrangements of traditional songs**. Arranging usually involves harmonizing and adding accompaniment to a traditional tune, most often in a western choral style. These may also incorporate musical elements that are typical of the culture. Many arrangers are non-natives, but some are natives of the culture trained in western music.
- **Transcriptions**. A transcription is based on a careful analysis of one rendition as performed by natives of the culture. Transcriptions attempt to capture as many cultural elements as notation and comments will accommodate.
- **Compositions by natives of the culture**. Increasingly the creations of composers from around the globe are becoming available from choral music publishers.[1] Often these natives are choral conductors who study western choral music and composition.
- **Notated scores with audio recordings**. Publishers sometimes provide recordings on their websites. While some feature American choirs, those with choirs native to the culture provide stylistic details and vocal timbre.

From the beginning I knew wanted to minimize the number of "hands" the song passed through before it reached its published form, and to have more cultural information than most scores provided. Notes on covers of scores usually included the translation and transliteration, but I wanted an interpolation of the lyrics, to know where the song was performed and if and how the singers moved when they sang. Recognizing that publishers typically print the diverse music that is likely to appeal (and, of course, sell) to western-trained musicians, led me to question whether the enticing songs that end up in print are representative of music that is meaningful within the culture. Palmer

(1992) wrote, "Much like the foods from other countries that retain outward forms but lose the inner content in taste by substitution and omission of certain spices, a transplanted music also may suffer the loss of its most prized possessions, that of different tunings, timbres, language, and music expressions that make it unique and representative of a specific culture" (p. 32).

Furthermore, published music had to have been perceived, conceptualized, and symbolized according to western musical processing. Thus, only those aspects that are important to trained musicians and for which we have symbols are transmitted through the notation.

Therefore pitches are written in notes on a staff (regardless of scalar particularities, such as micro tones, bending of tones, etc.) in keys that accommodate standard vocal ranges (inferring *bel canto* technique). Rhythms are fitted into measures and notes, even when the groove is more subtle and nuanced than note values could ever convey. In short, unfamiliar elements are "lost in translation." In a later publication, Palmer (2002) wrote, "If it has been altered in some way, the music from another culture begins to lose its ability to carry that culture's messages . . . the music will not carry the same connotations that it needs to in order to reveal a specific set of human values" (p. 40). Concurring, Schippers (2010) stated that in transcriptions, "the music may well lose the . . . important aspect of authenticity: power of expression" (p. 51).

CONSIDERING AUTHENTICITY AND CONTEXT

The issue of authenticity occurred often in readings and my interactions with ethnomusicologists. Traditional songs from diverse cultures are often passed on aurally, then shaped and reshaped over time by the singers who hold them in their minds. The composers often have long since been forgotten, and their songs may exist in multiple versions. Even when a soloist or ensemble repeats a song, the rendition may be different from a previous performance. In his book, *Facing the Music,* Schippers (2002) wrote, "The desire for a static and clearly defined authenticity simply does not correspond to musical realities, in which various approaches to authenticity overlap and interact" (p. 53). Furthermore, few cultures exist in isolation, so their music reflects myriad influences, ranging from historical conquests to current exchanges via media. "With the change of musical tastes of second- and third-generation minorities, eclectic musical mixes, and new musical realities, it is increasingly difficult to establish what a culture as a whole considers authentic, so authenticity in the narrow sense is becoming an unsustainable position" (p. 51).

Beyond authenticity, there was the matter of context. For western-trained musicians, songs performed in new contexts by different musicians remain essentially the same music even when interpreted in a new way. But I learned that meaning embodied in some styles of diverse music is bound to the culture and context. Since I could not immerse the singers in the culture, how could I enhance the experience so they sensed what the song meant when it was sung in context? Schippers (2008) wrote, "There is no stock answer to the question of what and how much context should be included in teaching world music. Decisions can only be based on intelligently weighing the various arguments for each specific situation and the educational goals" (p. 57). He recommends a four-step procedure that "can make educators aware of the main points to consider when dealing with recontextualization."

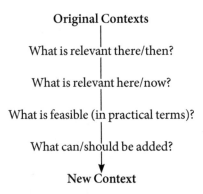

Original Contexts

What is relevant there/then?

What is relevant here/now?

What is feasible (in practical terms)?

What can/should be added?

New Context

Recontextualizing music in education: a dynamic approach

His discussion of context concludes with this proviso: "This leaves educators with a personal responsibility rather than a set of unambiguous guidelines for engaging with world music: the responsibility to deal intelligently with the dynamics of tradition and authenticity in order to create rewarding learning experiences in contemporary contexts" (Schippers, 2010, p. 60).

Re-creating and recontextualizing music

After wrestling with issues of authenticity and context, I decided that, even though there would be inevitable compromises, my ensemble would sing songs to the degree possible in the way they were sung in the culture, a process I call "re-creation." As part of this process, they would learn the music as it was learned in context; that is, unless notation was used in the culture, a song would be orally transmitted. I determined that the learning process would include details about the context and general information about the culture. Recognizing that musical expressions embody the emotions of the music's creators, I felt that re-creating vocal music could set the stage for singers to sense the music's essence and to *empathize* with the music's creators, their way of life, and in some cases their plight. For empathy to result, the process of learning needed to be *humanized*— something that would not happen with only a score or an audio recording.

Lakoff (2009) defines empathy as:

> A capacity to put oneself in the shoes of others—not just individuals, but whole categories of people: one's countrymen, those in other countries, other living beings, especially those who are in some way oppressed, threatened, or harmed. Empathy is the capacity to care, to feel what others feel, to understand what others are facing and what their lives are like. (p. 1)

Empathy elicited by works of art has been referred to as *aesthetic empathy*. About literature, Nussbaum (2008) wrote "Experience and culture shape many aspects of what is 'under the skin,' as we can easily see if we reflect and read. It is the political promise of literature that it can transport us, while remaining ourselves, into the life of another, revealing similarities but also profound differences between the life and thought of that other and myself and making them comprehensible, or at least more nearly comprehensible" (p. 156). Like literature, vocal music too has the capacity to "transport into the life of another," but the meaning and affect of words in songs are enhanced by the power of music—its power to express emotion. Moreover, choral musicians know well the bonds that develop when singers make music together, and I believe the kinesthetic experience of singing and moving simultaneously further enriches the experience. Current work on "mirror neurons" in neuroscience has reinforced the case for the re-creative process. Stueber (2014) wrote:

> Scientists refer to the fact that there is significant overlap between neural areas of excitation that underlie our observation of another person's action and areas that are stimulated when we execute the very same action. (Part 3, para.1)

Mirror neurons would contribute to our ability to match songs and movement when learning visually and aurally, and, as Stueber explains, to sense the affect of the music:

> If mirror neurons are indeed the primary underlying causal mechanisms for *cognitively* recognizing certain emotional states in others by looking at their facial expressions, then it is quite understandable how such an observation could also lead to the feeling of an emotion that is more congruent with the situation of the other; that is, to empathy in the affective sense. (Part 6)

In her book, *Rethinking Multicultural Education for the Next Generation: The New Empathy and Social Justice*, Dolby (2012) states, "Mirror neurons concretely demonstrate that our actions and our perceptions are not separate but instead are intimately joined. These neurons, which have also come to be known as 'empathy neurons,' allow us to 'feel' other's experiences" (p. 58).

I recognized that my singers needed to look into the face of people from the culture if my goal was to be achieved. The most reliable source for songs was the most obvious: I stopped looking for music from diverse cultures and started looking for *people* who could present the music live within a rehearsal. These culture-bearers, whom I called "informants," served to provide songs as well as the human connection I was searching.

Finding Informants

Finding informants turned out to be easier than I expected. When I began to look around me, people from diverse cultures were everywhere, both on my university campus, in my community, and in the region. And as diversity continues to increase across North America, it has become even easier to find cultural representatives. Often enclaves within urban areas organize to preserve their language and traditions, offering classes for their children, hosting festivals, and sponsoring concerts by local and touring musicians from their home country. Scratch the surface of almost any large city and you will discover the cultural riches that today's world offers.

As an outsider, I acknowledged that I was in no position to identify reliable informants from diverse cultures. I sought out the advice of natives and scholars of the culture and trusted their perspective. Most ethnomusicologists who specialize in the culture will have traveled to the country, lived with the people, and performed their music as part of their study. I joined the Society for Ethnomusicology and searched on the Internet for people and publications, such as *The Garland Encyclopedia of World Music Online* (http://glnd.alexanderstreet.com), a resource that provides access to research into "music of all the world's peoples."

Burton (2002) makes the following recommendations for identifying reliable informants.

- Is the source person (culture-bearer) a recognized performer/creator of music within the culture? This creator/ performer need not be "the best," but his or her performances must be considered acceptable by a reasonably representative element within the culture.
- Are the music and the performance of the music representative of an identifiable segment of the culture's musical mosaic? (p.164)

Within my university community, I was fortunate to find people whom I could consult regarding reliable culture bearers. My informants ranged from faculty to undergraduates on my own campus, often studying music or ethnomusicology; to Native American and African American artists from the region; to musicians native to other countries living in the United States; to recognized artists brought with grant money from their home countries. Below are some suggestions for locating them:

- At large universities, faculty and students from around the globe abound. The office providing services to these individuals can assist in identifying them. Often students from a country or region present events for the public featuring students singing, dancing, traditional clothing, and a taste of national cuisine. At Indiana

University, there is an annual celebration of Chinese New Year and Navruz by Central Asian students. African, Japanese, Indian culture nights provide an introduction to the aspects of their cultures they want to share. While these events are informative, they can also lead you to informants and music.

- Artists from around the globe tour North America each year, performing in cities large and small. Many participate in world music festivals—events with performances in a wide range of styles by native musicians. These performers also present educational workshops. By contacting the organizers of local events, it is sometimes possible to arrange for groups to visit a rehearsal. Using email, I worked with the artists in advance of their visit to choose several appropriate songs for the IVE. I prepared the singers for the visit by sharing information about the group and their country. When they arrived I had lyrics and translations ready to project during the session.
- Membership in international music organizations can connect directors with people from diverse cultures. Conferences held by the International Society for Music Education, the International Federation of Choral Musicians, and the Society of Ethnomusicology often include performances, sessions, and workshops with choral groups who want to establish professional relationships with directors from other countries. Attending such conferences can take you abroad to meet choral directors and educators face to face to plan collaborative projects.
- The Internet can serve in myriad ways to find informants or locate audio and video recordings of ensembles that are posted on websites. Joining the international organizations mentioned above allows you access to their websites where you can post messages, scour membership lists, and identify directors, choirs, or composers listed in past and upcoming conference programs.

Loving to travel, I had life-changing experiences when, following up on connections made at my university, international conferences, or through virtual media, I visited many countries myself. There, with the assistance of local music educators, I was able to experience the music in its context and enrich my understanding of the culture by seeing it first hand. I also made friends that last to this day. These trips, sometimes accompanied by members of the ensemble, led to reciprocal visits. As often as possible, my ensemble welcomed directors and traveling choirs to our rehearsals. All in all, the experiences I had traveling the globe heightened my commitment to the goals I had laid out for the ensemble.

Choosing repertory with informants

Once I found informants, I explained that their work with the IVE would be a chance for them to provide the singers with a portrait of their culture. We talked about what they wanted to share about their people, history, and country, and which songs might bring these aspects to life. With that in mind, the informants selected some songs. In settling on repertory, I was careful not to apply my own western aesthetic judgments to the music they suggested. (Dr. Sue Touhy, professor at Indiana University, stated: "That would be like applying the rules of basketball to a football game.") Together the informant and I chose songs that the IVE could re-create in a credible way. I knew the choir could not do justice to just any song in the rehearsal time available, and certainly not if they were overloaded with long texts in unfamiliar languages to memorize. Since the sheer amount of text to be learned needed to be limited, we chose songs that had musical and lyrical repetition. Songs with numerous verses and a recurring refrain were acceptable, but adaptations needed to be made. For those songs, the informant or small groups of singers would sing the verses and the ensemble sang the refrain. Or the verses would be divided among different vocal parts. In the process of song selection with the informant, I always learned a great deal about that culture's aesthetics and the reasons the song had special meaning to the informant. In preparation for rehearsals, the informant wrote out the lyrics and an English translation. In languages with characters, I requested the lyrics in the original language, then worked with the informant to assign symbols from the International Phonetic Alphabet (IPA) or create a transliteration of the lyrics.

Using technology

While people became the source of the songs that filled 24 semesters of enriched musical experiences for the IVE, the connection with these cultures was facilitated in countless ways by technology. Given the ubiquitousness of this medium, the group met informants via SKYPE over the Internet. I found that connecting by phone is not nearly as challenging as negotiating the time zones. That had to be arranged in advance and sometimes necessitated rescheduling rehearsals or requesting that the informant be available at times they might otherwise be sleeping. Video recordings served a multitude of purposes. I recorded the rehearsals in which informants presented the songs. If they were present for only one or two rehearsals, I carefully edited excerpts of the recording to assist the group in reviewing songs. I inserted the movies into software (such as PowerPoint or Keynote) for projection. Having had live interactions with the informant(s), the recording also recalled the spirit the informant brought to their music making. I often posted these movies and audio recordings along with the texts and translations of the songs on a website for students to practice. After several years, the media constituted a digital choral library, so I was able to reintroduce songs to fill out a program.

I also taught songs using video recordings of performances made at conferences, festivals, or during my travels. After explaining how I would use the recording, I always got permission and made a donation to the group. This list shows the essential elements beyond the complete performance to record so that songs could be recreated.

- An individual speaking the lyrics in rhythm at a slow tempo.
- A representative from each vocal part singing close to the microphone while the choir sings in the background.

- The informant speaking about the song, including
  - the literal and connotative meaning of the text.
  - where the song is sung.
  - how the person or ensemble learned the song.

While better than notation, I recognized that video recordings were nevertheless a compromise. As noted above, music is dynamic, and the recording is only one version. Plus the singers could not ask questions about the music, get clarification on ambiguities, and interact with the performers. In an interview for an ethnographic study by Matiure (1999), one IVE member stated "the idea is to connect people humanistically. The video is good but its not the same thing [as an informant]—it's plastic" (p. 56). Still recordings provided stylistic details of music and movement, and even though they were not live, the students could observe humans singing the songs they re-created.

To compensate, I searched for natives of the culture on my campus to provide a live human element. These informants relished the opportunity to share information about their culture and the music we were learning. To personalize the experience, I asked informants to share photos of their family, home, and community, and to talk about what was most similar and different from life here. While in the presence of trained musicians the informants were not always willing to sing for the ensemble, they enriched the cultural aspect of our experience.

Refashioning Rehearsal Procedures

Typically the IVE explored three cultures each semester with a resident informant from at least one of the cultures. Sometimes the guest would be there for only a few rehearsals, but when possible they joined the ensemble and attended all rehearsals. The other repertory was learned from video recording or over the Internet. At the beginning of each semester, I articulated the purpose of the IVE and held a discussion about the importance of connecting with people from diverse cultures. We discussed music as a vehicle for getting to know cultures. I explained the re-creative process and how learning music in this ensemble would be different from most other choirs. The students were excited at the prospect of meeting informants and learning about and singing music they had no prior opportunity to learn.

In rehearsals, I made extensive use of projections, both to play video recordings and to display the lyrics as they learned from the informant. To insure that they kept the translations in mind, the lyrics (in the original language and IPA or transliteration) and the translations were projected throughout the learning process. Sound files of spoken or sung lyrics, inserted into the presentation software, were played often to insure the association of the written symbols with the pronunciation.

John XIV

Ndebele Gospel Song from Zimbabwe
Sheasby Matiure,Informant

(Lead) John fotini

Vesi whani--Vesi whani

(Lead) Moyo yenyu kani

Ngairege kumanikidzwa

Tendaiwo kuna Baba

Motenda nekwandiri Vesi whani

(Lead) Ariko

Ariko munyaradzi Jesu

Translation:
Let not your hearts be troubled;
believe in God, believe also in me .

FIGURE 18.1 Typical Layout of Displays with Lyrics and Translation
(Audio files with pronunciation and voice parts were played by clicking on the sound icons.)

Rehearsing songs learned aurally differed from standard choral procedures (see Figure 18.1). After the first rehearsal, the lyrics were displayed and singers were asked to look at them and recall the song without singing aloud. Drawing upon what I call "group intelligence," they invariably succeeded in recalling more as a group than anyone could have sung alone. Having called upon their aural memory of the song, they often spontaneously sang the song in the key of the model performance. In her thesis based on the IVE, Zaretti (1998) included this comment about rehearsing with recordings: "With a video or audiotape, the rehearsal is more like a conversation among the members and the director of IVE. The students verify if someone heard the same thing as they did, debate a particular aspect of the music, and make decisions as to what to sing based on judgment calls. The re-creation becomes a collaboration between the members of the class" (p. 51). When songs were presented aurally, singers found memorization easier than when using scores. I facilitated memorization by displaying the lyrics as they sang, then on subsequent screens showing only first words of lines, key words, and eventually only the first letters of lines. However to insure accuracy, recordings were replayed even after songs were memorized. Whether learned from an informant or a recording, re-creating a song means the way it is sung in context serves as a *point of arrival*, while in most western choirs, choral scores serve as a *point of departure* for the choir's interpretation.

EXPLORING ALTERNATIVE
NOTATION SYSTEMS

When IVE did use scores, an informant and/or a recording provided stylistic details. I made an interesting observation about these musically trained singers. When presented with a score, they would sing the song as it was notated without appropriate elements of style, even when they had just heard it played or modeled by the informant. In an attempt to retain the cultural flavor, I explored various methods of using the scores. Sometimes I withheld the score until they had learned part or all of the song aurally. Interestingly, even then, when they sang from the printed music, the style was not retained. Only after the informant detailed the differences did they match the live or recorded model. Sometimes I recorded their rendition, then asked them to compare the way they sang the song with the model performance. Since their highly trained eyes superseded their ears, I found it was important for them to continue to listen to the model often and memorize the song early in the learning process.

While most of the scores were in standard notation, our informants introduced us to other systems of notation. Figures 18.2 and 18.3 are excerpts from such scores.

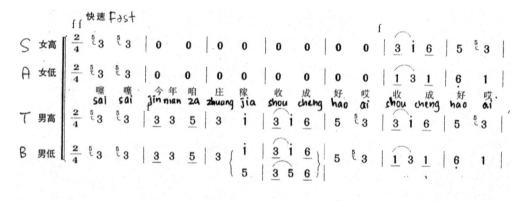

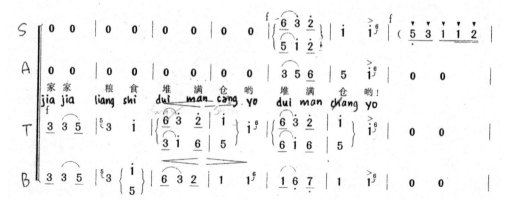

FIGURE 18.2 Chinese Choral Scores. (Scale degrees are represented by numbers and underscoring denotes beats and subdivisions.)

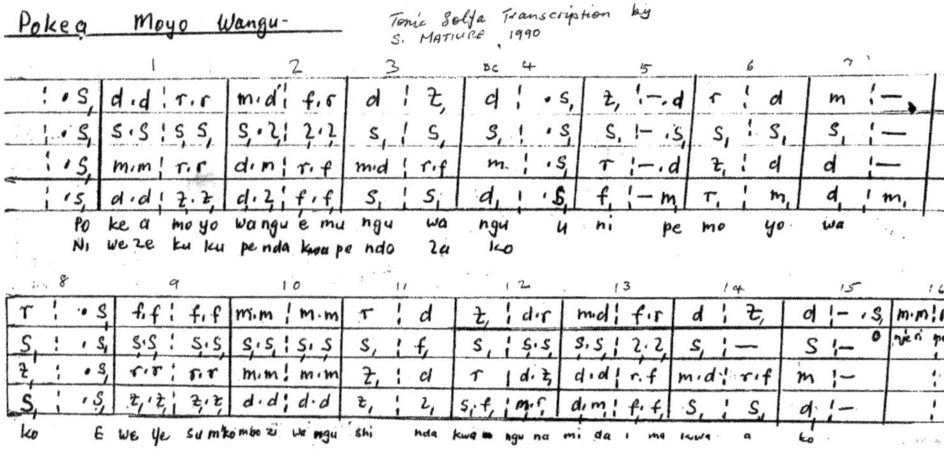

FIGURE 18.3 Zimbabwean Score in Tonic Solfa, notated by Sheasby Matiure.

We all found these different ways of notating music interesting and musically broadening. Since these systems are based on diatonic scales and meters, the choir was successful in realizing the scores, but repeated listening was essential for successful re-creation.

RETHINKING MY ROLE

The goal of re-creation along with the shift to aural/visual transmission from live informants or recorded sources led me to reinvent my role in rehearsals. In truth, I was only one step ahead of the singers in learning the songs in the unfamiliar styles of music we were singing. Thus I became a *facilitator* as I assisted the informant in communicating with the group. In helping the singers to understand and to succeed in learning, I often asked the informant questions in their behalf, and encouraged them to ask questions whenever they wanted clarification or additional information. In addition, I made occasional interjections, highlighting important ideas the informant made, pointing out similarities and differences, or relating what was said to ideas previously encountered in rehearsals.

The process was similar when using recorded models. The prepared slides were when the group needed to hear lyrics or vocal lines. When a question arose, I resisted providing answers or singing a part myself. Instead I replayed recordings so the entire group could arrive at the answer by listening and watching. My deference to the recorded or live source served not only to remind the singers that they were to re-create what they heard, but also to demonstrate my respect for the guest and the way the music was sung in the culture.

Given that I was not "in the driver's seat" when the informants were teaching, the rehearsals did not always go as I had envisioned. Sometimes the discussions even took time away from rehearsing the songs. But I reminded myself that the personal relationship singers formed with the informant, and the information gleaned from the discussion, was in complete alignment with my goal. I soon found that the music was always ready by the time it was shared, and the discussions informed the way the group sang, and fortified its emotional connection with the informant and the music's power of expression.

Matching Vocal Timbres

One of the challenges in re-creating music is matching the timbres that differ from the *bel canto* approach to singing. I assumed that if humans produce these timbres, then as humans, we too were capable of matching them. Since mastering a variety of vocal techniques was not realistic, my goal was for the group to *approximate* the vocal timbres; that is, basing vocal adjustments on the technique singers had already acquired. As a *bel canto*-trained singer I had little experience singing in any other way, so I explored matching recorded examples to see if it sounded externally the way I perceived it inside. When my attempt came close, I took note of how the physical changes I made differed from *bel canto*. I invoked my natural ability to imitate and left behind my inhibitions and everything I had learned in vocal training. Most approaches to singing varied in one or more of these aspects: laryngeal position, registration, resonators, and placement. Below I describe these and some of the ornaments and special techniques not typically used in western vocal music. [2]

Laryngeal position

While in *bel canto,* the larynx is lowered to enlarge the resonating space in the pharynx, but a raised larynx is used in other styles. The reduced space in the throat results in a brighter set of vowel colors that have less depth than those produced with a lowered larynx, and requires less breath to sustain a tone. (Place fingers on the larynx at rest, then say "uh-oh." While maintaining this high laryngeal position, sustain a tone and explore various vowels and pitches.)

Registration and pitch

In *bel canto* training, the head voice predominates while in many other cultures, the chest voice is used almost exclusively, even at higher pitch levels. In general, the vocal ranges for women are lower, often extending well below the treble clef. Other traditions call for the use of male falsetto, the upper limits of which are well beyond the top of the bass clef.

Resonators and placement

In general, it is the shape of the resonators that account for much of the variation in vowel colors and thus vocal timbres. The throat, mouth, and nose can be opened, closed, combined or shaped in a variety of ways. Exploring these adjustments when singing in either head or chest register yields a broad range of vocal timbres. Many cultures create far less space in the oropharynx when they sing. In Central Asia, the oral cavity has a horizontal shape during phonation, with the teeth close together and the corners of the mouth extended toward the cheeks. Nasality might be considered an extreme forward placement of sound. There are varying degrees of nasality possible, depending upon the size of the opening into the nasal resonators, and some of these require the lowering of the soft palate.

Special techniques

Ornamentation. Many traditions employ ornaments, such as trills and turns, but the character of the ornament differs with the fundamental vocal production—i.e. high or low larynx, chest or head voice. With the larynx raised, trills are more angular in character than the *bel canto* trill. The intervallic relationship of the pitches in ornaments may be wider than a half or whole step apart, and executed at various speeds and durations. Sometimes singers slide heavily between two pitches, rather than attack pitches in precise even slurs as in western art music.

Bleating and pulsations. In *bleating*, the sound wavers with minimal change of pitch. Similarly, *pulsations* involve repeated accents added to a sustained pitch. Variations in both pitch and dynamic level may occur on each of the pulses. The motion is usually slower than trills or bleats, and the pitch shift may be as wide as a third.

Yodeling. This ubiquitous practice involves an abrupt alternation typically between chest and head registers and is usually done by a soloist. Because *bel canto* training stresses a smooth transition between registers, yodeling may be more challenging for those with extensive voice training.

Overtone singing. Also known as *Khöömii* or *Xöömei*, overtone singing is common in the steppes of Central Asia. There are several distinctly different styles, involving various resonators and placements. In the one typically used in choral compositions, the fundamental is muted and the high overtones are amplified in the oropharynx. Typically the pitch of the fundamental is constant while adjustments are made in oropharynx.

Naturally, the best way to learn vocal timbre is from a singer from the culture who can serve as a live vocal model. But whether live or recorded, encourage your singers to share their impressions and physical sensations with one another as they explore matching vocal timbres. As part of your rehearsals, it is informative to record the group, play the recording back, and compare their timbre to that of the model.

Voice Health

It is my firm belief that matching vocal timbres will not have a negative effect on trained vocalists. In fact, I believe there may even be benefits. Singing in various registrations, laryngeal positions, or placements is a way for singers to become acquainted with their vocal potential. With regard to registration, singing in only one register naturally tends to strengthen the muscles used in that register, while those used in the other registers may atrophy. Thus singing in all registers may serve singers in the same way cross training serves athletes.

That said, it is important for the director to move gradually from the familiar to new techniques. My rehearsals included a typical choral warm-up, establishing good posture, deep respiration, and phonation over a wide range. The warm-up began with vocalizing in the head register at various dynamic levels, and then moved into the range of the chest register. Other exercises were keyed to the challenges in the songs to be rehearsed, transitioning from *bel canto* to the specific aspects of singing discussed above. Until singers' voices are conditioned to using unfamiliar timbres and vocalisms, it is best to avoid exceeding moderate dynamic levels.

In addition, it is important to teach singers how to care for their voices, especially to recognize the signs of vocal fatigue so they know when to stop singing. The formation of phlegm is an early sign that the voice needs rest and hydration, so singers should be given permission to rest and drink water as needed within rehearsals.

Enabling Singers to Move

In stark contrast to western classical choruses who often wear black, stand still, and hold scores, gestures, actions, and dance are an inherent part of music in many diverse cultures. Without moving, the singing would lose its cultural relevance, its expressive power, and often its spirit. Hand and arm movements often reflect, symbolize, or dramatize the lyrics. Actions are unified, but often not as strictly regimented as in show choirs or marching bands.

Typically the entire IVE learned movement from the informant or by watching the video recordings. Sometimes they mirrored the movement before learning to sing a new song. Inexperienced dancers tended to focus on their feet at first, but with repeated observations and suggestions, they matched arm and upper body motions as well. Working in pairs, I asked them to compare their partner's movement to the model and help one another match details of style (see Figures 18.4 and 18.5).

When the movement was more complex, folk dance specialists assisted the group. In some traditions, only a small group performed the movement in front of the rest of the choir, so I adapted this practice when the movement or dance was complex. I would invite a small group of trained dancers or those willing to practice outside the rehearsal to be responsible for the movement.

FIGURE 18.4 Optional photos: Photos by Alain Barker. Used with permission. South African Gumboot Dancing with Muziwandile Hadebe.

FIGURE 18.5 Tinikling from the Philippines with Katherine Domingo.

Sharing the Music

The western classical choir usually performs on a stage, clearly separated from the audience. This is symbolic of the rarefied role musicians play in western culture. By contrast, in some music cultures, including jazz and popular music, the delineation between audience and performers is blurred. Audiences may stand up, clap, sing along, scream, or dance during the music, participating in an active way as part of the musical event. In Africa, when the music excites listeners, you are likely to hear the piercing high sound called *ululation* and in response, the performers will extend the song, singing with more intensity. As I considered bringing diverse music into concert halls, I recognized the need to reshape the expectations of the listeners and to facilitate a relationship between the listeners and the music and culture.

I revisited my purpose and pondered how the bridge built with the singers could extend to the people who gathered to hear the songs we learned. First I dubbed these public events as "informances" instead of performances, and the IVE "shared" music rather than performed. Extensive program notes provided translations of each song along with facts about the cultures, and I added comments from the stage as well. When the informants were in attendance, they spoke directly to the audience, sometimes inviting them to sing parts of a song. Sometimes I showed video recordings of the informant, or of the rendition of the song that had served as the model. Occasionally the group minimized the distance from the audience by going into the aisles to sing or dance. My musical role was based on the practices in the culture. Graduate assistants or I conducted only when it was traditional in the country. When the rhythmic movement preceded the singing, only a nod was needed. Sometimes I started a song in front and then walked to the side, sang, and moved along with the group, then returned to signal the end.

As for appearance, the group most often wore colorful shirts with black pants and shoes. Given our limited budget plus the complications of costuming and costume changes, there was no reasonable way to honor visually the three music cultures explored in informances. However, the informants always dressed in traditional clothing and occasionally the singers wore hats or scarves from the country (see Figures 18.6 and 18.7). If there was a small special dance group, they were sometimes clothed in cultural garb.

Lessons Learned

The experience outlined here was rife with "aha" moments. I gained many insights, not only into the cultures the IVE studied, but into western culture, western music, and education. I include relevant ones below.

FIGURE 18.6 Optional Photos. (Photos by Alain Barker. Used with permission.)
Marlui Miranda Leading IVE in a Brazilian Indian Ritual.

FIGURE 18.7 IVE with Srividhya Jeyaraman from India.

Music Is Sound

We western-trained musicians forget that music exists in any other than a printed form. Yet most of the world's music is never written down. As long as humans walked on the earth, songs have sprung forth from individuals and groups. Most songs exist exclusively in the minds of humans. I always reminded the singers of this simple, yet profound fact: When a song becomes a part of us, we also became a part of the song's existence and its future.

Aural/visual transmission complements training in western art music

Having to re-create what has been presented aurally and visually requires intense observation of music and movement. The measure of perception is not in transcribing music into notation, but in the complex act of reproducing what was heard and seen.

The value of repeated hearings

When I played recordings of music we had already memorized, it was not unusual for a student to hear something the entire group had missed in previous hearings. I realized how shortsighted it is to offer performances of music (and lectures only once) when so much more can be gleaned from rehearing. With repeated hearings our perception is enhanced, revealing that we are unaware of what we miss.

People as musical repositories

In contrast to western culture, vocal music in diverse cultures is integrated into life and everyone is included. This is borne out in the Zimbabwean saying, "If you can walk you can dance, and if you can talk you can sing." Many people hold in their memory a rich repertory of songs and are living, breathing musical repositories.

Mutual benefits

Sharing music with an ensemble is beneficial for informants and their musical tradition. By valuing the music of diverse cultures, we support practices and repertory that might otherwise become extinct. One informant who was at the university studying western music said, "I had forgotten I was an expert in my own music."

REFLECTING ON THE EXPERIENCE

Throughout my tenure with the IVE, the response of my informants, singers and audiences affirmed my commitment to my goal. While student responses at the end of the semester were consistently positive, it is impossible to determine whether the experience had an effect beyond their time in the ensemble. However, a number of students enrolled in ethnomusicology courses and several pursued graduate degrees in ethnomusicology. Others have reported back that they traveled to or chose to reside in other countries, some of which we had studied. Others have attended workshops to learn more about diverse music.

In 2012 for his master's thesis, Scott Armstrong conducted a longitudinal study entitled "The Influence of Participation in the International Vocal Ensemble of Indiana University on Music Teacher's World Music Choices and Attitudes." He surveyed music education alumni who had participated in the ensemble during their pre-service education between 1995 and 2007 when I was the director. From the 30 responses, he concluded, "the participants in the survey demonstrate a wide variety of knowledge and conviction when it comes to implementing world music in their own rehearsals, stressing that IVE was an important factor in their burgeoning multicultural teaching abilities … The majority of subjects positively responded that IVE had influenced their approach to world music in their classroom, and in other musical ways. Notably, almost half (47%) of the subjects 'agreed' that they utilize exercises or techniques that they learned in IVE in their classes or rehearsals" (p. 77).

He closes his study by writing,

> Considering the IVE alumni and their increased appreciation, knowledge, and implementation of multicultural music in their own classes coupled with the fact that nearly half of the subjects received their world music training solely from IVE demonstrates not only the importance of the ensemble, but also the ensemble's worthwhile potential for emulation at other university music departments. (Armstrong, 2008, pp. 82–83)

IN CONCLUSION

In this chapter I have shared the model for including diverse music in choral repertory that was developed in the IVE at Indiana University should others wish to emulate any aspect of it. It is one way of "Putting music to work for the betterment of other people's lives and social well-being" (Elliott, 2012, p. 22). The methods were informed by my goal of honoring cultures by re-creating their music respectfully to promote understanding and tolerance. In addition to sharing ways to find people who can bring songs to life for ensembles, I have to outlined methods for transmitting songs and sharing them publicly.

I Included issues that emerged in the process of developing these methods, such as the challenges of unfamiliar vocal techniques and movement that are integral to the musical expression. I have highlighted the relationship between my goal and the method that evolved. Throughout this richly rewarding journey, it was my goal—my commitment to building a bridge of understanding and respect between my singers and diverse cultures of the world—that served to guide me in making each decision.

Clearly including songs from diverse cultures, regardless of the way they are presented, is more appropriate in today's world than singing only western art music—and more important now than ever before. Experiences with diverse music are a way to reach out to ethnic and racial groups present in our communities. Including their music is a way of validating their presence and making them feel welcomed. Conversely, broadening the repertory with songs from cultures *not* present in communities may introduce choir members and audiences to the world beyond their parochial environment and replace fear with friendships. The process of connecting to people through meaningful encounters with them and their songs holds the potential for singers to identify and empathize with those who come from different cultures—the basis for tolerance and appreciation. Providing enriched and informed experiences with diverse repertory is a way the choral profession could make the world a better place and pave the way for a peaceful future. Isn't it worth the possibility?

Notes

1. Some directors search out diverse musical examples on the Internet. They contact the performing group or the leader to gain access to the composer, from whom they purchase the score and permission to copy it.
2. More detailed discussions of vocal issues are included in Goetze (2012) and in Sperry and Goetze (2014).

References

Armstrong, S. (2008). *The influence of participation in the international vocale Ensemble of Indiana University on music teachers' world music choices and attitudes.* (Unpublished master's thesis).Bloomington: Indiana University.

Burton, B. (2002). Weaving the tapestry of world music. In B. Reimer (Ed.), *World musics and music education: Facing the issues* (pp. 161–185). Reston, VA: MENC.

Dolby, N. (2012). *Rethinking multicultural education for the next generation.* New York: Routledge.

Elliott, D. J. (2012). Another perspective: Music education as/for artistic citizenship. *Music Educators Journal, 99*(1), 21–27.

Goetze, M. (2012). Exploring the universal voice. In André de Quadros (Ed.), *The Cambridge companion to choral music* (pp. 216–237). New York: Cambridge University Press.

Lakoff, G. (2009). Conservatives are waging a war on empathy: We can't let them win. *AlterNet.* Retrieved from http://www.alternet.org/story/140362/conservatives_are_waging_a_war_on_empathy_--_we_can%27t_let_them_win

Matiure, S. (1999). Multicultural music education: An ethnography of rhythm learning and performance of African music. (Unpublished master's thesis). Indiana University, Bloomington.

Nussbaum, M. (2008). Democratic citizenship and the narrative imagination. In D. Coulter &
J. Weins (Eds.), *Why do we education? Renewing the conversation* (p. 156). Malden, MA: The
Society for the Study of Education, Blackwell.

Palmer, A. J. (1992). World musics in music education: The matter of authenticity. *International
Journal of Music Education*, 19(1), 32–40.

Palmer, A. J. (2002). Multicultural music education: Pathways and byways, purpose and ser-
endipity. In B. Reimer (Ed.), *World musics and music education: Facing the Issues* (pp.15–53).
Reston, VA: MENC.

Schippers, H. (2010). *Facing the music.* New York: Oxford University Press.

Sperry, E., & Goetze, M. (2014). Vocal versatility. *Choral Journal*, 55(2), 61–65.

Stueber, K. (2014). Empathy. In E.N. Zalta (Ed.), *The Stanford encyclopedia of philosophy* (Spring
2014 ed.). Retrieved from http://plato.stanford.edu/archives/spr2014 /entries/empathy/.

Zaretti, J. L. (1998). *Multicultural music education: An ethnography of process in teaching and
learning.* (Unpublished master's thesis). Indiana University, Bloomington.

PART V

TEACHING AND CONDUCTING DIVERSE POPULATIONS

CHAPTER 19

....

ADULT COMMUNITY CHORUSES

A Lifespan Perspective

....

SUSAN AVERY

ALTHOUGH research focused on adult music making has grown immensely since the 1970's, it has a long way to go before it offers what is needed to understand and accommodate the fastest growing segment of the population. The many subsets of *adult music* research combine the specific preference for vocal or instrumental music with areas such as sociology, psychology, physiology, learning preferences, and aging. Much of the research in adult music involvement is qualitative in nature, narrative or self-reporting, and rich with personal stories that give insight into the adults who invest resources in the making of solo and ensemble music. While there is considerable information pertaining to community singing throughout the world, this chapter focuses on adult community choruses in the United States. Therefore, this chapter provides information for the director of adult community choruses regarding adult singers in order to reconcile the differences between conductors' preferred ways of directing and adults' preferences and needs, therefore enriching the experience for all.

First, the concept of the adult community chorus will be briefly examined along with descriptions of their unique aspects. The main thrust of the chapter will then shed light on adult music participation, characteristics and needs of adult learners and music learners, and to answer the following questions:

1. What are the different types of adult participators in music and what benefits do they report to receive? What are the goals of the various types of adult community chorus members and how can we help them meet their goals?
2. What are the characteristics of adult learners? What are the issues of adult music learning? Is working with adults different from working with school-age students? If so, how?

3. What has been studied and reported that offers insight to adult changing needs (e.g. physically, cognitively, vocally) and how can teachers of adult singers accommodate their changing needs?

Finally, I will offer a brief look at the importance today's music education in the public schools as well as music teacher preparation is to the future of adult community choruses.

Defining an Adult Community Chorus

Bell (2008) provides several definitions of a community choir from organizations such as the American Choral Directors Association (ACDA) and Chorus America and several dissertations and books and concludes "there is no consensus on what, exactly, is meant by a community chorus" (Bell, 2008, p. 231). For the purpose of this chapter however, a portrait of an adult community chorus is considered through its singers, artistic leadership, organizational structure, and musical purpose. Each chorus is unique in terms of its characteristics of joining and membership, literature, educational views, and performance venues (Avery, Hayes, & Bell, 2013). For the adults that are members of these choruses, the ensemble provides a source of aesthetic pleasure, physical and mental stimulation, an extended family, and joy.

Music as a Lifespan View

A lifespan perspective does not segment adult music education into a specialized practice of highly differentiated strategies from those of childhood; rather, it envisions seamless relationships among music learning in educational settings, people's self-initiated lifelong music experiences outside such settings, and the assurance of richly diverse and developmentally appropriate opportunities for continued music learning through adulthood.

(Myers, 2012, p. 75)

The relevance that singing in a community chorus has to one's worldview is a personal matter for each adult, yet it is that relevance to their lives that drives much music participation and learning. Therefore, in order to influence policy, arts educators must demonstrate the impact music has upon humans "by designing, implementing, and analyzing programmes [sic] that embody authentic relevance" and making that relevance overt by increasing "perceptions of its value and relationship to daily life among the public" (Myers, 2008, p. 2). Myers also suggests personal goals for participation and fulfillment rather than levels of expertise as lenses through which relevance should be examined

(2). For some adults, it is the end result of the performance that is of greatest importance; for some it is the process of learning.

In what he terms the performance-pedagogy paradox, Freer (2011) provides several arguments as to whether the performance is more important than the learning or vice-versa. He resolves the paradox of choral music relevance by suggesting we balance that duality in ways that can shift to accommodate specific teaching goals, literature, some performances, and pedagogies needed for individuals. If we as directors can create this balance for our ensembles, the relevance of the experience will certainly strengthen and inspire lifelong participation.

GOALS AND BENEFITS OF ADULT MUSIC PARTICIPATION

Adult participants in music are often characterized by the degree to which they value and engage in musical activities as well as actively share their interests socially (Busch, 2005). There is considerable interest in the musical lives of adults by several areas of the music industry as well as sociologists, anthropologists, the medical field, and a host of other disciplines. The music industry examines adults' participation in music through lenses such as concert attendance, audio and print music consumed, instrument purchases, and the adults' influence on future generations. In 1991 the National Association for Music Merchants (NAMM) funded the New Horizons International Music Association (NHIMA). This was a model program created by Dr. Roy Ernst at the Eastman School of Music in Rochester, NY. This groundbreaking program offered seniors the opportunity to begin or return to playing an instrument. In Dr. Ernst's words:

> In the 1980s, I was thinking about how being in a music group could improve the quality of life for seniors. They would have a constant opportunity to feel accomplishment and they would be important members of a group. They would also have events to anticipate in the future, like concerts and music camps. Since then, I have seen how music connects people to life: to the past through music that takes them back to other times, to the present through music they are working on right now, and to the future through music and events they work towards, and—most of all—it connects them to other people. People also give their brains a great workout when they participate in a musical group. They don't need computer programs or pills. (Ernst, personal communication, August 2014)

Since the inception of the New Horizon program, the age of participators has expanded greatly beyond the original concept of retirees and now includes band and orchestra musicians in their 30s. Choral ensembles and singing "classes" are often included at New Horizon camps as one of the many electives available.

Information about adult participation in music is widely available in the research journals of several disciplines and articles in professional periodicals such as the *Choral Journal* or the *Music Educators Journal*. Current research and writing on adult participation can be general or specific in regards to choral or instrumental interests. It is most often centered in informal and formal community music making and examines benefits in social, cognitive, and aesthetic areas (Bowles, 1991; Myers, 2008; Waldron, 2008; Southcott, 2009; Kennedy, 2009). Adult participation is also becoming an important topic in baccalaureate music teacher education so graduates are prepared to teach both school age students and adults. Both state and national music education organizations recognize the importance of catering to a large segment of the population with eager development of workshops and presentations on adult and community music.

For directors of adult community choruses, knowledge of our participants' purpose for joining and remaining in our ensembles will provide valuable information and ensure the best experience possible in regards to the difficulty and type of literature, seriousness of purpose, eagerness to improve, and other considerations. Knowledge of the received benefits will make them more visible to the directors and therefore provide opportunities for enhancement. Dewey's model of experiential learning posits that the responsibility of both the subject matter as well as knowledge of the learners lies directly with the teacher (Roberts, 2003, p. 7). While it is not possible to ascertain for certainty each singer's purpose for participation (as this is often mercurial), answers to a director's questionnaire may provide insight into individuals' motivation for attending. Gates (1991) exhorts us to delve into the motivation of our membership in the "rich contexts of their own lives rather than through the stencils we construct for them" (p. 27).

Desired Learning Goals

There is great variation in the reasons adults give for participating in community music, but certainly an oft-reported goal is broadly stated as "learning more about music." Directors of adult choruses, after familiarizing themselves with the types of participators in their ensemble (see next section for more detail), need to ascertain what learning is desired. Boardman's Generative Theory of Music Instruction encourages learning that originates from the music itself and reminds us that learning occurs in context. To answer the question *what should we teach?* Boardman tells us that "the content of the music curriculum consists of those concepts that form the structure of music, including primary concepts of the musical whole—expression, style, and form—as shaped by subsidiary conceptual categories related to basic musical elements of timbre, dynamics, articulation, rhythm, harmony, and texture" (Boardman, 2001, p. 4). Going beyond the printed page with information about the historical as well as the theoretical aspects of literature intrigues many adult learners as they continue to construct meaning of the experience holistically.

The skill of music reading is one of the most often requested areas of desired learning by adults. Composer Libby Larsen believes "reading and writing are the fundamental relevant dimensions of people's ability to become lifelong music participants" (Myers, 2008, p. 5). Literacy, according to a panel of experts that worked with The National Adult Literacy Survey in 1992, is "using printed and written information to function in society, to achieve one's goals, and to develop one's knowledge and potential" (Brown et al., 1996, p. 2). Perhaps an even more apt definition is offered by David Cooper as "we must view literacy as the ability to communicate in real-world situations, which involves the abilities of individuals to read, write, speak, listen, view, and think" (in Hansen et al., 2007, p. 2). VanWeelden and Walters (2004) question whether music literacy was encouraged in the adults' public school music education in ways that would support lifelong participation. This sentiment is echoed in Gudmundsdottir (2010) as she posits that methods for teaching music-reading skills to children are flawed and emphasizes the importance of understanding "all the cognitive components involved in music-reading tasks" (p. 336) to improve the teaching of those skills.

Certainly the skill of reading music must not overshadow the art of learning aurally (nor should the opposite be true). Both skills are crucial in a holistic choral experience; some choral traditions are created with one or the other more firmly utilized, yet it is the combination of both methods of learning that should be attained. Kennedy (2009) describes the benefits of aural learning (via the call-and-response method) to assist new members to begin singing confidently.

Reasons for Participation

Coffman (2002) describes three categories of adults' given reasons for music participation: personal motivations, musical motivations, and social motivations. He also states that no single reason emerges as most important except from those who are better performers report musical motivations most. Certainly each type of motivation holds personal meaning (for instance, personal motivation may embrace spirituality, cultural significance, a desire to learn something new, a remembrance of previously enjoyed musical experiences, and so on). Sometimes the true reason for the participation is not fully realized by the musician.

One of the most comprehensive theories of music participations is found in Gates' writing *Music Participation: Theory, Research, and Policy*. Gates (1991) first defines a music participant as someone "who directly or indirectly produce musical events for an audience, even in the audience is the performer him/herself, and even if the audience is not yet present as when an individual learns or composes music for an upcoming performance" (p. 6). After extensive research in the areas of music education, ethnomusicology, and sociology of leisure, he suggests there are six types of music participants that are distinguished by the participants in terms of cost versus benefit to participating in music.

Gates' typology differentiates the six types of music participants according to how they *view* music and how they are *reinforced*. The view of music as work, serious leisure, or play divides participants into professionals and apprentices (work), amateurs and hobbyists (serious leisure), and recreationists and dabblers (play). Professionals, apprentices, and amateurs are reinforced in a social system made up of music professionals, amateurs, and publics, while hobbyists, recreationists, and dabblers are reinforced idiosyncratically—not reinforced primarily by a sociomusical system (Gates, 1991).

By and large, most adult community chorus singers are member of the serious leisure and play categories. According to Gates (1991), those in the serious leisure group are willing to accept "high costs in knowledge, skill, time commitment, and persistence contrasted with those activities s/he regards as play" but the player "does not identify with the activity sufficiently to overcome its difficulties for long" (p. 13). The recreationists look for entertainment benefits in the activity while dabblers are curious about the activity but cease to participate when that curiosity is satisfied. Researchers need to obtain information from adults who do not participate in musical activities to help us understand why they choose not to be involved in musical activities (Rohwer, 2010).

The suggestions Gates (1991) offers regarding attracting and maintaining membership involve directors examining ways we attract members and select literature, and the methods we use to teach them, as well as our offered rewards and honors. He suggests that we can improve membership retention "(a) if we design our recruiting programs to appeal to music participants and ignore audience types, and (b) if in major parts of our programs, we systematically reinforce the values of at least five types of music participants: musical recreationists, hobbyists, amateurs, apprentices, and professionals" (p. 27).

BENEFITS OF PARTICIPATION

It stands to reason that if directors of adult community choruses understand the perceived benefits of choral singing and can capitalize upon them, the singers will continue to reap those benefits in more profound ways. The myriad of benefits reported by the adults in many research papers and writings span aspects such as physical health, social opportunities and feelings of belonging, mental acuity, acquisition of new skills, emotional health, confidence, self-esteem, and friendship. After surveying 500 older adult participants in both music and non-music activities, Hallam, Creech, Varvarigou, and McQueen (2012) wrote extensively on the perceived social, cognitive, emotional and mental health, and physical health benefits, as well as the realization that "public performance also enabled participants to feel that they were giving something back to the community" (p. 170).

After surveying 404 adult choristers, Baird (2008) found there were six beneficial aspects of choral singing indicated by the respondents (in the order of importance): musical, intellectual, emotional, physical, social, and spiritual. Examples of the benefits in the categories reported are as follows: musical (enjoyment of music and aesthetic pleasure, developing range and reading ability, development of musical culture); intellectual (keeping brain stimulated, setting of goals and achievement); emotional (enjoyment, relaxation, removal of worries, humility); physical (general health benefits, asthma relief, strengthening of back and stomach muscles, therapy for stress and depression); social (making of new friends, social interaction after rehearsals, personal closeness); and spiritual (supporting religious beliefs) (Baird, 2008). Southcott (2009) reports themes of increased sense of purpose, relationship formation, personal growth, and maintaining cognitive abilities from her case study.

Directors often realize the same benefits as the participants. Travis (2009) quotes New Horizons founder Dr. Ernst's recommendation that music educators should "try and find time to teach adults. You will find it is the most pure form of teaching and learning."

Characteristics of Adult Learners and Issues of Adult Learning

Adult learning preferences and theories

Overtly or covertly, choral singing infers learning on some level. Gates (1991) declares if someone desires to be a music performer, that person "must purposefully develop specific music skills and knowledge" (p. 8). To many conductors of adult community choruses (as well as many choristers), learning may simply take the form of preparing the literature for performance. It behooves us to examine the construct of learning for adults as they take meaning and satisfaction from the experience of choral singing so we as conductors become the pedagogues in tandem with the singers. In order to provide a rich environment, perhaps we must first ask *just what is learning?* Behaviorists tell us learning is adding to the repertoire of observable skills while cognitivists assert knowledge is constructed by the learner (Baumgartner, 2003). Conductors of adult ensembles should consider how they prefer to lead and teach their choristers by directly providing desired knowledge and skills versus creating an environment in which each participant is allowed to choose and create their learning.

Adult learning theories

The professional practice of adult education began in the 1920's. Since then adult learning has become an area of great interest to researchers, scholars, and professionals in many disciplines (Merriam, 2001). In 1968, Knowles (1984) defined the term *andragogy* as "the art and science of helping adults learn" (p. 43) and inferred that adults learn differently than children (*pedagogy*). Andragogy encompasses six core learning principles: 1) Adults need to know the reason for learning something before learning it; 2) The self-concept of adults is heavily dependent upon a move toward self-direction; 3) Prior experiences of the learner provide a rich resource for learning; 4) Adults typically become ready to learn when they experience a need to cope with a life situation or perform a task; 5) Adults' orientation to learning is life-centered—education is a process of developing increased competency levels to achieve their full potential; 6) The motivation for adult learners is internal rather than external (Knowles, 2005, p. 159). The concept of andragogy has been debated as to "whether it is an adult learning theory, a teaching method, a philosophical statement, or all of the above" (St. Clair, 2002, p. 3) or that it is merely a "set of assumptions about learners" (3). Kruse (2009) defines andragogy as encompassing "self-directed learning behaviours that may indicate that independent musicianship has evolved" (p. 216).

Hiemstra (1993) offers what he termed three "underdeveloped models for adult learning": first, Cross's model of characteristics of adult as learners, which utilizes personal characteristics (physiological, sociocultural, and psychological stages) and situational characteristics (part-time vs. full-time learning and voluntary vs. compulsory learning) (Cross, 1981, p. 235); McClusky's theory of margin, which suggests adulthood is a time of growth, change, and integration that seeks to balance energy needed and amount available (Merriam, 1999, p. 279); and Knox's proficiency theory of adult learning. Knox (1980a) defines proficiency as "the capability to perform given the opportunity" and uses this term "as a unifying concept to relate acquisition of knowledge, skills, and attitudes to improved *performance*, which motivates much adult learning" (p. 378—italics mine). Knox declares the fundamental concept of his theory to be "interest in enhanced proficiency facilitates persistence in adult learning activities that are satisfying and productive of personal growth" (p. 378). Of the three, perhaps the most interesting to directors of adult community choruses would be the proficiency theory, since the focus of ensembles is often on performing.

The proficiency theory encourages directors of adult community choruses to become effective facilitators of their members' learning by purposeful planning and providing "periodic assessment of discrepancies between current and desired proficiencies related to an area of performance, which provides the basis for needs assessment, objective, organization of learning activities, and evaluation" (Knox, 1980a, p. 382). In considering adults' past experiences and learning differences, Knox labels them as important, but asserts that characteristics such as their learning ability, physical condition, experience, openness of personality, and current proficiency are more relevant to current learning. One last reference to the proficiency theory for consideration by chorus directors: "almost all instances of enhanced proficiency entails practice and rehearsal and one contribution of a teacher is to provide varied and sequential learning tasks that encourage and enable the learner to engage in sufficient repetition to achieve the desired level of proficiency" (p. 396).

The idea that adults learn differently than children has been often questioned. Garrison (1994, p. 13) implies that adults may not need a separate teaching approach and Kerka declares all parts of the discussion itself to be ambiguous but believes offering "transformative learning demands a different approach by the educator" (Kerka, 2002, p. 3). Merriam (2001) states her belief that no single theory of adult learning will ever be able to "capture the complexity of this phenomenon" (p. 95). She declares labels like andragogy, self-directed learning, and transformational learning to be termed *foundational* or *traditional* instead of *old* and posits how all theories expand our understanding about "the learner, the learning process, and the context of learning" (p. 93).

Facilitation of adult learning

Merriam (2001) suggests that the above-mentioned understanding should inform and assist the adult community chorus director in the following: the adult *learner* needs to be viewed as a whole entity with all that s/he brings to the experience; the learning *process* is more than information acquisition, it is making sense of our lives with others; the learning *context* takes on increased importance, allowing for examination of how situation, race, gender, power, etc., shape the context and the learning. Serious consideration of these areas demands the choral conductor's attention to all aspects of the singing experience such as literature choice, rehearsal demeanor, an in-depth familiarization of the singers themselves, knowledge of the score and implications for learning and transference to other songs, and the acumen to create and deliver learning opportunities for the singers who desire them. However, Mantie (2012) cautions directors not to "favour learning over participation (because) we risk reducing what we do to either a neverending quest that permanently delays gratification, or, as has been the case with school music, we turn music into a 'subject' to be learned where participation is rendered unnecessary once the learning objectives have been attained" (p. 228).

Of great use to current and prospective directors of adult community choruses are what Wlodowski (2008) claims are the five pillars of motivational teaching: expertise, empathy, enthusiasm, clarity, and cultural responsiveness, all of which can be learned and honed. He explains "expertise" has three parts: we (*the director*) know something beneficial for adults; we know it well, and; we are prepared to convey or construct it with adults through an instructional process (p. 50). Wlodowski defines "empathy" as the power of understanding and compassion containing three parts: we have a realistic understanding of the learners' goals, perspectives, and expectations for what is being learned; we have adapted our instruction to the learners' levels of experience and skill development; and we continuously consider the learners' perspectives and feelings (p. 59). He next defines "enthusiasm" as the power of commitment and expressiveness that contains two parts: we value what we teach for ourselves as well as for the learner, and we display our commitment with appropriate degrees of emotion and expressiveness (p. 72). "Clarity," he continues, is the power of organization and language, and he asks us to consider two standards: we plan and conduct instruction so that all learners can follow and understand, and we provide a way for learners to comprehend what has been taught if it is not initially clear (p. 80). Finally, Wlodowski defines "cultural responsiveness" as the power of respect and social responsibility and suggests three guidelines: we create a safe, inclusive, and respectful learning environment; we engage the motivation of all learners; and we relate course content and learning to the social concerns of learners and the broader concerns of society (p. 87).

Attributes that adult learners expect to see in their directors are described in many scholarly writings. Among them are: concern for student learning, motivational leading, enthusiasm, clarity of instruction, dedication, adaptiveness to diverse needs, flexibility, secure knowledge of material and learning strategies, empathy, respect, and many others (Donaldson, Flannery, & Ross-Gordon, 1993; Flannery, 1991; Ross-Gordon, 1991; Baskas 2011; Allen & Wergin, 2009). Brookfield (1986) suggests the "task of the teacher of adults is to help them to realize that the bodies of knowledge, accepted truths, commonly held values, and customary behaviors comprising their worlds are contextually and culturally constructed" and warn that "challenging previously accepted and internalized beliefs and values . . . can be uncomfortable" (p. 125). Knox (1980b) posits the teacher qualities appreciated by adult learners are more likely found in teachers who themselves are lifelong learners.

Crucial to the rehearsal process is assisting the singers in cultivating strategies that teach them how to learn. Knox (1980b) tells us "the best way to help teachers of adults increase their effectiveness is to emphasize learning—their's and the participant's" (p. 73). He suggests teachers (in this chapter's focus, *directors*) attempt to obtain background information of the students' (*singers'*) proficiencies, expectations, barriers, resources, and interests in order to support planning for students' proficiency, which he defines as "the capability to perform if given the opportunity" (p. 78). It is this planning of objectives as well as evaluation strategies, he posits, that will enhance both proficiency and satisfaction of the participants.

Basic learning-to-learn skills are crucial (along with information processing) for effective learning. Without them, learning will be more arduous, if it occurs at all (Cornford, 2002). These learning-to-learn skills are the closely related cognitive and metacognitive processes the learner uses and controls. The cognitive learning strategies are "goal-directed, intentionally invoked, effortful and are not universally applicable, but situation specific" (p. 359). Metacognitive skills, however, are not situation specific, but involve more generic skills needed for thinking and problem solving. Cognitive and metacognitive skills are by nature, personal and covert. What Cornford calls a "metacurricular approach" (p. 365) includes teaching the thinking skills along with the subject matter, which is a major change from teaching exclusively the subject content. The need for teachers to understand the skills themselves as well as the ability to teach them ultimately will have major implication on the amount of content covered and effective learning that will occur. Strategies such as repetition, elaboration, and organization will assist storage of information into long-term memory (which will resonate with adult chorus directors), as will building new learning onto previously stored information.

Adult music learning

Coffman (2009) examines the subject of working with adults versus children in terms of teaching and learning issues by surveying New Horizons band and orchestra directors. He reports that the process of teaching adults musical instruments and notation is no different than to with young musicians. He also concludes that the musical expectations in directing adults are no different than with their younger counterparts. However, the respondents describe differences in teaching styles while working with adults and youth. A few principles Coffman discovered concerning adult learners through his survey of directors are: adults are influenced by their prior experience, adults need to view themselves as learners, adults adjust their learning throughout life, and adults tend to be self-directed (p. 236). VanWeelden (2002) suggests that choral directors who have more experience with younger performers might be frustrated as they attempt to meet the needs of older singers.

Bowles (2010) examined features such as characteristics, preparation, and practices of adult music teachers to discover what is needed to become truly effective. The study resulted in four requests to the music education profession: to create age-appropriate instructional materials, to provide relevant professional development experiences, to organize a task force to develop strategies for their specific needs, and to encourage more research to provide further insight and solutions to challenges.

Roulston (2010) offers four key ideas gleaned from adult education that she suggests teachers of adult learners might find useful:

- Adults' motivations to learn music and orientations to learning are multifaceted and complex, and change over time
- Learning in adulthood is distinctive from learning in childhood in multiple and complex ways that involve the learning context, the learner, and the learning process
- Adults draw upon a lifetime of experiences in their learning
- Music learning involves embodiment
- Music learning in adulthood can be informed by non-Western perspectives of learning (p. 349).

ACCOMMODATING ADULTS' CHANGING NEEDS

Radocy and Boyle (1997), presenting psychologist Abraham Maslow's thoughts on hierarchy of needs, states that "Maslow contends that aesthetic experience is a basic human need, albeit one with which people become involved only when their physiological, safety, and certain psychological needs are met" (p. 271). Considering these factors in terms of choral rehearsals and performances might translate the needs as good venti-lation and light (physiological), reaching the rehearsal site safely, security of property (safety), comfortable social setting, relationship with the director (belongingness), and confidence and achievement (esteem). As aging occurs, a natural progress of physical and cognitive changes can affect music participation and the director of adult choruses should be aware of those possibilities and solutions. Merely attending rehearsals may seem prohibitive if certain needs are not met.

Issues of physical and general needs

Coffman (2009) observes that directors of older adult learners comment on limita-tions due to physical age. Ernst (2001) mentions visual and aural problems and suggests enlarging music for visual acuity and placing performers strategically closer to direc-tor for instructions, comfortably surrounded by others in their section, and the use of closed-loop audio systems to aid in hearing. VanWeelden (2002) states that problems with dentures (because of changes to the oral cavity), hearing, menopause (due to estro-gen loss), as well as other age-related issues can all hamper the enjoyment of choral singing. She also posits hearing loss often encourages singers to over-sing, thus causing vocal strain, and that the taking of aspirin can cause hemorrhaging in the vocal folds.

Yinger (2014) examines sensory and perceptual changes as aging occurs and sug-gests modifications such as brightened rehearsal site lighting and enlarged conducting gestures to compensate for visual decline; the option to sit or stand at their choice; the placement of wires or floor mats outside the rehearsal area to assist those experiencing haptic (touch-related) or motor control decline; and the use of nonverbal cues and slow, clear speech to help those suffering from hearing decline. Avery (2004) suggests direc-tors consider rehearsal sites that are convenient and have adequate parking, good light-ing inside and out, handicapped accessibility, and are in safe areas of the town.

Issues of cognition changes

It would be difficult to find a director of an adult community chorus that disagrees with the idea that music participation provides a positive impact on cognition. One of the many studies in leisure activities concludes that "participation in both socially and cog-nitively complex leisure activities is associated with cognitive function independently of socioeconomic status and age in a middle aged cohort" (Singh-Manoux, Richards, & Marmot, 2003, p. 907). Rather than assume cognitive changes occur only in older adults, Salthouse (2004) asserts that declines in cognition accumulate across the lifespan and begin in early adulthood. Major findings in a study by John and Cole (1986) reveal and compare similarities between information-processing deficits of young children and elderly adults in areas such as ability to process information quickly, quantity of infor-mation handling, and use of efficient retrieval strategies. They determined that most problems occurred with large amounts of information given; information not provided in ideal formats (lacking instruction as to how to process); and use of difficult response formats. Yinger (2014) suggests cognitive changes to short-term memory, spatial cognition, and ability to multitask will require strategies such as a slower pace of instruction, minimized multistep directions, and selecting familiar music.

With possible implications to earlier music study and learning, Burke and MacKay (1997) posit that episodic memory decline (diminished ability to remember specific events situated in time and place) that is linked to aging applies primarily to new or recent events and not to experiences from a younger age (p. 1846). They continue that "older adults can maximize their cognitive functioning by using familiar skills and knowledge acquired over a lifetime" (p. 1853). Another possible connection to music learning is through a practitioner's lens. Erickson (1988) suggests motivation as important to the adult learner and describes an English-as-a-second-language learner who was not interested in developing basic reading and writing skills, but skills that would result in employment. Failure to see the connection between basic skills and employment resulted in the student's lack of success. She also recommends encouraging students to simply write without correction of grammar or punctuation until they feel comfortable with writing so as to not inflame their perception of "I can't write."

Issues of vocal changes

The adult (and therefore, aging) voice is an area of interest for voice researchers in the field of medicine as well as in vocal musical production. Ware (1998) tells us hormones and changes in the endocrine system are linked to the aging process and therefore the aging voice. Sataloff (1991), reports that body changes through aging bring about "breathiness, loss of range, change in the characteristics of vibrato, development of tremolo, loss of breath control, vocal fatigue, pitch inaccuracies, and other undesirable features" (p. 146). He comforts us by declaring the decline may not be as inevitable as once thought and many of the vocal mechanisms can be maintained and even strengthened through proper exercise for many more years than previously assumed (p. 147). Books such as Caldwell and Wall's 2001 *Excellence in Singing Volume 2* and VanWeelden's 2002 article *On the Voice: Working with the Senior Adult Choir* as well as many other voice-training textbooks provide many exercises to use when working with the voice in all areas of technique. VanWeelden cautions directors of adult choruses not to be biased because of media stereotypes of adult and older singers' voices; the negative impact might discourage directors and singers to make efforts to strengthen and improve their sound.

The importance of understanding and recognizing the possible changes in a maturing voice is crucial to both the singer and director, who may observe the onset of subtle changes in tone quality, vocal power, endurance, and range. Singing itself may be valuable in delaying some inevitable losses (Smith & Sataloff, 2013). Baroody and Smith

(2013) remind us that the singing instrument utilizes the entire body and impresses upon singers the importance of total body health for senescent singers. The authors reason that choral participation by aging singers is a relatively new phenomenon and conductors are not yet able to rely on a plethora of research and articles to assist them in working with the adult voice. There are many well-considered suggestions in this chapter, including recommending the choice of literature that demonstrates a "cooler, more intellectual nature" rather than "dramatic or emotive texts ... with expansive vocal ranges and harmonic structures that encourage less controlled singing" (p. 95) to lessen the possibility of a wider vibrato rate.

Barrier (1993) reports that respiration requires more effort as we age, but again recommends proper training along with repertoire selection and planned phrasing to mask any difficulties. The choice of literature for senescent voices is examined in considerable detail in Barrier's dissertation by measuring voice quality registration through phonetography and Gelfer acoustic-perceptual analysis (used primarily by speech pathologists and otolaryngologists). Suggestions were provided from the data and other studied issues (stamina, visual and hearing problems, etc.) for literature criteria and choice and conductor behaviors.

The importance of music education from today's schools through adult participation

> Many music teachers across this country every day provide pleasurable, enjoyable, creative music experiences for their students. Yet, it appears that many children and adults do not choose to continue many of these music experiences outside of school. Perhaps we need to plan more directly for the future musical lives of students. (Jellison, 2000, p. 135)

In order to accomplish the goal of involvement in meaningful music experiences throughout their lives, Jellison (2000) recommends we use the transition principle which infers all children receive "music experiences in school that are directly referenced to contexts for music experiences valued for adulthood" (Jellison, 2000, p. 121). Agreeing with her, Myers (2008) states that musical potential and drives over a lifetime are not necessarily grounded in successful ensemble performances in schools. He further explains this by stating "it is not so much the issue that ensembles are part of music education as it is how we position them within a lifespan perspective on learning and teaching" (p. 55).

While tackling the myriad of challenges current public school music educators face, Jorgensen reminds them to seek opportunities to not only revitalize school music, but to return music to the forefront of cultural life in the community (Jorgensen, 2010). The directors of adult community choruses who are also public or private school music teachers have a responsibility to reconcile this issue and close the chasm between P-12 music making and lifelong music participation.

Music teacher preparation

Lee Shulman (2005) tells us "if you wish to understand why professions develop as they do, study their nurseries, in this case, their forms of professional preparation" (p. 52). In his seminal writing, Myers (1992) suggests music teacher education programs should encourage candidates to think beyond the traditional view of education and be prepared to offer quality music programs for all ages. In order to achieve those goals, he tells us music teacher education programs should contain components such as: systematic strategies that promote an increasing degree of self-directed learning; greater emphasis on problem solving, reflective thinking, cooperative goal setting, and logical decision making; and greater relevance between university classrooms and learning beyond the classroom.

Conclusion

Myers (2012), tells us "a lifespan perspective considers the holistic question of how music learning in schools and music learning in life may unite around the common goal or ensured opportunities for all people, regardless of age, circumstances, or musical background" (p. 90). Choral pedagogy for adult community singers needs continued refinement in order to accommodate all who enjoy the life changing experience of singing.

References

Allen, S., & Wergin, J. (2009). Leadership and adult development theories: Overviews and overlaps. *Leadership Review 9*, 3–17.

Avery, S. (2004). How to start an adult community chorus. *Music Educators Journal, 90*(5), 38–41.

Avery, S., Hayes C., & Bell, C. (2013). Community choirs: Expressions of identity through vocal performance. In K. Veblen, S. Messenger, M. Silverman, & D. Elliott (Eds.), *Community music today* (pp. 249–260). New York: Rowman & Littlefield.

Baird, M. (2008). Perceived benefits of choral singing: Social, intellectual, and emotional aspects of group singing. (Master's thesis). McGill University, Montreal.

Baroody, M., & Smith, B. (2013). *Choral pedagogy* (3rd ed.). San Diego, CA: Plural.

Barrier, J. (1993). *The development of criteria for the selection of age-appropriate literature for the senescent voice*. (Doctoral dissertation). The University of Arizona. Retrieved from ProQuest Dissertations & Theses Global (UMI No. 9322680).

Baskas, R. (2011). Applying adult learning and development theories to educational practice. n.p. Retrieved from ERIC database (ED519926).

Baumgartner, L. M., Lee, M-Y., Birden, S., & Flowers, D. (2003). *Adult learning theory: A primer*. Center on Education and Training for Employment, College of Education, The Ohio State University, Information Series No. 392, 8–9.

Bell, C. (2008). Toward a definition of a community choir. *International Journal of Community Music*, 1(2), 229–241. doi: http://dx.doi.org/10.1386/ijcm.1.2.229_1

Boardman, E. (2001). Generating a theory of music instruction. *Music Educators Journal*, 88(2), 45–53.

Bowles, C. (1991). Self-expressed adult music education interests and music experiences. *Journal of Research in Music Education*, 39(3), 191–205.

Bowles, C. (2010). Teachers of adult music learners: An assessment of characteristics and instructional practices, preparation, and needs. *Update: Applications of Research in Music Education*, 28(2), 50–59.

Brookfield, S. (1986). *Understanding and facilitating adult learning*. San Francisco: Jossey-Bass.

Brown, H., Prisuta, R., Jacobs, B., & Campbell, A. (1996). *Literacy of older adults in America: Results from the National Adult Literacy Survey*. US Department of Education. Washington, DC: US Government Printing Office.

Burke, D., & MacKay, D. G. (1997). Memory, language, and ageing. *Philosophical Transactions: Biological Sciences*, 352(1363), 1845–1856.

Busch, M. (2005). Predictors of lifelong learning in music: A survey of individuals participating in performing ensembles at community colleges in Illinois. (Doctoral dissertation). Urbana: University of Illinois. Retrieved from ProQuest Dissertations & Theses Global. (UMI No. 3182229).

Caldwell, R., & Wall, J. (2001). *Excellence in singing: Vol. 2*. Redmond, WA: Caldwell.

Coffman, D. (2002). Adult education. In R. Colwell & C. Richardson (Eds.), *New handbook of research on music teaching and learning* (pp. 199–209). London: Oxford University Press.

Coffman, D. (2009). Learning from our elders: Survey of New Horizons International Music Association band and orchestra directors. *International Journal of Community Music*, 2(2–3), 227–240. doi: http://dx.doi.org/10.1386/ijcm.2.2-3.227_1

Cornford, I. (2002). Learning-to-learn strategies as a basis for effective lifelong learning. *International Journal of Lifelong Education*, 21(4), 357–368. doi: http://dx.doi.org/10.1080/02601370210141020

Cross, K. P. (1981). *Adults as learners*. San Francisco: Jossey-Bass.

Donaldson, J., Flannery, D., & Ross-Gordon, J. (1993). A triangulated study comparing adult college students' perceptions of effective teaching with those of traditional students. *Continuing Higher Education Review*, 57(3), 147–165.

Erickson, J. (1988). From research to practice: the practitioner's perspective. In R. Fellenz (Ed.), *Cognition and the adult learner; Selected papers presented at the meeting of a summer institute on adult cognition* (pp. 49–52). Battle Creek, MI: Kellogg Foundation. Retrieved from ERIC database (ED305426).

Ernst, R. (2001). Music for life. Grand Masters Series. *Music Educators Journal*, 88(1), 47–51.

Flannery, D. (1991). Adults' expectations of instructors: Criteria for hiring and evaluating instructors. *Continuing Higher Education Review*, 55(1–2), 38–48.

Freer, P. (2011). The performance-pedagogy paradox in choral music teaching. *Philosophy of Music Education Review*, 19(2), 164–178. doi: http://dx.doi.org/10.2979/philmusieducrevi.19.2.164

Garrison, D. R. (1994). An epistemological overview of the field. In D. R. Garrison (Ed.), *Research perspectives in adult education* (p. 13). Malabar, FL: Krieger.

Gates, J. T. (1991). Music participation: Theory, research, and policy. *Bulletin of the Council for Research in Music Education*, 109, 1–35.

Gudmundsdottir, H. (2010). Advances in music-reading research. *Music Education Research*, 12(4), 331–338. doi: http://dx.doi.org/10.1080/14613808.2010.504809

Hallam, S., Creech, A., Varvarigou, M., & McQueen, H. (2012). Perceived benefits of active engagement with making music in community settings. *International Journal of Community Music, 5* (2), 155–174. doi: http://dx.doi.org/10.1386/ijcm.5.2.155_1

Hansen, D., Bernstorf E., & Stuber. G. (2007). *The music and literacy connection.* Lanham, MD: Rowman & Littlefield Education.

Hiemstra, R. (1993). Three underdeveloped models for adult learning. *New Directions for Adult and Continuing Education, 57,* 37–46. doi: http://dx.doi.org/10.1002/ace.36719935706

Jellison, J. (2000). How can all people continue to be involved in meaningful music participation? In C. Madsen (Ed.), *Vision 2020—The Housewright symposium on the future of music education* (pp. 111–137). Reston, VA: MENC.

John, D., & Cole, C. (1986). Age differences in information processing: Understanding deficits in young and elderly consumers. *Journal of Consumer Research, 13*(3), 297–315.

Jorgensen, E. (2010). School music education and change. *Music Educators Journal, 96*(4), 21–27. doi: http://dx.doi.org/10.1177/0027432110369779

Kennedy, M. C. (2009). The Gettin' Higher Choir: Exploring culture, teaching, and learning in a community chorus. *International Journal of Community Music, 2* (2–3), 183–200.

Kerka, S. (2002). Teaching adults: Is it different? Myths and realities. ERIC Clearinghouse of Adult, Career, and Vocational Education, Columbus, OH: Retrieved from ERIC database (ED 468614).

Knox, A. (1980a). Proficiency theory of adult learning. *Contemporary Educational Psychology, 5*(4), 378–404. doi: http://dx.doi.org/10.1016/0361-476X(80)90059-4

Knox, A. (1980b). Helping teachers help adults learn. *New Directions for Continuing Education, 6.* DOI: http://dx.doi.org/10.1002/ace.36719800611

Knowles, M. S. (1984). *Andragogy in action.* San Francisco: Jossey-Bass.

Knowles, M. S., HoltonIII, E. F., & Swanson, R.A. (2005). *The adult learner.* (6th edition). Burlington, MA: Elsevier.

Kruse, N. B. (2009). "'An Elusive Bird': Perceptions of Music Learning among Canadian and American Adults." *International Journal of Community Music, 2*(2 and 3), 215–225.

Mantie, R. (2012). Learners or participants? The pros and cons of "lifelong learning." *International Journal of Community Music, 5*(3), 217–235. doi: http://dx.doi.org/10.1386/ijcm.5.3.217_1

Merriam, S. (2001). *The new update on adult learning theory.* San Francisco: Jossey-Bass.

Myers, D. (1992). Teaching learners of all ages. *Music Educators Journal, 79*(4), 23–26.

Myers, D. (2008). Lifespan engagement and the question of relevance: challenges for music education research in the twenty-first century. *Music Education Research, 10*(1), 1–14. doi: http://dx.doi.org/10.1080/14613800701871330

Myers, D. (2012). Including adulthood in music education perspectives and policy: A lifespan view. *Yearbook of the National Society for the Study of Education, 111*(1), 74–92.

Radocy, R., & Boyle, J. D. (1997). *Psychological foundations of musical behavior* (3rd ed.). Springfield, IL: Charles C. Thomas.

Roberts, T. G. (2003). An interpretation of Dewey's experiential learning theory. n.p. Retrieved from ERIC database (ED 481922).

Rohwer, D. (2010). Understanding adult interests and needs: the pitfalls in wanting to know. *International Journal of Community Music, 3*(2), 203–212. doi: http://dx.doi.org/10.1386/ijcm.3.2.203_1

Ross-Gordon, J. (1991). Critical incidents in the college classroom: What do adult undergraduates perceive as effective teaching? *Continuing Higher Education Review, 55*(1–2), 14–33.

Roulston, K. (2010). "There is no end to learning": Lifelong education and the joyful learner. *International Journal of Music Education, 28* (4), 341–352. doi: http://dx.doi.org/10.1177/0255761410381822

St. Clair, R. (2002). Andragogy revisited: Theory for the 21st century? *Myths and Realities 19.* ERIC Clearinghouse of Adult, Career, and Vocational Education, Columbus, OH: Retrieved from ERIC database. (ED 468612)

Salthouse, T. (2004). What and when of cognitive aging. *Current Directions in Psychological Science, 13*(4), 140–144. doi: http://dx.doi.org/10.1111/j.0963-7214.2004.00293.x

Sataloff, R. (1991). *Professional voice: The science and art of clinical care.* New York: Raven.

Shulman, L. (2005). Signature pedagogies in the professions. *Daedalus, 134*(3), 52–59. doi: http://dx.doi.org/10.1162/0011526054622015

Singh-Manoux, A., Richards, M., & Marmot, M. (2003). Leisure activities and cognitive function in middle age: Evidence from the Whitehall II Study. *Journal of Epidemiology and Community Health, 57*(11), 907–913. doi: http://dx.doi.org/10.1136/jech.57.11.907

Smith, B., & Sataloff, R. (2013). Singing for a lifetime: Perpetuating intergenerational choirs. *Choral Journal, 53*(10), 16–25. http://acda.org

Southcott, J. E. (2009). "And as I go, I love to sing": The Happy Wanderers, music, and positive aging. *International Journal of Community Music, 2*(2–3), 143–156. doi: http://dx.doi.org/10.1386/ijcm.2.2-3.143_1

Travis, H. (2009). "Learning is a lifelong process". Western News Online Librairies. [Education Library Blog], https://www.lib.uwo.ca/blogs/education/2009/06/learning-is-a-lifelong-process.html. Accessed July 12 2014.

VanWeelden, K. (2002). On the voice: Working with the senior adult choir: Strategies and techniques for a lifetime of healthy singing. *Choral Journal, 43*(5), 61–69.

VanWeelden, K., & Walters, S. (2004). A survey of adult music practices: Implications for secondary general music classes. *General Music Today, 17*(2): 28–31. doi: http://dx.doi.org/10.1177/10483713040170020105

Waldron, J. (2008). Once the beat gets going it really grooves: Informal music learning as experienced by two Irish traditional musicians. *International Journal of Community Music, 1*(1), 89–103. DOI: http://dx.doi.org/10.1386/ijcm.1.1.89/0

Ware, C. (1998). *Basics of vocal pedagogy: The foundations and process of singing.* Boston, MA: McGraw Hill.

Wlodowski, R. (2008). Characteristics and skills of a motivating instructor. In R. Wlodowski (Ed.), *Enhancing adult motivation to learn: a comprehensive guide for teaching all adults* (3rd ed., pp. 49–94). San Francisco: Jossey-Bass.

Yinger, O. (2014). Adapting choral singing experiences for older adults: The implications of sensory, perceptual, and cognitive changes. *International Journal of Music Education, 32*(2), 203–212. doi: http://dx.doi.org/10.1177/0255761413508064

CHAPTER 20

"A DIFFERENT KIND OF GOOSE BUMP"

Notes Toward an LGBTQ Choral Pedagogy

CHARLES BEALE

"THERE's a different kind of goose-bump that you get singing with your tribe."

The worldwide LGBTQ (Lesbian, Gay, Bisexual, Transgender, Queer) choral movement is a vibrant and growing choral scene, featuring thousands of singers in hundreds of groups large and small, across almost all continents of the world. It is also a fascinating and unexplored research area that has the potential to reveal new questions, both for LGBTQ choral singing and for choral pedagogy as a whole.

Choral pedagogy may be seen as the teaching and learning of choral singing. Smith and Sataloff (2013, vii) see choral pedagogy as the union of five areas: choral conducting, musicianship, vocal knowledge, educational skills and leadership. Choral conducting is less of a focus here, but all the other areas are included at some point. Central to this chapter is the proposition that choral pedagogy does not exist independent of its social context; that any social context will have embedded in it a set of underlying values, which define why we sing and what is important about it; and that these values will inflect the teaching and learning of choral singing in different ways. The social context and values under discussion here are those of the LGBTQ movement.

LGBTQ choruses are one example of a group that has in common a minority characteristic, such as age, ethnicity or sexual orientation. Such minorities are by implication in some way excluded, "other," or "subaltern" (Gramsci, quoted in Spivak, 1988). For Spivak, the "subaltern" are also the oppressed, in choral singing perhaps the voiceless. For de Kock (1992) they are agents of social change, excluded from the hegemonic discourse. Examples of "subaltern" choruses might include: minority choruses of older people such as the Young@Heart Chorus of Western Massachusetts or the UK's The Zimmers; ethnic minority and faith-based choruses such as The London Community Gospel Choir or the Harlem Gospel Choir; or LGBTQ minority choruses, such as One Voice Mixed Chorus in Minnesota or the New York City Gay Men's Chorus. LGBTQ choruses not only contain members from their LGBTQ communities but also claim to represent them by telling their stories through song. All these groups challenge perceptions that the communities they represent are in some way disempowered. All have a strong conviction born from exclusion that their stories should be heard.

Two other well established and fertile fields of study are relevant to this topic. The first is Gender or Queer Studies, which, to simplify, begins from the premise that the linked but separate concepts of gender and sexuality are contingent, constructed, and based on false dualities. These dualities, such as gay/straight and man/woman, are seen as grounded in structures of language (Butler, 1990). The second is Queer Musicology, which grows from the theoretical frameworks of critical musicology, and seeks to identify the queer voice in music. It critiques canonicity and other conventional analytical and historical frameworks around musical texts and procedures, because they have tended to exclude minority composers, performers, and styles (Whiteley & Recenga, 2006; Brett, Wood, & Thomas, 2006). While noting both these fields as significant and from time to time touching on topics that fall within their purview, this chapter for reasons of space and clarity limits itself to the domain of choral pedagogy.

There is considerable fluidity from country to country and even from city to city around the use of the acronym LGBTQ (Lesbian, Gay, Bisexual, Transgender, Queer). Others include LGBT, LGBT+, LGBTI, GLBT, and LGBTQISS. The word "queer" is also emerging at the time of writing no longer as a term of abuse, but as a term that encompasses them all. Aware of the historical and current debates around these contested terms, for simplicity I shall be using the acronym "LGBTQ" as a shorthand throughout this chapter, to mean all singers and singer groups that identify as gender-and-sexuality-nonconforming. The terms "choir" and "chorus" are used interchangeably here to mean any group of singers.

Having defined our terms, we can move on to our central question. To what extent is the teaching and learning of choral singing in LGBTQ choruses unique? Does the social context of LGBTQ choruses set up the conditions for a distinctive set of values, and so to a distinctive LGBTQ choral pedagogy? One example of such a value is inclusion, the idea that an LGBTQ group should be a safe space, welcoming and inclusive to all. Put simply, some might observe a need for inclusion in LGBTQ choruses that could sometimes be in tension with the need for musical quality. This is because the need for musical quality requires the group to audition singers, and so at times to actively *exclude* them! Could this tension be evidence of a unique choral pedagogy, a new set of decisions affecting the way singers are selected, the way musical quality is defined, the way songs are taught, the definition of vocal knowledge, the leadership style of the director, and so on?

To approach this question, accounts from the literature on choral pedagogy and a number of related fields are analyzed in relation to two long semistructured interviews with singers from LGBTQ choruses. Accounts from both of these sources are also contextualized by my own personal observations, as a writer who has also been the director of two LGBTQ choruses for a combined total of 14 years. The two interviewee singers were chosen because their individual cases were likely to provide relevant and richer data on the topics in hand. Neither was necessarily representative of all LGBTQ singers, though, as it turned out, their interviews also revealed that they were more representative of the majority of LGBTQ singers than I had suspected. A more systematic piece of work would have used a larger sample, and I am aware that I excluded both men and straight people, among many others. Both singers were outliers, indeed minorities, even within LGBTQ singing—a female tenor in one of the major Gay Men's Choruses, and an MtF transgender alto in a mixed LGBTQ group. The interviews focused on what singing in an LGBTQ ensemble meant to that interviewee, and attempted to reveal how the choral pedagogy of their ensemble was inflected by their role as LGBTQ choruses. Neither requested complete anonymity, but the names of both have nevertheless been changed, to ensure a level of confidentiality. We begin with a short historical overview of the field.

A GROWING WORLD MOVEMENT

The LGBTQ movement started small and, like all change, local. The modern LGBTQ choral movement began in Philadelphia in North America, with the birth of Anna Crusis Women's Choir in 1975 (GALA Choruses website, 2014). San Francisco Gay Men's Chorus began soon after. Their US national tour of major cities in 1979 led within weeks to the establishment of a small network of large all-male choruses, around which the core of the movement gradually grew in the early 1980s. The first US National Gay and Lesbian Choral Festival was held in 1983, and the organization that formed for that festival soon became GALA Choruses, which now oversees the US LGBTQ choral movement and has run a four-yearly festival ever since. By 2012, the Denver GALA Festival hosted 6,100 singers and delegates, representing 112 performing choruses, mainly from the United States and Canada but including several from across the world. The vast majority of these choruses are community choirs, broadly TTBB, SSAA and SATB, with annual budgets of under US $50,000, but there are also some that consist of only 5–10 singers. A large handful of choruses number over 250 singers and have also become major nonprofits, with annual budgets of over $1 million, dedicated outreach programs, and teams of full-time staff. The movement continues to grow, as legal structures and attitudes change and the community becomes more visible. According to the current Artistic Director of GALA, 12 new US GALA choruses joined the organization during 2014, and new choruses also appeared in Mexico City and Havana, Cuba in the last 12–18 months.

A similar movement gradually formed in Europe, with the foundation of, for example, the London Gay Men's Chorus in 1991 and Paris's Melomen in 1994. Europe's equivalent organization to GALA Choruses is called Various Voices, which held its first festival in Groningen in 1995 (Legato-choirs.com, 2016). Again jumping forward to the present, the 2009 Various Voices Festival in London featured 76 choirs and around 2,800 paying participants, of whom the majority were from Germany (Fruitvox.org, 2009). The most recent 2014 Various Voices Festival in Dublin increased to 86 choirs, with around 3,400 paying participants. This Festival was cheaper to attend, but even so, this shows that, as in the United States, the European LGBTQ choral movement is healthy and growing at a rapid pace. More European groups are SATB, and ensembles and budgets tend to be smaller than in the United States, largely because the US philanthropic climate is more favorable and European ensembles are newer.

Similar movements are forming in Australasia and the Far East, starting, predictably, in major cities. There are major choruses in Sydney, Melbourne, Canberra, Western Australia and Brisbane, and several in New Zealand, including GALS in Auckland and the Glamaphones in Wellington. "QTas" began in 2013 and is the newest Australasian choir from Hobart, Tasmania. Asian choruses have been emerging since the late '90s. The opening ceremony of the 2002 Gay Games in Sydney featured a single Asian chorus—Hiraya, from the Philippines. At the time of writing, the Proud Voices Asia website lists 10 Asian LGBTQ-identified choruses in Japan alone, some of professional quality, and other choruses in Beijing, Manila, Singapore, Seoul, Taipei, and Pattaya. If proof of significant progress in LGBTQ visibility were needed, the Proud Voices website also says that new (and courageous) choruses are emerging in Shanghai and Tianjin. This is an exciting time in the LGBTQ chorus world, and there is much to sing about.

THE PURPOSE OF SINGING

Inclusion, and an ecology of belonging

LGBTQ people have been excluded from the mainstream throughout history, and have fought since the late 1960s for the fundamental human rights to be visible, to love, to marry, to be protected under the law. It is perhaps no surprise, then, that the inclusion and sense of community that singers of all backgrounds feel in a choral group is something especially important to LGBTQ singers. Choral groups, it turns out, have a unique function in the LGBTQ community, as a safe space and a place of deep belonging.

If you asked singers in the two LGBTQ choruses the author has directed why they sing, 70%–80% would say "because these are my friends" or "this is my chosen family." The concept came up multiple times in both interviews. First, here is Francis, an LGBTQ choral singer of several years' experience:

> [My father] used to go to barbershop chorus every Monday night, and it was his community. . . . I suddenly realized I was going to my community on a Monday night, and it was quite similar. . .
>
> Minority communities look for opportunities to be with one another, right? . . . because they feel welcome, they feel like they belong. . .
>
> I wanted something else . . . that uniqueness, that 'club'ness, that lack of external judgment that certain minorities . . . feel from the world around them. . . there's a different kind of goose-bump that you get singing with your tribe. . .

People take the time, there is much more of a sense of care and compassion and empathy for one another, that I would guess is not part and parcel of what you would see in other choruses . . .

Likewise Jennifer, an MtF transgender woman and a relative newcomer to this world, reported:

There's just a great . . . sense of camaraderie, just by virtue of the fact that we are in this LGBTI part of the community . . . It's just great for all of us just to have somewhere where we know we are on even terms with everyone else . . .

[It was] such a disparate group of people . . . and everyone . . . there just wasn't an ounce of friction anywhere . . . in a group of people, you'd expect someone to rub someone up the wrong way. . . It's just a friendly group . . .

It was clear that everyone had a real level of comfort in being with people who have experienced similar things . . . either prejudices or just concerns . . . about how the so-called normal part of the community sees them. . .

It's not just having the group that you know and a place where you can go and be perfectly comfortable in yourself but . . . there's also a very real possibility that there'll be a genuine friend that you'll add to your circle of friends that already exists.

Jennifer also noted that socializing almost became too important in rehearsals:

we actually have had discussions about . . . we need to have someone to get up, when we have a break half way through . . . and say, "Right you lot, shut up and get back in your chairs!" . . . because everyone is getting on so well on a social basis. . . [laughs]

Here the interviewees are representative of the majority of LGBTQ singers. Their singing embodies and facilitates for them a vitally important fellowship. This fellowship takes place via the ad hoc conversations, dating opportunities, lifelong friendships, partnerships, and marriages that happen around it. Members of these groups are each other's "chosen family," and many in my chorus would rather spend major holidays such as Thanksgiving and Christmas with other chorus members than with their biological families. A number have been rejected by their families, but many more feel merely tolerated, or in some lesser way not entirely comfortable. This almost church-like feeling of belonging creates a solidarity, a teamwork, an ownership, and a sense of purpose that binds the musical processes of the ensemble together.

Turning now to choral pedagogy and especially to leadership, the role of the director becomes almost that of a church pastor, empowered to create the safe space and facilitate that sense of belonging, as well as direct a rehearsal. S/he explains and models the values underlying the social behavior in the room as well as teaching the songs. At times, if there is a marriage or a death in the chorus, it can become the director's role to use the singing to facilitate the community's celebrations or remembrances. At other times, the director can simply share personal stories about her or his own life, and lead other non-singing activities that bring the group together. The director guards and communicates the values as well as managing the singing, and the two reflect each other. Excellent musician colleagues of mine have even been fired from groups for failing to communicate or embody a group's values in this way.

Little has been written specifically from the LGBTQ or other minority perspective about the especially deep feeling of belonging felt by members of these groups. However, literature from the related field of community music strongly supports the existence of this general phenomenon. Small (2008) famously opened the door to the theory of community music with his concept of "musicking," and more recently, Hayes (2007) also sees LGBTQ choral singing as a form of community music. Higgins (2009, 2012) covers a huge selection of community music activity across the world, large and small—everything from at risk teenager groups to massive community samba bands, while Woodward and Pestano (2013) and Deane, Dawson, & McCab (2012) also write about community music programs for the marginalized. Higgins always focuses on the way in which the musical activity brings individuals, communities, performers, and audiences together.

Perhaps the most fascinating phenomenon is the way in which members, audiences, and directors alike experience musical processes and community processes as intertwined, even interchangeable. Though not explicitly discussing LGBTQ choruses, Ansdell (2010) summarizes this aptly:

> The group is performing for their organization, and to people from their local community ... As Christopher Small (1998) puts it, the group is performing not just the music, or themselves, but a whole ecology of relationships: to each other, to their context, to their culture and its many complexities and conflicts. They are creating community [sic] through their musical performance. Equally the audience... doesn't just sit there and listen: they join in. During and afterwards, there are congratulations, but also an advanced sense of connection and belonging for all involved. (2010, p. 37)

Music facilitates community and integrates members by giving them the song as a common purpose. The music also embodies that integration, through, for example, the sense of listening, the blending of voices, and the unity of the rhythm.

Turning now to writing about choral singing, "fellowship" is also a key finding noted by Langston and Barrett (2008) in their study of what they call "social capital" in a community choir. Likewise, in their campaign for "A Choir in Every Care home" SoundSense a leading UK community music provider and research organization, concludes on their 2016 website that "Singing can lift spirits, but it can also do so much more. There is now hard evidence to show that music participation can help those living with dementia to engage and remember; and more generally, alleviate the effects of breathing diseases; reduce stress and anxiety; and build relationships between residents, carers and staff."

Chorus America's 2009 study of the benefits of choral singing notes that it has a direct impact on team-building, the social skills of singers, and community participation. Of gospel singing, Davis (2013) acknowledges the same ability of music to pull a minority and oppressed ethnic community together:

> Gospel music is largely synonymous with Christian churches, specifically those where the membership is predominantly African American. This music is the tenure of the African American community who filled it with history and tradition. (2013, p. 6)

It would be a truism to state that most musical activity and choral singing fosters a sense of community. My observation here is that community and inclusion is an *especially* central value for members of these minority or "subaltern" choruses. For many LGBTQ members, community and inclusion are the very reason these choruses exist and this creates a unique social context, an ecology of belonging, which is expressed both through the musical practices and procedures and through the verbal language and other behavior of the group. Relationship and music unify as a single integrated phenomenon.

Activism

The second unique feature of the social context of LGBTQ choral groups is that members and ensembles often see themselves as activist. Choirs advocate for political change through their singing, and the music functions as a tool for expressing the values of the group and for changing hearts and minds. As we shall see, this activism varies in level and type much more than inclusion does. Singers and directors can take a variety of positions in relation to the activist function of their groups, but all are aware of the issue.

Jennifer's quieter activism takes the form of simply being visible:

> From a personal point of view, I am not a radical... But I like to make sure I'm seen, so that more people will just see that [this] clearly transgender person... doesn't look like Dame Edna Everage, does ordinary things... and hopefully just defuse the misconceptions that I think most people have... about certainly male-to-female transgender people. I'm not sure about the rest of the choir, I think there's a feeling of... yeah, getting out there... and just doing something that people can enjoy. And if you do something that they enjoy, then they tend not to dislike you [laughs] ... or tend to lose what misgivings they might have had.

By contrast, Francis sees her chorus as having a much deeper impact on the listener's attitudes and on society as a whole: "The chorus has the ability to be highly political... highly political... because you tell a story... that actually has the ability to affect someone's heart and mind." Indeed, Francis was initially critical of her chorus, because she felt the community emphasis of the group was much more evident than its political agenda:

> It seemed very social to me... which was fine... [but] I was surprised at the degree to which members were uninformed about the LGBT movement landscape... There

was a lack of knowledge and understanding about the players in the movement. . . they certainly would have called it an LGBT organization but I don't think that they would . . . label themselves politically active.

For her, high musical quality is key to effective activism:

Now, did I want gay people to be turned down? Not really. But at the same time, I want my audience who is hearing a message, not to just hear the message but to hear the message from a blue chip chorus.

This need for effective activism through singing can lead to a further tension between a need for "blue chip" musical quality and that all-important LGBTQ need for inclusion. Auditions can be a particular bone of contention. Some choruses, including for example the London Gay Men's Chorus or the Miami Gay Men's Chorus, especially value inclusion. No audition takes place. Instead, members are voice-tested and all can sing in the group. In rehearsal, the pedagogy of mixed ability is more likely here. More and less advanced members will sing side by side for much of the time, while extra challenges are given to more experienced singers and extra support offered, voluntarily or compulsorily, to others. Programming in these choruses is more likely to include material at a range of difficulty levels too, so that everyone can excel.

By contrast, others do audition, excluding, in some cases, over 50% of applicants. Even so, many of these auditioning groups explicitly state in their missions that they see themselves as representing the LGBTQ members in their cities. The 2014 iteration of the website of Seattle Mens' Chorus stated in the FAQ that:

Members of the chorus are representative of the large community in which we live in [*sic*]. Members range in age, size, color, profession, background and outside interests. Both singing and associate members share a common vision—a world that accepts and values its gay and lesbian citizens.

Others will explicitly prioritize musical quality over the values of both activism and inclusion, and can be even more competitive to get into. Golden Gate Men's Chorus in San Francisco is one example of this, describing itself, like any other non-LGBTQ choral group, as:

Committed to excellence and joyous music-making; providing a supportive and nurturing atmosphere for our members' artistic and social self-expression; and sharing and expanding the rich and continuing tradition of male choral music.

The all-important elements of inclusion and a sense of belonging are present here, but they are more in the background. Likewise, as with Jennifer's group, political activism, is hardly explicit at all.

Repertoire and Programming

Sometimes LGBTQ, but not always

From the varied approach to activism identified in the previous section, one would assume that a similarly varied approach would also appear in LGBTQ chorus programming, and it seems this is the case. Jennifer's group, for example, has its own broadly progressive artistic strategy, but she was at pains to emphasize that they do not always explicitly foreground LGBTQ issues. There is "a lot of original material" along with "original arrangements of classics" or "familiar tunes with a bit of a twist." Her group also see themselves as "giving voice to local writers . . . not necessarily on an LGBTI theme." When I asked whether there was nevertheless a particular political slant to the messages that the group sent out in its programs, she responded:

> I suppose we are largely but not entirely left of center politically. . . but only in terms of sensitivity to . . . environmental issues and . . . obviously gay rights issues and . . . probably women's issues as well . . . It's not something that we push, but it's clear that that's where the leaning of most of the choir is at. . . . It's not exclusive, there are a couple on the other side . . . certainly right of center.

For her, their programming is little different from that of the non-LGBTQ identified all-male chorus that she sang in before. Instead, their sole claim to LGBTQ uniqueness lies in their very presence: "No, I think just being there is our one claim to any uniqueness . . . Our being there as a symbol of the LGBTI community."

By contrast, Francis was very clear about the uniqueness of her LGBTQ chorus's repertoire and programming. Indeed, she felt it needed an explicitly LGBTQ component:

> "With the chorus, yes, I believe part of its mission is to communicate a message through its music . . . The goose-bumpiest songs to sing . . . were songs that were universal in nature, that went . . . that spoke to me as a member of the LGBT community in some really profound way . . . And not always in a . . . not always in a "beat you over the head" kind of way.

In a recent performance, her chorus had performed a piece that drew parallels between the oppression of the LGBTQ community and the oppression of the Jews. She felt that the piece was especially successful because it built "a bridge between that straight Jewish person in the audience and the two hundred and some odd member LGBT chorus . . . and . . . to me the repertoire at its best includes those moments."

We can again observe here the tension in LGBTQ groups between musical quality and activism, but this time expressed through repertoire choice. Some take the more mainstream route by choosing repertoire that is "purely musical"—that is at the right level, that entertains an audience, and that creates beautiful sound. Others choose repertoire that will educate an audience about LGBTQ issues, and that communicates an activist message. This tension seems to occur from beginner groups right up to those at semipro and pro levels.

What a song means—Stylistic diversity and heteronormative "re-use"

A song's meaning is often especially important to the singers in an LGBTQ chorus. Indeed, even if a song is audience friendly and fits with the theme of a show, members will sometimes refuse to sing it if it is not congruent with their personal, political, or religious beliefs. While this can clash with a director's artistic vision, this connection members feel to the programming can make the art of an LGBTQ chorus especially compelling to audiences, because it becomes evident in performance that the programming resonates or does not resonate with members' values. For example, while the Western tradition of Christian church music is massively important within the history of choral singing, songs with Christian connotations are sometimes excluded completely in LGBTQ contexts, because they are seen as homophobic. Other LGBTQ singers will feel very much at home in this repertoire. Some will take a less explicitly political and more spiritual position on what the song means, while others may choose to ignore any oppression they read into the music. Either way, the meaning of a Christian religious song in an LGBTQ context can fundamentally change.

A related phenomenon is the way in which a song can change meaning depending on the context in which it is sung, or where it sits in a program. One simple example would be Rodgers and Hammerstein's "We kiss in the shadow," which takes on new and darker meaning sung by an LGBTQ group unable to kiss in the light. To give another more extensive and necessarily personal example, the statistic in our city recently was that 68% of new HIV infections come from a primary or regular partner, someone we are especially close to. So my chorus programmed Beyoncé's "Crazy in Love" into a performance about living with HIV/AIDS, to highlight the "crazy" decisions some of us make about safer sex in the throes of passion. We used Morten Lauridsen's gorgeous "Sure on this Shining Night" at a later point in the same show, at the moment where a very sick and possibly dying HIV positive man faces the prospect of death, comes to terms with it, and is at peace. We felt these songs fitted together because of the unique LGBTQ purpose of the singing. These are of course personal and anecdotal data, and at every performance, all choirs and audiences construct a new performance and necessarily read fresh meaning into songs. Nevertheless, the LGBTQ purpose and context led directly to distinctive repertoire choices, to a distinctive program order that would have made no sense elsewhere, and to a distinctiveness in the vocal pedagogy required.

Beyoncé's "Crazy in Love" leads us on to stylistic diversity in LGBTQ choral singing. A number of factors are already influencing all choral directors to program in a wider range of musical styles. In the past 70 years, fundamental changes have taken place in the way mainstream choral music is produced, presented, and consumed. Since the advent of TV and radio in the 1930s and '40s, most music has often been a mass-produced, electronically mediated product (Middleton, 1990; Shuker, 1994; Frith, 1996), dominated by record companies and more recently social media platforms like YouTube, SoundCloud, and Vimeo. The role of web-based audio and video in recent years has also led to vast changes in musical tastes and a much-decreased role for live music generally. This has had its effect on choral publishing and choral repertoire, so that more popular music, jazz, musical theater and non-Western musics appear in choral programs of all kinds. Similar trends have also influenced how audiences expect singers to sound, through, for example, the use of microphones and amplification, changes in venue style and sound, and so on.

Maclachlan (2015) is currently the major piece of research on the topic of the distinctiveness of LGBTQ choral repertoire. Working mostly from interviews with choral directors, she proposes a definition with regard to GALA chorus (US-based) repertoire, consisting of three categories: '"works (commissioned pieces), appropriated mainstream works (community songs), and re-used mainstream works." On the subject of "re-using," she quotes David Halperin, who concludes *How To Be Gay* by offering the following definition of gay culture:

> [It] can refer to new works of literature, film, music, art, drama, dance and performance that are produced by queer people and that reflect on queer experience. Gay culture can also refer to mainstream works created mostly by heterosexual artists, plus some (closeted) ones, that queer people have selectively appropriated and re-used for anti-heteronormative purposes. (2012, p. 421)

My chorus was in that sense "re-using" the Beyoncé and the Lauridsen.

Whether or not a chorus identifies as LGBTQ, it can of course still specialize in repertoire in any style. At Various Voices 2014, for example, Dublin's major LGBTQ ensemble "Gloria" opened its set very conventionally (and beautifully) with Mozart's *Ave Verum*—they sing more mainstream or "standard" choral repertoire. By contrast, the US Columbus Gay Men's Chorus is known for its spectacular authentic renditions of popular music, complete with costumes and choreography. Lavender Light Gospel Choir in New York City is famous for its commitment to the upholding the tradition of gospel music in a praise context for the LGBTQ community. In addition, Maclachlan is right that US LGBTQ choruses are known for commissioning many new works from major (often white male) contemporary composers, including John Corigliano, Morten Lauridsen and Stephen Schwartz.

Finally, Jennifer identifies in her account a different but related tension between the needs of the audience and the needs of the members: "What do the guys want to sing, but what do I really want people to hear?" she asks. In my group, there is hot debate among the "guys" between, on the one hand, a feeling that we should sing "meaningful" songs about current issues, such as marriage equality or teen bullying, and on the other, simply singing songs "for their own sake." Members also enjoy repertoire that entertains them or is fun to learn, and I often program songs that I know will appeal to certain age groups of singers. Even so, a program that perfectly pleases our more invested membership may not necessarily also entertain or educate our audience members.

To summarize, what we have here is a rich and varied picture. Directors must often negotiate a distinctive path between more mainstream and more activism-minded members and audiences. Programming and repertoire choice are sometimes inflected by an activist intent in LGBTQ choruses, and by a uniquely strong sense of ownership over the repertoire sung. The data also reveals the need for some to sing songs that raise awareness of LGBTQ issues but that also resonate outside the community. This varies too, however, and other artistic strategies that have more in common with mainstream choruses are also in evidence—some sing standard repertoire or have other progressive artistic goals. A unique tension is revealed between the need to entertain and educate the LGBTQ singers in the group, and the need to entertain and educate a wider audience. Depending on the level of inclusion, an LGBTQ ensemble is also more likely to contain a wider range of singer experience and voice type than its mainstream equivalent, and this can affect repertoire choice. Some LGBTQ choruses have specialized successfully in particular areas of the choral repertoire, gay and non-gay. As Maclachlan (2014) notes, LGBTQ groups may not necessarily perform repertoire that is in itself distinctive, but when they do sing mainstream repertoire, it often changes meaning, is "re-used" and becomes "anti-heteronormative" because of the LGBTQ social context.

Vocal Technique and Resonance

We now move on to vocal sound itself, for many the heart of choral pedagogy, and here it is impossible to avoid the relationship between voice and gender. Francis sang tenor very successfully in a large, high-level all-male LGBTQ chorus for several years. An experienced singer, a key word for her was "blend":

> I found myself thinking that being a part of the chorus was going to force me to blend . . . it was going to FORCE me to blend . . . that it was going to stretch my ability to be an integral part of the community . . . and . . . that was critical to whether or not I was good at it . . . That said, it was for me in a lot of ways totally the best of both worlds, because I DID stick out . . . like I was able to stick out and stretch the blending muscles at the same time.

And later she defined the nature of her challenge with considerable self-awareness:

> I thought that my being able to blend as a singer was something I had never been able to do very well, and I didn't know if that was my ego . . . I didn't know if I just didn't *want* to blend . . . and I thought that this would be a very interesting way to explore that.

For her, the skills of choral "blend" relate directly to her ability to "blend" or "stick out" socially within the community of the group. Identifying as a lesbian woman, she sets herself the considerable challenge of gender "blending" too, as the only woman in a group of over 200 men. Gendered and community meanings specific to the LGBTQ context are articulated here through the musical process. Most crucially, it is this exploration of her social "blending" skills that is the driver for her being in the chorus at all.

Our other interviewee, Jennifer, used to be a tenor when she identified as a man in her previous all-male choir. Having now started her transition, she decided, in collaboration with her director, to sing alto in her LGBTQ one. She found it a challenge:

> It's proving pretty ... difficult ... [our] MD has a different approach to breathing and that's helping ... I can hit higher notes, but having control ... being able to run a sequence ... of those higher notes together is taking some work, shall we say ... It's just as well we live out in the country [laughs] ... If the little app on my phone is correct, I did hit a top D last week, but it did sound like a goose flying overhead [laughs].

That said, it was crucially important to her to continue:

> Now that I've made my bed, I want to continue lying in it until it's time someone comes up to me and says, "You are a complete waste of space, go back to the tenors!" [laughs]

Interestingly, her director continues to support her in this, both by providing singing lessons and allowing her to sing in the altos:

> She says, "Well, actually I'd like you to try moving up there now, because when the altos get into a lower part of their range, they might lose a bit of puff, and you're coming right into the heart of" ... the strength of my voice. ...She sees that as a little something to add to the choir so I'm ... as I say, I quite like a challenge.

Her director also takes a much looser approach to assigning a voice part than many would, both within the LGBTQ community and outside it: "She has let people find their own level ... let people have a bit of a go at it."

While there is some writing on the transgender voice in general (Adler, Hirsch, & Mordaunt, 2012; Seeley, 2007), the transgender singing voice has not so far received much attention. The nearest work of use is the writing of Cooksey and others, who in the 1980s and 1990s kickstarted a well known and seminal wave of systematic research on the changing adolescent voice. Harries, Griffith, Walker, and Hawkins (1996) and others significantly moved forward the debate on how the voice changes at the onset of puberty. Cooksey's 1999 book on the adolescent voice remains a standard for teachers, because, for example, it identifies clear stages in the process and offers practical advice. Especially useful in this gender nonconforming context, Cooksey also points out that teenage girls' voices can change too, as does Gackle (2006). Questions remain on many transgender voice issues, including, for example, whether the changing adolescent voice is in fact an analogue of FtM transgender change; the exact effect of hormones on the transgender male singing voice later in life; and vocal strategies for the transgender woman.

The transgender singing voice is increasingly a hot topic within the LGBTQ choral movement at the time of writing. From my own discussions with directors, best practice, as with Jennifer, is to work on a case-by-case basis. It is often best to place transgender members in their voice part on the basis of their actual vocal range. This is not only more practical and vocally comfortable and makes for better blend, but also facilitates a useful rethink of a simplistic relationship between gender and voice part generally. Some choirs with trans singers rename the vocal parts, and others configure them in a range of ways, to make those with narrower or wider ranges more vocally comfortable. Voice testing more often is advisable as transition continues. It is also worth differentiating between the FtM and MtF experiences. Conventionally, the FtM transition is accompanied by hormone therapy that effectively takes the soprano or alto voice down in pitch by changing the nature and thickness of the vocal folds. This is much easier for the choral director or vocal coach to negotiate with the singer, because the journey is, at least in some ways, similar to that of the changing male voice. It is also easier for the singer concerned, who can often end up with extra flexibility vocally that they did not have before. With the MtF transition, no similar change in the vocal instrument itself can happen to aid the process. The results, as Jennifer found, can be unpredictable and can fit less well within the SATB framework. Where the voice lands in its sound and pitch range is also dependent on many factors, including previous voice part, age, and level of vocal technique.

Here a gender-nonconforming choral pedagogy is badly needed, and would be useful to transgender singers in choirs of all kinds. Our growing awareness of trans people's needs presents a challenge to choral director trainers, very often schooled largely or solely in the vocal production techniques (and gender roles) of common-practice classical and church music from 18th to 20th centuries, or what I am labeling mainstream choral pedagogy. The issue of how to define a single good vocal resonance or technique for choral singers is thorny in all choral pedagogy, and as with repertoire, the mainstream is changing. For example, with regard only to higher men's voices, there are now many models to choose from of real excellence and refinement, including Freddie Mercury in the popular music realm, Bobbie McFerrin in jazz, and Andreas Scholl in early music. The vocal resonance and articulation techniques used by Take 6, for example, are strikingly different from those of The Sixteen, but are, I would argue, no less accomplished. In the Broadway/musical theater realm too, there are subgenres of vocal technique now circulating in New York City, relating to classic Broadway (Rodgers and Hammerstein), modern Broadway (Sondheim, Bernstein) and contemporary Broadway (*Book of Mormon, Rent*). Core repertoire for LGBTQ choruses in recent years is more likely to include songs like the 2011 Lady Gaga hit "Born This Way", Pitch Perfect's "Bella's Finals" or Judy Garland's "Somewhere Over the Rainbow." Such a range of repertoire demands a range of approaches to vocal resonance.

There is not the space for an in-depth analysis of these issues. Even so, it is possible to observe two phenomena relating to "good" vocal technique. First, mainstream choral singing increasingly includes a wider range of musical styles, and new models of vocal resonance are necessarily taking root in mainstream choral pedagogy, to enable safe and enjoyable singing in these styles. This wider range is also being reflected in LGBTQ choral singing. In addition, some of the stylistic diversity evident in LGBTQ groups may be unique to the context, though more research is needed. Second, the LGBTQ community is increasingly campaigning for the visibility of transgender and other gender-nonconforming people. This new visibility for trans singers is forcing directors to rethink key areas of their work.

Towards a LGBTQ Choral Pedagogy

So far, our premise has been to identify two separate mainstream and LGBTQ social contexts. Of course, LGBTQ people live in the mainstream too, so it would be more accurate to see these two contexts as overlapping. I and my colleagues were mostly trained in mainstream choirs, and have lived out the tension between these overlapping contexts since our movement began over 40 years ago. Over time, our goal is surely to integrate them.

It is clear that the needs of singers from LGBTQ choruses are not always being met by current solutions. While the best mainstream choral pedagogy will meet many of their needs (and is itself being challenged from within), it is unlikely to meet them all. Directing an LGBTQ group definitely involves a specific and different set of skills and understandings, both of the inclusive and activist values that motivate and underpin the musical processes, and of how those values impact musical and educational decisions in practice.

As transgender singers become more visible, all choral directors need these special-ist skills. Whatever choir she is in, gay or straight, Jennifer deserves the opportunity to "blend" without sounding like a tenor in the alto section. Her choral experience should be an accepting and happy one, and her director should have the analytical tools and teaching strategies to include her, and to help her to contribute and grow within the ensemble. It would be relatively simple, for example, to build a deeper understanding of the MtF and FtM transgender voice into all choral curricula, to establish it as an exciting area of current research and to gradually loosen the link between gender and voice part.

Further exciting research questions follow, some within choral pedagogy and some outside it. What would a truly inclusive and activist choral curriculum look like? What exactly is the balance of repertoire LGBTQ choirs use? How commonplace are the vocal issues identified here? How do we teach the leadership skills required? To what extent are these issues occurring in mainstream choral contexts too, and how are they dealt with currently? As many (but not all) countries have gradually become more accepting, how has this influenced the growth and artistic activity of LGBTQ ensembles? What were their goals when they began, and, as some enter their 40th season, how have they changed over time? What political impact have they really had, and what are the processes through which this has occurred? Above all, what can mainstream choruses learn from the their LGBTQ brothers and sisters, and vice versa?

Whether you are convinced that choral pedagogy is inflected by its social context or not, this research reveals some fundamental truths that all choral directors will recognize. Singing is a deep need within all of us, a force for the good that can transform the lives of singers, and lead to their personal growth and empowerment. In addition, singing is a means by which all of us, gay or straight, can articulate who we are and what we believe to the wider world. My insight is that the LGBTQ community understands these truths especially well. It is leading the way with an artistic vitality, a poised radicalism and a spiritual life force grounded in these truths, that I am convinced will help drive the whole choral singing movement forward in coming decades.

We sing not because we want to, but because we need to. This need, communicated through song, inspires our audiences to feel and think differently, and gives our performances purpose, relevance and joy. As Francis put it:

> LGBT people live in a world that is filled with dissonance, right? . . . And to come together and sing, and to hear . . . the complete lack of that [dissonance] . . . where everything just totally fits, and it sounds so beautiful . . . I bet there is something in that. We are the outliers, we are the ones that don't fit in . . . and to be in a place where you fit in, and is very harmonious is, I think, probably, interesting.

REFERENCES

Adler R. K., Hirsch, S., & Mordaunt, M. (2012). *Voice and communication therapy for the transgender/transsexual client: A comprehensive clinical guide.* San Diego, CA: Plural.

Ansdell, G. (2010). Action musicking on the edge: Musical minds in East London, England. In S. Brynjulf, G. Ansdell, C. Elefant, & M. Pavlicevic (Eds.), *Where music helps: Community music therapy in action and reflection* (pp. 33–40). Farnham, UK: Ashgate.

Brett, P., Wood, E., & Thomas, G. C. (2006). *Queering the pitch: The new gay and lesbian musicology.* (2nd ed.). New York: Routledge.

Butler, J. (1990). *Gender trouble.* New York: Routledge.

Chorus America (2009). The chorus impact study: How children, adults and communities benefit from choruses. Retrieved from https://www.chorusamerica.org/publications/research-reports/chorus-impact-study

Cooksey, John M. (1999). *Working with adolescent voices.* Saint Louis MO: Concordia.

Davis, G. A. (2013). *Fundamentals of an anointed gospel choir.* Oakland, CA: Director's Desk Publishing.

Deane K., Dawson E., & McCab, A. (2012). *The heroes inside: Building communities in community choirs.* Retrieved from Sound Sense website: http://www.soundsense.org/metadot/index.pl?id=28474&isa=Category&op=show

de Kock, L. (1992). Interview with Gayatri Chakravorty Spivak: New nation writers conference in South Africa. *ARIEL: A Review of International English Literature, 23*(3), 29–47. Retrieved from http://ariel.synergiesprairies.ca/ariel/index.php/ariel/article/viewFile/2505/2458.

Frith, S. (1996). *Performing rites: On the value of popular music.* Oxford: Oxford University Press.

Fruitvox. (2009). Various voices: London sings out! 2009 Evaluation. Retrieved from http://fruitvox.org/vvl2009/evaluation/

GALA Choruses (2014). History. Retrieved from http://www.galachoruses.org/about/history

Gackle, L. (2006). Finding Ophelia's voice: the female voice during adolescence. *The Choral Journal, 47*(5), 28–37.

Halperin, D.M. (2012). *How to be gay.* Cambridge: The Belknap Press of Harvard University Press.

Harries M., Griffith M., Walker J., and Hawkins, S. (1996) Changes in the male voice during puberty: speaking and singing voice parameters. *Logopedics Phonatrics Vocology, 21* (2), 95–100.

Hayes, C. (2007). Community music and the GLBT chorus. *International Journal of Community Music, 1*(1): 63–68.

Higgins, L. (2009). Representing practices: Community music and arts-based research. *Proceedings of the International Society for Music Education Conference.* Retrieved from https://yorksj.academia.edu/LeeHiggins

Higgins, L. (2012). *Community music: In theory and practice.* New York: Oxford University Press.

Langston T. W., & Barrett M. S. (2008). Capitalising on community music: A case study of the manifestation of social capital in a community choir. *Research Studies in Music Education, 30*(2), 118–138.

MacLachlan, H. (2015). Sincerity and Irony in the "Gay" music of GALA choruses. *Journal of American Culture, 38*(2), 89

Middleton R. (1990). *Studying popular music.* Philadelphia: Open University Press.

Proud Voices Asia. (2014). The choirs. Retrieved from http://asia.proudvoices.org/

Seeley, J. (2007). *The transgender companion (male to female): The complete guide to becoming the woman you want to be.* CreateSpace.

Shuker, R. (1994). *Understanding popular music.* London: Routledge.

Small, C. (1998). *Musicking: The meanings of performing and listening.* Hanover, NH: University Press of New England.

Smith B., & Sataloff, R. T. (2013). *Choral pedagogy.* (3rd ed.). San Diego: Plural.

Spivak, G. C. (1988). Can the subaltern speak? In C. Nelson & L. Grossberg (Eds.), *Marxism and the interpretation of culture* (pp. 271–313). Urbana: University of Illinois Press.

Various Voices. (2014). About. Retrieved from http://www.legato-choirs.com/variousvoices

Woodward, S., & Pestano, C. (2013). Marginalized communities: Reaching those falling outside socially accepted norms. In K. Veblen, S. J. Messenger, M. Silverman, & D. J. Elliot. *Community music today.* London: Rowman and Littlefield.

Whiteley, S., & Rycenga, J. (2006). *Queering the popular pitch.* New York: Routledge.

....

CHAPTER 21

THE INCLUSION CONUNDRUM AND COMMUNITY CHILDREN'S CHOIRS IN CANADA

....

DEBORAH BRADLEY

CANADA has established an international identity as a racially and culturally diverse society that prides itself on acceptance of difference. Since the nation's first policy of official multiculturalism was enacted in 1971, educational organizations, including many of Canada's community children's choirs, have sought to promote cultural diversity. Early attempts focused primarily on repertoire, and from today's cultural understanding may seem not only naive but also trivializing, and in some respects, colonizing. However, these initial attempts were congruent with the original goals for Canadian multiculturalism, which focused primarily on diversity of language, customs, and religion.

Over time, Canada's understandings of multiculturalism matured, eventually leading to the enactment of the Canadian Multiculturalism Act in 1988. This law broadened the perspective on multiculturalism to one that seeks in part to:

- Promote the full and equitable participation of individuals and communities of all origins in the continuing evolution and shaping of all aspects of Canadian society and assist them in the elimination of any barrier to that participation;
- Recognize the existence of communities whose members share a common origin and their historic contribution to Canadian society, and enhance their development;
- Ensure that all individuals receive equal treatment and equal protection under the law, while respecting and valuing their diversity;
- Encourage and assist the social, cultural, economic and political institutions of Canada to be both respectful and inclusive of Canada's multicultural character (*Canadian Multiculturalism Act*, 1988, Section 3.1).

George Dei (2000) describes Canadian multiculturalism as "a political doctrine officially promoting cultural diversity as an intrinsic component of the social, political and moral order" (p. 21). Children's choirs often view themselves as organizations that may be influential in developing both the social and moral orders within their memberships. Although not legally bound by the Canadian Multiculturalism Act, many choirs strive to promote the ideals articulated in that legislation.

The language of the Canadian Multiculturalism Act, along with the multicultural discourses that have emerged since the first act of 1971, encouraged those interested in social justice in community music groups to find ways to be more inclusive[1]. In some cases this involved singing a more diverse musical repertoire, and striving to make their memberships more diverse racially and culturally. Among children's choirs, efforts expanded to recruit singers who could reflect Canada's racial and cultural diversity.

While a few children's and youth choir organizations have successfully recruited singers representing the diversity of their local communities, more than 25 years since the passing of the Canadian Multiculturalism Act, other choirs continue to attract predominantly White memberships, despite their efforts to the contrary. Oftentimes, initial recruitment is successful, but the retention of culturally diverse members fails. One sees this in the obvious diversity of many organizations' entry-level choirs; yet the makeup of the most senior level groups in these organizations visually tells the story of the attrition of children of color (Gurgle, 2013; Gustafson, 2008). This paper seeks to explore "the inclusion conundrum"—tensions experienced by community children's choirs in Canada in attempts to achieve racial and cultural diversity within their memberships. The paper begins with a brief history of multiculturalism in Canada. I next explore the notion of children's choirs as "White space," focusing on membership fees and bursary assistance plans, as well as the role of repertoire in recruiting and retaining diverse memberships. The final section of the paper interrogates our "terminal naivety" (Vaugeois, 2013) related to issues of race and class that emerged during colonial rule, and recommends a course of action that may begin to make children's choirs in Canada truly inclusive.

Canadian Multiculturalism

A brief history of multiculturalism in Canada

While it is beyond the scope of this paper to describe in detail Canada's path to becoming an officially multicultural nation, a brief background about Canada's policies of multiculturalism provides a backdrop for the issues explored herein. Canada's first settlers were aboriginal peoples, who have lived on "Canadian soil" for at least 12,000 years ("First Peoples of Canada," 2007). Following the first voyage of Columbus to North America in 1492, Europeans began to explore the eastern coastal areas of Canada. The French came and settled in Nova Scotia, PEI, Newfoundland, New Brunswick and

Quebec. The British made various attempts to settle in Canada, but met with little success, establishing only some fishing stations in Newfoundland. The founding of the Hudson Bay Company in 1670, however, enabled the British to establish fur trading posts, ultimately moving north to Nova Scotia from the 13 colonies to the south. Friction between England and France in the 1600s eventually led to war, and territory within Canada continued to be contested until the defeat of the French at the battle of the Plains of Abraham (Quebec City) in 1759 ("Canada History," 2013). Although Canada was from this point forward "officially British," both French and English language and culture became (after much struggle) foundational to the project of nation building. However, Canada did not adopt the "two official languages" policy of English and French until 1968 (http://www.canadahistory.com/sections/documents/Primeministers/trudeau/docs-officiallanguagesact.htm).

The vast Canadian geography necessitated increasing its population rapidly in order to manage the expansive territory. This was accomplished through immigration, which since the time of Canadian Confederation in 1867 has been an important factor in the makeup both of Canada's population and its national culture. The earliest immigrants were predominantly from Europe, a trend that continued through the mid-20th century, although the transcontinental railroad project also brought Asian workers to the western part of the country. Many Asian railroad workers chose to remain in Canada once the railroad had been completed in 1885.

The end of World War II, along with the fall of colonialism worldwide, brought about a wave of global migration that continues to this day. Canada's open door policy of immigration throughout the 1960s and '70s, particularly that attributed to the Canadian Liberal party under Pierre Trudeau's leadership, brought many "people of color" (Bannerji, 2000b, p. 545)[2] to Canada. This policy not only allowed but actively pursued immigration from the formerly colonized "third-world" countries (p. 551).

Official multiculturalism first began to take form during Prime Minister Lester B. Pearson's government in the late 1960s, emerging as the recommendation of the Bilingualism and Biculturalism Commission. The commission's mandate was to "recommend what steps should be taken to develop the Canadian Confederation on the basis of an equal partnership between the two founding races taking into account the contributions made by other ethnic groups to the cultural enrichment of Canada" (Bumsted, 1992, cited in Mackey, 2002, p. 63). Pearson's commission attempted to restructure what had been seen as a mutually antagonistic dualism between British and French Canada. As the commission consulted with groups around the country, protests surrounding the commission's ethnocentric and exclusionary language from a number of "ethnic groups" and First Nations caused the government to slow down their work and begin to shift philosophically from biculturalism to multiculturalism. The commission eventually proposed a form of official multiculturalism, which was adopted and became official policy during the Trudeau government in 1971 (Mackey, 2002, p. 64).

Mackey posits that this shift to multiculturalism was "an attempt to redefine the symbolic system" of Canada as a way to manage the potentially dangerous political situation related to emergent Quebec separatism by recognizing and managing culture (p. 64).

Nonetheless, after Prime Minister Trudeau enacted the first official multicultural policy, the discourses of nation, community, and diversity began to be tied together within the Canadian context. It should be clarified here that the demands of the various ethnic groups and immigrant populations that led to the Pearson Commission's recommendation for multiculturalism were not particularly related to an ideology of multiculturalism; rather, their concerns were about racism and legal discrimination related to immigration and family reunification, job discrimination based on requirements for "Canadian experience," and various adjustment difficulties related to child care and language (Bannerji, 2000b, p. 553).

In 1988, Conservative Premier Brian Mulroney's government enacted the Official Multiculturalism Act, which remains as the guiding document for multicultural policy in Canada today. This law broadened and codified perspectives that had developed since 1971 (Dewing, 2013), focusing specifically on what were seen as shortcomings of the 1971 policy, adding updates believed necessary to adapt the original law to the population's increasing diversity. As such, the act sought to "promote the full and equitable participation of individuals and communities of all origins in the continuing evolution and shaping of all aspects of Canadian society" (*Canadian Multiculturalism Act*, 1988). The Act established legislation to protect ethnic, racial, linguistic and religious diversity within Canadian society.

Critiques of Canadian multicultural policies

While the policies related to multiculturalism have led to a common understanding worldwide of Canada as a multicultural nation, an understanding that most Canadians accept as part of the national identity, the policies themselves have come under sharp critique from those Canadians who view them as not having dealt effectively enough with the issues that originally led to their creation. The intention of critique in this case is to provide illumination:

> Critique is not a matter of saying that things are not right as they are. It is a matter of pointing out on what kinds of assumptions, what kinds of familiar, unchallenged, unconsidered modes of thought the practices we accept rest. (Foucault, 1998, cited in Mackey, 2002, p. 18)

It is in this sense of interrogating the assumptions and unchallenged modes of thought and practice that the following critiques have emerged; these are foundational to this chapter.

Although official multiculturalism differs greatly from the overt racism and assimilationist policies of early Canadian governments, Mackey (2002) argues that it evolved from patterns that had become entrenched during colonial times. In this respect, those patterns assumed that White people (the French and English settlers) were the only legitimate citizens of Canada. The relationship with First Nations, Inuit, and Métis peoples was overtly racist in the beginning, and even at the time of the Trudeau policy in 1971, many of Canada's First Peoples were forced to attend residential schools, where they often experienced physical, sexual, and medical abuses, in addition to the intentional erasure of aboriginal language and culture as part of the government's assimilation process. About 150,000 children attended residential schools over the 130-year period of their operation. Many children were forcibly removed from families and communities in the campaign to "take the Indian out of the child" (Galloway, 2013). Thus one may conclude that the entrenched colonial patterns at work at the time multiculturalism emerged were based upon a culture of White supremacy, understood here as a "racialized social system ... practices that reinforce white privilege" (Bonilla-Silva, 2003, p. 9). Under policies of official multiculturalism, cultural diversity has been allowed to proliferate (primarily for economic reasons to support a growing economy), but the power to "define, limit and tolerate differences still lies in the hands of the dominant group. Further, the degree and forms of *tolerable* differences are defined by the ever changing needs of the project of nation building" (Mackey, 2002, p. 70, italics in original).

Writing from an anti-racist philosophical perspective, Bannerji, too, critiques Canada's official multicultural policies. While the original policy may have been prompted by concerns for racism, over time:

> The concept of race lost its hard edges of criticality, class disappeared entirely, and colour gave a feeling of brightness, brilliance, or vividness, of a celebration of a difference which was disconnected from social relations of power. . . (Bannerji, 2000b, p. 545)

As Bannerji explains, the concept of celebrating difference has led to a "graying out" of race, and an erasure of cultural distinctiveness under the philosophy of "unity through diversity." Bannerji further argues that the notion of diversity has become an ideology that supports a process of surpassing and subsumption of culture (p. 547) in the so-called celebration of diversity. She further states that this is the "paradox" of multiculturalism in Canada—the concept of diversity allows for an emptying of actual social relations that presumes cultures can be described in concrete terms, while simultaneously obscuring any understanding that difference is a discourse related to power:

> In fact, it is this uncritical, de-materialized, seemingly de-politicized reading of culture through which culture becomes a political tool . . .. One can only conclude from all this that the discourse of diversity, as a complex systemically interpretive language of governing, cannot be read as an innocent pluralism. (p. 548)

As Bannerji explains, the discourse of multiculturalism has led to a situation where people cannot make a distinction between racist stereotypes and ordinary historical/cultural differences of everyday life and practices of people from different parts of the world (p. 548). Diversity discourse "portrays society as a horizontal space, in which there is no theoretical or analytical room for social relations of power ... and its ideological culture" (p. 555). Yet the discourse of diversity "is the staple discourse of arts and community projects, conditioning their working agendas as well as the politics of the funding bodies" (p. 548–549). The ability to secure grant funds often depends largely upon a choir's ability to demonstrate "talking the talk" of diversity, even if its membership fails to walk the diversity walk. This last point is key to what I have termed the inclusion conundrum within community children's choirs.

I wish to clarify here that my perspective on multiculturalism, joining with those articulated in the above critiques, seeks only to interrogate the assumptions upon which multicultural policies operate. These assumptions similarly influence the beliefs of Canadians who conduct, administer, write grants, and perform other functions related to the operation of community children's choirs. There is no intent here to suggest that official multiculturalism is "bad" for Canada; while far from perfect, I believe the official policies have brought significant and positive changes. Even so, the intent of the policy and the lived reality for many people of color in Canada differs greatly from the notions of equality put forth in policy language. Thus it is important to read these critiques as indicative of the ongoing difficulties people of color face in Canadian society.

It is with all the foregoing in mind that I next look at the community children's choir scene in Canada. My remarks focus primarily on choirs in the Greater Toronto Area (GTA), the fourth largest metropolitan area in North America and its most diverse. As a resident of the area, I am most familiar with local area choirs and their approaches to membership, repertoire, and other issues that contribute to the "inclusion conundrum." In addition, given that most of the diversity in Canada's population resides in its metropolitan areas (Malenfant, Lebel, & Martel, 2010), a close look at the choirs in the GTA allows for illumination of the issues related to increasing the diversity of memberships in those choirs.

CHILDREN'S CHOIRS IN THE GREATER TORONTO AREA (GTA)

Choirs Ontario (http://www.choirsontario.org/LinkManager/list) lists twenty-one[3] children's or youth choirs in the GTA that may be considered "community" choirs from the perspective of drawing their membership primarily from the immediately surrounding residential areas. Some of these choirs are small, averaging fewer than twenty-five members; others boast memberships in the hundreds of choristers (for example, the internationally-famous Toronto Children's Chorus, which has established satellite choirs throughout the city). There may well be more choirs in existence who do not subscribe to Choirs Ontario, and thus do not appear on the website's membership list. I have not included church or school choirs in this number, since they do not operate under the same basic structures as the community organizations. Based upon the Choirs Ontario website, however, one can assume that the GTA is musically thriving with respect to community children's and youth choirs.

My concerns about diversity across these organizations emerge from the understanding that currently in the GTA, the White population is only a little more than 50% of the total population (58% according to the 2006 national census; see http://statcan.gc.ca). Thus one might expect community children's choirs to mirror that diversity, particularly since many promote themselves as "inclusive" or actively engaged in outreach to their local communities. Population projections for the Toronto area emerging from the 2006 census suggest that by the year 2017, the White population of the GTA will officially be the minority, and that by 2031, "almost 63 per cent of the region's population will be from a visible minority community" (Javed, 2010). Since immigration drives ethnocultural diversity in Canada, that diversity tends to be concentrated in Canada's "census metropolitan areas" (CMAs), with Toronto and Vancouver representing the most diverse of the country's 33 CMAs. A study commissioned by Statistics Canada projects that the Toronto area will be the home of 43% of all the country's diversity by 2031 (Malenfant et al., 2010, pp. 27–28).

While the greater Toronto area is the most diverse metropolitan area in Canada (and by some accounts the most diverse in North America), children's choirs in the GTA do not, by and large, reflect that diversity. A quick check of choir websites around the GTA tells the story. Most of the websites feature individual pictures of two or three children whose appearance suggests the group has a diverse membership, yet when one looks closely at the group shots and pictures of the choir on stage, it becomes apparent that these individuals represent only a small percentage of the group's predominantly White membership.

The remainder of this chapter seeks to shed light on some of the reasons why so many children's choirs, who may sing joyfully about peace and love across the family of humanity, celebrate Canadian diversity, and sing poignant songs about issues of social justice, do not yet embody the ideals they promote musically. I will look at some of the undergirding realities of choirs in the GTA, based upon my own eighteen years of leadership experience with a youth choir in this region, informal conversations with other conductors, and the information gleaned from the websites of choirs in the GTA. The discussion will begin with operating costs and membership fees. I will then address the role of repertoire in the inclusion conundrum, closing with an exploration of how the activity of choir may be coded for whiteness, demonstrating our "terminal naivety" (Vaugeois, 2013) about race, ethnicity, and diversity within music education. The final section of the chapter will focus on the changes in perspective that may help to establish choir as a truly inclusive space for all children who want to sing.

The economics of children's choirs

Operating a children's choir can be an expensive undertaking. The organization must often rent rehearsal space, purchase or rent octavos, and pay the artistic staff (conductors, accompanists, assistants, interns) and administrative staff, even though these salaries or honoraria may be small. Thus it often comes as a surprise to parents investigating the possibility of enrolling a child in choir that not only will they need to pay a substantial membership fee, they may also need to pay deposits for music, purchase one or more uniforms, and actively take part in fundraising (or pay an additional fee in lieu of participating in fundraising). The membership fee may not cover the costs for all the activities offered by the organization: retreats and tours usually require significant additional expenditures. Parents are expected to purchase tickets to attend choir concerts, as well as actively fundraise to support the choir's finances. While most of these anticipated costs are not published on choir websites, a few do publish their yearly membership fees. In the GTA, these range from a low of $325 per child per year to over $1500 per child annually prior to any ancillary costs such as uniforms. Economies of scale do not appear to be applicable, since the largest choir organizations tend also to charge the highest membership fees.

Most of the choir websites I have studied make an attempt to ameliorate what may be perceived as prohibitive access costs by offering bursaries, scholarships, or tuition assistance. Typically, however, these financial aids are limited to only a few "deserving" choristers, or may be dependent upon total enrollments, funding sources such as grants and donations, fundraising, or other means. The procedures for accessing financial support vary from one choir to the next; some require only a short statement about why support is requested, while other choirs require proof of the family's annual income and other personal financial information. Given that many people may be reluctant to share such personal information with a board of directors comprised of other choir parents, the application process itself may prohibit some deserving families from applying for financial aid.

Occasionally the receipt of financial assistance requires a commitment to do volunteer work on behalf of the choir, which may pose hardships for working-class families, single-parent families, or those engaged in shift work (Lareau, 2003). This represents an issue for both middle-class and working-class families, yet choirs are often highly dependent upon the work performed by parent volunteers.

Race, ethnicity, and economics. The connection between socioeconomic status and race/ethnicity has been well documented both in the United States and in Canada (Zawilski, 2010). Recent Canadian research has focused on the relationships between immigration, class, and integration into Canadian society (Wu, Schimmele, & Feng, 2012). While many immigrants to Canada may have arrived as middle-class or even highly affluent citizens of their home countries, once in Canada, some families find themselves in an ongoing struggle to maintain class status and income levels (Bonikowska & Hou, 2011). Statistics Canada reports that since 2007, the income of immigrants in Ontario (based upon tax returns) has declined significantly, with the greatest percentage of decline among immigrants from Asia and Africa. Immigrants from the United States, Australia, and the United Kingdom seem to fare best in measures of income stability, although they, too, have seen an overall decline in income since the recession of 2008 (http://statcan.gc.ca). The study by Wu, et al. (2012) focuses on the extent to which immigrants to Canada experience subjective well-being. Their findings suggest that immigrants' "sense of belonging is a reflection of integration into social networks and institutions, and it fosters feelings of social solidarity with the core or socially predominant group" (p. 383). Thus one might expect that new immigrants to Canada would actively seek out activities such as choir to help their children integrate into local social networks. In her study about race and class in the United States, Lareau (2003) writes that working-class and low-income children often have the same interests as their middle-class peers with respect to participating in the arts, music, sports, and so forth, but are often prevented from doing so by "finances, a lack of transportation, and limited availability of programs" (p. 242). Thus the high cost of membership in children's choirs and the financial stress in which many immigrants in Canada find themselves prohibits the opportunity that choir represents for children's social integration.

As the founder and now member of the board of directors of a youth choir in the GTA, I have firsthand knowledge of the difficulties related to making membership fees affordable. The board attempts to make financial assistance available to as many potential choir members as may require it. However, this is considered to be the type of operating expense that few granting agencies will support, meaning that funding such financial assistance is dependent upon spreading those costs across the entire membership, relying on the goodwill of private donors, or diverting funds from other expense areas within the choir's operating budget. Without being able to make absolute guarantees to parents at the time of registration that membership costs will be subsidized, or to what extent, many parents opt for a path that avoids disappointing their children—they decline to join. The choir with which I am associated has one of the lowest membership fees in the GTA; still, nearly 25% of our membership receives some sort of financial assistance, ranging from discounted fees to full scholarships. This is perhaps one reason (but certainly not the only one) why we also have one of the most visibly diverse choirs in the area. Even so, every season, we know that many interested young singers do not join the choir because they simply cannot afford it.

Children's choir as an activity most easily fits with an affluent lifestyle and a philosophy of parenting that Lareau (2003) has termed *concerted cultivation,* wherein "middle-class parents are increasingly determined to make sure that their children are not excluded from any opportunity that might eventually contribute to their advancement" (p. 5). Concerted cultivation as a parenting philosophy is more closely aligned with class than with race. Both Black and White middle-class parents in Lareau's study practiced concerted cultivation, while working-class and poor parents tended to view their children's development as "unfolding spontaneously," provided they were able to provide the basic necessities of life related to food, clothing, shelter, and other basic support (p. 238).

CHOIR AS "WHITE SPACE"

The discussion above locates the concept of community children's choir as an activity that typically occurs within a middle-class norm and supported by a parenting philosophy of concerted cultivation. Since middle-class norms are not confined to White people, economics alone cannot explain the lack of diversity observable in so many of the GTA's children or youth choirs, given the population statistics cited earlier in this chapter. In other words, while people of color across Canada may earn less than their White counterparts overall when the entire population is taken into account, there is of course a substantial middle-class and affluent population drawn from all races and ethnicities. This begs the question: why do these affluent children of color not seek out community children's choirs in numbers proportionate to their White peers? The question becomes especially perplexing when asked within the context of Canada's multicultural policy and related discourses, in which "unity is posited in terms of diversity, with pictures of many facial types, languages and cultures—'together we are [Canadian] . . .'" (Bannerji, 2000b, p. 549). Bannerji's statement bears out within the children's choir community: a common notion across the GTA is that choir is a natural place to celebrate Canada's diversity through music. The next sections of this chapter investigate who is celebrating, how those celebrations are enacted, and how celebrations of diversity may be perceived within the multitude of ethnic communities found in the GTA.

Repertoire and the celebration of diversity: Who is celebrating?

I believe Bannerji is correct in her assertion that the discourse of diversity is a staple of arts and community projects in Canada. Because this discourse affects funding possibilities, it becomes critical for children's choirs to (at least) appear that they are not only actively promoting a multicultural perspective, but that their membership embodies multiculturality as well. As discussed previously, often the pictures of choir members on websites feature children of color to suggest a diverse membership, even though the group may be predominantly White. The appearance of supporting Canadian multiculturalism is also evident in the language of children's choir websites in the GTA, as the following examples illustrate:

- The choir's vast repertoire embraces diverse cultures and traditions and covers an extensive range of musical genres (http://torontochildrenschorus.com/about/);
- developing children's choral and musical ability, promoting inclusiveness, fun, teamwork, cultural diversity and choral excellence (http://youngvoicestoronto. com/about-us/);
- an inclusive, multicultural music education and performance program open to all youth in the community (http://mfyc.ca).

In many of the websites I searched, the language is less inclusive than in the above examples, focusing primarily on musical excellence rather than directing attention to multicultural repertoire. This, too, is part of the inclusion conundrum. Whether intended or not, the language of musical excellence may convey a bias toward "traditional" children's choir music that draws largely from the Euro-Canadian canon of repertoire. The following examples from websites are typical: "the choir is known throughout Toronto and across Canada for its musical sound and professional approach" (http://www.bachchildrenschorus.ca/); and offering youth "the opportunity to achieve artistic excellence through innovative education" (http://www.vivayouths-ingers.com/about-us/biography/).

While many choirs focus their energies on music that may be deemed "multi-cultural," and most choirs will include at least a few selections on concert programs from other cultures, or in languages other than French and English, memberships remain predominantly White. I believe that at least in part, this lack of diversity results from a perception of children's choirs as an activity representing cultural whiteness, which exists in tension with the ethic of inclusion and diversity articulated on various choir websites.

Defining whiteness. As Frantz Fanon demonstrated in *Black Skin, White Masks* (1968), many people understand whiteness, not for what it is, but for what it is not. In defining whiteness here, I shall attempt to avoid reliance on negative descriptions, instead bring-ing into focus the particular characteristics that may ultimately affect attempts to make Canadian children's choirs more inclusive racially and ethnically. Whiteness is herein understood as a racial discourse involving a particular racial perspective or worldview, supported by material practices and institutions that benefit White people. Whiteness is an "amalgamation of qualities including the cultures, histories, experiences, discourses, and privileges shared by Whites" (Marx, 2006, p. 6). Characteristics of whiteness include the unwillingness to name the contours of racism, the avoidance of identifying with a racial experience or group, the minimization of racist legacy, and other evasions (Leonardo, 2002, pp. 31–32).

While many White people have come to understand the benefits of being White, and with such understanding move beyond color-blind racism (Bonilla-Silva, 2003), it is impossible for White people not to benefit from being White (McIntosh, 1990). Because being perceived as White carries implicit benefits, many people operate from the cultural worldview of whiteness, in which White behaviors, perspectives, and cul-tural practices are the tacit societal norms. Whiteness, as an imagined racial collective, inserts itself into history and when this happens, material and discursive violence often accompanies it (Leonardo, 2002, p. 32). Bonilla-Silva's term *color-blind racism* speaks to the damaging effects of Whiteness; it is an unacknowledged form of racism that continues to disadvantage particular people and groups while simultaneously benefit-ting those who are White. Color-blind racism resides in such platitudes as "I don't see color, I see children," or "I'm not racist because some of my best friends are _____" (Thompson, 2003).

It is important to clarify that whiteness as a racial discourse and worldview is not the same as the concept of White people, which is a racial category. There are a great many White people who have disavowed whiteness, and who work against racial injus-tices worldwide. Some do this through their work with children's choirs; I count myself among these antiracist educators. However, in order to disavow whiteness, one must first recognize how it operates in society. Thus, this chapter seeks to foster an interrogation of the way whiteness infuses the operation of many Canadian children's choirs, even those proclaiming a commitment to multiculturalism and diversity.

Choir comportment: "acting White?" In forwarding the argument that children's choirs in Canada may be perceived as predominantly White spaces that discourage the membership of children from other races, I recognize that most choir directors and boards operate with the intent to be inclusive. They want to attract a more diverse membership. Their inability to do so is not the result of overt racism, but may indeed be a reflection of their ignorance of whiteness as color-blind racism, or the way certain cultural activities are coded as White. Gustafson (2008) examined the construction of racial boundaries by linking specific body comportments, hailed as "worthy" by music educators, to historically constructed notions of whiteness. She states, "cultural differences implicit in music pedagogy unwittingly insert demographic divides and create boundaries to meaningful participation" (p. 269). Look at any number of children's choir websites: the photographs usually depict children standing calmly on risers, facing forward, smiling (or mouths open in song), hands to their sides, uniform in dress. This is the behavior expected by both conductors and audiences. Despite recent efforts by some choirs to incorporate elements of movement and choreography into performances, the actual space available in performance venues often stifles these possibilities. Apart from a few choreographed movements, members of children's choirs generally stand still on stage; to do otherwise may elicit criticism from conductors and audiences alike. This typical configuration for children's choirs, however, implies an emphasis on comportment that embodies whiteness:

> Where the "lower races" express themselves physically, white music must be physically constrained. Where singing in black churches is physically expressive, musically ecstatic and improvisatory, white singers must be carefully disciplined to constrain their physical gestures and sing with a uniform tone colour. (Vaugeois, 2013, p. 153)

Colonialism and the canon. Notions of correct comportment link directly back to Canada's history as a British colony. Similarly, the concept of "appropriate music" has roots in colonial discourse in Canada. In the early days of Canadian public education, advocates believed that engagement in particular forms of music contributed to population management. Britain's John Hullah, for example, "worked tirelessly to bring 'choralism' to the British working classes as a means to 'initiate pupils into principles of order,' contain worker dissent, and produce subjects loyal to the British Empire" (Olwage, 2005, cited in Vaugeois, 2013, p. 141). As Vaugeois explains, by the mid-19th century, music had found a place in most sites of White education in Ontario, where middle and upper-class children learned the works of European masters, and also performed music composed especially for them: "a combination of hymns, patriotic songs, and bucolic songs intended to teach desirable behaviour" (p. 141). The special school repertoire sought to foster such characteristics as innocence, obedience, pleasure in work, emotional constraint, discipline, and the association of pleasure with moral lessons. The songs carefully nurtured the notion of "'childhood'—an identity of dependence and innocence that emerged in contrast to the independent attitudes and behaviours of young people" (p. 144). As Vaugeois posits, the music supporting this carefully nurtured notion of (White) childhood innocence stood in stark contrast to musics of other peoples:

> Where black musics might express anything from pain and anguish to sexual excitement to political rebellion, and Aboriginal musics might strive to achieve a heightened spiritual state of body and mind, white musics are carefully sanitized to express "cultivated," distanced relationships to the body, to emotion, and to the politically contested. (p. 153)

What is now considered traditional children's choir repertoire emerged from these early attitudes about music education, whose primary purpose appears to have been the creation of good (compliant) White citizens, paired with a concept of childhood that sought to protect them from real-world experiences. Many decades later, in response to the emergent community children's choir phenomenon of the 1980s, choral educators Doreen Rao, Henry Leck, and others spearheaded reforms in children's choir repertoire, to encourage the publication of music from more diverse genres and with meaningful texts that support a "holistic, real-life view of human development" (Rao, 1993a, p. 45). Despite the plethora of new choral compositions for children offering this more real-world view, the residue of colonial attitudes about childhood innocence lingers in both parental speech and some educational discourses. Similarly, the notion that choir is an experience that encourages children to become good citizens remains widespread:

> The unparalleled music education and life-changing opportunities to perform exceptional music in local, national, and international venues help to promote the personal welfare, growth and a portfolio of life skills that *prepare children to become effective citizens* (italics added.) (http://torontochildrenschorus.com/about/).

While no doubt the author of the above statement did not seek to exclude any children from the promised "life-changing opportunities," the linking of choir experience and citizenship contributes subtly to the (mis)perception that children's choirs and choir repertoire support an ideology of whiteness that first took root in colonial Canada.

Concerns for vocal health. Another residue of colonial thinking that has led to a perception of children's choirs as "White space" emerges from concerns for vocal health related to musical genres such as gospel, pop, and various world musics. In Canada, the "ideal" children's choir sound continues to draw from the British boy choir sound as a model—a head tone production that creates a flute-like tone quality. Since this head tone was not appropriate stylistically to many of the newly discovered musical cultures, the 1990s trend to incorporate world music into children's choir repertoire simultaneously fostered concerns about whether it was possible to sing such music with healthy vocal production. These concerns in large part derive from colonial biases against Black musics and the music of indigenous peoples. White colonial writings on Black choral singing, almost without fail, noted a difference in the Black voice. Olwage (2004) writes that one reviewer described the "native voice" as "harsh and disagreeable"; "the European voice [was] far more agreeable, far better qualified to render the sublime conceptions of great composers than the natives" (p. 208).

As interest in different styles of music increased among children's choir conductors, articles such as the one in *The Choral Journal* by Cleveland (2004) did little to alleviate fears about vocal health. The article reported research conducted with members of a gospel touring choir, and although near the end of the article the author provided strategies for healthy production of the gospel sound (as well as other tone qualities related to different genres), the article subtly implied that producing a legitimate gospel sound in a healthy way was not possible: ". . . in the traditional gospel style, a measure of a successful performance is the degree of hoarseness during and after the performance" (p. 45). Even those advocating for the inclusion of gospel and other musical forms in the choir repertoire sometimes conveyed an unacknowledged bias, for example, in O'Toole's (2005) description of her children's choir performance with a professional gospel artist: "Although I still heard children screaming, it was transformed from vocal abuse to screaming new identities" (p. 306). O'Toole's use of "screaming" to describe the children's vocal production conveys her bias, even as she acknowledges the importance of the music to the choir members' identity formation. Such attitudes are difficult to hide from children, particularly those who live with the daily micro-aggressions of whiteness and color-blind racism.

The repertoire conundrum. Most of the choirs with which I am familiar in the GTA make some room in their repertoire for world music, gospel, and popular genres of music. Some choirs, such as the Mississauga Festival Youth choir (www.mfyc.ca), have focused their repertoires predominantly in these areas, and have successfully attracted a diverse membership. Yet repertoire alone cannot resolve the conundrum related to diversity, since much of this repertoire carries its own colonial baggage. When music from other cultures is published in North America, many of the genre's distinguishing characteristics may be simplified beyond recognition (Bradley, 2009). Rhythms that may be accurately reproduced through oral transmission are difficult, if not impossible, to convey through western notation (Agawu, 2003). The result is a "whitening" of Black musics in conformity with standards of White propriety, possibly a throwback response to the criticisms leveled in the early twentieth century at ragtime and jazz by White musical authorities who fearfully argued that these rhythms were dangerous and degenerate (Vaugeois, 2013, p. 207). I would suggest that in the early 21st century, rap and hip-hop represent "dangerous and degenerate" musical expressions to some White parents and educators.

This whitening of Black musics is in part the result of music's commodification (Adorno, 1944; Feld, 1994, 2000). "World music" is itself a catch-all category, originally developed by the recording industry for marketing purposes (Frith, 2000), and while some choral music publishers conscientiously attempt to provide culture-specific information for their publications, many others rely on generic descriptions such as "African folksong," a woefully nondescript reference to a continent made up of 53 distinct countries and territories, hundreds of languages, and distinctive regional musical practices. Beyond this, many new publications in the choral world intentionally blend musical characteristics from several cultures, creating "world beat" (Feld, 2000) arrangements that erase race and culture. This diffusion of world music reflects and reifies simplistic constructions of ethnicity and diversity that are central to the production, marketing, and commodification of culture, in a somewhat naive and simplistic celebration of ethnic diversity (Connell & Gibson, 2004, p. 345).

Unfortunately, the graying out of distinctive musical features relieves much choral music of its potential to speak to ethnic minorities in a diverse society. Some arrangements may be perceived as borderline parody of the original musical culture. A child who has emigrated from West Africa to Canada, for example, may find little of that distinctive musical culture in some of the choral publications claiming to represent the region. Thus repertoire alone cannot serve as the panacea for the inclusion conundrum. The flattening of rhythms in many "world music" publications, the focus on head voice vocal production and body comportment, teacher-conductor fears related to vocal health, or anxieties about teaching such musics "authentically" (Schippers, 2010), combine to create a rehearsal climate that supports the perception that children's choirs represent "White space."

CONCLUSION: TOWARD GREATER INCLUSION IN CANADIAN CHILDREN'S CHOIRS

I have attempted in this chapter to point to what Bannerji (2000a, 2000b) has called the "paradox of diversity discourse." Canada's official policies of multiculturalism have led to a grassroots understanding that Canada is a "multicultural society" that has failed to interrogate why some public spaces remain as White terrain. I include, sadly, a majority of community children's choirs in the Greater Toronto Area (GTA) in this description, based upon my observations over the past eighteen years as a choral conductor in the area. Yet there are a few choirs who seem to have successfully alleviated "the color line" (Du Bois, 2005) in their recruiting and retention strategies, including the choir that I founded in 1997. In this final section of the chapter, I share some of the hard-learned lessons related to building an inclusive community children's choir.

While the inclusion of more diverse repertoire, and ensuring access to children whose families cannot afford the often hefty membership fees, does have some positive effect on inclusivity, I believe that, first and foremost, conductors must be fully committed to that goal. Actions speak louder than words, and website rhetoric that gives lip service to inclusion and diversity to meet requirements of funding agencies can be easily seen through by parents from ethnic minorities or those with real-life experiences of racism and the shortcomings of multicultural policies. As Bannerji (2000b) states, "it does not require much effort to realize that diversity is not equal to multiplied sameness" (p. 550), yet too many children's choirs take a color-blind approach that "superficially accepts diversity with the provision that it not be significantly different from the White norm and, most importantly, that it not *challenge* the White norm" (Marx, 2006, p. 17, italics in original). Thus the goal of greater diversity cannot be about numbers or a shell game of representation. Featuring a few Black or Asian children on a choir website, in an area that has a minority White population, does not reflect true diversity. Yet such tactics exhibit how the concept of diversity is thought of "in a socially abstract manner, which also wipes away its location in history, thus obscuring colonialism, capital, and slavery. It... averts our gaze from power relations or differences which continue to organize Canadian public life and culture" (Bannerji, 2000b, p. 555).

Vaugeois's (2013) dissertation investigates the lingering effects of colonialism on Canadian music education today. She writes of the way white privilege and colonial residue have created "terminal naivety" among music educators in Ontario, which she describes as "a lack of awareness of power relations and obsessions with individual self-improvement" (p. 217). Think of the rhetoric of so many children's choir conductors in North America, conductors who are secure in their beliefs about the exalted nature of their work (p. 218) and simultaneously blind to the issues of race and class that their work may perpetuate. As Vaugeois states:

> [w]e continue to embody the colonial subject as worldly, sophisticated, civilized, innocent, and entitled. This is the education of feeling we both receive and convey through our work as embodied representatives of race-class- and gender-based notions of civilizational advancement. ...We, like so many of our compatriots, continue to perform ourselves into a state of naivety and innocence. ... (p. 219)

If we believe that all children can learn to sing (Rao, 1993a, 1993b), then community choirs ought to be reflective of the populations in their local rehearsal areas. Unfortunately, this is not the case even in as diverse a place as Toronto or its surrounding communities. Yet given the diverse memberships of some of the GTA's choirs, it is an attainable goal if the desire exists. But to accomplish this, conductors who self-identify as racially White may need to do some hard work to unlearn their whiteness, to avoid performing themselves into a color-blind state of naivety and innocence. It is no easy task to admit that Canada's colonial legacy keeps the benefits of White privilege alive, making us terminally naive about its benefits and resultant exclusions. It is difficult to admit that practicing the choral art that we love with children may be a perpetuation of whiteness.

White educators, including children's choir conductors, must "look deeply and critically at the necessary changes and growth we ourselves must achieve if we are to work effectively with the real issues of race, equity, and social justice" (Howard, 2006, p. 5).

Choir can, and should be, a place where children learn about what it means to be human in a diverse world through the myriad of ways humans express themselves musically. If we can do the hard work of decolonizing our choral practices and ourselves, rather than settling for superficial celebrations of diversity, children's choirs in Canada may yet become truly vibrant spaces for exploring humanity's remarkable diversity—explored by children who reflect that diversity, not only sonically, but also visibly.

NOTES

1. While the term *inclusive* in education discourse usually refers specifically to the inclusion of people with disabilities, children's choirs tend to use the term to mean that no auditions are required to join the choir. Some choirs that hold auditions utilize the term to convey that the choir is open to all who pass the audition and can pay the membership fees.
2. The term *people of color* is commonly used in Canada when talking about races and ethnicities other than White. The official term used by the Canadian government in policy documents is *visible minorities,* which the United Nations declared to be a racist term in 2009. See Bannerji (2000a, 2000b) for explanations of how the term people of color came to be accepted in Canada by those to whom it refers.
3. This information is subject to change per website updates and membership cycles. Access date for the estimate of 21 choirs was August 20, 2014.

REFERENCES

Agawu, V. K. (2003). *Representing African music: Postcolonial notes, queries, positions.* New York: Routledge.

Bannerji, H. (2000a). *The dark side of the nation: Essays on multiculturalism, nationalism, and gender.* Toronto: Canadian Scholars' Press, Inc.

Bannerji, H. (2000b). The paradox of diversity: The construction of a multicultural Canada and "women of color". *Women's Studies International Forum, 23*(5), 537–560.

Bonikowska, A., & Hou, F. (2011). *Reversal of fortunes or continued success? Cohort differences in education and earnings of childhood immigrants.* Ottawa: Statistics Canada. Retrieved from http://www.statcan.gc.ca/pub/11f0019m/11f0019m2011330-eng.pdf.

Bonilla-Silva, E. (2003). *Racism without racists: Color-blind racism and the persistence of racial inequality in the United States.* Lanham, MD: Rowman & Littlefield.

Bradley, D. (2009). Global song, global citizens? The world constructed in world music choral publications. In E. Gould, J. Countryman, C. Morton & L. S. Rose (Eds.), *Exploring social justice: How music education might matter* (pp. 105–120). Toronto: Canadian Music Educators' Association.

Bumsted, J. M. (1992). *The peoples of Canada: A post-confederation history.* Toronto: Oxford.

Canada's First Peoples. (2007). Retrieved from http://firstpeoplesofcanada.com/fp_groups/fp_groups_overview.html

Canada History. (2013). Retrieved from www.canadahistory.com.

Canadian Multiculturalism Act. (1988). R.S.C., 1985, c. 24 (4th Supp.). Ottawa, ON: Government of Canada.

Cleveland, T. (2004). On the voice: An examination of sixty-four voices of a seventy-voice Gospel Choir: Implications for vocal health. *The Choral Journal, 44*(9), 45–49.

Connell, J., & Gibson, C. (2004). World music: deterritorializing place and identity. *Progress in Human Geography, 28*(3), 342–361.

Dei, G. J. S. (2000). *Power, knowledge and anti-racism education.* Halifax, NS: Fernwood.

Dewing, M. (2013). *Canadian Multiculturalism.* Ottawa, ON: Library of Parliament. Retrieved from http://www.lop.parl.gc.ca/content/lop/researchpublications/2009-20-e.pdf

Du Bois, W. E. B. (2005). *The souls of black folk: Essays and sketches.* New York: Barnes and Noble.

Fanon, F. (1968). *Black skin, white masks.* New York: Grove.

Feld, S. (1994). From schizophonia to schismogenesis. In C. Keil & Steven Feld (Eds.), *Music Grooves* (pp. 257–289). Chicago: University of Chicago Press.

Feld, S. (2000). A sweet lullaby for world music. *Public Culture, 12*(1), 145–171.

Frith, S. (2000). The discourse of world music. In G. Born & D. Hesmondhalgh (Eds.), *Western music and its others* (pp. 305–322). Berkeley: University of California Press.

Galloway, G. (2013, January 30). Ottawa ordered to find and release millions of Indian residential school records, *Globe and Mail.* Retrieved from http://www.theglobeandmail.com/news/politics/ottawa-ordered-to-find-and-release-millions-of-indian-residential-school-records/article8001068/.

Gurgle, R. E. (2013). *Levels of engagement in a racially diverse 7th grade choir class: Perceptions of "feeling it" and "blanked out".* Ph.D. Dissertation, University of Wisconsin-Madison.

Gustafson, R. (2008). Drifters and the dancing mad: The public school music curriculum and the fabrication of boundaries for participation. *Curriculum Inquiry, 38*(3), 267–297.

Horkheimer, M., & Adorno, T. W. (2002 [1944]). The culture industry: Enlightenment as mass deception (E. Jephcott, Trans.). In G. S. Noerr (Ed.), *Dialectic of enlightenment: Philosophical fragments* (pp. 94–136). Stanford, CA: Stanford University Press.

Howard, G. R. (2006). *We can't teach what we don't know: White teachers, multiracial schools* (2nd ed.). New York: Teachers College Press.

Javed, N. (2010, March 9). "Visible minority" will mean "white" by 2031. *Toronto Star.*

Lareau, A. (2003). *Unequal childhoods: Class, race, and family life.* Berkeley: University of California Press.

Leonardo, Z. (2002). The souls of white folk: Critical pedagogy, whiteness studies, and globalization discourse. *Race Ethnicity and Education, 5*(1), 29–50. doi: 10.1080/13613320120117180

Mackey, E. (2002). *The house of difference: Cultural politics and national identity in Canada.* Toronto: University of Toronto Press.

Malenfant, É. C., Lebel, A., & Martel, L. (2010). *Projections of the diversity of the Canadian population 2006 to 2031.* (Catalogue No. 91-551-X). Ottawa: Statistics Canada. Retrieved from http://www.statcan.gc.ca/pub/91-551-x/91-551-x2010001-eng.pdf.

Marx, S. (2006). *Revealing the invisible: Confronting passive racism in teacher education.* New York: Routledge.

McIntosh, P. (1990). White privilege: Unpacking the invisible knapsack. *Independent School, 49*(Winter 1990), 31–36.

Olwage, G. (2004). The class and colour of tone: An essay on the social history of vocal timbre. *Ethnomusicology Forum, 13*(2), 203–226.

Olwage, G. (2005). Discipline and choralism: The birth of musical colonialism. In A. J. Randall (Ed.), *Music, power, and politics* (pp. 25–46). London and New York: Routledge.

O'Toole, P. (2005). Why don't I feel included in these musics, or matters? In D. J. Elliott (Ed.), *Praxial music education: Reflections and dialogues* (pp. 297–307). New York: Oxford University Press. (Reprinted from: Bulletin of the Council of Research in Music Education *144*: 28–39).

Rao, D. (1993a). Children's choirs: A revolution from within. *Music Educators Journal,* *80*(3), 44–48.

Rao, D. (1993b). *We will sing! Choral music experience for classroom choirs.* New York: Boosey & Hawkes.

Schippers, H. (2010). *Facing the music: Shaping music education from a global perspective.* New York: Oxford University Press.

Thompson, A. (2003). Tiffany, friend of people of color: White investments in antiracism. *International Journal of Qualitative Studies in Education, 16*(1), 7–29. doi: 10.1080/0951839032000033509

Vaugeois, L. (2013). *Colonization and the institutionalization of hierarchies of the human through music education: Studies in the education of feeling.* Ph.D., University of Toronto.

Wu, Z., Schimmele, C. M., & Feng, H. (2012). Self-perceived integration of immigrants and their children. *Canadian Journal of Sociology, 37*(4), 381–408.

Zawilski, V. (2010). *Inequality in Canada: A reader on the intersections of gender, race, and class.* Don Mills, Ontario: Oxford University Press.

CHAPTER 22

....

PROFESSIONAL
ADULT CHOIRS

....

JASON VODICKA AND SIMON CARRINGTON

In the United States and Western Europe, the 20th century saw the rebirth, growth, and development of the professional choral ensemble into a viable source of part-time income for singers and a creative outlet for conductors. McGee (2007), Rugen (2013), and Smith and Young (n.d.) attributed this phenomenon to the growth of the recording industry, the influence of television and radio, increased performance standards of the early music movement, the vocal demands of contemporary composers, and the desire to preserve and promote the African American spiritual. While early professional ensembles were locally based or focused on recording and touring, the most recent generation of ensembles pulls its performers from across large geographic areas for performances in multiple locations, reflecting the placelessness and influence of social media. From a world practically devoid of professional choral ensembles has emerged a network of "professional choruses, either entrepreneurial or state supported, in virtually all countries in which the music of Western civilization is performed" (Smith & Young, para. 11) all in less than 100 years.

Chorus America, the leading advocacy, research, and leadership organization for choral music in the United States, defines a professional choir as one that pays either all or some of its singers for their work. The organization further defines three categories of professional choirs, depending on the number or percentage of singers paid, as preprofessional, professional core, and fully professional: A preprofessional choir is an emerging professional ensemble that pays some of its singers some of the time; a professional core ensemble is one that pays at least 12 of its singers (or at least 25% of its membership) all of the time; and a fully professional choir is one that pays all of its singers all of the time (Chorus America, n.d.). To meet the criteria of a fully professional ensemble, singers must also be paid at least a set minimum wage and have at least three different programs per season (Chorus America, n.d.). In September 2015, data from Chorus America reported having 22 preprofessional, 35 professional core, and 53 fully professional choirs in its membership database. For the purposes of this chapter, professional choirs will be defined as choirs that fit into Chorus America's three-tiered system of pre-professional, professional core, and fully professional choirs.

Although professional choirs have seen rapid growth in the United States and in Europe over the last 100 years, and though some recent research is devoted to the history and organization of these ensembles, many authors have claimed that there is nearly no existing research devoted to the pedagogy of professional choral ensembles (Lawlor, 2009; McGee, 2007; Morrow, 1993; Rugen, 2013; Shrock, 1990). Because the body of research is so severely limited, and because the research deals primarily with choirs in the United States, this chapter is limited to describing the history, structure, and current state of professional choral singing in the United States, with limited information about European professional choirs. The chapter will address the pedagogy of professional adult choirs using information gleaned from published sources; from coauthor Simon Carrington's experience as cofounder and performer in an all-male professional vocal ensemble; and from informal interviews with conductors of professional adult choirs and paid singers from professional choirs in the United States. Though anecdotal and far from comprehensive, it is hoped that the information presented in this chapter will stimulate future research into the rehearsal and performance practices of professional adult choral ensembles in the United States, Europe, and beyond.

The History of Professional Adult Choirs

Although choral singing is considered by many to be a primarily amateur endeavor, for much of history choirs were made up of professional singers. From the birth of choral music in the medieval era through the flourishing of polyphony in the Renaissance, noble patrons and the church supported professional choral ensembles. In the Baroque era, additional opportunities to perform choral music professionally came about through the birth of opera and oratorio; it was only in the 19th century that the focus of choral singing shifted to the amateur rather than the professional, mainly through large performances by singing societies in Europe and the United States. In the 20th century, amateur singing continued to flourish in community, school, and religiously affiliated choirs. At the same time, a new wave of professional choirs began to emerge, this time supported not by the nobility (though sometimes funded by the church and government), but most often as self-supporting entities reliant on donors, ticket sales, and recordings for financial support (see Smith & Young).

One of the earliest fully professional choirs in the United States was the Musical Art Society, established in New York in 1893. Frank Damrosch founded the ensemble as a personal artistic endeavor. Damrosch also hoped to expose New York audiences to unaccompanied choral singing and to expand the choral repertoire beyond "oratorio and light part-songs" (Kegerreis, 1970, p. 13). For 25 seasons, this 55-voice ensemble rehearsed one night each week, performing two public concerts per year. Singers received $20 for each concert, a rate that is still in line with Chorus America's guidelines for base pay (when accounting for inflation). Kegerreis wrote that the Musical Art Society was successful in influencing the repertoire not only of other community-based ensembles, but of college and high school choirs as well.

Kegerreis (1970) further stated that professional touring choirs from Europe also influenced the repertoire and style of American choirs in the early part of the 20th century. These ensembles include The Sistine Chapel Choir which brought a program of mainly Palestrina to the United States in 1923; the English Singers, a vocal sextet which toured three times from 1925 to 1928 and introduced one-on-a-part singing to American audiences; the Prague Teachers Chorus, which toured both Europe and America singing Czech folk tunes and contemporary works; and several Russian choirs that introduced Russian folk music, rich bass sonorities, and special vocal effects such as humming and explosive variation in dynamics.

The early to mid-20th century also saw the flourishing of a number of professional African American choirs in the United States. According to McGee (2007), these ensembles existed as artistic outlets for their conductors, but also more importantly as a means of promoting and preserving the Negro spiritual (although the repertoire of these ensembles typically included European music as well). Such ensembles include the Eva Jessye Choir, founded in 1927; the Hall Johnson Choir, in operation from 1930 to 1952; the Albert McNeil Jubilee Singers established in 1965; the Brazeal Dennard Chorale, established in 1972; and the Moses Hogan Singers, in operation from 1998 to 2003 (McGee, 2007; see also Hill, 1980). These choirs ranged in size from 12 to 45 or more singers and were fully paid ensembles. Some, like the Albert McNeill Jubilee Singers, were locally based and rehearsed on a weekly basis, while others, like the Moses Hogan Chorale, pulled performers from a wider geographic area (McGee, 2007). Each of these ensembles required a high level of vocal skill and music reading ability, particularly those with limited rehearsal time (McGee). McGee reported that rehearsal pedagogy among the groups varied, likely because of the wide variety of configurations of such ensembles: Johnson focused primarily on clarity in text and rhythm, using verbal communication to convey his musical interpretation to the singers, and Jessye included theatrical devices such as acting and choreography in preparing her ensemble.

In Europe, opera choruses and church choirs have provided a reliable source of employment for singers for hundreds of years. In the 1940s and '50s, professional choirs funded by government-owned media sprang up throughout Europe. The primary function of these ensembles was to perform on-air concerts rather than to perform in concert halls or churches. These ensembles, many still in existence today, perform a variety of repertoire dating back to the Renaissance era including a cappella choral music as well as oratorio and opera. In addition to providing music for state-funded media, these choruses also engage frequently in recording projects, symphonic collaborations, and music festival performances. Included in this group are the Hungarian Radio Choir, Netherlands Radio Choir, Swedish Radio choir, Lithuanian State Choir, MDR Radio Choir, Polish Radio Choir (n.d.; now private rather than state funded), the Latvian Radio

Choir, the BBC Singers, and the Helsinki Chamber Choir—founded as the Finnish Radio Choir. Each choir has anywhere from 17 to 45 singers, though this number has trended lower in recent years due to decreased government funding (see Rugen, 2013).

While some radio choirs (particularly those in Germany) provide full-time employment for their singers, most European radio choirs provide only a portion of their singers' income (DeFotis, 1994; Shrock, 1990). Other professional vocal activities round out the singers' professional livelihood. A 2013 study of the current, training, and associate members of the Netherlands Radio Choir showed that while almost all singers had graduated from a music conservatory, each relied on other sources of income, usually related to music (Berghs, Creylman, Avaux, Decoster, & de Jong, 2013). Most (88%) sing as soloists, while half (57%) participate in other vocal ensembles; only one singer did not participate in any other professional vocal activities (Berghs et al., 2013). Festival choruses like the annual 134-voice Bayreuth Festival chorus provide additional work to singers from radio and opera choruses in the less-busy summer months (Bayreuther Festspiele, 2015).

Other professional choruses in Europe that provide income to their singers include fully and semiprofessional church choirs; small vocal ensembles, such as The Kings Singers and The Sixteen; and autonomous chamber choirs such as Sweden's Eric Ericson Choir, which is the companion chamber ensemble of the larger Swedish Radio Choir (DeFotis, 1994). According to DeFotis (1994), Ericson founded the Eric Ericson Choir in 1945 as a volunteer ensemble specializing in early music and arrangements of Swedish folk songs. Singers began to receive payment for their services in 1960 once Ericson felt the quality of the group merited professional status. The focus of the ensemble then shifted to performing and commissioning contemporary choral music. Ericson (as quoted in DeFotis, 1994) stated that professional choirs like his are needed to perform challenging modern a cappella literature. This in turn spurs the compositional process of composers who can write knowing that the performers will be capable of virtuosic literature.

While professional radio choirs proliferated in Europe in the 1950s, it was professional touring and recording choirs that emerged in the United States at midcentury: Fred Waring and the Pennsylvanians (founded in 1938), the Roger Wagner Chorale (founded in 1946), the Robert Shaw Chorale (founded in 1948), the Norman Luboff Choir (founded in 1948), the Gregg Smith Singers (founded in 1962), the Robert de Cormier Singers (founded in 1963), and the Dale Warland Singers (active 1972 to 2004; Hill, 1980; Parish, 2013). According to Sigman (2011), "what these conductors did was to develop a professional ensemble whose sound and style could be replicated consistently at the highest standards of excellence" (para. 9). The ensembles used lighter repertoire with wide audience appeal to build their reputations, eventually coming to dominate the commercial touring and recording markets. Income from more populist projects then helped fund more artistically satisfying projects focusing on serious repertoire. Like Ericson in Europe, Warland sought to expand the choral repertoire by commissioning more than 270 new pieces of virtuosic choral music by composers such as Berger, Paulus, Shaw, Penderecki, Larsen, Barnett, Argento, and Whitacre (Parish, 2013).

The 1950s also saw the establishment of a number of professional choruses associated with prominent American orchestras. (Prior to this era, orchestras had relied on community and college choirs to provide singing forces for choral-orchestral works.) The success of conductors such as Robert Shaw, Margaret Hillis, and Roger Wagner led directly to the establishment of such ensembles (Shrock, 1990). The most prominent of the professional symphonic choruses is the Chicago Symphony Chorus, which was founded as a volunteer organization by Hillis in 1957 (Chicago Symphony Orchestra). In its nearly 60 years of existence, the chorus has not only provided singers for symphonic works, but has also recorded and toured in the United States and abroad. Though individual pay was only $2,500 per year in 1990, the Chicago Symphony Chorus is one of the country's largest employers of choral singers, historically paying anywhere from 105 to 165 of its 180 singers (Shrock, 1990). Other symphonic choruses with professional cores have been located in Baltimore, Los Angeles, Milwaukee, Pittsburgh, San Francisco, Washington, DC, Minneapolis/St. Paul, and Montreal, each paying approximately one third of their singers (Shrock, 1990).

Other autonomous professional choirs more loosely associated with professional orchestras emerged in the 1950s to 1970s. The Los Angeles Master Chorale (2015), now in its 52nd season, presents its own series of concerts each year. The ensemble's repertoire ranges from Renaissance polyphony to newly commissioned works. In addition to touring and recording, the ensemble has performed more than 500 concerts with the Los Angeles Philharmonic. In 1990, a Los Angeles singer could expect approximately $15,000 in compensation if they sang in all performances during the year (Shrock, 1990). The late Michael Korn founded a similar organization, The Philadelphia Singers, which operated from 1972 to 2014. It too was an autonomous choral organization, which in addition to its own series of seasonal concerts collaborated with organizations such as the Philadelphia Orchestra and Philadelphia Ballet. According to one member, singers in the core ensemble were paid for up to 11 different concerts per year. Additional volunteer singers were added for ballet and orchestral collaborations, up to two volunteers for each paid singer.

Korn helped found the Association of Professional Vocal Ensembles (APVE) in 1977 in order to support and promote professional choruses like his Philadelphia Singers (Shrock, 1990). He stated in a 1990 interview with Shrock that the impetus to organize came from a desire to create and support professional choral ensembles on par with professional orchestras in the United States. Korn felt that such ensembles could provide a place for college- and conservatory-trained singers to continue to refine their craft while receiving compensation for their education and their work. APVE was also established in order to secure grants from the National Endowment for the Arts, which requires the existence of an industry (professional choral singing) in order to grant funds (see Shrock, 1990). Now known as Chorus America, APVE has since expanded its focus to support all autonomous choral organizations through advocacy, research, and leadership development. Its membership has grown from 17 in 1977, to 90 in 1990, to more than 4,500 today, of which 110 are considered professional choral ensembles (Chorus America website.). This number is significantly higher than the 32 preprofessional, professional core, and fully professional ensembles Hill reported in 1980.

The newest generation of North American professional ensembles emerged in the late 1970s around the time of the founding of APVE and continues to thrive today. In this group are ensembles such as Seraphic Fire (Miami), Phoenix Chorale, Santa Fe Desert Chorale, Kansas City Chorale, Cincinnati Vocal Arts Ensemble, Conspirare (Austin), VocalEssence (Minneapolis), and The Crossing (Philadelphia). This generation differs from its predecessors in several ways. First, whereas professional choirs of the mid-20th century were likely to earn a good part of their living by touring, most of these ensembles are based in a particular city (many are named for their location). This resident status differs from the recording and touring choirs of the 1950s and '60s who had no specific home base for financial support and concert attendance. Of these new ensembles, Korn (in Shrock, 1990, p. 9) said their basic structure may be the same, but success comes to those who can read the climate of their particular area and provide musical experiences that correspond.

A second difference is in the fluctuating membership of such ensembles and the sharing of singers by multiple ensembles. Although some choirs have regular rosters of locally based singers, it is not uncommon for other singers to regularly perform with these local ensembles in places as far apart as Miami, Philadelphia, and Sante Fe. While many of these choirs may audition singers, equally important seems to be recommendation by other singers in the group. Finally, rather than having a stable roster of singers, the membership of many of these ensembles is built on a gig-by-gig basis. Singers typically rehearse for four to five days, followed by five to six concerts in multiple locations within the same geographic region.

CURRENT TRENDS IN PROFESSIONAL CHORAL SINGING

Due to a dearth of research on this topic, the majority of this section is based on information gleaned anecdotally and from interviews with five professional working musicians: Andrew Megill is the conductor of the Montreal Symphony Chorus and several college, professional core, and fully professional choruses in North America; Donald Nally is a conductor of college and fully professional ensembles; Allen Crowell is a former conductor of the US Army Chorus and several collegiate choral ensembles; Diana Grabowski is a soprano who sings with four professional ensembles; and Timothy Coombs is a tenor with the US Army Chorus.

Full-time

The New York professional choral scene is unique in that its singers can piece together nearly a full-time living in one geographic area. In addition to steady church choir and symphonic work, numerous independent professional choral ensembles produce 5 to 6 concerts each season, also hiring on a gig-by-gig basis. None of the choruses in New York has a consistent core of singers; rather the ensembles rely on union contractors to hire their singers for the particular concert. "Most come from the same pool of about 150 singers. You will see the same faces in multiple ensembles," stated Dougherty. Because of the large number of professional choral singers in the area, contractors are able to specifically tailor the ensemble based on repertoire and based on the conductor's preferences. A singer who is hired to sing Bach, for example, may not be hired for a concert of opera choruses presented by the same ensemble.

Small vocal ensembles like Cantus, Chanticleer, and The King's Singers also provide full-time employment for singers, though because of their small number and small membership these positions are fairly limited (Sigman, 2011). While opera choruses typically provide only part time work for choral singers, choristers in New York's Metropolitan Opera Chorus ("the MET") are union represented and make a living wage solely from operatic choral singing. When especially busy, this 125-member group works six days per week, with two rehearsals during the day followed by a performance at night. During the 2013 season, which was unusually busy, choristers at the MET were paid an average of $200,000 plus $100,000 in benefits due to overtime payments (Swarns, 2014; Wise, 2014).

The largest employer of full time choral singers in North America is the United States military. The US Army, Navy, and Air Force all support fully professional choral and instrumental ensembles. These ensembles provide music for government functions in Washington and may tour for up to ten weeks per year. Singers audition for the ensembles as civilians, and if accepted must enlist before passing basic training and security clearances. Enlisted singers receive a housing allowance, salary, medical benefits, and pension in accordance with military standards. Many continue their musical studies while enlisted and therefore have advanced degrees in music, partially funded by the government. Because of the financial stability provided by both the MET chorus and military ensembles, each has an incredibly high rate of singer retention (Young, 1998; also Allen Crowell; Timothy Coombs).

Part-time

While some opportunities exist for full-time choral singing in small vocal ensembles, in New York, or in a military ensemble, the reality of professional choral singing for most is that it is not a source of full-time income. This has changed little since 1980 when Paul Hill wrote, "There are virtually no choruses at the present time that have fifty-two weeks of work each year for their singers" (p. 13), though some of the major touring ensembles offer 6 to 30 weeks per year. "Other revenue usually comes from music teaching, church and synagogue singing, opera choruses, employment in music shops, and non-musical responsibilities" (Hill, 1980, p. 13). Sigman (2011) wrote that:

> Reality (then as now) turned out to be a patchwork of church jobs, teaching, and the occasional solo opportunity, all the while studying with a vocal coach . . . Even core members of leading professional ensembles rarely yield as much as a third of their income from their primary chorus job, and usually much less. (para. 1)

Singing in or conducting multiple choirs, public school and private music teaching, coaching, and solo performing all help supplement income, while full- or part-time positions outside of music may provide necessary medical and retirement benefits. Megill stated that even the top choral singers in smaller markets often have day jobs outside of music, even though they may be as highly trained as fully professional musicians.

Church choirs also continue to provide steady employment for choral singers, though few if any in North America are considered full-time employment. Choristers in major metropolitan areas such as New York City or Washington, DC can make up to $140 per appearance, sometimes being called for up to 15 appearances in a week including Sunday services, evensong services, special concerts, and weekly rehearsals (Megill; Coombs). Symphonic choruses also continue to provide income for part-time choral singers. Singers in the San Francisco Symphony Chorus can be hired for up to eight major works annually plus seasonal concerts. While the total possible income for a singer in this ensemble was only $6,000 in 1990, singers in the LA Master Chorale made up to $15,000 if they sang for all performances in the same year (Shrock, 1990). Finally, summer residence organizations such as the Arizona Bach Festival, Oregon Bach Festival, and Carmel Bach Festival all support fully professional choral ensembles, providing another source of part-time employment for professional choral singers.

Rehearsal pedagogy

Research on the pedagogy of professional choirs is notably lacking. What evidence does exist in print is typically tangential to the main topic of the publication. Due to this nearly complete lack of research, the rehearsal pedagogy of professional choral ensembles will be described here based on a small number of interviews with current singers and conductors of professional choral ensembles. A complete investigation of the pedagogy of professional choirs is outside of the scope of this chapter. It is hoped however that this section will inspire future research into the pedagogy of such ensembles.

Although each professional ensemble differs in its pedagogy based on purpose and structure of the organization, several common strains can be found across most professional vocal ensembles, especially those in the United States and England. Major differences in pedagogy seem to be related to the size of the ensemble more than any other factor. Korn (see Shrock, 1990), Dougherty, and Carrington each compared professional vocal ensembles to their parallel professional instrumental ensembles: small vocal ensembles of approximately 6 to 12 singers are likened to the string quartet, while larger ensembles are compared to professional orchestras. In this section, the pedagogy of small ensembles will be described based on Carrington's experience as a founding and performing member of the Kings Singers. The pedagogy of larger groups will be described based on the small body of information gleaned from the literature, with heavy reliance on interviews with current conductors and singers.

Small professional vocal ensembles: The King's Singers

The King's Singers was conceived and founded by co-author Simon Carrington and five of his fellow students at King's College Cambridge in 1968. It is still "one of the world's most celebrated vocal ensembles" (The King's Singers, n.d., homepage) known particularly for the singers' interpretive and communicative skills. In such small ensembles, the level of personal responsibility goes beyond that of a typical choral singer because there is typically only one person singing each part. While a more or less consistent repertoire lessens the necessity to read music at a rapid pace, the interpretive demands of being both a co-creator and the sole performer on a part require each member to operate at full capacity at all times. Every minute of rehearsal time is made more valuable because of the demands of frequent performances.

Small vocal ensembles can operate with or without a designated music director. In the King's Singers, Carrington began as music director of the group, leading rehearsals by "lightly conducting" from within the ensemble. As time passed, the necessity for a conductor diminished, with each performer contributing more or less equally to the rehearsal process. Under this system, the manner of rehearsing is similar to that of a string quartet. Each member is solely responsible for their own part while having to listen and respond to the other members of the ensemble. Working in this manner requires a high level of collegiality, as all members' ideas are equally important in creating the musical product. Perhaps most importantly, each singer must be open to the ideas and constructive criticisms of the other group members. In order to function in such an ensemble, personal ego takes a back seat to sharing in both the responsibility and the accomplishment of the ensemble.

Consensus was the guiding principle during Carrington's tenure with The King's Singers. Rehearsals consisted of sharp, active periods of singing mixed with periods of discussion about which passages to sing through again, as well as discussion of stylistic and vocal considerations. While dialogue was a necessary tool in building consensus, it also allowed all members of the group to contribute their wealth of individual knowledge. Members who specialized in the music of particular genres or composers could bring insight to music within their area of specialization. Even the repertoire itself was selected through a consensus-building process. Although Carrington frequently proposed repertoire for the group, he had to convince the other singers of its worthiness. This sharing of ideas might not have happened as comfortably with one designated conductor. Finally, while working on a consensus basis took more time than typical director-led rehearsals, the process almost always yielded a result that musically satisfied each singer and valued individual contributions.

Small ensembles differ most greatly from large ensembles because singers are creators of their own artistic expression rather than re-creators of the conductor's musical ideas. Perfection is attained through individual responsibility rather than through a slow, repetitive, drawn-out rehearsal process. Working in such a manner negates the need for overrehearsing choral music, which according to Carrington is frequently the cause of stale, lifeless performances in large ensembles. Spontaneity and organic musicality are especially likely to thrive in the small group setting.

Although small vocal ensembles feature one singer on a part, they do still require consensus on basics such as vocal production and sound concept. In the King's Singers, a lean, "silvery" sound was used as a departure point. This silvery tone is flexible but with a consistent intensity, and can be colored by a controlled vibrato ranging from none to moderate. It is tall and unified through vowel shape rather than "blended" (a term which implies a complete ironing out of both individuality and meaning), and should "live" in the front of the face where communication happens most clearly (via the pronunciation of text and facial expression). From this default sound, singers can then change their vocal color to reflect the text. Spectrums of bright to dark, cold to warm, and hard to soft can be used to bring out expressive elements in the words and music. Such a sound concept is, according to Carrington, typical of many small vocal ensembles to this day.

An important feature of small vocal ensembles is individual communication through the text with the audience. Communication with the audience is a skill that must be developed along with sight-reading, tone, and stylistic interpretation. In addition to its concrete and interpretive meanings, text brings with it an implied atmosphere, emotional power, vocal color, and a natural pattern of stress and release. Additionally, in a well-crafted piece, the text and the music cannot be considered apart, as they inform each other at every turn. As such, rehearsals without text are avoided in small ensembles except where deemed absolutely essential to the correct learning of pitches and rhythms in difficult passages.

Singing texted music persuasively particularly involves bringing out the natural stresses of each word and each phrase. Doing so creates multiple layers of ebb and flow in the musical line. Reading the text aloud and bringing out the important words helps singers focus on the stress and flow of each sentence structure. Considering the importance of individual nouns, verbs, prepositions, conjunctions, adjectives, adverbs, and their poetic significance is also crucial to understanding the structure of each sentence. Using these natural stresses that are within each word and that pertain to important and unimportant words (*an*, *the*, etc.) is one of the small ensemble's most basic tools for building expressive musical line (see Carrington, 2012).

Large choruses

One of the purposes behind the founding Association of Professional Vocal Ensembles (APVE) in 1977 was to provide singers the opportunity to continue singing at a high artistic level after college. Large professional choirs vary greatly in their size, function, and ratio of professional to amateur singers. Even so, interviews with several professional singers and conductors revealed several common threads worthy of further research.

Vocal production. One of the most obvious differences between volunteer and professional choruses is the level of solo voice training. Even professional choirs that provide only a portion of their singers' annual income boast of conservatory or university trained musicians, while volunteer ensembles are more likely to be made up of trained and untrained voices. Megill said that the role of the volunteer choir director is both to teach the singers diagnostic skills and to equip them with the musical and vocal skills necessary. He stated, "In the professional ensemble, there is still some level of educating that goes on, but I always assume the singers know more about vocal production than I do." Put simply, in the professional ensemble it's about deciding what the music should sound like and communicating that to the singers, but not instructing singers on how to do it. Nally agreed, saying, "The college choir is about teaching techniques for the singers to unlock their own musical ideas," while the professional ensemble assumes an incredibly high level of vocal proficiency.

Practically speaking, a higher level of vocal responsibility means that professional choirs rarely warm up together as is common in amateur choruses. Singers are expected to arrive ready to sing and to know how to use their instruments wisely in rehearsal, although Nally will occasionally use "warm-up type exercises" designed to address specific tuning challenges. Grabowski noted that in her experience, singers are expected to have "incredibly versatile voices capable of singing a wide variety of repertoire." Furthermore, she noted that her colleagues all have the ability to sing both soloistically and as a chorister as the performance demands. Megill and Doughtery also indicated that professional singers are expected to have a basic understanding of style as appropriate to the repertoire at hand, and be able to implement that style vocally.

Sight-reading and basic musicianship expectations. Just as the expectation of vocal training is greater in a professional choir than it is in an amateur ensemble, so is the expectation for basic musicianship skills. This is most evident in the level of music reading expected of singers. Dougherty noted that in New York ensembles, music is typically distributed at the first rehearsal as it is typically in orchestral ensembles. It is generally expected that singers will be able to read the music on the first or second pass, and if not, come to the second rehearsal with all notes and rhythms learned. Dougherty felt this was reasonable as much of the music programmed in New York ensembles is familiar to the singers, or at least familiar in style. In the US Army's vocal ensembles, Crowell and Coombs report that music is also distributed in rehearsal, often with the conductor's markings in place. Here too singers are expected to read the score correctly the first time, get it on the second pass, or go home and learn it on their own. When music is mailed ahead of time in professional ensembles, singers are expected to arrive with notes and rhythms completely learned. The legendary Fred Waring, conductor of The Pennsylvanians, also reported having sent marked scores to professional singers before working with them as an ensemble in order to ensure a highly detailed performance:

> I'm a great attention-to-detail person—where you breathe, balance, everything that goes into making really fine music. Until all the essential details are in place, you cannot really begin making music. You don't want to waste time telling everyone where to breathe or how to pronounce any given word. All the markings should be done first, then insist that the singers follow them when you do rehearse and perform.

> I always send markings ahead of time. When I say "markings," I don't just mean only where you breathe but also exact pronunciation, dynamics changes, all the phrasing, the divisi assignments, et cetera. All of those go out before I arrive on the scene. I try to instill what I would term basic or fundamental expectations. These are essential to start with before you can even think of making great music. (as quoted in Parish, 2013)

Megill noted that while nonunion singers may be expected to work on music outside of rehearsal, union rules often prevent this practice.

Pacing. A higher level of vocal training, musical skill, and possibly preparation ahead of time naturally leads to faster-paced rehearsals than typically occur in the amateur ensemble. Charles Bruffy, conductor of both the Kansas City Chorale and Phoenix Chorale, stated "professional singers have reading skills that allow us to work at a velocity not possible with volunteer singers . . . and they have developed techniques such that a conductor can depend on replication" (as quoted in Sigman, 2011). Megill stated that fast-paced rehearsals are a financial reality, particularly when a larger percentage of singers are being paid or when travel is involved, as is now often the case. Crowell and Coombs reported that military choruses typically rehearse just two hours each day, partially because they are able to do so due to the high level of musicianship and training, and partially in order to keep voices sounding fresh for frequent performances. Donald Palumbo, chorus master of the Metropolitan Opera Chorus, noted that especially on busy days, much of rehearsal time is spent marking. Palumbo stated:

> The danger with marking is that when you pull back a little bit on the energy [while] singing, what usually tends to happen is musically things can also get a little lazy or a little sloppy, so you have to be very careful that when you mark you don't destroy any of the musical exactness that you've been working on so hard in all of the rehearsals. (Palumbo, 2015)

With up to 150 singers spread out across multileveled sets at one time, musical exactness is understandably a top priority for Palumbo's MET Opera chorus.

Finding ensemble. The professional singers interviewed for this chapter reported varying degrees of conductor-led detail work in professional ensembles, stating that instead much of the work in professional choirs is in dealing with building ensemble within the group. Coombs stated:

> It's not the same [director-led] detail work that you'd get in a college choir. We deal with larger sections of music at a time, and since we rehearse together every day, and since there is so much retention in the group from year to year, a lot of the detail work gets figured out. If we breathe together really well, we pretty much get to know what the other people in the room are going to do. (personal communication, September 11, 2015)

Rehearsals in other professional ensembles seem to be run in a similar fashion, relying on repetition as an important rehearsal method. Because singers are capable of self-diagnosis and correction, less talk is required from the conductor than in other types of choirs. Nally reported that since his professional singers are so experienced, much of his rehearsals are about "just getting on the same page chorally," particularly when singers come from different educational backgrounds or different parts of the country. Megill calls this rehearsing "ensemble skills" which include language work, rhythmic work, and also coming to a unified point of view toward both the music and the text. Grabowski stated that in her experience, conductors of professional ensembles work on ensemble through tuning, language, style, articulation, use of vibrato (especially for sopranos), and occasionally tone production. Much of Palumbo's work at the MET dealt with creating ensemble through unified vowel shapes. While a solo voice can modify vowels greatly for technical or expressive purposes, he stated that unified vowels are necessary to create a unified sound in the chorus. Canadian conductor Jon Washburn stated that it is ensemble that truly sets the professional choir apart: "The difference is in the ensemble. You are likely to have a higher and more consistent sound. When singers are all the same level they all make each other sound better" (as quoted in Sigman, 2011).

Intermusician relationships. Grabowski compared the work environment of the professional choir to that of an elite sports team with everyone working together at an incredibly high level. This is partially due to the fact that singers know they must pull their weight, otherwise they will not be asked back. She said that rather than creating a competitive atmosphere, this actually helps singers to remove their egos from the process. Rehearsals of the ensembles in which she sings are characterized by "generosity of spirit, a feeling of collaboration within each section, and a lack of hierarchy between singers." She also stated that though rehearsals are director-led rather than collaborative (as in small vocal ensembles), "rehearsals are characterized by a high level of mutual respect between singers and the conductor." She felt that rehearsals must be conductor-led with so many highly trained choral musicians in the room together; otherwise, there would be too many opinions at once. "And the conductors have very specific ideas about how they want the music to sound," she added.

Dougherty said that in his experience, there are "varying levels of interest in gathering input from the choir," but that conductors are all at least open to questions from the ensemble. In military choral ensembles, the relationship between conductor and singer is partially defined by military structures. In the US Army choruses in particular, the conductors are all officers, while the singers are noncommissioned officers. Coombs stated that while there is a good atmosphere of collaboration in these ensembles and a high level of respect coming from both sides of the podium, "there must always be an etiquette behind musical questions."

Megill saw the relationship between conductor and professional singer as different than the bond that is often created in amateur ensembles due to the lack of a teacher/student relationship. In professional ensembles, he felt that conductors and singers are more or less equal, coming from similar backgrounds and training. While conductors and professional singers can still have a close relationship, it is not the same as the bond typically formed between an amateur choir and their conductor. Crowell added that unlike professional choirs, the focus of college choirs must also include preparing the singers to become future music leaders. Megill also noted this difference in responsibility. In educational ensembles, he stated:

> The director is primarily responsible to the singers and their musical growth with performance being an important outgrowth of the process. In a professional ensemble, the responsibility of both the director and the singers is to the backers and the audience. (Megill)

Conclusion

This chapter has provided an overview of the history and current state of professional singing in adult choirs. This endeavor was limited by the small body of research pertaining to professional choral singing, with most information pertaining to choirs in the United States. This chapter was further limited in that the existing literature deals primarily with the history and structure of professional ensembles without addressing their pedagogy. While a written history of professional choirs was achieved through published sources, the overview of pedagogy for this chapter was only possible through interviews with a limited number of singers and conductors. Though anecdotal, and though coming from a small number of sources, certain trends emerged which show commonality in professional choral pedagogy that could form the basis for much needed research.

References

Bayreuther Festspiele. (2016). Festival chorus 2015. Retrieved from http://www.bayreuther-festspiele.de/english/performers/festival_chorus_2016_218.html

Berghs, G., Creylman, N., Avaux, M., Decoster, W., & de Jong, F. (2013, July). A lifetime of professional singing: Voice parameters and age in the Netherlands Radio Choir. *Logopedics Phoniatrics Vocology, 38*(2), 59–63. doi:10.3109/14015439.2012.731082

Carrington, S. (2012). Small ensemble rehearsal techniques for choirs of all sizes. In A. de Quadros (Ed.), *The Cambridge companion to choral music* (pp. 281–291). New York: Cambridge University Press.

Chicago Symphony Orchestra. (n.d.). History of the Chicago Symphony Chorus. Retrieved from http://cso.org/about/performers/chicago-symphony-chorus/chicago-symphony-chorus-history/

Chorus America. (n.d.). Chorus America. https://www.chorusamerica.org

DeFotis, C. (1994, March). An interview with Swedish choral conductor Eric Ericson. *The Choral Journal, 34*(8), 21–29.

Hill, P. (1980, April). The professional choir in America: A history and a report on present activity. *The Choral Journal, 20*(8), 10–16.

Kegerreis, R. (1970, October). History of the high school a cappella choir: Chapter 3: Professional choirs that influence the high school a cappella choir movement. *The Choral Journal, 11*(2), 13–17.

The King's Singers. (n.d.). *The King's Singers.* Retrieved September 13, 2014, from http://www.kingssingers.com

Latvian Radio Choir. (n.d.). Choir. Retrieved from http://radiokoris.lv/en/choir

Lawlor, M. F. (2009). *The fifty-year history of the Phoenix Bach Choir: From amateur to professional* (Doctoral dissertation). Arizona State University, Arizona.

Los Angeles Master Chorale. (2015). *About LAMC.* Retrieved from http://www.lamc.org/about/los-angeles-master-chorale

McGee, I. R. (2007). *The origin and historical development of prominent professional Black choirs in the United States* (Doctoral dissertation). Florida State University, Tallahassee. Retrieved from DigiNole http://purl.flvc.org/fsu/fd/FSU_migr_etd-2562

Morrow, P. (1993). *The influence of the Robert Shaw Chorale, the Roger Wagner Chorale and the Gregg Smith Singers on the professional chorus in the United States* (Unpublished doctoral dissertation). Southern Baptist Theological Seminary, Louisville, KY.

Parish, M. (2013, January). Changing the culture of professional choirs. *Choral Director, 10*(1), 10. Retrieved from GALE General OneFile database. (GALE|A320733934)

Palumbo, D. (2015, April 22). Interview by Terry Gross [Digital recording and article]. How the Met Opera's chorus master gets 150 to sound like one. Retrieved from http://www.npr.org

Rugen, K. Z. (2013). *The evolution of choral sound: In professional choirs from the 1970s to the twenty-first century* (Unpublished doctoral dissertation). Arizona State University, Arizona.

Shrock, D. (1990). An interview with Vance George, Michael Korn and Dale Warland: Professional choirs. *The Choral Journal, 30*(7), 5–11.

Sigman, M. (2011). The rise of the professional chorus. *Chorus America.* Retrieved from https://www.chorusamerica.org/conducting-performing/rise-professional-chorus

Smith, J. G., & Young, P. M. (n.d.). Chorus (i). In *Grove Music Online.* Oxford Music Online. Oxford University Press, Retrieved from http://www.oxfordmusiconline.com/subscriber/article/grove/music/05684

Swarns, R. L. (2014, April 20). Asking how much opera singers' work is worth. *New York Times.* Retrieved from http://www.nytimes.com/2014/04/21/nyregion/asking-how-much-an-opera-singers-work-is-worth.html?_r=0

Wise, B. (June 16, 2014). Metropolitan Opera's tax filing reveals salary details. *WQXR: Operavore.* Retrieved from http://www.wqxr.org/#!/story/metropolitan-operas-tax-filing-reveals-salary-details/

Young, J. A. (1998, November). Professional choirs: I can actually make a living? A look at selected military and orchestral singing opportunities and auditions. *The Choral Journal, 39*(4), 49–53.

CHAPTER 23

···

TEACHING AND CONDUCTING DIVERSE POPULATIONS

Boychoir

···

CRAIG DENISON

THE phenomenon of boychoir singing in the United States is an intersection of general choral pedagogy, male vocal physiology, and the social context of boys' singing. While many fine resources on male choral pedagogy and male vocal physiology exist, the social context of boychoir singing is not as well documented (Ashley, 2009; Williams, Welch, & Howard, 2005). This context is delineated by the documented historical past of European boys' singing (Ashley, 2009, 2013; Mould, 2007; Boynton & Rice, 2008) and American norms of choral performance, gender typing, and organizational structures (Abrahams, 2012; Abril, 2007; Ashley, 2011; Freer, 2006, 2009a, 2012b; Harrison, Welch, & Adler, 2012; Kennedy, 2002, 2004).

Boychoirs in the United States are characterized by four distinct factors: (1) they employ multistage singing in the diverse maturity levels of its member singers; (2) they allow for singing across registers as is suitable to its individual members; (3) they value traditional sacred repertory, and endeavor to connect the historical context with contemporary life; (4) they define their success by community and audience response more than adjudicated ratings.

This chapter describes and asserts the unique pedagogy of boychoir singing by these delineations. References to voice change will often utilize the terminology of vocal science: premutational in reference to unchanged voices, mutational to changing voices, and postmutational for changed voices. For those familiar with Cooksey's sequence of male voice change, these are Stage 1, Stages 2–4, and Stage 5 respectively (Cooksey, 2000a, 2000b; Thurman, 2012). Many of the assertions made in this chapter are supported by current American conductors of community boychoirs as reported in recent survey data (Denison, 2015). This survey will be referenced throughout the chapter.

What is a boychoir? In the United States, a boychoir is a choral group of young males whose voices can range anywhere from premutation through postmutation. In other words, the singers in a boychoir are those whose voices will change, are changing, and have changed (Denison, 2015). In the community boychoirs of North America, the postmutational singers are in their teens or early twenties, such as singers found in the American Boychoir, the Birmingham Boys' Choir, or the Pacific Boychoir. In some church and cathedral choirs, the changed voices are adult men, as can be heard in the Choir of Men and Boys at St. Thomas, New York City. In any case, these singers, in varying levels of maturity participate as artistic equals in performance (Higgenbottom, 1996), making the boychoir experience a multigenerational phenomenon. As a result, a boychoir can employ a wide variety of voicings. In a single boychoir concert, an audience member would certainly hear the Soprano-Alto (SA) singing of younger voices, but could also likely encounter Soprano-Alto-Tenor-Bass (SATB) from the whole choir, and even Tenor 1-Tenor 2-Bass 1-Bass 2 (TTBB) from the changed voices (Denison, 2015).

In the center of this variety is the maturing voice of the adolescent. Adolescents of both genders encounter complex change (Gackle, 2011). Because the manifestation of boys' vocal mutation is more overt, it attracts greater attention, especially from beginning teachers and directors. A great deal has been researched, written, and asserted about the change in boys' voices during maturation in middle school (Freer, 2009c; Barham, 2001; Collins, 1993; Collins, 2012; Cooksey, 1999; Dilworth, 2012; Friddle, 2005; Hollien, 2012; Leck, 2009a; McCoy; 2003; McKenzie, 1956; Palant, 2014; Phillips, 2014; Phillips, Williams, & Edwin, 2012; Reed, 2008; Swanson, 1961; Thurman, 2012; Welch, 2000; Williams, 2013). Hopefully, the rise of qualitative methodologies and greater precision in voice measurement will allow for a deeper understanding and explanation of female vocal mutation to correct this imbalance in the research.

Research and academic writing on male vocal mutation often presume a scholastic context for singing, creating a middle school pedagogy. Such research has provided new teachers and directors a valid framework on which to build their own approach to boys' singing. In particular, the research of John Cooksey (2000a, 2000b) has been valuable in confirming what many experienced boychoir directors know from oral tradition and experience: that neither chronological age nor visible physiological changes predict the onset of voice change. Inexperienced directors would be wise to familiarize themselves with his research and recommendations.

Boychoir pedagogy diverges from traditional middle school male voice pedagogy, particularly in its treatment of vocal registration. Most range charts, repertoire, and pedagogy manuals for middle school presume the use of lower register (Freer, 2009c; Barham, 2001; Collins, 1993, 2012; Cooksey, 1999; Dilworth, 2012; Friddle, 2005; Leck, 2009a). This register is often called chest voice or heavy mechanism and is characterized by thicker vocal folds with full vibration along the entire length of the vocal folds. Boychoirs, on the other hand, allow for lower and upper register singing.

Upper register singing is often referred to as head voice or light mechanism and is characterized by thinner vocal folds that continue to have full vibration along their entire length (Williams, 2013), possessing a vibrant and appealing quality for boychoir singing. Upper register notes that have only partial vibration are known as falsetto, which lacks the dynamic range of full fold vibration. Falsetto is frequently employed by boys as well, especially during mutation before vocal part reassignment, but should be used judiciously. A crescendo and diminuendo on a single pitch (messa di voce) can be employed to indicate whether full vibration is taking place in the upper register. While it is beyond the scope of this chapter to sufficiently address vocal registration in all its complexity and nuance, especially in regards to vocal formant, it is an ever-present concern for the director and the boys in a boychoir (Denison, 2015). This chapter will refer to the so-called head voice as upper register and chest voice as lower register. Both head voice and chest voice are subregisters of the modal range, and represent full vocal fold vibration (Thurman, Welch, Theimer, Grefsheim, & Feit, 2000).

The use of multiple registrations in boychoir singing complicate the applicability of the research situated in a middle school context. Middle school pedagogy asserts that the boys' voice change is a downward sequential shift of the singer's range (Freer, 2009c). Cooksey's stages of voice change (2000b) reflect this school of thought, and are supported by several studies (Rutkowski, 1982; Groom, 1984; Hollien, 2012; Tanner, 1969). The applicability of this research to boychoir, however, is limited to the boys' lower register singing. Since upper register singing has either not been included or has a minimal presence in these studies' data analyses, boychoir directors often feel that the models and ranges emerging from this research are not suitable to their boychoirs (Leck, 2009a). Cooksey acknowledged vocal registration as a valuable component of understanding male vocal mutation, but was not able to sufficiently quantify it to his satisfaction (2000a). As a result, upper register singing was excluded from analysis, although Cooksey accurately notes the emerging differentiation of registers as the voice matures and includes this differentiation in his description of vocal stages (2000b).

Boychoir pedagogy views the voice change more broadly. Often, conductors view vocal mutation as one of a growing range, where the lower register follows a path similar to the one delineated by Cooksey. The upper register is not only retained, but sometimes even expanded upward. Henry Leck (2009b), a children's choir director, first articulated this school of thought, and several children's and youth community choir directors share his view (Denison, 2015). The terminology is still being argued for this school of thought with some preferring the term "evolving" rather than "expanding" (Malvar-Ruiz, cited in Palant, 2014). While some children's and boychoir directors share this view, these directors are less in agreement on the lower register of a boys' changing voice. Many boychoir directors embrace the unique, rich vibrant color of the lower register, while others hear a timbre too different to be suitable.

I have thus far delineated the context of boychoir singing by its (1) multigenerational quality and (2) its use of singing across vocal registers. Another important factor in fully understanding boychoir singing is its history. Most musicians understand formal boys' singing as originating in the church centuries ago (Mould, 2007; Boynton & Rice, 2008). Through centuries, this practice generated a large body of sacred repertoire intended for boys' voices. Sacred music continues to be an important and valuable part of North American community boychoir core repertory even though most of them are nonsectarian choirs. Many boychoir conductors feel that boys value the sacred historical repertory because of its vocal fit, compositional style, and direct spirituality.

The final factor that differentiates boychoir singing is its relationship to the values of its audience. In other contexts of boys' singing, particularly in schools, an in-place assessment often defines what is musically valuable. These assessments may be standardized, such as Music Performance Assessments in Florida and Texas, or they may be unique to the corresponding competitive situations. While these adjudicated assessments may be useful for growth, their requirements are only recently beginning to allow for flexibility in key and voicing that boys' voices require. In the case of middle school, the evaluative tool is often a derivative of the high school measurement, which is not appropriate. Middle school is not 'high school lite'; it is a unique context unto itself. Furthermore, these assessments often measure how well a choir fits the evaluation model more than what an audience would value (Asmus, 2009). To be clear, assessment tools are not objectionable per se. To the contrary, they can provide a conductor a new framework with which to understand his or her choir. Audience surveys and formal music assessments have provided conductors with valuable information in the past. Certainly, a music assessment and an audience survey are not mutually exclusive; boychoir audiences can be very discerning. However, most audience members and judges by definition approach music making from two different experiential viewpoints.

Boychoirs in the United States are characterized by four distinct factors: (1) they employ multistage singing in the diverse maturity levels of its member singers; (2) they allow for singing across registers as is suitable to its individual members; (3) they value traditional sacred repertoire, and endeavor to connect the historical context with contemporary life; (4) they define their success by community and audience culture more than academic ratings.

The remainder of the chapter addresses pedagogical practices within boychoir: repertoire selection and preparation, rehearsal, and performance. The chapter closes with a consideration of the meanings of boys' singing from the viewpoint of American society, the individual boychoir community, and finally the boys themselves. The word "trebles" will be used to denote those boys whose singing is in a range similar to sopranos. Both words are used in the boychoir community, although most choirs use one over the other (Denison, 2015).

Choosing Repertoire

Boychoirs today sing all kinds of repertory in richly various historical, popular, and cultural styles. For many conductors, adapting the literature to the boys' voices is key. Rather than recommending what is good musical content for boys' singing, it is best to understand the voices of the boychoir and base repertoire decisions on that knowledge.

Boychoir repertoire needs to take into account the floaty qualities of trebles, and the timbres available to altos. A piece that is well-written for an SSA boychoir includes opportunities for trebles to sing very high, especially if the high notes are floaty. Many adult sopranos grapple with how to float, but boys tend to float with greater ease

(Denison, 2015). Boys' propensity for high, floaty notes should not be overused, however. Stamina is an important consideration in composing for the high pitches within the upper register. Some boys can also sing with great power in their extreme high, and those voices make great "finishers" in adding excitement to a final chord.

Some of the most effective compositions for today's boychoir treat alto voices like those of young baritones with upper register accessibility (Denison, 2015). Experienced boychoir singers have greater ease in managing the *passaggio* between upper and lower register than those with less experience (Denison, 2015), and altos are often asked to sing in this range. Second altos in a boychoir are more often pleased when their line goes down to D3 or E3, and many conductors agree that the unique color of these notes at this age is desirable (Denison, 2015). As the year progresses, many of them will have a useful Bb2. Second altos can still access upper register notes, although lines centered around D4 or E4 should be avoided when possible. They can do well and enjoy singing in unison with the trebles in certain works, but singing down the octave (via octave displacement) is also a pleasure for them to sing (Barham, 2001).

The interior voices, like treble 2 and alto 1, generally should be true to their "first name." Conductors often assign treble 2 to those boys who have better music literacy or struggle with extreme high notes (Denison, 2015). Alto 1 singers are often older boys who sometimes find the upper register uncomfortable. In addition to these older boys, boys whose premutational voice has a rich, warm color in the middle to low range make fine altos.

Teenage men in boychoirs are able to access some surprisingly high pitches within their lower register (Denison, 2015). These are often best heard as part of a rhythmic passage rather than a legato line. A slightly lower tessitura than is found in adult repertory is best for young tenors in singing lyrical SATB compositions. This is doubly true for young basses; sustained upper pitches in the lower register are difficult for them to execute well, although they can do quite well in accessing them in quick passages.

While the preceding is a good guide for composers and new conductors of boychoirs, those who have conducted boys for years know that boys consistently break generalities (Denison, 2015). With a strong foundation in vocal technique before the voice change, many boys are able to adroitly handle pitches near their *passaggio* and have an extended range far beyond what contemporary range charts express. Some teenage basses can sing remarkably low, especially if they had an early voice change. Sometimes, boys who were uninteresting as trebles become powerful and daunting tenors with remarkable upper extensions. Also, many high-school-age men raised in the boychoir context still have beautiful and powerful upper registers that can be of value in works that require power. Indeed, the vocal outliers that we find from year to year provide us with wonderful opportunities in program creation and repertoire.

Culture and repertoire

Outliers remind us that our choir is a unique cultural group, possessing its own dynamic qualities. Technical observations of range and voicing guide selection of repertoire and programming, but they are of no consequence if the social lives of the boys, their families, and the audience are not considered (Ashley, 2009; Harrison, Welch, & Adler, 2012). How boys feel about their voices and what they would like to do must inform repertoire selection.

Understanding boys' voices doesn't just mean their physiological voice, but their social one as well. A critical pedagogy approach allows all boys, outliers as well as typical singers, to express their experiences and preferences. Repertoire selection also involves using rehearsal time to have boy singers express and explain their voice as they understand it in that moment (Freer, 2006; Harrison, 2010; Kennedy, 2002, 2004). An atmosphere of inquiry in rehearsal can yield particularly powerful experiences for both singer and conductor, and valuable professional growth can come from these discussions.

Another way that a critical pedagogy can affect repertoire can be found in music making outside the usual rehearsal routine. Having a separate jam session, where the boys can freely create new music or improvise on the existing repertoire, can be a wonderful opportunity to hear music in a new way (Denison, 2012). In this environment, the conductor becomes the facilitator rather than instructor or director. This partnership with the boys has an important and vital benefit. The boys delineate their identity through the music rather than having it assigned or controlled by an adult (Ashley, 2011).

I agree with researchers and writers who assert that teenage singers want to explore their "possible selves" through music (Freer, 2009a, 2009b). The possible selves framework asserts that adolescents of both genders temporarily "try out" an identity as a means of exploring themselves and the world. In music, this means trying out identities by exploring new music of a wide variety: not just musical theater and popular styles, but also Renaissance polyphony, avant garde, and contemporary music. These genres in many ways can represent new aspects of the emerging self that I regularly see young singers explore and embrace (Freer, 2006). Younger singers learn from the older to adopt this positive, vibrant approach to diversity in music. For me, the music that I often favor for boys is music that is not only suitable for their voices, but also engages their imagination of what could be (Phillips & Doneski, 2011).

An expert boychoir conductor can take the boys' experiences and explorations and connect them to the larger culture of family and community. The values, desires, and preferences of families are important elements to consider when selecting repertoire. The same is true for the community-at-large. Arts and entertainment are words that differ by locale and culture, and the audience must be considered when repertoire is selected. Indeed, awareness of the audience is of great value to the singers in a boychoir as they prepare and perform their music. While it may not be necessary for the choir to strictly conform to these views, ignoring the specific culture surrounding the boys' singing is a mistake.

Historical repertoire

Upon first consideration, boychoirs seems to have a wealth of convenient and suitable music available. The Choral Public Domain Library (www.cpdl.org) has thousands of free works composed specifically for boys' voices, many of these with historical contexts.

Music from the past is a valuable part of the boychoir repertory, and plainchant, polyphony, and sacred works from the past are natural matches for boys' voices, as they are suitable for trebles and altos. Indeed, it could be argued that this music is the most suitable of all genres for boys.

Upon closer scrutiny, this repertoire presents several challenges. Some of these works have treble/alto lines that use extreme ranges or are highly florid, both of which require advance stamina and reading skills. A treble or alto line could be so florid (e.g., Bach, Cantata 147, mvt. 1) as to consume a great deal of rehearsal time in simply getting the counting and pitches correct. Also, younger trebles, around age 8–11, generally do not have the extreme upper range required by some of these works (Denison, 2015). Younger boys also have less stamina for longer lines and a narrower dynamic range (Cooksey, 2000a). Older trebles, approximately age 12–15, shine in the upper register, can sing long lines, and can have a remarkably wide dynamic range (Denison, 2015). However, many of them, particularly as they grow, lose dynamic power and core in lower pitches of their upper register, becoming somewhat airy in those pitches. Tenor and bass lines in these works can also be challenging for high-school-aged singers, especially since the works were composed principally with adult men in mind. Further complicating historical works is the contemporary use of *A* 440 Hz. For Baroque music, the use of the lower *A* 415 Hz is recommended, and Renaissance literature varied as much as a minor 3rd above and below our standard *A* 440 (Paulk, 2005).

An additional challenge in selecting boychoir repertory is that very few recent compositions have been written specifically for the contemporary boychoir, especially when compared with other choir types. As a result, boychoir concert programs can often be a collection of appropriations from other genres that are adapted to a boychoir's unique voicing (Denison, 2015).

Choosing the entire repertoire before a performance season begins is a luxury that many boychoir directors do not get an opportunity to enjoy (Denison, 2015). The onset and rate of voice change is not predictable, especially in the upper registers (Cooksey, 2000a). As a result, most boychoir directors often decide repertoire as the season unfolds. Many of their choices are based organically on the boys' psychology and physiology as they proceed through maturation (Denison, 2015).

Rehearsing Repertoire

Part assignment

Voice part assignment is also fluid in boychoir contexts. Multiple register singing allows the conductor to choose from a variety of timbres that can be judiciously applied to the style, genre, and performance space. For example, high school male singing in the upper register is generally more powerful but less flexible than premutational treble singing. In the large, resonant space of an old cathedral, high school treble singing of a festive anthem is thrilling to both the singer and the listener, but in a smaller space may seem rough and ungracious.

In a boychoir context, the director provides the singer with a general voice part, but as rehearsals proceed and balance becomes evident, he may change that part either wholly or in select passages (Denison, 2015; Herman, 1988). Opportunities for mutational and postmutational voices to sing down the octave, also known as octave displacement, are another tool in "on-the-fly" editing that conductors often can use to great effect (Barham, 2001; Dilworth, 2012). The part could change from piece to piece, or even measure to measure. The process of switching parts occurs with the understanding that the individual singer is a good music reader and able to manage such changes. These techniques are not unique to boychoirs; they are also an important part of middle school pedagogy (Killian, 2003). What is different in boychoir is that moving a boy up to a higher part than is assigned is more common, since the upper register is more highly valued in boychoir.

These processes of part-switching and octave displacement are valuable in several respects: (1) they strengthen the overall performance of the ensemble; (2) they allow flexibility for the singers to sing their voice as it exists not as it is notated on the page; (3) they reinforce the vocal abilities of the individual singer that may exist outside the assigned voice part. By filtering the music through the boys' own voices in the flux of voice part assignment, a culture of maturation drives the acquisition of knowledge and meaning expressed in the performance.

Rehearsal procedures

A meaningful boychoir rehearsal, then, is one in which the director is sometimes an authority, sometimes a collaborator. In both cases, the director leads the boychoir in the realization of meaning through music that can then be conveyed to an audience. Boychoir pedagogy includes elements of existing pedagogy as well as its own unique practices. Vocal warm-ups, sight singing, and music theory are present in boychoir pedagogy as well as typical rehearsal techniques. But because a boychoir is a culture of history, maturation, and performance, some adjustments and differences are present.

An expert boychoir warm-up accomplishes several goals in a short amount of time: (1) it assesses the emotional and physical state of boys; (2) it provides the exercises that create a desirable timbre for the repertoire to be rehearsed; (3) it teaches and reinforces healthy singing habits; (4) it sets the social tone appropriate to the genre to be sung; (5) it provides information valuable in determining part reassignment. While that may seem like a lot to do in a warm up, a well-chosen exercise can be the vehicle in realizing these goals. A deluge of choral warm-up books and methods exist to help, and a hybrid of these methods is recommended.

In general, boychoirs are music-reading ensembles. This follows the trajectory of performance established by centuries of boys' singing in sacred contexts, where a large rotating body of complex repertory had to be ready for performance on a daily or near-daily basis (Mould, 2007). As with warm-ups, boychoirs use and follow a wide variety of music literacy resources, some of them developed within the organization (Denison, 2015). Two are most common: Kodály-based instruction, with an emphasis on aural fluency utilizing solfège skills, and the Royal School of Church Music training method *Voice for Life*, which uses isolated intervals, dictation, and written composition to facilitate reading fluency. As new styles of music-making begin to make their way into concerts, particularly in non-Western and popular styles, conductors are beginning to explore a comprehensive training that involves movement, improvisation and by-ear singing. This trend is more established in children's choirs, but is beginning to make its way into boychoirs as well (Denison, 2015).

Movement

Also finding its way into boychoir rehearsal is the use of motion to engage musical understanding. Depending on the director's experience, the use of Dalcroze, conducting, and choreography are increasingly being employed to help connect boys to phrasing. In my own rehearsals, I encourage the boys to conduct themselves and find it very effective, especially when they are encouraged to eschew specific conducting patterns and let the gesture respond to and inform the music. On occasion, I will ask for them all to use the same gesture, but I find free movement more effective. The free and flowing body that results from movement in rehearsal should be encouraged to transfer to performance. This practice of body freedom in performance is supplanting the more uniform, and often rigid, stance of singing that has characterized many choirs in the past.

One movement that is unique to boychoirs is the practice of raising a hand for a mistake. This is a centuries-old practice, and one that was believed to be essential to rehearsal (Mould, 2007). In today's boychoir, a raised hand indicates several valuable bits of information to the conductor: (1) the singer is aware of the mistake, (2) the boys around the singer know that he is aware of the mistake, (3) he is committed to correcting the error. The result of this practice is a more efficient rehearsal, where the singing doesn't have to stop for an individual singer's mistake. So important was this to the ancient choir directors, that a chorister's failure to raise his hand resulted in corporal punishment! Happily, while the practice of hand-raising is still the norm, such punishment has long since disappeared.

Standing order

This hand-raising tradition signifies the trust and responsibility that is placed on the boy singer by the conductor. This relationship can also be seen in a long-standing choir formation, still used in many boychoir rehearsals, that is derived from the split chancel formation in high liturgy churches (Mould, 2007). In my organization, we called it "cathedral formation." In this formation the choir encircles the piano, where the conductor sits and plays: highest voices to the conductor's right to coincide with the piano's upper range. Singers are close to the conductor, and the best and most mature singers of each section are closest to the conductor, who is sitting at the same eye level as the singers. In many ways, the conductor, while still providing leadership, is creating music with the boys as an equal. While this set-up can also be construed as another structure that gives a conductor power, in honest and wise hands, this becomes a set-up of constructing music together in a more collaborative model. While this practice is disappearing in secular boychoirs, the use of circle singing is common, and echoes ancient practice (Denison, 2015).

Proximity is an especially important and powerful tool for younger singers. While older singers have a much wider circle of private space, younger singers are happy to stand close to the conductor and each other. Boychoir's use of proximity differs from the American norm of a conductor on a podium facing a distant choir in rows. The boychoir's more circular formation seen in the cathedral formation described earlier has been used for centuries and predates the use of singing in circles in rehearsals now used in other American choral ensembles (Denison, 2015).

Programming Repertoire

An engaging and expert concert for boychoir is one that includes a mixture of voicings and vocal timbres. It includes music of diverse styles that can be organized to share a unifying theme. It meets the audience's expectations of what a boychoir is, and expands its understanding through variety. It employs a visual component that reinforces the music, whether by fully employed choreography or simply a fluid body stance that interacts with the phrasing of the music.

For adults, the idea of boychoir singing indicates something spiritual and otherworldly (Ashley, 2009). The term "angel" and boy soprano can seem inseparable, and a music review of boychoir that doesn't use "angel" or "angelic" in regards to boys' singing is very rare. This expectation is completely contrary to how choirboys think of themselves or their music (Ashley, 2011). The music director has a unique challenge in programming a concert so that it fulfills the audience's expectation, and still portrays the culture and identity of the boys' singing authentically.

A good program includes elements that act within the "angel" paradigm, but also has selections that give the audience a new, possibly more genuine view of the boys. These selections could have elements of play that the boys enjoy. For example, in choreographing a piece of music, the boys should be encouraged to contribute moves, tricks, and acrobatics that could be applied to the piece.

Some selections can also have an element of what Estelle Jorgensen (2011) calls "transgression" against the angel image and the usual concert paradigm. Breaking the proscenium and singing within the audience is appreciated not only by the boys, who can consider this as play, but to the audience, who has an opportunity to appreciate the boys as individuals by their closer proximity. Transgression can also inform repertoire choice. "Revolting Children" from *Matilda,* Britten's "Golden Vanity," and "The Cremation of Sam McGee" by Ken Berg, are good examples of boys acting against the angel image. Varying the boy-angel archetypes in a program provides interest for the audience and allows for the boys perform in a range of roles.

Another source of variety can be found in the voicing of the music in the program. A boychoir program with treble, alto, tenor and bass singers offers a wide array of pitches and timbres for the audience. Consider a small program set about leaving and returning home: "Goodbye Then" (Timothy Takach), "Empty" (Takach), "Alister McAlpine's Lament" (Vaughan Williams), and "On My Journey Home" (arr. Jeffrey Douma). Within this program, we have TB, TBB, SATB, and SSAATTBB voicings as well as a diversity of timbres. In addition to the instruments (conga in "Empty," and clarinet in "Goodbye Then)," the contrast of vocal color between the Vaughan Williams, an English part-song, and "On My Journey Home," a Kentucky harmony spiritual, are important to adding variety.

Not only are there differences in timbre by style, but there are also variations in timbre by physiology. Aside from the obvious difference between changed and unchanged voices, young trebles (age 7–10) often have a different vocal color than older trebles (ages 11–15). A program that includes its younger singers wisely can delight an audience. Be wary of the "cute factor." Adults often find young singers appealing in a way that makes the boys' singing incidental. Conductors must ensure that the music selected and the participation of the singers is one that supersedes a simplistic display of their youth. By programming music of a wide age range that includes the youngest singers, conductors can ameliorate this "cute factor." In participating as equals in the music, the young singers can be understood by the audience as artists and musicians, and not merely children. Additionally, programming a work that allows family members to sing along with the choir reminds the audience that these boys are sons, grandsons, brothers, and neighbors, not just cute objects of attention.

Boychoir Community

Boychoir has a social fabric that begins with the choristers themselves, moves out to families, and extends to the community at large as well as boychoir alumni. Although there can be a democratic aspect to boychoir rehearsing as seen in circle and cathedral formation, most boychoirs retain the hierarchal structure they have inherited from the sacred traditions in which they arose (Mould, 2007). This is principally seen in the role of Head Boy or Head Chorister (Denison, 2015; Perona-Wright & Perona-Wright, 2004). The Head Chorister provides leadership by example in excellence and self-discipline. He and his assistants support the director in organization as well as in leading sectionals. Often the head boy is a soloist as well.

Some choirs have a highly organized and detailed leadership structure. In such contexts, a proctor is positioned in the hierarchy between the director and the Head Boy (Denison, 2015). The proctor's principal job is to oversee the organizational elements of the boys, namely in wardrobe, music library, tour preparation, and safety. Often the proctor is a college-aged young man who can function as a big brother-type or go-between, advocating for the boys' quality of life to the adult leadership. Similarly, he can advocate effectively for the organization's goals and aspirations to the boys in a way that the older adults may not.

In other boychoirs, parents fulfill the role of the proctor in maintaining wardrobe, music, and other organizational elements (Denison, 2015). These choir parents are usually trained specifically in the art of caring for other people's children in the same manner as a teacher may be trained in classroom management. They differ from proctors in that they advocate for their sons from a parental perspective rather than a fraternal one. The use of choir parents can be a rich source of ideas, resources, and energy, but without strong oversight can become a disproportionate presence. Individual boys can often be subtly bullied through innuendo and unprofessional backroom conversation by choir parents if the parents' training is inadequate or their authority unchecked.

Boychoirs seek to relate to the larger community that encircles it. Through touring, a boychoir contextualizes their music making on a state, national, and global scale. Boychoirs in the United States were touring decades before it became the norm for other choirs of young singers. In the past, boychoirs were very much like traveling performers with an agent that would book concerts in large cities and small towns where community concert series were common. The schedule was demanding with concerts and travel every day. Today, however, the choristers travel not just as performers but also as global students, who learn about the world through audience interaction, collaborative singing, and cultural activities (Denison, 2015). Touring is very appealing to these boys, and many recruitment efforts center on the spirit of adventure that touring evokes.

Most boychoirs have a fluid membership and graduate their singers. As a result, replenishing the choir through recruitment is an important part of the boychoir community. For most directors and administrators, it is a major concern. This is especially true in American culture where singing is usually gendered as feminine, and is losing ground as a shared activity in the general population. Americans are increasingly consumers of rather than participants in group singing. When speaking to prospective families about boychoir, conductors often use the vocabulary of advocacy: our singing builds character, collaborative skills, marketable skills, and correlates with academic achievement. To the boys, however, effective recruitment depicts an adventurous exploration of the world through music. In time, they learn that music is a unique world unto itself that they can know. Directors who convey music's meaning effectively to families are often the most successful in retaining boys and integrating them into the choir's community.

Conclusion

This chapter has focused largely on the contemporary social context of community boy-choirs of North America. Such a sociological framework may seem strange in a genre so rich in history; one might even argue that a historical framework would be more appropriate. Boychoir history's artifacts and traditions are important and valuable, but if boy-choirs are to remain vibrant, relevant, and life-changing, we must abandon attempts to strictly replicate the past.

We must be relevant by knowing and responding to our community of boys, their families, and neighbors. The so-called children's choir movement that began in the 1970s is now many decades old, and yet there is a body of research that shows that most Americans consider themselves non-singers (Stephens, 2012). We must ask ourselves if we have participated in creating a culture where people feel excluded from singing. This is particularly relevant in considering male voices where singing is gendered and discouraged (Green, 1997).

Do not misunderstand me. I find it unthinkable to not have great works by Byrd, Bach, Mozart, Mendelssohn, and Britten in our repertory. I do not, however, support their being depicted solely as artifacts, or the boys singing them as merely trained mes-sengers. A complete musical experience must have their voice. Benjamin Britten knew that and asked boys in choirs what they wanted him to compose for them (Holst, 1966).

I assert that if boychoir music is purely for adult benefit and not for the boys, we are working outside boys' lives and validating those who may see this genre as irrelevant. Instead, boychoirs needs to empower the voices lost in the din of mere enculturation that can pervade an ancient genre such as ours. That is why the pedagogy manifest in our rehearsals, our repertory, and our performances must aim not for a display of boys, but a meaningful meeting of singing artistry, boyhood, and community.

References

Abrahams, F. (2012). Changing voices—voices of change: Young men in middle school choirs. In S. D. Harrison, G. Welch, & A. Adler (Eds.), *Perspectives on males and singing* (pp. 79–94). New York: Springer.

Abril, C. R. (2007). I have a voice but I just can't sing: A narrative investigation of singing and social anxiety. *Music Education Research, 9*(1), 1–15.

Ashley, M. (2009) *How high should boys sing? Gender, authenticity, and credibility in the young male voice.* Burlington, VT: Ashgate.

Ashley, M. (2011). The angel enigma: Experienced boy singers' perceptual judgments of chang-ing voices. *Music Education Research, 13*(3), 343–354.

Asmus, E. P. (2009). Assuring the validity of teacher made assessments. In T. Brophy, et al. (Eds.), *The practice of assessment in music education: Frameworks, models, and designs.* (pp. 131–144). Chicago: GIA.

Barham, T. (2001). *Strategies for teaching junior high and middle school male singers: Master teachers speak.* Santa Barbara, CA: Santa Barbara Music Publishing.

Boynton, S. & Rice, E. (Eds.) (2008). *Young choristers: 650–1700.* Woodbridge, UK: Boydell.

Collins, D. L. (1993). *Teaching choral music.* Upper Saddle River, NJ: Prentice-Hall.

Collins, D. (2012). Using repertoire to teach vocal pedagogy in all-male changing voice choirs: Conversations with six master teachers. *The Choral Journal, 52*(9), 34–41.

Cooksey, J. M. (1999). *Working with adolescent voices.* St. Louis, MO: Concordia.

Cooksey, J. (2000a) Voice transformation in male adolescents. In L. Thurman & G. Welch (Eds.), *Bodymind and voice: Foundations of voice education. Vol. 3.* (pp., 718–738). Iowa City: The National Center for Speech and Voice.

Cooksey, J. (2000b) Male adolescent transforming voices: Voice classification, voice skill development, and music literature selection. In L. Thurman & G. Welch (Eds.), *Bodymind and voice: Foundations of voice education: Vol. 3* (pp. 821–841). Iowa City: The National Center for Speech and Voice.

Denison, C. (2015). A survey of community Boychoir conductors' pedagogical practices and beliefs. Unpublished raw data.

Denison, C. (2012). Jam sessions: Informal music making that can enrich your choral program. *ChorTeach, 5*(1), 7–9.

Denison, M. F. (2012). *Pediatric voice: Delineating the voice science and investigating child training methods toward pedagogical application.* (doctoral essay). University of Miami. Retrieved from http://scholarlyrepository.miami.edu/oa_dissertations/742

Dilworth, R. (2012). Working with male adolescent voices in the choral rehearsal: A survey of research-based strategies. *The Choral Journal, 52*(9), 22–33.

Freer, P. K. (2006). Hearing the voices of adolescent boys in choral music: A self-story. *Research Studies in Music Education, 27*(1), 69–81.

Freer, P. K. (2009a). Boys' descriptions of their experiences in choral music. *Research Studies in Music Education, 31*(2), 142–160.

Freer, P. K. (2009b). Boys' voices: inside and outside choral music. In J. L. Kerchner & C. R. Abril (Eds.), *Musical experience in our lives: Things we learn and the meanings we make* (pp. 217–237). Lanham, MD: Rowman & Littlefield.

Freer, P. K. (2009c). *Getting started with middle school chorus.* Lanham, MD: Rowman & Littlefield.

Freer, P. K. (2012). The successful transition and retention of boys from middle school to high school choral music. *The Choral Journal, 52*(10), 8–17.

Friddle, D. (2005). Changing bodies, changing voices: A brief survey of the literature and methods of working with adolescent changing voices. *The Choral Journal, 46*(6), 32–43.

Gackle, L. (2011). *Finding Ophelia's voice, opening Ophelia's heart: Nurturing the adolescent female voice.* Dayton, OH: Heritage Music Press.

Green, L. (1997). *Music, gender, education.* Cambridge, UK: Cambridge University Press.

Groom, M. (1984). A descriptive analysis of development in adolescent male voices during the summer time period. In E. M. Runfola (Ed.), *Proceedings: Research Symposium on the Male Adolescent Voice* (pp. 80–85). Buffalo: State University of New York at Buffalo.

Harries, M. L., Walker, J. M., Williams, D. M., Hawkins, S. M., & Hughes, I. A. (1997). Changes in the male voice at puberty. *Archives of Disease in Childhood, 77*(9711), 445–447.

Harrison, S. (2010). Boys on the outer: Themes in male engagement with music. *Thymos, 4*(1), 39–53.

Harrison, S. D., Welch, G., & Adler, A. (2012). *Perspectives on males and singing*. New York: Springer.

Herman, S. (1988). *Building a pyramid of musicianship*. San Diego, CA: Curtis Music Press.

Higgenbottom, E. Master class on Boychoir. American Boychoir School, Princeton, NJ.

Hollien, H. (2012). On pubescent voice change in males. *Journal of Voice, 26*(2), 29–40.

Holst, I. (1966). *Britten*. New York: T.Y. Crowell.

Jorgensen, E. R. (2011). *Pictures of music education*. Bloomington: Indiana University Press.

Kennedy, M. (2002). "It's cool because we like to sing:" Junior high boys' experience of choral music as an elective. *Research Studies in Music Education, 18*(1), 26–36.

Kennedy, M. (2004). "It's a metamorphosis": Guiding the voice change at the American Boychoir School. *Journal of Research in Music Education, 52*(3), 264–280.

Killian, J. N. (2003). Choral directors' self reports of accommodations made for boys' changing voices. *Reports of Research in Music Education Presented at the Annual Meetings of the Texas Music Educators Association San Antonio, Texas*. Austin, TX: Texas Music Education Research, 2–10.

Leck, H. (2009a). *Creating artistry through choral excellence*. Milwaukee, WI: Hal Leonard.

Leck, H. (2009b). The boy's expanding voice: Take the high road. *The Choral Journal, 49*(11), 49–60.

Leonard Paulk, J. (2005). *Preparing choral voices for historically guided vocalism in the Renaissance, Baroque, Classical, Romantic, and Contemporary styles*. University of Oklahoma. (Order No. 3203294).

Malvar-Ruiz, F. (2014). In J. Palant (Ed.), *Brothers, sing on! Conducting the tenor-bass choir* (p. 47). Milwaukee, WI: Hal Leonard.

McCoy, S. (2003). Falsetto and the male high voice. *Journal of Singing, 59*(5), 405–408.

McCoy, S. (2012). *Your voice: An inside view*. Delaware, OH: Inside View.

McKenzie, D. (1956). *Training the boys' changing voice*. New Brunswick, NJ: Rutgers University Press.

Mould, A. (2007). *The English chorister: A history*. New York: Continuum.

Palant, J. (2014). *Brothers, sing on! Conducting the tenor-bass choir*. Milwaukee, WI: Hal Leonard.

Perona-Wright, L., & Perona-Wright, H. (2004). *Voice for life choir trainer's book: An indispensable guide to choral training*. London: RSCM.

Phillips, K. H. (2004). *Directing the choral music program*. New York: Oxford University Press.

Phillips, K. H. (2014). *Teaching kids to sing* (2nd Ed.). Boston: Schirmer Cengage.

Phillips, K. H., & Doneski, S. M. (2011). Research on elementary and secondary school singing. In R. Colwell & P. R. Webster (Eds.), *MENC handbook of research on music learning: Vol. 2: Applications* (pp. 176–232). New York: Oxford University Press.

Phillips, K. H., Williams, J., & Edwin, R. (2012). The young singer. In G. E. McPherson, G. F. Welch & J. Nix (Eds.), *The Oxford handbook of music education: Vol. 1* (pp. 594–609). New York: Oxford University Press.

Reed, J. (2008). Working with male voices. In M. Holt & J. Jordan (Eds.), *The school choral program: Philosophy, planning, organizing, and teaching* (pp. 241–252). Chicago: GIA.

Rutkowski, J. (1982). Two year results of a longitudinal study investigating the validity of Cooksey's theory for training the adolescent male voice. In M. Runfola & L. Bash (Eds.), *Proceedings: Research symposium on the male adolescent voice* (pp. 71–79). Buffalo: State University of New York.

Stephens, E. G. (2012). *Formation and prediction of the singing perceptions of self-labeled singers and non-singers*. University of Miami: Miami, Florida. (Order No. 3511809). Available from Dissertations & Theses @ ProQuest Dissertations & Theses Full Text. (1023446799). Retrieved from http://search.proquest.com/docview/1023446799?accountid=14585

Swanson, F. (1959). Voice mutation in the adolescent male: An experiment in guiding the voice development of adolescent boys in general music classes. University of Wisconsin.

Swanson, F. (1961). The proper care and feeding of changing voices. *Music Educators Journal, 48*(2), 63–64+ 66.

Tanner, J. M. (1969). Growth and endocrinology in the adolescent. In L. Gardner (Ed.), *Endocrine and Genetic Diseases of Childhood and Adolescence*. Philadelphia: W. B. Saunders.

Thurman, L., Welch, G., Theimer, A., Grefsheim, E., & Feit, P. (2000). The voice qualities that are referred to as "vocal registers." In L. Thurman & G. Welch (Eds.), *Bodymind and voice: Foundations of voice education: Volume 2* (pp. 421–448). Iowa City: The National Center for Speech and Voice.

Thurman, L. (2012). Boys' changing voices: What do we know now? *The Choral Journal, 52*(9), 8–21.

Welch, G. F. (2000). The developing voice. In L. Thurman & G. Welch (Eds.), *Bodymind and voice: Foundations of voice education: Volume 3* (pp. 704–717). Iowa City: The National Center for Speech and Voice.

Williams, J. (2010). The implications of intensive singing training on the vocal health and development of boy choristers in an English cathedral choir. University of London.

Williams, J. (2012) Cathedral choirs in the United Kingdom: The professional boy chorister. In S. Harrison, G. Welch, & A. Adler (Eds.), *Perspectives on males and singing* (pp. 123–159). New York: Springer.

Williams, J. (2013). *Teaching singing to children and young adults*. Oxford: Compton.

Williams, J., Welch, G., & Howard, D. (2005). An exploratory baseline study of boy chorister vocal behaviour and development in an intensive professional context. *Logopedics Phoniatrics Vocology, 30*(3–4), 158–162.

CHAPTER 24

BLACK GOSPEL CHORAL MUSIC

Identity, Race, Religion, and Community

J. DONALD DUMPSON

BLACK GOSPEL MUSIC: AN OVERVIEW

BLACK[1] gospel music (BGM) is a form of American sacred music borne out of the experiences of African Americans. BGM influences other styles of music across racial, age, and gender boundaries. Although gospel music could be heard in New York City in the 1920s, particularly in the sanctified and Pentecostal churches of Harlem, Allgood (1990) identified Chicago as the birthplace of Black gospel music due to the creative genius of Thomas A. Dorsey, who promoted gospel there in the 1920s. BGM contributes to and borrows from the sacred and the secular, incorporating evolved elements of Negro spirituals or Black folk songs, blues, jazz, pop, rock and roll, rhythm and blues, and other sacred and secular forms of music. In cross-cultural church settings, BGM is used to stylize hymns and scared songs. Wise (2002) further delineated five gospel music eras, divided into ten distinct styles:

- Congregational—1900s to 1920s, hymn and quartet styles;
- Traditional—1920s to 1960s, early classic gospel and late classic gospel styles;
- Contemporary—1960s to 1980s, total, classical, and contemporary styles;
- Ministry—1980s to 1990s, contemporary jazz and blues styles; and
- Crossover—1990s to 2000s, urban style.

RACIAL and religious boundaries do not limit BGM—a variety of cultures appreciate and perform it. Educational institutions throughout the United States and abroad offer courses in African American sacred music, and performance groups devoted to gospel music, and Ph.D. and DMA candidates are successfully defending dissertations focused on a variety of research about Black and White Southern gospel music. Synder (2016) identified a college offering a bachelor's degree in gospel music.

BGM and other forms of Black musical experiences have been part of the informal music education experiences of many people from early childhood through adulthood (Dumpson, 2014). The informal music learning activities that take place in some Black churches and some schools encourage rote singing and improvisation. Those activities, coupled with traditional musical experiences, can help students bridge their musical worlds. In some cases, the paucity of BGM in formal educational experiences may foster identity conflicts, especially for Black students. For instance, if students are raised singing BGM, but experiences educational settings that make them feel that the music they valued throughout their lives is less valuable—or not of value at all—in their educational process, a conflict can develop. To this end, engaging BGM successfully requires the willingness for musickers[2] to acknowledge BGM's social and cultural implications. Musickers will become more comfortable with BGM when they interact with the music, the people who create it, and the settings in which the music naturally occurs.

Black Gospel Music: Race and Identity

Presenting BGM in a variety of settings over the past forty years took me from a small storefront church in North Philadelphia, Pennsylvania; to the esteemed halls of academia; to prestigious concert venues like Carnegie Hall and Lincoln Center. Each step of the way, colleagues, associates, and friends—of all racial backgrounds, including African American—tried to understand their identity in reference to various genres of music. Even though they were very competent in the field of music education or music performance, they wanted reassurance of their right to teach and perform BGM. Some wanted to know if their musical efforts would be considered insulting to the African American community: Do they have the tools and information needed to perform the music in an acceptable manner (Howard, 2006)? Would they be accused of inadvertently mocking the African American community if they did movements and gestures associated with some aspects of African American musical presentations (Crawford, 2001; Mahar, 1999)? Other inquires focused on a perceived lack of experience with the techniques and performance practices of BGM. In other words, would they honor the Black music and culture. Robinson-Martin (2010), Sellers (2009), and Thompson-Bradshaw (2014) offered concrete suggestions to address concerns about BGM pedagogy.

The racial implications inherent in gospel music can create additional barriers. Historically gospel music reflects dimensions of America's Black–White divide with Black gospel music and Southern (i.e., White) gospel musical output often compared. Often academics evaluate musics based on their experiences and exposure.

Devaluation of gospel music among traditionally trained professional musicians and educators has led to its sparse inclusion in textbooks and discourse (Dumpson, 2014). Phinney (2005) stated:

> The music that enriches our lives today—so much a part of our identities that we blare it from our cars; pipe it into our elevators, supermarkets, and offices; sing it at ballgames; and play it at funerals—would not exist as it does without contributions from both races. . . . Neither race can be removed from the equation without drastically changing the result. (p. 12)

Spirituals, field hollers, and call-and-response are components of BGM that represent the evolution of the sounds of the African diaspora from the slave trade to the Great Migration and the American Civil Rights Movement. While BGM is celebrated in other countries, many Americans resist the inclusion of gospel music in academia, certain worship settings, and performance contexts, citing the separation of church and state and questioning gospel music's perceived aesthetic, intrinsic, and extrinsic values in comparison with other forms of American and European music.

CREATING CULTURAL EXCHANGES THROUGH BLACK GOSPEL MUSIC

Gospel music provides teaching and learning contexts rich in sociocultural phenomena teachers can use to educate and develop sensitivity and understanding of others' experiences. Creating and sharing BGM offers opportunities for exciting cultural exchanges. For instance, BGM influences and is influenced by popular music (Burnim, 1980; Wise, 2002). While BGM's texts are generally sacred,[3] the accompaniments are often based on many different genres: the blues, as in Mahalia Jackson's version of "How I Got Over" (Ward, 1951/1996); the classically influenced music of Richard Smallwood, as realized in "Anthem of Praise" (Smallwood, 2001, track 2); the rhythm and blues and hip-hop influenced contemporary works of Kirk Franklin "Imagine Me" (Franklin, 2005, track 7), Yolanda Adams' "Open Up My Heart" (Jam, Lewis, & Adams, 1999, track 7), or Tye Tribbett's "If He Did It Before . . . Same God" (Tribbett, 2013, track 12) for which he was awarded Best Gospel Song at the 56th GRAMMY Awards in 2014.

BGM provides rich material for authentic teaching and performance. Its inclusion helps fulfill goals in multicultural music (Anderson & Campbell, 2010; Wilkinson, 1993). There are rich opportunities for educators and performers to deepen understanding of the background and cultural foundation for this music when performing or teaching BGM.

BGM provides opportunities for educators to bridge cultures through music by intentionally coupling gospel music with Western European and other American

choral genres. Introducing BGM and pairing it with other genres represents culturally relevant teaching; expanding repertoire options; and helping educators, students,
and audiences better understand how music from different genres relate to one another
(Jackson-Brown, 1990).

In addition, the inclusion of BGM can significantly impact how pre-service educators, practicing educators, graduate students, scholars, policymakers, and performers
think about teaching music (Choate, 1968; Howard, 2006). When teachers are exposed
to unfamiliar styles in their training, they are more likely to use those styles when
planning curricula and performances (Banfield, 2004; Bean, 1990; de Lerma, 1970;
Dumpson, 2014; Flandreau, 1998; Howard, 2006; Perlman, 1989; Taylor, 1984; Wyatt,
1996). BGM is a valuable consideration for sharing aspects of the African American
culture.

BLACK GOSPEL MUSIC'S SACRED TEXT:
IS IT TOO CHURCHY?

When one uses the term "Black gospel music," what comes to mind? Does the term
foster thoughts about church, religion, race, external emotional expressiveness, movement, or gestures? The words represent different things to different people, and one
of the major barriers to engaging BGM is its sacred religious context. BGM's sacred
messages may impact music directors' and teachers' desire to engage gospel music in
their choral, classroom, performance, or worship settings. Understanding, however,
gospel music's function, history, accessibility, and techniques and performance practices creates a basis for teaching Black gospel music as more than a hand-clapping,
toe-tapping selection at the end of a concert or the special song during a Black History
Month presentation. One of my colleagues expressed that "I feel totally comfortable
with the style of gospel music, and using it appropriately in a culturally respectful
manner, rather than as a style of music that closes a concert to get the most applause"
(J. Riss, personal communication, November 16, 2013). However, many music directors and teachers do not know how to address the intensity and emotional implications of BGM.

BGM is suited for classroom and secular settings (Bailey, 1978; Black Gospel Music
Restoration Project, [BGMRP], n.d.; Boyer, 1978; McCain, 1990; Walker, 1979).
However, BGM texts vary within styles and period of gospel music being performed.
Some songs have a direct overt focus on Jesus Christ while other Black gospel songs
may not mention Christ at all. Public school teachers and administrators may deem the
latter more appropriate. Gospel composers, artists, and communities continue to create musical experiences that incorporate dynamic BGM harmonic and rhythmic styles
while limiting the overt sacred text references, increasing the opportunities to program
BGM (BGMRP, n.d.; Bonner, 2010; Weekes, 2005).

Black Gospel Music and Other Sacred Texts in Educational Settings

Both solo and choral gospel vocal expressions cover a broad range of purposes in academic settings. Depending on the context, the music serves as a vehicle to foster cultural exchanges for students, family, faculty, staff, and community; provides opportunities to build community, exposing participants and audiences to music that speaks of hope during difficult times; and serves as a stabilizer for students of African American descent. Gospel choirs on college campuses may provide experiences familiar to students raised in Black church settings or Black communities who find themselves in settings, such as college campuses, unfamiliar to them. Involvement in a choir that sings gospel music may help people feel included in their environment.

Some educators may consider gospel music too churchy, too emotional, or too religious for inclusion in academic settings. While the music performed in worship settings is sometimes the same as the music used in educational contexts, its purpose can be very different (Weekes, 2005). Orchestras such as the Atlanta Symphony, Detroit Symphony, Los Angeles Philharmonic, Philadelphia Orchestra, and the St. Louis Symphony are presenting Black gospel or gospel-influenced performances. These concerts are not church events. Some of the music brings people to their feet and encourages clapping and singing along during the songs. This is not a negative act, and it is not unlike some pop concerts, holiday concerts, or concerts with popular artists as the special guests. They too can foster active participation from the audience.

Black Gospel Music Education

BGM provides a musical lens to learn from America's complex history in age-appropriate ways, revealing historical perspectives through the techniques and performance practices associated with gospel's inherent broad range of styles. The specific sounds of the genre, whether created by individual or communities of singers, compositional techniques employed by composers, improvisations, and tonal and harmonic patterns engaged through the aural/oral tradition or rote singing lend themselves to appropriate practices in vocal music education through BGM.

Sociocultural experiences impact perception. Wright (2010) identified categories or classes of music by defining them as low or popular/mass culture and high or elite culture. This way of viewing life and art challenges not only American history but also world history. Within our own country, significant sociocultural bias or preferences exist in diverse genres like blues, classical, country, gospel, hip-hop, jazz, and rock. In most contexts, the quality of a style has been associated with a perception of either educated or uneducated. The singing of African American concert spirituals has correlations to education, while singing field hollers or its "soulchild," gutbucket blues, has links to the uneducated. All three musical styles originated from the woe and pain of difficulties borne of the Atlantic slave trade and early American life, yet the sociocultural associations have created class system perceptions out of these lived experiences expressed through music. Jones (1963) believed that such outcomes impact society in profound ways.

PRACTICAL SUGGESTIONS WHEN TEACHING BLACK GOSPEL MUSIC

The Internet provides an excellent means of experiencing BGM through audio and visual recordings of professional musicians, churches, college ensembles, and performances by amateurs. However, recordings lack the spirit and energy present in a church or concert during a live performance. In addition, Appendix A provides several dissertations with well-developed reference sections and practical guides to aid in better understanding BGM.

Gospel music: Performance versus worship

> Dr. Edwin Gordon stated in an interview with Pinzino (1998):
> My best recommendation to music teachers of the next century is to improvise, improvise, improvise! Get rid of notation. Learn from music learning theory to teach children to make music without the aid of notation or music theory. Follow religiously the process the way we learn language. (para. 11)

There is a distinct difference between singing sacred music (of which gospel music is a genre) as an educational experience and singing it as a worship experience. Sacred music steeped in Western traditions dating back prior to Gregorian chant is perceived as having an intrinsic educational value. However, sacred music associated with the African diaspora and the lived experiences of African slaves and African Americans often is not. When becoming more comfortable with qualities associated with "being gospel," try not to be distracted or overwhelmed by the more flamboyant portrayals of gospel conducting styles, choral or solo singing, and movement approaches (Legg, 2010). There are various approaches to sharing BGM. It is important to select repertoire that is right for you and your situation.

Explore, relax, and engage with the music. For instance, play an up-tempo gospel song, such as "Every Praise" (Walker, 2013). Start by simply listening. Allow yourself to gradually move freely to the music. Try not to be critical of the music or your response or lack of response to the music. Notice the repetition. Try to acquaint yourself with the structure of the piece. Move and even dance freely to the piece. Do the lyrics resonate with you? Leach states, "you do not necessarily need to believe in the words, but you do eventually need to "be a storyteller" of the song text (Jacobson, Eaton, Connor-Moen, Leach, & Lloyd, 2007, p. 46).

Clap your hands freely. Do not worry about which beat is the correct beat to clap or move on. Relax, enjoy, feel the music.

Stop the music and reflect on what you experienced. It is ok to not feel how you imagine experienced performers feel when sharing the music. You do not have to be elated. It is helpful, though, if you are interested in exploring your feelings as they relate to BGM. Acknowledge whatever you are feeling. This will help as you continue to deepen your understanding of what either attracts or blocks you from engaging with BGM.

Now, at a moderate pace of quarter note = 55, establish cycles of four even macro beats per measure in your feet (Left – Right – Left – Right). Once you feel secure, add claps on beats one through four. Once your hands and feet are moving comfortably, start clapping on beats two and four only, while your feet continue to step on beats one through four. Now stop clapping and lean forward, lean backward, lift your hands—smile! Move and celebrate with the music. While doing so, identify the instruments (e.g., guitar, brass, drum set). Play those instruments in front of a mirror; if you have a tambourine,[4] take it out and substitute the handclaps with the tambourine. Try it on beats two and four, then try it using eighth notes. Now improvise, still in duple meter. Try some polyrhythms. Explore.

Know your audience

Leach (1993), a leading scholar on music of the African American experience, created a one-page guide to performing African American spirituals and gospel music, which provides several considerations for choral directors working with BGM. Following are five purposefully selected points from the guide:

1. Listen to performances of the following persons/choirs in order to understand aspects of the performance practice associated with this [gospel] music:
   - Essence of Joy, Penn State University
   - Sounds of Blackness
   - Morgan State University Concert Choir with Dr. Nathan Carter
2. Use choral editions by persons from the culture. It is an issue of authenticity not scholarship.
3. Vowels are generally darker in color and formation to better reflect the sound of speech by African Americans.
4. Vibrato may/may not be emphasized. A free vocal sound with warmth, especially from the male voices, should always be encouraged.
5. Lena McLin shared her 'take' with me on the African American spiritual. She stated, "The spiritual was the slaves' therapeutic response to the conditions

in which he/she found themselves. The gospel song is contemporary African American's therapeutic response to the conditions in which we find ourselves." (Leach, 1993, pp. 11–15)

Accompaniment styles

Blues, jazz, and other forms of popular music have inherent qualities that connect well with gospel music. Remember, gospel music's sacred text is often accompanied by secular sounds. Therefore, if you can play boogie-woogie, to some extent you can provide an accompaniment for blues forms of gospel music. If you are able to play various forms of jazz, hip-hop, or classical music, you will be able to transfer those skills to successfully play gospel music styles influenced by those genres. Strong sight-readers may be able to play accompaniments by gospel artists such as Richard Smallwood, Kirk Franklin, Andrae Crouch, and Walter and Edwin Hawkins, whose pieces are engraved with notation that accurately represents the recordings. These notated accompaniments are accessible to keyboardists with good music reading skills.

As with other genres of music, new performers need to listen, imitate, perform, and create to successfully play gospel keyboard accompaniments or to sing gospel music. Learning how to use electronic keyboards, also known as synthesizers, is essential to creating authentic musical accompaniments. For instance, if you cannot obtain a Hammond B3 organ, strings, brass, woodwinds, and other sound effects (or instrumentalists to play them), you can use patches, or electronic sound categories, to capture the authentic gospel sound. The gospel sound is not one specific sound; it is usually accompanied, but it can be a cappella. The accompaniment for BGM varies depending on the specific style. If the piece is traditional BGM, a three-piece rhythm section consisting of keyboard, often piano or Hammond Organ, bass guitar, and drums works beautifully. Guitar, brass, and strings, or other variations, can also successfully provide BGM accompaniments.

Accompanied BGM requires skillful instrumentalists, but even more importantly, it requires instrumentalists who understand the feel of the music. Feel in gospel music is not unlike the feel required to achieve a nuanced sound in classical music. For instance, musicians learn the differences in the music of early and late Beethoven, Ravel, and Debussy, or Andrae Crouch and Hezekiah Walker—two acclaimed gospel composers—by interacting with the music. Listening, studying, imitating, and developing the skillset to respond to the musical demands are central to building confidence performing BGM.

Typically, BGM keyboardists use acoustic pianos, electronic keyboards (synthesizers), and Hammond B3 organs to accompany BGM. While not optimal, certain styles of gospel music can be successfully accompanied by the pipe organ, especially compositions based on the classical style. Richard Smallwood is a good, classically influenced composer to study. For instance, Smallwood's (2001a, 2001c) pieces, "Anthem of Praise" and "Total Praise" have been arranged with orchestral accompaniments

(Smallwood, 2003b, 2003d). There are many other gospel works arranged for orchestra. Symphony orchestras are producing concerts with titles like "Gospel Meets Symphony." Gospel Christmas concerts are very popular and involve the symphony's collaboration with local church and community gospel choirs and regional choirs willing to include gospel music in their repertoire. These concerts are not necessarily sacred concerts, but instead acknowledge through programming the value of this literature and the potential of developing deeper connections with the communities associated with this music.

Conducting styles

As with the symphonic arrangements, BGM can be successfully performed using traditional Western conducting and singing techniques. It is important that you listen to the music, study DVDs representing a broad range of gospel performances, and seek to understand the sociocultural perspectives associated with the various styles of music. No matter your lens (conductor, singer, instrumentalist, or audience), explore and discuss BGM. Try not to be limited by any racial dynamics that may emerge. Instead, discuss them and allow the findings to enrich your continued exploration of BGM.

Conductors of all races who are not experienced with BGM may be challenged by the expectation that these ways of "being gospel" are indigenous to Black Americans or that they are the only ways gospel music can be fully experienced. This would be an inaccurate assessment.

Resisting stereotypes would prove very helpful here. There are people of African descent who find it very difficult to sing, conduct, or accompany on instruments in the "gospel style." Clapping in duple on beats two and four and in triple on beats two and three can be difficult. Exposure to these rhythmic and systematic lessons to break down the patterns in ways that combine movement, chanting, and singing activities can help build these skills. This is not unlike designing lesson plans to assist conductors and singers in performing complex polyrhythms or movements associated with some nongospel contemporary music.

The voice

Basic core vocal building techniques provide an excellent foundation for singing gospel music authentically. However, selecting appropriate repertoire within the gospel genre is equally important, and can be achieved by developing a broad understanding of the various styles of gospel music. Some repertoire is more appropriate for performances in educational settings than others. Characteristics of worship music have more to do with the text than the music itself. A song with the lyrics "Bow down and worship Him" is very different from a song that says, "Lord don't move this mountain, but give me the strength to climb." The former directs the singer to worship God, and the latter expresses a desire for perseverance through difficult times. This type of differentiation makes a significant difference in a song's perceived influence on non-Christian participants. Careful attention to song texts is very important when selecting music in non-Christian or nonreligious contexts.

The mechanics of singing gospel music require the same assessment given to other forms of singing. A thorough evaluation of the tessitura and vocal character of the particular gospel piece is necessary. Different styles of BGM present different performance requirements. For instance, the *hard gospel music* style requires belting and reaches its climax with the singers singing at a very high volume, often with very heavy vibrato. The "jaw-shaking" technique is a typical practice for hard gospel singers, although it is generally a practice of imitation rather than an instruction from directors to shake the jaws to create a dark, heavy vibrato sound. This is only one style of gospel singing. I do not recommend this style, but celebrate its role in the whole of gospel music.

As with any choral music, building a healthy choral sound requires knowledge that supports quality, healthy singing. Central to this is not necessarily the genre, but the selection of repertoire within given styles. For instance, while you might want to have your choir sing Bach or Mozart, not all Bach or Mozart compositions will necessarily be appropriate for your choir. You must take into account the age of the singers, the exposure the singers have had to the style, overall musicianship, and the voice types. There are gospel pieces that work beautifully toward this end with some gospel arrangements including a bass part (much of the BGM you may hear on the radio or experience in churches is written for Soprano, Alto, and Tenor). GIA Publications and N Time Gospel Music provide a wide selection of printed BGM written for Soprano, Alto, Tenor, and Bass. There are many BGM pieces for Soprano, Soprano, and Alto (SSA) configurations. Some gospel music is written in a range that can be too high for the male voice, but when assigned to SSA can work quite beautifully. Most gospel music by female ensembles like the Clark Sisters or Trin-i-tee 5:7 can work well.

Choral movement

Choirs marching and swaying, bending, and twisting are recognizable aspects of certain forms of BGM, but are not the sole or central attributes of its performance practices. For instance, you can observe or participate in BGM at three different Black churches, and each experience may reveal a different, yet authentic, representation of the music. Whether traditional or contemporary, styles of BGM, vocal sonority, accompaniment, and social climate reflect the eras in which the music was generated. The ability to replicate the essence of any era of BGM has everything to do with exposure to the songs and genres and much less to do with being African American. The same is true for African

Americans singing classical music. It is not a style of singing exclusive to everyone other than people of African descent born in America. With the vocal gift and appropriate training, singing classical music is very possible.

Experiencing various styles of BGM by observing, listening, performing, and creating is the best way to embody authentic gospel techniques and performing practices. You will be able to develop your personalized approaches to performing the music over time. For instance movement is characteristic of gospel music, and the character of the movement is based on the style of the music. If the music is very rhythmic, the choral movement will mirror that energy. One methodology to teach gestures used while singing gospel is adapted from a dance tool called *opposition*, or mirroring. For example, when you ask the singers to raise their left hands, you raise your right. This tool can be effectively engaged intergenerationally.

When working with singers it is important to help them understand the difference between swaying and rocking.[5] Swaying tends to be more fluid or legato in nature and it often more focused on the upper body with limited foot movement (step left, step right). Rocking on the other hand is suggestive of fuller rhythmic intention. The feet often move from side to side, the knees bend, and the upper body pulsates in a backward and forward motion while the feet move stepwise side to side.

When rocking, the upper body should not anticipate the left or right direction. This creates a swaying effect verses a solid rhythmic rocking motion. When rocking, the movement involves the entire body. However, please note that not all BGM requires movement. Rocking or swaying would be a distraction in some styles of gospel singing. For instance, there are gospel arrangements involving complex, a cappella harmonies (e.g., music by the group Take 6), which are best performed without uniform choral movement.

Table 24.1

FIGURE 4

The Rock/Sway Movement in Duple Meter

Beat 1	Beat 2	Beat 1 (or Beat 3)	Beat 2 (or Beat 4)
Step left (Lean left)	Clap (Right touch)	Step right (Lean right)	Clap (Left touch)

FIGURE 5

The Rock/Sway Movement in Triple Meter

Beat 1	Beat 2	Beat 3	Beat 1		Beat 2	Beat 3
Step left (Lean left)	Clap	Clap	Step right (Lean right)		Clap	Clap

Note: This pattern is also used for 6/8. Both patterns can be modified for various time signatures (Turner, 2008, p. 67).

On the other hand, if it is a rhythmic piece (e.g., music in the gospel style of Manhattan Transfer, big bands, or New Orleans), expressive movement is expected. As with the musical style, the movement styles tend to correlate between the sacred performance practices and the secular performance practices. The body language of the gospel rapper reflects the hand and body gestures, mic use, and even attire of the secular rap artists. The correlations tend to align with the performance practices of positive rappers versus gangsta rappers, though examples of either can be found. During the sharing of life experiences, also known as testimonies, before becoming a born-again Christian, some former secular gangsta rappers begin using their talents to rap about God or Jesus instead of women, men, sex, drugs, killing, or other typical subjects.

It is important to note that all of these perspectives are subjective and can change based on the setting of the presentation. BGM styles and its secular correlations are being experienced from the sanctuary to the orchestral hall. The merging of aesthetics is creating a new aesthetic; one where symphony and gospel choir coexist for select programming in very significant ways.

An honest self-assessment of your feelings about BGM may be the starting point to gain clarity about what inspires you or keeps you from tapping into your agency ability to succeed with this extraordinary music. Whatever your nationality, race, age, gender, or religious background, there is a form of BGM for you to consider. For conductors, teachers, and choristers, BGM provides an avenue for engaging cultural repertoire that is rich in informal and formal teaching and learning opportunities. Through BGM, we can gain insights into how we are impacted by our understanding of our identity as it relates to our perceptions, stereotypes, preferences, and influences generated by unfamiliar music that reflects race and religion.

National Association for Music Education (2015) continues to use the slogan "Music for every child, every child for music." Without the intentional inclusion of musical experiences like Black gospel music, students, performers, and audiences who are not part of the African American sacred community will not have the opportunity to engage in this wonderful music. Including diverse musical styles, genres, and cultural expressions in our teaching from Black gospel choral music will help bring cultures together by providing opportunities to deepen understanding of the rich history and musical output of Black gospel music.

APPENDIX A

DISSERTATIONS: BLACK GOSPEL

Choral Pedagogy and Music Education

Alwes, C. L., Jr. (1982). *Georg Otto's opus musicum novum (1604) and Valentin Geuck's novum et insigne opus (1604): A musico-liturgical analysis of two collections of gospel music from the court of Hessen-Kassel. Part I: Historical, textual, and musical analysis. Part*

II: Musical supplement (Doctoral dissertation). Urbana: University of Illinois. Retrieved from ProQuest Dissertations and Theses database (UMI No. 8302793).

Baker, B. (1978). *Black gospel music styles, 1942–1975: Analysis and implications for music education* (Doctoral dissertation). University of Maryland. Retrieved from ProQuest Dissertations and Theses database (UMI No. 0530134).

Burnim, M. V. (1980). *The Black gospel music tradition: Symbol of ethnicity.* (Doctoral dissertation). Indiana University. Retrieved from ProQuest Dissertations and Theses database (UMI No. 8105956).

Cox, D. M. M. (1986). *A descriptive analysis of selected choral works of Lena Johnson McLin* (Ph. D. dissertation). Washington University. Retrieved from ProQuest Dissertations and Theses database (UMI No. 8626372).

Deller, D. C. (1999). *Sing me home to gloryland: Arkansas songbook gospel music in the twentieth century* (Doctoral dissertation). University of Arkansas, Fayetteville. Retrieved from ProQuest Dissertations and Theses database (UMI No. 9959417).

Feyen, J. (2013). *"O lead us on, thou gentle Shepherd": A historical and musical survey of Black Canadian sacred and gospel music in Ontario* (Doctoral dissertation). Retrieved from ProQuest Dissertations and Theses database (UMI No. NS00138).

Gilchrist, C. H. (1980). *An assessment of the preparation of North Carolina public school music teachers in performance practices of Black gospel music: Implications for curriculum revisions in higher education* (Doctoral dissertation). York University, Ontario. Retrieved from ProQuest Dissertations and Theses database (UMI No. 8101502).

Hillsman, J. R. (1978). *Sequential instructional plans for administering gospel music lessons in the classroom, grades four through six* (Doctoral dissertation). Union Institute and University. Retrieved from ProQuest Dissertations and Theses database (UMI No. DP10651).

Holmes, M. (1998). *The music of the St. Brigid Catholic Church Choir: African-American gospel in a Catholic liturgy* (Doctoral dissertation). University of California, Los Angeles. Retrieved from ProQuest Dissertations and Theses database (UMI No. 9906771).

Jackson, I. V. (1974). *Afro-American gospel music and its social setting with special attention to Roberta Martin* (Doctoral dissertation). Wesleyan University. Middletown, CT. Retrieved from ProQuest Dissertations and Theses database (UMI No. 7423025).

Jefferson, R. L. (2010). *Spirituals and gospel music performance practice: A dual curriculum that bridges the cultural divide.* (Doctoral dissertation). University of Maryland. Retrieved from ProQuest Dissertations and Theses database (UMI No. 3426259).

Lewis, M. W. (2008). *The diffusion of Black gospel music in postmodern Denmark: With implications for evangelization, meaning construction, and Christian identity.* (Doctoral dissertation). Asbury Theological Seminary. Retrieved from ProQuest Dissertations and Theses database (UMI No. 3313400).

McNair, D. T. (2007). *Memphis gospel choir music, 1990–2006.* (Doctoral dissertation). University of Memphis. Retrieved from ProQuest Dissertations and Theses database (UMI No. 3276721).

Powell, W. C. (1993). *Performance and literature of African American gospel music as observed in gospel choirs of universities and four-year colleges in Alabama, Florida, and Georgia* (Doctoral dissertation). Florida State University, Retrieved from ProQuest Dissertations and Theses database (UMI No. 9334285).

Robinson-Martin, T. M. (2010). *Developing a pedagogy for gospel singing: Understanding the cultural aesthetics and performance components of a vocal performance in gospel music*

(Doctoral dissertation). Columbia University, New York. Retrieved from ProQuest Dissertations and Theses database (UMI No. 3424907).

Sellers, C. Y. (2009). *I sing because I'm free: Developing a systematic vocal pedagogy for the modern gospel singer* (Doctoral dissertation). Ohio State University, Columbus. Retrieved from ProQuest Dissertations and Theses database (UMI No. 3377650).

Smucker, D. J. (1981). *Philip Paul Bliss and the musical, cultural and religious sources of the gospel music tradition in the United Stated, 1850–1876* (Doctoral dissertation). Boston University. Retrieved from ProQuest Dissertations and Theses database (UMI No. 8126811).

Taylor, C. C. (1984). *The first decade of the Black music caucus of the music educators national conference.* New York, NY: Columbia University Teachers College.

Thompson-Bradshaw, A. L. (2014). *The impact of race on perceptions of authenticity in the delivery and reception of African American gospel music* (Unpublished doctoral dissertation). Bowling Green State University, Bowling Green, OH.

Turner, P. E. (2009). *Mentoring music educators in gospel music pedagogy in the classroom* (Doctoral dissertation). Columbia University, New York. Retrieved from ProQuest Dissertations and Theses database (UMI No. 3391753).

Weston, R. (2012). *It's not like going to church and singing a hymn: Performance, identity, and Canadian gospel music* (Doctoral dissertation). Wilfrid Laurier University, Ontario. Retrieved from ProQuest (UMI No. NR92007).

Whaley, V. M. (1992). *Trends in gospel music publishing: 1940 to 1960* (Doctoral dissertation). Liberty University. Retrieved from ProQuest Dissertations and Theses database (UMI No. 9305965).

Wise, R. (2002). *Defining African American gospel music by tracing its historical and musical development from 1900 to 2000* (Doctoral dissertation). Ohio State University. Retrieved from ProQuest Dissertations and Theses database (UMI No. 3059350).

Wong, C. O.-Y. (2006). *Singing the gospel Chinese style: "Praise and worship" music in the Asian Pacific* (Doctoral dissertation). University of California, Los Angeles. Retrieved from ProQuest Dissertations and Theses database (UMI No. 3247459).

Wyatt, L. R. (1996). The inclusion of concert music of African-American composers in music history courses. *Black Music Research Journal: Educational Philosophy and Pedagogy, 16*(2), 239–257. Retrieved from http://www.jstor.org.

APPENDIX B

BLACK GOSPEL MUSIC INFORMATION RESOURCES

ORGANIZATIONS AND PUBLISHING COMPANIES

allmusic.com	All Music
blackgospel.com	Black Gospel Music
giamusic.com	GIA Publications – African American Church Music
gospelmusic.org	Gospel Music Association
gmwanational.net	Gospel Music Workshop of America, Inc.
igccb.com	It's God's Choice Christian Bookstore
ncgccinc.com	National Convention of Gospel Choirs and Choruses
ntimemusic.com	N Time Music

GOSPEL CHORAL AND ORCHESTRAL MUSIC ARRANGEMENTS
Darin Atwater – soulful-song.org
Rev. Nolan Williams – neworks.us
Dr. Raymond Wise – raiseonline.com

PROMINENT BLACK GOSPEL ARTISTS

Solo Traditional
Shirley Caesar
Andrae Crouch
Al Green
Aretha Franklin
Tramaine Hawkins
Mahalia Jackson
Dottie Peoples
Albertina Walker
Vickie Winans

Solo Contemporary
Yolanda Adams
Karen Clark-Sheard
Kirk Franklin
Donnie McClurkin
Smokie Norful
Richard Smallwood
Ty Tribbett

Duos
Mary Mary
BeBe and CeCe
Winans

Small Vocal Ensembles
Take 6
The Edwin Hawkins
   Singers
The Staple Singers
Trin-i-tee 5:7
The Winans

Male Ensembles
The Original Five
   Blind Boys of
   Alabama
The Fairfield Four
The Dixie
   Hummingbirds

The Mighty Clouds
   of Joy

Choirs
Milton Brunson and
   the Thompson
   Community
   Singers
James Cleveland and
   the Cleveland
   Singers
Walter Hawkins and
   the Love Alive
   Choir
Mississippi Mass
Choir
Hezekiah Walker
   and the Love
   Fellowship
   Tabernacle Choir
Thomas Whitfield
   and Company

Important Terms Relevant to Gospel Singing and the Black Church Experience (Sellers, 2009, pp. 131-134).

Crystal Yvonne Sellers complied a list of terms in her dissertation, *"I Sing Because I'm Free": Developing a Systematic Vocal Pedagogy for the Modern Gospel Singer*. I have modified some of the points with bold, underlined, or italicized words.

Baptist Lining Hymns - A leader speaking or chanting a line of text, which is then sung by the congregation. The history behind lining hymns goes as far back as 17th-century England, where church pastors were required to recite the text of a hymn line by line due to lack of literacy in their congregations. Notable hymnist Isaac Watts decried the fact that hymn singing in church was "horrendous and lamentable." To improve this condition he began composing hymns in basic poetic meters that allowed them to be sung to familiar tunes. Thus, it was up to the pastor to recite the text of a hymn line by line and the congregation to sing it to a tune that was either suggested in the hymnbook or agreed upon beforehand.

Belting – using chest voice qualities, thick vocal fold mass and/or full voice qualities, especially in the upper register of the voice by both men and women

Bluesy vocal passages – vocal passages based on the blues or the pentatonic scale

Bridge – the transitional part of a song that separates the beginning of the song from the ending or vamp (see vamp)

Cadenza – florid passages or extremely long held notes used just before the final chord of a song

Contemporary Christian Music (CCM) – **sacred lyrics based on contemporary secular musical styles. It is often referred to as inspirational music.**

Dove Awards - annual awards ceremony celebrating achievement in Contemporary Christian Music (CCM)

Getting the spirit (also known *as catching the spirit* or *going in*) – showing outward expressions of praise by crying, shouting, or speaking in tongues (see glossolalia and shouts)

Glossolalia (also known as *speaking in tongues*) – the ability to utter words or sounds in a language not known by the speaker as a religious expression and used as a secret language in conversation with God

Head Voice/Falsetto – the Classical-sounding singing in the upper register of the voice, often called falsetto for both men and women in Gospel contrary to it being called head voice in women and falsetto in men in the Classical arena

High tessitura – singing in the upper pitch extremes of the voice during *solo* and choral singing. This is usually the result of the key in which the piece is composed

Melismas/runs/*riffs* – highly florid vocal passages used as an indication of virtuosic vocal ability (runs **or riffs** in Gospel music)

Moans – reminiscent of Blues singing, *but can be traced back to the Black folk spirituals and field hollers and chants, wherein* the singer departs from the words and uses a pressed hum while vocalizing

Modulation – change of key usually occurring by upward motion by either half or whole step key progression

Christian Rap (Holy Hip Hop, Gospel Rap, Gospel Hip Hop and even Christ Hop). Christian Rap has many names but as with other forms of CCM presents sacred texts on a secular music landscape.

Scat – singing on nonsense syllables in improvising in the Jazz style but used for artistic expression in Gospel music

Sermonette – small sermon often included in a song

Shouts – 1. Physical movement or dance as a form of praise, or; 2. Loud outbursts of praise

Southern Gospel – a form of Gospel music, with roots in bluegrass and country music

Stellar Awards – annual awards ceremony, celebrating achievements in Gospel music

Testimony – recalling a story or event where God has made a significant impact. *Often spoken, but can be sung*

Transitions between speech and singing – shifting from singing into testimony or sermonette

Vamp – repeated section at the end of a song

Vibrato manipulations – there are three types of Gospel music vibrato manipulations
1. **Delayed** – reminiscent of jazz singing – maintaining a note without vibrato and slowly introducing vibrato at the end of the note
2. **Eliminated** – vibrato is not used at all, used especially in choral or group singing to assist with intricate harmonies
3. **Exaggerated** – using of lots of vibrato either naturally created or by manipulation of the lower jaw to create a larger sound

Yells – loud vocal outbursts of either expression of praise or song lyrics

APPENDIX C

ADDITIONAL LITERATURE IMPACTING

BLACK GOSPEL CHORAL MUSIC APPLIED AND RELATED ISSUES

Boyer, H. C. (1995). *How sweet the sound: The golden age of gospel*. Washington, DC: Elliott & Clark.

Carpenter, B. (2005). *Uncloudy days: The gospel music encyclopedia*. San Francisco: Backbeat Books.

Cone, J. H. (1972). *The spirituals and the blues: An interpretation*. Maryknoll, NY: Seabury.

Curtis, M. V. (1988). Understanding the Black aesthetic experience. *Music Educators Journal, 75*(2), 23–26.

Delpit, L. D. (2002). No kinda sense. In L. D. Delpit & J. K. Dowdy (Eds.), *The skin that we speak: Thoughts on language and culture in the classroom* (pp. 31–48). New York, NY: New Press.

Floyd, S. A. (1995). *The power of black music: Interpreting its history from Africa to the United States*. New York: Oxford University Press.

Gay, G. (2010). Culturally responsive teaching: Theory, research, and practice (2nd ed.). New York: Teachers College Press.

Gaylor, A. L. (2009). Religious music in public schools. Retrieved from http://ffrf.org/outreach/item/14027-religious-music-in-public-schools

Grimmel, B. (n.d.). Gospel around the world: Germany (Part I: History). *Gospelflava.com Articles*. Retrieved from http://www.gospelflava.com/articles/gospelaroundtheworld-germany1.html

Greer, A. (2012, August 21). White Boy, Black Gospel: How African-American music got under my lily White skin. *Christianity Today*. Retrieved from http://www.christianitytoday.com/ct/2012/august-web-only/white-boy-black-gospel.html?paging=off

Gospel Music Workshop of America. (n.d.). *Our history.* Retrieved from http://www.gmwanational.net/about-gmwa/history/

Heilbut, A. (1971). *The gospel sound: Good news and bad times.* New York: Simon and Schuster.

Koza, J. E. (2008). Listening for whiteness: Hearing racial politics in undergraduate school music. *Philosophy of Music Education Review, 16*(2), 145–155.

Leach, A. T. (1993). Does gospel music have a place in general music? *General Music Today, 6*(2), 11–15.

Marti, G. (2011). *Worship across the racial divide: Religious music and the multiracial congregation* [Kindle Edition]. Oxford: Oxford University Press. Retrieved from Amazon.com.

Music Educators National Conference. (1996). Sacred music in schools [Position statement]. Retrieved from http://www.nafme.org/

Race Relations on Campus. (2006). *The Journal of Blacks in Higher Education, 54,* 110–111.

Rarus, S. (2008, October 1). Sacred music: Forbidden or essential? *National Association for Music Education.* Retrieved from http://www.nafme.org/sacred-music-forbidden-or-essential/

Shaw, J. (2012). The skin that we sing: Culturally responsive choral music education. *Music Educators Journal, 98*(4), 75–81.

Southern, E. (1997). *The music of Black Americans: A history* (3rd ed.). New York: W. W. Norton.

Szwed, J. F. (1970). Afro-American musical adaptation. In N. E. Whitten (Ed.), *Afro-American anthropology: Contemporary perspectives* (pp. 219–228). New York: The Free Press.

Tallahassee Florida Department of Education (1993). *Multicultural arts education: Guidelines, instructional units and resources for arts, dance, music, and theater, grades K–12.* Tallahassee, FL: Department of Education, Division of Public Schools.

West, C. (1993). The new cultural politics of difference. In C. West (Ed.), *Keeping faith: Philosophy and race in America* (pp. 3–32). New York: Routledge.

West, C. (2001). *Race matters.* New York: Vintage.

West, C. (2008). *Hope on a tightrope: "Words and wisdom."* Carlsbad, CA: Smiley Books.

Wise, T. (2010). *Color blind: The rise of post-racial politics and the retreat from racial equity.* San Francisco: City Lights Books.

Notes

1. I use *Black* and *African American* interchangeably throughout this chapter. The term *Black* generally describes any person of a dark color, and the term *African American* applies specifically to Black people of African descent who were born in America.

2. Small (1998) defines musicking as "taking part in any capacity in a musical performance, whether by performing, by listening, by rehearsing or practicing, by providing material for performance (what is called composing), or by dancing" (p. 9).

3. There are Black gospel compositions that do not mention God directly, however, God is implied. This is a popular approach to sacred text setting when artists want their music to have crossover, music industry appeal.

4. While the tambourine is an instrument traditionally used in some BGM, explore using other percussion instruments as well. There is not one way to perform BGM, and it is typical for BGM performers to use whatever instruments they have available. An appropriate assessment of your context includes the age and demographics of the singers, previous experience with the literature, selecting appropriate pieces for the singers, and the context in which they will be sharing the music.

5. Front and back swaying or rocking movements are rarely used in BGM because they can be interpreted as too secular or sensuous in nature.

References

Allgood, B. D. (1990). Black gospel in New York City and Joe William Bostic, Sr. *The Black Perspective in Music, 18*(1–2), 101–115.

Anderson, W. M., & Campbell, P. S. (Eds.). (2010). *Multicultural perspectives in music education* (3rd ed.). Lanham, MD: Rowman & Littlefield.

Bean, C. (1990). The Black composers series. *Black Music Research Journal, 10*(1), 97–102.

Bailey, B. E. (1978). The lined-hymn tradition in black Mississippi churches. *The Black Perspective in Music, 6*(1), 3–17.

Banfield, W. C. (2004). Black artistic invisibility: A black composer talking 'bout taking care of the souls of black folk while losing much ground fast. *Journal of Black Studies, 35*(2), 195–209.

Bean, C. (1990). The Black composers series. *Black Music Research Journal, 10*(1), 97–102.

Black Gospel Music Restoration Project: Royce-Darden Collection. (n.d.). *Black gospel music restoration project.* Baylor University. Retrieved from http://www.baylor.edu/lib/gospel/

Bonner, G. (2010). Secular vs. gospel: The next chapter. *Gospelflava.com.* Retrieved from http://www.gospelflava.com/articles/editorial-secular.html

Boyer, H. C. (1978). Gospel music. *Music Educators Journal, 64*(9), 34–43.

Burnim, M. (1980). Gospel music research. *Black Music Research Journal, 1,* 63–70.

Choate, R. A. (Ed.). (1968). *Music in American society: Documentary report of the Tanglewood symposium.* Washington, DC: Music Educators National Conference.

Crawford, R. (2001). *America's musical life: A history.* New York: W.W. Norton.

de Lerma, D.-R. (1970). Black music in our culture: Curricular ideas on the subjects, materials, and problems. Kent, OH: Kent State University Press.

Dumpson, J. D. (2014). *Four scholars' engagement of works by classical composers of African descent: A collective case study.* Temple University, Philadelphia (Doctoral dissertation). Retrieved from ProQuest Dissertations and Theses database (UMI No. 3623145)

Flandreau, S. (1998). Black music in the academy: The center for Black music research. *Notes, Second Series, 55*(1), 26–36.

Franklin, K. (2005). *Imagine Me* [Recorded by Kirk Franklin]. On *Hero* [CD]. Inglewood, CA: Zomba Gospel.

Howard, G. R. (2006). We can't teach what we don't know: White teachers, multiracial schools (2nd ed.). New York: Teachers College Press.

Jackson-Brown, I. (1990). Developments in black gospel performance and scholarship. *Black Music Research Journal, 10*(1), 36–42.

Jacobson, J. R., Eaton, R. P., Connor-Moen, C., Leach, L., & Lloyd, L. (2007). Approaches to teaching sacred music in a secular context. *The Choral Journal, 47*(9), 40–47.

Jam, J., Lewis, T., & Adams, Y. (1999). *Open My Heart* [Recorded by Yolanda Adams]. On *Mountain High . . . Valley Low* [CD]. New York: Elektra Records.

Leach, A. (1993). Does gospel music have a place in general music? *General Music Today, 6*(2), 11–15.

Legg, A. (2010). A taxonomy of musical gesture in African American gospel music. *Popular Music, 29*(1), 103–129.

Mahar, W. J. (1999). *Behind the burnt cork mask: Early blackface, minstrelsy, and antebellum American popular culture.* Urbana, IL: University of Chicago Press.

McCain, W. B. (1990). *Come Sunday: The liturgy of Zion.* Nashville, TN: Abingdon Press.

National Association for Music Education. (2015). *2016 National Conference.* Retrieved from http://www.nafme.org

Perlman, S. (1989). Black music in college texts. *Center For Black Music Research: Register, 2*(2), 1–3.

Phinney, K. (2005). *Souled America: How Black music transformed White culture.* New York: Watson-Guptill.

Pinzino, M. E. (1998). A conversation with Edwin Gordon. *Come Children, Sing! Online Teacher Education Center.* Retrieved from http://comechildrensing.com/teachers/articles.php

Robinson-Martin, T. M. (2010). *Developing a pedagogy for gospel singing: Understanding the cultural aesthetics and performance components of a vocal performance in gospel music* (Doctoral dissertation). Columbia University, New York. Retrieved from ProQuest Dissertations and Theses database. (UMI No. 3424907)

Sellers, C. Y. (2009). *I sing because I'm free: Developing a systematic vocal pedagogy for the modern gospel singer* (Doctoral dissertation). Ohio State University, Columbus. Retrieved from ProQuest Dissertations and Theses database. (UMI No. 3377650)

Small, C. (1998). *Musicking: The meanings of performing and listening* [Kindle ed.]. Middletown, CT: Wesleyan University Press. Retrieved from Amazon.com.

Smallwood, R. (2001a). Anthem of Praise. [Recorded by Richard Smallwood with Vision]. On Persuaded: Live in DC [CD]. New York: Verity Records.

Smallwood, R. (2003b). *Anthem of praise.* Milwaukee, WI: Hal Leonard.

Smallwood, R. (2001c). Total praise. [Recorded by Richard Smallwood with Vision]. On Persuaded: Live in DC [CD]. New York: Verity Records.

Smallwood, R. (2003d). *Total praise.* Milwaukee, WI: Hal Leonard.

Snyder, A. (2016, March 3) Getting a bachelor's degree in gospel music requires study – and soul. *The Washington Post.* Retrieved from https://www.washingtonpost.com

Taylor, C. C. (1984). *The first decade of the Black music caucus of the music educators national conference.* New York, NY: Columbia University Teachers College.

Thompson-Bradshaw, A. L. (2014). *The impact of race on perceptions of authenticity in the delivery and reception of African American gospel music* (Unpublished doctoral dissertation). Bowling Green State University, Bowling Green, OH.

Tribbett, T. (2013). *If He did it before . . . Same God (live).* [MP3 file]. Greater Than. Brentwood, TN: Motown Gospel (2013).

Turner, P. E. (2008). Getting gospel going. *Music Educators Journal, 95*(2), 62–68.

Walker, H. (2013). Every praise. On *Azusa the Next Generation* [MP3 file]. New York: RCA Records.

Walker, W. T. (1979). *Somebody's calling my name: Black sacred music and social change.* Valley Forge, PA: Judson Press.

Ward, C. (1951). *How I Got Over.* [Recorded by Mahalia Jackson]. On *16 most requested songs: Mahalia Jackson* [CD]. New York: Columbia Records. (1996)

Wyatt, L. R. (1996). The inclusion of concert music of African-American composers in music history courses. *Black Music Research Journal: Educational Philosophy and Pedagogy, 16*(2), 239–257. Retrieved from http://www.jstor.org

Weekes, M. E. (2005). This house, this music: Exploring the interdependent interpretive relationship between the contemporary black church and contemporary gospel music. *Black Music Research Journal, 25*(1–2), 43–72.

Wilkinson, C. (1993). Teaching the cultural diversity of America's musics: Methods and consequences. In *Proceedings of the National Association of Schools of Music, the 68th annual meeting* (pp. 125–135). Reston, VA: NASM.

Wise, R. (2002). *Defining African American gospel music by tracing its historical and musical development from 1900 to 2000* (Doctoral dissertation). Ohio State University, Columbus. Retrieved from ProQuest Dissertations and Theses database. (UMI No. 3059350)

Wright, R. (Ed.). (2010). *Sociology for music educators.* Burlington, VT: Ashgate.

Wyatt, L. R. (1996). The inclusion of concert music of African-American composers in music history courses. *Black Music Research Journal: Educational philosophy and pedagogy, 16*(2), 239–257. Retrieved from http://www.jstor.org

....

CHAPTER 25

THE GANG MENTALITY
OF CHOIRS

How Choirs Have the Capacity to Change Lives

....

ARREON HARLEY

ESCAPING THE LIFE YOU ARE BORN INTO

STATISTICS drive today's world. The science of mathematics provides the skills needed to draw conclusions from data, to track and predict economic trends, and even to predict the futures of children.

A provocative title in *The Washington Post*, "What Your First Grade Life Says About the Rest of It," attracted the attention of this author. The content was captivating:

> Researchers at Johns Hopkins University followed for years a generation of children who began first grade in the Baltimore public school system in 1982. The stories (and data) about their lives tell us much about what it's like to grow up poor in urban American—and what it takes to escape those odds. (Badger, 2014, para. 2)

In the study, Karl Alexander and Doris Entwisle tracked 790 children who began first grade in 1982. This group included children from the middle class as well as students from impoverished backgrounds. Over the years, the researchers remained in contact with the 790 students and watched as their lives were "constrained—or cushioned—by the circumstances they were born into, by the employment and education prospects of their parents, by the addictions or job contacts that would become their economic inheritance" (para. 6). By the time the cohort reached age 18, 40% of the black girls from low income had given birth to children. 10% of the black men in this study were incarcerated. And, sadly, at the conclusion of the study (after 25 years) only four percent of students who were classified as urban disadvantaged had completed a college degree.

What can be learned from these statistics? This study demonstrates that it is nearly impossible for disenfranchised youth to escape the disadvantaged lives they are born into. In a country that constantly talks about the American Dream of pulling oneself up by his or her own bootstraps, these facts demonstrate that the American Dream is not afforded to all Americans. In actuality, the American Dream is, more often, a privilege of birth.

A SEARCH FOR ANSWERS

The author of this chapter grew up in Baltimore City, Maryland, or "Bmore" (as it was affectionately called by its residents). Less fortuitously, the city was also dubbed "Bodymore Murderland," a city with a plummeting quality of life. There are blocks and blocks of abandoned buildings, projects, and ghettos.

The author is happy to report that he falls into that category of students who have been fortunate enough to complete a college degree. Following graduation from Goucher College with degrees in Vocal Performance and Music Theory & Composition, he went on to study at the University of Delaware, receiving a Master of Music degree in Choral Conducting and Vocal Performance two years later.

Reflecting on *The Washington Post* article, he finds his success a rather miraculous outcome. His mother, a victim of domestic abuse, left his father and was determined to make a better life for her children. His first childhood memories are of living in a shelter for battered women and children. Somehow or other, his mother worked hard, earned her CPA, and eventually was able to move her children out to the suburbs. To this day, her success is beyond comprehension.

It was not a childhood that he would have labeled as disadvantaged. Certainly some people had more things, but the author never seemed bothered or demoralized. That childhood was rich, full of family, and full of music. Based on central family values, being involved in music was important. Thus he and his brother were both enrolled in the Peabody Conservatory's Preparatory Program.

The author's trajectory of life changed when he joined the Peabody Conservatory Children's Chorus under the direction of Doreen Falby. It was there that he heard traditional choral music for the first time. He had listened to many great gospel choirs in church as a child, but never heard choirs quite like this. The roundness and purity of those sounds is something that will always resonate with him. Not knowing how to describe this style of traditional choral music, the family dubbed it as singing "Peabody Style." One treasured memory is being asked to sing songs heard in weekly church services "Peabody Style."

Singing in the Peabody's Children's Chorus provided an uplifting sense of purpose. It gave choristers something to cling onto. It was a utopian society in direct contrast to the chaos in Baltimore.

Today, the author is honored to serve as the Director of Music and Operations for the Cathedral Choir School of Delaware, an after-school outreach program. The Cathedral Choir School of Delaware, a 501(c)(3) organization, provides professional music training, leadership development, academic support, and mentoring in an intergenerational environment for youth in Wilmington, Delaware and the surrounding region. Choir School staff and volunteers serve as advocates for these students to help guide them to success in their academic, musical, and social endeavors.

The Choir School is special: it offers urban students in another violence-torn city the hope and help that the author received as a child. The Choir School program continues to achieve a 100% graduation rate from high school, which is absolutely incredible given the statistics for Wilmington.

The Choir School is an intergenerational choir, born of the Anglican Cathedral Choir tradition. It was founded in 1883 as the Cathedral Choir of Men and Boys. Much like Kings College, the Choir School performs works by Anglican composers such as Stanford, Stainer, and Bairstow as well as secular works by other master composers and modern composers.

What is amazing is how significantly this choral music speaks to the Choir School students. Even given the similar childhood experience of the author, who found choral music compelling as a child, it is remarkable that our choristers who are primarily black and from disadvantaged neighborhoods gravitate to choral music although they are inundated by hip-hop, R&B, gospel, and other popular genres on the street.

After much thought and research, the author concluded that it is not necessarily the choral genre that speaks to these youth—it is the choral community.

THE GANG MENTALITY OF CHOIRS

Choirs function very similarly to street gangs. Thus a choir has the power to radically transform the lives of poor, disenfranchised youths.

If a survey were conducted to define the meaning and purpose of a gang, the replies would certainly be diverse and contradictory: some would identify a gang as a "group of individuals who engage in organized crime"; others might state, "I know one when I see one" (Yearwood & Hayes, 2000, pp. 1–2). This lack of consensus around deriving a standard definition still exists today among researchers, criminal justice professionals, and policymakers. In his book *The Boy and His Gang*, Joseph Puffer writes, "A gang is one of the three primary social groups formed in response to deep-seated but unconscious need" (Puffer, 1912, p. 7).

Why do adolescents join gangs? For the same reason that adults join social organizations—to meet their needs. To understand these needs, psychologists and sociologists look to the writings and studies of Abraham Maslow, a psychologist who studied positive human qualities and the lives of exemplary individuals. In his book, *Motivation and Personality*, Maslow introduces his pyramid and hierarchy of needs. From the bottom of the pyramid moving up the hierarchy these needs are: physiological, safety, love/belonging, esteem, and self-actualization (Maslow, 1987).

Humans are innately one-stop shoppers who want to fulfill their needs in one place. Adolescents generally receive the most, if not all, of their needs fulfillment from their parents. If an adolescent does not feel those needs are fulfilled, then he or she must go outside the familial unit. The next place that an adolescent will look to fulfill needs is school. If the school does not fulfill the need, then the adolescent begins seeking what he or she needs from the larger community. This search for fulfillment of needs is at the crux of the issue of why adolescents join gangs in the inner city. Often in underserved neighborhoods, the familial unit is unable to fulfill the basic needs of the children; schools are under-performing and underfunded; and community centers are often not in a position to offer the holistic nature of the needs dictated by Maslow's hierarchy.

Outlined in this chapter are ways in which choral communities do fulfill the needs of an individual. This chapter examines several choral programs that provide and/or supplement four basic needs (physiological, safety, love/belonging, and esteem) and lead adolescents to a healthy and constructive place of self-actualization through mentoring. Most importantly, this study explores how and why choral music has the power to transform lives of disenfranchised youth, leading them to higher education, and better lives that contrast with their upbringing.

Maslow's Hierarchy of Needs

Maslow (1987) stated that people are motivated to meet their needs. When one need is fulfilled, a person is motivated to fulfill the next need, and each level thereafter (p. 17).

The earliest and most widespread version of Maslow's hierarchy of needs was originally published in 1943, with five groupings of needs depicted in a pyramid (see Figure 25.1).

FIGURE 25.1 Maslow's Hierarchy of Needs

This five-stage model can be divided into basic (or deficiency) needs (physiological, safety, love, and self-esteem) and growth needs (self-actualization).

Unmet needs provoke behavior. The urgency to fulfill such needs will become stronger the longer they go unmet. For example, the longer a person goes without food, the more hungry and desperate they are to find a solution. A person can become so hungry that he or she may exhibit extreme behavior to satisfy the need for food. In nature, animals can be observed eating their own species—even their own offspring—because their need for food is so desperate.

Individuals must satisfy basic needs before progressing on to meet higher-level growth needs. Once these needs have been reasonably met, a person continues to develop. This is called self-actualization.

Everyone is capable and wants to move up the hierarchy to a level of self-actualization. In reality, however, progress is often disrupted by a failure (or continual failure) to meet the lower level, basic needs. Life circumstances such as marriage, divorce, or loss of job can cause an individual to oscillate between or to regress to more basic levels of the hierarchy.

Physiological needs

Physiological needs are basic, primal essentials that all species must have to sustain life. These needs include such things as food, shelter, air, regeneration (sleep), and reproduction (sex) (Maslow, 1987). Although most choral communities do not provide all these physiological needs for their singers, they do have the capacity to offer many.

For many students who belong to choir, it is a regular activity, something that they participate in at least once or twice a week. Their choral conductors do not necessarily see themselves as providing shelter for choristers, but, in fact, it is most certainly true. Rehearsal spaces range from dimly lit rooms with fold-up chairs to state-of-the-art facilities with smart boards and collapsible risers. Whether a rehearsal space is state-of-the-art or not, it is certainly what would be considered a shelter even if it is only for a few hours, once or twice a week.

The Cathedral Choir School of Delaware provides nourishment of the soul and nourishment of the body. Since the majority of our choristers come from at-risk neighborhoods, the Choir School partners with the Food Bank of Delaware, which delivers a meal each afternoon for the choristers. These meals, much like school lunches, are high-calorie meals that are intended to sustain a child or teenager if food is not available at home. In addition to the meal that is provided by the Food Bank, the Choir School supplements each meal with additional fruits, carbs and, occasionally, sweets. The Choir School of East Texas, a program that is modeled after the Cathedral Choir School of Delaware (Harmon, 2014), has also found success in providing an afternoon meal or early supper to its choristers.

It is imperative that choral communities, particularly those who serve disadvantaged populations, consider how they are providing, or how they can potentially provide, some of these basic physiological needs. Maslow (1987, p. 17) explains that we all have a hierarchy of needs ranging from lowest to highest. Higher needs emerge after lower needs are met. Until one addresses his or her physiological needs, the higher needs will go unrealized, and the individual will make lateral moves in life until these needs can be achieved. This is how gangs draw their power. They have the means to provide the many of those basic needs. If a gang is able to provide the most basic needs, particularly physiological and safety, an individual is likely to engage in or continue an affiliation with the gang because the gang has a proven track record of fulfilling needs.

Safety needs

After physiological needs, the second block in Maslow's hierarchy includes safety and security. These needs include shelter from the elements, job security, security of health and well-being, and a general freedom from fear (Maslow, 1987, p. 18).

Gangs are possibly best known for their ability to provide safety and protection for their members. Choral communities can also provide safety and protection but in different and arguably more constructive ways.

When young singers come to the Choir School's rehearsal room they do so because they feel that it is a safe place. Certainly, in spite of the occasionally leaky ceiling and broken air conditioner, the choristers recognize that they are protected from the elements. Fortunately for choral directors, schools, churches, and landlords are generally responsible for addressing these needs.

Choral communities also provide a sense of job security. Most choirs are volunteer-based with singers receiving no monetary compensation. Choral conductors are always in need of singers. A choir of one cannot succeed on any level after all! This need for singers gives our choristers a sense of job security. Singers feel confident that they will be invited to return yet again for the next rehearsal. In an economy torn by layoffs, job cuts, and school budget cuts, our singers relish the security of knowing that they can continue to sing in choir. It is simple, but powerful compensation.

Although choral conductors are not in a position to provide healthcare, most care deeply about the health of their singers, if only because it directly impacts the performance of their choirs. Choral directors urge their singers to stay healthy, to wear scarves, to drink water, and to zip up their coats. Directors do this to care for their singers whose instruments, in actuality, are their entire bodies. This is what makes singing so personal, so intimate. When conductors nag singers to take care of themselves, the singers certainly understand that choral conductors want the best for the choir. In addition, it gives singers a sense of the care and love that conductors have for the ensemble.

Humans also use clothing as a means of protection and security. It protects the skin from cuts and bruises, and helps keep the body warm. Many students also feel a sense of security through the uniform (clothing) that they wear for performances, whether the chorister purchases it or it is provided. There is something that is safe and comforting about the idea of uniformity. In our performances, everyone looks the same. A student at the Choir School once told me how much she loved our uniform. She said, "whether your dad has five millions dollars, five dollars or five nickels to his name, our uniforms make us all look and feel good." The author will have to admit that he never heard a student mention loving a uniform before, but with more reflection the more the value of a uniform as a measure of security became clear.

One of the Choir School choristers who was asked to speak to small group of potential supporters was asked the question, "Why do you like coming here?" In his simple but sincere way, he looked out of the nearest window and responded, "Because I am not out there." How simple. How powerful. Just inviting someone to sing with the Choir School provided shelter from the dangers of a threatening neighborhood in an imperfect world.

Needs for love and belonging

Another reason why something as simple as a choir uniform can make one feel safe and secure is that the uniform serves as a reminder of membership, of being part of something, of *belonging* to something that is valued.

Everyone has a need for love and belonging. We need intimacy, friendships, and affection. Most individuals find these emotional links in significant others, family and friends.

Choral communities are often known for providing love and a sense of belonging. From beginning warm-ups with choral massages to ending rehearsals with singing an intimate piece while holding hands, choirs often create and revel in love-filled communities.

Researchers Roy Baumeister and Mark Leary (1995) wrote extensively on the topic of belonging. In their 1995 article entitled, "The Need to Belong: Desire for Interpersonal Attachments as a Fundamental Human Motivation," the pair states that humans have a basic and fundamental psychological need to have relationships with others, and that caring, affectionate relationships are a major part of human behavior. In their research, five points particularly relate to the choral conductor and choral singer:

1. Forming social bonds—Humans form relationships with others without being forced to do so even when they are in less than ideal circumstances (Baumeister & Leary, 1995, p. 501). This is certainly seen in the context of choirs. Chorister bond with each other over a musical experience. Even when choristers may be displeased with a conductor or his or her choice of repertoire, most singers still bond with their fellow choristers and the conductor.

2. Not breaking bonds—Humans are eager to have close relationships and do not want to break them once they are formed, even when the relationship is less than healthy. Furthermore, a human avoids permanent separation such as divorce, even when the costs of staying in the relationship takes a measureable toll on the individual (Baumeister & Leary, 1995, p. 503). This is the aspect of human nature that makes it difficult to say no to a choral conductor. Declining to sing in a concert is often cause for anguish, even when the singer has a valid reason. At the same

time, everyone has experienced this pain! Once a person makes a commitment to an organization, be it choral or otherwise, he or she a has a time detaching or even taking a temporary leave.

3. Emotional highs and lows—All relationships come with strings attached. This emotional weight can be both positive (love, joy, content) and negative (frustrating, stressful, depressing) (Baumeister & Leary, 1995, p. 505). All conductors must accept duality. Though singing in choir brings joy and happiness, it also brings frustration and dismay. Singers become exasperated when conductors repeatedly rehearse the same section of a piece because they perceive little progress or no progress is being made. Singers and conductors alike also can become irritated with one another when the bass section sings behind the beat or the soprano section sings a passage sharp yet again. These things are to be expected in the course of the rehearsal process and, in fact, are a part of building a strong and lasting relationship.

4. Consequences of deprivation—When humans are deprived of relationships with others, they suffer (Baumeister & Leary, 1995, p. 508). This phenomenon is seen in the natural world as well. Animals without a pack cannot last long in the wild. Data shows that married persons live longer than single persons (Baumeister & Leary, 1995, p. 508). When a singer does not sing with the choir, he or she experiences physical, emotional, and social setbacks. The vocal mechanism is made up of muscles. When these muscles are not regularly exercised, they tire prematurely. After the summer break, all choirs, no matter how mature or experienced, are somewhat rusty! Their tone quality is not at the level it had reached at the end of the program year, and there seems to be a widespread lack of breath support in the singing. Conductors are also voice teachers, so they must recondition all choirs after breaks. Similarly, singers who have been missing from the choral ensemble for some time often need to be reconditioned to match vowels and tone colors. Singers also experience emotional setbacks when they are not involved in choir. For many of the choristers at the Choir School, singing is one important way that they can and do express themselves. One student reported that every day she knows that she is coming to the Choir School, whether she has rehearsal or not, she has a better day at school. Just knowing that there is something to look forward to in a day or during the week helps motivate individuals and stabilize their emotions. When any individual steps away from a choir for a while, it takes time to reintegrate into the social community of the choir. Singers who have been absent have missed community experiences that the other members of the choir now share. These experiences can never be totally shared by the individual who has had an absence from the choral community.

5. Partial deprivation—Separation from or limited interactions with people we have a relationship causes a loss of satisfaction (Baumeister & Leary, 1995, p. 511). When married couples are separated due to distance, work, or even marital friction, they report more dissatisfaction (Baumeister & Leary, 1995, pp. 511–512). Those who are even missing from choir just temporarily often feel a sense of loss. On the occasion when a singer must miss a performance or a tour, he or she feels a sense of loss. Even when absent for a single rehearsal, Choir School singers miss the choral experience.

It is of the utmost importance that choral conductors create a community where the singers feel that they not only belong, but also that they are loved. One of the best ways that conductors can show choristers that they care deeply is by having high artistic and technical expectations. By asking the best of the singers in a choir, the conductor conveys both the message that the singer has yet to reach his or her full potential and the heartfelt belief that he or she can absolutely attain and exceed those expectations.

In creating a choral community, it is important to build in opportunities for the choristers to feel a sense of belonging outside the rehearsal room. The author believes this is the key to the widely acknowledged success of programs such as the Young People's Chorus of New York, the Cathedral Choir School of Delaware, and the East Texas Choir School. In these programs, choristers spend a significant amount of time together inside and outside the rehearsal room. These three programs also have structured afterschool programs linked with them that include: homework help, tutoring, one-on-one mentoring, and other group activities. As discussed previously, humans have a pack mentality and that has beneficial qualities. Youngsters and adults want to belong a group. When someone is part of a group, that individual begins to behave in harmony with the others who belong. In the case of these three successful afterschool programs, a culture of hard work along with expectations for excellence elevates the performance (musically, socially, and academically) of all of the students involved.

Self-esteem needs

To fully realize their potential, all humans need stable self-esteem (Maslow, 1987, p. 21). In 1968–1969, researchers studied the correlation between music and self-esteem. This study took place at an all-black elementary school. The protocol examined fourteen boys in the fourth, fifth, and sixth grades who were classified by the county psychologist as having behavioral problems, a lack of motivation to succeed, and conflict with others at school. These students also had multiple reports of failing academically. The purpose of this study was to "determine whether or not the learning of simple musical performance skills would affect self-esteem in such boys" (Michel & Farrell, 1973, p. 80). At the end of the study, the researchers concluded that music performance did in fact increase the self-esteem of disadvantaged students. Not only was self-esteem improved, the students also developed "on-task time commitment" that was transferable outside the rehearsal room into other academic classrooms (Michel & Farrell, 1973, p. 83).

The arts, similar to athletics, have long been recognized as a wonderful way to boost one's self-esteem. Maslow includes achievement, mastery, independence,, and respect from others as contributing factors that amount to self-esteem (Maslow, 1987). Choral conductors and their choirs have the ability to reinforce these contributing factors:

1. Achievement—One aspect of music performance that may not be thought about often is that performing is an act of instant gratification. When something sounds good, a chorister immediately hears it and emotionally responds to it. When the

choir performs well, each singer feels an immediate sense of accomplishment, of achievement. It is the responsibility of every choral conductor to make sure that his or her choir has at least one musical moment each rehearsal. A musical moment is a time when the singers can hear the progress that they have made and can emotionally respond to the musical achievement. For instance, when a choir is rehearsing a Bach fugue, the conductor must certainly break things down and do a bit of woodshedding. The advanced conductor knows that his or her time is better spent breaking the fugue into parts, possibly just rehearsing the exposition, subject, answer, and counter-subject. Instead of plunging ahead into the first episode, the conductor should discontinue woodshedding and allow the choir to rehearse the first part of the fugue. After proper rehearsal technique has been used and the choir has tackled a manageable chunk, the choir can sing through the first part of the fugue accurately. This sing-through certainly is satisfying for the choir, though the wise conductor will now go back to make the passage really *sing* by adding phrasing, dynamics, and other enriching measures. After the choir sings this passage musically (and accurately), the choir can hear its progress. The instant gratification creates a sense of pride, a sense of achievement.

2. Mastery—Once a choir has been able to sing through a piece accurately and with musicality, it is ready to reach for a higher level of mastery. Signs of this level engagement are kinesthetic movement within the choir (the singers are able to feel rhythms and phrases and are able to coordinate the breath with these kinesthetic sensations) and a heightened sensitivity to the conductor's gesture. It is important to be clear that mastery of a piece does not necessarily translate to memorization, although memorization is certainly an effective tool to motivate singers to attain this level of engagement. One cannot sing to his or her fullest potential while remaining physically still. In fact, the very nature of breathing elicits physical movement. One very significant difference between being a singer and being an instrumentalist is that the entire body, not just the vocal mechanism, is the instrument. The body as a whole works as one large resonating instrument. When there is a heighted sensitivity to a conductor's gesture, the choir makes musical and artistic decisions along with the conductor. The conductor is, at this level of engagement, able to convey an aural concept that is evoked by gesture and anticipated by the choir *before* the gesture is actually made. This stage is only possible after a conductor and choir have worked together intimately on a piece of music in focused rehearsals. At this level of singing, the choir feels more than just a sense of achievement: they feel mastery. They feel as though the notation were just the first layer in the artistic endeavor and that musical and artistic interpretation is the primary objective of the music making.

3. Independence—Being in choir is complex because one must be an individual in the context of a unified community. How can one be both an individual and part of the whole? Being in an ensemble is so very challenging because it calls for this paradox. On the one hand, participating in any ensemble is gratifying because it gives us a sense of belonging. One of the reasons for this sense of belonging is

that we recognize intellectually and emotionally that we have something to contribute to the group or ensemble. On the other hand, even though a conductor leads a choral ensemble and drives a unified aural mapping of a piece, it is up to each singer to interpret the conductor's gesture and the composer's notation. Each singer crescendos at a slightly different pace even if it seems imperceptible; each singer supports every phrase with a different amount of air; each singer colors each vowel slightly differently. The job of conductors is not only to create a unified aural perception in our singers, but also to foster a sense of ownership and independence. The conductor cannot and should not expect them to respond to each component of the music in the same way that the director does. Each singer brings his or her own life experiences into a personal approach to each piece of music. Having set this expectation with the singers, the conductor shows them that it motivates them to be independent singers.At the Choir School, conductors build the important skill of error detection by encouraging young choristers to fix their own errors. When something goes wrong in the context of a phrase, the conductor will stop and ask them to look first and listen second before re-singing the passage. Amazingly enough, this seems to fix the problems far more often than not. It is absolutely critical to build this independence; otherwise an unhealthy dependence on the conductor is established, eliminating the possibility of mastering the music. Working with these students has also clarified how incredibly effective it is to ask young singers to do learn parts or memorize music outside the rehearsal. Assessing this work through a part-test is also critical. It demonstrates to the singers that their independent work is being reviewed and measured much as a teacher would review a paper or homework assignment. It is a mistake to ask singers of any age to interface with repertoire only in the context of a rehearsal. The singer needs alone time with the music to fully digest it. These times of private score study build independence.

4. Respect from Others—Being a part of a group such as a choir—or a gang—garners respect. An audience admires, if not reveres, performers. Performers feel a sense of pride and prestige when they sing for high-capacity audiences and when audiences show appreciation through applause. Performing in front of others is something that takes courage and nerve! Audiences recognize that fact and respect it. In the best choirs, each member respects every other member. Singers in a choir respect each other for many reasons, ranging from one's technical musical ability to another's musicality, and another's aptitude for languages. Members of a choir also respect each other because they understand the commitment, time, and energy that each person invests to make the choir successful.Although not mentioned in Maslow's writings, self-respect is an important part of one's self-esteem. Members of a choir want the choir to be successful in performance. No one wants to sing in a choir that is not performing well. This is something that conductors must always keep in mind. It is amazing how time and time again choirs seem to pull themselves together just before a performance. Why and how does this happen? The members of the choir realize that they will be associated with what

the ensemble produces. They want that product to be of the highest quality. In a mature choir, the members are internally motivated to perform well. The singers want to do the music justice for reasons of self-respect and knowing that they have mastered the work. Conductors who require excellence in everything that they do teach their choirs to want more for themselves. This is not very different from a gang leader who sets the tone, culture, and expectations for his gang.

A person cannot be psychologically healthy unless he or she is valued and respected by others and is valued and respected by himself or herself. It is important to remember that we are not born with self-esteem. We are born with a desire for belonging. We yearn for and crave respect from others, but we are not born with the skills to value ourselves or to make ourselves valued by others. Children learn self-esteem first from the familial unit and then from outside communities who reinforce the lessons and values learned at home. As choral conductors and creators of choral communities (particularly those working with disadvantaged students), it is critical that singers are taught to value themselves. Conductors can clearly communicate how valuable each singer is. It is impossible to *force* children to have high self-esteem, but it is certainly possible to give them the tools and opportunities they need to become an integral and valued part of our choral communities.

Self-actualization needs

What exactly is self-actualization? Maslow (1987) writes, "What humans *can* be, they *must* be. [. . .] This need we may call self-actualization . . . It refers to people's desire for self-fulfillment, namely, the tendency for them to become actualized in what they are potentially. This tendency might be phrased as the desire to become more and more what one idiosyncratically is, to become everything that one is capable of becoming" (p. 22).

Maslow viewed self-actualization as a desire that one would fulfill once all other needs were met (Maslow, 1987). He believed that there were many characteristics that self-actualizers exhibit. Some of these characteristics that directly relate to the work of choral conductors include: perceptions of reality, acceptance, human kinship, problem centering, and peak experiences.

1. Perceptions of Reality—Self-actualized persons have the ability to correctly judge themselves, others, and the world around them (Maslow, 1987, p. 128). This is something that singers train to do within the choral community. Members of a choir are taught simultaneously to monitor and analyze their own singing and the singing of the choir as a whole. During the course of a rehearsal, mature choral singers listen louder than they sing. They listen closely to their aural perception of a piece of music, the conductor's aural perception of that piece as indicated by his or her gestures, their own singing, and the singing of the entire choir. Choral

singers also make decisions regularly about which passages to sing in head voice, falsetto, chest voice, or which passages to leave out altogether. In instances such as these, choral singers evaluate their strengths and weaknesses as they really are and make decisions that ultimately lead to the success of the choir as a whole.

2. Acceptance—This concept is closely related to one having an efficient perception of reality. When we perceive ourselves accurately, we perceive others, the world, and ourselves in both positive and negative lights. Having a sense of belonging in any group, and most certainly a choir, hinges on what an individual can contribute to the whole. Unlike perceiving reality as it actually is, the ability to *accept* those realities is a discipline of its own. For example, one soprano might be an expert at singing a floating, pianissimo high C at the end of a piece, whereas another soprano might be able to might be able to sing a high C at the end of a Moses Hogan spiritual. Both of these voices are valuable and are needed in order to have a well-balanced, well-rounded choir. In a healthy choral environment, the singers understand their shortcomings, recognize their strengths, and accept them. Choirs also help us accept people of all different cultural and socioeconomic backgrounds because they reflect the diversities of the communities they serve. This trains our singers to share their cultures with others while also being able to appreciate and enjoy the differences in the culture of their peers.

3. Human Kinship—Self-actualizers are connected to their humanity. They have the ability to empathize and a desire to better the human condition. A study published in 2012 concluded that long-term participation in a music ensemble improves empathy in children (Tal-Chen Rabinowitch, 2012). It is impossible to be an artist without the ability to empathize and relate to the human condition, because art is a product of the human condition. Above all, participating in choir teaches vulnerability. Since the instrument is the entire body, singing is intimate and personal. When one shares singing, one shares his or her entire self. Art is so personal that it cannot be shared in its entirety unless the giver and the recipient are vulnerable. This allows us to build into one another and form bonds of human kinship.

4. Problem Centering—Individuals who are self-actualized often want to solve problems beyond their own. These individuals help others solve problems in their communities and in the larger global community. The motivation to solve these problems is often moral or ethical (Maslow, 1987, pp. 133–134). In February 2015, *The Telegraph*, a United Kingdom newspaper, published an article entitled, "Perfect Harmony: How Singing in a Choir Can Make Us More 'Moral' ". In this article, the author presents research from 10,000 British children and 250 teachers at the Jubilee Centre, an academic unit at Birmingham University dedicated to studying issues such as character education (Bingham, 2015). The study concluded that children who participate in ensembles such as orchestra or choir are more likely to make choices that are more moral (Bingham, 2015). In fact, those who participated in choir were 17% more likely to make moral choices than their non-music participating counterparts (Bingham, 2015). Those who are more moral are certainly more likely to be problem centered.

5. Peak Experiences—These experiences can are characterized as moments of intense joy, ecstasy, and awe. Choirs often experience these moments together. One of the author's strongest memories is of the first meaningful standing ovation that he ever received. He was ten years old and had completed a concert with the Peabody's Children's Chorus and the Baltimore Symphony Orchestra. He had never worked as so hard on piece of music, and to have a high-capacity audience all on their feet felt exhilarating. To performers, the most powerful moment during a piece of music is the silence between the last note of a performance and first sound of applause. This precious moment is the closest experience that humans can have to nirvana. In this moment, after it is all on the line, the performers are proud of what they have accomplished. They are caught-up in a frenzy of ecstasy and completely vulnerable to the audience. Performing is all about those precious moments, not in anticipation of applause, but in anticipation of accomplishment, that is pure ecstasy.

Those who belong to gangs may fulfill the four basic needs, but they can never truly be self-actualizers, because they cannot perceive themselves as they really are. They particularly lack the ability to see themselves through the eyes of the larger community.

It is important to realize that self-actualization is not a destination point. It is rather a catapult, a psychological state that propels and thrusts individuals and organizations towards their goals, expectations, and dreams. This is why self-actualizers are successful.

It is the goal of every human to reach his or her fullest potential and to become fully self-actualized. Even if a person does not comprehend it, this motivates his or her actions. However, it is essential to remember that self-actualization cannot occur unless other needs have been met.

One must ask: why is it that a Stanford motet has the power to pull a disadvantaged "kid" off the street? It clearly does not have the power to do that on its own. The choral community, however, does have the power to pull a youngster off the street. Although the Stanford motet might be the finished product, the journey of how that singer could be rescued from his or her predetermined, first grade destiny is why he or she was able to become a success story.

It is difficult to deny the certain correlation between music and success. Music majors make up the most likely group of college graduates to be admitted into medical school, with 66% of music majors being accepted compared to 44% of biology and pre-med majors (Miller & Coen, 1994). Those who participate in choral ensembles are successful because they excel in cooperative and group learning. In this collaborative learning process, individuals have responsibilities to the group as well as obligations to themselves (Miller & Coen, 1994) much like in the expectations of the professional world.

The choral community offers particular benefits to disadvantaged students. It opens up to them the opportunity to escape the life that they were born into and to achieve peak experiences similar to their more affluent counterparts. The choral community is a gang for good, one that not only provides many critical needs to its members, but also leads its members to realize their fullest potential inside and outside the rehearsal room.

References

Badger, E. (2014, December 27). What your first grade life says about the rest of it. *The Washington Post*. Retrieved February 7, 2015, from http://www.washingtonpost.com/blogs/wonkblog/wp/2014/12/27/what-your-first-grade-life-says-about-the-rest-of-it/

Baumeister, R., & Leary, M. (1995). The need to belong: Desire for interpersonal attachments as a fundamental human motivation. *Psychological Bulletin, 117*(3), 497–529.

Bingham, J. (2015, February 27). Perfect harmony: How singing in a choir can make us more "moral." *The Telegraph*. Retrieved February 27, 2015: http://www.telegraph.co.uk/news/religion/11437624/Perfect-harmony-how-singing-in-a-choir-can-make-us-more-moral.html

Harmon, C. (2014, May). A successful choir school in an unlikely place. *The American Organist, 48*(5), 46–48.

Maslow, A. (1987). *Motivation and personality* (3rd ed.). New York: Harper and Row.

Michel, D. E., & Farrell, D. (1973). Music and self-esteem: Disadvantaged problem boys in an all-black elementary school. *Journal of Research in Music Education, 21*(1), 80–84.

Miller, A., & Coen, D. (1994). The case for music in the schools. *The Phi Delta Kappan, 75*(6), 459–461.

Puffer, J. (1912). *The Boy and His Gang*. Boston, New York: Houghton Mifflin company.

Tal-Chen Rabinowitch, I. C. (2012, April). Long-term musical group interaction has a positive influence on empathy in children. *Psychology of Music, 41*(4), 484–498.

Yearwood, D., & Hayes, R. (2000). Perceptions of youth crime and youth gangs: A statewide systemic investigation. North Carolina Criminal Justice Analysis Center. Retrieved January 5, 2015, from https://www.ncdps.gov/div/gcc/Gangstudy.htm

....

BUILDING SOUND AND SKILLS IN THE MEN'S CHORUS AT COLLEGES AND UNIVERSITIES IN THE UNITED STATES

....

PAUL RARDIN

IMAGINE a choir of collegiate singers called *Cappella Perfecta*. All 50 members of this brilliant ensemble have the same exact set of choral skills: all have studied for the same amount of time with the same voice teacher; all have studied music theory and music history with the same professors for the same amount of time; all sight-sing equally well; and all have sung in choirs for the same number of years. The ensemble derives its name in part from the fact that all members also have perfect pitch.

Would this not be ideal? The conductor would know exactly how challenging the repertoire could be, how detailed the rehearsal vocabulary could be, and how quick the rehearsal pace could be. The amount of guesswork at gauging a choir's success would be minimal to zero, and the group's performance potential would be enormous.

Of course, *Cappella Perfecta* exists only in the imagination. Singers in even the least experienced choirs, where we might expect children to begin with a similar set of skills, and the most experienced where we might expect grown professionals to have equal acumen, move at different individual speeds in the course of the collective rehearsal. Yet it is part of the challenge and part of the joy of the conducting profession to find the right repertoire, the right vocabulary, and the right pace to get unified beauty out of diverse individual sounds and brains.

Collegiate conductors may experience this disparity in choral skills most often in ensembles with high percentages of non-music majors. Even auditioned ensembles of this type may yield a large gap between the ensemble's most accomplished singer and its least accomplished. This is particularly true for men's ensembles in colleges and universities in the United States. Extensive research has offered numerous reasons that boys drop out of choirs during their middle- and high-school years,[1] past which time they may be less likely or less qualified to join a collegiate choir. The collegiate men's chorus, which is likely to consist of a high percentage, if not in fact outright majority, of non-music majors, may be more likely to have a wider skill disparity than any other choir on campus.

The challenge here requires conductors to aim high in their expectations. After surveying the musical gap between the most experienced singer and the least experienced singer, a conductor must:

- rehearse with enough pace to keep the most experienced singer engaged, and
- rehearse with enough patience to keep the least experienced singer from falling behind

Finding this "golden average"—that unique level of choral challenge (in repertoire, rehearsal pacing, and vocal understanding) that is above the average of these two hypothetical students—is an exciting process that invites conductors to think of themselves as much as teachers as a conductors. Finding even modest success with *Cappella Typica* should bring far greater satisfaction than coasting pristinely with *Cappella Perfecta*.

Conductors may help reach this "golden average" in non-musical means as well. They may benefit from honing critical social and political skills, particularly in cases in which the ensemble bears the name "glee club." Many men's choirs boast decades and even centuries of traditions, and many include student leaders that share governance with the conductor. In such cases, conductors may find that their voices and vote in governance is but one among many, and may need to develop effective working rapport with student leaders in order to further musical initiatives. They may also need to acknowledge that the social fabric of singing is the draw for many of the students, more so than the music, and to honor and support this element.

Does catering to our less-experienced singers slow us down? Does sharing important decisions with students impede musical progress? Does accepting the importance of social gatherings weaken the ensemble's musical identity? The conductor of the collegiate men's chorus learns quickly that the flip sides of inexperience and inability are energy and curiosity, and that many other non-musical attributes—computer expertise, graphic design, public speaking, finance expertise—can fuel musical excellence through that one component that members of all choirs desperately seek: Belonging.

BUILDING FOUNDATION: "SEEING" THE INVISIBLE INSTRUMENT

The conductor of the collegiate men's chorus is likely to be the de facto voice teacher for the majority of the singers, and should embrace this fact as both opportunity and responsibility. While conductors are likely to have had regular voice study in their own college background, conductors may or may not have had vocal pedagogy—training in the teaching of voice—and might benefit from even the most basic refresher course in this area.[2] This is particularly important if the conductor's collegiate choral experience focused primarily on choral issues such as blend, vowels, intonation, and less on vocal issues that include breathing, phonation, and tone. Paradoxically, the conductor whose college choral experience was rigorous and outstanding may or may not have learned much about the vocal mechanism; any conductor who wishes to teach non-music majors would do well to develop her own understanding of the "solo" instrument before delving into issues of the ensemble.

A useful first step in this teaching process is an introduction to the mechanics of the human voice, which can take place most effectively as a separate mini-lecture during rehearsal, or as a series of successive warm-up exercises. Ideally, the conductor uses both approaches to both introduce early and remind often during the semester.

Since the human voice is the sole musical instrument invisible to the naked eye, it will always prove somewhat elusive: We can't see, touch, or assemble our instrument the way a flutist can. At some point, verbal description of the vocal mechanism falls short, and the singer must use his imagination to comprehend the components of breathing, phonation, resonation, and articulation. The conductor should consider rehearsal exercises that help the singers "see" the inner workings of the invisible instrument. For students who learn primarily by seeing, these exercises will be especially useful.

Exercises to help "see" the invisible instrument

Many of the exercises below may be both demonstrated by the conductor (visual) and mimicked by the singer (kinesthetic).

Breathing

1. "Eight-handed breathing" (see James Jordan)[3];

The conductor invites four singers to demonstrate:
INHALATION

- One person imitates the ribs of the back, holding hands in front of own (front) ribs, thumbs and first two fingers outstretched towards each other horizontally and separated slightly; upon inhalation (ask the ensemble to inhale quietly through nose), hands rotate outward; thumbs stay gently attached while fingers pull away from each other
- One person imitates diaphragm, holding hands shaped as an upside-down bowl, in front of sternum; upon inhalation, bowl changes from more domed to less domed
- One person imitates abdominal walls, holding hands facing and parallel to stomach; upon inhalation, hands move outward to sides (following expanding stomach)
- One person imitates pelvic floor, holding hands parallel to floor, facing ceiling, one hand atop the other, in front of waistline; upon inhalation, hands extend downward slightly

EXHALATION

- Upon exhalation (ask singers to blow air out quietly and evenly as if through a straw), hands imitating ribs travel inward, returning to original position in front of ribs
- Hands imitating diaphragm travel from less-domed to more-domed position
- Hands imitating abdominal walls return inward to original position in front of abdomen
- Hands imitating pelvic floor return upwards to original position in front of waistline

This exercise provides an immediate view of the vast body-space required to produce beautiful singing. The singers see at an instant that effective breathing requires activity from the topmost rib to below the waist, which subtly reminds the singer of the importance of excellent body alignment.

It also provides the conductor the opportunity to teach the functions of these critical body parts in the breathing process—namely, that they all have the vital task of making room for the lungs to inflate. The ribs travel to make room for the upper end of the lungs; the diaphragm, a muscle, flattens and descends to push the viscera out of the way of the lower end of the lungs; the abdominal muscles create room for the displaced viscera, as does the pelvic floor. The process might include a gentle reminder that the diaphragm is an involuntary muscle, and though many well-meaning voice teachers and choir directors ask singers to "sing from the diaphragm," they do so believing, erroneously, that the diaphragm is a voluntary muscle and therefore controllable.[4]

2. Da Vinci's *Vitruvian Man*[5]

The conductor models this exercise for the singers, beginning with arms relaxed by side, with shoulders relaxed and aligned with ears and hips, and ribs tall.
INHALATION

- Inhale air gently and evenly as if through the vowel "u" as arms complete these three motions:
  - Arms lift slowly and gently, always outstretched, directly in front of body and with palms facing down, until parallel to the floor ("Frankenstein" position)
  - Arms move slowly outward, remaining parallel to the floor and with palms facing down, until outstretched at either side of body ("T" position)
  - Arms move slowly upward again, in an arc (tracing Da Vinci's *Vitruvian Man* circle) and with palms up, remaining outstretched until converging at a point directly above the head ("high-diver" position)

EXHALATION

- Exhale air on a soft hiss as arms complete this motion:

- Arms lower slowly and gently, with palms now facing outward (away from each other), re-tracing the complete *Vitruvian Man* circle until they return to their initial, relaxed position by the sides of the body.

This exercise offers a full-body visual analogy of the expansion of the lungs that is necessary for effective singing. In subsequent iterations future the conductor should point out to the singers the great expansion of the ribs that takes place with the upward motion of the arms, and remind the singers to maintain this "inflated" position through the descent of the arms. The conductor should listen to make sure that both the inhalation and exhalation are smooth and even. Repetitions of this exercise over the course of the semester, especially if adding time to both the ascent and descent, will result in an increased breathing stamina on the part of the singers.

Phonation

Using fingers to imitate the vocal folds, the conductor can demonstrate three types of vocal phonation: aspirate (lax) phonation, which results in a breathy sound; pressed (tense) phonation, which results in a tight, belting sound; and coordinated (balanced) phonation, which results in a more pleasing sound and more efficient use of air.[6]

- Holding index fingers outstretched and touching at tips, facing the ground in an V shape (a "cross-section" look at the vocal folds), the conductor brings the fingers together to mimic three different types of phonation:
  - For aspirate phonation, the conductor brings fingers together weakly so that they do not quite touch; singers sing breathy vowel [a] to demonstrate
  - For pressed phonation, the conductor brings fingers together strongly and tensely; singers sing belted vowel [a] to demonstrate
  - For balanced phonation, the conductor brings fingers together gently but firmly; singers sing free, balanced vowel [a] to demonstrate

Like many effective choral techniques, this one helps to clarify a concept by demonstrating both it and its opposite. By reminding the singers of what ugliness sounds like (and the singers will be familiar with many examples of popular music that uses both pressed and lax phonation), the conductor can help the singers "see" what beautiful phonation looks, feels, and sounds like.

Resonance—arching the tongue

- For warmer sounds to brighter: with singers singing the vowel [a], place the hands on either side of each ear, about one foot away, with palms facing forward (dark, diffuse sound), then bring them forward toward a single point forward, about one foot in front of you, slightly above your head, and palms facing each other (bright, focused sound). Singers should mimic these hand motions as they sing. Repeat this process for other vowels as desired.[7]

This gesture mimics what some singers call "forward placement" by gently lifting the soft palate and creating a forward, higher hump in the tongue.[8] The result is a larger resonating cavity in the mouth and a pleasing audible ring to the sound, one that lends a sense of presence and vitality. Its opposite is a dark, hooty, nebulous sound.

Resonance—lifting the soft palate

- Pull imaginary taffy, vertically and in front of the conductor's face (image: stretching the vowel north-south)[9]
- Set the left hand out horizontally (palm facing floor) in front of the conductor's chest; gently place the right hand flat on top it; and slowly lift the right palm away while leaving the right fingertips gently touching the left hand (image: a jellyfish rising); right hand is mimicking the movement of the soft palate; complete this exercise while singing the vowel [a], noticing the increased warmth and resonance with the higher soft-palate position[10]
- Place an imaginary cookie inside the mouth in horizontal alignment (parallel to ground); singers sing the vowel [a] in this position, then gradually rotate cookie to vertical alignment (perpendicular to ground), instructing the singers to make sure that the cookie never touches the roof of the mouth[11]

There are dozens of published and otherwise circulating exercises that accomplish the same goal—offering a visual analogy for the raising of the soft palate.[12] The raised soft palate creates tall, "vertical" vowels that increase the size of the resonance chamber, and which are preferable for most types of classical choral music. Its opposite is a spread, twangy, "smily" sound that may have a more child-like quality.

Taken together, the arched tongue and lifted soft palate—along with lowering the larynx and releasing the jaw—provide the choral holy grail of choral sound: The golden combination of brightness and warmth. One might think of the lifted soft palate as the ceiling of a great cathedral,[13] and higher/more forward hump in the tongue as the stained glass window high on its front wall; the high ceiling permits grandeur and "height" in the sound, while the stained glass is a hard surface that reflects sound from a fixed point. More succinctly, these concepts might be referred to as "point" and "dome,"[14] twin ideals that help the conductor focus her attention on the specifics of the sound she's hearing, and modify it until it has the sound she desires. Point and Dome will serve as focal points for our discussion of rehearsal techniques later in this chapter.

Resonance—navigating registers

This is an issue more easily heard and felt than "seen," but none is more vital in working effectively with men's voices. College-aged men have a very impressive range—it can easily cover three octaves from their highest head-register notes to their lowest chest-register notes. Connecting their three primary registers—head voice (falsetto), middle voice, and chest voice—is one of their most important tasks in singing men's music. One example helps the students feel, physically, the sensation of register:

- "Holy moley"; singers place right hand on ribs and speak "holy moley" in a very low register; then singers place right index and middle fingertips onto right cheekbone (just below eye) and speak "mm-hmm" (as in, "yes, I agree with you") in middle-to-high register; then singers place same fingertips onto side of forehead and speak "oo oo oo" in high head-voice (falsetto) register (a happy monkey?); finally singers place right hand on back of head and speak "oh, no!" in their highest possible falsetto register.[15]

This playful exercise helps male singers differentiate their chest voice ("holy moley") from their middle voice ("mm-hmm") from their head voice ("oo oo oo"). (The hyper-falsetto "oh no" is unlikely to find use in most men's-chorus concerts, but it provides a humorous dose of recognition that the male voice is capable of very high pitches.) It allows students to feel with their hands the sensations taking place in the hard-surface resonators (bones) in which the sound is vibrating. For much classical music, the middle voice ("mm-hmm") is the most useful starting register for sound. This register is usually higher than men's normal speaking voices, so making the adjustment from everyday speaking to classical singing requires effective pedagogy and regular reminders.

Armed with a "visual" sense of what's happening inside the body during singing, the singers are now in a good position to make good, healthy, resonant sound. The effective conductor finds ways to refer back to these exercises to remind the singers that supported breathing, beautiful resonance, and tall space—foundational concepts that, taken together, are sometimes referred to as "core"—must be the rule and not the exception. As the Listener-in-Chief, the conductor must diligently track these elements and address them as needed.

BUILDING SOUND: ESTABLISHING CORE IN REHEARSAL

As conductors and singers we take for granted the necessity of the printed page. While some choirs incorporate music taught by rote—such as gospel or folk songs—most have printed sheet music as the vehicle for the majority of their repertoire. It is easy to forget just what an obstacle to beautiful singing that printed page can be: Just when the singer is beginning to grasp the foundational concepts of breathing, resonance, and space—this foundation is sometimes referred to as "core"—he is handed a document that floods him with dozens of musical elements—pitch, rhythm, text, dynamics, articulation, tone quality, meaning, and many others.

In rehearsal, and particularly in the first rehearsals of a season, the conductor must assume that the brain cannot possibly remember all of these elements at once, and must find ways to reinforce these foundational concepts regularly throughout the process. Singers who are less confident as music readers may find themselves especially vulnerable to unsupported singing—whether through lack of confidence or poor body alignment (sheet music in one's lap)—in the early stages of rehearsing a new piece.

The effective conductor finds ways to help the ensemble build sound even during the preliminary stages of rehearsing. Absent any reminders from the conductor, the singers may view the above exercises as mere "warm-ups," necessary drill-work that is separate from the actual rehearsal process. The conductor should incorporate rehearsal techniques that help the choir build its foundational sound—built, again, on breathing, resonance ("point"), and space ("dome")—throughout the music-learning process.

Building breath: Supported sound

A colleague recently described an answer given by a brilliant choral conductor on what he felt to be the ten most important components of effective singing: his response was to utter the word "alignment" ten times.[16] Virtually every major textbook on singing and choral conducting rightly points to the minimum requirement of correct body alignment—it's worth noting that this word may have more positive connotation than its somehow patronizing cousin "posture"—in beautiful singing.

- Sing printed part on lip trills
  - Lip trills involve forcing air through closed lips, causing them to vibrate/flap in a way that sounds like a motorcycle engine. Lip trills require significantly more airflow than sung words. Like the *Vitruvian Man* exercise, this technique is superb for developing breath stamina in young singers.

This exercise provides a useful reminder that both forward placement and superb breath support are required for beautiful intonation and sound.

Building "point": Focused sound

Focused sound has shimmer, vitality, and presence. A choir might imagine the analogy of beautiful landscape, as seen in a photograph that is slightly out of focus: We can discern hills, grass, and flowers in a general, distant, hazy way, but only when the photo is brought into focus can we appreciate the clarity of color, contour, and texture. Focused sound is the polish that gives shine to a beautiful silver vase.

Focused choral sound is rich with upper partials of the overtone series.[17] The presence of these partials gives choral sound a sense of vitality, brightness, and presence, even in soft music. The singer can enhance these higher partials in part by allowing the sound to live in the "mask," a common term for the area "around the eyes and the bridge of the nose."[18] This maximizes use of the hard surfaces of the cheekbones as reflecting resonators.

Singers can find this space effectively in several ways during the rehearsal process:

- Sing printed part on "ng"
  - This consonant combination requires the tongue to be arched and the soft palate to be lowered, against the hard palette, effectively changing the resonating shape of the mouth and creating a buzzing sensation in the mask. Alternating between "ng" and a neutral syllable helps the singers transition maintain this "forward" sound once the soft palate is lifted and the tongue lowered.
- Sing printed parts on the neutral syllable [bi]
  - Both the consonant "b" and the arched tongue required for the vowel [i] encourage the sound into the mask. This exercise can be an extremely useful tool even after a piece has been learned thoroughly. Is the choir's sound dull or woofy on the phrase "A-ve Ma-ri-a," one so loaded with the most open of all vowels, [a]? Have the choir sing the same pitches on [bi-bi bi-bi-bi], then return to the actual text, but "remembering" the sensation of the buzzier, more forward [i] vowel. The sound should change instantly and for the better. As with "ng," use caution or modify the vowel to [bu] or [ba] for higher passages.

These exercises build core in multiple ways, establishing not only focus but also excellent intonation, as the upper partials help the singers distinguish the correct pitch.

Building "dome": Tall sound

Achieving tall sound relies on creating resonant space inside the mouth and throat. Singers can achieve tall sound primarily by lifting the soft palate—the fleshy portion of the roof of the mouth, toward the back. Through gentle yawn-sighs or mock expressions of surprise, singers realize their ability to lift the soft palate through everyday gestures. Raising this "dome" of space maximizes the physical resonating space inside the mouth and results in a pleasant, full sound. Its opposite is a spread, flat, perhaps child-like sound—one which may in fact be useful for certain types of popular or world musics, but for standard works may seem thin or unsupported.

Singers can achieve choral dome in rehearsal through numerous exercises:

- Sing using the "vowelometer"
  - While singing a learned passage of music, singers place their free hand several inches in front of their mouth, palm to the side and thumb closest to face, first in

"north-south" configuration (hand perpendicular to the ground, bisecting face from forehead to chin). The singers then sing the same passage with their hands in the "east-west" position (hand parallel to the ground, palm facing floor, bisecting face from cheek to cheek). The vowelometer's "north-south" position results in a lifted soft palate and tall, warm vowels; the "east-west" position results in a lowered soft palate and wide, spread vowels. The vowelometer is a useful tool for adjusting individual vowels—tilting from one position to the other and back on a single vowel—or for simply establishing dome during the choral warm-up.

- Sing with hands on cheeks
  - While singing a memorized passage of music, singers place the backs of their hands on their cheeks, gently massaging the cheeks in upward strokes with the backs of the fingers. This upward motion of the hands coaxes the soft palate into its lifted position and results in height and warmth in the sound.
- "Grow" 20 years in 20 seconds
  - Singers sing a memorized passage of music five different times, each time imitating the sound of hypothetical choir at a different age groups:
    - Elementary school
    - Middle school
    - High school
    - College
    - Professional/"Russian Army Chorus"

This light-hearted exercise uses the singers' collective imagination to "grow" their sound across the age range, from a youthful, spread, and perhaps twangy elementary-school sound to a robust, tall, and perhaps woofy professional sound. (The conductor would do well to remind her singers that excellent choirs at all age levels sing with beautiful and supported sound, and that this exercise relies on playful exaggeration.) Usually the desired timbre will fall exactly where it should: college-choir sound.

- Sing an octave above where printed[19]
  - Singers sing a short passage three times: first as printed, then one octave higher than printed, then immediately again as printed. Singers may be surprised to see just how high their voices can go, and in the process realize how much they must lift the soft palate to achieve this. Upon returning to passage as printed, singers bring a new, more lifted and freer sound, realizing that music that may have been in an awkward register or range for them is now easier in the more lifted position.

The concept of tall sound may well be new to college-age singers, particularly those whose vocal ideals are rooted in rock and popular music. These "dome" exercises help such singers see, hear, and feel the beauty and warmth in tall sound, and should be a regular part of the rehearsal diet. They must also take place in concert with "point" exercises, so that singers are always doing two things: creating focus, and creating space. It

BUILDING SOUND AND SKILLS IN THE MEN'S CHORUS   481

is the happy marriage of seeming opposites brightness and warmth that makes for the most beautiful choral sound possible.

Connecting registers: Using the "clutch"

Effective breathing, focus, and space will greatly assist collegiate male singers in navigating their three primary registers: head voice (falsetto), middle voice, and chest voice. Young singers' default register is their chest voice—rock, popular, and gospel musics make almost exclusive use of this powerful, robust resonating space. The difficulty in this default arises when untrained singers move from lower notes to higher notes that cause them to need to shift registers; even if the shift is made cleanly, without regular exercises there can be audible shifts in tone quality, beauty, and resonance.

If the human voice is a manual-transmission engine, and if its registers are different gears in that engine, the singers need to use an imaginary clutch to help shift vocal registers in an even and inaudible way. The conductor's approach should consist of 1) guiding the singers' default register (whether speaking or singing) from chest voice to middle and head voice, particularly when speaking, and 2) heightening awareness of the middle and head voices as viable, beautiful, and necessary registers for choral singing.

The following exercises help singers develop the head and middle registers:

- Speak in head voice
  - When speaking in rehearsal (in learning a new text, or answering a conductor's pronunciation of a word), singers use head voice. This helps singers make the shift from their daily, default speaking register (usually chest voice) to their classical singing voice. Imitating Julia Child or Mrs. Doubtfire while speaking a text[20] develops awareness of this important register.
- Bring the head voice down
  - Singers sing a descending 5-4-3-2-1 major scale on the syllable [nu], beginning in a high register (such as b2 down to e2). Most singers will need to begin this exercise in their head register, and many (especially basses and baritones) will need to stay there for the entire exercise. As the exercise modulates down by half-steps, singers discover those pitches on which they need to "shift gears" into their middle and chest voices, and learn to do so smoothly and inaudibly.[21] Singers tend to find success by "bringing their head voice down"—that is, singing longer in their head voice than they might normally do, and introducing their middle register only when it can match the timbre of an adjacent head-register pitch. This is a very effective exercise and an equally effective diagnostic tool in rehearsal: If there is an e2 on the vowel [a] that is sounding under pitch or heavy, it is probably due to tension caused by excessive chest voice. If the conductor applies this exercise to this pitch—starting on B arriving on the E on the syllable [u] before gently morphing to the printed vowel [a]—the resulting sound should now be freer, more lifted (by virtue of having had to begin in head voice), and more in tune.

In collegiate men's choirs, it is usually the tenor 2 part that benefits most from these exercises. The pitches of this part often live in the *passaggio* (range of pitches at which a register shift occurs), requiring them to have to make constant decisions about when to shift registers, which can result in vocal fatigue. (The tenor 1 part, by contrast, often lives above the passaggio, which makes these decisions easier by requiring more head and middle registers than chest register.) At some point, particularly in unison music, all parts will need to be comfortable shifting registers, so these exercises should be a regular part of the rehearsal experience for all parts.

A test case for rehearsal: René Clausen, *A Jubilant Song*

Just as the printed score can serve as a distraction or even impediment to the singer, it can serve as a crutch to the conductor. The conductor's primary musical responsibilities are arguably rhythm and pitch: Our ears must constantly answer the questions "Was it in time?" and "Was it in tune?"; therefore we often keep our eyes on the score to monitor its every detail. Answering these questions with minimal effort takes years of experience, so it is understandable that conductors may overlook the seemingly secondary concerns of "point" and "dome" as they rehearse.

Yet "point" and "dome" address not only the quality of the sound but also its frequency: They contribute to pitch as well as to timbre and resonance. They therefore are integral parts of the answer to "Was it in tune?" The effective conductor learns to train her ear toward the related questions "Do I hear core in the sound?" and "Is the sound full and resonant?" and gears her rehearsals toward building and maintaining these virtues.

René Clausen's *A Jubilant Song* is an excellent, joyous work that makes for a fine program opener or closer. As arranged for men's chorus by James Rodde, this spirited setting of a famous Walt Whitman poem presents immediate challenges to the conductor in its frequent change of time signatures. The conductor is forced to master this score—as she should do of course with all scores—before rehearsals begin in order to have her ears open to the ensemble's sound as it learns the piece. Accurate pitches and rhythms are important, but must never come at the expense of breathing, resonance, space, and register shifts. Indeed, reinforcing good choral habits will intrinsically improve its musical elements.

The sample rehearsal plan below, covering the piece's opening section, is designed to instill excellent choral habits in singers while learning the score.

Measures 1-33: possible rehearsal plan:

- Sing the excerpt, unaccompanied if possible, well under tempo and on the neutral syllable [bi]; this immediately encourages forward placement, improving both resonance and pitch
- Sing the excerpt again on lip trills; this builds breathing stamina and improves pitch (in some cases, improving it to the point of sharping)

- Speak the text in rhythm, staccato, in head or middle register; this builds rhythmic excellence, saves the voice by avoiding sustained tones, and introduces text without concern for pitch

To this point, the conductor is building vocal excellence before putting the music and text together. The singers have gradually acquired pitches and rhythms while also building breath and focus. The next logical rehearsal step:

- Sing the excerpt with text, under tempo

The conductor may notice challenges the minute the singers combine music and text: poor intonation, lack of focus, and inability to connect registers. Carefully tailored exercises address each of these issues. Over time, the conductor learns to anticipate where such issues might present themselves, and plan rehearsal strategies to address them.

Below are a few passages where such challenges may occur, and suggestions for how to rehearse them:

- Issue: m. 1 plus upbeat ("Make a song"): choir sound is overly dark
  - Remedy: choir sings these two beats on "ng" combination, bringing the sound immediately forward
- Issue: m. 1 plus upbeat: choir low D has too much chest voice, making the high D also chest-y, too heavy, and under pitch
  - Remedy: choir sings these two beats at pitch, then up an octave, then again at pitch, immediately lifting the soft palette and making both the low D and the high D more connected to the head voice
- Issue: m. 4 downbeat, the word "make": B1 and B2 sound is too dark, muffled, and under pitch
  - Remedy: choir sings the diphthong [ei] instead of [ɛi], thereby brightening and lifting the sound to a more "forward" position
  - Remedy 2: choir sings the preceding measure with a diminuendo, easing the voices' registers from chest sound to head-chest mixture
- Issue: m. 16–17: T2 leaps create uneven shifts in register; lower notes are too dark (chest register), higher notes either too heavy and under pitch (chest), or too weak and unfocused (head register) to create a seamless line
  - Remedy 1: choir sings the excerpt with all chest register (quasi-belted), then with all head register (falsetto), then with all middle register (balanced); this helps singers hear and feel the difference between the outer extremes and find the more pleasing midpoint
  - Remedy 2: choir sustains the e2 in m. 17 (it may well be heavy and/or under pitch); choir then sings descending 5-4-3-2-1 on the syllable [nu], beginning on b2 and ending on the e2 in question, then shifts pitch to printed [ʌ] vowel; by this

point sound should be in middle register, and therefore freer, more beautiful, and more in tune; choir then sings whole excerpt in their middle register

- Issue: m. 32–33: choir sound is muffled, lacks resonance (too dark)
  - Remedy 1: choir sings chord on [ng] combination, then switches to vowels in question
  - Remedy 2: choirs sings first syllable "light" very dark, with hands by ears pointing sound backward and upward, like flaps on an airplane wing, then points sound forward and upward; repeat process for "ning"; then sing both syllables in dark, "back-flap" position, then both syllables in brighter, more resonant "forward-flap" position.
- Issue: m. 32–33: choir vowels are spread and twangy (too bright)
  - Remedy: choir sings with vowelometer east–west (nasal and spread, to exaggerate the twang), then with vowelometer north–south (tall and full)

These and similar exercises accomplish learning the musical piece while shining a very important spotlight on airflow, resonance, and space. While rehearsing individual parts, the conductor may wish to keep the other parts mentally and musically engaged, by tapping rhythms, humming parts, or singing parts softly on staccato [du].

The process requires the conductor's diligence and patience. Her diverse constituency of singers needs this training, and needs to be reminded weekly of its importance. Even for the more accomplished singers—those who reside above the "golden average" of the ensemble membership—these exercises will resonate with their own training as useful, voice-friendly, and critical for bringing unity to the choral sound.

BUILDING COMMUNITY: THE VIRTUE
OF THE NON-MAJOR

Building vocal excellence is, in and of itself, a means of building community. Singers sing in choirs because they enjoy the process of joining their unique voice to dozens of other unique voices to create a common sound. Developing breath and sound, using the necessary exercises such as those listed above, help the conductor create that seeming miracle of a single voice out of many. Robert Shaw's published letters include dozens of statements that mark the joining of voice to voice as not merely a musical journey but also a spiritual one:

> That music is always a community enterprise. The solo performance does not exist. Even its creation is an attempt to communicate, and every performance an effort to unite the minds of men even of different generations.[22]

For some students in choir, the draw to the ensemble is more social than musical. For others, the draw may be the leadership opportunities that a shared-governance model—one in which both students and the conductor share leadership responsibilities—provides. Many men's choirs in the United States have long and distinguished histories, and their social fabrics and student leadership have helped to perpetuate and build upon these histories.

The conductor may imagine these social and political components to be somehow foreign to, or adversarial to, good music-making. Should not the ensemble's primary focus be musical excellence? Should not the conductor have complete authority over the ensemble, both in its music and its operations? Won't an excess of group parties and student meddling in choir governance distract from the musical goals?

Here there is a parallel between the ensemble's musical diversity and its human diversity. Just as a collegiate men's ensemble is likely to have a wide range of musical ability, it is also likely to have a wide range of interests, races, political views, hobbies, and career ambitions. Musically, this diversity presents a challenge: Help the weakest singer catch up to the strongest singer, and help them and all of the singers in between create a unified sound. Humanistically, this diversity is strength: Here are dozens of young men who bring a wide array of gifts and interests, many of which can help the ensemble to grow.

Ultimately, what may first appear to be limitations may well prove to be assets. The non-music major is less skilled than the music major, but brings more curiosity and energy to rehearsal—"I do this for enjoyment" instead of "I need the credit." The social activity increases time demands on the singers, but also strengthens bonds between them and therefore loyalty to the ensemble. And the student leader who is skeptical about the conductor's brilliant new initiative is likely to be an intelligent, dedicated, and respected member of the ensemble who will respond thoughtfully to well-crafted proposals. In short, the collegiate men's chorus consists of amateurs—people who, as Robert Shaw reminded us, are ones who love, not ones who can't do.

Cappella imperfecta

Choirs are wonderful reminders of many things that human beings share, including breath and voice. Whether or not a young man in a collegiate men's ensemble sings as well as the students on either side of him, he shares with them the ability to breathe and to phonate, and is therefore capable of growing in both capacities. And whether or not his neighbors are highly advanced singers, they may still gain equal benefit from exercises that introduce and maintain musical core. The sense of community between these vastly different singers exists at this very basic physical level.

Similarly, these singers likely bring diverse extramusical wishes to the table. The singer who is a choral 8 out of 10 brings great musical contributions but may be disengaged socially or administratively from the group; the singer who is a choral 2 out of 10 brings less musicianship but likely greater excitement and energy to rehearsals, and may also contribute to the ensemble in nonmusical ways. Both of these young men are vital components of a successful choir, and both need to be embraced. By teaching and reteaching the basic building blocks of effective singing, the conductor helps the 2 catch up with the 8, keeps the 8 in shape, and grows the ensemble's technical and musical prowess. By accepting responsibility as principal voice teacher and by supporting the social and administrative involvement of the students, the conductor of the collegiate men's chorus has the opportunity to build something meaningful, lasting, and excellent.

Notes

1. From Intersectionalities: exploring qualitative research, music education, and diversity, by Bruce Carter, 2014, in *The Oxford Companion of Qualitative Research in American Music Education*, edited by C. Conway. Oxford, England: Oxford University Press, p. 548.
2. An excellent refresher course on the mechanism of the voice can be found in Clifton Ware (1998), *Adventures in Singing* (2nd ed.). Boston: MacGraw-Hill.
3. From *The Musician's Breath: The Role of Breathing in Human* by James Jordan, 2011, pp. 52–55. Chicago: GIA.
4. From "Choral Directors are from Mars and Voice Teachers are from Venus: Sing from the Diaphragm and other Vocal Misstructions," by Sharon Hansen et al., panel discussion: American Choral Directors Association, Eastern Division Conference, February 2012, Providence, RI.
5. This the first of numerous notes citing not a publication but a technique observed in a rehearsal. The DaVinci *Vitruvian Man* exercise comes from Randy Wagner, currently professor of voice at Eastern Washington University, at a workshop given at Towson University in Maryland in the mid-1990s. The name for the exercise is my own.
6. Ware, p. 48.
7. Miller, Joe, professor of conducting and director of choral activities, Westminster College of Rider University, in rehearsal.
8. From *Vocal technique: A guide for conductors, teachers, and singers*, by J. Davids & S. LaTour, S. 2012, p. 81. Long Grove, IL: Waveland.
9. Blackstone, Jerry, director of choirs and chair of the conducting department, University of Michigan, in rehearsal.
10. Eichenberger, Rodney, professor of choral music, Florida State University, in rehearsal.
11. From *Daily Workout for a Beautiful Voice*, by Charlotte Adams, DVD. Santa Barbara, CA: Santa Barbara Music Publishing, 1998.
12. Ware and Davids both offer numerous exercises for achieving a lifted soft palate.
13. Nicosia, Judith, associate professor at Rutgers University, in workshop.
14. Case, George, director of choral activities, Boston University, in conversation.
15. Turk, James, formerly director of the Women's Glee Club at the US Naval Academy, in workshop.
16. Bass, Christine, director of Women's Chorus at Temple University, in workshop.
17. A detailed discussion of the acoustic energy of singing—formants, overtones, registers—occurs in Davids, pp. 67–72.
18. Ware, p. 9.
19. Blackstone, in workshop.
20. Blackstone, in rehearsal.

21. Blackstone, in rehearsal. Dr. Blackstone says to his singers "When you shift gears, don't let me hear you."
22. From *The Robert Shaw Reader*, by Dan Blocker (Ed.), (2004). New Haven: Yale University Press.

REFERENCES

Adams, C. (Producer-performer) (1998). *Daily workout for a beautiful voice.* [DVD]. Santa Barbara, CA: Santa Barbara Music Publishing.

Blocker, R. (Ed.) (2004). *The Robert Shaw Reader.* New Haven: Yale University Press.

Carter, B. (2014). Intersectionalities: Exploring qualitative research, music education, and diversity. In C. Conway (Ed.), *The Oxford Handbook of Qualitative Research in American Music Education* (pp. 538–553). Oxford: Oxford University Press.

Davids, J., & LaTour, S. (2012). *Vocal technique: A guide for conductors, teachers, and singers.* Long Grove, IL: Waveland.

Hansen, S., et. al. (2012, February) [Slide share] *Choral directors are from Mars and voice teachers are from Venus: Sing from the diaphragm and other vocal misstructions.* Panel discussion conducted at the Eastern Division Conference of the American Choral Directors Association, Providence, RI. Retrieved from http://www.slideshare.net/OfficialNATS/vocal-mistructions-presented-by-nats-at-acda-handout.

Jordan, J. (2011). *The musician's breath: The role of breathing in human expression.* Chicago: GIA.

Ware, C. (1998). *Adventures in singing* (2nd ed.). Boston: McGraw-Hill.

PART VI

CHORAL PEDAGOGY
AND THE VOICE

CHAPTER 27

VOCAL PEDAGOGY IN THE CHORAL REHEARSAL

DUANE COTTRELL

A choral director plays a significant role in the vocal development of singers under his or her direction, often being the only vocal instructor with whom a singer has contact. Using fundamentally sound vocal pedagogy is an absolute necessity for all choral directors in order to ensure the success, health, and enjoyment of the voice for all singers.

There are a great number of voice training methods and techniques among teachers of singing, but because there is little agreement over a standard practice, it becomes difficult to know which methods and techniques are helpful, which are harmful, and which are of no use. This chapter relies significantly on well-documented historical treatises when possible, particularly those from notable teachers whose methods were used successfully for generations. By examining a breadth of historical sources, it is possible to recognize agreement in multiple sources as a sign of validity of a particular method. These historical sources reveal what has worked in the past, helping to determine what will continue to work in the present day.

Modern science also gives us a lens through which to view voice training. Recent discoveries regarding the anatomy, physiology, and acoustics of the vocal mechanism have confirmed some time-tested pedagogical methods, and have disproved some techniques from the past that were incorrect. This chapter relies on scientific understanding not because it has given us new vocal training methods, but because it has given us the means to evaluate the effectiveness of the methods we already use.

Ultimately, this chapter is based on the idea that the fundamental concepts of a well-produced tone have remained largely unchanged through time, and these fundamental concepts can be taught within the context of a choral rehearsal. The ideas presented in this chapter will be focused on achieving an ideal tone quality which throughout the historical literature has been called *chiaroscuro*, or *voce chiusa*. *Chiaroscuro* is a balance between darkness and brightness, and has warmth and roundness along with the brilliance and ring associated with classical singing. This beautiful tone quality can be achieved by most singers in any choral setting, and if achieved, will contribute to an overall choral sound that is robust, well balanced, and unified.

PRINCIPLES OF PHONATION

Using vocal pedagogy in choral rehearsal requires a basic familiarity with the anatomy and physiology of the vocal mechanism, as well as a rudimentary understanding of acoustics. In this chapter, fundamental concepts will be reviewed in the context of discussing practical application of pedagogical principles. To begin with, basic functionality of the vocal mechanism will be reviewed within the context of a presentation of several exercises that can be used in choral rehearsals to promote healthy phonation. Sustained tones, portamento exercises, onset exercises, and occlusion exercises all contribute to the ideal vocal sound and can be used for developing voices in a choral setting.

Sustained tones

Sustained tone exercises can be found in singing treatises from the 18th century to the present day, and were often prescribed as the first step of vocal training. By using sustained tones in rehearsals, choral directors can build strength in the vocal mechanism itself (Austin, 2007b). Sustained tones are to singing what weight training is to fitness—they build muscle tone and develop strength in the core of the voice, most specifically, the thyroarytenoid (TA) muscles. Richard Miller states, "Where voice technique is founded on systematically acquired skills, sostenuto fills its role as a builder of the instrument. Sustaining power will increase vocal stamina and ensure vocal health" (Miller, 1986, p. 108). Further discussion of the benefits of sustained tones will be aided by a brief discussion of vocal fold physiology.

The vocal folds each have a body and a cover that are loosely coupled together (McCoy, 2004, p. 108). The body consists of the thyroarytenoid muscle at its core, and a multilayered area of soft tissue called the lamina propria. The cover is a thin layer of skin cells called the epithelium, or mucosa (Figure 27.1).

During phonation in chest voice, the thyroarytenoid muscles are engaged, the vocal folds are brought together, and air that is forced out between the vocal folds causes the mucosa to open and close very rapidly in a wavelike manner (Vennard, 1967, pp. 64–65) (Figure 27.2).

While the vocal folds are oscillating, the thyroarytenoid muscle remains steadily engaged throughout phonation. The ability of the TA muscle to remain engaged throughout phonation is dependent on the strength and tone of the muscle itself, which can be improved by sustained tones. Over time, sustained tones in the low register can build greater strength in the TA muscle resulting in stronger tone quality, greater resonance, increased vocal stamina, and even expanded range.

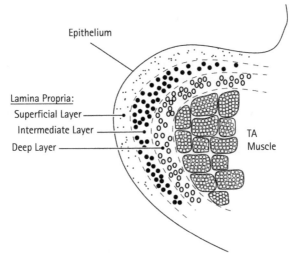

FIGURE 27.1. The structure of the vocal fold (Titze, 1991).

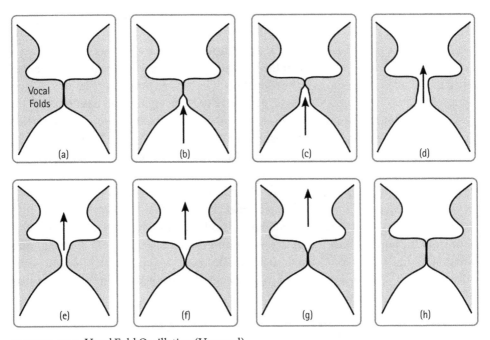

FIGURE 27.2 Vocal Fold Oscillation (Vennard).

The historical literature contains numerous examples of sustained tone pedagogy, from Mancini in the 1770s to Cinti-Damoreau in the 1830s (Austin, 2007b). Sustained tones are used in clinical vocal rehabilitation such as Joseph Stemple's "vocal function exercises," which improve vocal function in patients exhibiting vocal dysfunction (Stemple, Lee, D'Amico, & Pickup, 1994). Others have prescribed his exercises for singers and achieved improvement in vocal quality and efficiency (Sabol, Lee, & Stemple, 1995). Sustained tones have also been utilized in choral settings to improve vocal resonance and glottal closure (Cottrell, 2009a). Choral directors can employ these simple exercises at the beginning of rehearsal during vocal warm-ups, either a cappella or with any type of piano accompaniment. Singing sustained tones on each scale degree for a full octave, both ascending and descending, is a surprisingly demanding task but will yield significant results over the long-term if practiced on a regular basis. Historical, clinical, and scientific data suggest that beginning rehearsal with the sustained tone is a very effective way to improve vocal function and quality in singers.

Portamento

While sustained tones increase the strength of the thyroarytenoid (TA) muscles, using portamento exercises will develop the cricothyroid (CT) muscles. The action of the CT and TA muscles together lengthen and shorten the vocal folds, affecting both the pitch and timbre of the voice (Hirano, Vennard, & Ohala, 1970).

Portamento is the act of singing from one pitch to another, "with a continuity of tone that changes pitch in a way that is evenly distributed from the first to the second note" (Austin, 2007a, p. 59). If done properly, this will gently stretch and relax the CT muscles and promote coordination between the CT and TA muscles. Historical treatises advocated the use of portamento as an introduction to legato and other articulations (Austin 2004). Mancini considered it necessary in every type of singing, and defined it as "the passing and blending of the voice from one tone to another, with perfect proportion and union, in ascending as well as descending" (Mancini, 1923, p. 111). Manuel Garcia's *The Complete Treatise on the Art of Singing* also included portamento exercises (Garcia, 1984, p. 63). Using portamento exercises of this type develops true *legato* singing, which requires register equalization, carefully controlled subglottal breath pressure, stability of vertical laryngeal position, and other beneficial vocal qualities (Stark, 1999, p. 165). Looking again to clinical practice, Stemple's vocal function exercises use a long vocal slide from the bottom of the range to the top, and vice-versa (Stemple et al., 1994). This works in a similar way to portamento singing in that it requires stretching and relaxation of the CT and TA muscles, and trains a smooth coordination throughout a range of pitches, all with a sustained breath.

Using portamento exercises in choral voice building trains singers to utilize a constant and well-supported breath flow. Because the CT and TA muscles are working together, singing with portamento over a moderately wide interval while concentrating on a unified tone quality helps coordinate the action of these two muscle pairs. The portamento was also utilized throughout historical practice for register unification. In the low register, portamento gestures can bring the rich robust quality of the chest voice into the middle voice, along with clarity and breath efficiency. Portamento also allows singers to bring the lighter qualities of the upper register into the middle voice to balance the weight of the lower voice. This allows the singer to develop a fuller, robust middle voice, combating the breathiness so often experienced by singers in this part of their range.

To introduce portamento exercises in a choral rehearsal, have singers start on a moderately low pitch and ascend to a perfect fifth above, without any break in tone, and then back down to the original pitch. The director should be able to hear a "slide" from one note to the next without any hint of distinct scale degrees in between. Move to the next note in the scale and repeat the slide up and down. The simplicity of this exercise allows the singer to focus on maintaining the same tone quality and vowel for both notes. Once singers are comfortable with a fifth, the interval may be decreased or increased as the technique is developed. This has been a well-documented approach to voice training through the historical literature, and continues to be used with great success today.

Onset

There are three types of vocal onset commonly recognized today: the aspirate onset, the plosive onset, and the balanced onset (Miller, 1986, p. 1). In the aspirate onset the vocal folds are abducted when the airflow begins, and phonation occurs when the vocal folds are brought together resulting in an audible [h], incomplete adduction of the vocal folds, and a breathy sound. In the plosive onset the vocal folds are completely adducted just prior to phonation, there is a buildup of subglottal pressure below the larynx, and the vocal folds burst apart initiating phonation with a hard, glottal sound. The problem with the plosive onset is multifaceted: excessive muscular tension in the larynx can contribute to vocal disorders; the plosive sound is rarely attractive or artistic; and even though the vocal folds are completely adducted prior to phonation, loose glottal closure may result when the vocal folds are forcefully blown apart. The third, and most preferred type of onset recognized today is the balanced or coordinated onset. In this type of onset the vocal folds are abducted prior to phonation but at the precise moment the airflow begins, the vocal folds are brought into oscillation. The difficulty with the coordinated onset is the difficulty of adducting the phonatory muscles at the exact moment the airflow begins. Perhaps the most important reason the coordinated onset is incomplete is that is does not specify the type of glottal closure during phonation, and could allow for either firm or loose phonation (Stark, 1999, pp. 20–22).

In order to achieve the ideal firm phonation it is helpful to use a firmly adducted glottal setting before phonation begins (Stark, 1999, p. 31). Manuel Garcia discovered this over one hundred years ago and used it to train some of the best singers of the 19th century, as did many of his protégés. Unfortunately, many have completely overlooked his simple and effective technique for developing beautiful tone in young singers (Cottrell, 2009b, p. 40). Manuel Garcia's *coup de la glotte* is a type of firm onset, not an abrasive glottal plosive, and could be argued to be a separate type of onset altogether, clearly distinguished from the three types of onsets mentioned above. He describes the *coup de la glotte* as "similar to the action of the lips in pronouncing the consonant [p]" (Garcia, 1984, pp. 41–42). Although this seems similar to a hard or plosive onset, Garcia's *coup de la glotte* is entirely different in character. Garcia himself expressed this difference when he said "One must guard against confusing the stroke of the glottis with a stroke of the chest." The point of Garcia's *coup de la glotte* was firm adduction of the vocal folds leading to firm glottal closure during phonation.

Firm glottal closure leads to a tone that has brilliance and ring, while loose glottal closure produces a tone that is breathy, weak, and veiled. Loose glottal closure is a result of a lack of tension in both sets of muscles that control the movement of the arytenoid cartilages—the interarytenoids (IA) and the lateral crico-arytenoids (LCA) (McCoy, 2004, p. 115). Both are attached to, and define the movement of, the arytenoids—the pyramid-shaped cartilages, which are the posterior point of attachment for the vocal folds, and are crucial to the closure of the larynx (Figure 27.3). To initiate vocal phonation, the LCA muscles contract, rotating the arytenoids and bringing the vocal folds together. However, this medial compression only partially closes the glottis (Figure 27.4).

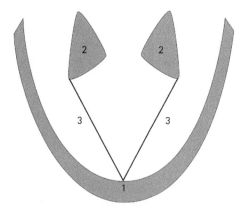

FIGURE 27.3 Breathing. Within the thyroid cartilage (1), the arytenoids (2) are apart and the vocal folds (3) are completely abducted for normal breathing.

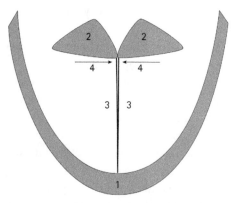

FIGURE 27.4 Medial Compression (Glottal "Chink"). Within the thyroid cartilage (1), the arytenoids (2) draw the vocal folds (3) together by the action of the lateral crico-arytenoids (4), leaving a triangular-shaped opening, or glottal "chink."

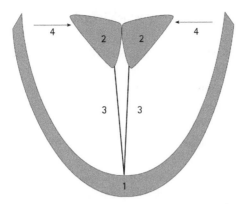

FIGURE 27.5 Loose Glottal Closure. Within the thyroid cartilage (1), the arytenoids (2) draw the vocal folds (3) together by the action of the interarytenoids (4), resulting in a loose glottal closure.

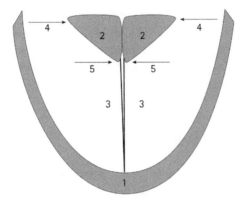

FIGURE 27.6 Firm Glottal Closure. Within the thyroid cartilage (1), the arytenoids (2) draw the vocal folds (3) together by the action of both the LCA (4) and the IA (5).

In order to completely adduct the vocal folds and eliminate the triangular shaped glottal "chink," the IA muscles must bring the arytenoids together (Figure 27.5); but without the medial compression provided by the LCA, there is only loose glottal closure. Firm glottal closure requires both the action of the IA plus the medial compression of the LCA (Figure 27.6).

Contracting the IA without the LCA results in a loose glottal closure (Figure 27.5), in which the vocal processes of the arytenoid cartilages participate in the vocal fold oscillation. This loose glottal closure is quite common in, and natural to, the speaking voice. By contracting the IA and the LCA together, the arytenoids are firmly adducted and do not participate in the oscillation. James Stark (1999) calls this the "three-fifths glottis," since only the anterior three-fifths of the glottis are participating in the oscillation when in this configuration. When this happens, "the resulting voice quality at the sound source is rich in high frequency components," which is to say the tone is resonant (Stark, 1999, p. 31).

The relationship of onset to phonation is vitally important. If the vocal folds are set loosely during phonatory onset they will retain that loose posture throughout phonation until the entire mechanism is reset with a new onset. The *coup de la glotte* is significant because it describes a type of onset that can not only eliminate breathiness, but also promote complete glottal closure and firm phonation. By firmly adducting the arytenoids prior to phonation, singers will be setting the vocal mechanism to produce a firm, brilliant, and efficient tone.

Incorporating the *coup de la glotte*, or glottal onset, into choral rehearsal is not difficult and, if done correctly, poses no risk to vocal health. Even Richard Miller (1986, p. 8), a strong advocate of the coordinated onset, suggests that a slight glottal onset would be wise and appropriate if the singer demonstrates a tendency toward breathiness. In order to teach choral singers the sensation of firm closure, have them sing the American English phrase, "uh-oh." While this light glottal onset is beneficial during voice building, it may be undesirable in performance since it can be hard to coordinate among many singers, and at higher pitch levels can create unnecessary tension in the vocal mechanism. But utilizing a light glottal onset during voice-building allows singers to learn the sensation of firm glottal closure, which is likely to translate into firmer, clearer tone quality in performance.

Semi-occluded vocal tract exercises

Exercises that utilize semi-occluded vocal tract postures have been widely used in speech and voice training because of numerous benefits to healthy vocal production. Exercises that partially occlude the vocal opening include humming, lip and tongue trills, voiced labiodental or bilabial fricatives ([v] and [ß]), and singing through a straw. These exercises can be used in choral settings to promote efficient vocal production among a number of other benefits (Titze, 2006, p. 457).

The acoustic benefits of a semi-occluded vocal tract are numerous: singers can achieve more acoustic output with less vocal effort; less pressure is required to initiate and sustain phonation; the vocal tract becomes highly "tuned," allowing greater opportunity to find the singer's formant; and there is a higher ratio of TA muscle activation to CT muscle activation (Nix & Simpson, 2008). There are also many practical benefits of semi-occluded postures: improved breath management due to greater resistance to the flow of breath; a high degree of sympathetic vibration, which mimics the sensation of resonant voice; habitual tensions in the tongue, lips, and jaw can be released; singers must let go of inhibitions and be more extraverted; and for all but the nasal consonants, the soft palate must be raised.

Incorporating humming, lip trills, and tongue trills into vocalizes is an easy way for choral directors to utilize semi-occluded postures. It may be helpful for singers to experience the immediate difference between the semi-occluded posture and a vowel, which can be accomplished by singing an entire vocalize or phrase of repertoire using a semi-occluded posture, immediately repeating it with a vowel. Beginning a warm up exercise or a musical phrase with a semi-occluded posture allows the singer to experience the sensation of moving from a semi-occluded posture into a vowel. Choral directors may be able to create a wide variety of beneficial scenarios utilizing semi-occluded vocal tract postures. These exercises greatly enhance the tone production and vocal health of singers and should be used liberally throughout rehearsals.

BREATH SUPPORT

Breath support is widely considered by choral conductors to be the foundation of good vocal tone (Darrow, 1975, p. 49). However, the current pedagogy of breathing for choral singing differs from prominent historical methods in that most early teachers of singing minimized the importance of breath "support" in favor of emphasizing glottal resistance (Austin, 2005b. p. 85). In addition, modern technology enables us to observe and measure vocal processes that were a mystery even a decade ago. Both modern scientific studies and historical literature reconfirm three useful principles that will help refine our pedagogy: first, that the use of both the chest and abdomen is necessary for breathing; second, that opposing muscular forces must be balanced during controlled expiration; and third, that breath support is dependent upon firm glottal closure (Emmons, 2006, p. 19).

The science of breathing

Breath support is best defined as control of subglottal pressure, so understanding breath support requires understanding the concepts of both airflow and subglottal pressure (Vennard, 1967). By way of example, turning a hose on at the spigot increases the *flow* of water. Partially obstructing the opening with your thumb increases the *pressure* just behind the opening, but also decreases the *flow*. Both concepts work together to yield greater velocity in the water coming out of the hose. With regard to singing, *airflow* is the measure of air flowing from the vocal opening, as managed by the musculature of the rib cage and abdomen. *Subglottal pressure* is the measure of air pressure just below the vocal mechanism, which is managed by the laryngeal structures. Airflow is related to subglottal pressure, just as with the garden hose, and good vocal tone is largely a result of the right balance of subglottal pressure and airflow (McCoy, 2004, p. 97). Increasing the airflow yields little result if there is insufficient resistance to increase the subglottal pressure. In order to manage subglottal pressure and airflow, singers must learn to manipulate both expiratory force and glottal resistance (Sonninen, Laukkanen, Karma, & Hurme, 2005, p. 236).

Expiratory force

The muscular processes that expel air from the lungs past the vocal folds are called *expiratory force*. Teaching singers to utilize abdominal muscles to support their tone has been a staple of choral pedagogy for much of the past century (Darrow, 1975, p. 54). This abdominal approach to breath support has often focused attention on the diaphragm, which is a component of the inspiratory process. The diaphragm—an inverted bowl-shaped muscle that forms the floor of the thorax and the roof of the abdominal cavity—contracts to draw air into the lungs, and relaxes during expiration (McCoy, 2004, p. 87). While abdominal breathing is necessary and valuable, ignoring the contribution made by the chest can rob singers of a significant amount of lung capacity and breathing power.

The intercostal muscles of the chest have received significantly less attention than the abdomen in the pedagogical literature of choral singing (Darrow, 1975, p. 56). These muscles expand and collapse the ribcage and play a vital role in breath support (Thomasson & Sundberg, 1999, p. 540). The external intercostals lift and expand the ribcage, drawing air into the lungs. During expiration, the internal intercostals contract the ribcage, decreasing its volume and forcing air out of the lungs. Because the surface area of the lungs attached to the ribcage greatly exceeds that attached to the diaphragm, utilizing the ribcage allows a greater volume of air to be processed. It should be noted that this kind of thoracic breathing—using the chest—is quite different from clavicular breathing, and the two should not be confused (Miller, 1986, pp. 28–29). Thoracic breathing expands the chest wall outward to increase the circumference of the chest and the volume of the lungs, and does not involve the shoulders and clavicles. Choral singers should be taught to utilize the chest without adding unnecessary tension by raising the shoulders.

Studies have indicated a complex interaction between the thoracic and abdominal muscle groups during singing (Sonninen et al., 2005; Watson & Hixson, 1985). Inspiration begins with contraction of the diaphragm and relaxation of the abdominals, which is followed by an expansion of the chest cavity by the action of the external intercostals. This combination of abdominal and thoracic expansion is the most significant way to increase the volume of the lungs (Thomasson & Sundberg, 2001). As the singer begins to sing, the balance of power shifts to the muscles of expiration. The diaphragm relaxes slightly, and the abdominals and internal intercostals contract, putting pressure on the lungs and expelling air. During expiration, the external intercostals and diaphragm remain slightly contracted in order to provide resistance to the internal intercostals and abdominals. This resistance keeps the expiratory muscles from contracting too quickly and air from being forced out too rapidly. When supporting a tone using this method, the abdominal muscles exert pressure on the lower portion of the lungs while the intercostals exert pressure on the upper portion of the lungs, resulting in maximum expiratory force (Watson, Hoit, Lansing, & Hixon, 1989). Many choral conductors commonly employ the abdominal breathing technique, but the balanced breathing approach described here provides the singer with more direct control over airflow and subglottal pressure, and is the best method for consistent breath support (Sonninen et al., 2005). Singers should be trained to control and balance all these muscular forces in order to maintain the correct level of airflow and subglottal pressure.

Glottal resistance

Expiratory force must be accompanied by glottal resistance if there is to be any improvement in tone quality or maximum phonation time. Glottal configuration has a significant impact on subglottal pressure, but has been conspicuously absent from the literature of choral pedagogy (Darrow, 1975, p. 50). Without a correct vocal fold configuration the tone will sound breathy and weak regardless of expiratory force (Austin, 2007b). Recall that firm glottal closure is the result of the contraction of two sets of laryngeal muscles—the interarytenoids and the lateral cricoarytenoids (Cottrell, 2009a, p. 38). Contracting both sets of muscles brings the arytenoid cartilages together while the remaining three-fifths of the vocal folds oscillate (Stark, 1999, p. 11). Engaging only one of these sets of muscles results in either a loose glottal configuration or a posterior glottal "chink," both of which cause breathiness and weak tone quality, which is common among many young singers. A study from 2000 revealed that 76% of female subjects showed an incomplete glottal closure during soft phonation, both speaking and singing (Schneider & Bigenzahn, 2004). Additional studies indicate that a well-supported tone is the result of firm glottal closure in addition to a raised rib cage, active ribs, and a reduced airflow (Thorpe, Cala, Chapman, & Davis, 2001). Developing complete glottal closure and firm phonation should be part of the breath-support training process.

Historical approaches

Pedagogy of the 18th and 19th centuries provides valuable insights and techniques that were not carried forward in the tradition of choral singing. In his *Complete Treatise on the Art of Singing*, Manuel Garcia devoted very little time to breathing (only about one-half of a page) and a great deal more to the production of tone (Stark, 1999, p. 47). In spite of this absence of breathing instruction in his treatise, Garcia suggested that singers should take a quiet breath with a raised chest and lowered diaphragm. He continued "to advise the abdominal breathing exclusively would reduce by one half the element of strength most indispensable to the singer, the breath" (Garcia, 1984, p. 33). Garcia understood that breathing power was related to glottal resistance. He advocated firm glottal closure and the use of the *coup de la glotte* or glottal onset in training glottal closure (Cottrell, 2009a). Following Garcia, the physician Louis Mandl (1812–1881) taught the *lutte vocale*, or "vocal struggle," which was a balance between inspiratory and expiratory muscular forces (Austin, 2007b, p. 87). Francisco Lamperti (1813–1892) advocated abdominal (belly-out) breathing only. He taught reduced airflow by placing a lit candle in front of the lips of a singer to reveal whether the singer was expelling too much air.

Lamperti also popularized the term *appoggio*, which means, "to lean," and is still used today to describe a balanced approach to respiration with a high level of muscular control. His son Giovanni Lamperti (1839–1910) departed slightly from his ideas by teaching singers to use the top and bottom of the lungs. The younger Lamperti stated that the voice controls the breath, not the other way around, which is an early way of describing the role of glottal resistance in breath support. He went on to state that the breath is held back by glottal resistance and muscular tension, foreshadowing the scientific concept of airflow. Lamperti taught that insufficient pressure makes the tone unsteady. In his teaching, nearly 150 years old and well before modern science defined them, the principles of glottal resistance, airflow, and subglottal pressure were clearly present. Finally, singing teacher William Shakespeare (1849–1931) taught a breathing method that combined ribcage breathing with diaphragmatic breathing (Stark, 1999, pp. 102–105). He also advocated the same balance of inspiratory and expiratory forces described in the *lutte vocale* and *appoggio* techniques. As Garcia before him, Shakespeare rejected the use of loose glottal closure in all singing.

Pedagogical literature from the *bel canto* period illustrates that the concepts of expiratory force and glottal resistance have been taught throughout the past few centuries. A return to a balanced focus on glottal resistance and expiratory force would be a best practice for teaching breath support in choral singing.

In rehearsal

Focusing instruction on muscular action and expiratory force will not yield a desirable tone quality unless there is firm glottal closure (Lundy et al., 2000, p. 183). In addition to teaching the mechanics of abdominal and thoracic breathing, as well as the balance between the two that is the result of *appoggio*, we must introduce singers to the sensation of firm glottal closure. Exercises that facilitate this type of glottal configuration will also develop breath support. Light glottal onsets, staccato exercises, or the imagery of Lamperti's candle can all work toward eliminating loose glottal closure or posterior glottal chink in singing.

Exercises that partially occlude the vocal opening provide an effective means of fostering efficient vocal production. These exercises include, in order of effectiveness, nasal consonants such as [m], [n], and [ŋ]; lip or tongue trills; bilabial [ß] or labiodental [v] voiced fricatives; and singing through a straw. The partial occlusion at the opening alters the pressure within the vocal tract, which encourages firm phonation and greater vocal efficiency (Titze, 2006). Singing teachers and voice therapy professionals use these exercises for their effectiveness in training and rehabilitation of the voice.

Firm glottal closure must be coupled with expiratory force, and there is no shortage of literature on training choral singers to support the airflow with muscular control. However, some singers may constrict their chests in a raised or expanded position in order to use only the abdomen for breathing. The chest should be allowed to expand and collapse freely while singing, without any raising of the shoulders or clavicles, which increases breath capacity. Breathing exercises should be focused on the muscular sensation of a full breath and strong expiratory force. (One simple way to achieve this is to have singers pant, which is rapid inhalation and exhalation that draws attention to the muscle areas involved in the breathing process.) This sensation should quickly be transferred to singing, so the connection is readily apparent. Exercises with sustained hissing or other unvoiced fricatives help only insofar as the singer is able to generate a similar level of resistance with the vocal folds as with the teeth, lips, or tongue. A singer who is able to hiss for 30 seconds may only be able to sing a sustained note for 10. In any case, it is important to remember that breathing is one area of singing that can be improved by consistent and methodical training (Phillips & Aitchison, 1997, p. 195).

One final application of these concepts is the use of the sustained tone in voice building. Using arpeggiated or scalar "warm-up" patterns can make it difficult for a singer to coordinate proper management of breath with the production of good tone, due to rapid intervallic changes. Many historical methods such as those by Franz Abt (1893), Frederick Root (1873), or D. A. Clippinger (1932), reserve these exercises for more advanced training and begin instead with a long sustained tone on a vowel conducive to a low laryngeal posture. Beginning with a sustained tone allows a singer to concentrate on breath management and tone production, making corrections and adjustments as necessary. The benefit of such an approach is that a singer must continuously coordinate the breath with the resistance offered by the vocal folds (Austin, 2007b, p. 92). By using sustained tones to begin each rehearsal, choral conductors are standing on centuries of vocal pedagogy, and choral singers reap the benefits of increased glottal resistance and greater breath support, leading to a more beautiful tone and the ability to sustain a legato phrase.

The Low Larynx

Few things influence vocal tone quality more than laryngeal position. Because the larynx houses the vocal folds—the source of all vocal sounds—altering its position has a tremendous impact on the length of the vocal tract, which significantly alters the tone quality. In addition, a low larynx encourages relaxation in certain muscles of the neck and throat, and aids in the production of good vowel sounds.

Tone quality

Since at least the 18th century, teachers have used the Italian word *chiaroscuro* to describe the quality of an ideal tone. *Chiaroscuro* means "bright-dark," and refers to the balance between bright, resonant singing, and darker, warmer color (Stark, 1999, p. 33). Others have used the term *voce chiusa*, or "closed voice," and others talk about the "covered" sound of classical singing. Though described in many ways, the ideal sound contains the same elements—brightness, or ring, balanced with warmth. Regardless of slight preferences, when it comes to tone color and quality some balance of bright and dark is almost universally appropriate.

The relative brightness or darkness of tone quality is determined by the size and shape of the vocal tract. According to the source-filter theory of voice production, vibration of the vocal folds is the source of the sound and the vocal tract—which is the airspace between the vocal folds and the lips—modifies, or filters, that sound (McCoy, 2004, p. 38). Adjustments to the lips, tongue, soft palate, pharynx, and larynx alter the size and shape of the vocal tract, which modifies the sound originating from the vocal folds through free resonance. Free resonance occurs when a sound travels through an enclosed airspace with an open end, such as a tube. When the sound waves reach the end of the tube, some of the energy is reflected back into the tube in the opposite direction. When those waves meet the sound source at the precise moment a new compression wave is produced, the effect is an amplification of that particular wave. Because of this, the length of the tube makes a significant impact on which periodic waves (frequencies) are reinforced. A simple experiment with two tubes of different lengths will demonstrate that a sound introduced in the longer tube will resonate at a lower frequency than the same sound introduced into a shorter tube. This is analogous to the way a trombone works. By extending the slide and lengthening the tube, the trombone resonates a lower frequency.

Of all the modifications we can make to the vocal tract, the position of the larynx has the most significant impact on the tone quality. Because the larynx houses the vocal folds, which are the source of vocal sound, raising or lowering the larynx shortens or lengthens the vocal tract, which in turn alters the resonance frequencies. When the larynx is lowered and the vocal tract is elongated, lower frequencies will be reinforced. While not altering the perceived pitch, this will enhance the lower frequencies on the spectrum, a similar effect to turning up the lower bands of a graphic equalizer on a stereo system. The overall result is a tone quality that could be characterized as warm, rich, and dark. This is the starting point for an ideal tone quality in both solo and choral singing. A tone produced with a raised larynx can be bright, brassy, and have a "spread" sound. Conversely, a tone produced with a lowered larynx has acoustical properties better suited to the blend and balance required in a choral ensemble.

Relaxation

In addition to creating a desirable tone quality, a lowered larynx also encourages relaxation in the neck and jaw. The movement of the larynx is controlled by two muscle groups, the infrahyoids and the suprahyoids. The infrahyoid muscles connect the sternum to the larynx at the point of the hyoid bone, and lower the larynx (Figure 27.7). The suprahyoid muscles connect the hyoid bone to the mandible (jawbone) and the base of the skull behind the ears, and raise the larynx (Figure 27.8). When one of these sets of muscles is engaged, the other is relatively passive. When lowering the larynx by engaging the infrahyoid muscles, the result will be a relaxation of the suprahyoid muscles

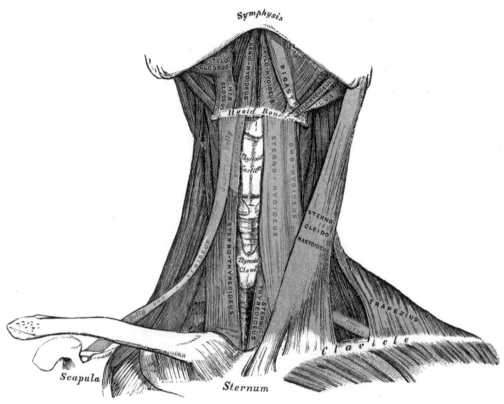

FIGURE 27.7 Infrahyoid Muscles (Gray). H. Gray (1918). *Anatomy of the Human Body* (20th ed.). Philadelphia: Lea & Febiger.

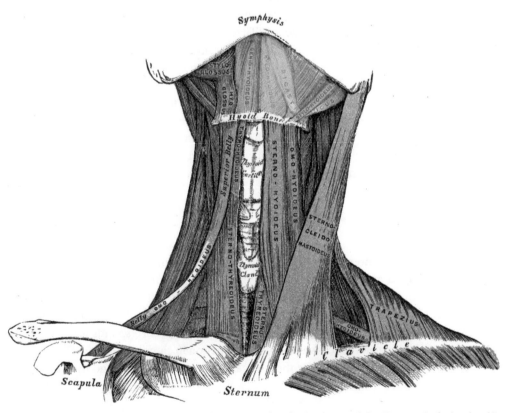

FIGURE 27.8 Suprahyoid Muscles (Gray). H. Gray (1918). *Anatomy of the Human Body* (20th ed.). Philadelphia: Lea & Febiger.

connected to the jawbone—one of the areas where singers often battle excess tension. By singing with a comfortably lowered larynx a singer may be able to alleviate some of the neck, jaw, and facial tension that is counterproductive in singing (Vennard, 1967).

Good vowels

Laryngeal position has a significant effect on the quality of vowels. According to the source-filter theory, vowels are created by specific resonances of the vocal tract called formants. When the vocal folds vibrate, they produce a complex tone at the source that includes a fundamental frequency (F0), as well as additional frequencies called overtones. As this complex tone is filtered through the vocal tract, certain overtone frequencies are selectively reinforced depending on the size and shape of the airspace as determined primarily by the position of the tongue (Figure 27.9).

The resulting output has distinct resonances called formants, and the frequency of the first two formants determines the perceived vowel. For example, when the first formant is near 800 Hz and the second formant is near 1100 Hz the perceived vowel is [a]. When the first formant is near 300 Hz and the second formant is near 2500 Hz the perceived vowel is [i] (Figure 27.10).

Lowering the larynx lengthens the vocal tract and will lower all formant frequencies so that vowel sounds becomes warmer and richer, what some refer to as "tall vowels." These "tall vowel" sounds are produced by a lowered larynx, extended lips, and a slightly closed mouth, not by dropping the jaw. A wide-open jaw actually brightens the sound by raising the first formant frequency (Titze & Worley, 2009). (The primary exception to this is for sopranos as they sing pitches at or above the top of the treble clef. Due to the acoustic nature of these higher notes in relation to vowel formants, it is helpful for sopranos to drop the jaw as they ascend to the uppermost part of their range. In some vowels, the first formant is quite low and it is possible for a soprano to be asked to sing a pitch that is higher than the required vowel formant. In these cases it is acoustically impossible for the soprano to produce the correct vowel without modification. The vowels [i] and [u] have especially low first formants, and sopranos would be better asked to modify to a vowel closer to [ʌ].)

In rehearsal

The comfortably lowered larynx has long been a significant part of vocal pedagogy, from Manuel Garcia and Julius Stockhausen in the 19th century to William Vennard and Richard Miller in the 20th. Some have called this a "yawn-sigh," or an "open throat," but the goal has always been a tone with warm, rich, and supple colors balanced with brilliance and ring. In choral singing, a lowered larynx often corresponds to the sensation of a raised soft palate, which is a common instruction in choral rehearsals (Darrow, 1975, p. 41). When instructed to raise the soft palate, singers often respond by lowering the

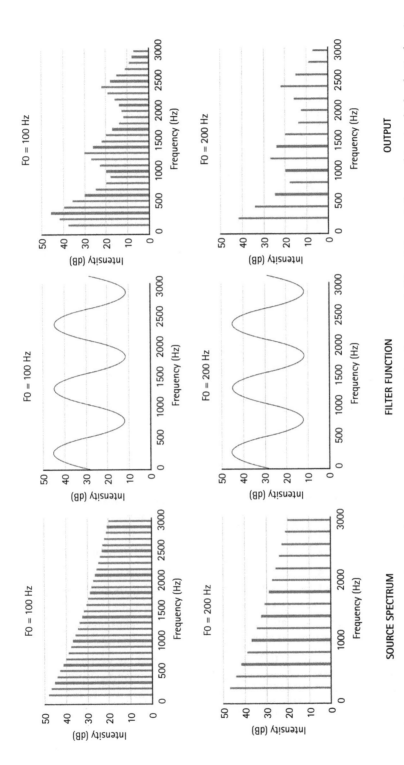

FIGURE 27.9 Source-Filter Theory of Voice: The acoustic spectrum generated at the source is filtered through the vocal tract, which selectively reinforces certain frequencies, resulting in an output with measurable resonances called "formants."

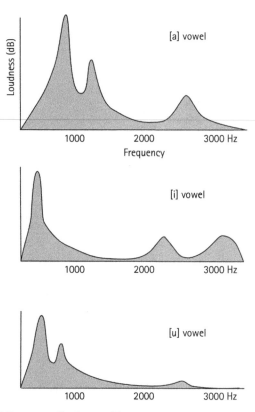

FIGURE 27.10 Vowel Formants. Each vowel has a unique acoustic signature measured by the frequency of the first two formants.

larynx, which produces the desired tone quality. The only function of the soft palate is to open or close the passage into the nasal cavity, which remains closed during most singing, and the "open throat" sensation and resultant tone quality is the result of a lowered larynx and elongated vocal tract, not a raised soft palate.

There are a variety of techniques to encourage a lowered larynx in choral rehearsals, but simply understanding the position and sensation of a lowered larynx is primary. As one of the few components of the singing mechanism we can see and touch, the thyroid cartilage is an important means of understanding this concept. Singers can lightly palpate (touch) their Adam's apple and feel it rise when they swallow and lower when they yawn. Teachers like Richard Miller advocate singing with a "yawn-sigh" sensation. In a choral rehearsal, singers can use this yawn-sigh as a stretching exercise, with a portamento or a glissando gesture. Alternatively, directors can encourage singers to sing any vocalize through the position of a beginning yawn. Another way to teach this sensation is to ask singers to close their lips, open their teeth, and inhale slowly and deeply through the nose. Most often, singers will instinctively lower the larynx to open the airway as wide as possible, and singers can return to this relaxing breath gesture throughout rehearsal as often as necessary to be reminded of the sensation of a lowered larynx.

Voice building exercises using [o] and [u] vowels can encourage a lowered laryngeal position, particularly in the mid to low range. Also, portamento gestures help singers keep the larynx low while ascending in pitch. Starting with a lowered larynx on an [o] vowel in the low voice, slide up a perfect fifth or even an octave. Once singers become aware of the natural tendency of the larynx to rise with pitch, they can work toward keeping the larynx comfortably low even when ascending.

Singers can also learn to hear the difference in tone quality produced by a low larynx. To illustrate this, ask a choir to sing as if they were significantly younger, and almost without exception singers will raise the larynx and sing with a shallow, bright tone quality. Once they have experienced that sound, ask them to sing as if they were significantly older, and most singers will likely exaggerate a depressed laryngeal position. By exploring those two extremes in a vocally healthy way, directors can guide singers to find the ideal balance between them.

It is most important for choral directors to learn to hear the difference between a low larynx and a raised larynx. Once the director can identify a raised larynx in singing, steps can be taken to encourage the ideal laryngeal posture through whatever means are most effective for the choir. It may be helpful to alter some terminology, since phrases like "tall vowels" and "drop your jaw" may produce a brighter sound than what is desired. Experiment with phrases like "open throat," "yawn-sigh," or "more space in the back." There is no exercise that is universally effective—directors should use what works best for their choir.

Resonance

Achieving *chiaroscuro* requires a balance of both dark and bright elements. A comfortably low larynx contributes to the darkness of tone due to the elongation of the vocal tract and the resulting effect on the acoustic spectrum. The brightness in tone quality, often referred to as "resonant tone," is produced by a specific configuration of the vocal tract that yields significant acoustic energy in the upper partials of the spectrum.

The human voice is amplified and enhanced by an acoustic process called free resonance (McCoy, 2004, pp. 27–28). When the vocal folds oscillate, they open and close rapidly which produces traveling waves of pressure. These pressure waves are reflected back and forth from the closed end of the airspace (at the vocal folds) to the open end of the airspace (at the mouth). Specific frequencies are reinforced, or resonated, depending on the size and shape of the airspace as determined by the configuration of the vocal tract. Tone quality is identified as "resonant," or "brilliant," when frequencies in the range of 2500–3500 Hz are reinforced. In order for this type of brilliant tone to occur, singers must make adjustments to the vocal tract that include lowering the larynx, narrowing the epilarynx tube, widening the pharynx, slightly closing the mouth, keeping the soft palate raised, and perhaps most significantly, singing with firm glottal closure.

Vocal tract configuration

A lowered larynx contributes darkness and warmth to vocal tone, but also helps foster resonance in the voice. A low larynx has a narrowing effect on the epilarynx tube, a small vestibule located above the larynx and below the epiglottis. Along with a low larynx, a narrow epilarynx tube and a widened pharynx create the necessary conditions for vocal resonance to occur (Titze & Story, 1997). This narrowing of the epilarynx tube functions much like the mouthpiece of a brass instrument. When the pharynx is wider than the epilarynx tube by a 6-to-1 ratio or greater, the resulting vocal quality is resonant (Sundberg, 1974). One further modification to the vocal tract that is helpful to achieving maximum resonance is a slightly closed mouth. Together with a low larynx and wide pharynx, this configuration is what Ingo Titze refers to as the "inverted megaphone shape" (Titze, 2009, p. 1530). The "inverted megaphone" (Figure 27.11) is a vocal tract configuration that includes a low larynx, narrow epilarynx tube, wide pharynx, and partially closed mouth, and yields acoustic properties ideal for classical and choral singing. The "megaphone shape" (Figure 27.12) is a vocal tract configuration that includes a raised larynx, a speech-like pharynx and epilarynx tube, and a wide-open mouth, and yields acoustic properties ideal for belting and other styles of singing.

Soft palate

The opening between the oral cavity and the nasal cavity, called the velopharyngeal port, is regulated by the position of the soft palate, which should be raised during singing. The soft palate is the posterior area of the roof of the mouth just behind the hard palate and acts as a valve that, when raised, closes off the nasal cavity from the oral cavity, pharynx,

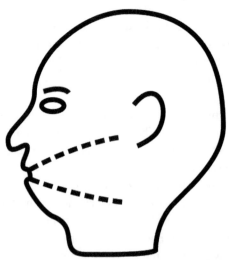

FIGURE 27.11 Inverted Megaphone Shape (Titze 1997). In the inverted megaphone shaped vocal tract, the larynx is low and the jaw is slightly closed, creating a classical tone quality.

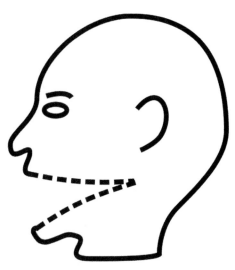

FIGURE 27.12 Megaphone Shape (Titze 1997). In the megaphone shaped vocal tract, the larynx is high and the jaw is opened wide, brightening the tone and creating a belt quality.

and larynx (Austin, 2000, p. 34). Singing with a lowered soft palate allows air to pass freely through the nasal cavity, resulting in a nasalized tone, while a raised soft palate seals off the nasal cavity from the airflow eliminating nasality.

Studies have indicated that resonance does not occur in the nasal cavity. Wooldridge (1956) occluded singers' nasal cavity with damp cotton to show that "neither the nasal cavities nor the sinuses furnish any part of the vocal tone," and that all vocal resonance is produced in the oropharynx and the oral cavity. G.O. Russell used x-rays to study the soft palate of singers, revealing that the great tenor Caruso was singing with a raised soft palate and a completely closed velopharyngeal port (Austin, 1997). Austin (1997) discovered that singers raised the soft palate when singing, and that "Singers learn that the quality of sound that is most appreciated and desirable is produced with the soft palate high, eliminating any resonance in the nasal passages." Even Vennard prefers the use of the nasal cavity be eliminated entirely (Vennard, 1967, p. 228).

There are also significant negative acoustic effects of singing with a lowered soft palate. When the nasal cavity is coupled to the vocal tract, it acts as a "side-branch resonator," much like the muffler on a car (Austin, 2000). This dampening effect occurs because the nasal cavity introduces a series of antiresonances, or zeroes, into the acoustic spectrum (Figure 27.13), causing a loss of intensity at or near the frequency of these antiresonances, resulting in vowel distortion, a loss of carrying power in the voice, and a significant loss of intensity in the singer's formant, the source of the "ring" in the classical voice. Even if the singer's formant is less prominent in choral singing, as Rossing, Sundberg, & Ternström (1986) suggest, evidence presented by Ternström and Sundberg (1989) indicates that choral singers match formant frequencies when tuning and blending in the ensemble, so the acoustical zeros introduced by a low soft palate could hinder the overall blending of the ensemble, particularly when it comes to vowel intelligibility.

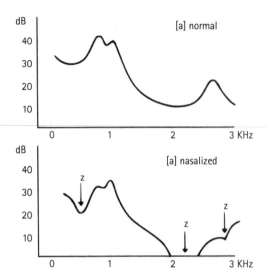

FIGURE 27.13 The acoustic effect of a lowered soft palate (Austin, 1997). The top graph is the formant envelope of the [a] vowel with the nasal port closed. The bottom graph shows the effect of opening the nasal port. Note the areas of antiresonance, marked with the letter *z*.

In order for singers to achieve the maximum potential resonance of the voice, the soft palate should be raised and the velopharyngeal port closed.

Firm glottal closure

The configuration of the vocal folds during vibration is a significant contributor to resonant tone. Manuel Garcia believed brilliance in vocal tone was a direct result of firm glottal closure. You will recall that firm glottal closure requires the arytenoid cartilages be firmly adducted during phonation, resulting in a three-fifths glottis. Acoustically speaking, firm glottal closure yields increased energy in the higher overtone frequencies, while loose closure results in fewer and weaker overtones. Austin comments "it is common knowledge that when the vocal folds close firmly and are completely adducted during each glottal cycle the air flow cuts off suddenly and the energy in the source spectrum is much higher than when a 'loose glottis' is allowed" (Austin, 2005a).

In rehearsal

Teaching an ideal vocal tract configuration is challenging since there is no conscious control over many of the adjustments that must be made. The larynx and the mouth are the only adjustments that can be consciously controlled by the singer and viewed by an outside observer. Adjustments to the pharynx and the epilarynx tube, while highly influential on the tone quality produced, are not easily made by singers and are not observable by the teacher. For this reason, many choral directors have used creative imagery to foster correct vocal tract configuration and tone quality (Phillips, 2004, p. 243–244). Instructing singers to place the tone "in the mask," "in the front of the face," or "in the forehead" can be helpful, but only insofar as it indirectly causes singers to alter the resonating airspace in such a way as to achieve the vocal tone choral directors are seeking.

The inherent danger in using imagery is that a singer's perception may not match the reality of the vocal tract configuration or acoustic properties of the tone produced. Often nasality can mimic the sensation of resonant tone (Titze, 1991, p. 244). Even though a well-produced tone with brilliance and ring may cause a buzzing phenomenon in the nose and face, this is a result of sympathetic vibration of the bony and soft tissue surrounding the nasal cavity, not the source of the resonant quality (Sundberg, 1987). As Richard Miller observes, "a major source of misunderstanding with regard to 'resonance' in singing stems from confusing the source of the sound with the sensation of sound" (Miller, 1986, p. 56). Studies have also shown that in areas of the vocal tract where acoustical pressure is greatest it is possible to feel a distinct sensation of that pressure, contributing to the notion that the tone is being placed or directed in a specific area (Titze et al., 1991). In his text, Neuen describes a process of instructing singers to use creative imagination to place the tone in specific locations of the face (Neuen, 2002, p. 34). Although he makes it clear that this is merely helpful imagery, not physiologically correct vocal pedagogy, confusion arises when choral directors do not make this distinction and singers are left thinking that the brilliance of the tone actually comes from the vibrating parts of the face and skull. As Austin points out, "Suggesting to a student singer that when his or her voice is well produced he or she may feel resonance in the vicinity of the nasal passages is very different from telling him or her to actually let the sound go through the nose" (Austin, 1997, p. 220). Imagery in choral rehearsals is of vital importance to singers' tone production, and choral directors must be careful to choose imagery that will encourage a low larynx, a slightly closed mouth, and the right configuration of the pharynx and epilarynx tube, all of which is the true source of brilliance and ring in the tone.

Using [p] or [t] consonants encourages singers to keep the soft palate high and maximize resonant tone. Although nasal consonants such as [m] or [n] encourage efficient vocal fold vibration, they also dampen resonance (Titze, 2006). William Vennard (1967) taught his students to pinch their nose while singing in order to detect a nasalized tone. Have singers pinch their nose and say the word "running" to hear nasality. Then have singers pinch their nose and say the word "pit," which should have no nasality at all. For more advanced singers with an understanding of French diction, try alternating French nasal vowels with their non-nasal counterparts on a single sustained tone, for example [ã] and [a]. Teaching singers to feel a raised soft palate will help them to produce a tone that is more resonant in all their singing.

Encouraging firm glottal closure in rehearsal is possible, although great care must be taken not to induce vocal hyperfunction in singers. As previously discussed, Manuel Garcia (1984) used the *coup de la glotte*, which is not a hard plosive with excessive

FIGURE 27.14 Staccato 5-Note Chromatic Scale. This is an exercise that was advocated by Homer Henley to encourage firm glottal closure.

tension, but a soft glottal onset that is used hundreds of times daily in spoken English with no ill-effects on vocal health. Similar to a [p] made with the lips, the vocal folds are completely adducted, after which there is a slight buildup of subglottal pressure followed by a quick onset of sound, just like saying the phrase "uh-oh." Because this onset begins with the arytenoid cartilages completely adducted, it fosters firm glottal closure by its prephonatory setting (Stark, 1999, p. 22). Utilizing a light glottal onset during voice-building teaches the sensation of firm glottal closure, which is likely to translate into firmer, clearer tone quality (Cottrell, 2009a). Staccato gestures also help encourage firm glottal closure, as in a technique described by Homer Henley (1931). By singing groups of five semitones in sharply struck staccato on the vowel [o] or [i], the vocal folds are made to reengage with each note, rather than remain loosely adducted in a legato gesture. Again, a light glottal onset is the key, as using an aspirate 'h' will not yield the type of closure desired (Figure 27.14). Resonance in the singing voice can be taught in choral rehearsals simply with the right vocal exercises (Cottrell, 2009a). Choral directors can foster this kind of tone by choosing the right imagery and techniques and reinforcing the ideal sound in each rehearsal.

Summary

The use of vocal pedagogy in the choral rehearsal is no longer optional, nor is it a luxury. Every interaction with singers carries the potential to either build or harm the voice. A thorough understanding of the anatomy, physiology, and acoustics related to singing should be a prerequisite for every choral director, whether professional or amateur. Though it is difficult to present such a complex subject in a short space, this chapter has touched on enough historical and scientific material to provide a sufficient starting point for choral directors to gain a working knowledge of vocal pedagogy for their choral setting.

Building a healthy approach to phonation in a choral rehearsal begins with using sustained tones and portamento exercises, encouraging a firm onset, and regularly singing with a semi-occluded vocal tract. Breath support must involve both the abdomen and the rib cage, but the primary factor in a well-supported sound is the regulation of the breath by the glottis. Encouraging firm glottal closure is a key component of proper breath management. Keeping the larynx in a comfortably low position during choral singing will not only enhance the tone quality, it will also help relax the neck and throat and encourage proper vowel sounds. And to maximize resonance in the voice, choral directors must encourage the optimal vocal tract configuration, including a low larynx, firm glottal closure, raised soft palate, and slightly closed mouth.

These are lofty goals to add to the already monumental tasks that choral directors face: singing choral repertoire with accuracy of pitch and rhythm, beauty, engagement, and expressiveness. But the fact is that singers are already learning and practicing their vocal technique in choral rehearsals, whether the director is aware of it or not. Developing an understanding of basic vocal pedagogy will only help singers toward a vocal technique that is healthier and more beautiful, which ultimately will serve the goals of the choir, the director, and the music itself.

References

Abt, F. (1893). *Practical singing tutor: For all voices*. New York: Schirmer.

Austin, S. F. (1997). Movement of the velum during speech and singing in classically trained singers. *Journal of Voice, 11*, 212–221.

Austin, S. F. (2000). Nasal resonance—Fact or fiction? *Journal of Singing, 57*(2), 33–41.

Austin, S. F. (2004). Provenance. *Journal of Singing, 60*(3), 301.

Austin, S. F. (2005a). The attack on the *coup de la glotte. Journal of Singing, 61*(5), 526–528.

Austin, S. F. (2005b). Two-headed llamas and the *lutte vocale. Journal of Singing, 62*(1), 85–89.

Austin, S. F. (2007a). Building strong voices: Twelve different ways! *Choral Journal, 48*(8), 55–66.

Austin, S. F. (2007b). First things first. *Journal of Singing, 64*(1), 89–93.

Clippinger, D. A. (1932). *The Clippinger class method of voice production*. Philadelphia: Oliver Ditson.

Cottrell, D. C. (2009a). *Increasing glottal closure in an untrained male chorus by integrating historical, scientific, and clinical practice into choral voice building exercises*. D.M.A. University of North Texas. (Order No. 3385779). Available from ProQuest Dissertations & Theses A&I. (304963511). Retrieved from http://search.proquest.com/docview/304963511?accountid=10457

Cottrell, D. C. (2009b). Voice science in the choral rehearsal: Examining glottal onset. *The Choral Scholar, 1*(1), 31–40.

Darrow, G. F. (1975). *Four decades of choral training*. Metuchen, N.J.: The Scarecrow Press, Inc.

Emmons, S. (2006). *Prescriptions for choral excellence*. Oxford: Oxford University Press.

Garcia, M. (1984). *Complete treatise on the art of singing: Part I*. D. Paschke (Ed. And Trans.). New York: Da Capo.

Gray, H. (1918). *Anatomy of the Human Body* (20th ed.). Philadelphia: Lea & Febiger.

Henley, H. (1931, May). Garcia's second discovery. *Etude, 49*(5), 361.

Hirano, M., Vennard, W., & Ohala, J. (1970). Regulation of register, pitch and intensity of voice. *Folia Phoniatrica 22*, 1–20.

Lundy, D. S., Roy, S., Casiano, R. R., Evans, J., Sullivan, P. A., & Xue, J. W. (2000). Relationship between aerodynamic measures of glottal efficiency and stroboscopic findings in asymptomatic singing students. *Journal of Voice, 14*(2), 178–183.

Mancini, G. (1923). *Practical reflections on the figurative art of singing*. R.G. Badger (Ed.) & P. Buzzi (Trans.). Boston: Gorham.

McCoy, S. (2004). *Your voice: An inside view*. Delaware, OH: Inside View.

Miller, R. (1986). *The structure of singing*. New York: Schirmer.

Neuen, D. (2002). *Choral concepts*. Belmont, CA: Schirmer/Thomson Learning.

Nix, J., & Simpson, C. B. (2008). Semi-occluded vocal tract postures and their application in the singing voice studio. *Journal of Singing, 64*(3), 339–342.

Phillips, K. (2004). *Directing the choral music program*. New York: Oxford University Press.

Phillips, K. H., & Aitchison, R. E. (1997). Effects of psychomotor instruction on elementary general music students' singing performance. *Journal of Research in Music Education, 45*(2), 185–196.

Root, F. W. (1873). *F. W. Root's School of singing*. Chicago: Geo. F. Root & Sons.

Rossing T. D., Sundberg, J., & Ternström, S. (1986). Acoustic comparison of voice use in solo and choir singing. *Journal of the Acoustical Society of America, 79*(6), 1975–1981.

Sabol, J., Lee, L., & Stemple, J. C. (1995). The value of vocal function exercises in the practice regimen of singers. *Journal of Voice, 9*(1), 27–36.

Schneider, B., & Bigenzahn, W. (2004). Influence of glottal closure configuration on vocal efficacy in young normal-speaking women. *Journal of Voice, 17*(4), 468–480.

Sonninen, A., Laukkanen, A.-M., Karma, K., & Hurme, P. (2005). Evaluation of support in singing. *Journal of Voice, 19*(2), 223–237.

Stark, J. (1999). *Bel Canto: A history of vocal pedagogy*. Toronto: University of Toronto Press.

Stemple, J. C., Lee, L., D'Amico, B., & Pickup, B. (1994). Efficacy of vocal function exercises as a method of improving voice production. *Journal of Voice, 8*(3), 271–278.

Sundberg, J. (1974). Articulatory interpretation of the "singing formant." *Journal of the Acoustical Society of America, 55*(4), 838–844.

Sundberg, J. (1987). *The science of the singing voice*. DeKalb: Northern Illinois University Press.

Ternström, S., & Sundberg, J. (1989). Formant frequencies of choir singers. *Journal of the Acoustical Society of America, 86*(2), 517–522.

Thomasson, M., & Sundberg, J. (1999). Consistency of phonatory breathing patterns in professional operatic singers. *Journal of Voice, 13*(4), 529–541.

Thomasson, M., & Sundberg, J. (2001). Consistency of inhalatory breathing patterns in professional operatic singers. *Journal of Voice, 15*(3), 373–383.

Thorpe, C. W., Cala, S. J., Chapman, J., & Davis, P. J. (2001). Patterns of breath support in projection of the singing voice. *Journal of Voice, 15*(1), 86–104.

Titze, I., et al. (1991). *Vocal health and science*. Jacksonville, FL: NATS.

Titze, I. (2006). Voice training and therapy with a semi-occluded vocal tract: Rationale and scientific underpinnings. *Journal of Speech, Language, and Hearing Research, 49*(2), 448–459.

Titze, I. R., & Story, B. H. (1997). Acoustic interactions of the voice source with the lower vocal tract. *Journal of the Acoustical Society of America, 101*(4), 2234–2243.

Titze, I. R., & Worley, A. S. (2009). Modeling source-filter interaction in belting and high-pitched operatic male singing. *Journal of the Acoustical Society of America, 126*(3), 1530–1540.

Vennard, W. (1967). *Singing: The mechanism and the technique*. New York: Carl Fischer.

Watson, P. J., & Hixon, T. J. (1985). Respiratory kinematics in classical (opera) singers. *Journal of Speech and Hearing Research, 28*(1), 104–122.

Watson, P. J., Hoit, J. D., Lansing, R. W., & Hixon, T. J. (1989). Abdominal muscle activity during classical singing. *Journal of Voice, 3*(1), 24–31.

Wooldridge, W. B. (1956). Is there nasal resonance? *NATS Bulletin, 13*, 28–29.

Index